# A Mind
## of Her Own

WISCONSIN LAND AND LIFE

# A Mind
# of Her Own

❧

## HELEN CONNOR LAIRD AND FAMILY
## 1888–1982

*Helen Laird*

THE UNIVERSITY OF WISCONSIN PRESS
TERRACE BOOKS

The University of Wisconsin Press
1930 Monroe Street
Madison, Wisconsin 53711

www.wisc.edu/wisconsinpress/

3 Henrietta Street
London WC2E 8LU, England

5   4   3   2   1

Printed in the United States of America

Library of Congress Cataloging-in-Publication Data
Laird, Helen, 1933–
A mind of her own Helen Connor Laird and family, 1888–1982 / Helen Laird.
p. cm.—(Wisconsin land and life)
Includes bibliographical references and index.
ISBN 0-299-21450-8 (cloth: alk. paper)
1. Laird, Helen Connor, 1888–1982. 2. Connor family. 3. Laird family.
4. Pioneers—Wisconsin—Biography. 5. Frontier and pioneer life—Wisconsin.
6. Women political activists—Wisconsin—Biography. 7. Political activists—
Wisconsin—Biography. 8. Wisconsin—Biography. I. Title. II. Series.
CT275.L245L35 2005

2005010204

Terrace Books, a division of the University of Wisconsin Press, takes its name from
the Memorial Union Terrace, located at the University of Wisconsin–Madison.
Since its inception in 1907, the Wisconsin Union has provided a venue for students,
faculty, staff, and alumni to debate art, music, politics, and the issues of the day.
It is a place where theater, music, drama, dance, outdoor activities, and major
speakers are made available to the campus and the community.
To learn more about the Union, visit www.union.wisc.edu.

*For*

JULIAN AND EDMOND
LAIRD-RAYLOR

## Our Best People

Our best people are able to discriminate between what is best and what is mediocre or common and they are also wise enough to hold onto the best of all time, even though it be the past. They are not "the first by which the new is tried, nor yet the last to lay the old aside." That is, they do not dash ahead until they are pretty sure they have something better. They believe in old-fashioned virtues such as honesty, fair play in the home as well as in the nation's affairs. They believe in justice, in consideration of others, in the saving grace of kindness and hospitality, and they usually have some faith in their fellow man and rejoice that, in spite of difficulties, he still aspires. Our best people are usually quite modest, unassuming people whose influence sometimes permeates a community rather than directs it, but they are the great stabilizers and in them lives the real worth, the hope of our nation.

—HELEN CONNOR LAIRD

# Contents

# Illustrations

# Prologue

In 1923, Helen Connor Laird delivered a brief autobiographical sketch to a group of ministers' wives. The "great popularity" of several current autobiographies made her think that even her "humdrum life might have something of interest to others." A thirty-five-year-old "homemaker," member of the "restless" generation of college-educated women, she had no crystal ball. She did not know that history would largely ignore her father, W.D. Connor, a pioneer in Wisconsin's hardwood lumber industry, and an important figure in state politics during the period 1903–12; that her husband, Melvin Robert Laird, a Presbyterian minister, would become an esteemed state senator; that she would become a regent of the University of Wisconsin; or that her son Melvin R. Laird Jr. would become "one of the great leaders Wisconsin has produced," whose name would appear in the indexes of numerous political histories. Great achievements and great sorrows lay ahead in the life that proved to be not at all "humdrum."

Her long life's journey, which began in 1888 and ended in 1982, reflects the proud and painful American twentieth century. Her personal story, interwoven with that of the exceptional men in her life, including her competitive brothers, speaks to the way we were and are: a stridently materialistic nation with a deep and persistent spiritual component. This is her story and theirs, the telling of which would not have been possible had she not been a keeper of records, a "closet historian" as well as "closet poet," and had not those with whom she was most closely associated also been keepers of records. The progressive movement and the La Follette name have become almost synonymous with Wisconsin history. This saga of one of the state's leading moderate Republican families over three generations broadens the scope of that history.

# Acknowledgments

Helen Connor Laird, my mother-in-law, saved scrapbooks and diaries, her own and her husband's, as well as business and political documents, newspaper clippings, notes, essays, stories, speeches, poems, and letters. Disorganized as they all were—and scattered throughout her home, garage, and attic—they, the Helen Connor Laird family collection, became the basis for this biography. My brother-in-law Melvin R. Laird, "Bom," graciously shared the personal letters he received from his mother and granted me permission to review family letters in the Melvin R. Laird Collection in the archives of the Wisconsin Historical Society. My husband, David Laird, has been supportive of this project over many years. I am grateful for his patience, his willingness to respond to hundreds of questions (to be interrupted in his work to "listen to this"), and am deeply humbled by his conviction that his family story was in good hands. That he sustained that conviction, following the manuscript's acceptance by the University of Wisconsin Press and his careful scrutiny of it, confirms my belief in miracles.

Many other members of the Connor and Laird families, some now deceased, contributed oral testimony and/or written material: Patricia (Laird) Thomas, Jessica Doyle, Lissa Laird, Angie Connor, William Duncan Connor Jr., Andy and Thelma Connor, Mary Roddis Connor, Gordon Phelps Connor, Sara Connor, Elizabeth Connor Campbell, and Jean Connor Evans.

The Connor Lumber and Land Company materials located in the archives of the Wisconsin Historical Library provided insight into the family's turbulent business and personal history. The university archives located in the University of Wisconsin Memorial Library enabled me to trace Helen's distinguished career as a regent.

Augusta Roddis shared her memories, and Edwin Witter Jr. shared his work of many years tracing the genealogical lines and history of the Witter and Phelps families. Lloyd Listle steered me to "Lower Town." Walt and Agnes Carter and "Bud" and Marian Hanson, Connor Company employees, shared their stories about life in Laona in the "old days." Arlett Spector, former editor of the *Forest Republican,* welcomed me into the back office where I spent many summer afternoons reading the back editions she kindly provided. Kent Calder and Michael Stevens gave much-needed encouragement. Vanessa Laird and Timothy Raylor read the manuscript with great sensitivity, corrected errors, and gave good advice.

# A Note on Some Family Names

Mary or Mame is Huldah Maybelle Witter Connor.

W.D. is William Duncan Connor.

William is William Duncan Connor II.

Billie is William Duncan Connor III.

Richard is W.D.'s son.

Dickens is Richard's son.

Dick is Richard Laird.

Bom or Bam is Melvin R. Laird Jr.

Rob is Robert Connor, W.D.'s brother.

Aunt Florence is Rob's wife.

*A Mind*
*of Her Own*

❧

# CHAPTER I

# To Wisconsin

Fragments of our past become our mirrors.

—ANONYMOUS

In 1854, Helen's paternal great-grandparents William and Mary Connor emigrated with their four sons, Robert, William, John, and James, from Johnstone, Renfrewshire, Scotland, and settled in the Scots-English colony around Stratford in Perth County, Canada. The promise of bounty drew the Connor brothers (along with some fifty thousand other Canadian volunteers) into the United States to fight in the Civil War. They obtained several bounties, avoided the fighting, looked over the great virgin forests of central and northern Wisconsin, and returned to Canada with enough funds to establish farms and homes for the families they had left behind.

The rigorous, marginal life of the Canadian farmer did not satisfy the strong, ambitious Connors. In 1872, Helen's grandfather, Robert, his wife, Mary McLeish, and their four children—Margaret, Jessica, Anne, and eight-year-old William Duncan, who became Helen's father—joined the Connor migration into central Wisconsin, which the railroad was just beginning to open to people and trade. They halted their wagons in a region inhabited by Chippewa and Potawatomi Indians who slept in wigwams made of bark and skin, hunted muskrats, skunks, fox, raccoons, weasels, and mink, and gathered ginseng, wild blueberries, and cranberries. They halted in that land of dogs, ponies, wolves, and bears crossed by footpaths skirting pine trunks, following the easiest route around swamps and hills. They settled in a little clearing in the wilderness near Point 32 by a rudimentary sawmill and began to build the town Robert and John would each later claim to have named after his own auburn-haired daughters: Auburndale.

Auburndale is now a small community of a few shops, a few orderly, well-painted, well-built houses, most of them wooden, and a fine grade school, which draws students from neighboring Milladore, Blenker, and Sherry. On the outskirts, on State Highway 10, a large, modern, gasoline station links the small community with Everywhere Else America. The highway runs east and west through Main Street. A brick building, facing it, bears the name Connor and the year 1876, but Auburndale otherwise gives few hints of its origins. Railroad tracks still cross the town, paralleling Main Street; and the pioneers, including Robert Connor, rest under marked stones in a neat little cemetery near the tracks. The Indians left long ago, with scarcely a trace, moving westward or retreating farther north into Forest County. The mill and the woods are gone, the surrounding land transformed into farms.

Auburndale and Marshfield (their origins date from the same time) lie in a county called Wood, where Helen Connor Laird spent almost all of her ninety-three years. Long after the reasonableness and appropriateness of the county's name has been forgotten, it bears witness to its beginnings.[1]

Grand Rapids (Wisconsin Rapids), the county seat, located on the Wisconsin River, open to commerce and settlement fifteen years before the land-locked areas around Auburndale and Marshfield, was home to the Witters, Helen Connor Laird's maternal grandparents. George Franklin Witter and Frances Phelps Witter had deep roots in America, their lineage proudly tracing back through minister and officer, craftsman and farmer, to John Howland, who arrived on the *Mayflower* as an indentured servant and survived to become one of the three leading citizens in Massachusetts.

George F. Witter, the youngest of carpenter Squire Porter Witter's eleven children, was born in Brookfield, Madison County, New York, in 1831. Trained as a teacher in New York, receiving his certificate at age sixteen, he was able to save enough money to continue his education, and in 1856 he received a degree in medicine at the University of Michigan, after which he began to practice in the outpost community of Wautoma, Wisconsin. Two cousins also migrated from New York into the new state, George W. Witter to teach school in Dexterville before enlisting in the 43d Regiment of the Wisconsin Volunteers, and Jeremiah Delos Witter.

In 1858, the latter, who flattered himself to be a "nice young man" who didn't "get drunk oftner than once a week," rode over from Wautoma to the Rapids. He thought he might remain there for some time—perhaps all winter—reading law. (A typical Yankee, Jeremiah was ready to move along if new and better possibilities presented themselves.) And though he found the undomesticated society "generally poor—hardly a man but what smokes and chews tobacco, drinks whiskey and swears,"[2] he remained anyway. In 1859, Dr. George Witter joined him. George and Jeremiah reached back to New

York for their brides, cousins Frances Louisa Phelps and Emily Phelps, who traced a proud ancestry back to Puritans who arrived aboard the *Mary and John* in 1630 from Plymouth, Devonshire.[3]

The Witters brought education, law, banking, and medicine to the frontier community. George Witter became the county's first superintendent of education in 1862; in 1863 he organized an institute for teachers; in 1873 he was the leading force behind the creation of a State Normal School in the Rapids. He became mayor; was a member of, and eventually president, the State Board of Health; a founding member of the American Medical Association; president of the Northwestern Medical Association; examining surgeon for pensions; and postmaster during the administrations of Grant, Hayes, and Arthur. This "very useful citizen," whose handsome but frail wife suffered several miscarriages, was the father of three surviving children, sons George Jr. and Willis Guy and daughter Huldah Maybelle. Called Mary or Mame, the pioneer's daughter was to be Helen Connor Laird's mother.

In her youth, during that expansive post–Civil War time, Mame was her father's companion and assistant, often going out with him on calls to the homes of the sick and dying. In spite of her fair skin, bright brown eyes, and luxurious brown hair, she was not conventionally pretty, having inherited the large Witter nose and a tendency to be heavy. She was known for her earnestness and good humor, and she was a gifted painter. From her girlhood, and throughout her life, she played the piano "loudly, very loudly." Like other members of her family and most of her community, Mame was a Christian, tolerant of all religions and an active member of the Presbyterian church.

She grew to maturity within an extended society of intelligent, well-regarded friends and relatives: cousins Isaac and Ruth, Aunt Emily, and Uncle Jeremiah (Jere), who did not, after all, go further west. Jere, the family lawyer, a brilliant businessman with far-ranging interests in Wisconsin lumber, Texas cattle, and Louisiana rice, organized the First National Bank in Grand Rapids, joined with Henry Sherry, Lewis Nash, John Arpin, George Hiles, and J. W. Cameron to construct the Centralia Railroad to haul people and lumber. Most important for the area, he obtained water rights on the Wisconsin River. His son Isaac Phelps Witter and son-in-law George Mead realized Jeremiah's plan of building a dam across the river at the Rapids and developed what became one of Wisconsin's great industries: the Consolidated Water Power and Paper Company. Jeremiah gave a Free Traveling Library to the town and bequeathed $1,000 "to every regularly organized church within the limits of the city of Grand Rapids."

The pioneers who settled in Wood County, Wisconsin, developed the farms,

homes, churches, schools, libraries, roads, financial institutions, and businesses
that allowed them to survive and prosper not only through the perseverance,
intelligence, and ambition of the men and women who saw and seized the
opportunity in the wilderness but through their prayers. The little wooden
churches that dot the landscape still are powerful reminders of the faith that
bound them, the beliefs that sustained them and let them grow.

While Helen Connor Laird's mother experienced perhaps an ideal childhood
in a highly respected family where affection was constant, responsibility gladly
learned and easily carried, and no family trauma marred an innocent, developing consciousness, her father's childhood was far from ideal. William Duncan
Connor early, through actions of his parents and strangers, suffered the "slings
and arrows of outrageous fortune." His survival and eventual enormous successes cannot be traced to a favored childhood. For him the essential challenge
lay not in the wilderness, which he could conquer, but in a wounded pride he
had to assuage.

In *Men of Progress*, a book published in 1897 as tribute to Wisconsin's leading citizens, father and son, Robert Connor and William Duncan Connor,
are linked together as "notable examples of the courage, enterprise, business
sagacity and inflexible perseverance by which the northern part of the state
has been developed, and fortunes have been made—men who not only carved
out their own fortunes, but at the same time have laid deep the foundations
of many beneficent local institutions."

William Duncan paid tribute to his father as "the leading, dominating spirit
of the pioneer settlement [of Auburndale] and its business," as "not only a
man of culture but one of indomitable perseverance, of great energy and enterprise." The son loyally admired his father for venturing into the wilderness,
for constructing the log cabin where they lived and the store with its post
office, which marked the beginning of the new town. He admired the hard
work that enabled him to purchase the rudimentary saw mill and in 1878 to
build a planing mill in connection with it; for his ability to handle ox, plow,
and saw; for toughing it out alone in lean times when his brothers moved on
with their families to seek other opportunities in Iowa and on the Nebraska
prairie. He admired him for the things he taught him: to fearlessly meet the
wilderness understanding that in those woods his fortune lay; to negotiate
lumber rafts down the Wisconsin River through the rocky, treacherous Dells
into the Mississippi River and down to St. Louis; to evaluate timber, survey
land, construct houses and roads; to judge men and to rule them; to dig a well,
raise animals, rotate crops. He admired him for the organizational abilities that

led him to form the R. Connor Lumber Company; for his political sagacity; for his election to the state assembly where he was "credited with being one of the most sensible members"[4]; for the intellectual curiosity he passed on to all his children, daughters as well as sons.

That Robert Connor had less admirable characteristics, that he was, like so many other survivors in the wilderness of whom life demanded almost super-human energy, endurance, and will, a heavy drinker (often his horse brought him home dead drunk from Marshfield tied onto his buggy) is not mentioned in *Men of Progress*. That he was probably unfaithful, that his frail wife, Mary McLeish, was unhappy, is also not recorded.

Six years after the family's arrival in Wood County, on September 12, 1878, when her eldest son, William Duncan, was fourteen years old, and her youngest, Robert, not quite eight months, Mary McLeish Connor hanged herself by a horse halter from the rafters of the family barn. Overworked and debilitated; weary of the care of her aged, blind mother-in-law; weary of childbearing (two more daughters, Molly and Agnes, were born in Auburndale); weary of the hard-ships, the extreme isolation, and the deep loneliness in the second new world she had known, life didn't seem worth the candle anymore to the small, delicate woman who, herself the child of a broken marriage, had perhaps never known ease or happiness. She was thirty-six years old when she turned out the light.

The family tragedy, never forgotten but whispered about by female rela-tives from behind closed doors, played a part in moving players in the next generation to accomplish the things they did, to be what they were.

A less traumatic but significant violation of a child's psyche became the subject of a confidence William Duncan shared with his youngest daughter, Constance, when the two were out in the buggy and the day was fine and reminiscence came easily to the civic leader and lumber tycoon. He recalled another day, a blustery winter day when he was six years old and trudging through deep snow to Broksden School, the little one-room wooden school-house he attended in North Easthope, Perth County, Canada. A lady passing by in her buggy invited him to ride with her. She put warm lap robes over him and was very cordial until he told her his name. Then, she abruptly stopped the carriage and ordered him out. He trudged on in the bitter cold. The motto above the schoolhouse door, "Knowledge Is Power," burned into his memory that day, along with the insult, and he vowed that he should not suffer such humiliation again.

A mother's death is a deeper wound, the consequences of which condition everything. But while skeletons rattle, life moves on: the aged, blind grand-mother to Scotland to be cared for by relatives there; William Duncan to study at Oshkosh Normal from his fifteenth through his seventeenth year; his sisters Margaret, Jessica, and Anne to take over a mother's chores and raise a baby brother and younger sisters; his father to manage farm, mill, and store and, in a year, to remarry. His second wife, Rebecca Waite, had been the family maid and perhaps his mistress. On May 31, 1880, Reuben Connor, first child of this marriage, was born in Auburndale.

In Oshkosh, a mature lumber town, William Duncan learned from books and life. Philetus Sawyer—Oshkosh's self-made millionaire lumberman with extensive land holdings in northeastern Wisconsin and other midwestern states, banker and politician, Republican leader in Wisconsin and in Washington, D.C., spokesman for large land-owning corporations, powerful dispenser of patronage, and civic benefactor—provided an even more stirring role model than had Henry Sherry, owner of 60 million feet of white pine and two saw mills in Wood County and developer of the town adjacent to Auburndale, which bore his name.[5] With his eye out for the main chance, William Duncan quickly perceived the links between land, power, and politics. He wanted to study law and had completed his first year at Lake Forest Academy when, at the age of eighteen, he was called back to Auburndale to help his father with his expanding lumber business.

William Duncan showed remarkable aptitude; the business thrived; his sisters went to college and traveled to Europe. With the arrival of three additional children in his second family—Wallace, Craig, and Ruth—Robert built another house. By the mid-1880s log cabin days were over for the Connors. Two handsome Connor homes with finished wood siding stood near one another in Auburndale, a tribute to the planing mill and emblems of the swift rise in the family's fortune.

In 1884, William Duncan became, at age twenty, a member of the Wood County Board, a position he held for twenty years, serving twice as its chairman. He rendered the Republican Party, the party of the lumber barons and for years Wisconsin's winning party, "much service in the conducting of its local campaigns."

In 1885, Mary Witter, the first female from Wood County to graduate from the University of Wisconsin, arrived in Auburndale to teach in the village school. The village's rail-thin, fair-haired, most eligible bachelor was soon seen regularly carrying wood into the schoolhouse for this very proper and very strict young woman. The only daughter of the distinguished family in the Rapids and William Duncan Connor were married in the Presbyterian church in the

Rapids on August 16, 1886. Mame and W.D. set up housekeeping in Auburndale in their new home next to their Connor relatives.

A first child, delivered by a midwife in Auburndale on June 23, 1887, did not survive; a second, delivered in the Rapids on August 22, 1888, by her grandfather, Dr. George F. Witter, did. Her parents named her Helen Melissa Connor, and their "hearts were singing." She was three weeks old when her mother brought her to Auburndale. Born into a world still linked to the frontier yet rapidly moving into new times, the perfect baby with the Connor golden hair and light-blue eyes, the first of a new generation of Connors in the new world, was loved, sheltered, and taught by a large circle of caring relatives in the Rapids and in Auburndale. Her ten-year-old Uncle Robert, called Rob, became her special friend.

On December 21, 1890, her brother, Donald, was born. As they grew, the two became the companions their mother hoped they would be. Together they traveled to Marshfield in the family surrey drawn by a beautiful pair of drivers and camped along the shores of Lake Monona with their parents as well as their Aunts Mollie, Bessie, and Agnes and their Uncle Rob and his Newfoundland puppy. Together they rode ponies, saw short-horned cattle being milked, and watched the "river pigs" (lumberjacks who rode logs downstream) show off as they strutted along the plank sidewalks digging in their spiked boots, making splinters fly. They observed the "girls," daughters of immigrant Germans and Scandinavians, haul water, bake, cook and clean, and make soap and candles and the "boys," wiry muscular men, who worked long and hard with the assistance of powerful Belgian shires, plowing fields, hauling loads, pulling stumps out of the ground and scrapers across newly cleared ground to make roads where none had ever been. Together they observed the blackness of those unelectrified nights, the sharpness of starlight, sunlight clear, through mist and rain, and the seasons' passing, the earth sleeping and awakening.

By the time she was five years old, Helen could read and write. GrandMa F. L. Witter received her first letter. "Your nice little letter came yesterday with its invitation. We—GrandPa and I—would be most happy to be there as you desire. But we cannot go twice and cannot well stay so long; so we think it best to wait until Christmas when we hope to find you and Donald well and as bright and happy as pretty birds, with your dear Mama and Papa. I will write a few lines to your Mama to enclose with this and bid you a loving good by."[6]

Helen spent the first eight years of her life in Auburndale, and her grandmother's wish for her came true. She was well and bright and happy as a pretty bird. She bonded to her people and her land so that forever after longing and homesickness filled her when she was away, and she could never stay away from Wood County long. Yet, as a very old woman, when she looked at her early years, she confided that she wondered why her little soul was inside her particular body and suspected that she was an orphan.

Helen Melissa Connor, ca. 1891.

CHAPTER 2

# Getting Ahead

He had the greed of a wolf and the temper of an aging bear, and yet his business ability admittedly commanded respect. He despised the small revenges; but in a strife with his equals he was inexorable—he pushed his adversaries to the ditch. All his faith in goodness and virtue, he reserved for his home.

—HAMLIN GARLAND

The first generation of lumber barons in the Wisconsin northwoods, Isaac Stephenson, Frederick Weyerhaeuser, and Philetus Sawyer, amassed enormous acreage of the public domain loaded with virgin pine and made fortunes sending floatable logs down river to market. By the end of the 1880s, the railroads were well established throughout central Wisconsin, providing passenger and freight service from the small towns to the midwestern financial, industrial, and political centers in Minneapolis, Milwaukee, Madison, and Chicago and beginning to spread their tentacles north into every corner where profit might be realized. They had land for sale—government grants to them of alternate sections for opening up the country at give-away prices—fifty cents, a dollar, a dollar and a half an acre. In that time of unchecked possibility in America, when individual aggrandizement was often viewed as a social good and hungry men from eastern states and many nations drifted over the land seeking opportunity in this ever-expanding, increasingly powerful country, W.D. Connor assembled his fiefs.

Two factors enabled him to become one of "the big lumber people [who] stole the whole north country."[1] His father, a state assemblyman in 1889, served on the State Road and Railroad Committee and provided insider information on the direction and the timing of the northern expansion of the Chicago and Northwestern and the Soo Lines, and W.D. had the ambition, drive, and skills to use that information.

His first major expansion, in 1892, was to a heavily wooded area twelve miles north of Marshfield, a day's trip with a good team. Although no English

Avon flowed there—instead, a French Eau Pleine—W.D. named the site Stratford. He built a band sawmill, a store, roads, a track of railroad (the Marathon County Road) to connect with the Soo Line, and houses for his workers,
many of whom came from Auburndale, where the timber had almost all been
harvested.

Bent on expanding, and constantly on the move, he needed dependable
agents to look after his interests. To manage his mill and the woods he chose
"keen-eyed" Sam Smith and Jerry Hughes, a farmer, butcher, and all-around
hustler who hauled for the company.[2] To secure his interests in the township,
he chose a sober Anglo-Saxon family man of enormous physical stature and
strength and promised him "great things if [he] would play ball with him."[3]
Leonard Sargent's son recounts how W.D. immediately maneuvered to make
his father the town chairman. Farmers believed their candidate outnumbered
Connor's men in the township; but when election day came, a new population
brought in by W.D. a few weeks before the election (a man became eligible
to vote after ten days) tipped the balance in Sargent's favor. After the election,
W.D. fired the newcomers.[4] He did not need the lumberjacks in the warm
weather, but he did need to control the town. Assessments could make or break
an entrepreneur.

As W.D.'s "tool," Sargent became town chairman, clerk of the school board,
and manager of the only hotel and tavern, Stratford House, and in that capacity received discount prices for provisions at the company store and held the
saloon license, an important benefit. The liquor trade—at five cents a shot for
the throat-searing blended barrel whiskey that the laborers drank and ten cents
a shot for the twenty-year-old branded bottle whiskey for the few who could
afford to drink it—brought good profits. Sometimes as many as fifty workmen crowded into the Sargent bar.

Fighting, gambling, drinking, hunting—unrestricted then by any law—and
an occasional barn dance, horse race, or mandolin performance provided
almost the only entertainment. Occasionally, someone would pull into town
with a wagon, hang up a gasoline lamp, announce a curiosity, and ask a fee
for a look. When a wagon with a "Petrified Man" the owner claimed to have
found near Peshtigo stopped in town, Mrs. Sargent wanted to know if W.D.
didn't want to pay the ten cents for a glimpse. "No, Mrs. Sargent," Mr. Connor replied. "If I want to see any petrified men, all I have to do is visit my
lumber yard." Or, he might have added, look in the window of Mr. Laemle's
clothing store in Marshfield, where "a mummified squaw and papoose" attracted
"a great deal of attention."[5]

Helen's father had a quick tongue, a knowledge of prevailing business practices in the lumber game, a relentless ambition, and not a great deal of respect for many of the men, the "counts and no accounts," who labored twelve-hour days or nights for him.[6] Many of the men had little respect for themselves. They drifted from camp to camp living on temporary labor, companionship, and booze. Young ladies attempting to settle them down to the hard routine of raising families were not often successful.

As he enlarged his timber empire, W.D. borrowed heavily, delayed payment of bills to suppliers, and paid his workmen with scrip, paper money issued by the company in 5-, 10-, 25-, and 50-cent and one and two dollar denominations. While the scrip was illegal, it kept "real" money available for expansion and essential "outside" charges. A new engineer at the sawmill who was smart enough to know the rules, upon finding that scrip was used to buy postage stamps at the post office, which was located in the company office, notified the post office inspector, who dropped in and put an end to the practice. The fact that the engineer lost his job did not go unremarked. W.D.'s reputation as a man bent on getting ahead and willing to bend the rules spread.[7]

In 1896, the year of his father's death, with successful operations in Auburndale and Stratford, W.D. pursued his aggressive march to fortune. Together with his eighteen-year-old brother, Rob, and a cruiser, Herman Langer, by foot and horseback, he explored the timberlands north of Gillett, then the Northwestern's northernmost point. He judged timber values, calculated costs, and bought from the railroad corporation about 100,000 acres of alternate sections in anticipation of the railroad's coming.

In the almost roadless land inhabited by Indians, wild cats, bear, and timber wolves, he discovered what became his principal fiefdom: the great virgin hardwood forests east of Crandon surrounding the tiny settlement called Laona in the county aptly named Forest. The county was "at the end of the world" in those days.[8] The area, almost as full of streams and lakes as woods, was an ideal location for a major mill, and in the heart of the great forests lay Birch Lake. Deep and clear, it was fed by underground streams and bordered by towering pine and graceful white birch. The men camped by its shores, and W.D. declared that lake, with its island at the center (which the Indians refused to visit thinking it rested on a serpent's back and would turn over), his own into perpetuity for his family's personal use.

Having scouted the land and sized up the population—the impoverished Chippewas and Potawatomies, who had not relocated further west but stayed on, or returned, to starve and freeze in the meager acreage the government allotted to them; the drifters, European castoffs, "Kaintucks," the few Swedish farmers; the railroad "boys," the camp suppliers—W.D. strove to establish order, to build a new community according to his enlightened self-interest. Seeking greater financial flexibility, he incorporated a new company: the Connor Lumber and Land Company, whose stock, like stock of the R. Connor Company and other of the nation's major lumber companies, was held in family hands.

Over the next few years, he cleared land for "his" Laona on the forty he owned north of the original railroad settlement known as Lower Town, where a few independent saloon owners, shopkeepers, and railroad workers lived. He dug wells, filled in marsh land, cleared land for a company farm, brought in pigs and cattle, and built a round barn, slaughterhouse, blacksmith shop, electric utility, lumber yard, mill, roads, dams, and railroad tracks for his own feeder line, the Laona and Northern. (It ran parallel with the Chicago and Northwestern and linked with the Minneapolis, St. Paul and Sault Ste. Marie Railroad and the Soo Line at Laona Junction.)

He gave the land and lumber for Presbyterian, Catholic, and Lutheran churches and brought trusted family men from Auburndale to Laona, including Albert Schuette, Jes Derme, Sam Smith, John Kissinger, and the Baltuses, Aschenbrenners, and Maedenwalds. He moved his faithful agent, Len Sargent, from Stratford to run his new town and put his young brother Rob, finished with his studies at Hanover College, a Presbyterian institution in Indiana, in charge at Stratford. He built another company store where, once again, his employees spent the money he issued. He built a boardinghouse, which the workers called the Prune House, and a hundred company houses with no waterworks, where the soot and cold winds blew through the primitive structures, and he collected the rent. No one working for Connor could buy in any store but Connor's or rent a room in Lower Town after 1900, when Sargent's thirty-room hotel went up in W.D.'s town.

No detail in W.D.'s empire was too minute to attract his interest, no scheme too grand. He built dozens of logging camps in the woods surrounding Laona, simple wooden shacks where meals were eaten swiftly and silently and men slept short nights and worked long days and were so filthy and so cold in the below-zero winters that lumberjacks claimed that, although they were all loaded with lice, not a head louse could be found among them; they were all down on their bodies where it was warmer.

Word of the new town and work in northern Wisconsin spread. Charles (Charlie) Edward Barney heard about it and came from southern Michigan, where the woods had been cleared and everything had turned to farms, and he didn't like farming. He came into Laona with his wife and children, four hundred pounds of household goods, seven dollars, and a canary, and there he settled in for life. As a young man he worked in the woods and the mill and hauled wood, coal, and groceries to the camps around Laona. Sometimes it got so cold (52 degrees below zero) that the only things moving were those head lice going south. The sleigh runners wouldn't slide until they doubled up the team. The potatoes froze in the open sleigh. But the men got the meat they needed to keep them going. When he got old, Charlie became W.D.'s caretaker at Birch Lake, keeping poachers away from the walleyes.

The Forest County operation grew enormous. Over the years, W.D. replaced his wooden buildings, store, and bank with brick buildings and added a three-story brick hotel with a billiard and pool room and a bowling alley in the basement, making it "one of the finest in Northern Wisconsin."[9] There no alcohol was served; it was a genteel place attractive to moneyed people. He invited Ernest Ovitz, the fearless doctor on horseback who loved medicine, hunting, and fishing equally, to be the company doctor and built a brick hospital for him. The first public library in Forest County was housed in the brick school building he built.

In the winters, hundreds of men were in Connor's woods; many, if not most, of them, had been "caught" by the "mancatchers" W.D. hired to stake out the saloons in Minneapolis, St. Paul, Duluth, Superior, and Chicago to trap likely men. They loaded the drunks in cars and delivered them to Laona, where at least half sobered up and stayed on to work. Most worked long enough to pay off the fare owed the company; some wandered off before doing so, leaving behind their gunny sacks with family pictures and a few possessions. The unclaimed sacks, called "turkeys" by the townspeople, periodically were gathered in a pile and burned.

Many of these ensnared wanderers—Finns, Russians, and Poles—came down with smallpox, prevalent among the Indians living in the woods. The "Bohunks," as the Anglos called them, were sequestered then, quarantined in the "Pest House" on Mill Street, the main street running west to the mill and mill pond and east to Birch Lake. The children and workers' wives living on Mill Street watched as food was taken up to the sick men, but none ventured out to the cemetery at night when the corpses were buried.[10]

No labor laws protected the workers, many of whom would wake up after a night of heavy drinking at Sargent's Bar in the "snake room" of his hotel. Nothing prohibited child labor. The work was dangerous, the logging work, and the work in the mill. Men were crushed under logs; sparks from machinery lighting on dust in the mill caused horrible fires; a body moving among the line shafts could get caught in one of many turning belts. But if a man were mutilated, and many were, it was too bad for him.

It was too bad for one "green foreigner" who got his foot caught in a conveyor chain and had his toes on one foot cut off. The doctor trimmed the end of his foot, folded the sole up, and sewed it. But he couldn't work anymore, and his wages stopped, and as soon as his accumulated wages were used up for board, he was kicked out of the Prune House. He went to the parish priest, as he would have "in the old country." Father John J. Loerke put him on the train and sent him to Green Bay with a personal message to Joe Martin, "one of Wisconsin's most famous attorneys." The young man's pitiful condition, along with the informative letter about labor conditions in Laona prompted Martin to write a stinging letter to W.D.

Learning that Father Loerke was responsible for the employee's seeking outside help, W.D. ordered the priest to come into the company office. Father Loerke responded: "If you want to see me, you come over to my office." Instead of going, W.D. "ordered the company to shut off the electric lights at the church and parsonage." By candlelight, the priest "delivered a sermon that was a sizzler." Shortly thereafter, he was transferred to Green Bay.[11]

Everyone in Laona knew W.D. showed more concern for his horses than his workers and would fire a man on the spot for beating one of them. Horses were harder to get and cost more.

W.D.'s control over the hard place was complete. Through that control he prospered, helped develop an undeveloped area of the state, provided livelihoods, however marginal, for many. Known among his fellow lumbermen in the hardwood business as "a thinker from way back," a philosopher and orator who had "a facial resemblance to Demosthenes and the calm, unostentatious manner of a supreme court judge,"[12] he was called the "high mucky muck" by his workers and "King William the Silent" by journalists. As W.D. carved out his fortune and his place in the history of the young state, he was feared and respected, admired and hated. At home, he was the handsome, loving, devoted, fascinating father whom Helen adored.

# CHAPTER 3

# Marshfield

Our country is perpetually renewed by the sudden making of fortunes, and by the absence of a hereditary, reigning set. Our political system alone, where the lowest may rise to the highest preferment, upsets in a measure all that the Old World insists upon in matters of precedence and formality.

—MRS. JOHN SHERWOOD

In 1895, William Duncan Connor moved his family to Marshfield. Ten miles northwest of Auburndale, begun at about the same time as a wild, whiskey-soaked clearing in the wilderness with a log cabin inn, saloon, a log shack store and fewer than a dozen families, the settlement had survived almost total destruction by fire in 1887 to become a boom town.

William Henry Upham, twenty-five years W.D.'s senior, served a term as governor in 1894 and was the town's leading citizen, owner not only of a saw mill and shingle mill but veneer, flour, and grist mills; a general merchandise store; a furniture factory; and an electric power facility. Thanks to Upham, Marshfield had electricity in 1885, a year before Milwaukee. Backed by the financial resources of his friends Charles Pfister and Marshall Field, Upham rebuilt after the fire, which began in his lumberyard, and added a waterworks to his enterprises.

By the time W.D. moved his family, a number of well-educated men lived in Marshfield. Most, like the first physicians in the area, C. L. Vedder, H. A. Lathrop, Andrew Sexton, Harry Vedder, and Henry Wahle, were Yankees. Karl W. Doege, probably the most illustrious of them, was German. Like other early settlers—Robert L. Kraus, William Noll, Edgar M. Deming, J. S. Marsh, Philip Adler, B. F. Wing, Eli Winch, Charles E. Blodgett, W. D. Pors, and William Henry Roddis—the prominent citizens had fingers in several pies: real estate, banking, and local politics as well as lumber, medicine, law, and merchandising.

Two banks, the German American, which W.D. incorporated in 1891, and the First National, in which William Henry Roddis, another of the town's leading lumbermen, and William Henry Upham held controlling interests; three newspapers (including a German language paper); and a six-bed hospital, St. Joseph's, run by Catholic sisters, were well established.

Hundreds of German Catholic and Lutheran families moved to the area in the 1880s and 1890s enticed by the railroads and the churches, which, advertising in Europe as well as America, promised a healthy climate, good water, churches, schools, German neighbors, and cheap, prime land ideally suited for dairy farming and cheese making. Many of the new immigrants' daughters worked in town as live-in maids for the Anglo families.

Upham's wife, Mary, brought a chapter of the Women's Temperance Union to Marshfield in 1882. While she and the other wives of the town's leading citizens sought to cultivate the rough garden in which their husbands planted them, they pondered the social problems of the day, presenting papers to one another bearing such titles as "What is Being Done for Railroad Men?" "Lumber Camp Work," "Sabbath Work and Work Among the Children," "Practical Value of Literature," "Gleanings from Great Britain," "What is Being Done for Social Purity?" and "Equal Suffrage."

The ladies pledged "to abstain from all distilled and malt liquors, as a beverage, and to do all I can to discourage their use." The Marshfield Brewing Company solicited business through inelegant advertisements: "shut up! and drink the Marshfield Brewing Co's Extra-Fine lager," while those of a more refined temperament were urged to try the Sunday dinner menu at the Blodgett Hotel on Main Street, which featured "claret punch, Burgundy, and Champagne" along with "roast prime ribs, calves sweet breads with mushroom sauce, and lobster salad."[1]

The new town, like all the others opening up across America in the last quarter of the nineteenth century, was a small place of great contrasts where high culture and frontier lawlessness, western extravagance and eastern refinement jostled. Intensely religious wives and their aggressive nonbelieving husbands did more than jostle, providing the underpopulated area—only one child of school age in 1875—with the numerous children that soon made new houses, roads, libraries, and schools essential.

Railroads supplied the shipping facilities and the thirty daily passenger trains that gave Marshfield national recognition as a railroad center and as the most important hub city in the central portion of the state. By 1895, Marshfield's population of 4,586 surpassed central Wisconsin's older river cities—Stevens Point and Wisconsin Rapids—and settlers predicated its further development into a city of steel-girded skyscrapers. Railroads brought traveling troops of thespians playing the circuit from Chicago to Minneapolis and points further west to the Adler Opera House. Most entertainment was, however, home made. Talented amateurs—readers, singers, violinists, mandolin, guitar and piano players, including Helen's very attractive aunts—performed for one another in homes and churches and occasionally at the Opera House.

Prominent men showed off their talents in a vaudeville production of "Burnt Corkers, a Monstrous, Marvelous and Meritorious Aggregation of Mirth Provoking Provokers." "Knute" Kinney played a "Svenska klerka . . . sellin snuss an alcohol har at ma store by Maister Upham." E. E. Finney, Upham's son-in-law, sang "I'll Make Dat Black Gal Mine." L. Voelker sang an Irish song and became "positively the only German . . . in a nigger show ever to have done so." Unselfconsciously they mocked blacks and immigrants. They were also intensely patriotic. Programs ended with actors and audience joining in ringing renditions of "The Star Spangled Banner."[2]

When Marshfield's Company A, 2d Wisconsin Volunteer Regiment, home from the Spanish-American War, mustered out in December 1898, the town provided a three-day "jubilee" celebration with a grand march, reception, speeches by B. F. McMillan (another leading lumberman) and Upham, a duet by songbirds Messrs. Finney and Mason, a reading by Mary Connor, and a grand ball open and free to everyone.[3]

W.D. installed his family in a large, rambling clapboard house[4] located in a parklike setting in a community of comfortable houses where the town's lawyers, doctors, and leading businessmen settled. Known as Pleasant Hill, this district of stately homes (and a number of modest dwellings, representative of the less grand ambitions and limited funds of most of the first inhabitants) was safely and conveniently located on a well-drained rise of land near the downtown within easy walking distance of churches, post office, banks, shops, industries, and the opera house. The Soo Line depot on Central and First was the natural heart of the district and of Marshfield. Train whistles regularly punctuated the quiet nights, promising families the connection with distant parts that the sound of the ship's foghorn gave shore dwellers on the eastern seaboard.

William Duncan set up his own telephone lines from Auburndale to Marshfield and Marshfield to Stratford. In 1900, he constructed a brick building to house the R. Connor Company on Central and Fourth Street. He changed the name of the German National Bank to the American National, and the bank received its national charter. Friends and neighbors E. E. Winch, R. L. Kraus, William Noll, E. M. Deming, C. S. Vedder, W. A. Pors, Philip Adler, B. F. Wing, K. W. Doege, and W.D.'s brother Rob were major stockholders— all men who knew how to make things work and how money was made. The city was on the move. In 1900, a brick city hall with a clock tower rose majestically on Maple and Second Streets, and a new $20,000 accredited high school, considered one of the most modern in the state, replaced the old school, formerly housed with the fire department and city hall in a wooden building on Cedar and Second.

Large and loyal congregations supported Lutheran, Catholic, Baptist, Presbyterian, and Episcopalian churches. Everyone belonged to a domination, and everyone knew where everyone belonged. The Roddises belonged to the Episcopalian church, Upham and Connor to the Presbyterian. Anglo-Saxons all, both the Roddises and Upham, who were good friends, competed with Connor for logs and political, social, and financial power. Formally correct in public, they were enemies, and soon everyone in town knew it.

W.D.'s home, like his bowler hat, immaculate wardrobe, soft-spoken voice and elegant manners, revealed his standing as a "millionaire" businessman and one of the county's leading citizens. In the spring, the lilac bushes and bridal wreath he planted about his large house opened into masses of purple

Ready for the parade in front of the Connor home, Marshfield, ca.1902. Richard M. Connor and Marian Elizabeth Connor face the camera.

The R. Connor Company Farm, Auburndale, Wisconsin, ca. 1900.

and white blossoms, while the native, majestic elms lining the broad street spread their green and welcome shade. In the inclement weather, Mame and her children enjoyed the large verandah that circled the front half of the house beckoning neighborly visits.

Inside, in generously proportioned, high-ceilinged rooms, the beautiful and the practical merged. Hand-woven carpets, Chinese and Oriental, lay strewn over hand-worked and polished oak floors. A parlor, closed off from the large vestibule by a massive oak door, unless there were visitors, featured a porcelain lamp and a mahogany table and chairs and a sofa covered in plush velvet and silk brocade. An example of the German woodcarver's art—a three-dimensional walnut tableau depicting a group of men merrily eating and drinking—stood on the mantle of the Italian marble fireplace. Mame's oil of pansies hung above; her hand-painted screen of lilacs rested beneath.

Mame had her music room, her piano, her collection of music books, which included hymnals, English ballads, Scottish folk songs, Stephen Foster tunes, Schubert's Lieder, *Songs for Little People*, as well as her collection of the historical romances of Louisa Muhlbach (translated from the German) and bound collections of the poems and novels of Wordsworth, Scott, Dickens, Austin,

Eliot, Hardy, and Thackeray. W.D. had in his library his reading chair, sofa, desk, and in barrister's bookcases stacked one over the other, volumes of American history, geography, economics, biographies of famous American men, and an 1881 twelve-volume leather-bound limited edition of the biographies of famous European men written by France and England's notable authors, among them Thackeray, Lamartine, Arnold, Macaulay, Michelet, Gibbon, and Carlyle.

A watercolor of an exotic Middle Eastern rug market, a colored engraving of a poised aristocratic young Englishwoman seated beside her dog in a sylvan landscape, and a large chromo litho of a bleak domestic interior where a worn working-class European American grandfather sits, pipe in mouth, gazing abstractly at the doll in his granddaughter's arms provided evidence of an American eclecticism, self–assurance, and broad interests of the inhabitants. Friends and visitors dropped calling cards in the small silver dish in the entrance hall.

The home supported a harmonious, class-conscious, sentimental view of the world. While tragedies abounded and death and heart-sickness were as

The W.D. Connor home, Marshfield, ca. 1900.

bountiful in song and story as everyone knew them to be in life, a pattern held during Helen's formative years, an old notion of redemption, of life as a continuum related in the end to an overarching, orderly, and hopeful scheme. Difficulties could be overcome; the good and the reasonable were related and, in the end, triumphant.

Home was the center of life for the Connors. From that center they all traveled, W.D. most of all. Helen wrote Mame on March 28, 1900, "We all got up at 5:45 because papa went away at 7:15. I have all of my practicing in and Donald has ten minutes more to put in. Last week we did go to Milwaukee and had an awfully good time. While we were there Aunt Mollie got me a lovely little cape and a Tamoshanter cap. My cape cost five dollars and cap one dollar. . . . Aunt Anne went to Chicago Monday night."

Helen already understood the importance of keeping records—and that money was not to be taken for granted. She also had a clear sense of her family's standing and no insecurity about her place in the democratic, but nonetheless class-conscious society. Assigned by her teacher to write an expository

Helen, ca. 1902. "I do not set the table. The girl does it."

composition, "The Setting of a Table," she began: "In setting a table, I have but little difficulty. I seldom do it for the cook or other girl does it. You use silver, knapkins, china, chairs, table, table-cloth, and edibles. The girl has charge of it or is engaged in it."[5] Having properly located herself in the social hierarchy, desiring to be accurate, she went on to carefully describe the task she had no interest in or need to undertake.

Her teachers taught technical skills, instilled patriotism, and indoctrinated moral "truths." In the sixth grade she parsed difficult sentences: "If we do not plant knowledge when young, it will give us no shade when we are old"; "To know by rote is no knowledge; it is only a retention of what is intrusted to the memory"; "What a man truly knows may be disposed of without regard to the author, or reference to the book whence he had it." She could recite the poem "The Battle of Trenton," which told of the band of half-clothed, starving, patriot soldiers who followed America's "loved and honored leader" and write a practical business letter.

Box 315
Providence, R.I.
May 21, 1900

Mr. L. Mason,
Sharon, Mass.

Sir:
Seeing your advertisement I write to inquire farther.
    I would like to know the exact cost. Are there any modern improvements on the farm?
    Please write and locate the farm as near as possible.
Yours respectfully,
Edward Poorman

By the time she was twelve, Helen understood that men could be heroic, that men conducted business, that a man in search of property kept his worth to himself. Men achieved while women looked on. Yet, while she and her friend Fanny Cole could not join the boys' Cuban Cadets club and play soldier, they were invited to play baseball because they could run and hit and didn't act silly.

Like most of his neighbors, W.D. kept riding and carriage horses in the large stable adjacent to his home. Helen often rode to Auburndale with him, where, at the Connors' 1,300-acre farm, he raised crops, cattle, and the Clydesdales he needed for woods work as well as the prize animals he showed at national and international fairs. A judge of oratorical contests and of the free-trotting and carriage racing events at the Marshfield fair, he taught her how to sharpen a speech and why one animal or team was superior to another.

In spite of her enthusiasm for horses and baseball, Helen was no tomboy. She helped her mother with chores at home, helped care for her younger siblings, and practiced the piano dutifully. She was not good with a needle, but neither was her mother. She watched how Mame administered aid, drawing on the limited tools in the black doctor's bag her father gave her, and the way she opened her purse to those needing that kind of help.

The church was central to her life. Years later, when asked by the congregation to "turn back the wheels of time" and speak about her girlhood memories of the "old church," Helen said she remembered the Bible school classes Mrs. Hinman, Mrs. Rewey, and Mrs. Brown gave and longing to be old enough to be a teacher herself. She remembered people sitting in the same pews every Sunday, Mrs. Upham's "pretty bonnets and dresses," the midweek prayer services she attended with her mother, "the thrill of certain Christmas Eves," Mrs. Riley "in times of trouble about the neighborhood quietly taking charge of things," and Mr. Elvis, who seemed "such a cultured gentleman."[6]

W.D. believed in the essential function of religion to provide an organizational foundation and ideal of conduct in national and family life, but he was not a religious man. He depended on Helen's mother to take religion seriously, to faithfully follow the commandments, to exemplify Christian virtue in her behavior, and to teach the moral consciousness. Secure in her faith and truly believing, Mame guided her daughter; by word and action, Helen's father also guided her.

From their parents the Connor children received a schizophrenic education, their world split between the real, dominated by aggressive egoism where the prize was private, personal, and worldly, and the ideal, where ego surrender gave a different prize: community, continuity, transcendence. Throughout her adult life, Helen sought to achieve harmony, to balance the reasonable and the ideal elements within herself. She yearned for the ideal but enjoyed the power of a "masculine" mind and developed a rapier's wit, like her father's, to express her observations of hard and tangled realities.

When Helen was young, reality was not so tangled. She accepted her parents' different spheres of activity, saw no essential discord, and observed that both worked hard. She saw that her mother was pleased with her life, with her home and children—which by 1900 included not only Helen and Donald but Marian Elizabeth, William Duncan, and Richard Malcolm—and with her association with other educated women. While W.D. never played a character in anyone's script but his own, Mame was an enthusiastic thespian, a great reader, and very sociable. In Marshfield, she had a chance to exercise her considerable talents as a member of the Ladies' Travel Class, where all the travel was mental. The close-knit group of educated women[7] carefully prepared for meetings by studying ancient and medieval history; the Renaissance; eighteenth-century Italy, Germany, Austria, Bavaria, and Russia. They gave book reports. Mame delivered one on *Anna Karenina*, a book she would not allow in her home because it was immoral, and another on the works of Schiller. They dressed in costumes and presented scenes from plays. They formed opinions, one being that American citizens differed from the ancients because "today no one man makes the history of his time. The ancients were like a flock of geese—one mind led many—therefore were centered the epoch around the man of greatest influence."[8] They enjoyed debating. Mame argued successfully for the affirmative on the proposition "Russian nihilism considered as a political movement is unjustifiable."

While they took themselves seriously as students of history, the women did not think of themselves as making history. Nonetheless, they believed that through their united efforts they could achieve some social good. For Helen, as a twelve-year-old, it was a great lesson when the Travel Class pushed for a public library. The women had well-stocked personal libraries. They could get along borrowing each others' books, but in 1900 they decided the time had come to build and support a public library. Committed to a society based on ability rather than birth, with social improvement their goal and no federal government interested in providing it, they were convinced that a public library in a public building would benefit not only those "of leisure and education, but those of all classes, occupation and conditions." The results of a library would be far reaching, "leavening for the whole lump, . . . an intellectual and moral salvation."

W.D., an immediate and principal benefactor of the project, promised to support the free public library movement to the tune of $2,500 a year for five years if the city organized a Public Library Board according to state law. He hoped that the board would "make an effort to furnish the library with a fair supply of the class of books that are attractive to the children of our city."[9] The mayor quickly established the necessary board, appointing W.D. and his friends and neighbors Dr. H. Wahle, Dr. K. W. Doege, E. E. Winch, and J. F. Cole to the board. Mrs. W. H. Upham was the sole representative from the Ladies' Travel Class. W.D. was unanimously elected president, a position he held for ten years. And in 1900, his star rose even higher, and not only in his daughter's eyes, when he also became president of the Wood County

School Board. Public honors went to W.D., but both of Helen's able parents provided powerful models for her. She inherited their commitment to education, their sense of "noblesse oblige," and their leadership drive.

Having succeeded in their quest to establish Marshfield's public library,[10] in 1901 the women decided on a motto for their club: "They can, who think they can."

# CHAPTER 4

❧

# *Laona*

It is rare, in this world of trouble that such an apparently ideal and happy state of existence is without a canker.

—WINSTON CHURCHILL

Public displays of guns and drunkenness had all but disappeared from Marshfield by 1902. When W.D.'s good-looking brother Rob, a self-styled "jollier," brought his bride, Florence Glasner, to town and proclaimed he was finished with his "nomadic life" and the "long winter evenings spent out in the woods somewhere wrapped in a fur coat," and would henceforth be a "true man" and spend his evenings "before the grate" with his wife by his side,[1] the town was as prosperous and tidy as he declared he had become. Further north, in Forest County, white man's civilization had made few inroads. "Criminal statutes" were "not very dangerous to the criminals and the criminal class knows it," and impoverished Potawatomies, many of them tubercular, still lived in the woods and tracked through settlements on ponies, males in front and females behind.[2]

Nonetheless, every summer, beginning at the turn of the century, when W.D. constructed a summer cottage on the western shore of Birch Lake, the Connor family left Wood County for Forest County's cool northwoods. A boxcar loaded with riding horses, ponies, chickens, a couple of pigs, a milk cow, family pets, and several trunks full of clothes, linens, blankets, and plated silver preceded them. While the Connors eagerly looked forward to the yearly migration, their hired girls reluctantly went along. Most had never left home before. For them the deep woods and the isolation were terrifying. The pearl-handled revolver Mame kept was not reassuring.

Built in the midst of virgin pines and hemlocks at the water's edge, W.D.'s white clapboard cottage was comfortable, big enough to accommodate the large family, hired girls and hired man, and guests but not at all ostentatious. W.D. had a porch constructed around the second floor "in anticipation of a large number of visitors who were going to be there for some time and the porch was divided into three rooms and it worked out fairly good. Of course, it was true that the occupants of the porch had to climb through the window out of the different rooms."[3] Mame never complained about the lack of doors onto the sleeping porches, or even the lack of a decent step. She didn't go out there, and the young people, who did, never complained that the only way to get there was by stepping on a chunk of wood and climbing through the window. When it rained, which it often did, they dropped awnings to keep themselves dry.

The older generation slept in proper bedrooms in massive mahogany beds with chamber pots conveniently and discretely located beneath, and Meaken ironstone bowls and pitchers full of ice-cold, mineral-laden well water were at hand for washing up. In the early 1900s, the Connors's city house had indoor plumbing; the country house did not. An outhouse and an icehouse, where great chunks of ice were stored in burlap and covered with sawdust, stood not far from the cabin. No one went out there late at night.

Mame served tea to members of the Presbyterian Ladies' Club and watermelon to the Potawatomi chief Shabodock whenever he paid one of his regular visits to the lake, sometimes with a good pony or some beadwork to sell. If a tramp, walking the Cavour military road, which ran behind the cottage, stopped for a handout, he invariably got it in food not money. W.D. greeted visitors as though he were a politician running for office—which he, in fact, became. Everyone admired his flowers—the magnificent red ones that were his favorites; the salvia, cannas, and geraniums planted near the large vegetable garden in the clearing at the water's edge at the end of the sandy road through the thick woods; and the long trail of flowers leading to the cottage. They were signs of care and cultivation in the wilderness.

Occasionally, when the weather was fine, following the custom of the lumber barons, W.D. provided his foremen and their families diversion while ensuring their loyalty, taking them for leisurely rides about the lake in his excursion boat. Powered by an industrial Chrysler motor with long wooden benches on either side, the boat seated thirty people. The boat house, built on piers, stood a few feet from the cottage.

The children paddled about in wooden rowboats or canvas-covered canoes. They and their parents fished from the shore with long bamboo poles. The children swam, but W.D., who usually left running house and children up to Mame, ordered them never to swim alone, after meals, in the cold or the rain, after five o'clock, or for too long. (He believed Marian had contracted polio because she had stayed in the water too long.)

W.D was a gentle and devoted father, soft spoken before Mame and the children. His word was, nonetheless, law, and he was as confident that he knew what was best for his family as he was certain of his judgment in business, where the vocabulary shifted to strong and expletive laden. (William recalled the shock he experienced one day when his father forgot his presence while speaking to another lumberman, Mr. Flanner, about the killing they were making in the shingle market. He had never heard such language at home, and he never would.)

Donald and Helen rode horses deep into the woods along trails richly carpeted with pine needles dropped by the trees towering over a hundred feet above them and down the sand-covered trail to town to pick up provisions at their father's store or mail at the post office located inside. They did not socialize with the town's children but played with one another and the summer guests, friends, and relatives who came, as W.D. anticipated they would,

After church, Laona, 1904. Standing, from left: Florence, Robert Connor's wife; three unidentified women; Helen, holding parasol; W.D. In front: Marian, Donald, Mame, and Dr. George Witter. The little girl is Katty Connor, Rob's daughter, and Richard and William Connor are beside her.

for extended stays. In the evenings, Mame played the piano brought out from the hotel, and everyone sang. She may have been a poor housekeeper, as Rob told his bride (probably because Mame had admonished him sternly to be a "KIND, faithful husband"), but she kept a happy home.

Children and guests joined in taffy pulls and in making the ice cream that took so much effort and vanished so quickly. They picnicked on the island, with W.D. occasionally joining them and making his special "cannonball eggs," so called because the eggs, cracked and dropped into the pan half-full of grease, came out round. The children explored the island from end to end picking wild raspberries and blackberries along the way. They watched eagles circling the lake looking for prey, returning finally to their high nests, observed their long wooden dock jutting far into the water and their cottage white and secure, hugging the shore, the only house among the towering trees.

Wary of sudden, violent storms, no one ventured far from shore when the weather was uncertain, which it often was, but on fine evenings Helen and Donald happily went along with Mr. Harris, a Scotsman and W.D.'s cruiser, who took them on overnight pack trips to the Oconto and Peshtigo Rivers. He knew how to spread a bed of pine branches and make them comfortable by a cheering fire under a brilliant canopy of stars. On rainy days they made balsam pillows from the needles of the boughs the hired man brought in, and puzzles, games, and books came out. While Donald picked up his father's interest in biography and autobiography and read about Napoleon, Lincoln, and Grant and the younger children worked through the "Twin" series (*The Eskimo Twins, The Scottish Twins, The Chinese Twins),* Helen and her mother read the enormously popular novels of the prolific, socially prominent American author Winston Churchill: *Richard Carvel, Mr. Crewe's Career, Coniston.*

Largely addressed to middle-class women of leisure, but also read by many men, including President Teddy Roosevelt and historian John Ford Rhodes, Churchill's entertaining and keenly observed descriptive early novels reveal a central issue of the day: the tension in American society between ideal social behavior as exemplified by the heroines, who invariably live in great estates on the eastern seaboard and are beautiful, intelligent, Christian women who represent the spiritual aspect of human life and wish to serve the larger social good, and the behavior of the aggressive men they love, who represent society's increasing materialism and selfishness. In the novels an occasional "good" man, reflecting principles set down by the Founding Fathers, also acts as foil to the self-serving, power-hungry men—the politicians, businessmen, railroad magnates—with whom the women are associated. As Churchill's plots unfold, the anguished heroine discovers the ruthless behavior of her beloved. Her distress finally enables him to perceive the folly and wickedness of his ways. Raising the loved one's social consciousness, the heroine succeeds in reestablishing basic principles of decent social behavior. American virtue and idealism are restored, selfish individualism abandoned, male and female and national unity reaffirmed.

While the Connor women immersed themselves in Churchill's novels on rainy days at Birch Lake, another saga, paralleling to an astonishing degree Churchill's fictional accounts of tensions in eastern society, unfolded in the Middle West. Unbeknownst to them, W.D. played the prototypical male role in the Connors's own "Churchillian" story in Forest County.

The idyllic summers Helen experienced at the lake in that magical time of faith and possibility, before the First World War, when she was a teenager and became a young woman, reflected one reality. Life in the mill and the town, little more than a mile away, reflected another.

Harry Messer, and his fun-loving wife, W.D.'s sister, Agnes (Ick), a favorite among the hard-working lumberjacks and mill hands, lived year-round in the rough, frontier community overseeing the work and joining in the little entertainment there was. Messer, whom W.D. not only made manager of the Laona operation and a member of the board of the R. Connor Company but a member of the Laona town board and postmaster of the unincorporated village, "forgot his obligations to W.D. and the company and made the mistake of listening to the sweet music that came from Sargent—a shrewd fellow—and his bar room." Sargent saw the money Connor was making in timber, wanted to move into the business himself, and persuaded Messer to join him in bidding against W.D. for a tract of timberland. When W.D. learned about it, "even though he knew there would be hard feelings in the family, he knocked Messer out of the company."[4]

Sargent's son tells another version. "Everyone knew W.D. was timber land crazy and bought all that the traffic would bear," and he had had the opportunity to buy the tract but declined. Messer and Sargent then joined to purchase the four-hundred-odd acres of timberland from the railroad company. They had not owned the land long before Messer came to Sargent. "He said that W.D. was madder than a wet hen because he had bought that land in his own name" and begged Sargent to buy him out, which Sargent did, accepting a quit claim from Messer.

Papers were soon served on Sargent "to the effect that he held certain land, timber, etc. illegally and same must be deeded over to the Connor Lumber and Land Company pronto." The document was typewritten, on legal-sized paper, bound and stapled to a cover, but it had not been notarized. Recognizing it as a bluff, but not wishing to cross W.D., Sargent did as he was instructed and deeded the land over to the Connor Lumber and Land Company. That did not put things right between the men.

When Sargent opened a blacksmith shop and started to sell furnaces and hot water heating systems, Connor moved in on him, putting in a full line of machinery at the company store and driving Sargent out of business. "Why did W.D. Connor do this to us? It was the consensus of opinion that Len Sargent was getting too big for Laona, and had to be cut down and destroyed like Connor would cut down a scrub tree that was in the way." When an explosion occurred in the liquor room in the basement of the hotel where Sargent had stored the packages left by two strangers who said they were walking to Crandon, and burned the hotel almost killing Mrs. Sargent, the Sargents stayed around only long enough to sell their farms and lots to the Connor company.[5]

W.D.'s son Gordon said of his father: "He knew men, recognizing their strength and weakness. Great satisfaction came to him through teaching and encouraging a lesser man and no greater disappointment than when that man might fail him." In Laona people put it more simply: "If you didn't go his way, you didn't go."[6]

CHAPTER 5

∾

# A Meeting of Titans

## Robert La Follette and W.D. Connor

A busy, clever useful man, who has been at work all his life, finds that his own progress towards success demands from him that he shall be a politician.

—ANTHONY TROLLOPE

Helen was fifteen when politics began to dominate life in the Connor home. During the 1890s, W.D. had been a minor and "safe" member of the Republican Party led by business-oriented Stalwarts Charles F. Pfister, John Coit Spooner, and Henry Clay Payne. He attended state conventions, and as chairman of the enormous Eighth Congressional district, which spanned almost all of central and northeastern Wisconsin,[1] he supplied the Republican Central Committee with lists of "the doubtful, the careless and the stay at home voters" and lists of superintendents of lumber and mining camps, who could instruct the men on how to vote. Following the depression and panic of 1893, when public outrage over the appalling treatment of labor was running high, he organized the distribution "to workers who could read" of *Milwaukee Sentinel* articles exposing "the hypocrisy of democratic concern for the wage earners." In 1896, hoping to sway "doubtful Germans" to the Republican camp, his agents distributed German- language copies of the eloquent speeches calling for reform written by the well-known German American Republican Carl Schurz. An impressive orator himself, W.D. assisted on the stump in that campaign and again in 1898.

Until 1903 he took no side in the increasingly heated battle between the two competing factions of the Republican Party: the conservative Stalwarts bent on maintaining entrenched privileges and the insurgent Half-Breeds bent on reforms. When, in his third run for governor, Robert La Follette picked up the popular issue of railroad reform and led a well-publicized regulation crusade,[2] W.D.'s interests and La Follette's merged. He was at his most eloquent as he explained to his family why he was going to Neillsville to meet with La Follette and offer his services to the reformers.

As a newcomer in the state's millionaire club, and as yet having insufficient political pull, his bid for regular rail service into Laona had been rejected. As he explained to La Follette and his family, he could not develop his business in Forest County with "one irregular train a day with inexact number of cars." He had been "extremely fortunate" in being able to secure credit with which to build the seventeen miles of his own road at a cost of $10,000 per mile, "enabling us to retain our manufacturing business and remain free and independent citizens without submitting to any arbitrary dictation from any source or be driven from the field by deplorable service furnished by railroad companies which administer their service often in very peculiar economy regardless of the wishes or the success or failure of the people who are so absolutely dependent on railroad transportation." (He did not explain that his good fortune in securing credit came about because he controlled three banks.)

The high-handedness of the Chicago and Northwestern galled W.D., who was not one "to lie down to be walked over by the crushing combination."[3] In the railroad's response to him he perceived a personal affront and an outrageous social injustice. The thirty-four hours it took him to cover the two hundred rail miles from Marshfield to Laona gave him "time for reflection." He studied the issue and learned that the company had received a grant of every odd numbered section from the government "way back in 1864," that the road had not been built until 1899, that the grant was "of sufficient value today to build and equip at least one double-track road between Laona and Milwaukee," that "the company sold millions of feet of the choicest kind of timber off this immense tract of land long before they ever thought of building a railroad through the grant, [and that] they were not compelled to construct the road until they got ready." Moreover, with the Chicago and Northwestern owning "so large a proportion of land and timber, no other railroad would care to enter the territory and independent land owners were obliged to let their lands lay idle and the development of all that portion of the state wait the pleasure of the railroad holding the grant."[4]

Enthralled by the history her father recounted, and his determination to undo the railroad's tyrannical control, Helen saw him as a hero, a challenger of the status quo, a spokesman for democratic progress. W. H. Chynoweth, a former member of the University of Wisconsin Board of Regents and La Follette's "undaunted, immovable, legal adviser and heavy hitter,"[5] saw the slender, quiet, soft-spoken man with the piercing blue eyes, the bowler hat, and mysterious air as someone who could be useful.[6] Recognized for his phenomenal success in large business enterprises, Connor could give the lie to the charge that La Follette was antibusiness. On May 17, 1904, the *Wisconsin State Journal* announced: "W.D. Connor, the Marshfield millionaire, is the choice of the Governor for the position of chairman of the Republican State Central Committee."

W.D. was not offering himself free of charge. For his money and his service he anticipated a reward, the same reward sought by his fellow Scotsman, the aged multimillionaire lumber king from Marinette, Isaac Stephenson: a seat in the U.S. Senate, a prize granted at that time not by popular vote but by vote of the legislature, whose members could be expected to follow the directions of the majority party's leader. If La Follette won, he would make W.D. a senator. He had La Follette's word for it, and told family and friends that he would be heading for Washington, D.C.[7]

From May until December 1904, Connor, "an expert manipulator of men and measures,"[8] worked tirelessly on behalf of Governor La Follette and his programs: to provide for direct primary elections of candidates, to regulate the railroads, to reform taxes. Helen enlisted in the cause, carrying La Follette posters across town and putting them up everywhere, even on the tree in Fanny Cole's front yard, in spite of the fact that (or perhaps because) the Coles were active Stalwarts. The ideals and goals were noble, but the campaign of 1904 was "the most villainous and disgraceful political campaign on record in the State of Wisconsin."[9]

The party split. It held two conventions, presented two slates of delegates to the national convention, two slates of candidates for state office. Connor spent his money, set up "the most careful organization of the state ever known in its history,"[10] and secured an unprecedented publicity campaign for the Half-Breed cause. In the pamphlets he distributed, written in English, Italian, Polish, German, and Norwegian, and in the speeches he made throughout the state, W.D. hammered through La Follette's message: this was the most important campaign that had yet taken place in Wisconsin; the future of the party of Lincoln, Grant, McKinley, and Roosevelt was at stake; issues in Wisconsin had become national issues, and Wisconsin was leading the way. "The rest of the country is awaiting the outcome," claimed the *Eureka Californian.*[11]

He traveled to Washington, D.C., to plead, unsuccessfully, the legitimacy of the Half-Breed cause to President Roosevelt,[12] and he caused a sensation at the party's national convention in Chicago when, observing the impossibility of getting the Half-Breed delegation recognized in the face of intransigent Stalwarts, he dramatically withdrew without a challenge.[13] He set up Half-Breed offices in Madison and Milwaukee, wrote and distributed a two-thousand-word "Statement of Facts" describing the events of the national convention, the Stalwart falsification of facts. He fought the Stalwart faction on his home

turf by initiating legal proceedings "to prevent the fostering upon the munic-
ipality [of Marshfield]—at a munificent price of $150,000—of a water works
and an electric light plant considered to be worth about $40,000." The whole
plant, including the land, had been on the assessment rolls valued at less than
five thousand dollars. He charged that the deal had been "worked through the
city council largely through the aid of E. E. Finney, former Governor Upham's
son-in-law, a member of the city council and the board of works."[14] (The alle-
gation of corruption against the old Stalwart Upham, a good friend of Charles
Pfister, owner and publisher of the Stalwarts' *Milwaukee Sentinel*, probably
caused the liver attack and cold the former governor suffered in the summer
of 1904. Mary Upham attributed her husband's six weeks of illness to "business worries . . . and the sinfulness of it all evidenced."[15]) In September, W.D.
made a sensational appearance, pleading the Half-Breed case before the Wisconsin Supreme Court. Quietly, firmly, holding the delegate count, he convincingly presented the legitimacy of the Half-Breed claim that they represented
the majority interests of the Republican Party of Wisconsin.

The Stalwarts withdrew their candidates.[16] On October 12, W.D. received
a telegram from the National Committee affirming "the La Follette organization as the regular one in Wisconsin" and requesting him to prepare for the
reception of Vice President Charles W. Fairbanks.[17]

In November, when La Follette won the governorship and control of the
legislature, he guardedly acknowledged his debt to W.D. "You have conducted
a clean, able campaign, remarkable for thoroughness and freedom from error.
You successfully applied your wide experience in business to the field of politics. I congratulate you most heartily and express without reserve my profound obligation to you for the great personal sacrifices you have made to our
cause."[18]

Chynoweth gave Connor greater credit for his "great victory over overwhelming odds."

> I do not think that it is or will be thoroughly understood as to the fullness of
> the conquest. I know that your best efforts have been directed toward the elec-
> tion of the governor, and when you understand that the money and every influ-
> ence of not only the railroad companies but the insurance, and other wealthy
> corporations have been sent out to encompass his defeat, it is indeed almost
> beyond belief that you should have carried him through with 60,000 plurality.
> I don't believe that any such campaign has heretofore been carried on in this
> state, or that anywhere near such results have been accomplished by anyone else.
> We all owe you a debt of lasting gratitude.

The 60,000 plurality of votes "means the absolute control of the state.[19]

La Follette was now in the position to determine Senator V. Quarles's successor. Newspaper reports, perhaps leaked by Connor, that La Follette favored him immediately began circulating.[20] People in Marshfield "firmly believed that Mr. Connor is a candidate for the Senate." In December, an article published in the *Milwaukee Sentinel* struck the only cautious note: "Up to this time in the senatorial campaign now progressing . . . in their Sphinx-like attitude, Chairman Connor can be compared to Governor La Follette. These two master politicians, either from design or because of a possible conflict in ambitions, coupled with the uncertainty of their power to accomplish their purposes, distrust political conjecture. . . . While discussing Connor as a senatorial possibility, it may as well be said here, that he is the enigma of Wisconsin politics."[21]

On December 15, 1904, Connor dined with La Follette's private secretary, Colonel John Hannon, at the Plankinton house in Milwaukee. On January 2, 1905, Mr. and Mrs. Connor attended the victory celebration at the inaugural ball. "The crush in the rear of the hall was so great that W.D. Connor was heard to mutter that he was more than ever impressed with the advantages of a good wire fence."[22] On January 6, Mrs. Connor assisted Mrs. La Follette at an informal reception held at the executive mansion in Madison.

Mrs. La Follette "would not claim that in meeting the exigencies of politics, Bob was always consistent."[23] In pursuing his personal ambitions, however, he was. On January 25, the friendship between the Connors and the La Follettes and the spirit of unity in the Half-Breed camp came to an abrupt end. Less than a month into his new administration, La Follette accepted the appointment to the United States Senate. Although he declared that he would not leave the state before seeing his legislative program through to a successful conclusion, Connor and Stephenson, rejected suitors for the same seat, were not impressed. La Follette, in his "all consuming ambition to rise as high as he possibly could,"[24] had betrayed them both. The elderly lumberman turned to words: "the bitter experience cost me many an illusion—perhaps the greatest loss I had sustained—and shook my faith in human kind."[25] Connor, in the full flower of a vibrant middle age, returned to his many business responsibilities as president of the R. Connor Company, the Connor Lumber and Land Company, and the American National Bank of Marshfield and as director of the First National Bank of Stevens Point and director and vice-president of the Consolidated Water and Power Company.[26] He resumed his civic responsibilities as president of the Marshfield Free Library, member of the Marshfield School Board, trustee and treasurer of the Wood County training school for teachers, and trustee of Carroll College, a Presbyterian institution. And he plotted his revenge.

A junior in high school in 1905, and trained by her parents to think clearly and speak well, to anticipate the day, which was surely coming, when women would vote, Helen followed her father's triumph and his loss. Dressed in the costume of the day—the highly starched, cinch-waist ankle-length dresses with hand-crocheted collars and layers of petticoats and sporting fine gold rings on her small hands, with her thick, naturally wavy hair tied behind with a wide satin bow—she was both a model of ideal, privileged femininity and an earnest, questioning person whose firm jaw belied her identification with the gentler sex. Like her father, who liked to confide in her, her mind held many chambers.

Her school compositions anticipated her lifelong interests in women's role, politics, civic responsibility, religion, and nature. Her lyrical essay "Spring in Wisconsin" reflects every Wisconsinite's love of spring. Two other essays, one on women and the other on religion, reflect her belief in social progress. She celebrated traditional feminine virtues but also women who found their way into a man's world: Joan of Arc, the "quiet, unassuming maiden," who led an army and suffered martyrdom; the women during the American revolution who installed "lofty ideals in manly beings" and took the part of men when occasion demanded, hoeing the fields, driving the herds, arming themselves with guns and ammunition, pitchforks and shovels. When she grappled with a dominant turn-of-the-century issue, religion, she again took a historical per-spective, noting that while Thomas Jefferson's age was one of "narrowness in religious matters," Jefferson was determined to say nothing of his religion, declaring it a matter between himself and God. "The evidence of a person's religion should be found in his or her life," Helen declared.

Her oration against trusts, "the greatest evil of the day," reflects not only her mastery of the cadences of her father's speeches but her absorption and identification with his present goals. She quoted from Washington's farewell address: "However combinations may now and then answer popular ends they are likely in the course of time and things to become patent engines by which cunning ambitious and unprincipled men will be enabled to subvert the power of the people and to usurp the reins of government for themselves." People had to act against the trusts, or the day would soon come when "the very basis of our government will be swept away and the power in this coun-try in the hands of a few to wield it as they wish." At the time Helen was wax-ing eloquent about the danger of ambitious men usurping power from the people, the Chicago and Northwestern, acknowledging that W.D. had become a significant political power in Wisconsin, quietly granted him an impressive 25 percent rebate on his shipping out of his Wabeno mill in Forest County to Chicago.[27] While Helen had no knowledge of this development, she learned from La Follette's broken promise to her father that some politicians, as well as some businessmen, might act unscrupulously.

While W.D.'s split with La Follette was whispered about in inner Republican circles (much to the delight of the Stalwart camp), he continued to deny it publicly. His family, however, saw that his anger had shifted from his former desire to wreck revenge on the railroad to a desire to thwart La Follette's ambitions.

With La Follette heading for the U.S. Senate, the governorship would be open in 1906. Irvine Lenroot, a young Swedish lawyer from Superior, and La Follette's choice to succeed him, approached W.D. in July asking for a meeting with him and "our friends." W.D. replied in a four-page letter that was at once cordial and subtly threatening, touching on the possibility that he might be ready to break with the Half-Breeds and letting Lenroot know that he could count on the support in his district should Lenroot decide to run for Congress. There was, W.D. pointed out, "considerable talk over the state regarding the future of our organization. The problem is . . . to hold our forces together in common understanding in order that no chance may be offered the opposition to get a new foot-hold in the state." He then touched on the most sensitive area. Having been told by "many of our friends" that they were for him, and that he should be candidate for governor, W.D. had just about concluded that he indeed should be, but he wanted to have a conference with Lenroot and the governor before deciding. He knew, he added pointedly, that "the governor is out of the state much of the time," but W.D.'s "aim for the party will be that which will strengthen and make more lasting and complete, if that is possible, the results of the work that has been originated and carried to such success up to the present time by the governor and friends."[28] It was a brilliant, foxy letter and was bound to trouble La Follette.

The relationship between Connor and La Follette, who in more congenial times recited Robert Burns's poetry to one another,[29] remained publicly unclear until December. Then, during a special session called by the governor, Connor succeeded in blocking La Follette's desired legislation to amend the newly passed Primary Law to allow for an alternate choice. Pulling on all the opponents of the administration—Stalwarts, Democrats, and Social Democrats—and gaining defections by senators La Follette had counted on,[30] W.D. succeeded in killing the measure.

On December 15, 1905, the *Milwaukee Sentinel* headlined Connor's victory and La Follette's defeat: "Connor Wins First Fight. Is The New Leader. Becomes Head of Opposition to Dictatorship and Scores Big Victory." The defeat of the "Mary Ann" bill (a derisive label hung on the measure to suggest it allowed men to behave like women who couldn't make up their minds) was "the first blood for Chairman Connor." On that date *Fond du Lac Reporter* printed a "special" from Madison: "The defeat of the 'Mary Ann' bill . . . points out clearly that Chairman W.D. Connor of the Republican State Central Committee is no longer an instrument in the political movement of Governor and Senator Robert M. La Follette. . . . It is evident that he does not like the treatment he has received at the hands of the governor." The *Milwaukee Wisconsin* broke a front-page story the next day: "Connor declares war personally upon the chief executive—says he was treated unfairly."

Reporters had overheard an angry conversation in the governor's office. Wagging fingers at one another, the outraged La Follette claimed that he did not think it right or fair of Connor to use the means at his command as state chairman to defeat a measure desired by the administration while an equally enraged Connor indignantly replied that he had as much right as a citizen to work and use his influence to protect his interests as La Follette as governor had to work and advance his. Connor claimed that the bill was an attempt on La Follette's part "to shuffle him out of the cut" so that he would be ruled out of the game. "You told me six years ago, Governor La Follette, and you repeated it four years ago, that I was the shrewdest political observer in the state of Wisconsin. Do you remember? Well, I am just as shrewd now as I was then and I have learned a great many things since that time. I told you then and I have repeated it since, that unless you treated me fairly, you would rue it. Now perhaps you realize what I meant."

If he wanted an elective office himself—and he did—W.D. could not be seen as the enemy of the governor he had helped to elect. His break with La Follette was final, but again he denied allegations of a split. He had not, he told reporters, been in Madison to defeat the governor's primary amendment; he had not gone to see the governor for any other reason than to pay his respects.[31]

Helen's father was famous. Journalists hung on his words. He might be devious, but he was always quotable. Christmas at the Connors was more festive than usual in 1905, not only because of W.D.'s victory over La Follette but because Mame had delivered another son, Gordon Robert Phelps. Born on December 12, in the midst of W.D.'s intense preoccupation with Madison politics, child and mother were thriving. The family's oldest daughter observed her parents' disparate roles, listened to her father, helped her mother, and felt enormously proud of them both.

CHAPTER 6

❧

# Business, Politics, and Family

## 1906–1907

The faith of Americans in their own country is religious. . . . It pervades the air we breathe. . . . We may distrust and dislike much, but our country itself, its democratic system, and its prosperous future are above suspicion.

—HERBERT CROWLEY

During the winter of 1906, a terrible winter for logging, with only three feet of snow on the level and no frost in the ground, when seven hundred men at W.D.'s Laona camps with a hundred team of horses could only bring in 350,000 board feet a day instead of the usual half-million, W.D. went north to oversee his operations in Forest County and weigh his chances while rumors circulated that he was or was not in the gubernatorial race.[1] La Follette's decision to ignore the natural prior claims of his loyal and popular Norwegian Lieutenant Governor James Davidson and to back Irvine Lenroot became public knowledge, causing yet again turmoil in Republican ranks.

W.D. had not made up his mind by mid-April when, exhausted and in need of a holiday, he took his family for a fortnight's vacation to Hot Springs, Arkansas. There he put the finishing touches on a speech he had been asked to deliver in Milwaukee on May 15, when Republicans gathered for the annual Lincoln Day dinner. Reflecting on his chances, recognizing that if he challenged Davidson, and three candidates entered the primary La Follette's man would win, he decided to join Davidson's team and run as his lieutenant governor. He would then be in line for the governorship or a seat in the U.S. Senate. He planned to make his decision public after delivering his speech.

The Lincoln Day address thrilled Helen and surprised his all-male audience. "Silent William Connor" could talk. "In one brief hour or less, he lost the title of sphinx of the Wisconsin Republicans," a title that had been "a misnomer."[2] Beginning with an overview of American history, he declared that each epoch "has been characterized by some mighty achievement which has brought about a better government, broader ideas of citizenship, greater liberty to the people and a firmer conviction in the minds of thinking men the world over that the American republic is a permanent institution."

W.D. Connor, "The Sphinx of the Republican Party," ca. 1906.

He struck a theme that permanently embedded itself in Helen's mind. Evil had crept into the national system because the people "absorbed in clearing forests, opening up new agricultural districts and establishing industrial enterprises" had been "more or less indifferent to the affairs of the country." Yet nothing was more vital to the Republic than "a citizenry committed to taking a personal interest in the affairs of the city, state and nation."[3]

Having spoken of the need for a vigilant, participatory citizenry, the need for a civil service and for a respect for the law and the courts, Connor, an insider in the world of corporate structures who understood that as "corporations" men almost routinely abandon the moral standards they claim to hold, cautioned the State of Wisconsin not to issue or set its great seal of approval on charters granting companies the opportunity of doing business in the state without restrictions. "Beautifully engraved certificates of stock with gilded borders, bearing the seal of incorporation, can be made mighty attractive to the investor by agents receiving large commissions for disposing of the shares. The officers of the company may be wealthy and prominent citizens and while the corporation has been authorized by the state [upon simple payment of a small sum into the state treasury] that very authority, relieves the individual from legal responsibility."

Like handsome John Allan, an ancestor on his mother's side, a Scottish Chartist repeatedly imprisoned in the late 1830s and early 1840s for speaking out at large open-air gatherings, demanding repeal of the Corn Laws and fairer labor conditions,[4] Connor could hold an audience. La Follette had good reason to be concerned, and Helen thought she had good reason to regard her father as a man of heroic stature. An idealistic young woman, she took him at his word.

Two weeks after delivering his address, which friendly newspapers claimed made him not only a find as an after-dinner speaker but "the new power in Wisconsin politics,"[5] W.D. attended her high school graduation. As the school's outstanding student in English and history, Helen delivered the first oration, "The Noblest of Shakespeare's Heroes," a study of the character of Hamlet. The prince, she asserted, "was a conflicted individual [who] could not reconcile the idea of revenge with the divine law of which he was a student. . . . There is a struggle between his Christian and his pagan nature. The latter says 'Strike the blow,' the former says, 'Take care, revenge is the Lord's.'" She concluded by praising Hamlet as "above all . . . a man. Though he was a scholar, a writer, an actor, it is for his sterling qualities of manhood that we admire him the most. He was a man among men, a favorite among his companions, a friend to his friends. He loved as a man, he died like a man." W.D.

would not have recognized any Christian-pagan struggle within himself, but behind his daughter's ringing conclusion he must have perceived her tribute to himself, the most significant male in her life and her standard for manliness.

Her parents gave her a small diamond pendant and a copy of Fannie Merritt Farmer's *The Boston Cooking School Cook Book* as graduation presents. The cookbook was dedicated to Mrs. William B. Sewall, president of the Boston Cooking School, for "promoting the work of scientific cookery, which means the elevation of the human race." In the fall, it would be left behind when Helen traveled to upstate New York to continue her education—before then, however, the summer holiday and a further education in Wisconsin.

W.D. warned his family that La Follette would do his best to knock him out. They could expect it to be a rough game, and it was. A comment from W.D.'s widely circulated Lincoln Day's address was challenged by Ed Hayes, a farmer from the town of Cleveland in Marathon County. W.D. had claimed that "if the people of the cities could have a few practical lessons in the management of affairs in the country towns, where every citizen and taxpayer on town meeting day attends the meetings and listens eagerly to the reading of the report of the expenditures of the town's money, where every act of the town officers is carefully considered, dishonest officials would find no place in city affairs."[6] Hayes thought "city folks" should hear the truth.

This town is run by a mill company, who completely dominates and controls the affairs of the town by their working men. Men in their employ hold nearly all the town offices, and no farmer tax payer can hold a town office unless he is agreeable to the company's wishes. A ticket is made up each year by the bosses, and on town meeting day their logging train is run out into this and adjoining towns, and they gather up their working men and others and the saw mill is shut down for the afternoon. Their men are brought in squads to the town meeting and kept there to vote on motions of levying taxes, building roads, bridges and so forth. . . . This company owns a large amount of real estate and personal property in the town of Cleveland, and the town officers can see very little value in saw logs along their railroad or lumber in their yard. About the only place they find value in lumber is when it is nailed onto some farmer's barn, or other building. . . . Records will show that as fast as the company disposes of their lands, the value of the land is raised at the next assessment, and then other parties have to pay the tax.

If city folks wanted a few practical lessons in conducting town hall meetings, they shouldn't expect them at any town meeting where the Connor Company owned property and controlled the town.[7]

The exposé, published and distributed by La Follette's paper, the *Milwaukee Journal,* brought no investigation, nor did a series of other charges accusing W.D. of arrogance, personal corruption, and "bossism." The *Journal* editorialized, "When one man delegates to himself the right to sit up and talk of what he intends to do, just as if he was the whole state, something is liable to happen to him."[8] Helen, along with the rest of her family, shrugged the charges off as politically inspired misrepresentations. Her father was a devoted and brilliant champion of just causes, and La Follette was an ambitious liar.

Helen believed that her father, newly reelected chairman of the Republican State Central Committee, was dedicated to the public good. In Ladysmith, a small town in northern Wisconsin, people were not so sure. An article in the *Ladysmith Journal* described "the young and serene looking" candidate, owner of one of Wisconsin's largest hardwood lumber corporations, as among the most ruthless in exploiting the underclass. "Such a calm and benignant countenance, such a placid exterior, but, as we know, with force enough back of it to run five sawmills."[9]

Another attack on W.D. appeared in thee *Milwaukee Journal* as an astonishing appeal to Governor James O. Davidson to disassociate himself from Connor and "pull out" of the governor's race, because, although Davidson was "a good man" and "a good citizen," he was "not a statesman. You know you're not. You are not a leader. You never have been. You never will be."[10] Connor was too shrewd for Davidson, who had unwittingly become part of a conspiracy to destroy the Progressive movement. "Think you that he cares the snap of his finger about your being elected governor, except as your election would be a step towards the realization of his own ambition which is to join the Millionaires' club at Washington." The Half-Breed field was not big enough for both Connor and La Follette. "Mr. Connor is not the man to play second fiddle. When you are governor and Connor is senator and La Follette is down and out—as he will be if Mr. Connor's hopes are realized—what then? Things will be beyond your control. . . . Pull out. That is sound advice, given with sincere admiration for you as a citizen and as a man, and with the kindliest good-will." The article, W.D. assured his family with a look of mischievous delight on his face, showed how desperate the opposition had become.

In the midst of the excitement, Helen prepared to leave Wisconsin for Wells College in upstate New York. The second-oldest women's college in America (Vassar was older), Wells was founded by a Presbyterian minister in 1868. There she could be assured of receiving sound instruction in music, language, history, and the arts in association with other young women from the "best" homes on the eastern seaboard and other midwestern states.

Stopping off in Madison with her father en route by train to New York, Helen mailed her mother a picture postcard of the old Chadbourne Hall, the women's dormitory at the University of Wisconsin, with the message: "Arrived safely—pleasant trip—Uncle Rob and Mr. and Mrs. Bebee on. Papa very busy. The University enthusiasm makes me almost want to start right in here."

Letters from home soon made her wish she had remained in Wisconsin where her father continued to be front page news. She kept a clipping from the *Sentinel* Donald sent describing La Follette's reaction to an unexpected question hurled at him by someone sitting on the platform behind him while he addressed a large crowd in Milwaukee: "What about Connor?" A hush fell over the audience as it waited to hear "the first public announcement of the feeling of Robert M. La Follette toward William D. Connor." Finally he said, "I have never flinched and I am not going to now. . . . For nearly one year— ever since Mr. Connor appeared before the legislature and opposed the perfection of the primary election law—I have distrusted him. I must hew straight to the right and that is my position." The remark caused "a sensation."[11]

Referring to La Follette as "that gentleman," Connor acknowledged that he had appeared before the legislature. "He asked me to appear before the joint committee to discuss the railroad rate. I did so appear and I used every effort and the practical knowledge I possessed to help frame a positive, forceful rate law that would serve the people best. If he refers to the now famous Mary Ann bill—now dead and gone—which was presented to the legislature at the special session, and which I have been accused of defeating, I want to say that . . . I was not at Madison when the bill was presented to the legislature."

Davidson, the honest man, and Connor, the shrewd one, using an automobile in order to make as many towns as possible during the day,[12] mounted a vigorous campaign and won by more than fifty thousand votes. When word reached Helen, she should have been jubilant, but she was not. Although not provincial (at thirteen she traveled with her Uncle Rob to the Dakotas to visit her Aunt Betty, newly married and a missionary wife in the Sioux Reservation), Helen had never been away from everything and everyone familiar. Seemingly a strong and independent young woman and eager for new experiences, Helen and her family had not anticipated her reaction to the separation. Her loneliness became so intense that not her studies, the beauty of the college's setting at the edge of Cayuga Lake, the congenial young ladies, or sympathetic teachers saved her from the morbid homesickness that rendered everything meaningless. She fell into an almost catatonic depression, refusing to eat, speak, dress, or wash. Her state roused others to action and led to her almost immediate return to Wisconsin.

In the midst of her family, all pressures relieved, her loneliness broken, Helen's depression quickly lifted. After the holidays, the lieutenant governor moved his family to a large house on Pinckney Street in Madison. When her mother, occupied with the younger children, could not act as hostess, Helen did. Life in the capital was never dull. Helen thrived there.

Throughout the 1907 legislative session, W.D. relished outwitting La Follette. While he never publicly acknowledged his dispute with the crusader, the intensity with which he sought revenge worried La Follette's supporters. In a very slightly veiled allusion to the La Follette–Connor split, the press pursued the story of the politicians' enmity. "Mr. Connor is undoubtedly a shrewd politician and a resourceful organizer, but he is not constructed along broad enough lines to be a successful public man. No man can afford to hold fierce and unrelenting enmities who aspires to greatness for if he does it will inevitably lead to disaster. He must learn to forgive and forget and that is a faculty, which seems to have remained undeveloped in Mr. Connor's character."[13]

The political jockeying began at once. With the help of Isaac Stephenson and other friends, W.D. marshaled the forces to defeat the Keppel bill, which would have made it unlawful for a man to serve both as lieutenant governor and chairman of the state's Central Committee. While serving both as state chairman and as lieutenant governor, he blocked La Follette from securing his choice of candidate for the United State's Senate seat left vacant by the resignation of John C. Spooner on March 4, 1907, two years before the completion of his term. The "toga fight," with John J. Esch, Isaac Stephenson, W. H. Hatten, and Irvine Lenroot the leading contenders, lasted eight weeks and required eighty-five ballots, making it the longest deadlock in the state's history.

A cartoon published in the *Milwaukee Free Press* on March 12 depicts the Wisconsin legislature as a young girl playing ring-a-round-a-rosy about a circle of candidates: Lenroot, Stephenson, Hatten, Esch, Davidson, and Connor. Where the handkerchief will drop is anyone's guess. On April 23, Max Otto's cartoon in the *State Journal* showed a race track in the background with, off to the left, three horses running almost neck and neck and a fourth whose head is just visible. In the foreground, in the center of the cartoon, Connor, in a jockey's outfit, stands holding the tether of an unbridled masked horse he gently strokes to keep him patient. "About Time to Trot Him Out, Mr. Connor," the caption reads.[14] But "crafty" Connor did not think it was.

On May 15, three contenders remained: Esch with twenty-eight votes, Hatten with twenty-six, and Stephenson with forty-four. Fifty-two were needed to nominate. Esch's backers decided to throw in with Hatten. "This with the scattering vote would have given Hatten the caucus nomination and the election . . . but when the evening joint session was called and the recess called that the Republicans might caucus, two of the men pledged at the afternoon conference to vote for Hatten—[C. R. Goldsworthy of Wood County and Elwyn F. Nelson of Langlade County]—did not show up. The best Hatten could secure was fifty votes."[15] Asked by Hatten why they reneged on their pledges, Goldsworthy and Nelson told him "they were under obligations to Mr. Connor and were tied up."[16]

"Wiley William" had handed his enemies another defeat. He had kept to himself his determination to prevent Hatten's nomination, pulling his trumps only when the game was almost over and there would be neither time nor will for the opposition to reorganize. Reporters began to piece together at least part of the story. Connor "hated Hatten" because Hatten had broken pledges, because Hatten's business partner Senator W. D. Dick had opposed him for the chairmanship,[17] and because the leader of the Hatten forces and the anti-Stephenson forces was Senator A. W. Sanborn, an enemy from the campaign that sent La Follette to the senate.[18] Hatten, Dick, and Sanborn were La Follette men. La Follette desired Hatten's election. The fight was only personal.

W.D.'s maneuvering in swinging the vote for "Uncle Ike Stevenson" made it seem Helen's father was "in the deal for long term." His admiring daughter, thrilled by his victory, took even greater satisfaction in the knowledge that her father presided over the longest and busiest legislative session in Wisconsin's history.

More bills were introduced in each house and passed into law than ever before: fire and police pension bills; bills creating an office of waterways commissioner and a state board of immigration; bills limiting the number of working hours for children and telegraph operators and the number of saloons to one per 250 people; bills prohibiting the sale of tobacco to boys under eighteen; bills lengthening the school year from seven to eight months, increasing state aid to rural schools, establishing a correspondence course at the university, increasing the state board of medical examiners control over physicians; bills requiring all railroads to be equipped with safety appliances and providing for inspection of those appliances; fish and game bills; a bill increasing the amount of money that could be raised for highway taxes; and bills of particular interest to Connor, the lumberman who loved horses, exempting from taxation lands planted to forest trees and making it a misdemeanor to mistreat a livery horse. Total appropriations exceeded any other legislative session.

As president of the senate, W.D. cast the deciding vote to place the women's suffrage bill before the electorate (it failed); the deciding vote on important bills regulating insurance companies (its passage had the unanticipated effect of driving many insurance firms out of the state); the deciding vote on a measure that raised railroad liability for a death caused by negligence from five thousand to ten thousand dollars; and the deciding vote to establish a uniform two-cent railway passenger rate.

As one of her prized possessions, Helen preserved the seven-page handwritten statement her father wrote describing the "close and exciting contest" that finally saw enactment of the hotly contested railroad bill, the passage of which W.D. saw as a personal triumph. His pleasure in overhearing one senator say to another, "I was very anxious for this legislation but would almost as soon see it defeated as to have the Record of the Senate show that it was saved by Mr. Connor's vote,"[19] matched his pleasure in reading another reporter's statement that "it must make poor Bob La Follette feel bad these days to see . . . W.D. Connor playing dry nurse for the reform infant."[20]

La Follette's men promulgated a series of negative articles blasting W.D. in the summer of 1907 for personally violating laws he helped put on the books: "Connor's Road Is Roasted,"[21] screamed one headline when the Railroad Commission found that the lieutenant governor's Marathon County Railroad, because of "its practice of carrying some passengers and certain freight free of charge, [was] in contravention of law besides being inequitable and socially and economically unsound."[22] After investigation, however, the commission was persuaded what people in the county already knew. The order to run regular service on the line was unwarranted. The Marathon County line was primarily for hauling lumber. The few passengers, who rode the line, might continue to ride in the caboose free of charge, and the engineer might continue his practice of tossing candy out to farm children along the route.

His road in Forest County, however, the Laona and Northern Railroad, did in fact haul people in addition to lumber, and there Connor paid no attention to the uniform rate law he helped put on the books. Privileged employees, supervisors, and their relatives rode free while others paid.[23] In the neighboring town of Wabeno he also disregarded the law. John Barnes, a lawyer from Rhinelander, one of the few people who knew how things stood in Forest County, tendered his resignation as a railroad commissioner when the uniform rate bill passed, charging that Connor cared

> as much for the plain people as he did for the dirt on his shoes. And while you are telling the people how they have been wronged by the railroads and neglected by the railroad commission, haven't you succeeded in faring pretty well at the hands of the railroads for a reformer. Aren't you the Connor who owns a

large manufacturing plant at Wabeno, . . . and don't you own a roadbed of a
railroad about ½ of a mile long connecting with the tracks of the Chicago and
Northwestern Railroad Company? . . . And are you not the identical person
who gets for every carload of freight loaded at your plant in its cars and hauled
over its rails for this ½ a mile, 20% of the freight on such car when shipped to
Chicago or to points taking a rate not in excess of that to Chicago? And as to
other commodities carried by you, don't you ever get a greater portion of the
entire hauling cost? And if the freight on a carload of manufactured product is
forty dollars for a haul of 290 miles, do you think you earn ten dollars of that
sum for hauling that car one-half a mile? While you are so vigorously twisting
the tails of the railroads publicly, how do you manage to so advantage yourself
privately?[24]

W.D. answered: "I would be glad to discuss railway freight rates or passenger rates with him [Barnes] though I have not been trained in the law and
would lack that finer discernment that go with highly cultured minds in legal
attainment. . . . I refuse, however, to discuss with the learned and dignified
commissioner any politics. . . . Any lawyer would plead in court that [political
questions] were 'irrelevant, incompetent, and immaterial,' hence not proper
questions."[25]

The correspondence, seized on by the papers, gave "promise of causing a
rise in the price of ice in Wisconsin, and that in the dog days too." They were
indeed "memorable days in old Wisconsin."[26]

At the top of his form, W.D. attracted headlines by buying and naming a
prize bull Sir Donald[27] after his eighteen-year-old son. But he was being
watched. A "representative" of the *Daily Herald* visited Stratford and "found
conditions there similar to those of years ago when certain big lumber concerns paid off their men in scrip instead of money and the scrip was good only
at the company store. . . . Employees of the company receive their wages in
the Connor brand of money and must be content."[28] The negative publicity
was finally becoming something W.D. and his family had to reckon with even
though he explained the attacks away: "You cannot break the status quo, take
on entrenched powers, do battle with the railroads, paid lobbyists, and the
politicians in whose pocket they are, without expecting to make enemies."

In the fall of 1907, Mame sent Helen and William to California, where her
parents and her brothers and their families had migrated in 1894. Absent from
Wisconsin for some years, in 1904 the widowed Dr. Witter returned to spend
several weeks at Birch Lake. Receiving her letter indicating her concern about

William's chronic bronchitis, he urged her to send William to him in Helen's care. The thirteen-year-old had a better chance of recovering in the benign California climate, and the children should become acquainted with their mother's family.

Helen's eagerness to partake in the adventure, to meet her Uncles George and Willis Witter[29] and her many Witter cousins, was tempered by her concern that her brother might die en route. She was enormously relieved to see her tall, heavily bearded grandfather on the platform when the train arrived in San Francisco.

While William convalesced in his grandfather's home in San Jose, Helen lived with her uncles' families in Oakland and Berkeley. Willis Witter had six children—Dean, Margaret, Willis Guy, Elizabeth, Charles, and John—and George four, Jean, Esther, Edwin, and Guy Phelps. Helen and Dean Witter, whose name became almost synonymous with stock market trading, hit it off immediately. Born in Wausau, Wisconsin, on August 2, 1887, a year older than Helen, Dean, a student at the University of California, Berkeley, was a tall, handsome, highly intelligent, and confident young man. They rode horseback for hours together in the Oakland hills among the tall, sweet-smelling, shaggy-barked Eucalyptus trees exchanging stories about their lives and relatives.

Timothy Guy Phelps, their grandmother's brother, who had been responsible for the Witters' move to the coast, exemplified the "manly" beings both admired. Deceased when Helen arrived in California, she already knew his story by heart. Among the countless failed miners in forty nine, he survived misfortune and illness to make a fortune in merchandizing and real estate. Politically active in the Republican Party, he served as a state senator in 1856 and as congressman in 1861.[30] He was credited with breaking up an attempt by Southern officers to seize California and with saving the state for the Union.[31] The first president of the California Board of Regents, he served the board for twenty years.

While Helen was proud to count Timothy Guy among her ancestors, she "was crazy about Dean," Fanny Cole Purdy recalled seventy years later. Although he and her other Witter cousins came to Birch Lake for an extended visit the following summer, long distance separated the families. Dean and Helen remained life-long correspondents, however, and from time to time their paths crossed.

∽

# CHAPTER 7

# Risky Business

## 1908–1909

Business cares and state cares are too much to promise health much
longer.

—MARY UPHAM

Helen's sister, Constance Jane Victoria, was born on February 13, 1908. More
sister than daughter to her forty-three-year-old mother, Helen shared in the
nursery and household chores as well as in the social and cultural opportunities Marshfield offered. She accompanied her mother to meetings of the
Woman's Club and to meetings of the newly organized chapter of the Daughters of the American Revolution (DAR), which studied American history;
the Woman's Club (formerly the Travel Class) affiliated with the Federation
of Women's Clubs. The club reflected the greater twentieth–century self-
consciousness of women identifying themselves nationally by sex rather than
class, a growing recognition that in order to effect social change, including
obtaining the right to vote, they had to band together. Where the aim of the
Travel Class had been self-improvement, the aim of the Woman's Club was
"to promote intellectual and social culture and to advance whatever related to
public welfare."[1]

While the meetings were open to any interested woman, the educated "Yankee" women in the Pleasant Hill area, most of them also members of the DAR,
dominated the association. The monthly meetings were held at St. Alban's
Guild Hall, a short walk from their homes, and their programs were reported
as social news in the *Marshfield News Herald.* Club, church, and home remained
the pivots about which the women's lives revolved, but the real stimulation for
Helen came from her father's lively accounts of his political battles.

As chairman of the state central committee, blocking La Follette's ambitions,
W.D. prevented the senator's supporters from putting up a slate of delegates
to the Republican National Convention committed to him. The attorney

general concurred; delegates would have to be elected in the April primary without previous convention endorsement. Putting up a La Follette slate violated the Primary Law.

When La Follette's delegates lost the primary, his supporters accused W.D. of pretending to support and speak on behalf of La Follette throughout the state while secretly entering into a deal with the powerful Business Men's Taft Club in Milwaukee, committed to presidential candidate Robert Taft. They accused him of throwing his strength to the Taft district and state delegates, opening voter lists to the Secretary of War's backers and offering to send out, at cost, envelopes addressed to Republican voters in any district. Isaac Stephenson was also accused of taking part in the campaign for Taft and against his "colleague" in United States Senate.[2]

Running foul of La Follette was a risky business. And so the list of those opposing W.D. grew longer, and the negative publicity he endured following the 1907 legislative session escalated in 1908. A public figure, he could not operate his business or his personal affairs secretively. He had sent agents into Milwaukee in the winter of 1908, a winter as remarkable for snow and ice as 1907 had proved deficient, to hire some of the five hundred to seven hundred loggers needed in his camps. The men paid $1.50 for the privilege of working, but when they arrived most were turned away. The law firm of Sheridan and Meuller filed suit on behalf of a number of them "for damages for alleged breach of contract and the damages asked will be the rail fare to and from Laona and pay for the time consumed in the trip."[3] Two of the men, having no funds, walked back to Milwaukee. Not everyone believed W.D.'s explanation that the call had been for experienced sawyers and cant hook men who could speak English. "Most of those sent to us could not. . . . Had I known that they had no money, I surely would have paid their fare."[4]

And the suit filed by J. Howard Clement and John F. Williams for payment of $1,087 for work and materials contracted for in the decoration of the Connor home in Marshfield would undoubtedly have gone unnoticed had Connor not been a public figure.

While the suits embarrassed his family, they were more concerned about the obvious toll the dual pressures of business and politics were taking on him. While W.D. went after a target like a Yorkshire terrier and enjoyed the adrenaline rush of confronting challenges, his body rebelled at the excessive, unrelenting expenditure of nervous energy. He suffered from frequent migraines and digestive problems. Mame finally declared the situation intolerable and insisted that for all their sakes he temper his ambition.

Helen's voice joined her mother's: "Here father is a quotation from Lloyd

George for you who in warning against excessive ambition said: 'The mountain of fame has great responsibility; the higher you climb, the colder and lonelier it becomes; you are exposed to every attack of the elements: also it is necessary to deny your self *The Comforts of Peaceful Home Life.*'"

The news that Connor was "out of politics" made headlines in the summer of 1908 and came as "a great surprise to all."[5] He told reporters, "My health has been such the past six months that I have found it necessary to change my ideas about the amount of work I can take care of." He was "satisfied" that he could not attend to business and politics at the same time; his family urged him "very strongly" to lighten his load. He would serve out his term as state chairman, which, while "very trying and at times a severe physical strain," had been the most pleasant of his political tasks, but he would not again be a candidate for lieutenant governor or any other political office.[6]

Helen enrolled in Milwaukee Downer Seminary for young women in the fall of 1908. The school prided itself on a curriculum that "protected and emphasized sound academic studies . . . [in] languages, literature, the social sciences, pure sciences and philosophy" while maintaining that "a woman's education should prepare her for her chief vocation, and that the science and art of home-making, which is a business most complex and most significant, should form a recognized part of her training for life."[7] She was among the advantaged students, whose tendency to wear "expensive costumes of the merry widow order surmounted with sumptuous 'confections' to class" caused the school's president, Ellen C. Sabin, to threaten to establish "a college uniform of gingham" so that no "false and mischievous line of distinction between the poor girls and their wealthier schoolmates" could be drawn.[8] While she was as interested as any girl in a pretty costume, Helen often wore gingham to school. If she had a choice between showing off her clothes and showing of her intellect, she came down on the side of intellect.

In one of his last acts as chairman of the Republican Central Committee, W.D. organized Taft's visit to Wisconsin scheduling stops in Janesville, Evansville, Waukesha, West Allis, and Racine as well as a noontime speech in Madison and a night speech in Milwaukee. (As a final act, he called Wisconsin Republican leaders together in Madison to elect a new chairman. Stephenson's campaign manager, E. A. Edmonds, was elected over La Follette's candidate, A. C. Backus.[9]) Helen picked up his enthusiasm for the candidate and played Taft when Milwaukee Downer held a mock election, replete with "Women's Votes" signs and banners on canes and umbrellas. "There was a tremendous burst of cheers and applause when Miss Helen Connor, Marshfield, daughter of Lieutenant Governor W.D. Connor took the platform. For some

Helen Melissa Connor, "a child of privilege," 1908.

Helen with classmates at Milwaukee Downer, 1908. Helen, wearing a hat, has her arm around her life-long friend Maybel Pick. In 1971, Helen wrote on the back of this photo, "I like this—H.C.L."

moments speaking was impossible, until curiosity finally conquered enthusiasm. Taft began by stating in a matter of fact way 'I'm not an orator, I'm not a vote getter, but I'm a conviction getter,' and the audience responded with shouts of: 'I should say you are.'" Cheers rattled the windows of the college chapel. "Taft" won by a vote of 181 to 55 for Bryan.[10]

When Wisconsin voters elected Taft and reelected Governor Davidson, W.D., who had hoped to bow out of the public eye, discovered he remained a subject of interest. His six-cylinder "locomobile, an expensive car," was burned in a fire that started in the Crescent Auto and Machine Company garage in Fond du Lac a few minutes after it had been garaged there. The fire swept out of control and burned $250,000 worth of property, including the Presbyterian, Lutheran, Methodist, and Catholic churches. The *Fond du Lac News* reported that "it is not believed his car had anything to do with it."[11] The *Milwaukee Free Press* suggested the "fire might have started in his Machine."[12]

Although the incident occurred in September, the day after he had turned over the chairmanship of the Republican state committee to his successor, it was not until Taft's victory in November, and the revelation of the letter W.D. wrote to the insurance agency George H. Russell and Company complimenting them for being prompt to pay, that newspapers throughout the state carried an identical suggestive report. The policy "good anywhere" was a "valued" policy, "which means that the amount named in the policy shall be paid in full in case of total loss, regardless of depreciation or second hand value at the time the loss may occur, a comparatively new thing in automobile fire insurance."[13]

W.D.'s promise of withdrawal from politics had not yet offered him the desired anonymity.

At Downer, Helen continued to enjoy her position in the limelight. In May 1909, when the school presented an evening program for parents and the public, "The Peace and Arbitration Movement," she delivered a speech. "Militarism," she declared, "has no place in a representative government"; war, she claimed, was "a survival of old feudal days. The soldier is going down, and the economist is going up."

Jane Addams, a friend of Downer's president, Ellen Sabin,[14] and a role model for women of Helen's class and generation, delivered the school's commencement address. An inspired spokesperson for women's rights and involvement in social causes, Addams's high-minded idealism, her efforts to return to the simple charity of early Christianity and to help the poor at a time when there were no welfare programs in America and anarchy threatened, had driven her to the speaker's platform and culminated in her establishment of Hull House, a settlement house in Chicago.[15] Women of wealth and standing in Wisconsin and Illinois, including Mrs. Hall McCormick, wife of the publisher of the *Chicago Tribune*, longing for a connection with "the real life of the world," supported Miss Addams's work.[16] Addams's talk was entitled "Woman's Education and Modern Life."

In thought, Helen had been trained to "go out," but she and most of her fellow students also understood that they came from social classes that would allow them to marry well and "stay in." While the year she spent in Milwaukee undoubtedly reinforced her desire and need for independent achievement, and she certainly looked forward to entering the university in Madison in September, home was still very much the center of life's security and happiness for Helen, and her mother's life was still exemplary of a woman's satisfaction in her "career" and her father's an example of the heroic male's.

In August 1908, W.D. bonded his Laona property with the Wisconsin Trust Company, Milwaukee, and secured a loan of $500,000 to rebuild the mill with modern machinery run by electric power generated at his plant. He began to construct "an immense addition . . . for manufacturing hardwood flooring and moulding" and to build additional homes for an expanded workforce and streets to accommodate the automobiles, which were beginning to enter the picture even in Forest County. He not only had plans for a major expansion in Forest County but plans to secure additional timberlands in Michigan to ensure his supply of logs as he depleted his sources in central Wisconsin. In these projects he was successful. He was not successful, however, in transferring the county seat from Crandon to Laona and in ensuring the building of the new courthouse in Laona. He had competitors in Crandon as willing as he to bend the rules.[17] This fact, however, was part of the secret world of business about which Helen knew almost nothing.

CHAPTER 8

॰॰

# Promising Years

## 1909–1913

The sudden and very general expansion of the girl's horizon is manifest to everyone. . . . The education of to-day cries out to them "never mind other people; make the most of your own life. Never mind marriage: it is an incident; men have proved it for themselves; it is just the same for women. Never mind social laws; do what your temperament dictates—art, affairs, enjoyment even. But do your duty to yourself."

—MARGARET DELAND, "The Change in the Feminine Ideal," 1910

In the fall of 1909, while her father, Governor Davidson's appointee to the Lakes to the Gulf Waterways convention, traveled from St. Louis to New Orleans with President Taft and a group of the "most representative men of our country,"[1] Helen was enjoying student life in Madison. Only the year before, the university had given up the notion that strenuous mental activity might endanger women's health and began admitting them "to membership in all classes."[2] Not only to the sociologist, but "to any ordinary observer, it is becoming evident that women have come into the public life of the world to stay."[3] When an anti-coed club formed in Helen's first year, the women quickly labeled it "ridiculous" and "silly," its members "sad birds" and "lemons." "Miss Helen Connor, daughter of W.D. Connor, former lieutenant governor [declared] 'Such a movement seems very silly at a state university. The women have as much right as the men, and I should like to know what lot of fellows is behind it. If they don't like women, let them get out, and leave the women alone.'"[4]

She studied French, history, philosophy, education, English, and sociology. She read Gissing's *Aphorisms and Reflections,* thought about the influence of science on literature, and read Royce and William James. She wrote out the plots of the twenty English plays that were required reading for Professor Young's class, English 36; she studied the Elizabethan age, could rattle off the various acting companies, and copied her professor's assertion that Shakespeare was a "good money maker, not sentimentally interested in art."

She studied the Romantics, who "turned to the past, realized the continuity of thoughts," and learned to show the relation of the Romantic movement to the Oxford Movement and the scientific movement and the direct, indirect, and reactionary effects of the French Revolution. Her professors taught that "the Victorian poets wanted to tame Pegasus and make him eat common oats"; that lyric poetry was "crippled with increase of realism"; that the mid-nineteenth-century Victorian period was one "of goody-goody mediocrity, an era of harmless, useless productions."

She learned to contrast romantic ideals and methods with the realistic, to trace the development of the idea of individual reason from Luther, Descartes, Mill, and Arnold; to trace the inductive, empirical idea from Bacon to Darwin to Huxley; to understand how the "evolutionary theory" corrected "the fallacious reasoning of the Revolutionists and 18th century democratic ideals." Her professors taught that it was "the fate of all movements to begin as heresies and to end as superstitions." She learned to "apply the law of action and reaction to the history of thought from 16th to 20th century, and to illustrate the eclectic character of modern thought."

She read *The Doll's House, Pillars of Society, Hedda Gabler, The Master Builder, Rosmersholm,* and heard her professor say the English considered Ibsen "immoral." Ibsen's men were "hum-bugs" who made "a present of [their] opinions"; the society Ibsen presented was based on "organized hum-bug." Nobility of character and will would not come from "the humbugs" who were the ostensible "pillars of society" but from the "new order," coming from "women and workmen," whose futures were intertwined.

Her professors asked her to understand that there were probably two sides to an argument, that "a person without any convictions is neither wanted in heaven or hell." In the turbulent sea of change in which they were living, they advised her to hold fast to the twin lighthouses of "character" and "will."

Helen already believed that "mere democracy cannot solve the social problem; aristocracy of character must be introduced." She had already resolved by her character and her will to be among her country's virtuous leaders, an American aristocrat.

Among her copious notes, a couple of quotations suggest the presence of traditional ideas nestled among the radical new ones: "woman will be the last thing civilized by man"; "in the midst of the mighty drama . . . girls and their blind visions . . . are the yea or nay of that good for which men are enduring and fighting. In these delicate vessels is borne onward through the ages the treasure of human affections." Perhaps the women as "delicate vessels" phrase led Helen to remark, much later in life, that tiring of the "flowery writing" she was getting in English, which was not what she wanted, she switched her major to journalism. "I wanted some straight writing."[5]

Helen studied sociology, a new field, and just opened to women, with Professor Edward Alsworth Ross. A tall, handsome, and prolific scholar, this Scots-Presbyterian born into a pioneer family in Illinois in 1866 was esteemed nationally throughout the academic community. He had been dismissed from Stanford University for political reasons.[6] His former instructor at Johns Hopkins University, the economist Richard T. Ely, also under suspicion for radical ideas (he lectured at Hull House on the "Labor Movement in Chicago"), brought him to Madison.

With Ross, Helen studied English and American labor movements and the histories of money and banking. She read about the "causes of poverty" in the *American Journal of Sociology* and the "economic causes of pauperism" in the *Westminster Review* and learned that credit had become essential because of the "round about capitalistic methods of production and the increased area of commerce." She also learned that divorce had become "democratized" and was increasing three times as fast as the population in America, that juvenile courts were an American creation twelve years old and that juvenile delinquency among immigrants could be traced to certain causes: congestion, incompetent parents, impaired family ties, illegitimacy, want of industrial training, the gang, lack of places for boys to play. Ross taught that "hard, thoughtless justice makes criminals"; that experts, "scientific observers," were needed to study causes of social defects; and that almshouses were "temporary places of abode for a dangerous population where the aged and vicious are placed together." Muckraking literature was helping to bring about the social changes—among them direct legislation, popular choice of U.S. Senators, direct primaries, corrupt practices acts, publicity of campaign expenditures, and commission forms of government for cities—crucial to keeping the nation from experiencing "a huge futile social blow-up . . . followed by iron military repression."

Ross insisted his students not only read about but observe conditions, engage in "scientific observation." Helen visited and reported her observations of the Boys Industrial School in Waukesha where "some good is really being done." It was "not a penal institution but a school and as such is trying not to punish but to instill better ideas of living into the boys and to make them more capable citizens." Her report on the Milwaukee County Alms-House was not as favorable. There, some 435 people "were just sitting around waiting to die."

It seemed "pretty weird to think of some of these people at work making their own coffins."

When Ross announced to his classes that anarchist Emma Goldman was in Madison and would speak on the difference between Russian and American higher education and suggested they take the opportunity to hear her, some members of the academic and political community criticized him. Helen did not. She relished the opportunity of thinking over the opposing views of Addams and Goldman, both strong women who preached social reform, the one idealistically through a spiritual association between classes, the other through class confrontation, workers united in opposition to capitalists. Goldman, who "had always found university towns the most indifferent to the social struggle," was surprised to discover at the University of Wisconsin "professors and students vitally interested in social ideas, and a library containing the best selection of books, papers, and magazines."[7] Familiar with the capital city, the battles in the legislature, the controversies at the university, Helen was not surprised at the wide range of views the university's extensive collections represented. She expected diversity and, intellectually, reveled in it.

Her father's prominence in state politics, guaranteed that the attractive, articulate daughter would be a noteworthy young woman on campus. The notice that "Miss Helen Connor is in Marshfield for the weekend," appeared in the student paper, *The Daily Cardinal*,[8] along with her articles as an early campus "sob-sister." She labeled exams "a good dumping ground for a lot of things you don't care anything about knowing anyway"; was initiated into the Pi Beta Phi sorority; became a founding member of the Beta chapter of Theta Sigma Phi, the woman's journalism society, and a member of the Mortar Board Society (the women's honor society). No one seriously "courted" her, but she was friendly with a number of young men, including her French instructor, and enjoyed the company of friends from Marshfield, among them Edward Kohl, business manager of the *Cardinal*, and Wayne Deming. Her brother Donald, also a student, drove her home on weekends and holidays.

During the summer holiday of 1910, in spite of W.D.'s declaration that he was out of politics, his presence hovered over the political scene. That La Follette's supporters had cause to fear him became evident when he attended a state convention of conservative Republicans (all Taft supporters opposed to La Follette's presidential ambitions). On that occasion, Governor Davidson greeted Vice President "Sunny Sam" Sherman, and W.D. Connor delivered an address, the implications of which were clear. He had come to Milwaukee and had agreed to speak because "I am a Republican, because I believe in the things that the Republican party has enacted into law during its existence in this country, and also because I have confidence that in the future of the United States no one can stop its progress if the Republican party rules. . . . I am an organization Republican. . . . There is no place, no place in Republican politics in this country for the individual to set himself above the party organization."

His speech caused the usual "sensation." Emanuel I. Philipp nominated Connor to be chairman of the state executive committee with power to appoint five men to assist him and to call a state convention at any time. When he was unanimously elected, E. I. Philipp and J. G. Monahan escorted him to the platform while the delegates cried "Connor, Connor" and "the band failed to drown the deafening cheering."[9] Senator Stephenson sent a telegram indicating that it was "peculiarly fitting that Republicans of Wisconsin should meet . . . to renew their pledge to the party and to profess their loyalty to their chosen leader," Taft. Not a whisper of support for La Follette's candidacy came from Wisconsin Republicans assembled in Milwaukee in June 1910.

The Connor family, 1908. At back, from left: Helen, Marian, Donald, William; at front, from left: Richard, Mame, Constance, Gordon, W.D.

The *Milwaukee Sentinel* published an exuberant description of the convention and a highly flattering full-length portrait of Connor on its front page on June 10; the next day, the *Milwaukee Journal* initiated a campaign to ridicule the conservatives and undermine Connor's reemergence on the political scene by publishing a satirical cartoon on its front page and an ironic article describing the event and Connor's performance. In the cartoon, King Connor sits on his throne, draped in royal robes and with a crown on his head. He is waited on by subordinates, including Emanuel Philipp and former Governor Upham, who, as keeper of the sacred word, bears a document entitled "Love Your Neighbors," a reference to the notorious Upham-Connor enmity.

"My faithful subjects," King William the Silent is quoted as saying in a tearful voice. "I am deeply moved by the honor that has been shown me. I, who was down and out, am now put in my place again. My ancestral estates have been restored to me. My dignities and renown are mine most unexpectedly. Merit has its reward. I, who was content to live in retirement beneath the silent pines, now have been called to my rightful station. I will accept. But I must consult my wife."

With his health restored, his plans for expansion in Laona nearing completion, and the slow summer months about to begin, W.D. thought he could handle the chairmanship of the Republican committee to reelect Taft. Convinced that the temporary position would not entail more than her husband could handle, ruin his health, or mean his reemergence as an office seeker—and that he was eager to accept the position that would be his final thrust against his enemy—Mame supported his decision to accept the chairmanship of the Republican committee. A wife had to know when to use her force and when to retreat. Besides, one cartoon depicting him as henpecked was enough.

In the midst of a threatening typhoid epidemic in Milwaukee, Connor announced his decision to take on the state chairmanship of the Republican Party, to "direct the campaign the national administration will put up against the insurgency as exemplified in the actions of Senator La Follette." The *Sentinel* promised that with "Mr. Connor at the head, the new organization will be of such strength as to cope with insurgency in all its phases."[10] In spite of rumors circulated by La Follette supporters alleging that the Taft Republican Committee, under Connor's leadership, "employed 1,200 Milwaukee residents at $6 and $60 a week principally for services of an unspecified nature,"[11] Taft bested La Follette, and W.D. retreated from the political main stage as he promised he would.

He remained, however, "ready to help push along the welfare and best interests of the Republican party"[12] and kept a sharp eye out for political developments that could affect his business. Occasionally, he picked up his pen to deliver an eloquent appeal for, or condemnation of, pending legislation, but he never again became a major, controversial political figure in the state. He had succeeded in blocking La Follette's ambitions and in doing so pretty well cleansed himself of his imperative need for revenge.

Helen graduated in 1912. As toastmaster at a first Mortar Board Society luncheon honoring female journalism graduates, her introductions suggest social changes. "If, as Dr. Sargent claims, men are degenerating into pigmies while women are gaining Herculean strength and stature, it would be interesting to investigate some of the causes. . . . A husband returning from the theater with his wife asked her how she liked the play. 'Very much,' she replied, 'There's only one improbable thing about it. The second act takes place two years after the first and they still have the same servant.'"

President Van Hise's commencement speech was made to address attacks on Professor Max Otto of the philosophy department for his anti-theistic position in his course "Man and Nature," which emphasized the changing nature of the world in which they lived. Truth was not static, he declared, but had to be constantly reexamined in the light of new knowledge because "nowhere is there fixity or completeness."[13]

Having "satisfactorily completed the course of professional instruction prescribed by the university for all persons who intend to teach English as a major subject," Helen was licensed for a year to teach in any public school in Wisconsin. An offer came from Hurley, a lumber and mining town in northeastern Wisconsin, a town even wilder than Laona where dull and difficult times were too often punctuated with reports of violence and drunkenness and even murder, even "on Christmas when all are supposed to have peaceful inclinations."[14] Iron miners and lumberjacks from northern Michigan and Wisconsin, unrestrained and desperate for relief from the backbreaking, muscle-wearying, brain-numbing routine of their poorly paid, dangerous labor, met together in town and, with few other available "amusements," drank and brawled and visited the brothels. Hundreds of girls had been brought to Hurley "for the worst of purposes, some of them not knowing to what they were coming. A large house of immorality [stood] just in the edge of town."[15] With its reputation for vice and violence, professional men, ministers, and lawyers reluctantly accepted assignments there.

W.D. would not let his daughter accept the appointment. He also rejected her suggestions that she either join Jane Addams at Hull House or accept the job as a reporter for the *Milwaukee Sentinel*. He wanted her safely married.

She was bright, gifted as a writer and orator, and ambitious. She had, none-theless, essentially been brought up, like her mother, for marriage and mother-hood. Besides, she had received what her parents considered an eminently suitable offer of marriage in her junior year. She had written to her father then, describing herself as fickle and changeable and uncertain. On December 16, 1911, he answered at length.

I have so much wanted to see you the past few days. I felt that I would like to get away and come down for a day but many things have detained me here. I so hope your affairs will work out for the best and to your happiness and future enjoyment of the greatest possible that life can bring to you for surely you deserve everything that is possible to bring to anyone. . . . You can be fair and straight forward with Mr. Laird even if you cannot decide now for a little while what you want to do. He can not object if you do ask him to wait a little. If you feel that you do not wish to decide either way on so short NOTICE or on so short acquaintance. Miss Miller sat across the table from me tonight at the Episcopal supper. Though as yet I have not had the honor of her acquaintance. She surely is waiting to make the sacrifice and how nicely she would fit into the sur-roundings. Things could go right along. She would make a captain of industry in the community, right here. The Family circle that is so potent in Church affairs would have a firmer hold and all working for the uplift of the commu-nity—and then too the lifting would all be right certainly for the Upham fam-ily would be doing it. Mrs. Frank [Upham] would be so busy that she would not find time to sit down not even during service hour—but then all that would seem so nice and appropriate that I fear Fates will scarce permit lives in this here disjointed world to get fitted into such smooth and harmonious grooves. . . . I hope THAT YOU WILL BE HAPPY—and your being happy, WE ALL WILL. And your admirers passing content to accept of the best they can get and wait and hope.

As usual, W.D. provided a double perspective, slipping from a sincere con-cern to be fatherly and helpful to undercutting the very conventions and institutions he upheld. Irreverent and cynical as he often was, W.D. did not then, or ever, find any reason to mock Melvin R. Laird, "a man of very pleas-ing personality, about six feet in height, with a frank, open face, a perfect gen-tleman in appearance and manner and culture, and one of the cleanest, most sincere and earnest men that I know."[16]

Helen lived at home after graduation, helping her fifty-year-old mother with the children, participating in Woman's Club meetings where the subjects, some at least, were those she had studied at the university: parole laws, labor

*The Ladies Speak Last,* 1912. From left: Mrs. W. D. Connor as Juliet, Mrs. Vollmar as narrator, Mrs. Lathrop as Lady Macbeth, Mrs. Robert Connor as Ophelia, and Mrs. Hayward as Gertrude.

unions, recent strikes, child labor, pure food laws, anti-trust laws, and "Some Possible Solutions of the Race Problem."[17] She helped her mother prepare her costume and practice her lines for the Shakespeare and the Woman's Club joint presentation of the comedy-drama *The Ladies Speak Last.* Mame, a portly mother of seven draped in roses, played Juliet, while Aunt Florence, a slightly more probable candidate, played the mad Ophelia.[18]

Helen moved between her father's world and her mother's as she contemplated her future. She read proof of the essay W.D. distributed to the papers describing the dangers in proposed legislation to enact a state income tax, a bill he claimed was designed by "a few shrewd politicians" who, while calling it a "people's law," exempted themselves from paying a tax on their salaries. Conceding that a national income tax might be necessary and just, he claimed a Wisconsin state income tax would discourage industry. "The best protection a new and struggling enterprise has is to conceal in large measure the success of its operations. Under the Wisconsin Income Tax, it is utterly impossible, except by perjury, to accomplish this concealment."

He spoke and wrote as an oracle. "We can look forward and see the end of the lumber trade in Wisconsin." Wisconsin's future development lay in manufacturing. "What," he asked, neatly distancing himself from any notion that his interest in squelching the state income tax might have a personal component, "with the passing of the lumber trade, will be the future of Wisconsin workingmen?" He also wrote as a statesman, a student of history, who could sound a warning.

> In connection with the public right of taking from each individual part of his property or part of his earnings with which to pay the expenses of government, two things must always be borne in mind. First, that the right of taxation, which, as Chief Justice Marshall says, is the power to destroy, derives its legitimate basis from the necessity of taxation, and that the levying and collection of taxes beyond the necessities of the government is robbery. And second, that nothing so surely foretells the downfall of any form of government as the indiscriminate and reckless exercise of the taxing power far beyond all legitimate necessities, leading, as indiscriminate and reckless taxation always does, to reckless and inordinate expenditure of public money, and thence, by easy gradation, to corruption.[19]

This was probably the compelling argument that kept Helen in the Republican camp throughout her long life.

As the days, weeks, and months passed, as she approached her twenty-fifth birthday, Helen came to feel that she should become a wife. Her suitor lived in the neighborhood, in a rented apartment in the widowed Mrs. Lathrop's home on Second and Cherry and was a frequent dinner guest in the Connor home. Mame and W.D. were convinced that Melvin had the necessary "great strength" to help their daughter "meet all the problems" with which she would have to contend and the breadth of intellect and experience to keep her interested.[20]

Donald admitted in the letter he wrote to Mr. Laird on March 20, 1913, that "it is a rather hard thing to ask a fellow to take part in the wedding of his sister. Helen has always been a *sister of sisters* to me and I do not know what we will do without her."

On Wednesday, April 16, 1913, at seven o'clock in the evening, the "young lady whose modesty and winning ways make her the idol of many admiring friends," was married to Melvin R. Laird at the First Presbyterian Church in Marshfield. The *Marshfield Herald* described the wedding as "one of the largest and most brilliant social functions that has ever taken place in this city," and the bride as "possessed of a lovable disposition and the best qualities of womanhood." Helen's brother Gordon stretched white ribbons down the west aisle for the wedding party; Mayor Robert Connor and Donald served as ushers. Her sister Marian sang "O Promise Me" while "little Constance Connor acted as flower girl" and scattered sweet peas in the bride's path. Helen, exquisitely dressed in a court-style gown of white charmeuse covered with "real lace," walked down the aisle, her arm linked in her father's. The ceremony was performed by Melvin's close friend, Dr. George Hunt of Christ Presbyterian Church in Madison. A supper for out-of-town guests and a formal reception followed at the bride's home.

Melvin and Helen left Marshfield aboard the Velvet Special, the overnight sleeper that took them to Chicago. After a short honeymoon at the Blackstone Hotel, they traveled on to Lincoln, Illinois, where the Reverend Melvin Robert Laird, "one of the best men in the whole world," had accepted a pastorate.

CHAPTER 9

❧

# *Melvin Robert Laird*

Religion was instilled onto them betimes, which grew up and mixed
itself with their ordinary labors and recreations.

——HORACE BUSHNELL

On March 26, 1911, after the evening service at the First Presbyterian Church
in Marshfield, F. R. Upham called the congregation to order and presented
the name of Melvin R. Laird for pastor. W.D. Connor told the ballot. The
vote, seventy-four for and two against, was made unanimous. Another motion
was made and passed granting the reverend a month's vacation, the use of the
manse, and a salary of $1,400 "to free [him] from worldly cares and avoca-
tions." The church leaders, those eminently successful businessmen, called Mr.
Laird to their service in the hopes that his ministrations would be "profitable
to the spiritual interests" of the community.

He was a child of the Middle West, a descendant of Scots-Irish Presbyterian immigrants who had settled in Pennsylvania, where they had glorified
God and farmed the land since colonial days. In 1846, Samuel Laird, Melvin's
grandfather, came over the arduous Allegheny trail by wagon with his wife,
Jane Magee Laird, and their three children, Joseph, William, and Elizabeth.
They came up river to St. Louis and on into Illinois, to Griggsville Landing;
they came on one of Captain Samuel Rider's famous, dangerous steamboats,
whose boilers, fired by wood, threatened to explode.

Melvin's ancestors do not figure in books celebrating the leading men of
Illinois. Their reputations extended no further than the borders of Pike County,
the undulant, creek-strewn, fertile land bound by the Mississippi on the west
and the Illinois River on the east, in which they settled. They prospered in
that local world settled predominately by Scots-Irish and English Presbyterians
who, like earlier generations of pioneers in New England, were grateful for
an opportunity to own property and have a voice in shaping their common

destiny. In a Pike County atlas published in 1872, and a Pike County history published in 1880, Melvin's grandfather and father are celebrated as prominent, well-known citizens who were "active in extending the business and agricultural interests of [the] section, and in its public life."

Melvin's grandfather, Samuel Laird, founded a town on the old stage route between Quincy and Naples and named it Maysville. He opened the first store there, became first postmaster, and kept a hotel, stage stop, and horses. As increasing numbers of settlers raised land values and the country pulled in new directions with the development of the railroads, he adapted to the shifting times. He sold his properties (except for the family homestead and farm where he raised wheat, corn, cattle, and hogs on his four hundred acres in New Salem township) and began to deal in real estate. Active in the state's majority Democratic Party, this upright, almost entirely self-taught pioneer was a frequent delegate to conventions. He was a school director and also served as justice of the peace for eight years and as deacon of the Presbyterian church.

His youngest son, William, Melvin's father, born March 12, 1839, inherited his father's talents and his enthusiasm for Pike County. Educated in subscription schools and at a select school at Griggsville, he lived in the old homestead with his parents until their death, took charge of their farm, and, as the years progressed, moved into the leadership roles formerly occupied by his father. He became school director and trustee of schools and a notary public. He exercised considerable power as commissioner of highways and as a representative of the New Salem township on the County Board of Supervisors. Following in his grandfather's and father's steps, he was active in Democratic politics and in the Presbyterian church, where he was a ruling elder and trustee and superintendent of the Sunday school. A tall, heavily bearded patriarch, with a "strong, sturdy character . . . of fine mental capacity," he was dignified in his bearing, conservative in his views, liberal in regard to money matters, kind, pleasant, well liked, "straight forward and upright in all his relations." He followed the pattern of the times and in 1869 married within his neighborhood, his church, and his ethnic group.

His wife, Anna Osborne Laird, Melvin's mother, was the daughter of Samuel Osborne, another "worthy representative of the agricultural class of Pike County," a "quiet, unassuming man who never pushed himself forward in public affairs but was always ready to assist those who were in need, morally or materially." In "a calling which is sometimes considered ill-paid drudgery," the Osbornes succeeded in surrounding themselves and their families with all the comforts of life; they wore "their religion as an everyday garment, reared their children to the habits of usefulness, gave them every opportunity possible to obtain an education, [and] earned the respect of their fellow-men."

Melvin's maternal grandmother, Margaret Osborne, bore twelve children, six of whom survived. His mother bore ten and all survived. Born in 1877, Melvin was a middle child. After the death of her husband, Margaret Osborne came to live with the Lairds. A corn-cob pipe in her mouth and mending on her lap, the elderly lady, almost blind, sat in her chair by the fire and recited verses from the Bible. The children were asked to locate the verse in the book and the passage. Family prayers were said each evening as well as prayers for food, health, happiness, and sorrow. Theirs was one of those "fine old families where father and mother and children are all God-fearing and of a clean splendid type of people."[1] Melvin's sister Margaret remembered her home as "the very essence of Heaven. Love was the word in our home."

The three-storied clapboard house in which they lived was an unostentatious, utilitarian box with no furnace or plumbing. The children hauled water into the house from the nearby well or cistern, carried wood from the wood shed and ice from the icehouse near the barn and meat from the smokehouse north of the summer kitchen. Depending on the season, they picked vegetables from garden and apples and pears from the large orchard east of the house or fetched them, carefully preserved, from the damp, unfinished root cellar built of local stone. In the buggy shed (not grand enough to be called a carriage house), located far enough from the main house to keep the flies away, the phaeton and surrey waited, covered with sheets until called into use. The outbuildings—hog shed, chicken house, hay barn, ice house, stable, and buggy shed—were plain structures built of wood from the Lairds' woods, as was the main house, where the hand-carved oak doors and intricately wrought porch cornices suggested the work of a master craftsman.

Secure in the land his ancestors tamed and in the house his grandfather built and his father added on to, Melvin Robert Laird responded to the call of prayer and chores. He helped with the planting and the harvesting, the splitting of wood and feeding of cattle. He rode to the junction to pick up the mail; fished and swam in Big Stew Creek; watched the steam boat traffic, listened to the river sounds, and enjoyed an occasional overnight holiday on the Ferrands' houseboat on the Illinois River. He attended country schools and a little Presbyterian church in New Salem. A few hundred feet from his home his kin lay buried under modest stones. Melvin's serenity and faith were rooted in that supportive Illinois childhood.

By the time he was a lanky teenager, it was clear that he was intellectually gifted and had a calling. Ministers and teachers encouraged his parents to let him pursue a higher education and study for the ministry. His brothers remained on the farm where they were needed. Melvin attended two church colleges in Illinois: Carthage College, a small (185 students) highly respected Lutheran College located in a grassy meadow some ninety miles north of Maysville, and Illinois College at Jacksonville, a Presbyterian College some thirty

Melvin R. Laird's high school graduating class, Griggsville, Illinois, 1895. Melvin is seated in the front row, right; his sister Annetta "Nettie" stands behind him.

miles east of Maysville founded in 1830 by the Reverend John Millot Ellis and a band of dedicated Yale divinity students, "friends of religion and literature" who accompanied him into the western wilderness to establish a seminary of learning on the beautiful hill site overlooking town and rolling hills.[2] Thirteen students, all male, were members of Melvin's graduating class in 1899. After a stint teaching in Griggsville, Melvin left the prairie state to continue his education at Princeton, the country's leading Presbyterian institution.

Life in America was radically and rapidly changing as the frontier closed, populations shifted, immigration expanded, technology advanced, and old "truths" were increasingly subjected to skeptical analysis. But the gentle scholar studied his Greek, Latin, and Hebrew texts, history, and philosophy with the same conviction held by those earlier theological scholars: education and religion must go hand in hand to make a man, and while man moves in a changing world, he also exists transcendentally in harmony with the everlasting. Melvin returned to Illinois to continue his graduate studies at the University of Chicago and to complete his training for the ministry at McCormick Theological Seminary in Chicago.

On April 6, 1905, Herrick Johnson wrote Mr. E. C. Moore, the First Presbyterian Church in Prairie du Sac, Wisconsin, "to say that Melvin R. Laird of our Senior Class will preach for you on the 23 of this month. He is not a flaming, fiery orator, but of the conventional style and he is a very fine spirit in every way, a good student, a clear thinker, a faithful servant of God, whom to know is to love." The congregation approved of the tall, brown-eyed farmer's son who wore his erudition so modestly, and on June 8, 1905, the Reverend George E. Hunt of Madison officiated at his installation.

Prairie du Sac's location along the Wisconsin River in Sauk County, some thirty miles northwest of Madison, recalled for Melvin his childhood by the Illinois. Black Hawk Bluff, visible from his window, was named after the last great Indian chief who had made a heroic stand there but from whom the land was finally wrested.

Melvin preached to his congregation, baptized and buried them, gave them reasons for their pain, and sustained them in their emotional deserts. "The spirit of the Lord God is upon me; because the lord hath anointed me to preach good tidings unto the meek; he hath sent me to bind the broken hearted; to comfort all that mourn, to give unto them a garland for ashes."

The words of Isaiah were needed then. And the young prairie son spoke them often during his tenure in Prairie du Sac. Many young wives died in childbirth, including, in the first few months of his service, Mrs. Wallburg and Mrs. Giegerick, who were both just twenty-two years old, and Mrs. Cora

Just, wife of the editor of the *Prairie du Sac News*, whose tribute read that she "was a faithful wife, loving her home and her husband and devoting herself to them." Melvin reminded his congregation that "nothing occurs by chance. All things are under the dominion of the Law." Tuberculosis took others, men and women, young and old, those from established families and wanderers. Gust Guast, a woodman, had no relatives to mourn him. His death "pointed out more clearly in Prairie du Sac as ever before the brotherly love which exists in the Modern Woodmen of America" who saw that his "funeral was not that of a pauper, but that he was buried with the same degree of honor of the average man of today."[3]

While the reaper claimed his harvest, Cupid shot his arrows. Celebration and sorrow, Melvin's ministerial duties called on him to phrase the things that bound men and women to each other, to their community, and to their God. He also entered into the civic life of the community. There was no separation for Laird, as there had been none for his parents or for earlier generations of pioneers in the new world, between God's work and man's. God's was only of another and higher order. For Laird, through man's work God's will might be done. A good man could not abstain from the rare privilege of exercising civic responsibility that America afforded.

He found among Prairie du Sac's predominantly German settlers, whose ancestors had fled persecution in Germany in the 1840s, men and women of high intelligence and broad education, though they might be essentially self-taught. When the Free Thinkers invited him to speak on the theme "Jesus Christ's Life on Earth," he indicated that he was glad to speak to a society of free thinkers because he liked to think that he was himself a free thinker. "A free thinker is one who is determined to be guided by his reason and his enlightened conscience." He stood, he said, as a representative of a religion that put emphasis on freedom of thought: "The ultimate test of a human life is its fidelity to known truth. Jesus believed in God, prayed to God; worshipped regularly in God's temples; and taught men that there was a life hereafter. Strange isn't it, that if such beliefs are false and superstitious that they should produce the best character that the world has ever known. His masterful self control; His magnificent heroism; His pure unselfishness. Can you face these facts and not feel you ought to know and to love him."

Melvin joined the free thinkers' social and business club, the Twin City (Sauk and Prairie du Sac) Twilight Club. On one occasion the men discussed the location and building of a dam across the Wisconsin River with representatives from the Wisconsin Hydro Electric Company; on another, Chinese and Japanese delegations spoke of developments in their countries. Mr. Obata indicated that Japan was "trying to improve its business world with all its might," and Mr. Gwk-tsai Chao, a native of China, spoke on the real China. "China is awakening and the whole nation is eager for education," he told them. "Schools and universities are being established all over the empire. Opium smoking and bound feet, social evils of old China, have practically been abolished." Female drudgery in India was the topic on another occasion.

The Twin City Club meetings were dinner meetings. The men feasted on substantial German American food with a dish or two disguised under a French label, a nod to the cook's sophistication. Women, excluded from club membership, prepared and served the meals.

While writers like Owen Wister, whose popular novel *Lady Baltimore* Melvin purchased, read, and marked up when it appeared in 1906, claimed that Americans were no longer "a small people living and dying for a great idea, [but] a big people living and dying for money" and that "nothing united the states anymore except Standard Oil and discontent," in Prairie du Sac a sense of community and fierce patriotism persisted. The heroic pioneer past was the common heritage that bound those who gathered on August 8, 1907, to hear Dr. A. O. Kendall reminisce about early days in Wisconsin when

rain and snow drifted through the roofs and fell upon floor and beds. There were no barns; stock had to be kept in rail pens with straw about them. Everything about farming was disagreeable. There was no leisure—it was all weariness and vexation of spirit—but we lived and were happy in spite of it. . . . Our flag and the nation before the [Civil] war was not thought much of; we were a second rate nation. . . . Oxen were the only teams and no fresh German could drive an ox team. Nobody but a Yankee could drive an ox team successfully. Six yoke of oxen on a plough to break the ground. We used to have to go 40 miles to mill and haul wheat to Milwaukee and sell it for 35 and 40 cents. . . . There was no money in the country; why, as late as 1860 the government paid 12 per cent interest and the paper money was often not good over night. Banks going down all over the country. . . . Those were times that would make a man weep. People lived upon corn and bacon. . . . Eating was a necessity, not a pleasure. It was hard on the cooks.[4]

Similarly, Melvin's Memorial Day address voiced a patriotism he shared with those for whom the Civil War was more than a distant chapter of American history: "To peril life in the national defense is the severest test of patriotism," that "noble sentiment . . . which is the only security for the continuous life of the nation. So long as its sons are willing to die for their motherland, so long will it endure to shelter and bless them and their children. . . . The best patriot is he who gives the best manhood to his country."[5]

Laird made frequent trips by rail to Illinois to preach at Quincy, visiting his aging parents, performing the wedding ceremonies for his sisters and brothers, baptizing their children, burying family friends and relatives. He visited friends and attended concerts, services, and lectures in Chicago and Madison, where he saw a good deal of the Reverend George Hunt and Max Otto, the Presbyterian cartoonist turned "free thinker" who was beginning to pursue his career as a lecturer in philosophy at the university.

In 1909, Ira M. Price, a professor at the University of Chicago, invited Melvin to join the student group he was guiding through Egypt and Palestine. Granted a six-month leave of absence without salary, and promising to send back an occasional letter for publication in the *Sauk County News*, on February 13, 1909, he sailed from Boston on a White Star Line's twin-screw steamship.

After eighteen days in Alexandria, the class traveled on to Cairo, Heliopolis, and Memphis. He went up the Nile to Aswan, Edfu, Luxor, Karnak, and Thebes, taking notes and hundreds of Kodak photographs. On March 26, he embarked for Palestine, reaching Jaffa the following morning. For forty days he traveled in Palestine and Syria, visiting historic sites already familiar to him through years of study: Bethlehem, Hebron, Jericho; the Jordan River and the Dead Sea; the Mount of Olives and Gethsemane; Samaria, the plain of Esdraelon, and Tiberius on the Sea of Galilee. He journeyed by mule and slept in tents.

The class disbanded in Naples, and he went on alone to visit Rome, Florence, and Paris and then spent some weeks in Germany before returning to Sauk County in August. One hundred parishioners attended the ice cream social welcoming the young educator-preacher back. He gave them an illustrated lecture, beginning with views of Germany before turning to the region closest to his heart and imagination: Nazareth. He located it along the highway between Acre and the Decapolis along which Roman legions and Greek culture and gossip about taxes, Gentiles, the emperor, and the "loose living" in Rome traveled, the place in which "the culture, the tendencies, the delinquencies of His age, were open to the greatest student of the life of men." Nazareth was, he said, "a great university, a fitting and proper school for the Saviour of the World."

His Sunday sermons on his return, drawn from his experiences in the Holy Land, were published in the editorial pages of the *Sauk County News*. "The foundation truth of Christianity," he said, after interpreting the text of "Jacob's Well and the Samaritans," is "the infinite worth of man."[6]

After seven years of outstanding service to the community in Prairie du Sac, the thirty-four-year-old minister accepted the call to Marshfield. Smitten from the moment he saw Helen seated by her parents in the Connor pew, he proposed before the year was out, was finally accepted, and began to look for another pastorate. The Reverend George E. Hunt wrote on his behalf.

Your committee may wonder why he should be ready to leave his present charge after only two years. I can quickly satisfy your committee that the reasons are good and sufficient. He has never married, but in his present charge he has become engaged to one of the finest young women in that city. She is a graduate of the University of Wisconsin and a very earnest and beautiful girl. But unfortunately for the prospects of union, she is the daughter of one of the wealthy and leading citizens of that community. Now that community has had a long-standing feud, not of the Kentucky variety, between the two leading families of the city. They are the leaders in politics, in business, in society, and in the church. That little town of seven or eight thousand is divided between these two families in a rivalry and jealousy that makes for constant division among the citizens of that town. . . . The two previous pastors of that church have always had great difficulty in keeping the balance and maintaining the peace within the church between these two factions. Mr. Laird has completely won the confidence and hearty support of both factions, but he has done the fatal thing of falling in love and becoming engaged to the daughter of the leader of one of these factions, which will make it psychologically and practically impossible for him to remain in that church, when he marries that girl.[7]

෴

# CHAPTER 10

# Illinois versus Wisconsin

## 1913–1916

If I were a man, I shouldn't stay here. I'd be somebody. I'd make a national reputation for myself. . . . That's the worst of being a woman—we have to sit still until something happens to us. . . . It's dreadful to feel that one has power and not to be able to use it.

—WINSTON CHURCHILL, *A Modern Chronicle.*

In the heart of the northern Illinois prairie some hundred miles southwest of Chicago, Lincoln was home to a small college affiliated with the First United Presbyterian Church, a Coca-Cola bottling company, a number of shops, shopkeepers, retired farmers, lawyers, ministers, doctors, and educators. With a student body of 308 and ten full-time faculty members whose aim was "to lead rather than drive the students to a higher and better life,"[1] the college provided courses in domestic science for a few female students and courses in history, rhetoric, and classical languages for the men.

The manse on Pekin Street, an enormously scaled-down version of Helen's home on Cherry, was located a half-block from the church and within easy walking distance of the Illinois Central station and the town center where the post office, bank, and small shops surrounded the green. Churches—the First United Presbyterian, the First United Episcopalian, the First United Methodist, and the First Baptist—dominated the area. Helen's new home had a small front yard shaded by a single maple, a rear garden, and side yards barely wide enough to accommodate a carriage or an automobile. Helen decorated her high-ceilinged living room comfortably and tastefully. Her upright piano, on which she liked to play popular tunes and the classics for at least a little while every day, stood against one wall. Velvet drapes framed and lace curtains covered floor-to-ceiling windows. Family photographs and original landscapes in oil and watercolor decorated the papered walls. Mahogany coffee and end tables held books, magazines—*Harper's, The Atlantic,* the *New Republic,* and

*The Outlook*—and wedding gifts, including a slender Tiffany vase from her cousin Ruth Witter Mead and her husband George and a silver coffee service from Donald. ("Say, you better get some burglar insurance on all your silver valuables and your rings!! Right away," Donald advised, and "you better get some fair slave to do the rougher of your domestic duties."[2])

Although Helen's home was as modest as the minister's $1,800 annual salary, her small formal dining room featured a bell on the floor under the dining room table, which Helen used to call the "girl" who prepared and served the meals Helen prescribed and cleared and washed the dishes and handled the "rougher domestic chores." Melvin's brothers, who were pig and grain farmers, like their father, and construction workers, and his sisters, homemakers and home economics teachers, speculated that even with a bell on the floor to call a servant, it must have been "quite a come-down to come to a little place like Lincoln."

Eager to support and encourage her in the new situation in which they had been eager to place her, Helen's parents sent white potatoes from Laona and other root vegetables and apples from the Auburndale farm in spite of the fact that Lincoln lay in the heart of fine farming country. They wrote, telephoned, and visited, applauding her creation of a tasteful home and commending her new friends, people associated with the church and college, including the Vaughns, who ran the Coca-Cola plant, and the Diffenderfers and Woodses, people W.D. called "the right kind."

Donald, who after graduating from the University of Wisconsin had returned to Marshfield to take charge of sales in the Connor office, wrote on May 25 expressing the hope that Helen would "get acquainted and take more pleasure in being there at Lincoln." Although he had "very little enjoyment here outside of the business," Donald made himself believe that Marshfield was "quite a place . . . and then too, when we, or rather the family, are up at the Lake, we are very easily satisfied with the deal life gives us if we exert a little amount of mental persuasion to that way of thinking. . . . Write to me when you have time. Just get a tablet . . . and scribble what you think." Two weeks later he was dead, fatally injured in an automobile accident near Fremont, Wisconsin. "If Marshfield citizens ever were shocked, they probably never experienced one of such severity as was occasioned by the sad news of this young man's untimely end. The news spread rapidly over the city and the citizens are bowed in sorrow."

Donald had driven his father to pick up orders in Rockford and Elgin and a new car in Chicago, "one of the finest cars on the market, a six cylinder high powered roadster." After dropping his father off in Milwaukee, he drove on

Donald, the Connors' first-born son, ca. 1912, age 22.

alone. Driving too fast over roads not yet paved or engineered for powerful automobiles, he abruptly hit the brakes when he came on a curve obscured by trees. The car ran on two wheels, leapt into the air, and turned over, throwing him clear. A witness, who ran to the scene, perceived his agony and heard him say, "God save me if the doctor's can't. Poor father, poor mother. Tell them to pray for me and I will too."[3]

With the insurance money, W.D. erected a massive, sternly plain mausoleum in the aptly named Hillside Cemetery on the northern edge of Marshfield. Across the face, etched deep in the stone was a single word, "Connor." Inside, for many years, the mausoleum contained only the remains of his firstborn son.

For Anglo-Saxons, emotional display is in bad taste; pride demands self-control. Mame, however, shared her pain with Helen. "This morning has been so full of Donald. Everywhere I saw and felt him. And the very air breathed his sayings so antic and funny until I thought I could not stand it." She tried "to think perhaps Donald was permitted to see a heavenly vision which softened and made easier the way of his going—and that there is much work somewhere for such a busy, energetic soul."

Pregnant and craving activity as an antidote to depression, Helen plunged into community betterment projects. While the milk supply was recognized as "a source of disease, not alone typhoid, but of many infantile troubles,"[4] and the role of bacteria in disease had been established, milk was not yet uniformly inspected or pasteurized. Lincoln, moreover, like most other American towns, did not have closed sewers or proper garbage disposal, and while sputum was now suspect as a carrier of the tuberculosis bacteria, and ordinances against spitting existed, they were not enforced. Helen wrote letters to the State Board of Health and the State Food Commission and delivered public speeches before women's groups and church groups calling for safe water and pure milk, clean and safe streets, sanitary schools, inspected meat, cheap gas. With her university anthropology professor Edward Ross's lectures, and the example of the successful establishment of social centers in Milwaukee in mind,[5] she urged town leaders to develop a public playground for the children and a YMCA "where men and boys of all classes will find a welcome; where they can have reading rooms, a gymnasium, swimming tanks, shower baths, etc." She spoke publicly on behalf of the temperance movement and most passionately on behalf of female suffrage.

That women were different from men was, she pointed out, "the very reason they should vote. They do not look at things in exactly the same way. Both have contributions to make to every subject, *which concerns them both.*"

(italics added). The objection that "women would have to associate in politics with rough men" could not withstand scrutiny. Nor could the argument that men would lose their chivalrous attitude toward women. "The chivalry, which satisfies itself in meaningless forms to women of the fortunate classes and permits other women to drudge their lives out is not worth having. Real chivalry is founded on respect and understanding. How can a man respect a person whose ideas of what is good for herself and her children he does not consider worth expressing at the ballot box?" The well-publicized argument that "bad" women would vote and that "respectable women would have to face the class that is not respectable, a thing appalling to modest women,"[6] could not stand up to scrutiny either. "There are more 'fallen' men than 'fallen' women; chastity is not imposed upon *men* as a qualification for voting." Besides, she said, "women of underworld do not want to register. They are constantly moving away."

Outraged that the one thousand representatives of the thirty thousand striking shirtwaist workers in New York who marched to see the mayor and complain of mistreatment at the hands of police and judges were turned away, she argued that the mayor would not have turned them away had they represented thirty thousand voters. Privileged women would also benefit from suffrage. Most of them craved to do more than darn stockings, play bridge, and drink pink tea. "A hand in government will make a woman a truer, more active being with a broader horizon."

When the "Female Suffrage in Presidential and Municipal Election" bill passed in Illinois in 1913, and Illinois became the fourth state in the Union to grant limited female suffrage, W.D. wrote Helen a long letter crackling with cynicism for the way men ran things. He looked to women voters "to rid the country of the greatest danger"—liquor. It was "sad to see so very, very many of our strongest and most capable men carried away with this stuff. The laws and law makers have helped protect the traffic. It bought the politician at once. The nucleus of a political organization, the Brewers and Distillers all powerful with their line of agencies and saloons, and immense wealth accumulated from the profits, ever ready to help any party, any faction that would place them on a surer footing. They want business. They have no political principles any more than moral principles. They want money."[7]

He knew how impressive a public speaker she was but advised, "if you are going to take part in public meetings, you first want to have a press agent. That means so much. The press with one issue properly handled can get started for anyone a favorable or unfavorable current of feeling in any community. . . . It is necessary for anyone to deal carefully with the news gatherers."

He drew on personal experience. The wave of sympathy that had united Marshfield when Donald was killed shattered abruptly when Frank Upham and Hamilton Roddis spearheaded a well-publicized drive to recall Mayor Robert Connor, charging negligence and inefficiency in the performance of his duties. On October 15, the headline of the *Marshfield Times* proclaimed: "Recall of Connor Possible Through Special Election."

In a move that looks very much like payback time for Connor's previous attack on Upham, Roddis, who served on the judiciary committee, alleged that the company books of the Marshfield Water, Electric Power and Light Company were short $4,000. He implied that the mayor was in on the take; that he knowingly permitted Louis Carl, who oversaw charges and payments, to skim the receipts; and that the mayor was, at the very least, negligent. The Connors claimed they'd been framed; the books were sequestered in the offices of the Roddis Lumber and Veneer Company, kept in their vaults and not at the City Hall; the shortage was not $4,000 but $100. Mr. Carl made good on the amount with a check drawn on the First National Bank in Marshfield, and the mayor had therefore not seen fit to press charges.

The Upham-Roddis faction won the round. The Connors suffered the humiliation of seeing Rob recalled. On December 3, headlines proclaimed, "Marshfield Has New Mayor." A Roddis supporter, Arnold Felker, who had lost the election to Connor the year before, became mayor. The humiliation of Rob's recall passed. The pain of Donald's death lingered. W.D. wrote, encouraging Helen, "We simply must try to go on the way, not simply existing, but striving our utmost to accomplish something worthwhile."

Accomplishing something worthwhile for W.D. meant accumulating wealth, property, standing. In sermons and in the advice he gave to students and to Helen, Melvin emphasized something else. With Mammon flexing his muscles in America, education, traditionally believed to be for the enlightenment of character and intellect, was rapidly giving way to the notion that a college education "pays."[8] Melvin cautioned students, "Money is not success. Of course a person has a right to make his occupation or profession bring him money for bread and butter if he does it honestly. To make money rapidly is not to make a success of your life. . . . A young man should consider his opportunities for doing good along with his opportunities to make a good living when choosing a profession or occupation."

While her husband held firm to his religious beliefs, like so many of her generation brought up as a Christian, Helen had doubts about Christian doctrines. As a thoughtful, conscientious person, and someone also married to a minister, she could not slough them off. The letter in which she raised questions has been lost, but she saved Melvin's response. It reveals his outlook and suggests hers. In 1913, he was optimistic that his sheltering faith would eventually become hers. To her expressed interest in a Unitarian minister's sermon, he told her, "his creed is pagan." Across the ages, many people have said the world could be saved by education. "Educate people, and they will see that it is folly to do wrong and they will cease doing it." He did not believe that. In his experience, "equip a man with all the powers that education can equip him and you simply give him power with which he can carry on selfishness more skillfully than before. The most wicked people I know are the educated." The world's greatest need, Melvin was convinced, was for "a miracle—the miracle of grace." Nothing could be gained by "breathing into men's minds a distrust of all stories of the miraculous."

Helen had probed. Did one have to believe or have unshaken faith in spiritual things in order to enter the kingdom of heaven? Melvin thought one had to have "faith in unseen spiritual things—goodness, love, kindness, character" but did not have to have faith in theological statements such as the trinity. She was right in saying "that actual living and our deeds are the things upon which the emphasis should be placed," but he was convinced that "those things are determined by our faith in goodness, in God, in spiritual things." Love was mysterious.

The last word of paganism was "self-reliance," Melvin concluded, and the first word of Christianity was "God-reliance. I love you still, but you are a pagan. I'm going to make you see some day that a person must have the Christ ideal, the Christ motive and the Christ power to get the most out of life. I'm not saying that I have realized all this in my own life, but I see it all very clearly."

Helen spent Christmas quietly in Lincoln anticipating the birth of her child. Mame filled her in on the family gossip. W.D.'s sisters' Christmas gifts demonstrated their Scots parsimony. "Aunt Anne sent Jess a *little* plant in a funny paper jardiniere. It looked like one of her ten cent presents; Aunt Molly limbered up to the extent of a pair of gloves; Aunt Bess a handkerchief." Mame also touched on the first instance of conflict over the inheritance of family wealth. Observing their brother's rapid rise in fortune, feeling that they had not been adequately compensated for the shares of Robert Connor stock they had sold to him, W.D.'s sisters hired accountants to go over the books. "They have had *two* men over at Stratfold for *three weeks*. They have gotten down to *1892*. They have been called in to Milwaukee. It is *comical*. Then they have the same to do with these books [in Marshfield] and the Auburndale books. It will be some bill for Aunt Anne and Molly. I just laughed to see

Aunt Anne's face when she saw the bill. She will be getting *smaller* plants."
Mame thought Aunt Jessica, who was then showing signs of the schizophre-
nia for which she would soon be permanently institutionalized, seemed better, and if Jessica's sisters would "keep away, she will keep all right."

On Sunday, December 28, 1913, Helen's first child was born. Baptized
William Connor, he was called "Con Con" as a baby and thereafter known as
Connor. W.D., desiring that "they start the boy right and have him know
good music from the first," had a Victrola shipped out from Chicago. Mame
went to Lincoln to be with her daughter. She remained long enough to feel
certain that Helen had sufficiently recovered from childbirth to take on her
new duties without assistance and returned home to supply her daughter with
the gossip and family news. "This Mrs. Harry Vedder is a wonder, I think, so
calm and sweet. They have lost their Baby Boy three years old. . . . They think
it was tuberculosis of bowel. Anyway, their Darling is gone. . . . Funeral from
the house tomorrow afternoon. William to be one of the pall bearers. I rather
hated to have him, but they asked." "Daddy" had not been home in a long
time, two days short of three weeks. "I joshed him a little about being gone
so long, telling him I had gleaned from his letters that there were show people
staying at the hotel and a teachers' meeting and so many exciting things to
hold him" at Laona. She had probably not heard the gossip circulating in
Laona that her husband had a relationship with a schoolteacher, but chance
or instinct or merely a desire to prove to her daughter that she too was a
"modern" woman led her to tell Helen, jokingly, that she was "on the point
of a divorce."

Seeking his daughter's sympathy, W.D. wrote Helen. "We must try and
keep as close as possible. We must keep cheer and confidence. I try to but
mask a failure. Sometimes I get a little discouraged. Seems as though all the
little disappointments and obstacles look bigger. Business has been such a trial
the last six months, so many changes in conditions, such a change in finance,
but then we simply must make things straighten out and hope for better
times."

Finally extricating himself from the Northwoods, W.D. took his wife to
New York, combining business with pleasure. They spent "lovely days" walking along Fifth Avenue, taking pleasant rides along Riverside Drive "on one
of those high top buses," and visiting churches. Mame was "glad papa can be
away a little and have some change" and willing to stay away "unless papa gets
uneasy and gets fever for home."

With her easy tattle, lighting briefly on one subject and another, Mame
sought to support and encourage her daughter. She knew Helen's character,

was confident that she would be a conscientious mother. She was, as the Reverend Hunt said, an "earnest" woman, who took her responsibilities seriously. Less certain that Helen was happy, or that she would sufficiently value the role into which she had so swiftly been thrust, along with her newsy letters, Mame sent a book she had found inspirational.

*A Study of Child-Nature* celebrated "one of the greatest lines of the world's work": raising children. Published by the Chicago Kindergarten Training School in 1891, it addressed a class of elite, educated American women who, in the pre–"great books" era could be expected to share a common culture based on the texts of Homer, Goethe, Shakespeare, Byron, and Carlyle. Urged to train their children "so that the unseen things in life shall be as real as the seen," they were also to understand the prevailing "scientific fact" that "nervous power is expended by the infant in tossing his limbs about in creeping and crawling; by the growing boy, in climbing and running; by the young girl—who must not climb or run as such conduct is not ladylike—in twisting, squirming, and giggling; thus gaining for her muscles, in spite of prohibition, some of the needed exercise."[9]

Helen left no comment about the "twisting, squirming, and giggling" prescribed for girls. She performed her duties as mother and minister's wife gracefully but not uncritically. She appreciated the familiar church services, the music and prayer; attended her husband's instructive stereopticon lectures; supported the Home Missions' work, because "Home Missions is a synonym for patriotism, for progress, for prosperity and the perpetuity of the Nation." She joined in the Tuesday Ladies' Aid Society meetings in the parlors of the church and welcomed newcomers.

She required more solitude than a minister's wife often gets. Fortunately, she had an automobile, her "fair slave" to look after the house, and some independence. When pressures became too great, and irritation overwhelmed her, she drove into the countryside. Gazing out on the vast Illinois horizon she relaxed. Nature took away her restlessness, briefly.

"I wish there were things I might say that would make things seem easier for you," Mame wrote after receiving Helen's letter indicating she was again expecting. "*Perhaps* I in my loneliness then in Auburndale idealized motherhood more." Many of the moments Mame might have devoted to Helen were given to Donald, and she often grew tired as Helen did. "How many mothers do!!! and have *so* little of comfort from husband or other loved ones to help them over the hard places." She had "*never thought* to rail" against her lot as a mother, though many times it seemed hard. "The best mothers and fathers have had to give up for others-*much.*" Mame wished she could have the child for Helen, "but that I am denied. But I can pray for you," and told her that anytime she wished to come, their home would be open to her. She could be made "very comfortable there. The children will be lovely! and you will be at *Home.*"

Helen accepted her mother's invitation and made frequent visits to Wisconsin, taking Connor with her and noting afterwards her return "from home." While she "railed" against the second pregnancy coming so soon after the first, Connor's development interested her, and she kept a record of it in her "Baby Book." At eleven months, when asked "Who loves the baby?" he answered "da da." At a year and a half he began to put words into sentences. "I ove my mamie all to pieces." "Dadie peach at church tell people how be good. Con Con tell people how be nauny." "I know one hing-sweetest boy in countie—

Helen with Connor, 1914.

Dadie say dot to Con Con owt in tudy." Soon, Helen reported, "Connor says everything—uses long sentences. 'Don't go to Springfield, Mamie, isn't necessary.' 'I think you're a pity nice woman.' 'I'm sprised at you mamie.' 'Do you love dadie tonight mamie? I just wanted to know.'"

Connor's "dove ou" was, Helen thought, "the nicest thing in the world," and sometimes that love was enough to make her happy. At other times it was not. Then, restless, like the women in the stories she read in *Harper's* and the *Atlantic*,[10] she chafed at the predictable pattern of her days in the small house in the small town.

In June 1915, when she was almost eight months pregnant, taking Connor along, Helen returned to Marshfield to await the birth of her second child. An even-tempered, friendly, brown-haired toddler with his father's soft brown eyes, Connor was already well established as the family favorite. Rob's daughter, Angie, only a year and a half older than he, and his ten-year-old Uncle Gordo and seven-year-old Aunt Constie instantly took over as his teachers, protectors, and friends. Connor liked living in the big house with the big yard and being the center of so much attention from so many caring relatives. On July 28, 1915, Richard Malcolm was born. Soon after Connor advised his mother, "Don't call me Con Con, call me sweetheart" and proclaimed "baby

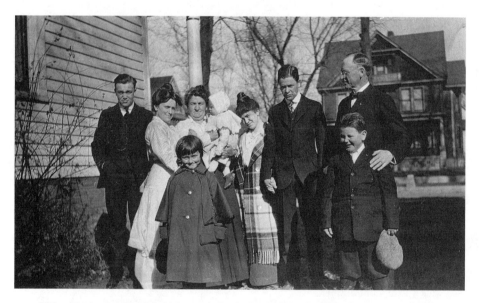

Helen visiting in Marshfield, 1914. At back, from left : Richard, Helen, Mame holding Connor, Marian, William, W.D.; Constance and Gordon are in the front.

Dick and Con Con two nice boys." Helen and her boys did not return to Lincoln until three and a half months had passed.

On August 18, 1915, the *Marshfield Times* ran a headline: "Germany Has the Lead. Gives Kaiser's Kingdom Laurels Up to Date." Germany had won "mighty and memorable triumphs" on the field of battle. "Allied offenses [are] in retreat. Today her [German] armies occupy all of Belgium and 8,000 square miles in France. . . . In the East amazing victories." Germany's rapid advance or possible eventual victory sounded no alarms in Marshfield. The concerns of the Connors and Lairds, in spite of the Hearst press's loud outcry when the British announced a total embargo on trade with Germany and when Germany threatened a submarine blockage of the British Isles, seemed to be entirely domestic. Only Helen's action in clipping Ellen Kay's article, "War and the Sexes," from the *Atlantic* indicates she followed the war, which had been raging in Europe for over a year.

The article ignores the war's threat to American meat, cotton, copper, and munitions interests and the increasing number of nations involved, but it deals with the effect the swelling number of dead and wounded men would have on "woman's prospects from the point of view of her natural duty—motherhood." That would "be dark indeed after the war." Germans planned to deal with the shortage of men by opening a marriage department to further early marriages and by giving invalids homes, wives, and stipends. The English proposed a "society for the marrying of wounded heroes," which appealed to "woman's self sacrifice and patriotism to make the lives of these men bearable and to propagate children who will inherit their father's qualities of patriotism." A committee of clergymen and physicians would link physically strong women with men who needed to be carried or pushed in a chair. Blind men, who could still at least enjoy good food, would be married to good cooks. Helen underlined the author's conclusion. Those who regretted that the war would restrict woman's ability "to produce future soldiers," should look upon the matter in a more human way: "*as a condition for future development that women resolutely refuse mass production of children,* and more consistently seek to improve the quality of humanity, while they, at the same time, try more energetically to procure the right to have a share in dictating the politics on which the lives of their sons and daughters are so dependent."

The issue gnawing at the conscience of American Christians, Melvin said, speaking from the pulpit in January 1916, was neither the role of women, whom he believed to be "frail by nature" and in need of protection, nor the European war but the accumulation and display of extraordinary wealth by some Americans and the equally extreme and visible poverty of so many others. The love of money was "as old as the race," and the "scramble to get it has always been widespread and furious," but the contemporary age was a wealth-producing age compared to which the fiction of Arabian Nights was tame. He told his congregation that "no other nation is growing rich so rapidly as our own. The wealth is flowing into the cities and in the cities it is accumulating in the hands of the few." Fewer than 25,000 people possessed more than half the wealth of the country. An "enormous literature," written in "feverish vehemence and with exaggerated phrases" by "badly frightened radicals," but also by serious scholars and thinkers, warned that "money has become one of the dangers of our time." He cited Professor William Graham Sumner of Yale, who claimed that "the real issue that men of the future have yet to meet is the struggle between plutocracy and democracy," and Professor Albion Small of the University of Chicago, who spoke of the danger inherent in making capital accumulation an end in itself: "Whether we realize it or not, our vision of freedom is passing into the eclipse of universal compulsion in the interest of capital. The march of human progress is getting reduced to marking time in the lockstep of capital's chain gang."

Melvin reassured his congregation that one did not have to renounce one's wealth to be a good Christian, but "a rich man is constantly tempted to be arbitrary, or domineering, or autocratic, or tyrannical or self-indulgent, or inhuman or mean." Christianity had words of warning for both rich and poor. "Accursed is the dishonest man whether he steals pennies or millions."

In another sermon, Melvin called upon his congregation to work for the glory of God and not for one's own glory, to make the same self-denial for moral ends that business men make for personal gain. He described businessmen who, "from early morning till late at night," were "straining and striving, figuring and calculating, exhausting their nerve-force and their vitality until they are ready to break down." His father-in-law was the prototype.

Shortly after La Follette's arrival in Marshfield on a campaign swing during which he delivered his popular diatribe against the railroads and all the lumber men who had "tainted money,"[11] W.D. was subject to a potentially devastating lawsuit. The Interstate Commerce Committee indicted the Laona and Northern Railway and the Connor Lumber and Land Company for violating the Elkins Law by falsely billing hardwood and maple flooring as cedar posts and soft wood. The latter two carried a significantly lower rate than hardwood, "thereby denying railroads the just compensation as called for under tariffs." The Interstate Commerce Department's "great interest" in the case, which led to their sending a special assistant U. S. district attorney from Washington to Milwaukee to work on it, had as much to do, W.D. believed, with his running feud with La Follette as with the fact that it was the first case of its kind in Wisconsin and the outcome was of "some concern to the department of justice."[12]

W.D. had faced a crippling thirty-thousand-dollar fine and two years imprisonment. He escaped with a fine of $1,000 on six counts (a considerable sum in the days when a man could stay at any of Marshfield's three hotels on Central Avenue, the Majestic, the Eagle, or the Northwestern, for a dollar a day or at the "strictly first class and modern" Hotel Blodgett for two dollars), but his health broke. He was hospitalized with pneumonia.

On January 30, Rob wrote Helen to tell her that her father looked much better, and if he could be quiet and build himself up again, he would be all right. "You know a fellow goes along every day and never stops to think about some things but believe I did when we took your father to the hospital for it would have gone pretty hard with me had anything happened to him. . . . He is almost the only 'blood relative' that speaks to me and for the last twenty years have been with him in so many ways that I would have been lost for a long while without him."

By mid-February, W.D. was sufficiently recovered to go to the office for a short while. In March, leaving Rob in charge, the family left for Florida. As they traversed the country by rail, Mame told the children to "keep the blinds down, or Papa will be off buying more land." She hoped he could put business out of mind and concentrate on recuperating, but he kept them moving, arranging for them "to stop off to see each large city in Florida." And he did buy more land. In one of his moods where he saw possibility everywhere, he bought several hundred acres of the inland waterways. He asked his sons William, a nineteen-year-old student at the university in Madison, and Richard, a junior at Marshfield High, if they would like to go to Cuba. While W.D. remained behind with his wife and the two younger children, Richard and William sailed to Havana.

On their return to Marshfield, Mame wrote glowingly of W.D.'s restoration to health and the new spirit of cooperation in town, prompted largely by W.D., who, in responding to Governor Philipp's order for an immediate increase in the Wisconsin National Guard, because of the outbreak of violence along the Texas-Mexican border, had delivered a magnificent speech advocating "association, united action and unity of purpose." For men to make progress, there had to be team work, with every man doing his very best, as in the old log-rolling days. It was "now or never with the present generation of men in Marshfield and there has never been a time in the history of the city when there was greater need for patriotic and united effort."[13]

The European war was Europe's business, but America's border was America's. The Marshfield guard grew to include 150 men. Rob, who had resigned his commission as captain when his brother became ill and he had to shoulder many of his responsibilities, reenlisted as a private. He felt, he wrote Helen, he "had to go with the outfit" and wished to prove himself "no tin soldier, but a real one."[14] He was thirty-nine years old.

Assuming his old place as leader, Rob drilled the unit in Marshfield, instructing the first-generation Americans and new immigrants, conditioned by the European class system, that they should be aware that in America "no officer humbles himself by giving due courtesy to one of inferior rank for that is the part of the business of an officer no matter how high his rank." Helen, in Marshfield with her children on June 21, when the unit prepared to depart by special train for Camp Douglas, joined the early-morning crowd at Columbia Park. W.D. was on the speaker's platform with other dignitaries: Mayor Felker, former governor W. H. Upham, and attorney E. C. Pors.

"A month ago," W.D. said," it was possible to criticize our president, our governor or any other official. Today, we are confronted by a serious problem.

The Reverend and Mrs. Melvin R. Laird with Dick and Connor, Marshfield, 1916.

Today we should stand by every one of them—one country, one flag, one president." The men could have "no better encouragement than to know that the people of their home-town [were] standing by them," not only in voice and sympathy but also financially. "Unless we are willing to fill the pockets they are unable to fill, our words here mean nothing." The soldiers, whose salary was a meager fifty dollars a month, had to know "that on every one of those hot nights across the alkali sands every heart in Marshfield throbs for you."[15] Those who stayed behind would "proffer financial aid, good counsel and advice to the dependents of these soldier boys."

W.D., president of the Marshfield Executive Committee of the Wisconsin National Guard Relief Fund, and Rob, who had "quickly risen to the rank of battalion sargeant major, the highest noncommissioned rank in the regiment,"[16] secured columns of favorable publicity.

W.D. with Connor in
Marshfield, 1916.

Rob's wife, Florence, along with W.D. and hundreds of others conquered muddy roads to see the Wisconsin regiments off when they departed Camp Douglas on June 28. It had been hard to see Rob go, Florence wrote Helen. "It just seemed as if he was gone from us forever." Everyone had been "so dear and kind and want to do everything for us and their prayers with yours and Melvin's are going to do so much good. Your father did the sweetest thing at the train. He put his arm around Rob and kissed him just as he would have done to any of you children."

"Guess the only people I know in the world who have not written me are my own sisters," Rob wrote Helen from Texas, letting her know how welcome her letters were. "Maybe they don't care and if so, am glad they don't write."[17] His letter reached her at Birch Lake, where she and the boys spent the summer in the simple, roomy, one-story cabin W.D. built for her growing family adjacent his own.

A narrow concrete walkway linked the white clapboard cottages built out of wood from the Connor mill. Between them, a tall wooden flagpole, also painted white, supported an enormous American flag. A hill, rising a few feet behind the cabin and thickly covered with virgin pine and hemlock, cast it in deep shadow by four in the afternoon. Consisting of a large, rectangular living room, two bedrooms, and a screened in porch (no kitchen), the cottage, a few feet from the water, seemed, when it stormed, to ride in the lake, more boat than house. The families took their meals together in the big cottage, swam and fished off the Connors' long wooden dock, and pumped water from the same pump. They shared the outhouse and icehouse and the family cow, which had been brought up from Auburndale and was milked by Otto Maedenwald, who for many years, until he came to live permanently in Laona, made the same annual migration from Auburndale to Laona to take care of the cow and the children.

Publicity photographs, distributed primarily in Milwaukee and Madison but also in Chicago, advertised "W.D. Connor Summer Cottages, Birch Lake, Laona." but W.D. wasn't offering property on that lake for sale. Profit could be made, however, selling lots on the cut-over around Silver Lake and other clear, fish-filled lakes in Forest County and by filling the Gordon Hotel, which advertised fifty-five rooms, steam heat, electric light, a barbershop, an amusement room, and a knotted-rope fire escape hanging from the third floor.

The Connors were flourishing. In Marshfield, W.D. advertised the American National Bank, of which he was president and his family the principal stock holders, as "one of the sound financial headquarters of Wood County" in which "financially responsible men" whose affiliation means prestige and

The Connor cottages at Birch Lake, Laona, 1917. W.D. advertised lake lots in the cut-over in Forest County. He did not sell lots around Birch Lake.

strength are interested." At a meeting of the newly formed Marshfield Chamber of Commerce, he asserted his new theme: "Now, in all lines great and small our maxim is co-operation." The town's doctors—William Hipke, V. A. Mason, W. G. Sexton, R. P. Potter, Karl Doege, and H. H. Milbee—proved it by forming the Marshfield Clinic.[18]

With the public feuding between the Upham-Roddis faction and the Connors apparently a thing of the past now that the raw pioneer days were over, W.D. waxed enthusiastic. There was room for a big town in Marshfield. If everyone did his share, he forecast, in forty years they would have "from 20,000 to 30,000 people, the best stores in the territory, smoking factories, beautiful school buildings, the finest churches, and, at the upper end of the street, a great monument to the memory of all those who served in '61 to '65; on that monument we shall inscribe the names of the Grand Army, and of those who followed Company A to Charleston and Puerto Rico in '98, and add those of the Company A of 1916 who went out and answered the call of the country to do service." He said that in 1946, if the country called, another Company A would respond from Marshfield and "go with light hearts knowing that those at home will have their burdens made lighter by those around them."

The Connor reputation was restored and business was booming, and when the Methodist minister asked him to speak from the pulpit, W.D. wrote Helen, "*So it goes. They kan't* keep Them Connors Down."[19]

༼

# CHAPTER II

# War

## 1917–1919

The plunge of civilization into this abyss of blood and darkness . . . is
a thing that so gives away the whole long age during which we have
supposed to be, with whatever abatement, generally bettering that to
have to take it all now for what the treacherous years were all the while
really making for and MEANING is too tragic for words.

—HENRY JAMES

When Marshfield's Company A came home on February 28, 1917, the flags
went up all over town, and the city held a banquet. The boys had not seen
any action. At the Texas-Mexico border Rob had "trained them into a pretty
good outfit," and they had been exposed to "some of the different kinds of
people this country is made of." They thought they had come home to stay.
Headlines, however, no longer hailed German advances but the demoraliza-
tion and exhaustion of the English and French troops.

All the horrible news of the "civilized" world gone mad coming through in
1914, 1915, and 1916[1] had not engaged America's attention, but when American financial and industrial leaders, their fortunes interlocked with those of
the Allies, recognized the possibility that the battle on the Continent would
be lost, and American interests forfeited if America remained neutral, they
persuaded Wilson to enter the war. He immediately launched a compelling
propaganda campaign. The "Boche" became the enemy, and America became
responsible for supporting freedom and democracy, for upholding the foundations of civilization.

The "Order of Service" Melvin handed out to parishioners now included
the statement: "That which is to be is conditioned by that which has been.
Some time, somewhere, the plan that the centuries have brooded over will
come perfect out of the shell of time. I am not afraid that humanity will stop

short of its inevitable climax, but I am so jealous for the glory of my country that I long for America to retain the leadership."

La Follette's March fillibuster of a bill permitting the protective arming of American ships became moot on April 2, when President Wilson asked Congress for a Declaration of War. The declaration was ratified on April 6, and America moved rapidly forward to develop the enormously efficient and powerful war machine that has continued to affect everyone since. Woodrow Wilson delivered an inspirational call to service of "every man who can think straight and act effectively,"[2] and most American men felt called upon and honored to serve a noble cause, and most women believed they should.

Rob, respected by the men for his leadership on the border, had just won the race for alderman of Marshfield's fourth ward against Upham's son-in-law, E. E. Finney, by a wide margin of 197 to 96 when the war declaration came. He immediately volunteered for duty, writing Helen that "nearly every Sammy will have to go across that can be outfitted in order to bring the thing to a successful ending for us. It seems hard, but it would be a good deal harder if we sat idly home and the war should be brought to our own country and this is what it means as affairs stand right now. . . . It seems as tho Kaiser Bill started something that woke the whole world up."[3]

Marshfield's German-born gave up their firearms to the chief of police, able-bodied men aged twenty-one to thirty signed up for the draft, and the town celebrated Loyalty Day with a big parade. W.D. wrote Helen of going to Milwaukee for a meeting of the executive committee of the Wisconsin Defense League. The governor asked him to organize Wood County. He had $5,000 to work with to establish committees and subcommittees on military affairs, Red Cross, finance, planting, publicity, automobiles, and loyalty. He advised everyone to get busy and grow a garden and urged that the ordinance forbidding raising pigs within city limits be dropped "and let all those who want to raise pigs raise them. 'Pigs is pigs' and they are money getters right now."[4]

Melvin, as acting president of Lincoln College, encouraged the boys to give up studying for the time being and enlist, saying it was their "patriotic duty." William and Richard joined the navy and served stateside. Dean Witter enlisted. His sister Elizabeth joined the Red Cross and both, separately, went to France. Connor hoped the war wouldn't be over before he could get in it.

Buying Liberty Bonds became a moral duty, and anyone shirking that duty was subject to public humiliation. Mr. McMillan failed to show the required patriotism, and for that he was criticized, labeled an "abominable slacker" by Julian S. Nolan, director of the bond drive at the Federal Reserve Bank,

Chicago. W.D. saw that copies of Nolan's letter were spread around town and sent copies to Helen and to Rob as well.[5]

From Fort Sheridan, Illinois, Rob wrote on September 3: "Everyone here from Marshfield has his [McMillan's] number by this time. If the Marshfield newspapers were American they would publish this letter and show that fellow up in his true light." The 32d Division bought nearly a million in bonds.[6] Everything from Wisconsin was "being changed and reorganized and the old Regiments are suffering about as much as we are." A "pretty sober crowd of soldiers," which six bands had not been able to keep from "thinking pretty hard," gathered to say goodbye to Companies E, F, and G leaving "to go East to some place near Long Island." Young Edmund Arpin, a member of the prominent Wisconsin Rapids lumber family, was among the Wisconsin men leaving that day.

Another vast movement from Fort Sheridan on September 20, when six Wisconsin regiments were condensed into three, and from each of the three new regiments three officers received their orders to France: Colonel McCoy (head of the Wisconsin National Guard), Captain Leadbetter of the 4th, and Rob. He wired Helen on September 22 that he expected "to go through Lincoln tonight about midnight but may not stop." She would know he was going through anyway and could think of him.

In Waco, Texas, the next organizational point for many Wisconsin boys, Marshfield's Fred Rhyner, Bill Pors, Wayne Deming, Leo Schoenhofin, Cobby Kraus, and Charles Normington were together, Kraus and Normington going into Company A as 2d lieutenants. "Pretty nice for both of them to get into their old company again and guess they are glad to get back here with the Wisconsin troops." It was nice to be among friends, but less nice was Leo Schoenhofin's revelation that Fred Kohl was spreading a rumor back home that Rob had refused to go to France and was locked up in Texas for fifteen years. "Probably started by the pro-Germans[7] and of course that old gang there helped along all they could as it would just suit them if I were locked up or killed off." Rob hoped his brother would "get after Kohl and at least scares him good." Rob had been ordered to go on ahead to Camp Merritt to "pave the way so to speak" for the division.[8] W.D. would see that the information got spread around.

The country was on the move (it took eighty railroad cars to move the Wisconsin division to the coast), and business was booming. "For the first time in eight years," W.D. wrote Helen, even with the changes the war was making in the labor market (men wanted higher wages, less work, and better conditions), the lumber business showed "signs of giving the manufacturer a chance." They had "a great crew at the farm in Laona, twenty five to twenty eight men—only one or two of whom could speak English—and eight to twelve teams"; W.D. had had to send a good cook up from Marshfield to replace a bad one but not, unfortunately, before some men had left the camps because not enough potatoes were served. Even with all the high prices of supplies and labor, the flooring business was the best it had ever been, and the paper business was "clear out of all bounds." There was no possible excuse for the Consolidated not making $1.5 million in clear cash. The stock could go to $300 a share.

Speculating further on economic conditions, W.D. explained to Helen in his letters that "money came to this country in such abundance that property jumped in price very fast. I do not know how that will work out. With all the rapid changes in conditions, it is difficult to figure. For a year it has seemed to me when a person had debts at fixed sums, it ought to be easier to pay them when money, as compared to property, has been getting more plentiful so fast."[9] Having filled Helen in on business conditions, with which he certainly didn't believe she should actively concern herself, he wrote of his pride in Rob and in himself. "So many things they have for me to do. Along with the usual business keeps me busy." He was not too busy, however, to accompany Florence and her daughters, Angie and Katty, to New Jersey to say goodbye to Rob before he embarked for Europe.

Rob sent word that the two Marshfield men on board the torpedoed *Tuscania* had both been saved and, on March 2, that "young Riethus" (one of the many Wisconsin boys with German surnames) was "the first one from Marshfield to go." On March 11, the eve of his departure, Rob's only prayer, he wrote his wife, who shared his letters with the family, was to acquit himself as a soldier should and "if it is fated that I become only a memory"; he hoped it would be one she and their children need not be ashamed of. He had just received a message from Will. "Tell him goodbye for me. He has been so good and kind." She was to go to Will at once if anything happened to him. But, somehow, he had "the feeling that the Boche won't get me and that I'll get back to the U.S. all right."

He wrote Helen of his safe arrival in England. Canadians, who were there in great numbers, seemed like "someone from home," but he didn't like the English. He liked the French village from which his next letters came and admired the "picturesque old country" with its very winding good roads, which Caesar had laid out in his invasion of Gaul. He was "glad to be among the crowd he knew." The division headquarters was located in an old chateau that each village seemed to have—"a relic of the old days and customs."

For a time, Rob's letters seemed like those a tourist might write. They took a more serious tone, however, once the first soldier from their division fell on German soil. "The Huns," who had taken another offensive drive, would be held, he wrote, but if they had "a few million more Sammies" the thing would be over. They were far from their base, and it took time. "One thing I will wager on and that is that every Sammy who gets over here will be a continuous booster for the U.S. if he ever gets back as we do not realize what a country and people we have until we see some of the others. As for me, if I ever get back to Wisconsin I don't think I will ever go outside of the State again for there is no place that compares with our own country as to people and general conditions."[10] The boys had celebrated when word reached them that Hamilton Roddis was defeated in his bid for reelection from the Fourth Ward and that Henry Kalsched, a Connor loyalist, had been elected mayor. Roddis protested that the election was illegally obtained,[11] but it held.

W.D. wrote Helen boasting about the Connor faction's win and about further honors to himself. He had been asked by the Wisconsin War History Commission to chair the Wood County History Committee[12] and by "New York interests" to take over a bankrupt logging operation at the Jordan River in British Columbia. He had made an exploratory visit to the Pacific coast and was seriously considering taking on the presidency of the Canadian Puget Sound Timber and Lumber Company (CPS). There was a lot of virgin timber in Puget Sound, and plans were afoot to dredge harbors in Victoria. With harbors close to source, they could ship logs and lumber by sea to markets on the East Coast and in Europe through the Panama Canal, which finally opened in 1913.

Rob's experiences were also broadening. In a letter to Florence, he boasted about being plucked out of his division and sent to Army Staff College: "When they put a lumberjack like me up against majors and colonels, I feel handicapped in this game." His time wasn't all locked in study, however. He rode horseback almost every day and thought about bringing home a little French boy—"so many have lost their father and mother, a nice boy whose father was an officer in the French Army."[13] With the Sammies finally arriving in droves, he thought "the Huns will have something awful happen to them in a few months."[14]

While the men in Company A "covered themselves with glory" in the Battle of the Somme, where the German high command had mounted an offensive they thought would win the war and "everyone realized the awful punch the Sammie has, and the inspiration he is to the sorely tried troops of the allies," the "other side" of the story came home forcibly to Rob, who wrote of the "many friends and comrades of years I will never see again." His feelings toward

Robert Connor, 1917. He received the Croix de Guerre for valiant service during
World War I.

the "Boche" hardened: "The people at home better get busy and clean out the Boche newspapers and the language in the U.S. or the returning Sammies will do that too on their return—for we won't stand for any of it—too many of our friends have given their lives in the cause."[15]

Helen sent Rob copies of *The Outlook*, a magazine subscribed to by Protestant-American intellectuals, thinking that the numerous articles concerning the Russian Revolution, the Kerensky government's efforts to survive in the face of the destructive work of German agents and "Bolsheviki" agitators might interest him and hoping that the article "Immortality and a Personal God" might comfort him.

The author of that article "in common with most university graduates, regarded immortality as a rather interesting speculative problem" until he became a soldier fighting on the French front. Then it became a live question,[16] as it must, Helen thought, for Rob. Rob, however, who had warned Florence before their marriage that he would accompany her anywhere but church, was interested neither in religion nor in the afterlife. He had no time to read the *Outlook* but appreciated Helen's sweet letters and thought it "too bad all the women in America are not as patriotic as you are for you show it in every word of your letters." One of Helen's letters, Rob wrote Florence, made it seem "as though she hoped to see Melvin get into the service and be doing his share in the war."[17]

Melvin R. Laird reported for duty on July 31, 1918, to the commanding general of the 84th Division, Camp Sheridan, Ohio. In spite of his forty years and his obligations to his young family, he felt he could not in good conscience remain at home, and with Helen's enthusiastic approval, he had volunteered. Commissioned as chaplain, with rank of 1st lieutenant, he studied his army-issued pocket dictionary *For the Man Who Is Going to the Front*. He memorized the words and phrases useful to a soldier: *prendre les prisonniers* (to take prisoners), *se livrer* (to give up), *le sabre* (sword), *la puissance* (power), *la guerre* (war), *la blessure* (wound), etc. And he wrote a love poem to his wife.

Hands, you have caressed it
Lips, you've known its thrill:
Eyes, you have beheld it—
Soul of mine, be still.
But oh, my soul is sateless;
It will not give me rest—
Forever and forever,
I hunger and I quest.

It had been like a spring day and it had gone to his head when Helen's "foolishly affectionate husband" begged permission "to be sentimental for a few minutes." He promised to add another stanza to "The Beauty of My Wife" when he saw her. "The last stanza must be the climax when I get you in my arms. I shall be happy to see you for I do hunger for your hugs and kisses. Now, will you forgive your foolish husband. Tell me, do you think he is foolish. I always have told you I had to do the love making, but I can't help it. It is in me and I have to let it go sometimes. I do love you, passionately dear."

As Rob, on temporary assignment from the Army Staff College, moved to the front, Melvin, after a short farewell visit with Helen at Birch Lake, moved across the sea. The reflective and the active, the North and South Poles of human experience, moved in heightened measure through Helen's mind as she vicariously participated in her uncle's and husband's experiences. In letters written to Helen in the form of diary entries, Melvin told of his love—"I thought I loved you when we were married and I did, but my love for you is a million times greater now. You seem a very part of me, of my soul. The boys are in fact a very part of me and I love them as my own life"—and shared his thoughts and experiences.

The fleet in which Melvin sailed across the Atlantic—troop boats, submarine destroyers, armored cruises, and a dirigible balloon—gave him a feeling of safety. The 335th Infantry was on the ship, as well as a number of "colored troops," whose singing he enjoyed. He conducted a burial service for one of the black soldiers, who died of pneumonia and was buried at sea, and wrote a letter to the boy's parents, explaining to Helen, "They are colored people but they have feelings like us and are doing their share in defense of this country."

He wrote about the officers with whom he ate: a football player from Illinois, a railroad engineer, a "man of silence," "a garrulous cuss," a farmer from Missouri, a sarcastic jollier, and a Baptist minister's son. They had "very good accommodations," he told Helen, but the sea was rough. "The boat rolling. Many sea sick. At night the other boats of our fleet have a weird appearance. Against a starlit sky you see them as great black objects moving across the surface of the water—no lights, flashlights, matches. No smoking after dark. The nights are long. It is easier to plan for the day. Not permitted to write much about our convoy. . . . We are the flag ship."

On September 18, Melvin was "in the midst of the excitement and glory and pomp of military life" and on his way to Birmingham with "the regimental officers and three companies to give a parade before the nobility and distinguished officials of England." He thought the men needed "every help and encouragement that can be extended to them in morals." The young women hanging about the camps distracted them. But the stone fences, hawthorn hedges, quaint low homes hidden in shrubbery appealed to him strongly. He had time for an hour's walk around Lord Derby's estate and observed the wonderful and varied trees, swans in the lake, deer grazing on slopes, short-horn cattle, thoroughbred shires and Southdown blacklegged, black-faced sheep in the meadows, and the deserted stables. "Lord Derby you will recall is Ambassador to France having two sons in the service and devoting much time and money to winning the war." His superintendent told him "Lord Derby not only entertained the King and the Lords [at his thirty-thousand-acre estate] but often opened the place to the public. He said, incidentally, that these large estates would never again be as they were before the war. England is a sad ruined nation."

On September 24, Melvin arrived in a "beautiful part of France," where the shrubbery and trees indicated it never got very cold. Again he had "some anxiety" about the boys. "It is the grape section of France," and wine was abundant and easily secured. The women dressed in black, the wooden shoes, two-wheeled carts, ox teams, donkeys, stone houses, narrow streets seemed "old fashioned and primitive" to him, but the people were "so gracious, hospitable and courteous." Old people and children were in the fields and the old kept up the places of business. The young men were all at the front. Officers were billeted in the better homes. He wished Helen could meet the people with whom he was staying, people of "some means and much refinement and education." They had a son, "an only child, who had been made a prisoner by the Germans."

He had received his gas mask. "It is just this thing . . . that reminds us of the serious work before us. We are not deceived over here. The American army has a tremendous task to perform."

On October 6, with Helen's letters of September 3, 5, 7, and 9 before him, which he read and reread, Melvin wrote of feeling her nearness "and a new pride in my wife and boys came to me. You know how to write the kind of letters that make a man in the army glad that he is in the service. Sometimes when I permit myself to think that you and the boys may need me at home, I get very lonesome and regret that I joined the army. Your letters have made me feel that everything is all right at home and I am turning to my work with new interest and purpose."

While Helen's letters reassured Melvin that everything was all right at home, everything was not all right. She tried to be the dutiful soldier's wife, to find sufficient satisfaction in living vicariously through the letters of her male relatives who were doing the exciting things. She tried to be content in Lincoln,

to find fulfillment in caring for her children and writing letters and reading
Fosdick's steadying essays, books, and sermons and socializing with a few good
friends, the Diffenderfers and the Woodses. But it was not in her—and not,
certainly, when she heard that a faction in the church thought she should
not be living in the manse rent-free when the minister was away. The small-
mindedness offended her.

Melvin R. Laird, 1918. He served as a chaplain in France during World War I.

Alone in the small town, her life dominated by the little chores that wore her down, she became increasingly frustrated and depressed. While she had sufficient funds and could have survived in Lincoln financially, emotionally she decided she could not. Before the month was out, she took matters into her own hands and left the alien place and went back home. "In September 1918, we broke up our home in Lincoln. The boys were very good during the process and didn't seem to realize much what it meant. We went over to Maysville for nearly a week and then returned to Lincoln for a few days at Mrs. Diffenderfers, and returned to Marshfield where we will await Mr. Laird's return from France."[18]

Rob, who heard the news from Florence, conceded that "it would be hard for her living there alone with the children" but thought that "she would want to keep up her home."[19] Helen, however, felt no attachment to the Pekin Street house. Her rejection of Lincoln signaled the beginning of her rejection of her lot as a minister's wife. When Melvin received her letter informing him that she had moved, he wrote that he was sorry. They had good friends in Lincoln. He would have to do a lot of hard work as a chaplain to make up for the trouble he had caused her and the inconvenience in which she had been placed. "When I return you and the boys shall hereafter come first. Nothing shall ever separate us again." He was determined, he wrote, to make the best use of his opportunity, but he was "full of sentiment and heartache" and worried about Helen.

But with the children safely installed in their grandmother's house, and with cousins to amuse them and plenty of grown up female help to look after them, Helen enjoyed a memorable holiday with her father. The trip they made to Victoria, where the Canadian Puget Sound Timber and Lumber Company had its headquarters and mill, remained a high point in both their lives. They lived at the Empress Hotel, which opened in 1913 and was a magnificent palace built to honor Queen Victoria, the empress who had ruled the world. Helen expressed her pleasure in being there in a poem deeply gratifying to W.D., who continued to take great pride in her "wonderful command of English," wishing, he said, he had the same gift himself.

During those idyllic days, Helen luxuriated in the elegant surroundings, the cultivated ambiance, and in her father's company. On later visits to Victoria, W.D. invariably reminded Helen of their mutual love of the place. "Too bad we can't move the climate, the scenery, the timber and the sea over into Wisconsin."[20]

In Marshfield, Mame, Helen, and Marian, who had graduated from Milwaukee Downer, quickly fell into familiar routines: taking charge of house and children; keeping up correspondence; sharing the news from Europe and studying maps to see where the men were; and attending women's meetings at the church, the Woman's Club, the DAR, and the Fortnightly Musical Club, where both Florence and Marian frequently starred as vocalists. As usual, Mame ruled over her big house with love and conviction. "Again I can see Mother at the old upright piano playing 'Onward Christian Soldiers' so that Connor and Dick could march from room to room and there is Connor leading the way laughing happily as he looks back over his shoulder at his grandmother!"[21]

The happy children marching about the house pretending to be soldiers provided relief from the news reported by letter and in the press. Everyone knew the intensity of the war had increased; no one knew when the carnage would end. The draft age had been extended to include all men between the ages of eighteen and forty-five; strangers were sent to jail for disloyal remarks; the German language was banished from city schools.

Rob wrote of the "beaucoup souvenirs" he wanted to send home so they could be displayed as a warning to all Boche in Marshfield. He boasted that they "needed seven league boots more than anything else so we could keep up with Fritz as he don't wait for the Americans to get close up." On September 15, he wrote of being in a "big show," the first "all American show," when they took the St. Mihiel Salient. It was "a fine piece of work. We have few casualties and captured about 20,000 Boche, the latter seeming dead anxious to surrender as soon as the Americans got close to them. The Outfit I was with went in from just South of Verdun and went so fast they kept the Boche running to get away. It rained most of the time and that made it disagreeable but it was a good stroke of business and was glad to be in it." He said that in talking with the Germans as they were herded to the rear, they seemed glad of capture and "think that since America stepped in the war has gone against them."

In Verdun not a house was left. In St. Mihiel, the day after the Americans got it back, "it was like the 4th of July in the states, with American and French flags everywhere and the President of France and many of their prominent men there. The Huns occupied this city for four years to a day and were chased out so fast that they did not have time to burn it as they did everything else in our front." The six thousand French people the Germans released certainly were "surprised to see the Americans as the Boche had told them that t he submarines had prevented any Americans from coming over to France." Rob predicted that "our wonderful troops will make this war the last."

At the end of September, Rob was back with the greatly changed 32nd, "Red Arrow," Division as battalion commander of the 127th Infantry, nicknamed "les Terribles" by the French for their fighting ferocity. Dean Witter, whom Rob had encouraged to try to get appointed to the Army Staff College's next course, had begun his studies at the college, but Rob thought "he has no idea of this game and has a lot to learn."[22] He and Dean corresponded and followed each other's movements but did not meet; nor did Melvin and Rob, although they hoped to.

By October 4, Rob had been back and "on the go" with the old division for nearly two weeks, living in dugouts. The one they had just taken from the Germans was "a fine place with electric lights and stove so am very comfortable and feel fine." He was on General Haan's staff. "Never cared anything for staff work, but they seem bound to have me do it and hope I may be able to deliver the goods. Am very busy as we are in the midst of operations and don't know how long it will last. . . . Everyone here seemed glad to see me and it was like coming back home to be here."[23]

During the early days of the Oisne-Aisne offensive, Rob wrote enthusiastically about "having lots of fun with the Boche who are getting their fill of the Americans and the boys certainly are giving a good account of themselves." By October 10, however, after "living in dugouts etc. for a couple of weeks," he hoped to "go back as there are too many rats around here and one gets enuf of this in a short time." The weather was rotten. It rained all the time. By October 19, he was feeling desperate to "get cleaned up again as have been living like a human rat." Everyone hoped the war was about finished, but no one wanted to quit until it was really over.

Writing on the night of October 26, as the "impolite Boche" were dropping shells, and "one don't exactly feel like sleeping," he declared that he knew "all this part of France as well as I do the country around Stratford. Can go anywhere night or day in my car, and, at night we don't use any lights as Fritz might be watching. All the country around Verdun is just like around home to me and I know every town and city and road in it and as we push Fritz back I enlarge my territory every day."

While Rob described the soldier's life in the trenches, Melvin described life in Bordeaux. The pace of the war also accelerated for him as the end drew near. Bordeaux was a busy city, he wrote on October 8. A constant stream of American troops, nurses, YMCA men, and Red Cross passed through the port. "When the American engineers presented the specification for the building of the docks at this place to the French engineers for their approval, the French replied that they could not be built in three years; the Americans built them in three months. When they were finished, the chief of the French engineers looked them over and said to the American chief, 'They will not stand ten years.' . . . The American engineer replied, "Well, who the Hell wants them to?"

Death, the leveler, worked overtime on the battle front and at home. On October 23, 1918, the headline in the *Marshfield Times* proclaimed, "Death Rate Increasing Influenza and Pneumonia." When Angie became critically ill, an exhausted Dr. Karl Doege could not bring himself to go to the hospital yet again until Florence protested: "And what am I to tell Rob? That she died because you were too tired to see her?" And Dr. Doege knew he would go even though, for civilians as for soldiers, chance usually determined who survived.

With Bulgaria, Turkey, and Austria out of it, the Germans could not hope for success. Rob's letter of November 6 indicated that the end could not come too soon for him. He was "tired of roaming and don't think I want any more," but he was also "curious to see how the Germans at home, who always said the Boche could never be whipped, are going to account for the fact that it was thoroughly done by men who only had a few months experience at the fighting game." On November 11 he wrote, "Finis la guerre. Armistice was signed this morning at 5:00 and went into effect at 11:00 A.M. today, the eleventh hour of the eleventh day of the eleventh month. Things are very quiet since then. The usual sound of firing is not heard and guess it is the end as the Boche has had enuf and we have been fighting and following him since September 26th." They had crossed the Meuse, and he expected the 32nd would "be part of the outfit that follows up to the Rhine to see that the Boche lives up to all terms of the Armistice."

Rob had risked his life by moving out to the front lines to tell the men that the attack order had been called off, the war over, the armistice signed. While he did not write about that, his troops, many Marshfield boys among them, lived to tell the story. Young Edmund Arpin told a sadder tale on his return to Wisconsin Rapids. His regiment, which had not been informed of the cancellation of the attack order, suffered "a tremendous loss of an inexcusable nature on Armistice Day." They had "penetrated the German line to a depth of a couple of miles against a concentration of enemy artillery fire, with German infantry and machine-gun units closing in on their flanks and rear. When they finally cut their way out in a fighting retreat, there were not many survivors left to tell the tale."[24]

Of the twenty-nine battle divisions, the 32nd, with 2,660 men killed and wounded, stood fourth in the number of battle deaths,[25] but, thanks to Rob, none of those deaths occurred after the war. He felt he had "made good and done the work under the hardest trials that the Division has had in France."[26]

On November 13, in spite of the pneumonia and the influenza that struck every family and usually more than once, the whole town turned out to "celebrate the Downfall of the Kaiser." The Marshfield band, different local orders, the fire department, children from the city schools, and hundreds of citizens on foot and in automobiles, all of them displaying old glory, paraded down Central Avenue. The remains of Kaiser Wilhelm were hauled on "a manure spreader" and inscribed with "may he rest in h——!" The flag was raised and "a few short remarks fitting the occasion were made by Reverend Jordon, Mrs. Melvin Laird and C.B. Edwards." Standing before the service flag in front of the Hotel Blodgett, E. C. Pors paid tribute to the boys who gave "their all" for the noble cause. "Taps" was then sounded, and a volley by Company 1 ended the program of "the biggest day in history."[27]

On November 24, a recovered Angie, whom her father had not seen in almost three years, celebrated her sixth birthday. As Rob anticipated, the 32nd followed the retreating German army from the Meuse River north of Verdun through Marville, Longuizon, and Longvey to the French border and then through the Duchy of Luxembourg, "a beautiful country, very clean and well kept" that showed no signs of war and the people all spoke German and seemed glad to see them. A recipient of the Croix de Guerre, Rob was "proud to be of the chosen few for the March to the Rhine which I imagine will be famous in history."[28]

Rob's wife and daughters celebrated a happy Thanksgiving with Helen and her boys at the Connors'. The period of rejoicing was shortlived. In December, illness struck in Marshfield again. Helen was the first to succumb. Suffering from depression and physically ill with tonsillitis, she entered a hospital in Chicago on December 8. On December 20, while "still in the hospital after having tonsils removed, [she] received word little Dick was ill [and] hurried home. He had had a short run of pneumonia. In less than a week, Connor was taken ill with what the doctor said was infection of some kind—probably intestines." The infection was not in the intestines but in the mastoids. Dr. Copps, one of the surgeons in the newly formed Marshfield Clinic, performed a mastoidectomy. Aunt Florence comforted Connor at St. Joseph's Hospital while Mame took charge of the ill at home: Helen, who had not fully recovered, and little Dick and Gordon, who had come down with the mumps.[29]

Helen wrote a short entry in Connor's baby book to describe the Christmas of 1918. "Both boys ill and daddy in France. Enough said. Otherwise it would have been a happy day for William and Richard were home, William released from, and Dick on furlough from the Navy so all the Connor family was together." She entertained her recovering five-year-old by reading "many of the books at home here. The Eskimo Stories interest him greatly and we read many animal stories."

Connor's verbal skills, the droll, funny things he said, gave her pleasure, and she continued to write them down. "What kind of a car is this? A street car or a freight train?" "I'm waiting for my horse-radish to get cold." "I dreamed of cows in the meadow, Jesus in the manger, and daddy on the train." "Isn't baby Dick cute? I just love him when he's sleeping cause he doesn't bother me." To Helen's admonition in reference to some candy he was eating, "Oh, Connor, don't eat that trash," he replied: "Well, it came from the church and surely the church people wouldn't give out trash."[30]

Melvin and Rob spent Christmas 1918 in Europe; Melvin was in France, thinking of his wife and children, conducting services for the boys, and visiting the sick in the hospitals. In Rengsdorf, Germany, the four inches of snow that fell on Christmas Eve reminded Rob of home. He had dinner in Coblenz with his roommate, Major Scott, who hailed from Appelton, Wisconsin, but there was "not much doing." On Christmas Day he had a feast at noon with a wealthy German family and a second feast at the general's mess. But everyone was "getting more and more homesick. Nothing to keep one interested unless one is a professional soldier." He was eager to get home but had no complaints about his accommodations, his Cadillac car, or his orderly, a "fine little chap" who had been in his company on the border in 1916 and who took care of him "like a woman would." He also liked his office assistant from Arkansas, Captain Crandall, and his chief stenographer, an Indian who hailed from Haywood, Wisconsin, and "of course is a real American."

The arrival of Dean Witter's sister Elizabeth, whose path had crossed Rob's in Dijon and whose Red Cross unit followed the army into Germany, did not add any cheer to his life. She was "too like the English," not "sweet" like Helen. They "didn't step it off very well" in spite of the fact that they seemed "destined to be thrown together." Rob didn't hate the Germans anymore,[31] but when he and Fred Rhyner and Major Barnes visited their Marshfield friend Phil Schaefer's family, Rob anticipated showing "these people what a free people and nation means and how much better off they are without the Kaiser." The pleasant afternoon with the Schaefers convinced him, however, that Americans had something to learn from Germans. The wife was "some cook," and their two little girls played the violin beautifully together. He instructed Florence to make sure his daughters had music lessons. He had "come to realize how much it means to the girls when they grow up and go out and are called on to do things and people will expect things from them."[32] His sixteen-year-old Katty should "graduate from High School with a good record," but it was "more important that she become proficient in her music and French." It meant "so very, very much to her in the future." Angie, too, in spite of the fact that she didn't have any musical ability, "must get started on music so she will have at least one accomplishment or especially being a girl she will be entirely out of luck."[33]

Rob noted "a good many in the states getting rich thru the war" but did not perceive its effect on women. He remained fixed in his belief that women belonged in the domestic arena. But forty-one determined suffragists, picketing in front of the White House, made headlines when they were arrested, and in Great Britain, where women had already won the right to vote and to sit in the House of Commons, it was widely recognized that their war work had won them according to the newspaper headlines, "A BIG ROLE IN RECONSTRUCTION WORK".[34]

While Rob's older daughter, Katty, followed the traditional pattern of marriage and family, the war set Angie's course differently. "I made up my mind to study medicine at age five years. The teacher told me—'I am leaving for the war to be a nurse'—that had a great effect on me."

The war and time had an effect on Helen's first born as well. A self was taking shape. With his father away, perceiving himself a man, Connor began to assert his authority. His hair had been cut short in March 1918. In January 1919, he finally rebelled against the feminine attire in which little boys of the day were dressed. "This waist is so dog-gone girlish, I'm not going to wear it." He was not certain "whether to be an Esquimo or porter when I get big. I think a porter so I can stay up all night."

Melvin, meanwhile, was exploring the fields over which Rob in his "seven league boots" had pursued the enemy. Anticipating recounting the full story "some evening when I get back to you and have you on my knees with my arms around you," he "briefly" (in a ten-page letter) described for Helen the "wonderful trip" to the Bellum Woods, Soissons, the Argonne Forest, Verdun, Varennes, and St. Mihiel, from which he had just returned.[35] After the trip, after spending a night in a German dugout and viewing the devastation, he appreciated "more than ever the work of the American soldiers in this war. It was won largely by the courage and individual ingenuity of the dough boy. He is a wonder."

On February 12, W.D. threw a Lincoln's Birthday Dinner at the Marshfield Armory for six hundred attendees in honor of the returned soldiers and sailors of the 32nd Division. After W.D.'s welcoming address and short speeches celebrating Republican Party leaders Abraham Lincoln and Teddy Roosevelt, the "Boys of '61" and the "Boys of '98," three "boys" back from the World War spoke. Captain R. P. Potter, one of the founders of the Marshfield Clinic, talked about being "A Medico in the Army," Lieutenant Robert Bulmer about "The Flyers," and Corporal Glen Kraus about "The Teufelhunde" (Devildogs).

The printed program included an "Historical Record of the 32nd Division American Expeditionary Force," listing the fronts and the dates on which the division served, prisoners captured, material captured, number of casualties, officers and men, and the location of the division headquarters from February 16 to December 19, 1918. The chairman of the Wisconsin History Commission for Wood County maintained a meticulous record.

Learning about the celebration, Rob gloomily wrote W.D. that by the time they got home the welcome would be worn out. It didn't matter anyway. "I guess there are only about 75 or 80 out of all that went from Marshfield that have been through it all and will be back. Guess these will have seen enuf however, to make up for the rest."[36]

February came and went. Most divisions were already home or on the way, and most of the younger chaplains were gone. Dean Witter was back making money in California (his sister, Elizabeth, married a Frenchman, Henry Debost, and remained in France); Wayne Deming was back in Marshfield practicing law in his father's office. But still Rob and Melvin lingered. Melvin could not understand why they did not ship the older men out first, and Rob repeatedly urged his brother to arrange to get him home. Will, he thought, needed him a good deal more than the army. "His health is not the best and there is so many things to look after there."[37] The adventure over, home was what both men longed for.

On March 7, 1919, Melvin was honorably discharged from the United States Army at Camp Dix, New Jersey, and on his way to Marshfield. Rob was still in Germany, but his friends, anticipating his return, filed papers for his reelection as alderman of the Third Ward. On May 5, Company A and its band landed in New York; on May 13, and late in the afternoon, Major Robert Connor finally came home. The next day an announcement appeared on the first page of the *Marshfield Times*: "June 18 And 19 Are Designated as Red Arrow Days. Home-Coming Celebration for 32nd Division Is Now Being Planned. City to Be Wide Open. Band Concerts, Exhibition Drills, Military Review, Wrestling Matches, Barbeque, Dancing, Movies and Vaudeville Features Billed."

The survivors of the 32d received a raucous welcome. They had not, as Rob feared, been forgotten—nor were those many more who had not survived. Their names were engraved on little white stones arranged in rows in Flanders Field, an area of Hillside Cemetery set aside for them, and there the citizens of Marshfield gathered to stand quietly reflecting and remembering them.

Rob was immediately absorbed in the family lumber business, but Melvin's future was uncertain. He met with the trustees of Lincoln College and delivered an oration to the members of the congregation shortly after his return. Mrs. Charles H. (Norma) Woods wrote Helen and Melvin afterwards, urging their return. The church and the college needed Melvin. By their being away, they had "drawn the people who cared for you and the things you stood for closer to you. . . . If our Captain leaves us there are none from the ranks that can step into his shoes. The past months have proved that." She had "no faith in an outsider coming in and making it go. It would be the Lairds' personality that would have the pull."[38]

The offer interested Melvin, but he would not accept unless his wife could be happy in Lincoln. Helen doubted she could. Her mother strongly urged her to go back, feeling that her daughter's as well as her son-in-law's talents made them both ideally suited for work in education and the church. But Helen was conflicted and uncertain. She visited Lincoln briefly with her husband and the children in May and then took her boys to Laona, hoping, away from family pressures, to be able to decide. Baby Dick observed her distraction and begged for attention: "Would you like to begin training me?" "For what, Dick"? "Oh-just to be nice." Connor, the much more confident first-born, observed that his "Bampa [grandfather] can do anything in the world" and objected to his mother moving him around: "I no sooner get to learn people in one town than you move on to another." When men at the Gordon Hotel, Laona, asked him, "Say boy, where do you live?" he replied, "I don't live any place. I'm a travelling man." He offered his mother a word of advice: "The thing to do is to go back there and be content."

That was something Helen could not do.

◦◦

# CHAPTER 12

# Omaha

## *1919–1923*

> Often it happens that both the human and the natural worlds transform themselves so rapidly that they outrun men's ability to digest them. This undoubtedly is what has taken place since the Great War, with the rapid development of applied science, power machinery and mass production, the splendor and decay of capitalism and the growing self-awareness of the proletariat.
>
> —MALCOLM COWLEY

On October 3, 1919, the Reverend Melvin R. Laird preached to more than three hundred members of the Westminster Presbyterian Church in Omaha, the nation's "gate city." Organized in 1887 with forty-seven members, the church was, thanks to the railroads, the opening and settling of western lands, and the rapid industrialization fostered by the war, one of thirteen other Presbyterian churches in the bustling city of almost 200,000. A manufacturing center for paper products and asbestos and a packing and distribution center for grain farmers, cattle ranchers, sheep and hog farmers, the city celebrated its centennial in 1919. Among the stock yards, packing houses, factories, shops, universities, homes, hotels, brothels, and churches, the people went about their different lives.

There were "deadly serpents in the garden of life"[1] in this throbbing metropolis so different from the congenial small towns in which the Lairds had spent most of their lives. While members of the Westminster Church may well have followed Melvin's injunction to "somewhere, some way, some time each day . . . turn aside and pray that God [will show] the way of righteousness to men," many of Omaha's citizens did not. The times were tumultuous, and so was Omaha.

The Lairds arrived as a thousand men from the regular army patrolled the streets. The army had been in Omaha a week. It arrived too late to save Will

Brown, a black man accused of attacking a white woman in south Omaha. Racial tensions ran high and were fed by inflation, unemployment, poor wages, poor working conditions, and frequent newspaper reports of riots: "16 Dead in Race Riots"; "Murder Plot to Kill All Whites in Arkansas Community Uncovered"; "Violence in South Side—24 White Women Attacked by Negroes in 3 Months." The week before Melvin delivered his inaugural sermon in the Westminster Presbyterian Church, a mob stormed the courthouse, demanded Will Brown, got him, lynched him, and tossed his body in a bonfire as thunder clapped and a torrential rain poured down over the steaming city.

The mayor, Ed Smith, who had been elected on the promise of cleaning up a flagrantly corrupt municipal government and police force, tried to stop the mob and barely escaped lynching himself. The violence cost the honest, but inexperienced, Mr. Smith his chance for reelection. James Dahlman, Omaha's "perpetual" mayor since 1906, whose control over all aspects of Omaha's business community, from banks to brothels, had helped gain for the city a reputation for order as well as corruption, was reelected the following year and served until 1930. The International World Workers was blamed for stirring up the mob, and the city was smoldering from the news when the Lairds arrived.

On October 3 the *Omaha Bee* reported, "Rioting in Washington, Chicago, Boston and now this latest outbreak in Omaha, are exceedingly disquieting. They show the danger of a relapse into barbarism that exists in every community."[2] The city had been "disgraced and humiliated by a monstrous object lesson of what jungle rule means." "A wolf pack, . . . inflamed by the spirit of anarchy and license, of plunder and destruction" had run over the city, teaching its citizens "how frail is the barrier which divides civilization from the primal jungle."[3]

The alarm had been ringing for years. Members of the privileged classes had been told in soft voices and loud that workers lived in deplorable conditions, that class stratification and commercial imperialism threatened to destroy democracy, that laborers had to be redeemed from economic serfdom. Most businessmen and politicians accustomed to thinking in laissez-faire terms were not convinced and went about pursuing self-interest rather than social good, while the churches (although increasingly involved in social issues) and the women, in their charities and settlement work, barely touched the surface of the pervasive problems of immigration, industrialization, and poverty.

In 1919, strikes erupted all across America, from Boston to Seattle, Indiana to Missouri, general strikes and strikes among particular groups of workers: policemen, steel workers, coal miners, textile workers. Newspapers whipped up fear with reports that Russian madmen, advocating the violent overthrow of federal troops and government, were behind them, and "radical revolt" was spreading. Europe was a "seething scene of misery, torment and malevolence."[4] Germany was threatened by "Reds," Portugal by Bolsheviks, and Russia, the "world's great gaping wound," was gripped by a reign of terror following external wars and internal revolution.

In Marshfield, the community celebrated Thanksgiving with a service at the Adler Theater celebrating "The New America" of many peoples in one nation that would "be permeated with a patriotism so strong and loyal as to destroy all racial and religious prejudices" and where "every form of religion and sect, every color and every race will be at home . . . and 'do unto others as you would have them do unto you' will be the motto of all."[5] In larger cities, however, including Omaha, the prevailing sentiment was that "unprecedented immigration of ignorant Europeans to supply the labor demand," the "riff-raff" spilling into and out of Ellis Island, had ruined the country. Ministers, including Melvin, attempted to quell the hysteria sweeping the land, while the newly installed Republican administration of Warren Harding and Calvin Coolidge set up J. Edgar Hoover as a spy chaser and watch dog of the social order.

Hoover established a cross-indexed file with information on every known radical organization in the nation; Department of Justice agents raided suspected Bolshevik headquarters in eleven cities; the secretary of the Industrial Workers of the World, "Brick" Smith, was lynched[6]; 112 "Reds" were arrested in Chicago; 1,500 radicals were "bagged" in thirty three other cities; three hundred radicals were rounded up in New York and sent to Ellis Island.[7] Emma Goldman, accused of being an anarchist and a menace to law and order, was unceremoniously and illegally deported, while Jane Addams, despairing of domestic justice, sought social justice through international forums.

Leading American businessmen, including W.D., received pamphlets from the American Defense Society, Inc., 154 Nassau Street, New York, highlighting the Communist threat along with a copy of a letter Mr. Zinovieff, president of the Communist International, wrote instructing the Central Committee of the Communist Party of America "to direct its particular attention to the progress of the strike of the miners of America" and to send agitators and propagandists to arouse the striking coal miners to the point of armed insurrection. "Let them Blow Up and Flood the Shafts. Shower the strike regions with proclamations and appeals. THIS AROUSES THE REVOLUTIONARY SPIRIT of the WORKERS AND PREPARES THEM FOR THE COMING REVOLUTION IN AMERICA."

When the society began to crack, the Presbyterian church divided on causes. While the *Presbyterian Advance* claimed the Boston Police strike was "the nearest approach to Bolshevisim we have had in this country,"[8] a Commission of Inquiry of the Interchurch World Movement reported that most of the grievances suffered by the workers [in the steel strike in Gary, Indiana] were real, most of their demands just, and the strike failed only because management, using unscrupulous tactics, convinced the public that the strike was a bolshevist plot."[9] A report in the Federal Council of Churches *Bulletin* indicated that coal miners "have a real grievance and yet they were powerless to make a statement save through a strike" and asserted that government had "to secure its workers against exploitation . . . and to secure wages and hours of work that will make possible an American standard of living."[10]

While many thoughtful Americans rejected Christianity as outmoded and could not accept religion as a solution to social problems, others, including Herbert Croly, editor of the *New Republic,* and Lyman Abbott, editor-in-chief of *The Outlook,* and countless other Protestant intellectuals who identified with and felt a personal obligation to the country in which they and their ancestors had found spiritual and physical sustenance believed that only in the imitation of Christ, in following his message of love and reverence for human life, in affirming Christian truth, could Americans find their way out of the "morass" of the disturbed age.[11] That was Melvin's belief.

Helen pondered the tumultuous national and international times, but for her the situation was not so clear. Against the backdrop of social turmoil, in the land of drought, heat, wind, and thunderheads, and while Connor and Dick began school and became enthusiastic baseball players and Melvin ministered to his large flock, Helen picked up her life as a minister's wife.

Away from the factories, dumps, gambling halls, warehouses, and the blacks—all the crowded chaos of industrial south Omaha—the manse was located on 1323 South 35th Street across from a large park in an exclusive area of large homes near the Field Club, the scene of many social functions, including University of Omaha student dances. The house itself, built of brick, stood on a knoll surrounded by a luxurious expanse of lawn. On a salary of $3,000 a year, the minister and his wife were expected to be gracious hosts, making their home the obligatory setting for regular meetings, teas, dinners, and the traditional open-house for the entire congregation on New Year's Day.

For Melvin, coming to Omaha represented both a promotion to a larger parish and reunion with his sister Annette and her husband, John Pressly, his former classmate at Carthage College and a close friend. (Pressly, the state executive of the Presbyterian Synod of Nebraska, was undoubtedly instrumental in Melvin's having received the call to Omaha.) The Presslys' four children—Paul and Morey, students at the University of Omaha, and Elizabeth and Grace, teenagers who "had instant delight in [their] visible relatives"—were impressed that the Lairds, while waiting to move into the manse, stayed at the Blackstone Hotel, one of the city's most exclusive and expensive. Presidents McKinley, Taft, and Wilson had slept there. Ministers usually could not afford to.

Young and beautiful, Helen became a mentor for the girls. When Elizabeth bobbed her hair and her Uncle Melvin said she didn't need to come and see him, Helen comforted her, saying she was still loved and looked nice, and the next year she bobbed her own. Although Helen made efforts to fit in and be content, she was not. Suppressing her feelings under a cloak of proper behavior, she became an increasingly troubled woman. Seven years of marriage and motherhood had not brought her that "tremendous source of power and satisfaction: the peace of the untroubled heart." An even greater prey to homesickness in Omaha than she had been in Lincoln, in spite of, or perhaps because of, frequent letters and frequent gifts (including kindling, pecans, walnuts, and the inevitable white potatoes from Laona), she continued to be ambivalent about her role as wife and mother. She found great demands easy to cope with: "After all, it is not the big things of life that harass us. Most of us can be heroes in a crisis . . . but the little, unimportant things of every day life, . . . we let them sap our strength."[12] She both respected and resented her subordinate female role with its necessary repetition of small, unfulfilling, but essential chores: "There is no job in which the danger of losing oneself in petty details is so great." The "tired nerves" for which Helen had been treated several times by the prevailing method of "rest cure" and water therapy had always provided temporary relief in the past, but a little more than six months after their arrival in Omaha, she experienced a serious breakdown and Melvin sought medical help for her.

He turned to one of his parishoners, a psychiatrist of German descent trained in London, Gustave W. Dishong, a specialist in the treatment of nervous and mental diseases and head of the Department of Neurology and Psychiatry at Creighton University Medical School. From 1920 until 1939, when he retired, Dishong served as Helen's doctor and friend. Proud and notoriously close-mouthed throughout her life, Helen nonetheless needed and depended on a handful of others who, by training or the intuition of their sympathetic hearts, she believed, could help her.

Visiting in Omaha in June 1920 on one of his frequent trips to the West Coast, W.D. wrote William that he had seen Helen: "She was not nearly so well again. I was out today. She is some better again. I am going back in the morning. . . . I think when I come back from Victoria will take her to Birch Lake. Is there a first class man cook up there we could get for July and August?"

He wrote Connor urging him to be a good boy and help his father and mother: "Do not get into any argument with Dick. You are so much larger and older than Dick is and you know the argument disturbs your mother. Try and remember that, will you."

No one knows whether Helen's "neurotic eclipses" were caused by her inability to either trim or exercise her vast dreams, the result of a complex illness generated by an inherited chemical imbalance, the manifestation of deep unresolved conflicts, or a combination of several factors. In any event, her susceptibility to mental overload and illness was an effective control, a means by which she exerted power. Her father also exerted power, exercising his patriarchal right to assume responsibility for her. He showed no hesitancy either in guiding Helen or in continually using her as his confidante. Theirs was a relationship of intense reciprocal dependency. She had a husband, but he was gentle and bowed to W.D.'s greater experience and readiness to assume authority.

W.D. found the required help, and Helen and her boys returned to spend the summer months at Birch Lake. Helen's brothers William, married now to Kathryn Brown, and Richard, married to her cousin, Florence Brown, both members of a prominent Rhinelander lumber family and Smith College graduates, were year-round residents of Laona. W.D. set them up there. He made William president of the Laona Bank and general manager of the mill, the store, and the company houses, while he continued to issue orders about everything. Because it was "out of the question" to run up any bills with the packing houses, William should not to "make any checks unless it is for something that cannot be avoided. Every dollar we take in in Marshfield this month must go for other purposes." W.D. was expanding.

He recapitalized the Connor Lumber and Land Company to $1.5 million and turned over a block of Connor Lumber and Land Company stock to the R. Connor Company "to take up part at least of the indebtedness to that company." Realizing that if he turned over the stock at book value (about a half of the real value, as far as the timber and timber lands were concerned), the company would have to pay a profit's tax, he cooked the books, "figuring on turning the stock over at about $182." He carried on the statement 52,975 acres of timber exclusive of the land at $1,977,042.22: "That item should carry a valuation of $4,000,000.00 at least. That would only be around $80.00 an acre for the timber and . . . that is very ordinary price in Forest County at the present time."[13] While trees and land were real enough, numbers were fictions. W.D.'s sons listened and learned.

After old John Baltus, who couldn't "get around so well anymore, "acquainted Richard with the lands and the woods," W.D. put him in charge of the logging operations, advising him that in the old days, when there wasn't much value in timber, timber owners didn't pay much attention to cleaning up after logging. With the change in lumber values, W.D. wanted tops cleaned up, all the damaged timber cut and rounded up, and everyone around the camps to be on the lookout for fires.[14] He also made Richard responsible for the farm operation, for advertising and handling the correspondence regarding the sale of cut over land (which "we don't want to carry on our backs and pay taxes on"), and for looking after Birch Lake.

The townspeople thought W.D. worked his sons harder than he worked his horses. Mame's scolding prompted him to write a letter acknowledging that he may have "got after things pretty hard." If in his "eagerness to help" them, he caused "offense," he said, he was "truly sorry." He didn't want hard feelings. Only with "the closest co-operation, harmony and the greatest possible mutual confidence [could] things be kept going the easiest." He hoped his sons would never "seriously regret getting into the business." He felt "fortunate to have sons anxious to do things, desirous of making something of their time and ability and the business."[15]

Exempted from the pressures her brothers experienced, Helen felt fortunate to be back among the big trees, her people, and those familiar to her from the pioneer days of her Auburndale childhood. During the long, easy summer days in Laona, Helen became well again. Strikes and revolution seemed far away. The mill whistle and loon call dominated. The problems she heard about—the socialist farmers who didn't bring much business to the store, the number of stills in the county and the traffic in moonshine—were not world shaking, although W.D. thought the moonshine problem was serious enough for him to take it up with R. P. Hutton, the superintendent of the Anti-Saloon League, and James A. Stone, the federal prohibition officer for Wisconsin, a personal friend who promised to do anything in his power to help clean up the county.

The problem grew worse, not better. The Connors were aware that the "Kaintucks" had stills all over the woods and that Laona's Lower Town was "living and thriving off the manufacture of the stuff." Evidence was usually "smothered,"[16] but the largest still ever found in the state, containing "300 gallons of whiskey and a large amount of mash," was found in a log cabin near Crandon.[17]

Forest County, a summer refuge for Helen, was a problematic place for people who lived there year-round. The marshal in Crandon, Mr. McGlynn, the Republican and the only candidate for the office, was convicted by a jury of assault with intent to do bodily harm following the shooting and killing of

Joseph Breitkopf. He was in prison serving a two-year term. That information was not broadcast by the property owners and businessmen in the northwoods eager to sell the region as a mecca for tourists and summer residents. A group of 150 of them banded together to form an organization to publicize the ten northern Wisconsin counties.

W.D. kept the family news going when Helen returned to Omaha, letting her know that the business manager of the *Milwaukee Sentinel,* Mr. Cargill, who covered the meeting of business and property owners in the northwoods, said that "he never saw such a strong forceful personality [as William]. Always had the right thing to say. So much so that finally William was the unanimous choice for president of the Northwood's organization, which they named the Land O' Lakes, Inc." He missed Helen and the boys and hoped Connor, to whom he wrote a personal letter, would always remember his experiences at the lake and what he saw and learned about the woods and farm. "Get books at the library that tell about the woods—fishing, hunting and about the trees. Then you will feel more at home among them."

With William and Richard settled in Laona, British Columbia began to play an increasingly important part in W.D.'s life. In long letters to Helen he detailed his experiences as he struggled to make the bankrupt Puget Sound Timber and Lumber Company viable. He thought the New Yorkers, bankers and bondholders, might "get a little cool" when they heard what he wanted for himself, but he was "not entirely working for purely unselfish motives." He wanted cash, stock, and control. He planned to have the stock put in escrow so he could reach it any day—and planned to have "authority to vote the stock at any stock holder's meeting—even though it is in escrow. . . . I am not going to leave the way open for anyone to control against my wish."[18]

Maneuvering in the far West, he "got acquainted" with the big fir, western hemlock, and spruce (his survey revealed not the 3.5 billion feet reported by Brayton & Laubaugh, but 750 million). He let twenty-one square miles of valueless timber go for back charges and bought another piece of timber that was immediately accessible for cutting. He cleared up and sold off old logging equipment, engines, cars, and railroad rails that had lain scattered about in the woods and in different camps for years. "The logging outfit at Jordan River [was] in deplorable condition," as was the mill in Victoria. But, although it had not been easy to find "men that can do that kind of work in that country," by trying them out he had found the millwrights to repair the mill.

The financial report issued by the Canadian Puget Sound Timber and Lumber Company in 1921 indicated that old obligations had been cleared; the carrying charges on the entire property, the taxes on the timber and mill property, and the interest on the bonds that were issued to the stockholders who put in the new money had been paid. Securities issued by the new company were the first lien on all the property. Moreover, after taking care of depreciation and repairs, the company had a considerable sum to go into the working capital.[19] He transferred his faithful employee John Kissinger from Wisconsin to Canada and made him manager of CPS retaining for himself all decision making authority.

Lumber prices plummeted soon after Helen and the other stock- and bondholders received CPS's glowing financial report. Having come through a number of periods of "money stringency," W.D. was not overly upset, merely writing Helen that there had been "*some change*." Fir joist studding they were sawing and shipping at $42 and $43 at the mill was selling "if it is possible to sell at all at $18.–$20."[20] He took reversals in stride. In his fifties, his confidence seemed as boundless as his vigor.

His letterheads indicated that he was president of Canadian Puget Sound Timber and Lumber Company, R. Connor Company, Connor Lumber and Land Company, American National Bank, the newly chartered Cloverland Bank of Marshfield, and First National of Wisconsin Rapids. Rob was president of the Bank of Stratford, and William was president of the Laona Bank. "So that we can keep control of the organization without fail under any circumstances," W.D. purchased additional bank shares for Helen and Marian.

Helen read Sherman Rogers's condemnation of the use of unprotected Chinese labor in British Columbia, which, according to the *Outlook*'s industrial correspondent, had practically killed the American shingle industry, causing unemployment among the "high grade, substantial white population in Washington and Oregon" who worked eight hours a day and enjoyed good working conditions.[21] From W.D.'s letters to Connor and Dick, she also understood that "Chinks" were providing the cheap labor that helped make the Canadian Puget Sound Timber and Lumber (CPS) profitable and that her father was interested in making the logging business seem to his grandsons the great adventure it was to him. There were, W.D. wrote Helen's boys, a lot of "Chinamen" working out there and Chinese foremen. "Yesterday one Chinaman thought he did not have to do what the Chink foreman told him to do—the foreman is a little fellow. They had some words. The foreman tied into the fellow. Had him down and was beating him up before the fellow knew what was going on. Some of the Chinamen work pretty well, but others are stupid." He wrote the boys about the danger and the expertise required to bring in the rafts of logs from the Jordan River to the mill in Victoria. Heavy winds could force the long logs over the boom logs. They had tried three days to get away from one place where they were hiding from a storm before they finally made it. "The captain of the boat is responsible for the boat, the crew and the rafts and it hurts his reputation if he loses any logs."[22]

Friends and neighbors in Marshfield, hearing of the promising prospects in British Columbia and confident that the "millionaire" lumberman was putting them on to a good thing, readily put "new" money in the Canadian Puget Sound enterprise. Speculative fires were fueled when a Norwegian freighter, the S.S. *Bjornstjerne Bjornson,* one of the largest ships engaged in the lumber business, steamed into the newly dredged inner harbor in Victoria and, with the aid of two tugs, swung her majestic length of 410 feet along side the dock of the Canadian Puget Sound Timber and Lumber Company Ltd. The entry of the freighter marked "a new era in the lumber industry of the great Northwest." Hitherto, at great risk and expense all lumber had been loaded on scrows and towed to other points on Vancouver Island or across the straits to the city of Vancouver to be stowed and shipped by rail. Now the 175,000 board feet of lumber that rolled from the saws daily could be loaded directly onto cargo ships, thus cutting costs and ensuring "steady employment to a complement of over 400 men drawing a monthly payroll of over $30,000."[23] In letter after letter to Helen, W.D. boasted of his accomplishments. "We sold more than a 1,000,000 feet last month at retail around Victoria and vicinity. Last month we loaded 5,000,000 feet of lumber."[24]

"The ancients glorified the high spirited, independent, self-willed, assertive character . . . the crown winners, the rulers, the kings of the earth. Jesus, who delights in paradoxes says, No! The humble, the lowly-minded, the consciously dependent, are the truly happy . . . the true crown winners. To them belongs the kingdom of God."

"Blessedness belongs to character."

"Great things in religion cannot be reached by reason."[25]

The split between her father's worldview and her husband's remained an unreconciled constant in Helen's life. While her father's fulfillment lay in building a business empire, her husband's lay in building and sustaining faith in unseen, spiritual things. On Sundays Melvin preached a morning service and another, different service in the evenings. He conducted Wednesday-evening Bible study and prayer classes and led the young people's society of Christian Endeavor. In an effort to develop character in a cadre of responsible Presbyterians capable of taking leadership positions in a society growing increasingly indifferent to high moral standards, he spoke to the young people, including his sons, about Christ, courage, trust, compassion, loyalty—the ideals of the

Knight who was "free from the stain of a single lie or even equivocation, ready to help the weak and the distressed whether they be so by nature as in the case of women and children, or by circumstances."[26]

A pageant, "Voices That Call," distributed by the General Board of Education of the Presbyterian Church and presented by the young people's society of the Westminster Church on "vocation day," May 7, 1922, illustrated the church's and Melvin's identification with education and leadership—as well as the church's assumption of male superiority. "The Alien, preferably a woman, representative of one of the nationalities of Southeastern Europe now crowding our cities" speaks to the figure of Time: "My people are not happy, our children lose God and the Church in America. They have no Pilgrim Fathers! All they seek is money, money, money and there is badness everywhere." A representative of rural America speaks: "The patriotic pioneers pass, the churches die, the communities disintegrate, old ideals and purposes are no more!" The Spirit of Christian Education, a man in the academic robes of a college president, "including cap and gown and hood with a scroll in his hand," tells them: "The crying need of the world is for dependable personality in leadership!" He represents those "who are praying and planning to mobilize an army of trained leaders . . . ready to answer the call . . . with trained minds and noble ideals of consecrated service!" A young man says, "Take my life and let it be, Consecrated Lord to Thee"; a young woman adds, "O use me, Lord, use even me."[27] For Melvin, the church was "the home of my soul, the altar of my devotion, the hearth of my faith, the center of my affections and the foretaste of heaven."[28] Its unity, peace, and progress concerned his life, and its life was intimately tied to the whole, needy social fabric.

Still under Dishong's care, but sufficiently recovered to resume her duties as a minister's wife, Helen attended lectures, prayer meetings, and services; entertained members of the congregation, visiting clergymen, and their wives; hosted meetings of the Ladies' Society and the Women's Missionary Society; joined in the sometimes humorous, sometimes serious, always instructive skits; and, as always, avidly followed the news from "home."

Mame wrote that someone put out the rumor that W.D. was going to become a candidate for governor, but Rob squelched it. W.D. wrote that it would be difficult to sway voters from La Follette, who had merged "in an overwhelming personal constituency the anti-corporation agrarians, the wets, the Germans, the pro-bonus soldiers, the Socialists and the industrial workers of all shades."[29] A fair minority, however, was coming to the conclusion he and Lenroot came to years earlier: La Follette was "not to be trusted."[30] W.D. had taken Lenroot around the schools and factories in Marshfield. The speech he gave at the opera house was the best he ever heard him deliver, but changing "any of those fellows" from La Follette would be "a hard job." The senator stayed overnight with them before leaving for Oshkosh, and they had entertained "quite a few from the Rapids, Neillsville, etc."

W.D. boasted about his activities and criticized "those Methodists [who] worked very well all through the building" of the church on Second and Cedar, "but so soon as they could get inside and sit down, I guess they all did. Since then liens and all kinds of trouble." He hadn't received a cent for all the lumber he supplied. The Presbyterians also came in for criticism. The new minister could not be trusted, W.D. said. In his desire to please "the governor" and everyone else, Mr. Black lauded the Klan one Sunday, and "later he turned about face. He is traveling too fast for his weight." W.D. wondered whether the church had joined forces with the Klan or "has the Klan just taken the church over?" He thought "the first we know the whole outfit, Frank and Lill, Mrs. Hinman & all of them will get on the war path and get to stomping around with those black hoods on." [31]

The lively letters from "home" pulled Helen back to Wisconsin, however much she tried to be content in Omaha. In search of intellectual stimulation, occasionally with, but usually without, Melvin she attended meetings of the Omaha Society of Fine Arts at the Fontenelle Hotel. There she heard the American writer Vachel Lindsay give an interpretive reading; G. K. Chesterton, whose short stories she read in *Harper's*, say and prove that he "was one of those famous Englishmen who cannot lecture—and do"; Willa Cather speak on the "Standardization of Literature and Art"[32]; Dr. D.V. Bush, "America's greatest orator," lecture on "The Function of the Subconscious Mind"; and Sir Arthur Conan Doyle speak on ectoplasm and the spirit world, which was "all about us, but . . . expressed in colors and sounds which our senses were too gross to understand," where marriage was "on a higher level than on this plane" and "always happy."[33] And at the Brandeis Theater she saw D. W. Griffith's films *Birth of a Nation* and *God Help Poor Girls* and performances of Shakespeare's *The Merchant of Venice, Hamlet, Macbeth,* and *As You Like It.*

She attended football and basketball games at the university and followed current events in the *Omaha Bee,* in which she read how social advance and social upheaval seemed to be moving in tandem: the Omaha crime rate quadrupled in three years; the city passed an ordinance requiring the pasteurization of milk; Congress passed a bill requiring government supervision of the meat packing industry; insects infested grain in Omaha bins; J. Armour refused to answer questions but defended speculation claiming that grain marketing practices helped farmers;[34] a language bill passed the Nebraska Senate providing that foreign languages could only be taught on the Sabbath and fixing "a penalty on any organization or individuals who discriminate against the English language" (German might be "the language of the heart," but a state could not exist politically 50 percent German and 50 percent American, or 90 percent American and 10 percent German).

She joined the exclusive Mu Sigma Society, a woman's literary-philosophical society, and studied "the best of what had been thought and written in the past." The group of earnest likeminded women were not among the "new women" who smoked, used slang, chewed Wriggles Spearmint Gum, and called their "limbs" "legs" and showed them. This group studied Ralph Waldo Emerson, and they took turns leading discussion groups. Helen led the session "Emerson the Teacher of Ethics" and delivered a long (fifteen-page) and thoughtful report about "Compensation."

With a tinge of irony, and a hint of resentment, she said: "Had I been able to shut myself up and dwell in Emerson's thought world, or had I been able to spend my time drinking in the heavenly days and feeling myself absorbed in the glorious sunsets, I might in a small way have done justice to this essay." She was, however, a mother of boys and did not have the time. On hurriedly rereading Emerson's essay, she found it "absolutely impossible." After discussing Emerson and his essay with her husband, and reading more deeply what his contemporaries had to say about him, his life, manner, and work, she changed her attitude and came to see that the difficulties were due more to style than content. Judged by its literary style, "Compensation *is* impossible. If one reads it with idea of one paragraph leading up to another into a perfect whole, one is quickly lost in the shuffle." It had no logical sequence, no deductive reasoning, but the subject matter accounted for some of its obscurity. "Truths of spirit are brought out not so much by logic as revelation. Emerson had flashes of it. When some thought him mad, others [thought him] divine. He was subject to great ecstasies when his mind worked with phenomenal brilliancy. He was able to tap the invisible and bring man great gifts therefrom."

She appreciated Emerson's thought that "no one would be tired if he could see far enough"; she had herself experienced how quickly trivialities fell away when she went out and lost herself in a beautiful sunset or been in the open country and seen the horizon live. But she thought his might be "too dainty a touch for a world such as ours"; Emerson seemed "to have anticipated paradise before we have got there." Yet, what Emerson had to say about fear hit home in 1922. "We all hear so much today about fear being the great evil, undermining social relations, fear of the labor situation, fear among nations." Emerson called fear an "instructor of great sagacity and the herald of all revolutions.

One thing he always teaches that there is rottenness where fear appears. He is a carrion crow and though you see not well what he hovers for, there is death somewhere."

In other sessions, dealing with "Poems of Life," "Poems of Nature," "Poems of Faith," and "Representative Men," the women studied works by nineteenth-century English authors: Coleridge, Browning, Wordsworth, Carlyle. But the grip of England on America was lessening. A whole new group of writers was coming on the scene, and they were American, and some were women. With the poet Amy Lowell, Helen celebrated America's growing pride that "we are no more colonies of this or that other land, but ourselves, different from all other peoples whatsoever." Mrs. Thomas G. Winter, second vice president of the Federation of Woman's Clubs, claimed that the postwar literature merited women's "deepest thought for it is the literature of the democratic period."[35]

Of all those describing this "new" America, and many of them—Theodore Dreiser, Hamlin Garland, Sinclair Lewis, Sherwood Anderson, Harriet Monroe, Edgar Lee Masters, Carl Sandburg, Scott Fitzgerald, Zona Gale, and Willa Cather—midwesterners, Willa Cather inspired Helen's deepest interest and enthusiasm. Helen thought Cather wrote the "most excitingly exquisite prose in the English language" and taught that "realism need not be sordid." The music of Cather's formidably simple prose echoed her own thoughts, experiences, and feelings. She understood Cather's response to the land, to those who tamed it, the morally thin individuals, male or female, who lived on and by it, and the better sort who were also there.

Zona Gale, whose work was studied by Federation of Woman's Club members throughout America, elicited her admiration as a writer and political activist. (Gale was a member of the Council of the National Woman's Party.) Born and educated in the small central Wisconsin community of Portage, her play *Miss Lulu Bett* won the Pulitzer Prize in 1921, a year before Willa Cather won the Pulitzer for her novel *One of Ours*. Gale made the isolation and loneliness, which went along with the "protection" society afforded women, her principal theme. She saw and judged the small-town "lovely family," a patriarchal family with money, through the new lenses provided by "the new knowledge concerning renunciation and repression and hypocrisy and business and the Church."[36]

Gale's advocacy of women keeping their own surnames was not something Federation Club women supported, but they did admire her pamphlet "What Women Won in Wisconsin." Published in 1922, it forcefully presented the "need for specific laws which would remove civil and legal disabilities, inequalities of other discriminations of law against women by reason of sex or marriage."

The female suffrage amendment, ratified on August 26, 1920, was "a half way house on the road to equal civil, legal and political rights for women which will place them on an equality with men." In Wisconsin, Gale pointed out, unless women won the right to serve on juries (a special bill out of the judiciary committee of the Assembly in 1921 expressly forbad them to do so), it was incomplete. Many other states had laws requiring wives to turn over their earnings to their husbands and laws classifying women with children and the insane and as unable to contract on their own responsibility—which had to be changed before equality could be achieved.[37]

Tradition and legislative bars held women "in their place," but the news was full of achieving women. Madame Curie visited America and was honored with a gift of a gram of radium; the International Congress of Working Women held a meeting in Washington, D.C., making it "the first such meeting to take place in the history of the world"; Republican women in Chicago demanded equality on the national committee and representation by a fair delegation of women from each state; Miss Alice Lorraine, Madison, North Dakota, became the first woman to be nominated for governor in the United States; Mrs. A. K. Gault, a former Omaha woman prominent in the Nebraska DAR, became a Democratic Party nominee for Congress; a woman pharmacist, the first to be so honored in the United States, was elected president of the Minnesota Board of Pharmacy and was made delegate to the United States pharmacopoeial convention; Mrs. Murray donned khaki and, acting as scout, geologist, financier, and drilling superintendent, made a fortune in oil in Tulsa, Oklahoma.[38]

While the press covered women taking on new roles and the rise in the number of divorces granted women, the *Omaha Bee* published an editorial celebrating women's traditional role: "The women of Nebraska's homes are building up a citizenry of such character and splendid spiritual and intellectual endowment as makes the future certain. . . . [W]hen Mother is right the rest can not go wrong." Home, city, state, and nation, all depended on the mother.[39]

Helen's sister Marian, whose voice was "a joy to everyone," aspired to become one of the new women. At twenty-seven, with no marriage prospects and no longer satisfied with living at home and singing at Fortnightly Musical Club gatherings and in front of members of the Elks Club and their wives, she went East to continue her musical studies and pursue a career as a professional singer. On May 3, 1922, Marian and Mame left for New York City. They were still there on June 16, and on August 13 W.D. wrote William, "I do not know what their plans are at present. Marian is some lady. We surely move about some."

Mame had returned to Marshfield by the time Helen, leaving Connor and Dick behind in Wisconsin, returned to Omaha to await the birth of her third child. "Connor and Dick are surely good boys," W.D. wrote. "I do not believe I ever saw two boys their age who knew so well what to do and how to do it and I never saw boys so thoughtful and kind around the home. Good, clean, high minded boys. We all surely were proud of them and glad to have them with us."[40]

On September 1, while Omaha temperatures soared to 101 degrees, Helen gave birth to her third child. Perhaps as a gift to her devoted and patient husband, whose life she had not made easy, she named him Melvin Robert Laird. This "Bambino," coming almost seven years after the birth of her second child, was welcome. Marian, who traveled to Omaha to help her sister, observing Helen with her infant, sang Puccini's "O Mio Bambino," and "Bambino" became the baby's name until it was no longer suitable. Then it became and remained "Bam" for his mother and grandfather and "Bom" to the rest of the family, himself, and his friends.

When this baby, Melvin R. Laird Jr., became Secretary of Defense, Helen, speaking in the carefully controlled, unemotional manner that had become habitual, admitted to the reporter who interviewed her that she enjoyed him about as well as any of her sons. When he was her "bambino," she allowed, he meant a good deal more. Then, he was her "only tie to the great beyond, as well as the great before." With him nestling "warm and close," she felt "a part of the great unseen, at peace with the gods as they are."

Helen's "peace with the Gods as they are" did not last. Although she made efforts, she never established a connection with the big city or the broad Nebraska spaces. W.D. kept writing, drawing her into his world. From Victoria he expressed the hope that "the time will come when I will not have to tie down so close to business but I guess work does not hurt a person much." The lumber business looked "more encouraging than any time in past two years. There is fair demand and at better prices. Production costs are also higher. Wages in the mills and woods are higher. Timber stumpage and prices of logs if we went into the market to buy now would be near war time prices. Standing timber is getting valuable. . . . We are getting fairly good prices for most of our products."

From Laona he wrote that the snow in the woods was as strong and deep as at any time all winter and the ice roads firm. He had "had a little 'lay off,' and it continued longer than my most anxious desires." Mame was with him. He had not been out to the lake. "No chance to drive out with team. So much snow." Richard would attend to things out there, and everything would be ready when Helen and the boys came for the summer.

By the time Helen returned to Omaha after spending the summer of 1923 in Wisconsin, she had made up her mind that she could not and would not fit the mold of a minister's wife. Struggle as she might, she was unable, as the Reverend W. M. Hunter suggested at the turn of the century that ministers' wives must (the tradition had not changed much), "cross the threshold of affluence and ease," turn "from society delightful and in harmony with birth and education . . . [and] trusting her master to provide a comfortable [home], a hearty welcome, wise and judicious friends to fill the void, lay herself on the altar of self-denial." She could not agree to surrender her opinion to the wishes of female parishioners "kin to the most wealthy and influential members" and be satisfied to become known as "a tidy housekeeper, fertile of resources."[41] Her education at home and at the university had taught her to expect different things from life. Helen could no more walk among the meek and subservient than her father could.

In an essay, "Protests of a Parson's Wife," Helen confronts her situation head on and reveals her violent objection to the society in which she found herself and to the constraints imposed upon her. The great popularity of several autobiographies made her think that even her "hum-drum life might have something of interest to others. After all, it isn't the position which we have attained, the great men and women whom we have known, or the social and educational advantages we enjoy that awakens interest, but it is ourselves, the registers upon which these outside influences act and re-act, the impressions, repressions and expressions which they cause."

By expressing her feelings, she thought she "might amuse or even strengthen some fainting spirit among the sisters (how I dislike that term when applied collectively) of the cloth. Ten years ago, I was a care-free college girl in one of our big universities. I loved its very bigness, its mingling of races, its fusion of ideas. One was free to draw deep breaths, to express oneself as he liked." She recalled a history professor's interest in an essay she wrote, "drawing a most uncomplimentary parallel between Robespierre and a well known politician of the state [La Follette], under whose influence the university was reputed to be." She had felt free to express her opinions at the university, free intellectually and socially, "there was little pressure brought to bear either by tradition or existing conventions. In this atmosphere I lived and moved through some of the important years of my life and when, soon after my graduation I announced by intention of marrying a minister, my friends gasped. (I remember I even considered leaving out the Reverend on the wedding invitations to spare others the shock). I spoke of my approaching marriage to a former professor, also a friend of mine. He showed no enthusiasm and I said, 'Well, what's the trouble? Can't you imagine me as a minister's wife,' and he replied, 'I can't imagine you happy as one.'"

Analyzing her reasons for marrying her husband, the easy answer was that she married for love. But why, she asked, did she love him? She concluded that she loved Melvin because "all the ministers I had met up to that time were of an inferior sort." Melvin seemed a "new specie—not in comparison with other men but with other ministers." He had "youth, vitality, brains, a human interest. He had not lost his contact with men and affairs, but "used that contact to broaden his vision, intensify his motives and deepen his service." He "could have succeeded in any other line of work" but was "giving his life, and energy to the ministry; not like so many because he wasn't good for anything else." (Helen was markedly insensitive to the feelings of others. Many of her "sisters of the cloth" must have winced at her description of the inadequacy of "so many" of their husbands.)

As for being happy as a minister's wife, in her case it "devolved itself into the question of being happy, in spite of, rather than because of that circumstance." Some things bothered her. Not having been trained in the church, and having no preconceived notions regarding church matters, accustomed as she was to forming her own opinion, she applied the same standards to church matters as to any other business. Some methods were good, some "extremely bad."

In most lines of work, if a man wanted a job, he went after it, and people admired him for it. In the ministry, "he must hide behind his friends and get them to push, ostensibly without his knowledge, until some sleepy session deems him sufficiently disinterested to warrant a hearing." The church's "one salesman," the minister, was not given the automobile and gasoline necessary to carry on his work. Her father was "a business man and the firm in which he was interested, furnished their salesmen, numbers of them, with an automobile, gasoline, etc., to be used in advancing their sales. They certainly would never have expected for one moment that any of those men would run his own car at his own expense, in carrying on the firm's business and yet this is exactly the thing many churches take as a matter of course." A trivial complaint, she admitted, but it was symbolic of the inefficient, flawed methods in which the church conducted its "business."

Her greatest frustration lay in the triviality of the issues that confronted her. It afforded her "only amusement" to attend a meeting of an organization of ministers' wives where the consensus of opinion seemed to be that "a minister's

wife should have no intimate friendships, either within her own church or
without (jealousy would always arise), and that she should not under any circumstances entertain certain ones of the church to whom she was indebted,
unless she could have them all and so forth and so forth." But her reaction
had been more violent. "Everything and everybody began to get smaller and
smaller and more wizened, and I fled for the open country and a breath of
God's fresh air." If a timid woman who shunned friendship for fear of giving
offense were "the sort of person congregations like to have as the mistress of
the manse," she was "an insurgent."

She married a man whom she thought "capable of managing his own affairs,
and while [she] would gladly give any inspiration, help or cheer" that was in
her, she refused "to be bothered by any bickerings of that kind." She would
have to continue to manage herself, her children, her home, and her social
life, "much as if I were the wife of a man in any other line of work."

Asked by a friend a few months after her marriage how she liked being married to a minister, she replied, "About as well as to any other man. That has
always been my attitude, whether right or wrong, and as for always living in
the shadow of what some parishioner may say or think—I couldn't tolerate it."

While Helen vented her frustrations in forceful language without a single
word of praise to soften her blows, Melvin wrote an impassioned plea for the
recognition of the value of dedicated Christian service. Clearly they came at
their experiences from very different needs and perspectives. Perhaps Helen
heard his address delivered as a sermon in Omaha; perhaps she read it, or he
read it to her; perhaps he put it in his desk and she never saw it. The essay, a
heart's cry for recognition, asserts that "earnestness and enthusiasm in religion
is the highest rationality." He knew

a lady who has left her family and gone to Laos to live. Her parents stand second to none in the society where they dwell. She was the child of admiration.
On her was lavished everything that could be lavished in the culture of native
excellence. And she cheerfully took it all in her hand and joined herself to the
lot of a missionary and is living in the wilds of China surrounded by the poor
untutored creatures there. And men are either so indignant that she should have
thus thrown herself away that they will not speak of it, or else they hold up hands
of exclamation and amazement, weakly wondering how it is possible for anyone
to do such a thing as that.

If the man had gone after gold, and his wife had gone with him, that would
have been another thing. That man would have understood. . . . When men
deny themselves to become richer, to become luxurious, men think it is all right;

but when he denies himself to become better and nobler, that is what men do not understand.

Melvin believed in self-denial. In the fall of 1923, Helen was bent on self-preservation. As always, she confided in her father and turned to him for help. In the letter he wrote to her on October 24, 1923, he said he agreed with her, "in part at least, that self preservation is one of the first things taught or given by instinct to human beings as well as all other kinds of animals. We get neither credit nor thanks, neither is it the right thing to do to be always looking out for the other fellow. Those you help the most will appreciate it the least and by instinct will be your enemy if an occasion arises." He wanted to work on a time and a definite plan that would get Helen "to the place that will be most agreeable to you to live in—and best for the children for school and everything. And get into a home that will give you the conveniences that our daughter should have." With "all the banks, the retail yards and stores and other interests we are interested in, Melvin can make a choice of the work he would like best. And get into it."[42]

While Helen was convinced she had to bring her family back to Wisconsin and with her father's help recreate her husband in the image of a businessman, her mother did not greet the decision enthusiastically. W.D., who purchased the house across the street from his, Dr. Henry Wahle's house at 208 South Cherry, for her, with a small down payment and a mortgage from his bank, acknowledged that her mother did not know what to decide. She was thinking only of Helen's welfare and interests; "she thought all along that Melvin (and you) were specially adapted to the ministry, and that the pulpit and the church was losing their best workers. . . . Mother said the other day that she did not believe you wanted to come to Marshfield, that you only entertained such ideas because you thought I wanted it.——So the world goes."[43]

The congregation of the Westminster Presbyterian Church dedicated its new church on 35th and Woolworth Avenue (raised through Melvin's inspiration, determination, and effort) in September. In November, Melvin surprised his congregation by requesting that they consider his resignation. "I have been here long enough and it would be better to make a change. I have not accepted another call, but am considering two from larger fields, one at Maryville, Tennessee, and the other from the church at Evanston, Illinois, both of which have about one thousand members. Mrs. Laird's health has not been good here."

W.D. spent the Christmas of 1923 in Victoria. Mame traveled to Omaha to be with Helen and Melvin, to judge the situation for herself, to give her support and cheer, to help with the boys. She understood that not only would

Helen never be happy, but she would not survive as a minister's wife, and she saw that even for Melvin the world had grown darker and more complex and that he could not survive without Helen and his boys.

Melvin did not take another pulpit. His library of philosophical, theological, and historical texts purchased over the years and written in Latin, Greek, German, Hebrew, and English together with his sermons and copies of the weekly order of service were boxed and shipped to Marshfield, where most remained shelved out of the way in the attic of the Lairds' new home. The Lairds returned to Marshfield, and Melvin went to work for Helen's father.

# CHAPTER 13

# The Return

## 1924–1931

So far, what has been gained under the higher standard [of living]
is mostly material and what has been lost is mostly spiritual.

—JAMES TRUSLOW ADAMS

"The Lairds might not be entirely welcome in the church of the Andrews and
the Finneys," W.D. warned Helen, tongue in cheek. He alluded to the scandal that had made headlines throughout Wisconsin in 1923, when Lydia Ritt,
a former maid in the Roddis home, identified Robert Brown of Milwaukee as
Robert Connor of Marshfield. Private detectives, hired by Rob's "political enemies," and an attorney for the Federation of Church Women confirmed the
charge, and Rob and his unmarried "other wife," Bertha Gurtier, the mother
of three of his children,[1] had been arrested. Because Florence refused to press
charges, and Bertha's relatives in the Rapids knew of, and accepted, the arrangement, and because of Rob's distinguished service on the Texas border and
during the World War, he avoided prison. Mame, however, meted out the
punishment of the respectable. She led the little band of indignant wives who
forbade W.D.'s brother from crossing their thresholds. Ostracized by polite
society, Rob moved to Wakefield, Michigan, with his second family to look
after Connor operations there. W.D., who had known all along about the two
families, took the scandal in stride, as did a number of other men with "love
nests" of their own in the big cities.

Melvin quickly reestablished himself in town, rejoining the Masons, the
Elks, and the Rotary. He directed the men's Bible class at the First Presbyterian
Church, preached when asked to fill the pulpit there and in neighboring vil-
lages, and conducted wedding and funeral services for friends and neighbors.
"I am sure you have clarified many thoughts I have had and felt, but never
expressed even to myself," Dr. Karl W. Doege wrote in appreciation after
Melvin spoke at his wife Frieda's funeral.

Rob's office in the corporate headquarters of the R. Connor Building, and Rob's duties became Melvin's. Assuming the oversight of the Auburndale farm was no problem for the farmer's son. He was not a natural businessman, but, like many Americans of his generation, believed a man should be able to do anything. A quick learner experienced in the world of facts and figures, and with W.D. instructing him, he learned how to handle the Connor accounts. From the frequent dunning letters that crossed his desk from Carson Pirie Scott, Peters Shoe Company, Hart Schaffner and Marx, and other suppliers to the Connor stores in Auburndale, Stratford, and Laona and from the summonses for nonpayment or delinquent payment of bills, he learned that money, the essential commodity, was scarce, its distribution requiring a juggler's skill. He learned about the company products, the hardwood maple flooring for which the Connor Company had developed a reputation, the different grades and lengths of lumber. He became a master salesman, traveling the country, meeting customers, taking orders from the large distributors, collecting accounts due. Customers responded to the tall salesman with the honest face, old-fashioned vocabulary, and courteous manners.

If the business world did not appeal to Melvin's imagination, if he could never follow W.D.'s repeated admonition to "let's look to ourselves first," he very quickly became one of the inner circle of men W.D. trusted and depended on. People in town did as well. Dedicated to the welfare of the less well off, he soon became a trustee and chairman of the Wood County Hospital for the Insane, a working farm of a thousand acres within the borders of the city, and head of the Wood County Red Cross.

Helen furnished the house her father gave her with furniture brought from Omaha and the oriental rugs, carpets, draperies, gauze curtains, and yellow globes she located at John C. Stravrum's on Michigan Avenue in Chicago. The large, comfortable four-square white clapboard with its gracious entry, many ornamental spindles on the broad front porch, second-floor balcony, and widow's walk crowning the third floor (from which she might have watched the ships at sea had there been any in that inland port), lay directly across from the Connor home. She slipped back into place as one of the town's women of standing, though some privately criticized her for forcing her husband to abandon his calling but were too well bred to show any overt disapproval. Besides, they knew she was a help to her mother, and, with her intelligence and wit, she added a great deal to their little band. Connor and Dick were widely acknowledged to be very well brought up.

Helen, Mame, and Florence, who divorced Rob but remained close to the other Connors and the Lairds, were a familiar trio at teas and luncheons, DAR meetings, Ladies' Society meetings in the Presbyterian church parlors. Twice a month they could be seen walking the two blocks to St. Alban's Guild Hall to attend Woman's Club meetings. The women sang (the "How De Do Song" was popular), produced skits and plays, watched performances of aesthetic dances, and supported charities with the money they collected in their "Sunshine Box." They discussed bills introduced in Madison and current events, including the controversial subject as to whether the University of Wisconsin should accept money from the General Education Board, "tainted money" that came from the Rockefeller Standard Oil millions, the Duke tobacco millions, and the Carnegie steel mills.

Newspaper reports about labor unrest, mine explosions, murders, abductions, lynching, Al Capone's reign of terror in Chicago did not discourage the Club women from sticking to their ideals of elevating humanity and promoting "all movements looking toward the betterment of life." They supported traditional values. "I don't care if a woman has it in her to be the greatest success in the history of the world as a business woman, an artist, a singer or an actress," one of their members flatly stated. "All the success she may win that

The Laird family in Marshfield, 1925. From left: Connor, Melvin with Melvin Jr. (Bom) on his lap, Helen, and Dick.

way is but, as the Bible says, 'those husks that the swine did eat' as compared with the fulfillment of a woman's destiny and career as a wife, a home-maker, a mother."[2]

For Helen, wife, homemaker, mother were not enough. She added book reviewer, essayist, poet, and public speaker to the list. Signing herself "The Bookworm," she reviewed children's books for the *Marshfield News Herald,* advising youngsters that a book was a child's "very best friend of all. Books never get tired or cross." She also reviewed contemporary novels by American female authors for the Club. Willa Cather remained her favorite. In her review of *My Ántonia,* she praised her for making "poetry out of a life thitherto esteemed vulgar," for carrying "on the torch of living to others." She admired Zona Gale for having the courage to fashion herself from "a fragile, feminine character" to a woman "willing to cover murders, accidents, fires, anything to get writing experience," to become a "respected dramatist and novelist and public servant," but not her style in *Faint Perfume,* which was "too staccato." Nor did she admire the heroine, Leda, a "superior" woman of "high intuitive understanding and fine intelligence," who was forced by circumstance to leave a home of culture and refinement to live with cousins, the Crumbs, "ordinary, tiresome, commonplace . . . people." The Crumbs were universal and it was not their provincialism, but "their low thinking and dull feeling which oppresses." Helen identified with the heroine to the extent that she "wanted to scream at Leda to do differently." She thought "one might criticize her for not having the will to withstand." The book cut close.

Janet Ayer Fairbank, "a talented, interesting Chicago woman," covered "the whole panorama" of American history in her novels. In *The Smiths* Fairbank described a world familiar to Club women, where girls needed to be pretty, and men usually preferred a wife to be a "sweetly feminine little thing, entirely subservient [who] hadn't an opinion about anything." Occasionally a man married a "superior" woman who suffered periods when she "remained languid and totally uninterested in life," when she wanted to be let alone, the children tired her, the hot weather exhausted her, she slept poorly, and "felt entirely superfluous." Peter Smith, "a coming man" who founded a steel company in Chicago, had a "superior" wife. He also had something of the robber baron about him and brooked no curb to independence. He became a director of the Chicago National Bank because "it might be convenient to be connected with a bank which carried so much of his paper"; he went into iron mines in the Mesabi Range of Minnesota anticipating the business would amount to something big and he might be worth ten or twenty times more. He was not communicative about "the secret city where he lived his vital life." His wife's life became "duty, duty, duty." She grew stale and had her moments of rebellion, but there seemed to be nothing to do about it. "Life," the trapped "superior" woman decided, "is all very well to live . . . but it won't bear thinking about."

Like Fairbank's fictional Mr. Smith, W.D. pursued the heady adventure of increasing his fortune in the expansive twenties. The delegation of businessmen that arrived from Wakefield, Michigan, hoping to persuade him to build a mill in their city of 5,000, received favorable publicity. The news that the Connor company planned to start operations on a large tract of virgin timber, more than 500,000,000 feet adjacent to Lake Superior,[3] confirmed the general opinion that here was a businessman who could carry a number of them along on fortune's path. His wife, however, feared that he was carrying his family into "deep water."

His plans involved borrowing heavily from the banks (over $1,500,000 from the First Wisconsin Trust in First Mortgage 6 percent Sinking Fund Gold Bonds as well as additional funds from banks in Wisconsin, Michigan, and Illinois) and his calling back and reissuing the R. Connor Company stock he had recently turned over to family members.[4] His schemes did not sit right with Mame, and they quarreled. In the long "Dear Wife" letter he wrote Mame from the Hamilton Club, Chicago, after a day spent with the bankers, he tried to gain her approval. The trip home had been "a disappointment in some ways." He had her letter and felt he "should come home and try to talk with you about this business. . . . Seems as if we got no where, but into a word war over Robert, my brother." He wanted her and all the family to understand. "I so wish you would be patient with me and I need your co-operation. I need your help. I need your backing and confidence. I really feel I have the experience and the ability to put through some of these propositions and that I should be using some of the talents that have come to me by inheritance or by determined struggle against many odds to obtain."

He had owned the Michigan timber for many years, had borrowed money to obtain it; taxes and carrying charges had been "very heavy and continually increasing." He had also carried Robert's interest in the timber and owed the R. Connor Company large sums on the book and had also "to find so much money to put into British Columbia." He was "square" with the company in 1911 when he sold a block of timber in Minnesota, but at present he owed the company $300,000 "on the books." By his children turning their R. Connor Company stock to the Connor Lumber and Land Company, the debt would be paid, there would be no income taxes, and, if he got a fair value on the property, he would have credit or cash to help him finance some other properties. "The timber would be going to the company that myself and you and the immediate family own eighty percent of the stock in." He wanted to have all their real estate property in the hands of corporations because of the laws on inheritance taxes. People die; corporations, he asserted, go on forever. Money from the loans would go to new timber purchases. Large sums would not go into a new plant.

Helen comforted and reassured Mame as best she could. W.D. probably knew best. Besides, there was no stopping him. But she let her father know that her mother needed a holiday. The shame of Rob's duplicity, Marian's lack of success in either catching a husband or establishing a career, Richard's depression because his wife was having a difficult time adjusting to life in Laona, Melvin's sacrifice of his calling, W.D.'s long absences—all made her seem "used up." Helen knew how a woman could get driven down, all unobserved by a self-absorbed man who did not realize how she worked and worried and grew tired. Apologizing for spending so much time away from home, W.D. took Mame to Victoria, where she relaxed at the Empress while he looked things over at the Jordan River, and then to Michigan and the Battle Creek Sanitarium, where he met with bankers and she took the waters.

Not at first, but soon, Rob also began to worry about his brother's reorganization of the company assets and of what rapidly became clear was, in spite of W.D.'s initial denial, a major expansion of both the mill and the housing in Laona. Deflecting criticism, and seeking recognition for the many months he spent overseeing the project,[5] W.D. tried to ease his exiled brother's mind by boasting of his achievement in putting up a new plant for 50 percent of what such a plant would normally have cost and agreeing that "statements coming from the books [should be] made right and reasonable." His explanation that he wanted "to get the corporation business going in a different way, and all our finances and all our buying of everything" going through one channel, because "that is the way other people are doing," may not have reassured Rob.

Unilaterally, W.D. increased the boards of both the R. Connor and the Connor Lumber and Land Company, putting Melvin on the boards of both as secretary and W. W McCulloch of Marshfield, a stockholder, notary, friend, neighbor, and long-time business associate, as treasurer. He put William on the board of the Connor Lumber and Land Company and added Richard's name to the board of the R. Connor Company. W.D. remained president and Rob vice president of both companies. The reorganization "will look better and it will be more satisfactory to everyone connected with the Company." Perhaps not to Rob, however, who recalled how his sisters felt cheated out of their inheritance when W.D. reorganized the R. Connor Company and set up the Connor Lumber and Land Company at the turn of the century. He may have wondered if W.D. wasn't setting up his family dynasty for the long haul and he being squeezed out. No use complaining, however. The brothers had had a long relationship, and W.D. had always been the caring elder, the boss, who had always been fair to him.

Life, judging from the poem Helen wrote on her return from a trip to the East Coast, where she had taken Constance to look over the women's colleges and to visit Gordon at Andover and Marian in Boston, had not been fair to Helen.

> Seventeen full years have been yours, dear girl
> To frolic, to grow, to dream,
> Till soon you must measure things as they are
> By the yard stick of things as they seem.
>
> The glorious dreams are all right, my dear,
> Only build so you'll realize some
> Else the fog will thicken, the way grown dim,
> And gray days with misgivings will come.
>
> For every resolve have something to show
> Don't let things just slide and slip
> Play fair, aim true, hit sure my dear
> Make the rudder guide your ship.
>
> You've dreamed of some handsome prince charming, I know
> Or some Lochinvar brave and bold,
> But wait till he really comes, girl with the curls,
> Or the fires of your love will grow cold.
>
> Have the measuring stick you use in your life,
> As long as the one in your dreams,
> And you'll always be happier, girl with the curls,
> Making life turn out what it seems.

The return to Marshfield—her lovely home, travel, books, clubs, friends, family—had not stopped the fog from settling or the gray days from coming. Dream and reality continued to fight their wearing dual. Melvin performed his duties and was loved by all, it seemed. But as it also seemed, if her poem to "To Constance" provides a clue, he had not proven the right mate for Helen, for whom, perhaps, none existed. Perhaps no Prince Charming's kiss could have released her from her repeated depressions and sense of solitude.

Constance, the "girl with the curls," Marshfield, 1925. Helen urged her sister to be the director of her fate.

If I should die tonight, I wonder
When my body's torn asunder
Would come a thrill at life's conclusion,
Here, at new beginnings
Or only nothingness, a feelingless Nirvana?

I don't much care, if truth were known,
I'm tired of endless trails alone.
Alone, though always round about me
Are family, friends, and persons plenty.
The loneliness that's in my heart
Remains there, come what may.

W.D. had no time for introspection as he transformed himself from cunning businessman who would not give the Wisconsin Conservation Commission "the information [about cruise valuations] on the townships we don't want to give them information on," to loving father who enjoyed playing host at the Connor home to 130 of the most prominent members of central Wisconsin society gathered for a musical soiree to hear Marian sing, to savvy political pundit whose opinion was solicited and who was, on occasion, when he thought his help made a difference, active on behalf of Republican candidates. He rejected Coolidge appointee Federal Marshall Richard J. White's request that he come to Milwaukee to help develop a strategy to put up a candidate for the deceased Senator La Follette's expired term: "Talking big and sitting in comfortable chairs in a cool place around the hotels and clubs in the city won't bring the necessary results, you know that." He supported Senator Irvine Lenroot's 1926 gubernatorial campaign against three-term "opportunistic Governor John Blaine"[6] and enlisted Helen's help in bringing in the women's vote.

Helen was on the speakers' platform with Lenroot at the Silver Lake Pavilion on the brilliant August day when he campaigned in Forest County. The mosquito season was over, and the assembled crowd—including all the Connors, the Lairds, and Lew Sarett, the famous nature poet, Chautauqua lecturer, and Northwestern University professor—eagerly anticipated the speeches.[7]

Helen began by saying she was glad to see the people of Forest and surrounding counties and considered it an honor to appear on the same platform with Senator Lenroot, an intelligent, proven statesman. She recalled when Forest County was an isolated part of the state and she rode "on horse back over to Stone Lake (Lake Lucerne) and Crandon when there was little more than a trail over twenty years ago." She had been "interested wonderfully in the development of this part of the state" but was more interested in the people of this part of the country and in the record they would make in the coming election. "If ever there was a place where people should do some clear-minded thinking it is up here. Here in the broad open spaces where you can spend much time in God's out-of-doors, you haven't the confusion, the congestion of population like the great cities and there's little excuse for you to be muddled or side tracked in your thinking."

She campaigned for Lenroot because of "his fearless stand on many issues" and because the choice lay between "this statesman or a mere politician under the thumb of the ruling family of Wisconsin."[8] She had another reason for supporting Lenroot: he supported the World Court, "the most honest, conscientious effort thus far to prevent war." Finally, she said she was on the speaker's platform because "the time has come when women must speak when called upon and do more than speak. You women were included today because you are voters. Ten years ago you might have been invited out of courtesy, or to help feed the multitude, but today you're here for the same reason the men are, because you have a vote to cast and because it's up to you to get all the information you can on every public question before you cast that vote."

She spoke to the women, particularly, about the necessity of an international court because "it seems to me they thought more about the awfulness, the dumbness, the futility of the great war than the men." She was "raising three boys and the Lord knows I want them to serve their country every day of their lives, but I do not intend that they shall be used as fodder for cannons, or targets for big guns, or as victims of poisonous gas, until every possible means has been tried to prevent such a catastrophe." The World Court, she said, "may not be perfect, but I think it is one more step toward making it more difficult to get into a war."

Ideally, the broad open spaces of Forest County should have afforded the women who lived there the opportunity to think clearly and independently, but for some of them that possibility did not exist. Less than two miles from the Silver Lake Pavilion, as part of her father's "secret" world, W.D. had constructed in an area formerly occupied by pigs "the cheapest type of fairly safe, livable cottages," which he could rent cheaply "to the common laboring families." Mrs. Underwood, whose husband was an engineer in the fire hole, and Mrs. Carter, Mrs. Whiting, and Mrs. Jonvin, lived in "Pigville." They were picked up by Henry Pueschner, "a Connor man" and officer in the Laona bank, and driven to the polling place. On the way, Pueschner pointed out on his marked ballot the people the women should vote for. After voting, they were allowed a half-hour's time to shop in the company store before being driven home again, a useless treat when they had no money to buy anything anyway.[9]

Mercifully, the idealistic spokeswoman for social improvement remained ignorant of a host of other violations in her father's town, where workers could not order from the Sears catalog for fear of being reported and fired (the post office was in the Connor store, and the postman "a Connor man"); could not board in Lower Town but had to live in company housing; paid dues out of their pay checks to the company-owned insurance company; and paid their electric bills to the Connor-owned electric company. Employees mumbled among themselves that Lincoln freed the slaves but hadn't gotten far enough north to free them. They mumbled about their restricted lives and about the unsanitary conditions in town where the sewers from the hotel, boardinghouse, store, and school ran into the Rat River and sewage from the hospital came down an open ditch and emptied into a pond behind the Catholic church. In winter, effluent was collected in wooden boxes and hauled onto the ice. When the ice melted, the boxes sank. In the 1920s, they put up with it and told the lovely boss's daughter nothing.

Helen believed W.D. acted in the best interests of the workers and their families, that he was dedicated to the well being of the people in that remote county. Hadn't he repeatedly spoken of the need to "clean up the county" so that decent people would come in; hadn't he applied for help to the Anti-Saloon League and the state Federal Prohibition Office; hadn't he been irate when William reported that Otto Olson, Laona's constable, found a sixty-five-gallon moonshine still on property belonging to the supervisor of Caswell?[10]

As for the charges Herman Kronschnabl, the editor of the *Forest Republican*, made against W.D., that he fixed "the tax rate to suit himself" and that the Connors wanted "to control the legal machinery of the county so that whenever anyone crosses their path in their nefarious work of controlling politics they can throw him in jail,"[11] that was the same old dirty politics Helen had heard about when she was in her teens. Kronschnabl was a rabble-rousing Progressive bent on pushing his own agenda and the Crandon gang. W.D. was the good man trying to bring order to that part of the country. She knew how hard he worked.

None of the Kronschnabl-Connor quarrels bubbled to the surface when Governor Blaine, reelected in spite of the Connors' efforts, and his wife, along with other dignitaries, came to Forest County to celebrate the grand opening of the new mill. Their party stayed for dinner and overnight at the Gordon. A photographer from the Milwaukee Public Museum took pictures of the mill, a model of which was on display in the museum. This was a proud time for W.D. and his family. While most of the old mills in the "winter" part of the state—Hiles, Owen, Kaiser, Rice Lake, Eau Claire, Willow River, Hayward, Bissell, and others—had shut down, W.D. had succeeded in expanding and moving into new times. He had completed construction of the state's largest sawmill as well as of a wood flour mill to use hemlock waste to make a product sought by the burgeoning plastic industry;[12] he had acquired the forests to keep the operation going and built more rails to move his timber over longer distances. And he had trained sons, who eventually, when he was unable or unwilling to take charge of everything, could take over.

Where W.D. had once assumed that Wisconsin's timber industry would end, and the state would become a manufacturing state, new theories of forestry and the passage in Wisconsin of forest fire legislation and Forest Tax Bill 4595, for which W.D., "Wisconsin's best known conservationist" fought, led him to believe that the lumber business could be made permanent. He jubilantly noted the U.S. plan to buy back and reforest large tracts of land in Minnesota, Michigan, and northern Wisconsin in the newly created Ninth Forestry District (some 2,500,000 acres, 125,000 of which would be in the Oneida Unit comprising Oneida, Forest, and Villas Counties).[13]

Helen, having learned in childhood that politics was a rough game, absorbed another lesson in political reality when her father, after several long absences, shifted his focus back to Wood County: in the absence of a controlling figure, the opposition moves in. C. L. Hill, whose three-year contract as superintendent of the Wood County Normal School was about to expire, charged that W.D., a trustee of the school since its establishment in 1903 and president of the board, was a "cheap politician" who was inattentive to official duties and who wanted to move the school to Marshfield. W.D. counterattacked, accusing Hill, whom W.D. repeatedly referred to as "that bird" or "that gent," of spreading the word that "Connor is a dangerous man plotting the destruction of the school or its removal to Marshfield," whereas, W.D. claimed, Hill had called on him with maps and papers and a proposal for a combined Clark and Wood County training school to be located at Marshfield and had asked for W.D.'s support. "I refused to have anything to do with it, and told him to forget it. As he was leaving, I told him to leave the maps and papers with me, because if he had an accident on the way home and Wisconsin Rapids people should pick him up dead and find those papers on him, they would throw his body into the Wisconsin River."[14] W.D. defied anyone "to show that Connor has not always stood for the interests of the taxpayer and the masses of the people who have to make their way in Wood County."

The dust had barely settled when W.D. stirred things up again. The supervisor from the Rapids charged that "Connor had the right as a millionaire

politician and political boss of this county for 40 years to fire Hill," but when
he made "repairs to the county school buildings with funds voted for other
purposes, without being authorized to do so, he exceeded his authority and is
liable to a prison sentence and fine."[15] W.D. countercharged: for his corruption
in handling county roads, the supervisor from the Rapids deserved a prison
sentence. Reuben Connor, chairman of the Wood County Board, a calm man
of long experience, ruled the motion to present the education committee's
resolution to dismiss Connor out of order.[16] W.D.'s attorney, T. W. Brazeau,
saved the day, affirming that the statutes provided for a formal and fair hearing on any charge. "Mr. Connor requests you to file a criminal charge against
him and have it tried so evidence can be heard before a court."[17] P. J. Kraus,
Second Ward Marshfield supervisor, declared that it struck him that these were
largely personal affairs and that investigations would involve needless expenditures to the county. He had known Mr. Connor for years, he stated, "and
while he may have his faults," they would do well to put "this personal matter
into oblivion." Connor won again. Reporters described how his adversaries
"grew visibly angry as he talked and [their] arms gesticulated like pistons."[18]

Those not on the receiving end of W.D.'s barbs appreciated his eloquence,
the startling swoops he executed between "high" and "low" language, his ability to relate to the gutter and the court, but a growing list of the wounded neither forgave nor forgot.

Life around the sixty-three-year-old was never dull. His wit and brilliant ana-
lytical powers were a source of delight to Mame and Helen and, when reports
of his violent eruptions became public, a source of pain.

Helen's fourth son and last child was born on October 17, 1927. "A lovely
child," David's arrival took nothing away from her feeling for his five-year-old
brother, Bom, her "jolly little elf man," her "very best friend of all."

David was barely five months old when Bom became seriously ill. Kept at
home at first under the care of a private nurse, he eventually had to be hospitalized. The ordeal of coping with the potentially fatal illness of one child so
soon after giving birth and coping with a lively twelve- and fourteen-year-old,
even with Mame's help, exhausted Helen, who maintained her equilibrium until
Bom was out of danger. Then she collapsed. Melvin drove her to the sanitarium in Waukesha. On May 2, after ten days' rest, water treatments, and counseling, she came home, where the warm weather and Lew Sarett's letter saying
he looked forward to her return "with the warblers and vireos"[19] turned her
thoughts to Birch Lake, where Richard was already seeing to the turning of the
soil in the vegetable and flower gardens and the planting of the seeds.

Business expansion and family expansion came together in the twenties.

William and Kathryn provided W.D. and Mame with two more grandchildren, Mariana and William Duncan III, and Richard and Florence B. added Dorothy Jean, called Jean, and Charlotte Joanne, whom everyone called Joanne. W.D.'s sons built cottages at the lake for their families, and W.D. transferred the deed to the "Laird cottage" to Helen. The 100-foot lot on which the cottage stood kept her personal tax liability low. All the land surrounding the lake and the backlands, taxed on favorable forest crop basis, belonged to the company. And company was family.

Recognizing that Helen needed to have her duties lightened, and feeling that Connor would benefit from an eastern education, the Lairds enrolled him at Phillips Academy, Andover. Not at first enthusiastic about leaving home—he wrote his parents: "I would never send any child of mine to a boarding school because the years that a boy or girl should spend at home and the years that home will do the most good so far as character is concerned are from 8 to 18"—Connor was soon "in the swing of the school," enjoying his books, friends, "two or three swell gals," shows, and concerts at school and in Boston. He liked his jobs selling hot dogs and drying silver and glasses at Adams, where he got "wonderful food." He even enjoyed the obligatory chapel services. Dr. Drury of St. Paul's "delivered a perfect sermon at both services. The one on mothers had the school in tears." He became a "really big man" on campus, president of the Psi Upsilon fraternity, captain of the baseball team, and a member of the board of the Phillipean.

W.D. also had some positive news. From the Republican point of view, the political picture was looking brighter. "If there was someone who had the capacity and ability to make a reasonable, fair, intelligent talk and refute a lot of the things that are being said by Blaine and young Bob, they could turn the state upside down." He didn't believe, however, that George Mead was that "someone." According to W.D., there wasn't "much room for Mead in State or National politics at this time. The people of Wood County don't even owe Cousin George a complimentary vote." The Connors and Lairds went all-out for Walter J. Kohler in 1928. When he became governor, they thought that at long last the La Follette machine was showing some vulnerability.

As the 1920s ended, the country had its heroes—"Slim" Lindbergh of the skies, Babe Ruth of baseball—and its villains: accused anarchists Nicola Sacco and Bartolemeo Vanzetti (who were summarily executed) and Al "Scarface" Capone (who finally went to prison). Marshfield pioneers died, and the town began to know it had a history. News of the stock market and stock market quotations became as much a feature in the *Herald* as news of the locally raised cows and locally produced cheese. The market churned but reached new heights, assessments and bank deposits increased, an all-paved highway connected Wood County with Chicago and the Twin Cities. A few voices were raised in concern: the promise of the "machine age" was "in things rather than men" and "therefore a promise which may be *for* things rather than men"; American literature had become a literature of protest and discontent;[20] homes, stamped out by machines, were becoming standardized in a "monotonous sameness"; no "accepted view of life existed anymore but "a profusion of creeds and philosophies, fads and intellectual experiments"; the Wisconsin River was badly polluted, and pollution hurt fish life; John Adler worried that the motion picture industry might "experience severe setbacks by gigantic mergers for the purpose of monopolizing the industry."

For the Lairds and the Connors, however, there were reasons to celebrate, and they did. In 1928, they hosted a gala New Year's Eve dinner dance at St. Alban's Guild Hall, which was "the outstanding social event of the holiday season."[21] Covers were laid for about sixty at small tables decorated with holiday favors. Colored lights adorned the tiny trees set in the window boxes. Constance and Gordon stood in the receiving line with Mame and W.D. and Helen and Melvin. Mary Roddis was among the invited guests, as was Dick (Ritchie) Modrall, the Texas cowboy and a law student at the university, who was Constie's date (and who took care of her horse at the university stables). Connor also had a date, Betty Nash from the Rapids.

On July 20, 1929, the budding romance between Gordon Connor and Mary Roddis was sealed in an elaborate wedding in the garden of the Roddis home. Gordon's Psi Upsilon fraternity brother, Bernard Brazeau, son of W.D.'s lawyer, Theodore Brazeau, was best man. Little Miss Ellen Roddis, in a lace dress, and Melvin Laird Jr., wearing a cut-away jacket, striped trousers, bow tie, and the corrective glasses he wore to strengthen his "slip" eye, walked behind the bride carrying her long train.

Among the three hundred guests were George Mead, who had taken his political defeat in stride, and his wife. Robert Connor had not been invited. Respectful younger brother no longer, he had made headlines in April when he filed an action against W.D. in Bessemer, Michigan, for recovery of $10,000 from the R. Connor Company. Registered now as a Wisconsin corporation doing business in Michigan with headquarters in Ironwood and logging operations north of Wakefield, the R. Connor Company, Robert declared, was indebted to him for money lent and money due him. The papers were full of the story.[22]

Marian, married in June 1928, was there with her husband, Albert Rhyner.

No doubt she contrasted her brother's splendid wedding with her own. As W.D. feared, she had fallen in love with "a fortune hunting Italian artist in Boston" while studying voice and attempting a career as a singer. When the private detective W.D. hired to find out about the man uncovered a "bohemian" past, he refused to support her out East anymore and brought her home. Albert Rhyner, a former classmate in the Marshfield public schools, worked as a conductor for the Chicago, Milwaukee, North Shore Railroad. Their wedding, officiated by Melvin, with Helen serving as her sister's maid of honor, took place quietly in the Connor home and made the kind of headlines of which the family was not proud: "Weds Heiress But Clings to His Job," "Riches Didn't Count," "Bridegroom Keeps Job Running His Car." Albert was musical, a fine violinist, and, as the family learned to its sorrow, an alcoholic. W.D. built a small house for them on West Eighth Street, gave Albert a job, and, as some relatives thought, "took his manhood away from him."[23]

The Connor-Roddis wedding proved to be the final great family social event of the decade. In October the stock market crashed. Headlines proclaimed, "Stock Crash Will Not Hurt Business," but the six-story plunge to death from his offices on Wall Street of the sixty-year-old president of the Union Tobacco Company, which also made headlines, suggested another story.[24]

Alone in her front bedroom as the decade ended, her two-year-old asleep in his cot in the little room adjoining, as the winter sun's gray light fell over the pages, Helen read Miss Mathilde Weil's criticism of the poems she had sent her. (Miss Weil advertised in the *Atlantic* magazine's "Books and Art" section as someone who had worked as a consulting specialist and editor for major publishing houses, including Macmillan, Holt, Lippincott, Harcourt, and was in a position to help aspiring authors.) Helen aspired to greatness. Perhaps in her poetry, she could find her path. She sent a letter to Miss Weil's address at the Writer's Workshop, 849 Lexington Avenue, New York, requesting her brochure, and then took the first frightening step of sending Miss Weil her check with the packet of poems she hoped might be good enough.

Miss Weil began kindly, apologizing for her delay in sending her report. She encouraged Helen to keep on with the poetry in which she had made "so good a start." All her verses were "evidently based upon deep rooted feeling that makes them appeal . . . to one unfamiliar with the people and places on which they are based," and her lines were frequently musical, but few held appeal to a broad audience, and almost all seemed like first drafts rather than finished products.

"The Empress Hotel," while it would certainly be appreciated by the owners

Helen with David and Bom, Marshfield, 1928. Bom wore glasses to correct a "slip eye."

of the hotel, ran on too long and was not suited to the general public. "A Wisconsin Idyll," in which Helen described Birch Lake in a five-stanza poem as "lovely little laughing lonely lake set in the pines" that "put my winter in forgetfulness," was more general but too repetitious. Her essay "Spring in Northern Wisconsin" was beautifully written, but there was not now much demand for nature papers.[25] The poems "To Constance" and "To David" were too personal; "Memories," one of the three poems that Helen's "bambino" inspired, needed to be gone over, the rhyme and meter strengthened, but all the "bambino" poems were "very lovely in spirit."

*Memories*

I raise you in my arms dear little soldier
Your eyes a'sparkle and your cheeks aglow
And realize how I love you, near to heart-ache
How can I make you know I love you so?
When you are grown I'll have but pictures
To call you back from all along the line
To link up memory with memory
More real than things that happen at the time.

"Autumn" showed her love of nature "and that undercurrent of foreboding that gives depth to so many of your poems." It was, however, a mixture of free verse and lyric form and, like her other verses, required work. "Marriage" was Helen's most original poem. "Many wives would do well to heed the lesson it inculcates. I should say a husband was very fortunate to have such an understanding wife."

*Marriage*

Like two steeds woefully mated,
One restless, galloping fast,
The other patient, plodding gentle,
Our union seems at last.

Gladly would I have leaped forward
E'en to pull more of the load,
But that binding, hindering harness
Kept me slowly in the road.

I longed to dash over yon hill-top
To pastures green and new,

And never would have settled down
Were it not for the harness and you.

Some say why don't you dash ahead
And break the tugs called marriage?
But oh, my friends! 'twont do you know
To wreck a family carriage.

But do you really mean "woefully mated"? Miss Weil wanted to know.

The large check-mark Helen placed beside "Mountain Meadows," a short story she came across in the August 1930 issue of *Harper's,* indicates that, while she may once have considered herself to be "woefully mated," she no longer did. Mary Sheldon's story is told by a narrator, a midwestern schoolteacher who, on a trip to California, decides to stop off in Colorado, where a favorite former pupil lives. The teacher finds Mary, a woman of great promise in her youth for whom every study was a "joyous experience," married to a dour farmer and burdened with the care of an invalid mother and a severely retarded son. Her life, while lightened by the affection of two lively daughters, strikes her former teacher as appalling. Mary explains that she finds the strength to keep going by "going apart" for a while each day. "The great ones of the earth—Jesus, Laotse, the Buddha, the saints—always went apart!" Meditating upon the good, Mary thought she could grow good. She willed to see beauty, and while "reality" placed her on the "brown plain," she was sustained and inspired by the "mountain meadows" she inwardly perceived. Moreover, while she does not love her husband "in the way wives are expected to love their husbands. . . . there is another sort of love, larger, perhaps; farther seeing—and I think it has begun to grow in me."

Like the heroine in the short story, by 1930 Helen was a middle-aged woman committed to her husband and her children. Like the heroine, she was also sustained by the "mountain meadows" of her imagination. The story in *Harper's* may have put Helen in mind of her former English teacher at Milwaukee Downer. She invited Emily Brown, in whose classroom Helen "knew that rare experience of being transported into the realm of the intellect beyond time and space," to speak to the Woman's Club. Miss Brown also remembered Helen. "How I loved to hear you speak on the platform! I can never forget your fine utterance and poise." It was "a great joy" for her to come to Marshfield to visit her former pupil in her home. She wished she did not have to ask for $10 plus expenses, "for our values are other than that."

Helen read "plenty of the sordid" in the contemporary American novel,

"thinking that by going down through the valley [she] could better appreciate the hill top in American letters." She thought "it may not come in my day,
but it will come." She agreed with Melvin that while Sinclair Lewis had received
the Nobel Prize, his focus on the cheap and tawdry in American life indicated
that he had never experienced any great, authentic, formative experience at
home, in school, or in church.[26] She alluded to, but never reviewed, Lewis's
novels. Preferring to boost America, she wrote a fifteen-page paper celebrating the new American theater, the work of the Drama League of New York,
and Eva Le Gallienne's repertory theater, which produced "week after week
plays of great finish at a top price of $1.50." She wrote, "No vehicle [is] so
powerful and so competent to carry the meaning of America to our assimi-
lated and unassimilated population as the drama." Marc Connelly's *Green Pastures*, with its "all-Negro cast," this "divine comedy of the modern theater,"
barred in England as sacrilegious, was going to be read and performed by the
drama group the Woman's Club organized. Helen thought the women might
be encouraged in their efforts in "reading of a town in Iceland, not as large as
this, where there has been an amateur stock company for over 30 years."

She could not "emphasize too strongly the effort toward the esthetic in art
and in life—only those who cultivate it are really free. . . . . Until we ourselves
cultivate the seeing eye and the hearing ear the whole realm of esthetic expression is closed to us and we remain bound and oppressed by circumstances and
conditions about us, unable to escape into those other worlds."

Escape was becoming "more and more important in this country, for our
pioneering days are about over, physical adventure is closed to most of us, and
there is left only that field of free imagination of mental adventure. We must
learn to redeem the commonplace imaginatively. Some can do this through
religion, some through music, but in any case it involves an effort."

In her inaugural speech as Woman's Club president in 1931, she said, "There
is a place for this Club in the community to enrich the life of this community, to better understand history and international relations, to be of help in
the unemployment situation, to help in safeguarding the health of the community." She urged the women to recognize the important social side of the
Club, which provided "a meeting ground for strangers and new women."
"Remember," she said, "we are all lonely."

Including Melvin. Needing time to pursue her interests, Helen refused to
meet him in Chicago or to go with Dick to Madison so that the three of them
could visit the university together. Melvin hoped Dick, a "fine, thoughtful
boy," would not annoy his mother with his efforts to get her to come along.
By way of bolstering his son's wounded ego, he wrote of his pride "every day

Melvin with his four sons, ca. 1931: Dick, Melvin Jr. "Bom", David, and Connor.

as I watch you growing into manhood. We do want to help you get a splendid education and training for life. If you get the right kind of training and preparation now, the difficulties, which arise later in life, will seem small."

On August 30, in the alcove of the Connors' spacious living room, W.D. gave Constance Victoria Jane Connor in marriage to James Ritchie Modrall. Melvin read the marriage ceremony, and Helen stood as maid of honor. Fifty friends and relatives were in attendance. Keeping up the fiction that the Connors were not seriously perturbed by the economic downturn, the *Herald* reported: "Plans for a more elaborate wedding were curtailed owing to the fact that the bride was convalescing from an attack of pneumonia." The Connors' youngest daughter went off smiling to the frontier community of Las Vegas, New Mexico with her lawyer husband. It wasn't long before W.D. wrote Helen that he "had thoughts of how much she felt like the part she was trying to play."

# CHAPTER 14

# Surviving Losses

## 1932–1936

Five horsemen of this new apocalypse: Profligacy, Propaganda, Patronage, Politics, Power. Their other names are Pork-barrel, Poppy-cock, Privilege, Panaceas, Poverty.

—HERBERT HOOVER

W.D. ruled his family through love and dedication, his opponents by intimidation. He could not, however, intimidate Herman Kronschnabl, editor-publisher of Crandon's *Forest Republican,* who persisted in challenging W.D.'s stranglehold over Laona and Forest County. When his "anti-Connorite campaign" succeeded in bringing about the defeat of Judge Conway, the "last candidate of the Connor gang holding office in the court house," W.D. charged that Kronschnabl "never worked an honest day in his life" and was the brother-in-law of Paul E. Fauteck, convicted of disloyalty and sentenced to eighteen months in Leavenworth penitentiary for publishing pro-German propaganda during the World War. Kronschnabl retaliated with a $25,000 libel suit, which led to "one of the most serious and hard fought civil actions" ever tried in Wood County. The news that Connor lost the case and was fined $500 spread across Wood and Forest Counties,[1] and Kronschnabl kept hammering away at the Connors.

A front-page article described how people in Laona's Lower Town lost their homes when a fire broke out and the company's fire equipment wasn't brought out in timely fashion, and how only the arrival of the Crandon "pumper" prevented destruction of the entire south side. "Witnesses" overheard the fire chief remark that "he had a letter in his office to the effect that whenever a fire is not on company property to 'roll over and go to sleep.'" (Three weeks later another fire broke out in Laona, this time in W.D.'s town. Connor equipment and volunteer fire fighters saved Richard's home, which had been in "great danger," but the Laona bakery and the homes of E. Gutself, Adolph Manges,

Joe Ratty, all of them owned by the Connor Company, went up in flames.)[2] And when William Grumann, a Lower Town man, filed a formal complaint with the Public Service Commission and appealed for lower electric rates from the company-owned electric service, Kronschnabl made the story front-page news.[3]

Then, suddenly, there was no more fun in the fight. Not only was Kronschnabl elected an assemblyman on the Progressive ticket, but everyone knew the infallible Connors had slipped. The R. Connor Company and the Connor Lumber and Land Company defaulted on interest charges and fixed principal payments and were under the trusteeship of bond protective committees. Tears streamed down William's face as he stood before the large crowd of Indians, workers, and wives in Laona and explained the company's nonpayment of taxes. William Grumann beat CL&L Company candidate Reno Fletcher and was elected town chairman. The Federal Indian office closed in Laona and moved to Crandon. Kronschnabl's *Forest Republican* bought out the Connors' *Tribune* and the *News*.

The loss of local, company, and county control; the newspaper; and the Indian office were not the hardest blows the family suffered as the economy plunged and lumber production dropped to less than it had been in 1869, when the country had less than a third of the population. The hardest blow came when Robert Connor filed another civil suit, charging that "since July 25, 1929, W.D. Connor has exercised exclusive management, supervision and control of the affairs of the Connor Lumber and Land Company, and the R. Connor Company, and because of his mis-management of these companies each has become insolvent and the stock has become worthless or of little value." Rob sued W.D. for nonpayment for the sale of 1,259 shares of his common-capital stock in the Connor Lumber and Land Company and 460 shares of R. Connor Company stock and for making "transfers of property of great value to his wife, Mary, and other persons and corporations with intent and purpose not to perform or abide by the terms and conditions of his contract and supplemental agreements with Robert Connor." The suit made headlines.[4]

W.D.'s countersuit, alleging that Robert "repeatedly made false statements to bankers and other persons which injured the credit of the defendant and the two companies,"[5] also made headlines. He denied transferring property of value to his wife and other persons with the intent of not abiding by terms of the agreement. Foreseeing the fiscal crisis and his personal liability, he had, however, done just that, deeding timberlands, including hundreds of acres surrounding Birch Lake, to Mame and his stock in both the Connor Lumber and Land Company and the R. Connor Company to her, his children, and Melvin.

The American National and the Cloverland Bank in Marshfield, of which W.D. was president and family members major stockholders, closed. W.D., not unduly alarmed, analyzed the situation. "It develops that the small depositors all over the country when they move in the same direction dominate the situation." Not the fellows in Wall Street. If they passed laws preventing people from getting their money out, it would be "hard for the banks later on to get the confidence of the people." His solution was for "the Federal Government [to] fill the Reserve Bank with good currency. Those banks in turn pass out the actual currency so freely for every purpose that actual currency—not credit—would become so plentiful that people would begin thinking of turning their money into property. That cycle swings back and forth regularly, over every period in our economic history."[6]

Overlooking his own role as banker, albeit on a comparatively small scale, W.D. predicted that "banks and bankers won't be the 'big boys' for a while." Nothing had been run "so extravgently [*sic*] as the banks." Operating costs would have to be cut in two. It would "be a criminal offense for any banker to use the bank's office, stationery, heat and lights as the place from which to conduct *personal speculation* and sale of securities. The temptation is if the deal turns out all right the profit is his, if it turns badly then it is slipped into the banks."

Although he dealt with a number of those "dressed up wise city boys" at Baker, Fentress and Company, agents for Connor bonds, who had "so many bond issues go wrong," and they were "so near dead" their Chicago office began "to smell," he held the pioneer's disdain for the "fellow at the fancy desk."[7] He also ridiculed the manager of CPS for being so "afraid of these fellows in Victoria that he would give them all his eleven children if they suggested it."

A portly receiver, John Fordyce, arrived with his family to oversee the collapsed banks, and he remained for years. He settled into the Pleasant Hill neighborhood, on the corner of Second and Cherry, a few doors down from the Lairds, and his presence was a perpetual reminder of the family's personal financial difficulties and the disappointed depositors and creditors he represented, among them many friends and local people. A man of average height and a heavy drinker, his slightly disheveled appearance, his shirt invariably pulled out of his vest, contrasted with the tall, meticulously groomed Reverend Laird, whose appearance, language, and bearing indicated, even in the most discouraging days of the Depression, that here was an antique man of substance. Fordyce was, however, appearances to the contrary, a man of intelligence and wit who maintained a cordial relationship with his beleaguered neighbors.

Robert Baird of Milwaukee and George R. Birkeland of Chicago, the court-appointed trustees for the bankrupt Connor Lumber and Land Company, remained on good terms with W.D. The company had operated successfully in Wisconsin for many years, and W.D., Melvin, and Birkelund were granted the trusteeship of the stock. However, the R. Connor Bond Protective Committee and the United States District Court judge of the Western District of Wisconsin, Patrick T. Stone, removed the Connors from management of the R. Connor Company. In spite of W.D.'s assertion that he would not build a mill in Michigan, he had gone ahead and done so at Connorville, a swampy site near Wakefield and Thomaston. He had put Gordon in charge of what turned out to be, even with materials and rails from the defunct Stratford operation, an expensive, badly timed project that overwhelmed the company's debt obligation.

Men for whom W.D. had nothing but the greatest disdain, R. S. Peotter and Harold Smith, became the court-appointed director and comptroller of the R. Connor Company. They took over the R. Connor Building in Marshfield, forcing Melvin as well as Miss Lavinia Huber, W.D.'s loyal secretary, and several salesmen to set up the Connor Lumber and Land Company business office in rented quarters. W.D. accused Peotter and Smith of having "the money to chase around the country in all directions, live at the best of hotels in the most expensive way," while letting "the whole works go to pot in Michigan." Peotter "fixed himself up with a dude woods uniform, went in and said he was going to stay right there for all time. He stayed two days. The job was so strenuous, had to go to town and go to bed and has not been back since."[8] Getting control of his company and out from under the strangers' authority became an obsession for W.D.

As the Depression deepened, with the Connors no longer in charge in Michigan and with no real prospects for him elsewhere in company management, Gordon went to work for the Roddis Company at their Park Falls Division. Richard was sorry "to hear of Gordon's choice—he seems to have only his own interests in mind," but he supposed that Mary, expecting her first child, was "strong for the change. If it doesn't work out, it will be difficult for him to get back on the CL&L Co. and I don't think I would want to make the plea."[9]

Melvin, involved as he was in the Connor bankruptcy, as chairman of the county board and the county relief committee, also heard the hardship stories of many desperate farmers. With W.D.'s half-brother Reuben Connor, welfare administrator for Wood County, he set up a single welfare department handling all cases of relief, including WPA and CCC certification. Wood County, where every able-bodied relief client had to work for his or her maintenance, was "way ahead of the average county in the state in the way it handled welfare," Dr. Alfred W. Briggs, the State Welfare Department director claimed. With the vanished frontier no longer absorbing excess population, machine efficiency increasing, and an increase of 4.5 million persons in the labor market since 1929, the relief problem would be with them for some time.[10]

District Attorney Charles Pors, who at the beginning of 1933 was quoted as saying, "We are losing rapidly" by government going into the field of charity, changed his mind as the Depression deepened and soup became the national meal. When President Franklin D. Roosevelt appointed him the local chairman of the National Recovery Program, he no longer lamented the passage of the age of individualism. The "favored few must give way for the general good of all." There had been a "gradual evolution towards a more ideal existence in America." The time had come "when benefits of gainful work must be evenly divided. People must co-operate."[11]

Helen, reelected president of the Woman's Club, encouraged women to canvas homes and get pledges from heads of households to support and patronize employees and workers who were members of the National Recovery Act, a "great campaign" she likened to the wartime Liberty Loan drives. The blue eagles they distributed, symbols of participation, appeared on homes and businesses all over town. The women presented a petition to the Common Council demanding that employed women whose husbands had jobs relinquish their jobs to single women.[12]

Convinced that "to be intelligent with regard to the world point of view is an absolute essential of the day in which we live," that economic issues and political issues were linked, Helen formed and led, along with her friend Helen Doege, the club's international affairs study group and became active in the Wisconsin Committee on the Cause and Cure of War.

The downward spiral continued. A quarter of a million young men drifted across the United States, and revolution threatened at home and abroad. Communism represented hope for increasing numbers of the unemployed as well as for workers and intellectuals. In the midst of chaos, a family tragedy occurred. Marian Connor Rhyner died in May 1933, three days after giving birth by Cesarean-section to a daughter, Elizabeth. "She should never have died," said her doctor, Harry Vedder, who had successfully delivered her son William in 1931. "But she did not want to live." Not with a mate like Albert.

When sober, her husband was "meek as a lamb." Drunk, she had to fend him off with her cane until someone responded to her call for help. Mame immediately rushed in to take over the care of her daughter's toddler and her newborn,[13] climbing (the story goes) up the fire escape of St. Joseph's Hospital to take the infant from her bassinet before Alfred could claim her. W.D. obtained a court order preventing him from coming to the house.

Helen told her sister's story in a poem.

You sang when your heart was breaking
You smiled to keep back the tears
You fought for some compensation
To crowd back disappointment and fears.
One can die of a broken heart so they tell me
You lived with one first which is worse.

Marian's life was "no longer sharpened on the grindstone of pain." If Helen "could only know" she had "reached a realm" where she sang and smiled, their parting would not "seem so sad, nor yet so long." It took a trip to Massachusetts to attend Connor's graduation to, mercifully, pull Helen out of her grieving.

When Connor set off for the University of Chicago in the fall, if Helen were a woman of normal curiosity, which she was, she would have looked into the unlocked diary he left behind, written during his senior year at Andover. From its pages she would have gleaned his thoughts and understood his pride and vulnerability. He wrote of feeling "very exalted and old at times, and at other times very down and young." "Popular and well liked by everyone," he wished he "were different, more intelligent and not so damned superficial." He admired Philip in Somerset Maugham's *Of Human Bondage,* who didn't believe in God, but for him "it would be a useless world without God." He was "lazy and ambitious at the same time," wasn't "cut out to struggle and strive like Grandpa." He wanted "to have enough money to live happily and not to worry" but wasn't sure he was "capable of making a living." He had fallen "dreadfully in love," was "awfully afraid of facing life," and "quailed at the thought of making a new start, new friends, more books, especially at that Mecca of intelligence Chicago." He wrote that in ten years he expected to go over his diary and be able to answer the question as to whether something had been accomplished during his four years in the East to make him a better man. "It will be then a question which will mean whether or not my life will be on the high road or the low or on the misty flats drifting to and fro. I tremble at the thought, but haven't enough nerve to go out and change drastically the course it is taking now."

Nor could Helen change the course of hers. She had done that once when she linked her future with her parents rather than follow in Melvin's chosen path.

She had not seen Rob for many years, when, a little more than a year after Marian's death, she and W.D. traveled to Ironwood, Michigan, to attend his funeral. The fifty-six-year-old vice commander of the Michigan State Legion, who had indulged in all the free cigarettes the Red Cross and the army distributed during the Great War, had succumbed to lung cancer.[14] (His death imminent, Rob settled his suit with his brother out of court.) From Michigan, Helen and her father traveled to Chicago, where Mame was being treated for cervical cancer at Mercy Hospital. Having her daughter near by gave her "strength to make the fight."

While Helen and W.D. were visiting with Mame in Chicago on July 2, Melvin attended his mother's funeral in Griggsville. Helen celebrated Anna Osborne Laird in a poem as one who

> humbly, sweetly serving human kind
> upheld by faith as simple as a child's
> faithfully fulfilled her destiny as wife and mother
> unperturbed by life's changes and vicissitudes.

In September 1934, Minneapolis experienced a "Bloody Friday," during which police fired into a crowd of picketing Teamsters and the women supporting them. Governor Olson called out the National Guard in Minnesota at almost precisely the moment Governor Schmedeman called out the National Guard in Wisconsin to quell the violence that erupted in Sheboygan as workers and "agitators" struck the Kohler manufacturing plant.

And the free speech issue roiled the university as Helen assumed the presidency of the Seventh District Federation of Woman's Clubs. In her inaugural speech to representatives from the forty clubs in her ten-county district, Helen stressed the need for "open mindedness towards public questions" and the importance of debate and analysis. There was "already enough shoddy thinking. . . . Let us remember no one scapegoat is to blame for everything." She urged the women to make the community's needs their business and become "more and more awake to the increasing importance of our international relations." The hard questioning she subjected them to about current affairs seemed to contradict her claim that the women must not forget that "a sound judgment still needs an understanding heart." Her heart was absorbed in brightening her mother's days as she lay dying at home upstairs in the front bedroom.

In Madison, while attending the university, Dick earned a little money as chauffeur for the head of Wisconsin's National Guard, General George Immel, and by clerking in a men's clothing store, McNeil and Moore. He joined the Psi U fraternity and the debating team, where Jim Doyle Sr. usually argued the opposing view. His firsthand accounts of campus politics and issues echoed Helen's own experiences during her university years.

Helen's former sociology professor, Edward Ross, was again under attack. His comment that he "stood well" with authorities in Russia, where he proposed to lead a group of graduate students from Chicago and Madison to study the "Russian system," condemned him in the mind of Colonel Stephen A. Park, the principal witness at the hearings that Wisconsin state senator E. F. Brunette, the Joseph McCarthy of that era, was holding into political subversion. The "Red Scare" was in full throttle at both universities her older boys were attending, fueled by the Hearst newspapers, which headlined the story that Charles R. Walgreen had withdrawn his daughter from the University of Chicago because she was "acquiring new ideas as a result of the prevalence of communist doctrines."

On May 8, 1935, Helen told the more than two hundred delegates and guests gathered in Marshfield for the Seventh District Women's Club convention that peace was "a challenge to the Christian nations of the world— for peace is a fundamental Christian doctrine," and that "students striking in the cause of peace are not communistic. . . . They are merely showing their indignation against war to inform the world that they are more interested in scholarships than battleships." She urged club members to support university president Glenn Frank, a staunch defender of free speech.

Mame died on July 16, 1935. Leaving the oversight of his affairs in Marshfield to Melvin and Helen, W.D., secure in the knowledge he could depend on Florence to help out, hired a widowed lady in the neighborhood, Mrs. Mason, to look after Marian's babies and left town. He spent months out West trying to hold himself and his family together. Deeply distressed and lonely, the jaunty tone he adopted at the beginning of the Depression entirely disappeared. Yet he sought credit for achievement. He had had the foresight, in spite of the opposition of "the New York people and their friends," who held "quite a few bonds" but not enough to block him, to induce 65 percent of the bond holders of CPS to take preferred stock for their bonds. He had "just put that through in time,"[15] but the market collapsed before he could push through his plan to refinance and borrow a new $2.5 million. At least he had cut out the bond interest, and the holdings in the West were not all locked into receiverships.

He was proud of having held onto the Miami tract, by far the most valuable asset in the province. In the Renfrew District near the Jordan River, the property, which he had put in the name of "the boys," adjoined land owned by CPS.[16] He was also proud of having had the foresight to assign his CPS shares, with the exception of one qualifying share, to his family. When the IRS finally caught up with him and filed suit against him for nonreport of salary from the Canadian Puget Sound Timber and Lumber Company for the years 1920–30, it was too late to recover anything. On December 31, 1935, W.D.'s personal bankruptcy and sworn statement was filed in the office of the District Court of the United States for the Western District of Wisconsin. The Internal Revenue Service could not collect the $93,040.84 deficiency or the $42,962.29 penalty. Just as well Mame had not lived to suffer the indignity.

When, in January 1936, newspapers in Victoria printed "quite an article detailing his ruin," he was pleased to have people believe he had gone belly up. While there was some truth to the rumors—the mill hadn't operated since 1930, and most of the Canadian Puget Sound timber had gone for taxes and royalties—he had managed to hang onto the choicest timber in the province because the government inspectors "listen on the street to what some person, uninformed says" rather than conduct their own investigation. "When we keep quiet—make little show of intelligence, sort of harmless, these very noisy smart chaps don't discover what is happening until too late."[17] Peotter and Smith had stopped looking out there, believing "what they heard on the street."

"The problem is," he confided to Melvin, "can we hang on to it through all this strife and turmoil, keep our enemies from finding out what we have got?" He confided other worries. He could not climb the hills and over the logs quite as freely as he once could. A "little tumble" shook him up "quite a bit. Logs with bark off are very slippery." He missed his spike boots.[18]

Working for his family's economic survival was his passionate crusade. Working for peace became Helen's, but she was no lone crusader. Federation members all over America sang Longfellow's words: "I hear once more the voice of Christ say, 'Peace.'" Churchmen united with them. The Reverend F. W. Hyslop, who came over from the Rapids to address the Marshfield club, urged the women to talk, sleep, and dream peace and, above all, to vote for peace. Her two close friends, Helen Doege and Margaret Schorger, were deeply involved in the peace movement. Margaret, a former president of the Wisconsin League of Women Voters, was president of the Wisconsin Cause and Cure of War Committee.

Helen followed Eddie Cantor's "peace crusade" on the radio. The long letter she wrote to him traces her thinking about war as she became more involved in the Cause and Cure movement. Deciding "verbose talk" was of little use, she tried to clear her head by the question method: Were we convinced war was "wrong, unchristian, a sin against God and humanity"; Were we and the "people of the world" convinced war didn't pay; Have we given up "the old idea that war is inevitable"; Were we interested in "real neutrality" or did we want the right to decide who is the aggressor and to apply sanctions"; Did we "admit that our prosperity, our pursuit of happiness depends on our co-operation with other nations"?

She knew where she stood. Neutrality laws deepened "our illusion that a policy of complete isolation is desirable or possible. To save ourselves we must help prevent all war and what does that mean but a policy of co-operative effort with other nations to obtain security." Americans had to "begin training diplomats and stop handing out foreign posts as political plums," she said. "We have neglected this vastly important field, are often outwitted by shrewder, better trained men. Our citizens have lost confidence in this first line of defense where wars are made or prevented. This is the great challenge to our country and to our younger men and women to-day, that they shall be so trained and inspired that they shall help keep not only this country but all countries out of war. Last: Of politicians we have plenty—of statesmen few." (In 1974, she scrawled "A historical document now" over her letter.)

While Connor wrote of having "developed a sort of ancestor worship which makes my family the center of religion and belief,"[19] the essay he wrote for Thornton Wilder's course "Classics in Translation," one he had taken for "relief from the toils and troubles of the business school," reflects a growing cynicism. "The heroes [of the Greek world] died in splendor; we shall die in sophistication; our children may not die at all which will be even worse. The race, after Homer's golden age was growing soft; 'progress' had begun to raise its ugly head."[20] He accepted a job with Continental Can Company after graduation in order to be near his fiancée, Barbara Vail, and because his grandfather had not been able to offer him one. The company's prospects were too uncertain.

John Fordyce had lived on Cherry Street for "two years, three months and twenty days" when he and Melvin worked out the settlements for the notes drawn on the First National Bank by W.D. Connor Jr., W.D. Connor Sr., and the Canadian Puget Sound Timber and Lumber Company. When the family came up with $16,000 to settle the $37,000 William borrowed for the Laona operation, Fordyce wrote the Comptroller of the Currency, Division of Insolvent National Banks, Washington, D.C., that the amount was more than could be obtained in any other way. He recommended he be given authority to effect the compromise and reminded the comptroller that when the Reconstruction Finance Corporation agent was there appraising the assets of the bank, he classified the W.D. Connor Sr. paper as being doubtful with perhaps 10 percent recovery, and he made "no report on the Canadian Puget Sound Timber and Lumber Co. assets as he thought they were worthless." W.D. was in the courts of bankruptcy, and "there is no possible way of my trust to expect to recover one penny from the W.D. Connor Sr. estate, part of the reason being that he began two years before he declared himself bankrupt to get rid of his good properties and also that the government claims a big income tax lien against his estate." He saw "no possible hope of recovery from W.D. Connor Sr. or from the Canadian Puget Sound Timber and Lumber Company of which he is the guiding factor." His investigation told him that its assets consisted largely of "timber limits in the province of Victoria and that the rights have been eliminated by inability to keep up the taxes and payments."[21]

When Melvin relayed the news of Fordyce's action, W.D. wrote that he thought it "strange Fordyce has not tried harder to dig up the CPS out here. I suppose he has heard the plant is idle, going to be sold for taxes etc. People here they might write to only see what is here in the city in front of them. I always think more of the timber assets."

The "Miami contract" was his greatest asset in the West, and, when William, protesting that he had finally gotten out of the clutches of all the bankers and was reluctant to get back in, refused to wire the $5,000 that W.D. needed to hold on to it, he became frantic. The parties involved would be only too glad to close him out if he defaulted. "If I can't make this turn we are through here for good, no use trying again." When William finally came through, after several urgent telegrams, his mood soared. One of his "principal thoughts" was to have Brazeau draw up articles of incorporation for a new corporation that could handle matters like the "Miami," which "should run into a million dollars in dealing in timber and logs before it is closed out. We are just getting started. I do not think the business will be principally in Wisconsin—British Columbia, California, Michigan—[the articles of incorporation] should cover dealing in *all kinds of properties* including timber, manufacturing of lumber and sale of logs and lumber, also mining leases and mining shares and stocks."[22]

With things straightened out in the West, W.D. turned his attention to the fight to regain control over what was left of the R. Connor Company's assets. William acknowledged that he "knew so little about the Michigan timber" and claimed that "Richard does not seem to be interested,"[23] but W.D. knew what he had. The birch was as good or better than in Forest County, and the maple, which was there in great quantity, had gone up tremendously in value as compared to ash, birch, and basswood. For practical and emotional reasons, he wanted the R. Connor Company properties back under family control. He also wanted to bring Gordon back into the Connor Company where he belonged.

When the Wisconsin and the Michigan State Banking Departments ordered banks holding any R. Connor Bonds to charge them off, the Connors were eager to buy them up at $30 to $35 on the hundred before the R. Connor trustees or anyone else did.[24] Melvin wrote dozens of letters contacting general creditors of small accounts, offering to make settlements for return of R. Connor Company notes. But when the Reverend A. V. Ingham, pastor of the Methodist Episcopal Church in Belmont, wrote inquiring whether he should sell his bond, "Don't," came Melvin's answer. "There are some changes being made in the organization and if you can wait a few years for your money, I am sure you will realize more on the bond."[25]

Melvin was not successful in urging R. Connor Company general creditors, stockholders, and bondholders to protest W.D.'s removal from the management, but by October the Connors were close to closing a contract with the executive committee, which would enable them to cut the timber.

Chastened by the events of the past few years, and wanting no personal responsibility or liability, William was adamant about not being a party to any contract unless he signed as a member of the new corporation W.D. planned. He was, moreover, "definitely opposed to a policy of investment in real estate and other ventures *if we are going to attempt this contract*" and flatly stated his opposition to buying the old R. Connor Company building in Marshfield.

W.D. would not accept rule by his oldest son any more than he accepted rule by anyone else. When the money began coming in, he blithely disregarded William and bought the old R. Connor Company building, the old homestead in Auburndale, and the mill in Victoria.

Three years after Federal Judge Patrick Stone ended Connor management of the R. Connor Company, W.D., Melvin, Gordon, Richard, William, and their lawyer, Theodore Brazeau, appeared before him in Madison on their petition to resume control, claiming mismanagement by Peotter and Smith. Stunned when Peotter and Smith charged Melvin with handicapping their efforts, stealing vital R. Connor Company land and estimate records from the Marshfield office, and canceling the insurance held by the company at Connorville, Melvin stammered a reply, which he believed "peeved the court" and "worked great injury to the cause of the stockholders."[26] When the records he was accused of taking were found in the R. Connor Company vaults, and letters from the underwriting company proved that the insurance had been cancelled by Peotter and Smith themselves, the men were proven to be, as W.D. claimed, "absolute liars." As Melvin put it, "Their falsehoods put in the mind of the court a big question in regard to [their] veracity."[27]

Helen recognized the strain under which Melvin operated, the heavy responsibilities. She knew William resented Melvin's close relationship with their father and that he was offended that Mame had named Melvin trustee of her estate, an honor that should have been his as oldest son. With W.D. spending most of his time on the coast, William attempted to wrest control from the Marshfield office. Alerted by Melvin, W.D. wrote many letters asserting his authority. "Orders, no matter where they come from, the orders should go through this [Marshfield] office." Helen stayed out of the way but was aware of the growing tension and perceived that William's behavior troubled Melvin, who uncomplainingly fulfilled many uncongenial tasks on W.D.'s instructions.

The former minister and the lumberman were a strange pair, but they were close in age, only ten years apart, and each valued the gifts and achievements of the other. When the R. Connor trustees scheduled an auction of the property in Auburndale, W.D. returned from the coast to attend it with Melvin. It was "a farce," W.D. declared. Stuff was "given away."

> Peotter and Smith stood around and when something sold for a song, they had a good laugh. They went around [and] picked up everything there was on the place. Went into the barns, unfastened hangers and equipment that was bolted to the buildings and took the pumps out of the wells—stripped the place of everything—stuff that was part of the buildings. They went into the granary, into the slaughter house. There was a lot of brass hangers fastened to the wall, part of the building. Had men go in and take this out—must have taken five or six hours to take them down—and threw them into a bucket. The entire lot sold for a quarter. The auctioneer and finance people were part of that. Smith and Peotter had such a *big laugh* over that.[28]

The men were, W.D. raged, "deliberate crooks, degenerates in every way— mentally and morally."

Coming face to face with Harold Smith afterwards, the wiry old man socked the portly, urbane, rather pompous, middle-aged banker. He was back in Victoria when his lawyers informed him that because of their other work, they would not be able to handle Smith's charge of battery. They strongly advised him to accept an out-of-court settlement. The $500 the plaintiff was asking was unusually low because of the aggravated nature of the assault; $1,000 would have been reasonable. "About that Smith case," W.D. wrote Melvin, "you go to [attorney M. S.] King. Have him prepare an answer and let us get the answer filed in time. The usual denial of everything."

Melvin and Helen quietly settled the affair before it became another full-blown family scandal. Neither W.D.'s lawyers nor his family believed W.D.'s claim that "Smith started the row—started the bullying—rose up in his chair and swung back as if he was going to hit me." They recognized W.D's description of Smith as someone who "when he gets stirred up is an entirely different person from what he would have people believe. He becomes very angry, appears vicious, ready to devour anyone who is in his way" as a fair self-portrait of the "thoroughly tired" former president of the R. Connor Company who had just about lost everything he had worked for fifty years to build and was, against heavy odds, struggling again to "make it some way."

It seemed that he would. He'd managed to keep the best property out West, sold off rusty equipment for needed cash,[29] observed the West booming again. With the cash, he paid off taxes, fees, and other charges the government insisted on. With "the very great revival in business on the coast and specially in the Province," if they kept on, they would have all the property free of debt. "You know," he wrote Helen, "*some* folks told me more than once let us forget about Victoria. We will never get anything out of that property. They did not know. I was so sure they did not—of course it may to them have looked like a hope-less situation. I guess it was. The boys urged me. 'Let us save Laona' out of *the wreck.* 'Let Victoria go.' I must not now take any credit, do any boasting. I was responsible. I was to blame for the whole business."[30] But he also knew his worth. Helen, he was sure, would not "object" to receiving the "couple" of dollars credit he had been able to get on the books out in Victoria or "inquire too closely how these things are brought about."[31]

Everyone's spirits lifted. A "greeting" Melvin received from an old college friend, C. M. Stanley, editor of the *Alabama Journal* in Montgomery, brought him "more cheer" than anything else that had come to him in "recent days." Stanley's reference to their "Latin days" put Melvin in mind of the happier time—and of his third son, Bom, who was "having his first year of Latin in the Marshfield High School." He thought his former classmate might be inter-ested to know that he had four sons, "which are the four chief reasons why I am now working for a lumber company." The new deal had "put the lumber business on its feet again and the future for the father and four sons is brighter than it was three years ago."[32]

However, he added in a letter to his old friends in Lincoln, Illinois, the J. C. Diffenderfers, "Wisconsin, as you know, under the leadership of the La Follette family has become definitely Progressive, or Liberal, or Radical. Some partisans would like to say that the State is Communistic, but I do not think that would be quite fair. The La Follettes are working for the re-election of Roosevelt and that probably means that the State will go Democratic."

Assessing the political situation from the coast, W.D. also doubted that the Republicans could win in Wisconsin in spite of Landon's personal strengths and the support he had in Marshfield, where a lot of people were sporting his sunflower pin. W.D. heard Franklin W. Knox speak in Spokane. His history and W.D.'s had intertwined back in 1910–12 when Knox was chairman of Michigan's State Republican Committee and W.D. continued to keep abreast of political developments in Michigan. He believed the result in the Michigan primary had been a letdown for the Democrats, who had been "quarreling among themselves." They couldn't get any "Democrat of influence" to run in the Democratic primary, thinking that Norman Cousins would win the election. Brucker would make a good senator, and he hoped Fitzgerald would beat Murphy for governor. If Murphy were beaten, it would "leave the way open for Brewster and especially Vandenberg to have clear control of the state—and put the Senator in better position as a Presidential candidate four years from now if Landon fails to win this year."

W.D. did not like to think of Roosevelt being reelected; yet, he did not look forward to changes in business conditions, which were making "such improvement." Western prosperity was something marvelous to see. "The government has already spent twenty million on Grand Coolie."

Hugh Goggins's victory for the county judge seat in the Republican primary had been good news, but if Helen "and all the others who can be enlisted do not get busy and help Hugh—*he can't be elected.*" Fred A. Rhyner was running against him, and "we don't want those Rhyners to get in any more position of influence—anywhere."[33]

In November, tired and sick, an exhausted W.D. came home. Reassured that the charges would be reasonable if he had to have the prostate surgery Melvin had undergone in January, he allowed Helen and Melvin to drive him to Rochester. Helen lingered until his recovery seemed assured, then, with Constance on her way to look after him, returned to Marshfield. Recuperating at the Kahler Hotel, he wrote his "Dear, Dear Daughter": "You have been so good to me and thoughtful, but that has always been true." He didn't want Helen to "worry a minute." He would get along all right, but "the last three or four days that unfortunate sick headache came back. I just could not shake it, any more than their pills seemed to cure it." Anyway, he felt like eating a little. He would get along all right. How long he would stay would depend on some things. "What they try to do for my headaches. Whether they think, what they think they come from, my nerves, my eyes, from getting tired, and continual changes, and weather changes. To put everything in the show, seems as if that trouble in my hands got down in my right heel and ankle. For couple of days I could not get my foot on the floor. By having several ailments at the same time each sorta offsets the other. I do not think so continuously of any one."

Having encouraged her "not to worry a minute," W.D. gave Helen plenty to worry about. But he had always leaned on her. During his frequent, lengthy absences, he repeatedly pleaded with her to tell Marian's children "about their Grand Pa. Teach them some little songs. Tell them the right things to think about and do." "See that they learn the beauty in things," learn "to love the old Home and their Grand Pa." He admitted he might be selfish, but he did "not want to be deprived of their company and association." He would not let them go to any of the Rhyner family, would not let Constance take them as she offered. He hadn't wanted William to go to kindergarten, but Helen was adamant. He needed to be with other children. "You are so like your mother who had a mind of her own and at times could make clear what she meant."

W.D. was not the idol he had been, but she loved him, and he loved, admired, and depended on her. When he felt "so lonesome and a little tired of it all," and "the effort, the struggle to keep the pace that seems to be required" seemed almost too much, the calm and courage with which she "faced so many trying circumstances" sometimes made him feel ashamed. He said he understood the burdens that rested on her shoulders as she took "the humiliation, experienced the worry and grief being there right in it every day,"[34] but he did not consider that caring for her sister's children might be a burden.

Helen had made her peace with her father's complicated character long ago, and intermittently at least, with herself, if one can judge from the essay she wrote and delivered to her friends at the club. Birch Lake was the source of inspiration, a subject in her mature years, as it had been in her youth, of poems and talks.[35] In "Fruits of the Spirit," she wrote her "thoughts that pass through."

A friend of mine told me she was going to talk about the fruits of the spirit. It set me thinking. What are the fruits of the spirit? Big order. Is it a progressive thing—begin on one and lead to another. I immediately began to look for encouragement. Who doesn't need it these days. If I begin practicing one virtue will the others come? Patience. Through practicing that will I come to know the mind of God. Thought of great music, symphony of Beethoven's. Can I say that because I recognize certain great themes of Beethoven's, I know Beethoven.

Certainly not in his completion or fullness and yet I'm beginning to know Beethoven. I can love his work because of the little I do know. Is it all through personal effort this attaining the fruits of the spirit. Some of us may work too hard at it, and hope with Goethe's Faust to attain by continually searching, striving, "immer striebend." Something else enters in, a mysterious quality and I pass on this illustration for what it is worth in finding encouragement. The idea of reflection.

I looked out upon the lake this summer as it reflected the myriad of stars— a beautiful but apparently effortless thing, but I walked on down the path and here is the point I want to make—the encouragement—a puddle also reflected a star—not great numbers of stars, not with such brilliance, but it reflected a star. May it not be true of us, each of us reflects at times something of the fruits of the spirit.

Living had proved a humbling experience, but Helen persisted in her quest for transcendence and settled here for a share of reflected glory in a small and impure place.

❧

# CHAPTER 15

# The Divided House

## *1937–1939*

Why, America's the only free nation on earth. Besides! Country's too big for a revolution. No, no! Couldn't happen here.

—SINCLAIR LEWIS

Two stories dominated the *Herald*'s headlines on January 8: the dismissal of University of Wisconsin president Glenn Frank by La Follette's enlarged board of regents, which was dominated by Progressives, and the Wood County Income Tax Board of Review hearing into the "alleged non-payment of $25,000 in state income taxes by W.D. Connor between the years 1920–1935." The fired university president and bankrupt businessman were front-page news again on the January 9. Frank was quoted as saying he believed that "an alert press can recognize a political firing squad when it sees one," and Paul Burrill, the income tax assessor, assailed "the indefiniteness of testimony showing how Connor came into possession of notes and stock of the Canadian Puget Sound Company" and his transfer of stock in September 1933 to his "now deceased wife."

On January 10, Helen and Melvin left town with David and Bom in the family Packard to begin a long automobile trip through Illinois, Missouri, Arkansas, Texas, New Mexico, Oklahoma, Colorado, Kansas, Nebraska, and Iowa on the combined business-holiday W.D. authorized. Because it was Sunday, Melvin extemporized a short sermon from the Bible verse Helen chose, while Florence (along for the ride as far as St. Louis, where her daughter Katty Mullen lived), led the hymn singing.

They drove away from the snow and the numbing temperatures, their concerns about the firing of the university president, the dueling lawyers, and the negative publicity. They stopped in Madison for a brief visit with Dick, telephoned Connor from Rockford, spent a half-hour with the Diffenderfers in Lincoln, and arrived in St. Louis at 10:00 P.M. after what Helen described as a "bum trip in over bum McKinley Bridge." Everything looked green and fresh in Arkansas but God-forsaken in Texas, until they neared Dallas and the "rich sunset" made everything "pretty." The palm trees and cacti between Midland and El Paso interested David; the oil wells interested them all. The boys counted white horses in the fields and Burma Shave signs along the roads. Helen and Melvin danced a bit in the evening. After nine days, driving some-times through heavy wind and sand-storms, they arrived in Albuquerque, land of "the grandest sunshine one can imagine."

Melvin contacted the company's major customers en route, assuring them of the Connors' return to solvency, and returned with payments and healthy commitments for orders. Helen returned so refreshed, she wrote William, that she had "pep enough to do my own housework."

Family tensions put an end to her sense of well-being. Unperturbed by the tax assessor's charges, W.D., jubilant with the upturn in business, had gone ahead with plans for the new corporation. On January 13, 1937, the Connor Brothers partnership, the last of W.D.'s great schemes to hold and increase the family assets, was chartered. (Belying the corporation's name, Constance and Helen held the same 200 shares as their brothers, when Melvin's and Ritchie Mondrall's single qualifying shares were added to theirs. The brothers and brothers-in-law were the directors.)

Believing the Connor Brothers to be the vehicle by which W.D. was going to negotiate a cutting contract with the R. Connor Brothers, William left for the West Coast to solicit new business and renew contacts with customers. He sent enthusiastic reports about the boom in construction in San Diego, where "two growing aviation plants, and the base for the fleet which Roosevelt [was] operating at increasing efficiency [were] bringing a payroll of some $10,000,000 annually." His optimism and good spirits collapsed on his return, however, when he learned that, unilaterally, W.D. had taken the contract with the R. Connor Company in the name of the Connor Lumber and Land Company after Judge Patrick Stone rejected the Connor Brothers' application, declaring the new corporation's assets insufficient.

Industry watchers considered that with the purchase of 15,000 acres of R. Connor Company timberland in Gogebic and Ontonogan Counties in the upper peninsula,[1] the Connors had "effected probably the outstanding recent development in northern lumbering." The company may have "placed itself in a truly dominant position both as to current production and facilities and sustained, efficient life,"[2] but board meetings degenerated into the kind of bickering sessions only members of a family engaged in impossible competi-tive love-hate relationships can know, and the stage was set for future quarrels of bitter and finally destructive intensity.

In a series of long letters, while ostensibly attempting to convince the other of his rectitude and of the "reasonableness" of his position, William and W.D. leveled complaints revealing more emotional ego involvement than rational control. On his own initiative, without consultation, William accused W.D. of escalating the $40,000 he had been willing to chance in Michigan in November 1936 to $200,000 from Laona in 1937. In November, W.D. "wouldn't have put $8,500,000 [a Freudian slip; he meant $8,500] into a Manager's house [Gordon's], and they couldn't afford to now." He was "not going to work [his] head off 15 hours a day to build unnecessary houses in Michigan."[3] William believed the Michigan operation was for liquidation purposes only. W.D. believed Michigan would go on long after Laona blew the whistle. William's criticisms of his father were met by W.D.'s criticisms of William's management of Laona.[4]

William drew Helen into the quarrel, charging her with entering into a conspiracy against him. His accusation wasn't "even a joke," Helen wrote William, "You know I opposed that venture all along and said all I could against it. The only possible excuse was that unfortunately the two companies were tied up together in a way, but even at that I was thankful the Connor Lumber and Land was getting on so well and was not for *over* burdening it." She knew "something of the difficulties before in Michigan," and thought that now that the Connor Lumber and Land has taken it on, it should be under the full board of directors and expenses kept down. I tell father he is certainly tempting fate, after the good recovery he made, to jam back and forth up there as he does and stay out at that camp. He seemed miserable until he got another chance at it however, and now the deed is done, there's not much use bemoaning."[5]

Before returning to the coast, where W.D. saw his "only chance of income in any quantity," and forgetting Helen's low tolerance for emotional stress, W.D. charged William with being "a smart boy" who said things that were "entirely false," uttered things for "a malign purpose," "rudely assailed" him in an "insulting way," and had so many times lately taken the attitude that he would drive him out of the Connor Lumber and Land Company. He might have given his stock away, but W.D. was president of the Connor Lumber and Land Company, one of the three voting trustees (Melvin and George Birkelund were the others). William was "a subordinate, an employee. Every dollar, every piece of property he ever had in all his life he received from his father!"

However turbulent the Connor business, however frustrated and verbally abusive family members became, Melvin and Helen maintained an ordered house and continued to exemplify high standards. While lines of a poem Dick and David co-authored when the new high school was built—"It's not much to look at / It's square as a box / But how else could the school board / Line their socks?"—suggests their grandfather's influence, their parents exerted a contrary force. Feeling "very keenly" that the program adopted by the board of the Marshfield Country Club in allowing alcoholic beverages to be served did not make "for temperance and sobriety in our community,"[6] Melvin resigned from the board. He did not want his boys to witness alcohol-induced fellowship but was glad to have them observe the fellowship he enjoyed with books and good friends.

Melvin spoke of his admiration for American humanist Paul Elmer More, teacher, translator of Greek and Sanskrit, poet, and author of hundreds of essays tracing the history of ideas in literature and philosophy who had come near to being the first American to earn the Nobel Prize for literature in 1930, when the prize went to Sinclair Lewis.[7] More expressed beliefs Melvin held: the soul's assurance of truths was an intuition of veritable realities, and the test of the quality of a man's mind lay in the degree in which he felt the long-remembered past as one of the vital laws of his being. In the family business, Melvin ran up against daily insults to his idealism, but he held on, and by his words and example transmitted his positive view of the human enterprise as powerfully as W.D. transmitted his darker ones.

The Lairds formed an informal reading club among their friends, drawing newcomers Stephan Epstein, a renowned Polish-Jewish dermatologist, and his wife, Elsbeth, who had witnessed relatives being taken off to the death camps and had fled Nuremberg, into their little society. Helen read *Faust* in German with Elsbeth, a Quaker whose beliefs reinforced Helen's strong pacifist inclination.

When Harry Emerson Fosdick, chairman of the Emergency Peace Campaign, joined by Admiral Byrd and Eleanor Roosevelt, delivered a radio address on the twentieth anniversary of the United States's entry into World War I,[8] urging the organization of peace pressure groups in the smaller towns and villages, Helen helped organize the Emergency Peace Campaign in Wood County. Like the organization's national leaders, she advocated social progress at home and equality for Negroes and feared that another world war would be "a battle of big business in a sense more baldly unrelieved by redeeming motives than any other great war."[9] Together, Melvin and Helen grappled with the issue America's leading Protestant theologians grappled with: the essential conflict between Christianity and the ethics of capitalistic individualism—the divided house in which they lived.

W.D had spoken of labor problems in the McCormick, Weyerhaeuser and

Long-Bell Longview Companies on the West Coast in 1935 and 1936. In 1937, he acknowledged the unrest spreading over northern Wisconsin, Michigan, and Minnesota, but he did not anticipate trouble in the Connor camps or mills. The men had never gone out when there was a Connor around. Besides, they kept the men so busy they didn't have time to talk.[10] A strike in the Michigan camps and mill just as Gordon started them up again came as a surprise. No entrenched "spy system" forewarned the family, which now had a good deal more to worry about than its internal quarrels.

On June 2, Melvin and William were at the Palmer House in Chicago meeting with other midwestern mill operators, who formed a Gogebic County Wood Operators Association and agreed to unite and stand together in regard to wages, hours, and any other demands the union leaders made. By aggressive and collective resistance, they believed they could gradually dissipate the strikers' ranks and get the men back in the woods.[11] They were wrong. Three days later, Melvin wired W.D.: "Certain groups intimidating workers. Cannot load out orders without protection." If Michigan could not load out orders, the Connor Lumber and Land Company would not be able to meet its debt obligations. The family was once again thrown into a financially threatening situation.

Because she had "always been considered a self-sufficient person," Helen felt "impelled to confess" that she belonged "to the strap-hanger's league." As time went by, she needed "to hang on tighter and tighter" and did so by counting her blessings. She was grateful for God's care through the night; for her father, "with all the memories and connections with my old home he conjures up"; for her husband's "loving help"; for her "four boys, big and little, and for all the activities and interests with which they keep me in touch." She was "thankful for [her] home with its dear familiar belongings, and the life of the family which centers about it. In this mood of gratitude I start my day and I find one is much less likely to grow impatient later with persons for whom he has taken time to be thankful in the morning. It encourages an attitude of praise instead of criticism and encourages the art of appreciation." She was also grateful for Harry Emerson Fosdick, "whose writings and radio utterances" helped her "many times through cellar moods and heavenly"; for the "skilled physician and guide" who knew her in all her weakness and strength as no one else did, who inspired "pluck, valor, patience, faith and hope in others"; for the church and the old hymns. Helen wrote "The Strap-Hanger" in room 211 of Saint Joseph's Hospital, Omaha, in the psychiatric wing Dishong had established.[12]

She had sought Dishong's help during other periods of stress in the thirties, but only by long distance for reassurance, information, and medication. In January 1933, he felt she was "making improvement and better able to analyze and handle the situation in general." She had wanted to know about "unconscious conflicts," and Dishong explained, "of course, you realize that we all have them, but some have been more fortunate in their early training and the conditioning influences which enable them later in adult life to face the various life's situations with better poise and acceptance. I think you understand this fairly well, and I am inclined to think you will more and more come into complete control." That "the son" felt she was "hard boiled," Dishong was inclined to think an encouraging reaction. "Of course you will watch yourself to see that this particular reaction does not become over-emphasized, but here again I think your judgment will suffice." He asked Helen to supply "frequent brief reports" as she found time. Like Helen, he was listening to Dr. Fosdick's sermons, had "heard practically all of them. I enjoy him immensely, and it seems to me I can get more out of his sermons than any of the others being broadcast."[13]

Those outside the family circle believed Helen was visiting in Omaha. Dick and Connor understood their mother had gone to Omaha to recuperate and hoped she had a happy time. "She certainly deserves it." Aunt Florence took charge of nine-year-old David, while Melvin took Bom to Chicago where Connor and his roommate, John Stevens, a former fraternity brother and son of the vice president of Marathon Paper, kept him occupied, and he proved "a little soldier."

W.D., writing Melvin from Victoria, hoped Helen would not leave Omaha too soon and gave his opinion that "a few days won't help her case so much." Writing Helen, he began by keeping his letter light, describing the heavy rain and the antics of his grandchildren, seven-year-old William and four-year-old Elizabeth, whom he had taken West with him. But he ended on the usual self-pitying note. He regretted that he would not be able to attend Dick's graduation. "It seems I never can do what I want to do or should be doing. . . . I hear so little of what is going on at home. . . . . I guess I am not needed for the management of the business." He wished she could be with him. "I miss you so very much. You have always been so good, so thoughtful of me."[14]

After a month's hospitalization and daily visits by her faithful physician and medication (which "makes me feel so limp and pepless, I'd just as soon stay in bed all day and just about do"), Helen regained her equilibrium and began to be curious and interested in her home life again.

Dishong wrote Melvin. "Mrs. Laird has made a nice improvement." It was now "quite safe for her to leave the hospital." She had been looking forward to Dick's graduation and to meeting Melvin in Madison. He knew Melvin was "cooperating fully" and "willing to make most any sacrifice for Mrs. Laird who also realizes that you are trying to do everything in your power to make her comfortable." In confidence, he wanted Melvin to understand that his wife was "working against a lot of unconscious emotional fixations that amount to a considerable overload and have a tendency to throw her off balance, when she is tired or under prolonged stress. Naturally one would think that she should rest more at home," but this was not the solution. "We encourage such patients to find wholesome outlets for their interests, and then prevent emotionalism by attempting to understand their conflicts."

While Dishong found it "extremely difficult" to express himself in a letter, he could say that it would seem "advisable for Mrs. Laird to get away from the home situation for a week or ten days once or twice a year; and by this I mean she would really be alone. If you are with her in a hotel, for instance, allow her to have a separate room. Mrs. Laird is intelligent and is trying to work out more harmonious adjustments to her various situations, but she is forcing herself. If you can encourage frank discussion occasionally, allowing her to unburden her resistances, this might prove beneficial. But be very careful that you do not become annoyed when you realize that you have innocently given offense by an incident that appears trifling. I should be very glad to hear from you occasionally and advise with you by letter."[15]

"The props of humans," Helen wrote, were "hope, laughter, and sleep." She took a pill in the morning, a "capsule for sleep" at night, kept up a full schedule, and balanced her intellectual interests with a great deal of travel and sociability. She avoided, as best she could, hearing anything about the business. Constance noted on her visit to Birch Lake how "Father was eager to discuss" their problems, that Gordon joined in, and that "Father would have said something to Helen when she came in, but she sensed it, and left." "Father," Constance thought, was planning on returning soon to Victoria and "wants to spend most of his time out there . . . so as not to come in contact with William and the Laona business." She wished Gordon had stayed where he was with the Roddis Company and that William would calm down. "I hate to see a break in the family." She could see where Melvin and "Helen have a lot on your mind and I wish you were both out of it like we are."[16]

While her father and brothers prepared to do battle with the union organizers, Helen dedicated her efforts to world peace. She studied the program of the state convention of the Cause and Cure of War meeting, which she had missed.[17] The national leaders were honored: Zona Gale, an honorary member; Jane Addams, who had died two years before leaving "not only a heritage but a challenge"; and seventy-eight-year-old Carrie Chapman Catt, the organization's founder and honorary chairman of the convention. Carrie Catt provided the Cause and Cure of War's statement of principle: "Whatever may be the rumors of war, or the number of actual wars in operation, or however savage and barbaric individual nations appear to be, perpetual peace will come. No power can prevent it. The date of its coming, perhaps even the generation which first sees it, are not known, but come it will. The date will be earlier in exact ratio to the intelligence and the persistence of the work done by all those who have faith in its coming."[18] Helen assured Margaret Schorger of her eagerness to be involved in the conference's work.

Meanwhile, the Connors' troubles with labor intensified. Workers, emboldened by the Supreme Court's decision upholding the constitutionality of the Wagner Act (and the passage of the "Little Wagner Act" in Wisconsin), were determined to secure more of profit from their labor. In Kansas City, "they were over turning the lumber trucks and it was almost impossible to make deliveries."[19] In Michigan, the Connorville mill was operating with a company union hurriedly set up by Gordon, but the Industrial Workers of the World (IWW) were keeping the men out of the woods. Without a steady supply of logs, the mill would inevitably have to shut down, and the workers in that vagabond industry would drift away.

Faced with defaulting on debt obligations, and ignoring legislation prohibiting management interference with union organization, William sent Kenneth Allen to Michigan to help Gordon. Allen, he believed, had the "courage and aggressiveness," the vigilante eagerness, to maintain order. In other words, he was a thug. William instructed Gordon to authorize him "to maintain some police force in the camp and give the men protection." He also offered to "pick up some men" in Wisconsin and send them into the camps at night.

On June 30, 1937, Henry Paull and Luke Raik, Congress of International Workers (CIO) and American Federation of Labor (AFL) lawyers hired to represent the striking workers at a hearing to be held in Ironwood, Michigan, while gathering facts to present to the National Labor Relations Board, were "set upon, assaulted, beaten and threatened with torture and death by Kenneth Allen. . . . While suffering from wounds and injuries to the head, face, nose and other parts of the body, and while in a weakened condition from loss of blood and the beating administered to [them] by Kenneth Allen, and other members of a lawless mob," they were dragged down the public streets of the city of Ironwood, their bodies "prostrate and bleeding on the pavement." They were kidnapped, thrown into an automobile, and driven "for a long distance and for a long period of time out into the country, over parts of the states of Michigan and Wisconsin." They were dumped in the village of Saxon, Wisconsin, and warned that they would be killed if they ever returned to Michigan.[20]

Violence bred violence. Floating bands of workers directed by union organizers confronted the bands of vigilantes the operators sent in. A special five-man committee appointed by Michigan's governor to investigate the situation in the Upper Peninsula was of no help to Gordon. The investigation threatened to drag on for months. Meanwhile, although the Michigan police offered some protection, it was almost impossible to get lumberjacks back into the woods. "A crowd of hoodlums in Ironwood and other places in that section," Melvin wrote W.D., unaware of the Connors' own vigilante action, were "continuing their method of intimidation." All the best men had left that part of the country. "Only the worst element remains who are under the influence of the agitators and they are the ones that are trying to get in a position to represent all of the lumberjacks in that section." It was "a rather discouraging situation." Melvin would inform the court of the difficulties in Michigan and ask "some indulgence in the matter of payments."[21] He would also express his disappointment that the original stockholders did not yet have representation on the R. Connor Company board.

As predicted, the unions' competitive campaigns to organize workers spilled over into Wisconsin, where William, having put into effect a company union, credited himself with having things well in hand. AFL men bearing cards identifying themselves as members of the United Brotherhood of Carpenters and Joiners, International Timber Workers Local 2776, arrived at Menominee Bay Shore Lumber camps near Long Lake in Forest County on July 13. The organizers were polite.[22] They preferred "no strike" but could not guarantee that the CIO or the IWW organizers would not interfere in the event the men joined and the company signed an agreement. Roddis had signed up, but they expected "hard-boiled treatment at the Connor camps next door."[23]

The turbulent labor situation did not prevent W.D. from plotting. William attempted to block him from selling some property in Sawyer County by refusing to sign the necessary release unless W.D. agreed to use the funds to pay off the mortgage and interest obligations in Laona. W.D.'s threat to take action in the County Court to put the title back into Mame's estate did not have the desired effect, but when he revealed that he wanted the cash to buy back the Connor Lumber and Land Company stock Rob's widow held, stock whose value would become "more apparent to anyone that is at all interested as the months go by," and that if the deal went by the board, "that opportunity is going to be lost to get that stock back," William capitulated. W.D. got the funds he needed, played the gallant with Rob's widow, got her stock, and wiped her and her children out of memory.

The family tightened its control. From the business point of view, it seemed to be doing well. The board of review upheld the appraiser's finding that the Connor Lumber and Land Company stock held no value at the time of Mame's death. The labor situation, however, continued to deteriorate. In October, the International Woodworkers of America, Local 72, charged the Connor Lumber and Land Company with violation of the National Labor Relations Act by denying them the right to visit and talk to lumberjacks employed in their camps. After receiving the regional director of the National Labor Relation's Board warning—"Employees have the right to organize without interference"—William contacted company lawyers, Goggins, Brazeau and Graves, who asked for the chain of events leading to the warning. William explained that by setting up a local company union, "headed by a man by the name of Henry F. Pueschner, who is not in the employ of the company," posting their property, and establishing watchmen to keep radical organizers out, they thought they had secured themselves. The company union's application for a charter was not acted on, however, because state senator Glen Roberts, whom they had hired to look after their affairs in Madison, said the by-laws were not properly drawn "to get by the State Labor Board." The CIO then became more active. William attended the organizers' public meeting at the Silver Lake Pavilion, and when he heard some of their "absolute falsehoods," he rose to challenge them. William believed that was when the CIO people alerted the national board.

CIO organizers may, as William charged, have spoken some "absolute falsehoods." William certainly delivered one. This Henry F. Pueschner, suddenly actively involved in organizing a union "independent of management control," is the same Henry Pueschner who chauffeured the wives of Connor employees to the voting booth and told them how to vote; the same Henry Pueschner who was a repeated and successful candidate for the Laona Town Board; the same Henry Pueschner who was treasurer of the Laona Bank; the same Henry Pueschner who was identified back in 1932 by Herman Kronschnabl as the Connors' "sweetheart and protector." He may not have been on any company payroll, but Henry Pueschner was, in fact, a "tool of the Connor Company."

Helen pursued her own course. On scraps of paper, she copied down thoughts she came across in her prodigious reading, as though the very act of writing connected her with something solid she could hold on to. "Faith is the conscious co-operation with an unseen force." "If you love everything you will perceive the divine mystery in things. Once you perceive it, you will begin to comprehend it better every day. (The monk in Dostoevsky)." "Let me tell you this. I'd rather be a blasted neurotic woman and be spiritually alive than a blasted successful man—and spiritually dead. (*The Citadel,* p. 317)."

Her 1938 diary included a more flatly realistic statement: "Marriage is all right if you don't think too much about it." She had been married twenty-four years. Two of her sons were grown and out of the nest. Connor had moved up the ladder to a "darn good spot" at Continental Can as assistant to the art director for the central district, where the engraving was done, but he was not entirely satisfied either with his $135- a-month salary, or with prospects of a life in the canning business. Dick was out in Victoria with his grandfather learning the lumber business. David and his friends kept busy after school shooting BB-guns in the basement of the old Pulling house and smoking corn pipes filled with string. Bom and his friends gathered in W.D.'s enormous barn-garage to talk and work on the school yearbook and their orations.

From time to time, Melvin received welcome reminders of his former life. A former parishioner wrote asking if he would return to Prairie du Sac to deliver the last rites for Mrs. Cooper's son when the time came. Melvin said he would. He liked Mrs. Cooper's philosophy of life. It enabled her "in spite of every trial to face the future with courage and comfort." She held "to that sublime faith that back of all things and underneath all is the great love of God."

Melvin kept his faith against a barrage of negative publicity regarding the Connor company. On November 6, the *Sheboygan Press* reprinted as an editorial an article that was originally published on May 16, 1933. Charging that "the people [in Laona] are practically owned body and soul by the company," the article painted a gloomy picture of the workingman's life in the mill town. Improperly fed, sapped by long hours of work, "living in the most squalid conditions, . . . forced into health institutions, . . . dying early deaths," it was "no wonder these people lose interest in the United States."

The author could have added some current material to support his case. Ehtelyn Grey Fehl, who took charge of the Connor Lumber and Land Company boardinghouse in Laona in 1937, complained of the twenty or more doves, the dirt, the piles of straw, paper bags, and moldy corn in the attic. With the rain seeping in and the sun beating down, the result was not conducive to good health. Nor was the plumbing: "Living with and sharing your bathroom with thirty other people whose standards of living do not extend even to flushing the toilets has become unbearable." The situation in the basement was "terrible"; it was used by "everyone including the public who come in from the street. Some of the boys are using a pile of sand instead of the toilets. Even during the winter the odor permeates even the lobby and now [in

July] it becomes unbearable." As for the first floor, "the lobby is being used as a playground not only by the children in the building but by the children of the neighborhood. The noise is deafening and it is impossible to keep it clean."[24]

Not only was the boardinghouse filthy and the 150 company houses without running water, but in 1937 William still maintained the practice of controlling theft by holding court with Tom Rasmussen, company accountant.

> QUESTION: Now, Mrs. Bankert, you stated that you took from the Connor Company Department Store, one pair of Chippewa shoes and gave them to your Father. When did you do this?
>
> ANSWER: That was about in June, 1937.
>
> QUESTION: You did not make any purchase of these shoes then?
>
> ANSWER: No Sir.
>
> QUESTION: You mean you went into the store, picked them up and walked out with them without making the purchase?

The interrogation continued, with Mrs. Bankert finally admitting to having taken merchandise over two years without "any assistance from clerks or agents."

> QUESTION. This merchandise which you brought back to us today and which we are asking you to take away after paying us for it, plus the various articles which you admit having stolen which you did not bring back and all the articles which you stole and cannot remember in detail, will be sold to you for $150.00 is that satisfactory?
>
> ANSWER: Yes and furthermore, I am willing to sign a confession as follows.
>
> I, Lois Stenerson Bankert of Laona, Wisconsin, do hereby freely and voluntarily confess that I have stolen various articles of merchandise from a department store of the Connor Lumber and Land Company. I have made a list of many of these articles and turned it over to the Connor Company and also returned many of the articles and offered them to the Company. I feel the total of the merchandise which I have stolen in the last two years to be at least $150.00.

Lois Bankert made the confession of her "own free will and accord, not having been promised immunity or threatened by any person or persons." She promised "never to do this again" and fully understood that "if ever found so doing," the confession would be used against her.[25]

Neither Melvin nor Helen was aware of Ehtelyn Grey Fehl's portrait of the boardinghouse or of William's prosecution of Mrs. Bankert. Lacking knowledge of the company's closely held secrets, they believed the Sheboygan editorial unfair. Melvin wrote to the ten or twelve companies in Sheboygan with which the company did business, countering the "slanderous editorial." Claiming such benefits and satisfactions for the townspeople as school buildings with "splendid equipment"; a place of amusement "well managed by a workers' committee with opportunity each evening for wholesome pleasure and recreation, with games, movies and dances"; places of worship "in which a happy, reverent company of believers gather for services each Sunday"; a small hospital "adequate for the community where two of the best trained doctors . . . are always at the service of the employees and their families at the lowest possible cost," a medical service that "has no equal in the United States," Melvin made it more paradise than hell.

The CIO organizers, however, did not believe Laona was any paradise. They ignored no trespassing signs and locked gates. Driven off company grounds by George Britten, the plant foreman, William, and Richard, they immediately lodged another complaint, this time with the state's labor board, charging the company with "discrimination against organizers, unfair labor practices, unsanitary conditions at Connor camps and poor living conditions at Laona."[26] W.D. believed the union was "making a special effort in Laona." If they could force Laona to come to their terms, "all the other mills in that country will fall in line."[27]

On November 22, under Wisconsin Board of Labor supervision, Laona mill workers filed into the Laona high school gym to cast secret ballots. When the IWW, Local No. 125 affiliated with the CIO, lost, Darlie Patton, president of Local No. 125 IWA, Edwin G. Adams, vice president, and Edward J. Lambert, secretary, placed a protest with the Wisconsin Labor Relations Board, charging that the election was "unfair because there was coercion, intimidation, and other unfair methods, such as issuing leaflets on which foremen of the plant instructed in their own handwriting men to vote etc." and that "the local setup is company controlled."

Woodsworkers of America Federation of Labor (WAFL) infiltrators into CIO organizations provided William with the information that known Communists intent on overthrowing the government—among them Oscar Risberg, Ed Derwin, Walter LaFage and an Olson[28]—were involved in the CIO efforts to organize in Laona. Determined "at all costs" to keep the "very radical" organization out, William praised the "friendly attitude" of the AFL. Their "speakers" were "very conservative and warned the men against striking," asking them "to cooperate with the management in trying to secure greater efficiency, better

results, in order to get better wages when the time came." The versatile Henry
F. Pueschner, having given up his role as organizer of the "independent Company Union," was now district organizer for the AFL.

Dishong, who maintained his correspondence with Helen, thought she was
"naturally energetic and capable," and might take on more responsibilities
than she should. "But don't hesitate to say no at times, and be rather selfish
generally. You must look out for yourself first, but at the same time it is hard
for a mother to be selfish." He thought Melvin understood "the situation
fairly well" and advised her to talk over her conflicts rather frequently with
him and allow him to help her make decisions. "Please do not become discouraged. Keep trying and you are bound to win, but strive constantly to prevent over-reaction emotionally."[29] It was hard to keep from overreaction in
the disorderly world around—when Russia, a Communist totalitarian state,
and Germany, Italy and Portugal, fascist totalitarian states, threatened democratic systems everywhere, and anarchists, communists, and fascists were shooting it out in Spain and when President Roosevelt warned that if Americans
did not "end the misuse of the powers of capital," the capitalist system would
destroy itself in America. Labor wars threatened her family's future, she knew.
Yet, intellectually, she was strong and eager to pursue the political arguments
swirling about in the charged time.

While active in the Federation of Woman's Clubs' fight to outlaw war, and
the DAR's sponsorship of Americanism Committees, she also attended political scientist Howard McMurray's lectures at the Purdy with Melvin and other
concerned conservatives, anarchists, communists, and socialists, eager to hear
from all sides.

During the heated discussions following the lectures, Emil Leuchterhandt,
a German farmer and militant socialist from Medford, speaking with verve
and often so belligerently he had to be gaveled down, advocated an end to the
present system and a redistribution of wealth. Others, including Melvin, spoke
of the danger of government interference and the curtailing of individual freedoms and for the need for evolution rather than revolution. *Mobilize* was rapidly becoming the most heavily used verb in the language, but after driving
to Wausau "with Fanny Purdy and others," Helen chose another popular
word: "Personally, I find an *isolation* policy has its advantages" to indicate that
the women's prattle held no interest.

The state labor board confirmed CIO charges of election irregularities in
Laona and called for another election in February. Many workers were bitter,

convinced the election had been one of fear, with superintendents and fore-men threatening that if workers did not sign with the AFL, they would not have jobs. When William closed the mill for repairs and transferred some AFL workers to other jobs and, in violation of preelection agreements, laid off workers who had signed with the CIO, the CIO retaliated. "CIO picketed this morning, but sheriff opened the road and every department operating full force," William wired his father on March 28. W.D. anticipated violence. "If those radical fellows . . . become disappointed with their efforts, they may go to extremes." He warned Richard and William to "be careful not to be drawn into any controversy with any of those fellows," not to go around alone "where there would be any chance for two or three of those radicals to do [them] any harm." He would return from Victoria at once if he could be of any help.

William enlisted the help of the sheriff, the undersheriff, the police chief, their deputies, and the brazen Kenneth Allen. Men attempting to cross the picket lines faced fists, stones, lead pipes, clubs, and knives. Richard and William posted armed guards in front of their houses on "Silk Stocking Street" and warned their children not to walk out alone. No one knew for sure how far the ordinarily submissive people on "Flea Street," or the lumber-jacks from Northern Wisconsin, Michigan, and Minnesota who "closed in on the town to 'see what it was all about,'"[30] might go. On March 30, Henry Pueschner, in his capacity as town chairman, wired the Honorable Philip La Follette: "Urge you take action to pursue Law and Order here. Expect serious mob violence any time. Suggest you send militia at once."

On March 31, the violence in Laona escalated. Workers were knocked un-conscious, thrown into the Rat River, hospitalized. Sixteen new arrests made that morning brought the number to thirty-six in four days. While the situa-tion was serious, the breakdown of order also brought about a carnival atmos-phere. A crowd of six to seven hundred men, women, and children, unleashed from the usual hum-drum work-a-day world following outnumbered CIO pickets to their headquarters in Lower Town began a spontaneous "march of victory" through the streets of Laona yelling, "'Yea, boo!' in typical football fashion," honking horns, and shouting "Back to Russia, back to Kentucky with the Kaintucks."[31]

The CIO workers fought on, knowing they had the support of regional and national leaders, including the president of the International Woodwork-ers of America, Harold J. Pritchett, whose wire to B. J. Husting, assistant U.S. district attorney for the Eastern District, vigorously protesting the clubbing and arrest of their "legitimate pickets" in Laona, was turned over to the FBI for investigation. CIO organizer Harry Mayville, identified by an AFL "spy" as "Comrade Harry Mayville of Local No. 1313, International Association of Machinists, member of the Communist Party,"[32] wanted in Minnesota for violating parole, exhorted the disgruntled laborers to "break the chains of slavery." He joined the increasing number of men (including members of established Laona families: Donald Aschenbrenner, Steve Novak, and Fred Lemerand) filling the jails in Crandon, Rhinelander and Antigo.

Had W.D., who enjoyed history, been there to hear Mayville and in a reflective mood, he might have appreciated the irony in his having raised his family to membership in the "exploiting classes." He had, however, early in life viewed the opportunities afforded in the new world and decided he had what it took to join them.

On April 15, *Midwest Labor*, a Duluth, Minnesota, publication of the CIO (Oscar Risberg, one of the original "outside" CIO organizers in Laona was on the editorial board), proclaimed in two-inch headlines "TERROR LIFTS IN LAONA." Governor La Follette, the United States district attorney, and the state and national labor relations boards restored order. Spirit among the strikers was running high, and the picket line was lively. *Midwest Labor* made the strike its lead issue, featuring workers' stories illustrating the hard-heartedness of the Connors. One old man who worked in the "Fire Hole" for twelve years, seven days a week, eleven hours a day and never got a half-mile from the plant, was told by the "super" one day to "lay off a while" because "he might get sick workin' so steady." He never got back to work there again. That worker would have been a rich man if he had all the money he should have gotten for the extra, unpaid hours he worked. Sometimes down in the fire hole he'd "sort of think . . . if I quit this fire hole right here and now the whole works'll blow up," and sometimes he'd think he'd "like to let it go and blow off if the right ones was inside."

The most moving story of all (told by union organizers) told of a raw, wintry night in April 1935 when a truck stopped at the hospital of the little lumber town where the Connor family owned everything including the hospital, bank, stores, hotel, light plant, "the long black miles of virgin timber," and the 1,500 "wage slaves" who referred to themselves as "subjects of the Kingdom of Connor." Because "King" Connor left orders that the Laona hospital would take no more relief cases, when Joe, the driver, ran in begging for help because "Mrs. Kalata out there in the truck is having a baby," the head nurse looked coldly up at him and told him she would not admit the woman. She had her orders. And she wouldn't call the doctor or come outside to help either.

Employing the jackknife used an hour before to cut tar paper for a roofing job, the driver separated the infant from his profusely bleeding mother in the cab of the truck. "There were no bandages, not even a piece of string." With a piece of soiled yarn he unraveled from his sock, Joe tied the baby's cord. "Then the truck rolled on, leaving a trail of blood." Mrs. Kalata, almost dead from the loss of blood, tossed in a fever of infection for three weeks. "When she was well enough to talk they told her how Connor had her blood washed off the streets. 'He can wash my blood off the streets of Laona,' Rose Kalata smiled wryly, 'but he can never wash the blood off the Kingdom of Connors.'"

Stories were read and passed along. Emotions ran high, whipped up by writers and perhaps by preachers, even possibly by the Presbyterian minister in Laona. Word may well have reached W.D. that the minister's sympathies lay with the strikers, which would explain his instruction to Tom Rasmussen to discontinue at once deducting five dollars per month from his expense account and turning it to the Presbyterian church.[33] He did not, of course, share his decision to take this action with Helen or Melvin, or the grizzly stories either.

As the *Herald* splashed the news of the "labor war" at the Connor plant across its front pages, Melvin pulled Helen out of Wisconsin, driving her with David and Bom to Illinois. They called on the Diffenderfers, the Vaughns, and the Woods in Lincoln and on Melvin's relatives in Pike County. As usual, time away made it seem "nice to be home."

Helen pursued her high-minded interests. Kept from her was the knowledge, shared by the men in the family, that in setting up the "Connor Brothers," which involved the highly profitable "Miami" property in the West, W.D. had entangled the family in a financial web that bore potentially serious consequences. The bookkeeping for the partnership had been handled by W.D. As William put it after a conversation with James Ritchie Modrall, who had become an increasingly important person in New Mexican Democratic political circles and as assistant attorney general had drawn up the 1936 New Mexican Unemployment Security Act, if something should happen to W.D.— and at his age anything could—there was "a great danger of prosecution. . . . None of the family could answer one half the questions that might be put to us on the Miami matter, whether tax or bankruptcy matters. The whole business will be so tangled up that it will take years of litigation to unscramble it."[34] W.D. was mistaken if he thought he could get away with a pioneer mentality this far into the twentieth century.

Helen presented the DAR award to the outstanding high school student who best exemplified and understood American ideals and American history, entertained friends and relatives at a reception to introduce Connor's fiancée

Barbara Vail, and "stopped cleaning to drum up a speech" before driving to Madison with Helen Doege to attend the second statewide convention of the Cause and Cure of War. Mrs. L. A. Leadbetter, who opened the meeting, declared: "The organization of the world on a basis of law and order is the primary challenge." The delegates urged a revision of the neutrality policy of the United States through legislation to keep America out of war and to permit cooperation with other nations to prevent war. They supported positions taken by Secretary of State Cordell Hull in his "Eight Pillars of Peace" speech delivered at the July 1937 Buenos Aires Conference. The first of his pillars, "People must be educated for peace," as well as his conclusion that "moral law [is] the highest of all law," perfectly corresponded with their core beliefs. They issued policy statements and appointed Helen chairwoman of the Marathon Round Table of the state conference on the Cause and Cure of War. The meetings over, Helen and her friend Margaret Schorger addressed and mailed out hundreds of letters indicating their readiness to distribute study packets to "any organized groups in the community, men, women, or both." Almere Scott, secretary of the organization and former head of the Department of Debating and Public Discussion at the university and the director of the University of Wisconsin Extension Division, made use of WPA federal mimeographing funds to develop the "Loan Package Library," the largest in the nation. The WPA mimeographing funds enabled the Cause and Cure of War Committee to send educational materials throughout the state.

Birch Lake was no place for transcendent reflection in the summer of 1938, with the National Labor Board holding meetings in Laona. W.D. "spent everyday but one" overseeing the hearings.[35] When William ordered away a foreman W.D. was coaching over breakfast at the Gordon, W.D. erupted: "The company never before has been in such a nasty mess." The case needed "the greatest care." The other side was "working night and day preparing their witnesses." W.D. might get out of William's way in Laona, "but the moment I do, a stranger, a complete outsider will be the Responsible Head of the Connor Lumber and Land Company."[36]

Henry Pueschner's testimony that he had neither attempted to coerce lumberjacks into signing with the AFL nor given them whiskey, was contradicted by the sworn statements of Darlie Patton, Nick Carloss, and Joe Wilk, a "Russia Pole" who was "not a citizen," and Walter Haranpoh, a Russian, who testified that Pueschner gave whiskey while trying to get them to sign up. Other witnesses testified that company foremen threatened the men would lose their jobs if they voted CIO and that the company posted notices on company billboards charging that the CIO was Communist dominated.[37]

Theodore Brazeau, now a state senator, warned the Connors to be careful. The Wisconsin labor board, the governor, and the heavily Progressive state legislature were friendly with the CIO and working in tandem to reign in the industrialists. Moreover, the governor's brother, Robert La Follette Jr., was chair of the United States Senate's violently antibusiness Civil Liberties' Committee, which amassed a body of testimony constituting a damning indictment of the practices of the industrialists.

The CIO sang paeans to La Follette and Roosevelt. At their convention in Seattle in 1938 (a convention attended by two or three from the Connor camp), the CIO Committee on Legislation offered its grateful acknowledgment to the Civil Liberties' Committee for its tireless probing into the organized suppression of the rights of workers. "The entire convention approved a resolution stating that the La Follette Committee more than any committee in Senate history, deserved the appreciation of American workers."[38]

Industrialists were not without political friends of their own. In 1938, with leading American businessmen smarting under new federal regulations and shouting "conspiracy," Representative Martin Dies of Texas chaired a Special Committee on Un-American Activities, an investigative counterweight to the La Follette Committee. John P. Frey, president of the Metal Trades Department of the AFL, presented "a sweeping indictment of the CIO," tying it and the La Follette Committee to a Communist conspiracy." Rumors circulated in the press that the Dies Committee would consider a proposal to determine if "well known Communists" had conspired to create the La Follette Committee.[39] The Federation of Woman's Clubs, while disapproving of some of the Dies Committee's methods, adopted a resolution supporting the committee "in order to safeguard the American democratic system in the light of the growth of Fascism, Communism and Nazi-ism."

Communists or no, workers made progress. On August 25, W.D. called a meeting of Connor Lumber and Land Company managers and foremen to go over "things brought to notice during the six weeks hearing." "The time has passed," he said, "when the management can go out and put John here and Jim there. We have to have a record of it and be ready to show from the record that what has been done has been done wisely and fairly." He hoped they could "get along with the least possible amount of grind and difference between the company and the foremen and the union." They expected to get "a man to do a day's work." If he didn't, "get rid of him not in anger, but in an orderly way that fits into the new way that we are required to do things." Foremen should be careful to "keep away from talking with the men. If you have a Russian or a Polack in your crew that cannot talk English—don't try and talk

Russian to him and don't talk English to him. . . . Keep away from talking with these men about their buttons, the way they wear them, which union they belong to or which meeting they attend."[40] The men could file grievances.

The eminently serviceable Henry Pueschner left town and gave up his long service to the quarreling Connors. He opened a movie cinema in Greenfield County, Wisconsin. His wife and son went with him. Their departure deprived the women in the Laona Woman's Club of their leading soprano and William's son Andy of the companionship of Junior Pueschner, whom he had had to endure for many years as an example of what a good boy was. Junior Pueschner never swore, prepared his lessons, was polite to his elders, didn't harass the girls, and, most damning of all, "he loved his mother." For all this Andy forgave him the day that Junior Pueschner revealed himself related to the human race by carefully packing an ice ball and hurling it at Mrs. William Connor, hitting his proper mother squarely on the back of her neck.[41] The Peuschners departed, but they survived in memory, foul and fair, in Forest County.

The stressful summer took a toll on Helen. She reported "feeling bum," "not sleeping." Observing the frequency of her "not so good" days, sleepless nights, and increased irritability as warning signals of "overload," Melvin introduced the idea of sending Bom to Lake Forest Academy for his junior and senior years. With only David at home, she would have more time to devote to her interests, to her work as chairwoman of the state's Marathon Round Table Discussion Group, and the Seventh District Woman's Club Chairman of International Affairs.

Melvin had not anticipated Bom's strong negative reaction to the idea, or his own, as he explained that it was for Helen's sake that he proposed his son go away to boarding school, because Helen was not entirely well. When Melvin suddenly broke down and wept, Bom grasped something of his father's deep weariness, and the toll of the heavy burdens he quietly bore. When the school's letter of acceptance arrived, Bom pretended to be pleased, and they were all, Helen thought, "quite excited."

Bom's departure and Connor's marriage to Barbara Vail occurred simultaneously. Helen registered the presence of Norma Woods from Lincoln and Helen Doege, not of the two hundred others the *Herald* reported present at the wedding of "wide importance" held at the Joseph Bond Chapel at the University of Chicago. W.D. was not there but in Victoria, having once again managed to avoid a major social event. "I could not add to the ceremonies— to make the union more happy or more lasting." He also observed "this country [is] more affected by war scare than Wisconsin. Business from China and Japan has been entirely out. Now there is nothing going to Europe."

Helen spent time in Madison with the Wisconsin Library Association, preparing the study plan for the Marathon Round Tables and jotting notes for speeches on three-by-five cards. She would warm up her audience with a couple of jokes: "Husband tells his wife who is leaving for a meeting of The Cause and Cure of War organization: 'If civilization were in ashes there would still be women poking around trying to find the causes and cures of war.'" A "youngster asked where his mother was said 'off causing and curing wars.'" The women might be mocked for their effort, but they pursued their idealistic goal of preventing war. Helen's notes suggest what her contemporaries in the peace organizations were thinking: "Unless we chose the higher plane, we all go down together." "No convergence between science and religion although sincerity, truth, honesty are still ideals." "Need more believers and fewer belittlers." "Morality enlightened self-interest?"

The AFL struck Laona in October, demanding higher wages and a closed shop—a demand the company could not meet without risk of another lengthy hearing before the labor board. Production dropped 19 percent.[42] Adding to the family's problems, the CIO lawyers, Henry Paull of Minnesota and Luke Raik of Michigan, filed a lawsuit in federal court against the company for "authorizing and conspiring with Kenneth Allen . . . to perform acts of violence." The *Herald* ran the story of the $450,000 damage suit under the headline "CONNORS, LAIRD NAMED IN SUIT."[43]

That Melvin had been included with Kenneth Allen, Duane Statesil, the Connor Lumber and Land Company, Marathon Paper Mills Company, R. M. Connor, W.D. Connor Jr., D. C. Everest, and John Stevens Jr. (alleged leaders of the Gogebic County Wood Operators Association) in the long list of named defendants struck Helen as "unfair," the single word she used in her diary to describe the article.

William did not show the letter he had received from Allen, who had gone into hiding, to Helen or Melvin. Allen claimed he was ready to "face the music" because he had had enough of being "a monkey for the sake of 'loyalty to my employer,'" enough of being "a fool" and "taking the rap" for William and Gordon. "The whole business," Allen asserted, was their doing and they "ought to be ashamed." He was prepared to stay away and keep quiet, provided they kept their word and took care of his family, which they hadn't. His wife had been thrown on relief in Laona at five dollars a week and was threatening to divorce him unless she was taken care of. If they never believed anything else, Allen threatened, they could believe this: "Unless I hear from my wife before October 1st that everything is O.K. as far as the kids and she are concerned,

I am going to turn myself in and get it off my chest." He had been "such a monkey so far" he might as well "go the route." He had nothing to lose.[44]

W.D., to whom William sent the letter, surmised that Allen thought he had them "over the barrel. Nothing will satisfy him or his wife until he lands in the Pen." If Allen were found, his testimony would be "fatal." Some way had to "be worked out to keep him out of the way and silent." The Connors paid him off with the immediate $200 he demanded and sent him a weekly check for $15 and made sure Mrs. Allen had no reason to complain either. Townspeople watching her enter the company offices in Laona knew why she went there, and her satisfied air when she stepped out told them she got it. No one ratted to the authorities.

W.D. instructed William, now eager to listen to his father, to tell Allen not to write to his wife or to make any attempt to contact her. Government people, "determined to get hold of" and convict him, were "looking everywhere." Allen was the only witness they needed; he was the big shot. But others had been involved. Allen could, if he showed up as witness for the state, "immediately implicate" someone else. People in Ironwood were talking, saying that another vigilante by name of Weston was likely to draw three years; "the local people are so scared they crawl under the bed at night," W.D. pointed out, mocking, as was his custom, the frailty of "ordinary" people. Paull, one of the two "very bitter" lawyers who had been beaten and abducted in Ironwood, told W.D. they were "gradually taking these fellows into the CIO," and as soon as they got them, "they talk." That was one of the reasons W.D. was "anxious to keep one shift going at Connorville" in spite of the slow-down in sales and the pile up of lumber at Laona. "There were several there who were in the forefront" of the violence, and if they got "scattered around," they would get someone to talk.[45]

Frightened, William temporarily dropped his omniscient certitude and painful arrogance. Father and sons worked toward the same threatened end: to keep the Connor Lumber and Land Company going with Connors at the helm.

Melvin made the difficult presentation to Judge Stone and R. Connor Company trustees in Madison and received an extension of interest payments due on the Connor Lumber and Land Company Bonds. But harm had been done. Confidential reports issued by the First Wisconsin National Bank and Dun and Bradstreet made further borrowing all but impossible. The vice president of the City National Bank and Trust Company in Chicago wrote: "Our study of your company's situation as revealed by the audit . . . has led us so far to conclude that despite the admirable progress made since 1932 the immediate financial stability of the business is too much open to question because of the pressure of the maturing fixed debt. Unless a considerable relief from this pressure could be arranged, we would not be attracted to a loan on inventory."[46] Trauma for the Connors piled on like lumber in the yards, and yet orders were good, and most buyers agreed that the label the Connors put on their maple flooring, "The Best in the World," was about right.

Happy and doing well at Lake Forest, Bom was on the debating team working up a "Prince of Peace" speech. While Helen thought "mostly of Bom some days," she was closely following the news from abroad: Hitler's march into Austria was seen as a giant step toward his goal of taking all Europe into a Germanic confederation; the English were in gas masks, their children leaving London. Writing from Victoria on October 8, W.D. hoped she was "less disturbed about the war situation in Europe. Surely there has been a trying time for all the folks who think of world affairs. . . . You have had many things to think about. Yes, I am sure you think of Mother and with all the burdens how she carried on. Each one in turn will have to do their utmost to work out the life that they seem to be placed in." He and Richard (Laird) had spent a full day at Jordan River. "I was telling him yesterday that he surely would soon know more about this whole proposition than his grandfather." He thought "Richard would like to follow Connor soon by taking on a helpful mate. . . . He goes some with a girl here in Victoria. We were at dinner the other evening. She is all right I guess. Has been about quite a bit. Is a registered nurse. I think has worked five or six years in Los Angeles, Cal. *I think she is as old as Richard.* You should be more of a match-maker. Young and inexperienced boys and girls should not be left to themselves to decide such important problems."

He hoped Helen, who could not know how much he missed her, would try to see Elizabeth and William when she could. He was away from them "so very much. . . . I cannot do for either of them as I should. I must try and be with them more."

It wasn't only for the children's sake W.D. felt he "should be in Wood County and other places in Wisconsin in the fall of 1938. This is the first real chance that has come in forty years to give the *La Follettes a beating. They have it coming.* They have it coming. I understand *George Mead* is now for *Phil.* George and Phil had a secret conference at Camp Douglas six weeks ago. They spent two nights in one of the Cottages there together. *Phil* is in dire straits for money to *finance* his campaign. Phil is now for the Little Eau Plein Project. Assemblyman Vaughn has denounced the project at every opportunity up to a month ago. Now he is not opposing it."

"Melvin getting interested in politics," Helen observed after returning from the Rapids where the Lairds heard Republican gubernatorial candidate Julius

Heil speak. When the Milwaukee businessman, the choice of Democrats and Republicans united in their opposition to La Follette, won the November election, Melvin decided to run for the state senate in 1940.[47]

Helen, who admitted to feeling "bum to no purpose," felt better when she settled down to write a speech to deliver to the Missionary Society. Beginning with selections from St. Matthew, wherein she found a "great confirmation of faith," and Tolstoy's belief that "the reason of life is for each of us simply to grow in love," how, she wondered, could they make their patriotism and their religion less incongruous—the Christian flag and the Stars-and-Stripes? That question was "of particular interest to women." She spoke of the importance to their lives and the nation's of individuals who strove for both Christian and American values: Harry Emerson Fosdick, Muriel Lester, Rufus Jones—but, she claimed, the "human race slipped up somewhere, was moving elsewhere."

She listed things her audience should remember: their ancestors came to worship God not gold; Christianity was based on the importance of the individual; Democracy and Christianity were bound together. Democracy was not something handed out "perfected on a golden platter" but a "sacrificial obligation." Whether America deserved to be free depended on how she solved her social problems, Helen asserted. Unemployment was "part of that sixth column gnawing at our foundations." The great inequalities and flaws in the American system were the poll tax, crime, greed, poverty, corruption. For us to build up "great armaments supposedly in self-defense . . . would be to engage in a futile attempt at prosperity." Reciprocal trade treaties were "the only dove of peace this country has sent out. Why shoot it? Our greatest contribution to the world is to make democracy work here."

She attended the Cause and Cure of War meeting in Washington, D.C., in January 1939 with Helen Doege. They shared a room at the Mayflower, visited the monuments and the Episcopalian Church; had tea with Mrs. Roosevelt, who had been urging women for some time to pressure Congress to keep the profits out of war; met with Wisconsin senators and congressmen; listened to sessions in both the House and the Senate; and attended three days of meetings. The committee drew women from eleven national member organizations[48] and international organizations representing South America, Australia, China, Canada, Czechoslovakia, and England. The delegates demonstrated "the fact that all over the world women have interests in common, that they have a mutual abhorrence of war and aspire to help in finding a means of settling disputes in a more Christian manner and with greater justice." The conference, Helen thought, was "of a higher standard than any to which [she] had ever listened."[49]

Like Helen, most of the delegates had been involved with and taken leadership positions in women's organizations. Most had been active in the suffrage movement. The experience of the First World War convinced them of their larger task to look beyond themselves, their homes, and their communities to the world community. Buoyed by their numbers, their shared commitment, their history of achievement, and imbued with a forward-looking orientation and to reason as a method of solving problems, they believed that even in the vastly more complex arena of international relations they could exert a powerful, beneficial influence.

In Washington, Helen "thrilled to the strength of the vast nation"; her mind reverberated with Walter Scott's words, "This is my own, my native land."

She summarized her impressions of the conference in a lengthy article published in the *Herald*, and on February 14, with the thermometer registering 20 below zero, she drove to Stevens Point to deliver a radio address about the committee's work. In the speeches she gave to clubs throughout the Seventh District, she said that America held a position of leadership in "the chaotic world not only because of our resources, but because we have had no part in some of the questionable compromises in Europe." She urged women "to earnestly study peace and not just propagandize it," to realize that "an unjust, uneasy peace does not make for stability in the world." She drafted a series of questions for study groups, listed available source materials, and cautioned that the tremendous importance of foreign policy in no way diminished the importance of domestic problems but "intensified the absolute necessity of making democracy work here at home." She cited as the administration's "tragic failure" the lack of low-cost housing.

The headline in the *Herald* on May 23—DROP CASE AGAINST CONNOR LUMBER CO.—contributed to her high spirits. Federal judge Patrick T. Stone had dismissed the two damage suits filed by Henry Paull, Duluth labor attorney, and Luke Raik, representative of Lumber and Sawmill Workers Union AFL. The terms of the settlement were not disclosed. The Lairds were enormously relieved to have that sorry bit of family history behind them.

At the third annual Wisconsin program of the Conference on the Cause and Cure of War, held in Madison on June 9, Helen presided at one of the three roundtable luncheons during which the Midwest director of the League of Nations Association spoke about the recently held Pan-American conference in Lima, Peru. She took part in a panel discussion on the topic "What Role Can Democracy Play in Building a Better World?" and socialized with other participants at the tea University of Wisconsin president Clarence Dykstra hosted at his home afterwards. (Dykstra had many supporters, but the governor was not among them. Heil had already attacked Dykstra as "this stranger in our midst who is ambitious to make this University the largest school in America."[50] Rumors spread that Heil wanted to drive Dykstra out.)

Her meetings over, she joined Melvin, who, representing county boards, had advised the senate finance committee that county government could not continue to meet state-mandated obligations by raising property taxes. Together they attended the honors' convocation at Lake Forest. His proud parents watched as Bom received the Debate Medal and the Book Prize—*The Golden Treasury of the World's Wit and Wisdom*—for his outstanding work in plane geometry.

Spirits were high in Laona in July 1939, as people gathered to celebrate life among and by the big trees in the free nation. The Paul Bunyan Days celebration was an advertising stunt for the Connor Lumber and Land Company, which invited people to come by air to the air strip laid in near Laona, 100 feet wide and 1,200 feet long (the company provided cars to bring them to the village). Over four days it gave the company a chance to show off its world, what they, workers and owners, had done together, what they were doing. Catwalks built over the operations on the inside of the main building allowed visitors to watch the work at the "huge sawmill," and a living panorama presented the logging industry from oxen days to the motorized present. There were exhibitions and concerts and a parade with businessmen, representatives of the lumber industry, and the U.S. Forest Service marching.

W.D., dressed not in the customary navy wool suit, shirt, and tie he usually wore but in a bright-red flannel shirt borrowed from David, a broad-rimmed felt hat on his head, and trousers tucked in his spike boots, walked at the head of the parade. A switch in his left hand, and his right holding a rope, the seventy-five-year-old pioneer slowly, proudly led a plodding, sturdy ox pulling a heavy load of perfect logs down Mill Street. The event, according to the *Forest Republican,* vied with the World's Fair in New York.[51]

"Father left for Victoria day before Governor Heil comes to Wausau," Helen noted in her calendar on August 15. In a private dining room at the Wausau Club, Melvin met with the governor and Republican leaders, who had arrived in town ostensibly to celebrate the naming of the Marathon County Dairy Queen, but really to discuss strategy for the 1940 election.

On September 3, England and France declared war. Roosevelt addressed the nation, warning that while "it was easy to say that conflicts thousands of miles away did not seriously affect the Americas, every word that comes through the air, every ship that sails the seas, every battle that is fought does affect the American future."[52] Helen wrote in her diary: "The way to stay out of Europe is to stay out." Then Melvin, Helen, David, and Bom, who was going to remain home and take his senior year at Marshfield High, went to the fair.

Helen attended the Wisconsin Federation of Woman's Clubs' fall convention in Sheboygan. Mrs. A. L. Blackstone, "Dean of Directors" of the General Federation, wondered whether they, "the privileged women of the world," were "carrying the torch as high as we might, the torch tossed to us by the strong hands of Wisconsin club women of yesterday, who had such faith in the federation." Josephine Pierce claimed the home as "civilization's first line of defense" and urged "encouragement of early marriage and child rearing among the upper thirty percent of the population." The women declared Frank C. Klode "unqualified" and opposed his appointment as director of the state's Department of Public Welfare.[53] Helen chaired, and was the principal speaker at, the Federation's International Relations Town Hall session.

She had many questions and few answers. "Shall we go all out for Britain and take the consequences, or shall we give what we can safely spare?" "Why did we never secure islands and bases as payment for first world war debts?" "Whole question of Japanese aggression. Further war there would further complicate world problems. War is one. All part of same. Especially since Japan signed with Axis. Why so concerned? Strategic, essential materials, tin, rubber, gypsum. Southeastern Asia makes our ties in South America child's play." She urged the women to remember that "a war economy and a democracy can never form a permanent partnership"; "militarism is a dangerous foe to democracy"; "a great armament program is only a temporary stop to economic distress—no solution to problem." If Americans believed in the brotherhood of man, they had to see to it that a British victory did not become end in itself. These were the thoughts that occupied her when her life suddenly took a dramatic turn.

In the little pocket calendar she had neglected for months, on October 22, she wrote: "David suddenly taken to hospital. Operated at 1:30 P.M." The next entry, November 5, "M.R. in Washington. Stay at night with David," and the following entries reveal her consuming concern about her youngest son, whose appendix had burst and who was not recovering from the emergency surgery. November 8: "Upset begins in late afternoon. Night terrible." November 11: "no improvement. Can see Paul [Dr. Paul Doege] is alarmed. . . . . Operation decided upon 11:30 A.M. Transfusion in afternoon." November 15: "XXX." November 16: "Another Transfusion." November 17: Barbara and Connor come."

Day after day, night after night, Helen was at his side. Melvin donated several pints of blood and heard his twelve-year-old ask: "Man to man, am I going to die?" On December 5, David came home. "BIG DAY," she noted.

Emerging from her intense preoccupation with her sick son, Helen attended the final club meeting of the year, at which the local Episcopalian, Catholic, Presbyterian, and Methodist pastors gave a panel discussion comparing the "Great Religions"—Judaism, Islam, Buddhism, and Hinduism—with Christianity. Afterwards, engaged in preparations for the holiday, anticipating the return of her family, with many reasons to celebrate, she could not block the thoughts that came to mind. "The Lord reigneth, the Lord resigneth. Let earth rejoice," she wrote across the last page of her calendar. Not quite an appropriate line for a Christian and a leading spokeswoman for the Cause and Cure of War, but hope and reason had always pulled Helen in different directions.

CHAPTER 16

❧

# Endings and Beginnings

## 1940–1944

So the holidays are over, and America celebrated them with unique extravagance and festivity, as if to enjoy one last great party before the sharp encounter with destiny.

—DOROTHY THOMPSON

After a month spent with a recuperating David in St. Petersburg, Florida, Helen thought it nice to be home, to fall into familiar routines. She accepted an invitation to serve on the Wisconsin State Committee on Women's Participation in the New York World's Fair but declined an invitation to have her biography published in *Leading Women of America*.

She gave no public speeches about women's roles in society but made a note in her diary, "if you want to know something about the English woman's fight for suffrage read *Fame is the Spur* page 490 on,"[1] and clipped and saved articles regarding the status of women, one of which—"Office Women and Sex Antagonism"—addressed college-educated women who settled for low-paying jobs as secretaries and did not stop to reflect that in getting out from under the dictatorial influence of their kin, they would "be getting under the thumbs of other men who wouldn't be any appreciable improvement."[2] Another article addressed privileged club women who were "great educators and organizers" but knew little of the fundamentals of finance and economics. They recommended "spending large sums of money—other people's money, they think, but in reality their own—without questioning or analyzing the business judgment of inaugurating such projects." Women would wield "a tremendous power when they realized that in their hands reposes the biggest financial stake in all our national wealth."[3]

The "woman question" hit home when Rob's daughter, Angie Connor, asked W.D. for a job practicing medicine in Laona. He agonized over his decision. While a woman doctor at Sooke, about twenty miles from the Jordan River camps, did a good business among the people living in the area, he did not believe that if a man was "injured that they ever think of stopping at the woman doctor's office for treatment or call her to the camp." If he gave Angie the job, "possibly it would be the only place in the State of Wisconsin where there is a woman doctor, and I think the people would say, 'well, she picked out the roughest going place she could find.'"[4] He decided he could not do it.

In spite of his seventy-six years, and discounting rumors that there was a move to make a federal park in the area, he purchased additional major tracts from the Keweenaw Land Association and from the Porcupine Land Association, "which is Keweenaw in a way." Using Connor Brothers as the instrument by which to acquire the land, he allocated between $2,500 and $3,000 from the Connor Lumber and Land Company to the partnership under the fiction that the Connor Lumber and Land Company was, according to agreements worked out with the Reconstruction Finance Corporation (RFC) trustees, buying stumpage only as needed for the manufacture of lumber.

Less alert to the niceties of legal fictions, Melvin referred in correspondence to land purchases made by the Connor Lumber and Land Company. L. L. Beard, the company comptroller, reprimanded him. Using "Connor Brothers" was "a nice easy method" to make purchases without consulting anyone. For the Connor Lumber and Land Company to buy a tract of timber, even a little one, was something the RFC would have to weigh and might have to get Washington's approval on.

Working for the company, Melvin accepted its mores, but his deep interests had always been and remained elsewhere. Committed to public service, he explained his reasons for seeking the office of state senator. In old texts he found the grounding for his new career. In what probably was his last sermon, "Responsible Living," he drew on a "striking parable" taken from the ninth chapter of the Book of Judges in which "the trees went forth to anoint a king over them," all of whom refused to accept the duty until at last the bramble accepted. The bramble king had "neither timber, nor fruit, nor shade." "He is a useless man, and worse, he is dangerous. He is not substantial or fruitful, but he is combustible. He is capable of burning and setting other things on fire." Melvin did not name Hitler, but everyone knew to whom he referred when he said "another bramble king has risen in the world and lit another fire" and grasped his implied warning: America was not immune from what had happened elsewhere.

The nation had gone astray, had lost its sense of "ought," Melvin declared, affirming for the hundredth time that, while "not doctrinaire," he was religious. Religion helped man "to believe in himself." It enabled "a true prophet to see beyond what is to something which is not yet, but ought to be; he can dream of a new heaven, a new earth, and valiantly labor to achieve it." What would happen if during the chaotic times of intellectual and moral confusion through which they were passing, when Isaiah's words seemed like "the voice of a mocking bird calling from the midst of the dust and debris of a ruined world," there was "no institution, which had a high conception of human worth, an inspiring vision of human destiny?"

Melvin courteously but firmly declined W.D.'s offer to hire a man to go into the bars and spread the rumor that his primary opponent was a drunkard, but he counted on help from other family members. Bom and friends Nancy Barnes and Bob Froehlke plastered "Laird for Senate" posters on telephone poles, storefronts, and yards all over Clark, Taylor, and Wood Counties and stuck the large gray and white plywood elephant with Melvin's name and candidacy written in black in front of halls where he was scheduled to speak. If Melvin Sr. could not meet a speaking obligation, Melvin Jr. happily took his place. He was already a good speaker, and no one complained. David rang doorbells, smiled, and handed out three-by-five publicity cards listing Melvin's qualifications.[5] The card did not advertise that he was an ordained minister or that he was associated with the R. Connor, the Connor Lumber and Land Company, or the Canadian Puget Sound Timber and Lumber Company.

Helen and her friends founded the Wood County Republican Woman's Club. They held receptions for state senate candidates Melvin Laird and Alvin O'Konski and, just before he was killed when his car failed to round a curve, Glenn Frank, a candidate for the U.S. Senate. Melvin introduced Governor Julius Heil on the opening day of the Central State Fair on September 4, and the schools cooperated, as did many businesses and some industrial plants, by closing for the afternoon in order to allow larger than usual crowds to attend the unusual event.

Through letters Dean Witter forwarded from his sister, Elizabeth Witter Debost, the news from France became personal. Elizabeth wrote of German soldiers overrunning her adopted land, the fall of Amiens, the treachery of Leopold, and "finally the ghastly battle of the Flanders fields again and the magnificent performance of armies and navies in embarking 334,000 men from Dunkirk." German methods were "terrible, corruption first, well organized and financed, threats, bluff and finally the terrific advance with all sorts of motorized units. Worst of all, perhaps, has been the treatment of civils [sic], and if some people were beginning to forget the atrocities of the lst war, those of these few weeks will never be effaced." The "most demoralizing thing of all was to realize that Hitler and his evil workers had found so much complicity inside France and that maybe even the highest army officers were guilty of collusion with the enemy."

W.D. did not believe that the fall of France would mean an end to the war. "I think it means that the war will be carried down through over lower French soil and also the engagement of many more English soldiers and such equipment as Great Britain can furnish and apparently all the equipment that America possibly can get ready and get over there."[6] The government had placed a large order for lumber.

Congress narrowly passed a draft bill affecting young men ages twenty-one to thirty-five. Marshfield's Company C, 128th Infantry, received word to fall in. Dick who was toughing it out alone at Camp No. 2, Point-No-Point, Jordan River, rising at 4:30 A.M., cleaning up the logs in the water at the booming and sorting grounds at Beachy Bay, came home, registered for the draft, and declared he was eager to get into "something quite good on this national defense set up by taking up flying."[7] Helen wrote to Secretary of State Cordell Hull. She had had "considerable misgivings" when she read that "the embargo on machine tools to Russia had been lifted and that $60 million worth had been shipped" but was "sore distressed" when she "heard that the planes completed for Sweden were now also destined for Russia." She could "not understand it and would like authentic information. If, as rumored, 50 percent of all war supplies secured by Russia were going to Germany, then this was "a betrayal of our interests." She hoped she had been misinformed. Planning "some talks," she wanted "the truth."[8]

The war news was oppressive, but Melvin's election to the Wisconsin senate raised the couple's spirit. After undergoing minor surgical procedures at the Mayo Clinic, both Lairds looked forward to leaving health problems, and the old routines and responsibilities, behind. They planned to take David with them and live in a furnished apartment in the Kennedy Manor in Madison for the duration of the legislative session and anticipated a liberating time.

In a sober ceremony in keeping with "the present critical period of history,"[9] Julius Heil and the newly elected legislators (most of them Republicans) were sworn in on January 12, 1941. Melvin met with the leadership, received his assignment to the senate's prized labor and agricultural committee, and learned about the coming battle of the budget and the governor's wish to institute compulsory Reserve Officer Training Corps (ROTC) at the university. The gray-haired dean of the senate, President Pro-tem Conrad Shearer, called for cooperation "so we can get out of Madison at an early date," and Warren P. Knowles, a new senator, declared "the meeting of economy and efficiency can be demonstrated by a short business-like session." May 1 was the target con-cluding date for the part-time legislators whose principal income derived from other sources.

While David "tried a couple of classes" at Wisconsin High, Helen attended lectures and concerts at the university; hearings at the capitol; "fine" services and sermons by Dr. Kennedy at Christ Presbyterian Church; dinners at the Union, the Madison Club, the Loraine Hotel, and with the Sisks and the Schorgers; suppers at the Pi Phi House; teas at the home of university presi-dent Dr. and Mrs. Dykstra; and a study group at the Congregational Church. She drove into the countryside when she needed calm more than stimulation.

Helen and Margaret Schorger spent many afternoons together. Their talk ranged widely, as talk between old friends will: state affairs (Margaret was chair of the Madison Woman's Club legislative committee), world affairs, univer-sity affairs, family. Recalling their innocent student days, when they had both been members of the Pi Phi sorority, they compared themselves with the pres-ent toughened generation of students who, with the knowledge that weapons' manufacturers had made millions during the First World War, described them-selves as "morally weak" and "fanatically determined not to be suckers about ideals."[10] They talked about President Dykstra's—and their own—concern that if Americans did not "lay emphasis these days on responsibilities as well as privileges . . . our experiment in democracy will soon be ended."[11] Dyk-stra's appointment as chairman of the all-important eleven-member National Labor Mediation Board, organized to mediate between quarreling labor and management, and the governor's stated belief that Roosevelt should outlaw all strikes during "the period of emergency," meant that, with the positions reversed, the state's current political and educational leaders did not see any more eye-to-eye than did their predecessors.

The women talked about their sons. Margaret's two were conscientious objectors who could do CCC work. Helen's Dick had already gone off to Sikeston, Missouri, Air Force Training Detachment; Connor, a married man, was exempt from the draft; Bom would soon be required to register; David was only thirteen, and they hoped he would never have to register. They attended meetings of the League of Women Voters, on record as favoring the lend-lease agreement, which the defeated Republican presidential candidate Wendell Willkie declared would keep America out of war and jubilant Lon-doners declared meant the United States was in the war. They read Lindbergh's testimony before the House Foreign Affairs Committee in which he declared his sympathy for both sides and said the lend-lease was wrong.[12] Helen assumed the presidency of the Cause and Cure Committee.

A call from Aunt Florence sent her hurrying back to Marshfield in February the middle of the night. Barely recuperated from one severe bronchial infection, W.D. had come down with another and was coughing, feverish, weak, and calling for her. Angie, back from serving as head of the Harrington Harbor Hospital in Labrador, was there, diverting the family with her stories about her French, English, and Indian patients. (The latter lived in smoke-filled tents in an encampment at Romaine Bay and bled "patients through holes in their veins made by the insertion of ordinary nails.") She had traveled miles by dogsled across salt ice and through spruce forests heavy with snow and climbed the steep hills of Mutton Bay, her dogs "plodding, walking, sinking into the snow" to see patients.[13] Angie had not turned out as Rob hoped. She was not domesticated and couldn't play a musical instrument. She showed twentieth-century female pioneer courage and enterprise instead. W.D. liked her stories. With all the love and attention surrounding him, and with his own strong life impulse, he began a slow recovery.

Helen remained in Marshfield looking after David and her father, while Melvin lived in bachelor quarters at the Madison Club during the week and, unless some urgent business called, spent the weekends at home and at the Connor office. The "Madison sojourn already past history," she noted in her diary. She felt "bum," jotting down another of her potent phrases: "country right or wrong; mother, drunk or sober." She wasn't a drunken mother, but a dutiful daughter. She felt better when her father improved. "Love sun on Bakerville ski hill; father comfortable."

When Dick's flying instructor told him he didn't have the right coordination and would never make a flyer, he began preparing himself for a commission in the navy by taking a correspondence course in accounting from the much-maligned La Salle University and returned to work for his grandfather in Victoria. If he eventually had to go into the army, he wouldn't have any regrets about not trying the other branches first. He advised Bom, whom he had given the task of acting as his agent and investing some of his earnings in the stock market, since he could not legally do so from Canada, to keep his eyes open for "a good spot" for himself.

With customary objectivity, Helen studied the opposing views regarding the American position vis-à-vis the war. She appreciated the pacifist views of Fosdick, whose "old Baptist heritage about liberty of conscience vs. this whole totalitarian drift [was] aroused" by conscription,[14] and Norman Thomas. She heard the impassioned speech Charles Lindbergh made on the radio urging nonintervention in the European war and sent to the America First Committee, Chicago, for a copy of his address in order to think through his arguments:

America's army was untrained, her air force "deplorably lacking in modern fighting planes"; 100 million Americans opposed entering the war. "If we are forced into a war against the wishes of an overwhelming majority of our people, we will have proved Democracy such a failure at home that there will be little use fighting for it abroad."

Having absorbed the arguments for nonengagement, Helen studied the arguments propounded by Secretary of State Dean Acheson, principal spokesman for the Committee to Defend America by Aiding the Allies, one of the architects of the destroyers-for-bases agreement with Britain. She invited him to present his views at the Seventh District Convention of Women's Clubs. He was leaving for South America and, regretfully, his secretary wrote, had to decline.[15]

New friends, challenges, and chances to do public good made Melvin, friends and relatives agreed, a happier man. Always a serious student of state and national issues, he now saw the reason for study as directly purposeful. Always eager to help worthy people along, now his opportunities to do so greatly expanded. At sixty-three, he aligned with eager young Republican legislators: Warren P. Knowles and the twenty-seven-year-old senator from Green Bay, John W. Byrnes. He developed a reputation in Madison not only for his political skills but for his close links with both the religious and academic communities. He crossed, as probably no other contemporary politician could, dividing lines between churchmen and statesmen, academics and politicians.

Through conversations with friends Professors Max Otto, Bill Schorger, and E. B. Fred (dean of the Agricultural School), through University Club meetings and through information gleaned from the editorial pages of the *Daily Cardinal*, he followed the thoughts of academicians and a new generation of students excited, as he and Helen had been, by the free expression of ideas at the great and liberal institution.

In Walter Lippmann's article published first in the spring issue of the *American Scholar* and reprinted in part in the *Daily Cardinal* on March 21, 1941, he heard echoes of concerns he first voiced at Lincoln College in 1914. Lippmann proposed that universities throughout the country debate the proposition that those who were responsible for education had progressively removed the Western cultural tradition from the curriculum. Not only had schools become "a mere training ground for personal careers," the modern secular education had isolated the individual. It made him "a careerist who must make his way through a struggle in which there is no principle of order. This is the uprooted and incoherent modern 'free man.' This is what the free man—in reality merely the freed and uprooted and dispossessed man—has become."

Lippmann's message was dark. Melvin was not as pessimistic, although he agreed with both Lippmann and Bernard DeVoto that youth's "wretched ignorance of American history" was a factor in the society's decline.[16] And Melvin believed "the history of Wisconsin ought by law to be taught in every public school in Wisconsin, and that every public school in every state should be far more than now a teacher of patriotism as well as a trainer of intelligence."

When Germany escalated the war and German troops moved against the 2,000-mile front of the Russian army, Dick, who confessed he didn't know what to make of the fascist-communist confrontation, advised Helen not to take the war too seriously. "One news broadcast per day should be enough as we can't do anything about it but go along with any little duties as we see them. It's all part of our life and we should enjoy it so far as possible." He concluded with the inevitable worthless advice that she "get plenty of rest."

While Helen agonized over the chaos reigning over much of the globe, as businessmen the Connors had to be jubilant. After all the lean years, they were running three shifts twenty-four hours a day in their mills and could not keep up with demand. In the 1930s, the cry had been to "get rid of the stuff!"; in the 1940s it became "produce!"

They had cut everything on the west side of the Presque Isle River in Michigan, and W.D. had built a bridge using scrap iron to the east side where they had begun cutting. When the Michigan superintendent of the Board of County Road Commissioners requested a sixty-six- foot right-of-way for the construction of a highway through his property, he testily replied: He understood "the purpose of this highway down to the mouth of the Presque Isle River and down to Lake Superior is for the benefit largely of the city folks. People who want vacations and outings. We in the lumber business don't have any time for such things. We have to work continuously full time every day trying to get enough ahead to pay our taxes of the many different kinds that are being imposed on us." W.D.'s fighting instincts remained as strong as ever. The R. Connor Company might enjoin the highway people from trespassing on their property: "If those fellows have to run around in circles for 30 days or 60 days, they will be more civil when we try to talk to them about our rights and our property."

Out West, the operation at the Jordan River, the second largest truck job on Vancouver Island, was highly profitable. W.D.'s name as president of the Canadian Puget Sound Timber and Lumber Company, deleted in the thirties, had been restored. His letters and instructions seemed to come from a younger, happier man.

Informed by his lawyers that if 80 percent of the Connor Lumber and Land Company and the R. Connor Company were owned by the same parties, there would be no tax liability when the companies merged, he prepared the case for a loan of $150,000 that Melvin and Richard presented to the board of directors of the Reconstruction Finance Corporation in Minneapolis. The loan enabled the Connor Lumber and Land Company to purchase unsecured notes of the R. Connor Company at 65–75 percent of their face values. The notes were then tendered back to the R. Connor Company to offset the indebtedness of the Connor Lumber and Land Company to the R. Connor Company.[17]

Anticipating the arrival of IRS attorneys interested in determining whether any or all of the family had some property that might be liable to attachment, W.D. coached his family. The IRS would inquire about the ownership of stock in the Connor Lumber and Land Company and the R. Connor Company. He would take the position that "all our timber around Laona is going to be cut off in five or six years and all the assets of the Connor Lumber and Land Company then will be invested in what cut-over land we have left and in machinery and equipment. That we will try to realize on all we can. Possibly by that time most of our indebtedness may well be paid up and it might leave some value for the stock, but not much."[18]

The IRS attorneys believed him. W.D. relaxed. He wrote Edwin Kohl, who in his youth had heard W.D. speak about the older La Follette and Theodore Roosevelt, that he would never write a book called *Behind Closed Doors*, which Kohl hoped he would.[19] While he had spent "a good share" of his life taking "great pleasure in looking down over the seats in the U.S. Senate and thinking how comfortable they might be and how serviceable I could be if I occupied one of them to my folks back home," it was "so seldom in a life time that our 'dreams come true.' So that you know I have settled down very patiently and thoroughly trying to make a living handling the forest products and the products of our mills and also the farm."[20]

As he neared the end of the road, while he seldom referred to his political past, W.D. increasingly assumed "the voice of experience" mantle to recount some of the history of the lumber industry into which he had so "patiently" settled, hoping that in passing on the history, he could help shape his family's future. He told how he had seen the timber cut around Victoria. Fifty years ago "it looked as though there was timber for all time, but so much of it has disappeared." Mills going ten or fifteen years ago had disappeared. As the fir got "further away and in less quantities," the hemlock would take its place, and "with what the paper mills use, it won't take long to catch up with the hemlock. The same as has been true in this country."[21]

He turned to history again as he tried to convince William that now was the time for aggressive expansion. "The terrific crash" William anticipated was making him overly timid. They had had panics before, he said, "and I don't know how they can be prevented in the future." W.D. wanted production, immediate cash on hand so they could "go out and buy at great bargains, at panic prices." It had been his "experience in 1883, 1893, 1907, and 1908, that immediately after there has been any serious disturbance in the lumber market, the prices of stumpage were not affected. On the contrary, each time like that it was more apparent that the stumpage was in closer hands and people were more eager to buy and the same thing followed in the much longer depression and panic we had in 1930 to 1933. There were no real big good blocks of timber thrown on the market at great sacrifice." Lumber in pile "had to be moved at whatever the market would take it at. That isn't true of standing timber." In the ten-page letter he directed to William and submitted to the whole family, he could not resist pointing out how much William's temerity had cost them. Menasha hadn't known they had "60 to 65 million feet of the best timber that ever grew in Wisconsin." They estimated 20 million below W.D.'s estimate, and William let it go.[22]

On September 27, W.D., Melvin, Gordon, Richard, and their attorneys were in Judge Stone's chambers in Wausau meeting with the court-appointed directors and attorneys of the R. Connor Company. W.D. thought they would "come in for the kill" before they turned back control to the family but instructed his family "not to fight." The essential was to "dispose of all such accounts and claims" and get "that whole business . . . closed up."[23] On October 24, Richard, Gordon, Melvin, and W.D. met in Marshfield to discuss their petition to the federal court for turning back management of the R. Connor Company to the family. The important meetings took place while William was traveling. Helen was also away; after attending a Cause and Cure of War meeting in Madison, she visited Maybel Pick in West Bend and Connor and Barbara in Chicago. She could not this time be accused of conspiring against William.

It took W.D. another ten pages to explain to his namesake why the meetings, of "extreme importance" to the family, were held in his absence. Nothing was being done behind anyone's back. He had commissioned the Chicago accountants, Gore and Company, to go over the Connor Lumber and Land Company books and "prepare a firm, direct statement," because Mr. Clark of the RFC wanted the report.[24] William didn't believe it. In directing Gore and

Company to go over the Connor Lumber and Land Company books, his father had violated his authority as manager. Not only that, the report gave W.D. precisely the ammunition he needed to yet again criticize William's pet project: the furniture department. When it confirmed what W.D. had insisted on from the beginning, that the department was a drain on the other divisions, W.D. fired off the letter that, while disclaiming any wish to persecute his son, may well have been the trigger that set William careening off, at last, from his obligations to the Connor Lumber and Land Company, from Laona, and, perhaps, most of all, from his father.

The furniture department was the only department losing money in "these money-making times." Furniture was always a losing proposition, had been for Fish at Elcho, then Joannes of Green Bay, who also tried for three years to get out until a fire let them out. "However, that is all past history." W.D. gave William credit for working hard and doing "everything possible" to make the department go but undercut the crumb of praise by turning the dagger of wit into his vulnerable hide: "Personally I am not prejudiced against the furniture business. I have had wide experience in selling furniture factories in all the places where furniture is made, for fifty years, ninety percent of them have gone the same route—Rockford, Fond du Lac, Oshkosh, Sheboygan."[25]

In November 1941, William Duncan Connor Jr. accepted a position with the Federal Office of Production Management in Washington, D.C., as "Principal Industrialist Specialist" in charge of the lumber section of the Building and Lumber Material Division of the Civilian Supply Division. In the larger world, he hoped to find the ego satisfaction nobody granted him in Wisconsin. The position with the government suited his deep sense of patriotism as well as his need for recognition and independence. When William took a leave of absence from the Connor Lumber and Land Company "for the duration of the emergency," when he locked his desk, took the key, and closed up his affairs in Laona, he anticipated having a position to come back to. Perhaps, by then, his father would have given up instructing him.

Two weeks later the Japanese attacked Pearl Harbor.

Censorship and the mobilization of the nation's entire resources to the war effort began. Civilian Conservation Corps camps closed in Forest County; 62,000 national guardsmen from Illinois, Michigan, Wisconsin, Indiana, Kentucky, and West Virginia trained in base camps in Wisconsin; the *Forest Republican* began publishing international as well as local news; Governor Heil outlined civilian defense methods in a radio address; Brigadier General Ralph M. Immell became director of military and police activities under the governor's industrial antisabotage program; Herman Kronschnabl became a representative to the Wisconsin Committee on nondefense public spending; Richard became manager of the Laona Division of the Connor Lumber and Land Company and a member of the Forest County Council of Defense. Connor telephoned, asking Melvin for a copy of his birth certificate and diploma. It seemed inevitable that the draft would get him before many weeks passed, and the wise thing to do was to get a commission before that happened. Twenty physicians on the Marshfield Clinic staff also immediately volunteered for service.

The Lairds threw a holiday dancing party at St. Albans Guild Hall on December 27, a sudden inspiration to celebrate while the boys were home. David and Dick memorialized the night in a poem.

> T'was two nights after Xmas
> And all through Lairds' shack
> All creatures were stirring
> Especially out back
> Where the boys and the girls
> Were grabbing a snack
> And washing it down with straight Cognac.
> The bottles set down on the table with care
> In hopes the Senator wouldn't see them there. . . .
>
> T'was two nights after Xmas, And really a toot
> 'Till in walked the Cops who knew our repute.
> We saw the old man when things got rough,
> He said we'd sure have to cut out that stuff.
> And anyway boys, it's getting late.
> He looked at his watch, it was half past eight.
> Never again will we have such a ball
> So dash away, dash away, dash away all.

In the living room of the Epstein home where the tree alight with real candles symbolized for them all the peace that eluded mankind, the Lairds saw the new year in, talking quietly of the year past and the one that was coming. No one in the deeply reflective little party saw anything to cheer about in the thought that the war might "mark America's real coming of age as economic headquarters of the planet. Enormous technological advances, secrets until war's end, would inevitably flow from the war."[26] Those who had witnessed the First World War knew what else would inevitably flow. Still, the money was coming in. Construction in Marshfield topped $485,000.

William wrote Helen, "The company was never in better shape than when he left for Washington, D.C."[27] W.D. wrote, "William left us a nightmare in furniture and a labor mess."[28] He had had to hurry up to Laona to help prepare the company's case to take to the hearing that Secretary of Labor "Mme. Perkins" had called for in Washington, D.C. to defend against the CIO's claim that the company had violated federal law. W.D. had given the company lawyers the Communist literature Matt Savola, the CIO labor leader, had been spreading[29] and they were taking "that Paull book" along. The book included not only the two essays, "A Baby Born in a Sausage Truck" and "Justice in Connor's Kingdom," which Irene Paull ("Calamity Jane") wrote in 1937 at the time of the violent labor upheaval in the lumber camps and mills in Michigan, Minnesota, and Wisconsin, but new essays alleging that World War II was a class war. "Calamity Jane" incited the people of the world, including Americans, to unite against their rulers.[30] The Connors would show what those CIO fellows were really up to.

To counter the atmosphere of disillusion and cynicism, and unite a fractious nation, Roosevelt declared an "I am an American" day on March 14 and delivered a Fireside Chat on April 28: "This great war effort must be carried through to its victorious conclusion by the indomitable will and determination of the people. . . . It shall not be imperiled by the handful of noisy traitors—betrayers of America and Christianity itself."[31] Melvin told members of Marshfield's Professional Woman's Club to lobby for democracy. "With conscientious voters—people who studied, discussed and choose intelligently—good men and women in office would result, and democracy would take care of itself."[32]

During the early months of the war, unemployment remained a problem in central Wisconsin. Melvin, aware that the University of Wisconsin College of Agriculture had begun training women for farm work, asked W.D. if it might be feasible to give women work in the woods. W.D. didn't believe "the women out in those CCC Camps could do very much toward preventing fires or cleaning up getting ready to plant trees. Of course, there may be desirable. It would keep them off the streets in the city."[33]

During the interim legislative year, usually Melvin rose at six and walked to Central Avenue to have a cup of coffee at Trudeau's or the Coffee Cup and talk with "the regulars," who came there to visit, to express their opinions, to seek his. Afterwards he would walk over to the R. Connor Company office, work an hour or two, and then, at about nine o'clock, walk home for breakfast and a visit with Helen before going back to the office to pick up his correspondence as well as his work for the company and for the people of the city, county, and state. Unless a business or political meeting took him to Wausau, the Point, the Rapids, or one of the numerous smaller towns and villages in the district, he joined Helen and David for lunch. (There was no school cafeteria at Purdy Junior High). After lunch, while David walked back to school, Helen, having cleared the table, retreated to her second-floor bed/sitting room, and Melvin stretched out on the davenport, turned on the old Grunow, and dozed a while before slipping out to the office again.

As W.D. lingered in Laona preparing the company's case to present in Washington, D.C., Helen and Melvin worried about his not getting out of the winter climate. Yet, for the first time in years, he hadn't had his annual winter "lay off." He seemed to thrive, not having to expend energy fighting William, who apparently was having, as he wrote Helen, a "thrilling experience" in his new job. The Lairds felt for Richard, who had begun to feel some of the pressures William had rebelled against with W.D. breathing down his neck.

More things united the couple now that three of the children were grown and they had a shared history of almost thirty years. While Melvin would never lose his sense of being one of the world's obligated elect, and Helen would always remain a questing, idealistic realist, they shared a passionate commitment to family and America. Whenever Melvin could, he paid his 20 cents and joined Helen at the Wednesday-evening current affairs forums at Purdy auditorium.[34] Forum leader Leonard Haas predicted that the story of science would be "as enthralling and interesting in the next five years as any blood tingling account imaginable."[35]

Women marched forward, as they always did when the men were away, gaining increasing respect for themselves, taking all sorts of jobs they had never had before. Helen wrote Dean Witter, somewhat regretfully, that her job was probably to stay home, and the patronizing phrase "even women," which had pursued her all her life, continued to do so. "Even women" were told they played a part in the defense program "as the new interest in dietetics and nutrition revealed the importance of their jobs at kitchen sink and stove to the nation's welfare."[36] Aunt Betty confirmed Helen's membership in the "even women" brigade and consoled her for the personal sacrifices she made in being there. She wrote her "high brow niece" of "thinking gratefully and thankfully, oft times *tearfully* of how you have 'stood by' your father thru the hard years of your mother's illness and since she has gone. What would he do without you?"

Helen, however, continued to stretch the "even women" bars. After attending her thirtieth class reunion and the baccalaureate ceremonies in Madison, inspired by the address the Chinese ambassador to the United States, Dr. Hu Shish, made, she immediately turned journalist. Harold Quirt published her article covering the speech without a by-line, assuming that, "as usual," she preferred to remain anonymous. She quoted Hu Shish, saying, the "kind of peace that will follow the war will depend entirely upon the vision, the wisdom and the efforts which leaders of nations can apply to the task of making the peace and (equally important) the intelligent support which the leaders will receive from their peoples." "Students of history," Helen wrote, should find particularly significant his statement that they had "a better chance to win a just and effective peace this time than in Wilson's time," because this time there were "no secret treaties of intrigue and division of spoils." In 1919, "the transition from an imperialistic to an international outlook was too sudden."

Connor received orders to report to the Treasure Island Naval Base, and he and Barbara moved to San Francisco. When Dick, shortly afterwards, was ordered to report to the Bremerton Navy Yard in Seattle, Helen traveled west with him. She saw him settled in Bremerton and then traveled further down the coast to visit Connor and Barbara, who had moved into a small apartment on Telegraph Hill while Connor took courses in navigation, seamanship, ordinance and gunnery, naval administration, and communications on Treasure Island. Dean Witter, who received a commission as a colonel of ordnance in the army, true to his word, gave Helen, who, in his mind, would "always be a young lady of about twenty," a "hearty welcome."

Melvin, having received W.D.'s okay to "take the day off," taking David and Bom along, joined Helen in Denver for a few days' holiday at Troutdale in the Pines. He needed a respite from business—and politics. A holdover senator, he was not, as he suggested to J. Peters, "sitting in an easy chair and watching you men fight" but was listening to the concerns and complaints of constituents and getting up to speed on measures affecting the lumber industry and on farm problems caused by increased demands for high protein and high vitamin foods and on shortages of labor, machinery, equipment, nitrogen fertilizers, silage preservatives, and insecticides.

Dick's wedding plans materialized suddenly, as wedding plans invariably do as wars begin. On August 1 in Seattle, he married Patricia Burke, a Green Bay girl. Dean's daughter, Ann, a Vassar graduate, married a navy man, Lieutenant Edmond Stephen Gillette Jr., in a September wedding at Grace Chapel, San Francisco. Connor, who represented the family at Dick's small wedding, participated in Ann's grand wedding as well. He and Barbara, "an extremely popular couple," had "a very gay time, being wined and dined by the elite of San Francisco society." In spite of the champagne, music, and laughter, Connor experienced "terrible doubts" after turning down the chance of going to school in Newport, Rhode Island,[37] where Ritchie Modrall and Walter Kohler Jr. were headed.

Dick slid into a "quite definite spot" as a shipping clerk at the Bremerton Yard, but uncertainty hovered over Connor's life even after he completed (in the top 10 percent of his class) the eight-week program on Treasure Island. He thought he would probably eventually "be placed on a boat, sent some place for more training, or given some sort of a land job until enough boats become available."

Though a bad year for the parents of sons of draft age, 1942 was a proud year for W.D., who had emerged from defeat and pulled his family through—again. Melvin informed Dun and Bradstreet, Inc., in Green Bay that "the plan of re-organization of the R. Connor Company will put the former management and the former Board of Directors in charge of the business of the R. Connor Company. . . . Mr. W.D. Connor Sr. will be President and I will be the Secretary." The National Labor Board, on appeal, sided with the Connors on major issues. The pressure for hardwoods escalated, along with the inflation,[38] and the Connors owned the large tracts of timber that would keep their mills going for a long time. As happened periodically throughout his life after great exertion, W.D. suffered from migraines and from asthma. He needed to take it a little easier.

Helen wanted to do more. She accepted Mayor Leonhard's appointment to fill a vacancy on the Marshfield school board, visited classes, and littered her desk with magazine and newspaper articles relating to foreign policy and world government and with notes and drafts for speeches, fastening pages together with straight pins.[39]

"Those of you historically minded," she told her DAR friends, "have seen the set of volumes at the library entitled *The Chronicles of America 1920–1925*." She recommended another set of books: The *Pageant of America*, fifteen volumes published at intervals beginning in 1927, particularly Volume 6, which was based on the winning of freedom, and Volume 8, *Builders of the Republic*. She remembered an idealized American history the way W.D. recalled leaders who had risen against the odds from humble beginnings, individuals like himself. Helen emphasized character and leadership: "Washington: daring and brilliance at Trenton Princeton campaigns; character of leadership shown at Valley Forge; perfectly conceived and executed plan that led to Yorktown. . . . Metal from which our country is forged." Thoughts of the country's past, philosophical speculations, and current events ran through her mind, spilling out over innumerable scrawled pages and scraps of paper tucked in books and magazines. The "challenge of the persistent residue of evil in the world," coupled with the individual's "inner yearning towards the fascinating goal of perfection," was a "mind cracking problem." She urged the church to move "away from Sunday into politics" and fixed on Wendell Willkie, champion of civil liberties and an internationalist, as a leader.[40] A "new world order" would require work to achieve. It wasn't possible to "*drift* into anything desirable as enduring peace."

Following the November elections, Melvin was on the inside track planning the leadership and the agenda for the 1943 senate term,[41] which would be Republican dominated, although, to Melvin's surprise, Governor Heil had been defeated[42] by a young Progressive, Orland Loomis. He put politics aside, however, when Connor called to say he had received a temporary assignment on a minesweeper, a little 135-foot tug, "the roughest riding baby in the world," and would be based at Coos Bay, Oregon, for at least two weeks. He and Barbara, Dick and Pat would be able to celebrate Thanksgiving with their parents if they could come. In the letters he wrote Helen two or three times a week, Connor had dropped the "Dear Mother," for "Dearest Mommy." The Lairds would not miss the opportunity of a reunion.

Senator and Mrs. Melvin R. Laird, Victoria, British Columbia, November 1943.

Dick Laird, 1943. He served as a shipping clerk at the Bremerton Navy Yard during World War II.

Stories of lost boys were coming in. Margaret Schorger's son, serving in the ambulance corps in Tunisia, had felt "the wind from the grave" blow over him when a bomb dropped thirty feet from him demolishing his ambulance. He lived "in luck." Sad news came from Melvin's sister Grace, however, whose son was missing in action, and from Dean, whose twenty-four year-old nephew, Ensign Jean Carter Witter, a lieutenant junior grade who had married ten days before shipping out as a navigation officer on a cruiser, was reported killed. Across the envelope bearing that news, Helen scrawled: "A Modern Drama. 6 months. June wedding—father—gleam in eye, prosperous San Francisco."[43]

Bom came home from Carleton for the Christmas holidays. Other children did not come home because of the gas shortage or crowded trains and buses, or, because like Connor and Dick, they were in the service or, because like Leander Merkel, Reuben Steger, Caral Cherney, George Bores, former members of Company C of the Wisconsin National Guard, they had been killed in Papua, New Guinea, and would never come home again.

Neighbors watched as Bert the barber came to W.D.'s house each morning at 10:00 A.M., a sign that Mr. Connor was not well enough to walk the three blocks to Central Avenue for his morning shave. Helen came over two or three times a day to check on him and read to him as he recuperated from yet another severe bronchial attack and admitted to feeling "discouraged and disappointed." She herself needed help to get through the anxiety-ridden days when Melvin was in Madison four days out of seven and she was alone with time and duty, dependent on "capsules" to see her through. She wrote asking Dr. Dishong for a refill unless "one of the new drugs" might be better. He sent the old ones, along with word that he was helping with the examinations at the induction station at Fort Crook, "some days as high as three or even four hundred of these fine young fellows from the Midwest. All are eager to get in and do their bit."[44]

Even with bad news from Europe, a crisis in the Bethlehem steel mills, W.D.'s illness, and her concern about Connor, who was frustrated by on-again-off-again orders and his sense that chasing non-existent Japanese submarines in arctic waters might not be useful, exacerbated by Wisconsin's sunless, frigid winter days, which depressed her, she strove to overcome her darkening mood. "As program chairman," she wrote members of the Wisconsin Council on World Affairs, "I can only say what we hoped to emphasize and clarify. What was actually accomplished remains to be seen. In the first place there was the idea of the greater interdependence of nations in a new smaller shrunken world.

Air travel knows no continents or oceans. We are all part of the sphere. There is no denying that this is a tough war or that what may follow it can be tougher still."[45] She received Bom's dirty laundry in the mail and shipped his clean laundry back, as mothers with boys and girls in college did in those days. She wrote Connor the newsy letters he asked for, reporting "Wisconsin's political story with all the side lights."

"The Chief," who set off on Monday mornings in a car pool with Assemblyman W. W. Clark, a slight, rather prissy older gentleman, and Assemblyman Walter Cook, a large, flamboyant young man, was "not in the driver's seat," where Connor had him. He didn't become lieutenant governor as Connor thought he might when Walter Goodland, the octogenarian who had been elected to the office, became acting governor after Governor-elect Orland Loomis unexpectedly died before taking office. But Melvin was elected chairman of the Agricultural and Labor Committee and made a member of the Legislative Procedure Committee, and he was glad to be back among his good friends in the senate: Frank Panzer, William Freehoff, Jess Miller (older men also born on farms in the nineteenth century), Robert Robinson, and Gustave W. Buchen, whose long public service as schoolteachers, businessmen, aldermen, and community activists paralleled his own. He admired the young holdover senators—John Byrnes, the bright orator from Green Bay, and handsome Warren Knowles—and welcomed Arthur A. Lenroot Jr., the newly elected assemblyman from Superior, whose father's political career had intertwined with W.D.'s at the beginning of the century.

Acting-Governor Goodland's refusal to meet with the Senate Republican Steering Committee prior to delivering his message to the legislature struck Melvin as unfortunate, an indication that he intended to steer his own course. Goodland's choice of secretary, moreover, James J. Kerwin, a Milwaukee executive and attorney, and the man responsible for Goodland's run for lieutenant governor on both the Republican and Democratic "coalition ticket" in 1938, was a suspect Republican. Running as a Democrat, he was defeated in the 1942 congressional primary. His association with Goodland made Republicans wary. Representing largely rural districts, the senators were determined to check the power of the Milwaukee block and to adhere to Republican principles of keeping as much local control as possible. From the clippings and the news Helen sent, Connor could tell that the "Chief" was enjoying himself.

From Helen's letters he also knew something of the goings-on in the Wisconsin state legislature. The first senate bill of the new session rescinded a bill Robert La Follette Sr. sponsored in 1905 banning women from working as legislative employees.[46]

In the almost daily letters Connor wrote Helen, he kept his news positive. As commissary officer, he had ordered plenty of provisions, winter clothing, slickers, sheepskin, even fishing tackle. His crew was "a prize one." The engineering force could keep them going "under any circumstances"; two of the deck force had "spent most their lives in the Arctic," and the fourth officer was "a darn little nice guy from North Carolina." Only the captain, a Swede, was a "_____ _____*!?!!," but the navy had "incredibly enough" and finally caught up with him and relieved him of command. "How and why it finally came to pass is a mystery. . . . I'm sure if he had simply been a murderer, arsonist, saboteur, it would never have happened." That the hated Swede was gone, that Barbara and he had met some congenial people, that they had been comfortably at home in Marshfield, Oregon, outside Coos Bay, for a week, that the Pacific had been "pacifica" made it seem that everything was going well. Ironically, it was then, when he felt supremely at ease and reported "bountiful blessings," which made it seem that "everything this pen wants to write is tinged with a golden halo," that he went out, the ship capsized in heavy seas and he was lost in the dark.[47]

Melvin was at a senate meeting when Helen called at 4:00 P.M., Monday, February 22, with "bad news of Connor." He took the 5:00 P.M. train home. For two days they hoped he might be alive, but with the passing hours hope died. Word spread. The radio beamed the message and newspapers reported the tragedy of the navy minesweeper that capsized a quarter of a mile from the harbor entrance at Coos Bay, with the loss of five dead and thirteen missing. Hundreds of letters of condolences poured in from relatives, friends, former classmates, strangers. Believers wrote of their prayers that the Lairds might "be sustained in faith and in the realization that unless fine young men are willing to pay the full price to preserve freedom, we, all of us, and many generations to come would find living a terrible experience."[48] Expressions of sympathy were linked with words encouraging the Lairds to feel proud—proud that Connor was an exceptional boy, proud of his valor and courage, proud of his love for freedom and his devotion to duty.

W.D. wrote from Phoenix, "You could not have shaped things different if you tried." His "continual thought and wish was to hurry home. That is what I should have done. . . . Keep well. Keep your courage. . . . I hope I am going to get some better here, but up to now, I have been rather discouraged." Dean Witter took four pages to express his sorrow. Connor was "such a grand boy, so eager for active duty. . . . It always seems that the very best have to go. That makes the whole thing worse, not only for us, but for the world."

Connor Laird, 1943. After completing courses at Treasure Island Naval Base, San Francisco, he received temporary orders to serve aboard a minesweeper, searching for Japanese submarines off the northwest Pacific coast.

The director of admissions at the University of Chicago wrote that "thousands of students have passed through this office. I easily put Connor Laird in the top one hundred. I not only admired him, I loved him."

Bom wrote that Connor had been "so loved by us all." Dick wanted to do or say something that would make his mother's sadness easier to bear, but then a "wonderful letter" came from her, and it made him realize that her "thoughts and attitude couldn't be helped by anything he might add. You helped us, and I am sure that you will help each other." Most people thought her "so courageous," never speaking of her tribulations, but Elsbeth Epstein saw that she often felt "so deeply alone," and Melvin admitted to his brother Clement that she "found it hard to carry on."

March was a cruel month, frozen and gray, a month of death and whipping blizzards. Richard wrote of 30-below-zero temperatures in Laona; Gordon wrote of "real winter" in Michigan; fawns died in record numbers in Wisconsin, hogs in Illinois. Connor's death remained the open wound through the long and difficult winter and into the spring. The navy was slow in replying to requests for information, in confirming the death; Connor's body was not shipped to the Albinson Mortuary in Minneapolis until the end of March; the cremated body in the plain urn Melvin ordered was not shipped on the morning Soo to the Merkel and Ritger Funeral Home in Marshfield until May 22; and the plot at Hillside Cemetery was not prepared, with six cedars chosen to mark the site not in the ground, and the long, unadorned rose marble stone bearing the simple inscription "Ensign Connor Laird, 1913–1943" was not engraved or Connor's remains interred, until all the lawns in Marshfield were green again.

The return of warmth to the earth, the return of the pointy-headed, red-feathered cardinals to Cherry Street, did not lift Helen's spirits. Melvin encouraged her trips to Madison. She listened intently to Edwin Kennedy's sermons at Christ Presbyterian Church and Richard Hulbert's at the First Congregational Church and wrote letters afterwards probing both men, hoping for a way out of her pain. Dr. Kennedy, appreciating "the appalling sense of emptiness that sweeps over one at times," thought Helen was doing "wonderfully well to keep going at all." Dr. Hulbert wanted her to understand "that all that we have is *given* and if it is given it can be taken away. Money, food, clothes, property, wife, children—all these are but a trust. Whether we admit it or not, we are God's."

Helen dragged herself into life, tended to duties, remembered birthdays, kept up her correspondence with family members, canceled the annual meeting in Madison of the Wisconsin Council of World Affairs. Melvin was undoubtedly behind her appointment to the board of the Wisconsin War Fund, a newly formed organization created for the purpose of ensuring a "broader standard of giving" throughout the state. She was one of only two women on the board.[49] Family members tried to help with newsy, positive letters. Bom wrote of the army moving into Carleton in "full force," the more than 100 uniforms on the dance floor at the ladies' invitational, the Naval Reserve that would remain in school until July. William, revealing his endless capacity and need for self-promotion, wrote of having received his commission as lieutenant commander and his assignment to the General Inspector of Naval Aircraft, who put him in charge of an aircraft company with plants in Baltimore and in the south, a company that had not delivered on its contract for wood airplanes and was in a "bad mess." He had been chosen for the job, the general inspector told him, "because I had the reputation of being an expert organizer and millwork man. I felt like saying Captain, I have been called a specialist (who is nothing but a fool away from home) and a prophet (without honor in his home-land) and many other names, but never an expert." He had been "in the "Mars"—the world's largest airplane, capable of carrying cargo of 60,000 pounds 3,500 miles. "It is twice as large as the China Clippers." Constie wrote of packing up, taking her family to Texas to be with Ritchie while he trained in the naval reserve. W.D. wrote of "getting along without such awful coughing" and "sleeping good nights," of the crowds, of having urged Constie hard as he could to come to the old home with the children.

Much as he wanted to, however, he could not arrange his youngest daughter's life as he had arranged Helen's a generation earlier. Constie was determined not to follow her sister's example and return to the old home as Helen had done during the First War. It was not as it had been. Neither was W.D., nor Marshfield, nor anything else.

Richard's wife, Florence Brown, whose daughter Jean had taken "French leave" from Carleton to take a job as an apprentice chemist in the Squibb plant in New Brunswick, New Jersey, producing the vaccines the military needed in the exotic places they were fighting, thought Helen should follow her daughter's example, take "French leave" from her duties, come to the lake, which was at its most beautiful in the pre-summer season, and help plant the garden and open with her a private canning factory, provided, of course, they could "find some strong woman that knows her way around a stove."

Helen did not go to Laona. She remained home entertaining thoughts she could not prevent from crowding in. Among the hundreds of messages of condolences she received, only Gordon's wife, Mary Roddis Connor, touched the troubling truth. "Lairdie" was their "favorite person," his death "a bitter loss." From "Barbara's earlier accounts of Lairdie's trips and his recent letter, I had been appalled that so small a boat should be used by the Navy in such pounding weather, and it was a horrible and needless ending."

When Claude M. Fuess, headmaster at Phillips Academy, wrote that he had received word that Connor, "one of the outstanding boys at Andover in the Class of 1932, [whose] record of accomplishment probably surpasses that of any other undergraduate of his generation," had lost his life in an accident off Coos Bay, Oregon, and requested that Helen send some of the details,[50] Helen replied in pain and rage, attacking the clichés by which almost everyone had hurried to console her. She felt no pride, took no comfort in the thought his "sacrifice" had been an important contribution. Her son's death had been neither noble nor necessary. Human stupidity had made a mockery of all her care to raise a grand American boy. She named his virtues and railed at his needless end. The navy should have done better by her son.

If clichés irritated her, in the true poet she heard the perfect pitch that soothed her. She copied out Matthew Arnold's "Sohrab and Rustum" in the scrapbook she kept detailing Connor's life.

> For we are all like swimmers in the Sea
> Poised on the top of a huge wave of Fate
> Which hangs uncertain to which side to fall
> And whether it will heave us up to land
> Or whether it will roll us out to sea
> Back out to sea, to the deep waves of death
> We know not, and no search will make us know
> Only the event will teach us in its hour.

Melvin's almost illegible handwriting in his brief diary entries—"at office," "at home"—in the days immediately following his son's death strengthened as the days passed. He had work to do: company income tax reports to prepare for the accountants; caucuses and senate sessions to attend; an important meeting with a few select Republican senators, assemblymen, and nonelected power brokers with the governor and his staff to try to work out some cooperative plan on the legislative program and appointments procedures.[51] A scheduled speaker at the Midwestern Council of State Governments, to which Committee on Interstate Cooperation Governor Heil had appointed him in 1941, he left for Chicago on April 2, as did Senators Knowles and Fellenz, Acting-Governor Goodland, and Secretary of State Zimmerman.

The midwestern states' delegates agreed on the important postwar tasks: to

convert industries to peacetime production, to absorb into a peacetime economy those currently employed in the war industries and the services, to locate
and plan transcontinental highways. Some delegates argued that state treasuries should actively be building surpluses. Melvin argued the Republican point
of view: if you "want industry to build a program to meet postwar conditions,"
you "cannot bleed industry white in taxes." He was "utterly opposed" to building up "great surpluses in state treasuries."[52]

On their return to Madison, Melvin and his colleagues discovered that
Zimmerman had quietly left the meeting on April 3, returned to Madison, and
assumed the mantle of acting governor. In that capacity, he authorized the
purchase of a new automobile for the secretary of state—himself!—and also,
according to rumors circulating in the senate when it reconvened on April 6,
requested that all bills awaiting the governor's action be brought to him for
disposition, calling for a locksmith to unlock the executive vault in which
they were locked. He was particularly interested in obtaining Bill 56S, the
integrated bar bill, and Bill 58S, relating to the closing hours of taverns in
certain counties.

Laird, Byrnes, Knowles, and Fellenz, joined by two-term senators Republican Frank Panzer and Democrat Anthony Gawronski, drew up a resolution
that they presented to the senate on April 8. It demanded answers to questions regarding Zimmerman's trip to Chicago and his actions on his return to
Madison and requested that Goodland "countermand the approved authoriza-
tion for the purchase of a certain automobile for the Secretary of State signed
by the Secretary of State as Acting Governor during the temporary absence of
Governor Goodland."[53] The resolution passed the senate unanimously, and
Goodland countermanded Zimmerman's order.

Cashman, an old war horse in the senate with whom Melvin had clashed,
proclaimed the interrogation a "foolish act" inspired by "the younger members." Zimmerman, claiming separation of powers, refused to answer the
questions. The six senators responsible for the resolution, including Melvin
Laird, who at the age of sixty-five was not really a "younger" member, released
a letter to the press stating that "all members of the State Government, whether
in legislative or executive capacity, are morally bound to answer to the public
at large for acts which they perform during their stewardship." Because Zimmerman refused to furnish the information requested, they had to assume he
had "no proper explanation or answer to the questions propounded."

Zimmerman's actions had far-reaching consequences: legislators passed a
joint resolution relieving the secretary of state of the duty of acting as state
auditor and authorized the legislature to provide by law for the auditing of

state accounts; a bill, sponsored by Assemblyman Schmitz, which Byrnes steered through the senate, required a special election to fill the governor's office if the office should be vacant before the next general election (its primary function was to prevent Zimmerman from becoming governor in the event of the octogenarian Goodland's death);[54] and the legislature established an interim budget committee to investigate and report on the state budget system. Melvin was elected chairman of the bipartisan and bicameral committee.[55] John Wyngaard, Wisconsin's most influential journalist, claimed the need for reform was great but cautioned that entrenched bureaucratic interests would not take kindly to removal of budget idiosyncrasies and anachronisms.[56]

Republicans could look on achievements: they had passed a bill mandating that the state welfare director pass a Civil Service Examination and giving full Civil Service protection to all division heads serving under him. It meant, to the great satisfaction of Wisconsin's club women, who had gone on record opposing Frank Klode, that his days were numbered.[57] They overrode the governor's veto of the Laird-Downing Bill, which called for a repeal of the 60-percent surtax on individual incomes, a Depression carry-over measure, by a vote of 25 to 8 and passed an integrated bar bill, over violent opposition by a handful of attorneys and Progressives.[58] Melvin steered bills through the senate controlling Bang's disease in cattle and cornborers in corn and promised to reintroduce his failed lime bill in the next session. He and his friends increased funding to technical schools, clarified the duty of chairmen of county boards and the manner in which county boards issued bonds, and revoked the power of the superintendent of public instruction to initiate consolidation proceedings merging school districts without prior review by a committee of county boards.

Melvin developed a reputation as a hard worker. His accounts of the politics in Madison enlivened W.D.'s old age and helped Helen. Four months after the death of her oldest, she gave little outward evidence of having suffered the loss, although it lodged in her heart like a stone. When Bom began his navy career in the V-12 program at St. Mary's College, Winona, Minnesota, his parents hoped, "in view of his expressed preference for service in the Supply Corps," he might "be sent to some school of business."[59]

Grateful that Dick's duty kept him ashore, Helen sent him copies of Willkie's *One World* and Lippmann's *Foreign Policy.* In his subtly critical thank-you letter, Dick pointed out that she knew what a slow reader he was. "It's a wonder I get by at all as actually I must be pretty dumb. Persistence, I guess, is my only redeeming feature. But I will get to *Foreign Policy* yet." He wanted her to know that, albeit being a "slow reader," the captain had praised him in front of all the officers. "It has had a very good effect upon my morale to get a word of appreciation."

Two scrapbooks from the period—one all about Connor, and the other all about national and world affairs—reveal Helen's emotional and intellectual divide. She organized the list of books in the library's Victory Book Club; sent letters to members of the Wisconsin Council on World Affairs, indicating her support of the newly formed Women's Action Committee for Victory and a Lasting Peace; and read about and engaged with Melvin in the national debate over whether the United States should form an alliance with Britain after the war.

Winston Churchill advocated such an alliance with all his formidable rhetoric, claiming for the nations "common heritage," shared beliefs in "impartial justice" and "personal freedom." He preached "the doctrine of the fraternal association . . . not for any purpose of gaining indigenous material advantages for either of them, nor for territorial aggrandizement or the vain pomp or earthly domination, but for the sake of service to mankind and for the honor that comes to those who faithfully serve great causes." The rhetoric didn't convince W.D., other leading Republicans, or journalists. Alf Landon said, "By making an alliance, however temporary, with one country, America abandons her traditional impartial role of peacemaker"; Raymond Moley thought advocates of an alliance with Great Britain distorted history; Senator Robert A. Taft opposed the idea of an "international super-state"; Senator Arthur Vandenberg urged Congress to assume its constitutional authority over the administration's postwar planning and not permit "so difficult an issue" to be determined through an executive agreement[60]; Henry J. Taylor worried about the arrogance of American theoreticians "distributing promises everywhere" while its own cities were "in the most deplorable condition in their history."[61] The infamous lynchings in the south and race riots in the north were violations of the American promise of the equality of man.

W.D. looked at the future from a capitalist adventurer's perspective. Assuming his "voice of experience" role, he predicted that after the war the government would be owing billions of dollars. As had been the case in the past, it would have to pay off in cheap dollars. All commodities, timberlands, farm lands, everything "held in a strangle will blow." Any company or individual who wanted "to be happy" when those days came should get into debt now. Disregarding rumors that efforts were being made to develop a national park in the Porcupines, he bought heavily in the area.

Acquiring more land put him in good spirits, as did the publicity regarding Melvin's achievements in the political arena. John Wyngaard wrote a highly flattering syndicated article at the conclusion of the 1943 legislative session: "Political Reporter Sees Marshfield Senator as Gubernatorial Timber." In Wyngaard's opinion, Melvin R. Laird was "one of the members of the upper house . . . who has made a strong impression by reason of his earnestness, capacity for work and study, and temperament, and a man who has won the universal respect of his colleagues." He should not be overlooked as a gubernatorial candidate. "Never a narrow partisan, and yet a man who has effectively represented the Republican point of view in legislative activities this year," Melvin's rural birth, extensive education, rich background of professional work, his broad and thoughtful interest in public affairs, and, his most distinguishing characteristic, his "quiet dignity . . . ought to put him in the forefront of any list of potential candidates for the governorship."

"Good Republicans" wanted to replace Goodland not only because of his advanced age but because of his advisers. Following his appointment of James Kerwin, a "suspect" Republican as attorney general in Milwaukee, he named Roy L. Brecke (a twelve-year executive secretary of the Wisconsin Petroleum Association) as his personal secretary and Frank N. Graass his financial secretary. Republican legislators were no fonder of Brecke and Graass than they had been of Kerwin, and Goodland was not fond of the Republicans who gave him a lot of trouble and not enough respect.[62] (They overrode twenty-four of the thirty-six bills he vetoed.) Melvin, of all the names in circulation to replace Goodland, was "the candidate most likely to receive the nomination and election." He would also be "an ideal candidate for U.S. Senator"[63] should he prefer that post.

Melvin had no intention of leaving Wisconsin for Washington, D.C. As for throwing his hat in the governor's race, "As I see the picture, Goodland will be a candidate for Governor in the Republican primary. Frank Graass and others have had this in mind since they first came into the Governor's office as advisors. With six or more candidates in the field, Goodland would win the nomination."

Writing Helen from Victoria, where he had gone to "settle some things definitely" as soon as he felt well enough, W.D. dwelt on the past. His old room at the Empress, overlooking the gardens, seemed "quite familiar." The gardens had always given him "great pleasure," although "some of the most trying times in all my business and financial career were put in here about. There were times when it seemed almost cruel, when some of my own family were telling me, insisting I must come away—try and forget *the effort I had made, the money I had put in*—you can't hold on and recover—what has gone over the Dam—

the whole situation is against you—you are down and cannot get up. No one can realize the lonesome hours, the headaches, the heart aches—that in some way I cannot keep from sweeping over me today. I am, never was, any wizard of finance. That always seemed secondary to me. If I controlled the timber— the thought always was—I cannot lose out in the struggle. The only thing that saved me here—I knew the timber—in the great forests I was among friends— the others did not."[64]

He was sorry he had not pressed Helen harder to make the trip and "continually felt" he should have. "I wish you were here. Come on out. David can surely live at my house for a month. . . . Week from Sunday we could spend here, you, Richard, Patricia, myself. We could be visiting. I could be planning." He needed her; he expected Melvin to take care of himself, expected her to take care of him, and if she would not come, he expected her to take care of the youngsters,[65] to see that they were "always at Home on our own grounds as it begins to get dark, see that Elizabeth keeps up with her music and William his arithmetic."

David's sixteenth birthday, Helen noted in her diary, passed "without fuss," a sign that the house revolved more around mourning and duty than celebration, although the war news from the European theater, with Italy's surrender, was good, as was the news that Bom would be going to Wellesley for further training to become an officer in the Supply Corps.

There was "not much interest in politics," Melvin wrote Leo Miller, although he and his Republican friends were disturbed that the governor made appointments without consulting the wishes "particularly [of] the Senators on whom he must depend for confirmation of his appointments."[66] Interest suddenly quickened when Goodland published a financial report highly critical of the "youthful leadership" in the 1943 legislature.

The governor charged lawmakers with bowing to the whims of lobbyists, placing their personal welfare before that of the state, and squandering the state's money. The *Wisconsin State Journal* published the "good Republicans'" answer: "Goodland Charge Insult, Byrnes, Thomson Agree." "Both houses barred lobbyists from their chambers early in the session, but the executive who declares lobbyists are a menace still harbors two of the most clever lobbyists [Roy L. Brecke and Frank Graass] that the state has seen in years in his office as secretaries." Published "without authority" as an "official state publication," the financial report was "purely a political campaign booklet of the acting governor published exclusively for his own individual purpose at state expense."[67]

Melvin hoped the gates could be kept closed on new bills when they met on January 12, unless they clearly arose out of the war emergency. Otherwise, he wrote John Byrnes, they would be faced "with a flock of new bills" and "be in session two or three months." If that "unfortunate situation" should arise, "great harm" would be done to the Republican Party. At present, the farm bloc was favorable to them, and they would have its support in the coming election if they could avoid any discussion of the oleomargarine tax. "Perhaps my fears are not well founded. I have often boasted that I am a politician. The above expressed opinions will doubtless prove the contrary. At least I have a sincere interest and a deep love for the old Republican Party."

From Tucson, W.D. followed the proceedings of the Michigan Conservation Commission, which, having failed in its efforts in Congress to develop a national park in the Porcupines, was pursuing plans for a state park. The proposal involved taking 8,000 acres into which the Connors had already built roads and bridges and in which they were rapidly cutting. In letter after letter he offered Melvin and the lawyers advice. His "first thought" was that they had to get the case into federal court. The company could not expect a sympathetic jury in Gogebic County, or in the state of Michigan, where the entire population had been "systematically preached to" through the press and the politicians in favor of "the large park proposition." The head-waters of the Presque Isle River originated in Wisconsin. If there was any question over power rights, it was a question for the Interior Department.[68]

They could not have avoided the Lansing case, he reassured Helen, deflecting criticism for once again involving the family in a long, public, time-, and energy-consuming struggle, which added to Melvin's already overburdened schedule. He asked her again to join him, this time in Arizona and with David. They could fix up a place to stay where she would be "quite comfortable." It was "not easy [for him] to spend *so much of the days* in idleness."

The Connors had cut 798 acres within the Porcupine Mountain Park boundaries when Michigan's conservation commissioner, P. J. Hoffmaster, ordered them to halt. Condemnation proceedings began in Gogebic County Circuit Court, and W.D. began working out the figure Michigan would have to pay for taking the property. "It should add something to our values, the fact that they are undertaking these condemnation proceedings in the year when there is a favorable market for the products."

It had long since ceased to be essential for W.D. to make the news, but with a magnifying glass to assist his failing eyes, he read the fulsome letters Helen sent and copies of the *Marshfield Herald* and the *Forest Republican*. Helen reassured him that the children were well and reported on deaths of friends and neighbors, David's lead in the drama class play, the first prize he took in the extemporaneous speaking contest, Bom's passing his exams at the naval school, Dick's promotion to the rank of lieutenant, junior grade, his expectation of soon becoming a father, Kenneth Hoerl's return from the Pacific and his unwillingness to talk about his experience, Angie's enlistment in the Army Medical Corps, Florence and her friend Ruby Winch's opening a second-hand dress store above Wing's drugstore.

Melvin's news enlivened W.D.'s days on his return to Marshfield. During the interim session, the "good" Republicans had passed a bill requiring the immediate construction of new hospitals and improvement of the state's seven mental hospitals and tuberculosis sanitarium;[69] they succeeded in avoiding taking up the controversial issue of the oleomargarine tax, put a drag on Acting Governor Goodland by leaking the news of a ground swell to make Oscar Rennebohm the gubernatorial candidate, and exposed a serious misuse of public funds. Spending money secretly, without legislative approval, without records, without hearings, the State Emergency Board granted $30,000 to erect and furnish a home for the state prison warden and $4,000 to furnish the home of the president of Platteville State Teachers College, a neighbor in Grant County of Senator Lewis and Assemblyman McIntyre, who had two out of the three votes on the board.

W.D. thought the Republicans had done well and that Roosevelt, with his "New Bill of Rights," had probably done the nation harm. Promising what government could do would end by creating cynics, not believers. Besides, it did little good. "The selfish agitation" abroad in the land had not ceased after Roosevelt delivered his famous "rights" speech. Workers all over the country went on striking in spite of the call to patriotism and the promises. Public service workers, coal miners, electrical workers all struck. The strike by the electrical workers shut down 84 aircraft plants, 38 navy plants, 14 army service plants, and the army, which had earlier moved in to run the coal mines, had to move in again.

Helen did not discuss her work for the Council on Foreign Relations or the fact that she had joined the NAACP Legal Defense and Educational Fund after reading Walter White's and Thurgood Marshall's analysis of the Detroit race riots during which thirty-four Detroiters had been killed. When the Federation, acknowledging that women lived in a changing world, sponsored an essay contest asking women to say how the club would change in the postwar years, she didn't mention the fact or bother to provide an essay. Her energies turned elsewhere. Having enjoyed a term on the school board as the mayor's appointee, she was running for the office.

When "Cousin" George W. Mead, president of Consolidated Water Power and Paper Company, a would-be Willkie delegate, hosted a reception and put Willkie up overnight in his spacious brick home on an island in the middle of the Wisconsin River, Helen and Melvin, among those moderate Republicans who admired his "practical social vision and his fine conception of world wide humanitarianism,"[70] went to hear him. Vernon Thomson, another would-be Willkie delegate, gave a radio speech: "Willkie for President." W.D. predicted a Dewey victory because the liberal-moderate wing of the party was divided. Harold Stassen, the three-time governor of Minnesota and a lieutenant commander in the navy, while not actively seeking the nomination, said he would accept the nomination should he get it. His supporters held a major rallying dinner for him at the Wausau Hotel while Willkie stumped the neighboring towns.

Helen was elected to the school board, but George Mead, Vernon Thomson, and Wilbur Renk failed in their bids to become Willkie delegates. Wyngaard's claim that he was "cordially disliked and distrusted by Wisconsin liberals and Wisconsin conservatives" and "had scarcely any support within the stalwart and dominant Republican party machine"[71] surprised the Lairds and his other backers in Wood County.

"Very encouraging" radio and newspaper reports, along with the fear that these very positive reports could change, provided the background to the meeting of the Council on Foreign Relations Helen called to order at the Memorial Union in Madison. Operation Overload, the Normandy "invasion" or "liberation," had begun. The women divided on the course they wished the council to take. Some wished to merge with the Women's Action Committee for Victory and Lasting Peace, a politically active offshoot of the Cause and Cure organization; others felt very strongly that women's groups should educate and influence public opinion and not work in support of any definite legislation.

In the letter Helen sent to the membership afterwards, she summarized points on which they agreed: the council would continue its work "at least through the coming crucial year." It would make every effort to get out helpful information and suggestions, especially in the educational area. She asked members to contact the various education groups in their cities so that they could plan workshops and discussions groups to promote the necessity of full participation by the United States in an international organization to keep the peace. She urged members to study the Roosevelt proposal for a World Council, an organization strongly advocated by Sumner Welles, as soon as it was made public. She quoted Dr. Henry Sloane Coffin, whose words, she thought, "will be of interest to Church women. 'Had the Church succeeded in placing all nations on the heart of her people, we should never have been bedeviled by the hideous pagan isolationism.'"[72]

Melvin R. Laird Jr., "Bom," 1944. The dispersing officer in charge of money and stores aboard the destroyer USS *Maddox*, he saw action in the Pacific.

Helen saw W.D. through the crisis of another attack of pneumonia before leaving for Boston with Melvin and David. The *Maddox*, to which Bom had been assigned as disbursing officer in charge of money and stores, was about to disembark.

Bom took them through the newly completed destroyer, narrow as a cigar, and introduced them to the officers and the crew. The family had dinner the last night at the Copley Plaza, everyone's feelings heightened by the place and the reason for being there, everyone attentive to the news from Europe where the fighting in Warsaw was intense and the invasion armies were pushing inland and Patton's army was nearing Paris. Overjoyed at the promise of an ending to the European war, they were aware that Angie, from her vantage point in New Guinea, thought the Pacific war might go on until 1949, and the Pacific was where the *Maddox* was almost certainly heading.

W.D. headed for Laona as soon as he was strong enough to travel. No small child stood by his knee to distract him or to be entertained with the bear stories that had enthralled every one of his children and grandchildren at one time or another over the course of his long life. Yet, it was the year of the bear in Forest County, where one animal or another seems to come to prominence each summer. Some summers it's the skunk. Skunks will be found everywhere, under cabins, walking down paths. Dogs—and their owners—have a terrible time that year. Another time, it will be the year of the beaver. Then the lumberjacks have competition and streams and outlets get blocked and men are kept busy undoing their competitors' work. The year of the porcupine alerts both cabin owners and dogs. Only the Indians know how to use the porcupines, fashioning their quills into baskets and their bodies into food. Whites worry about damage to cabins and just shoot and bury the animals.

For one reason or another, 1944 was the year of the bear. Story after story appeared in the *Forest Republican* in W.D.'s last summer establishing the animal's dominance in the north. "Louis Grubb, who lives near Newald shot a 400 pound black bear in his pig pen on his farm." "On Monday night Warden Ernest Meress of Laona and District Attorney Allan Stranz went over to Blackwell to try and help Frank Gentz shoot a bear that had been raiding his bee hives." "A bear carried off one of Mr. Ritter's sheep and now Mrs. Ritter has an orphaned lamb to feed with a bottle." "Francis Marshall's sheep dog got his leg caught in a bear trap and broke it. The dog couldn't watch the sheep and the bear stole two more. Marshall is having a bad time." "C.K. Warbriton killed a 582 pound bear about 9:15 Saturday evening at the Cliff Murray farm. . . . The bear had been after the sheep, and in the past few weeks had killed 20." "Lewis Rasmussen, resort owner at Butternut, Franklin Lakes, shot a 500 pound bear last week at his resort. The bear had been raiding the resort garbage cans with regularity, and finally tried to get in the kitchen."

In the forests and across the seas, death reaped a plentiful harvest. Bear killed sheep; trains killed cattle that wandered down embankments and couldn't climb out; humans killed humans. Private Donald Pitts was killed in France, Grant Witt in New Guinea, aerial gunner Forest Shorey in Italy, Captain Edward McAllen in Germany, Richard Marvin in Holland. Mrs. Frank Bradle, a Laona pioneer and resident for forty-five years, born in Irensten, Germany, the mother of ten, died in Laona of natural causes. Lumberman John Jorgeson, a supervisor of timber crews, was run over by a Soo Line freight train. His death was judged a suicide, one of the county's long list; he heard the train but did not get out of the way. When the engine ran him down, it severed his body in two places. "A search of the man's clothing revealed a few papers, probably of little importance, and about two dollars in cash."[73]

Secretary of Agriculture Claude R. Wickard arrived in Forest County during his swing through the Midwest. His presence generated hope that timber from the Nicolet forest might become a steady source for permanent logging operations in the area and a source of employment for returning veterans.[74] Laona ranger Louis Tausch Jr. further encouraged the belief that the county would not become another American wasteland. While the "pressing need of lumber for war had stepped up the cut of timber in the forest beyond all expectations," a careful check of previous estimates of potential timber indicated the estimates were low. By cutting selectively and filling in with what the Nicolet forest offered, the mills could prolong their runs. The Connor Company, and the Cleerman-Jauquet Lumber Company in Newald, provided the best examples of selective logging.

Praise for the Connors in the *Forest Republican* couldn't have come at a better time as far as the old warrior was concerned. Once the arch enemy of the "Crandon gang," he had lived to see his Laona mill honored as "one of the largest hardwood sawmills in the world," running twenty-four hours a day and able to run indefinitely into the future with selectively cut timber.

News from Michigan was less favorable. The jury award of $211,646 for the Connor tract of 4,754 acres of virgin hardwoods, the key tract in the "Yellowstone of the Middle West," was not only far below the $1,200,000–$5,000,000 the Connors publicly demanded, but below the $600,000 W.D. was willing to settle for. The company asked that the jury's decision be set aside on the grounds that the sum was insufficient.

W.D.'s mind remained sharp. He was feeling "quite well. Had some cold for few days. I try to be careful—but seems to come on so easily. But I am very

W.D. Connor at Birch Lake, 1944, shortly before his death: "I have tried to take the load, the knocks, and keep going."

fortunate," he wrote Helen from Laona.[75] He thought about the international situation, hoping the allies would "refuse to negotiate with the Japs until they turn over everything they got in the way of war material and turn over all the properties that they have taken from the weaker peoples during the last 35 or 40 years." They had not recolonized but, putting their own people in charge, had taken control of the banks, the transportation systems, "every source of income in the territories." They "reap the benefits from the labor of all the people that they enslaved." There should be "no compromise—no let up on them until they turn back everything that they have taken from other nations or the smaller peoples in the Pacific and, of course, turn over all those islands that the Versailles Treaty authorized them to mandate."

On October 19, the eighty-year-old lumberman arrived in Albuquerque to help his ailing thirty-six-year-old daughter, who had begged him to come. Migraines, a battle with breast cancer, young children to care for alone, a husband in the Pacific to worry about——Constie's nerves were shattered. But the year, the trip, and life had worn down W.D. as well. When he got off the train, he had to sit down on his suitcase and wait for breath. On October 20, from his room at the Hilton Hotel, he wrote his "Dear Dear Children," William and Elizabeth, assuring them of his love. He had taken a little cold in the cars, he wrote Helen, and had to keep as quiet as possible, couldn't say just what his plans would be for the next few days. He knew he wasn't writing as often as he should, was uncertain as to how long he would stay, and hoped, but doubted, he could get Constie to return with him. The weather had not been best for him. He had a lounge car, a seat reserved on the 30th, that he hoped to change for a berth or roomette. The traffic going east was very heavy. "I will make it out some way."

He did not "make it out." His "little cold" developed into something more serious. He needed the old home more, perhaps, than the doctors realized. They gave Constie the assurances she wanted to hear, that it was better for him not to attempt to travel back to the Midwest but to remain in the Southwest, not in Albuquerque where the altitude aggravated his heart condition and his asthma but in Phoenix, where he would have a better chance of surviving the winter. In Phoenix Constie's health improved and W.D. became her patient.

His affairs were in order; his children held all the stocks in the companies he developed—all but his single qualifying share in each. He had deeded to Helen as a memorial the lot on the eastern shore of Birch Lake that Connor had hoped to buy on the installment plan and the lot on the hill at the northeast corner of Marshfield where she and Melvin hoped to build a new home. With the exception of his old home in Marshfield and the old cottage at the lake, the real property was in corporate name; he had no significant outstanding personal debts. His will provided that his estate be bequeathed to his children "share and share alike, the share of any deceased child to go to the heirs of his or her body per stirpes, and in the absence of any such heirs, to be divided equally between my surviving children." He named his three sons executors and hoped his grandchildren would all "keep acquainted and know each other—and all. All the time look after each other." He wanted the family to think that he had "tried to do what seemed best for all of them," had "never put [his] own personal interests first" but "tried to take the load—the knocks, and keep going."

Yanks raced for the Siegfried line; Marshfield merchants, anticipating the end of the war in Europe, prematurely agreed on a V-Day closing; Melvin was reelected to the senate; the papers were full of the strange names of places— the Bonins, the Volcanos, Celibes, Davao, Chichi, Jimi, Haka Jima, Iwo Jima; Nimitz's Pacific fleet was bombarding; and W.D. lay dying in Arizona. While Melvin, one of Wisconsin's twelve electors, concentrated on preparations for the coming legislative session,[76] Helen followed her father's uncertain dance toward death. He seemed better, then worse. Constance wired Gordon, hoping he would come. When W.D. understood that he would never make it back to the "old Home," politics and the Porcupines dissolved unfixed as clouds, but the children remained. "What will happen to the children?" Constance heard him repeat over and over, until she promised to look after them. On November 15, she wired Helen: "Father comfortable, but no better. I am getting along alright." Gordon had not come.

Conversation over Sunday-night supper at the Laird home on November 19 was subdued, weighted with thoughts of W.D. dying far from home. He died the next day. William was with him at the end. "You've come a long way," W.D. said, acknowledging his presence. William traveled with the body by train to Chicago, where Gordon and Richard waited to continue the trip together to Marshfield. Funeral services were held on Saturday, November 26, at the old Connor home. The *Herald* published the account under a headline: "Body of Pioneer Lumberman is laid to rest in Mausoleum Here."

The Northern Hemlock and Hardwood Manufacturers Association, in commemoration of their "respect and esteem" for W.D.'s "determined and aggressive character," inscribed a memorial in their records and sent a copy to the family.

W.D. Connor has been described as the last of his generation, one of those bold and stalwart pioneers who carved out a career in a new country. During his lifetime he saw and took part in the transition of Wisconsin from a primitive community to one of modern and cultural achievement.

Unlike many of his contemporaries who cut their timber holdings and moved on to other fields, Mr. Connor extended his roots into the soil of the North and made his welfare coincide with the opportunities it offered, leaving an ample heritage to be carried on by his family.

The examples of the past must guide the pattern of the future and we have much to learn from such a long and vigorous life, fraught with such varied experience.[77]

Following the funeral and Helen's very nice luncheon, the men got down to business. They elected Richard president of the Connor Lumber and Land Company and Melvin president of the Canadian Puget Sound Timber and Lumber Company. Richard hoped "the family, including you girls and us boys will be able to keep close enough at least in our thoughts and deeds to successfully carry the responsibilities that have come our way. I can say that there is no doubt in my mind that you [Helen] will do more than you should do to help!"[78]

Richard was "not unmindful of the many things" she had "done there these past years to help in the difficult situations that have come to us." The ideal solution for him, however, as far as the children Elizabeth and William Rhyner were concerned, until legal issues had been settled permitting their removal from the state and Ritchie Modrall gave his approval to taking them, was for Helen to make another sacrifice and move into the old home with David when Melvin assumed his legislative duties in Madison.[79]

From New Guinea, Angie wrote Helen *not* to consider moving across the street. "David needs his own home!" Aunt Betty, recognizing her niece's struggle with her conscience, urged her "to make haste slowly for so often problems will solve themselves if we give them just plain time." Fanny Cole Purdy, who had married late and had no children, was surprised and critical because Helen did not immediately volunteer to adopt her niece and nephew.

Helen willed herself not to anguish about unsettling problems. She wanted to shuck the past, rebelled against the idea of further selflessness, perhaps for years, just as her duty to her youngest would be discharged. There was Melvin to think of as well, ten years older than she. They both looked forward to a new life, a new house, away from the old neighborhood, obligations, heartaches, and burdensome memories.

She buried herself in her correspondence, writing endless thank-you letters to the many who sent condolences as word of W.D.'s death spread across the country and warm, encouraging letters to family members in the war, and letters to members of the board of the Council on World Affairs, reminding them that they had voted to cooperate with the Women's Action Committee for Victory and Lasting Peace.

As the newly elected president of the Canadian Puget Sound Timber and Lumber Company (CPS), preparing to leave for British Columbia to analyze the situation there, Melvin cleared his desk of political business, heavy now in anticipation of the coming session. Goodland would again be governor, and Oscar Rennebohm would be lieutenant governor and, sooner or later, was bound to replace the octogenarian. Melvin wrote Henry Baldwin, pleased to learn that Baldwin was taking on the job of strengthening the Wood County Republican organization and that the churches in the southern part of Wood County had joined the United Church Canvass movement sponsored by most of the Protestant churches on a national basis.[80] (Promoting Christian values and supporting racial equality, the movement was anathema to extreme conservatives, who considered it outrageously liberal.)

Melvin had not felt "a welcome visitor" when he attended the governor's budget meeting, as the governor did not invite him to take any part in the hearing. He regretted missing the State Welfare Department's Advisory Committee meeting on December 8 but planned to be back by December 18 when the electors met in Madison. He wrote his good friend Senator William A. Freehoff asking him "to discuss with Jess Miller the question of the organization of the State Senate."

Freehoff thought Melvin should not feel too badly about missing a meeting. "The day was a goldfish bowl, everybody was underfoot; the result is several got into the meeting who didn't belong." He suggested Melvin check with Jess Miller, "the shrewdest trader in the Senate and probably knows the boys better than we do" as to who should meet to determine committee chairmanships. Freehoff suggested Robinson, Buchen, Laird, McNeight, Miller, Hipke, Downing, and Freehoff for another meeting, asking Melvin to check the list with Miller. Several blocs were in the making. The "conniving" was "distasteful" to Freehoff, and it was only because he did "not want important committees to fall into incompetent hands" that he was "willing to discuss the matter at all. It is easy to throw harmony out of the window. The three men who will be picked on the committee on committees will have their work cut out. Heaven help them if they are thin skinned or spineless, or both."[81]

The Lairds received V-mail Christmas letters from Bom, Angie, and Barbara Vail Laird, who after Connor's death had taken a job with William Donovan's Organization of Strategic Services, the precursor to the CIA. Bom's letter came from "somewhere in the Pacific,"[82] Angie's from New Guinea, Barbara's from Egypt. Bom "looked forward to "Christmas '45 when the M.R. Laird Jr's will gather around your household for a good old Christmas." It would be up to all of them out there to see that the spirit of Christmas "Peace on Earth, Good Will Toward Men" remained in effect after the war. Angie wished Dave could drop over for a chat and looked forward to sitting by the Laird fireplace and talking about what she had seen, except by the time she came back she was sure none of them would want to talk about it. She worried more about the heat than the bullets and looked forward to spending a month at the Laird cottage and feeling the breezes blow. Barbara was having a "marvelous experience," had no feeling of homesickness and didn't expect to have any. "There are so many new things to do and so many new people to know that there hasn't been an opportunity to think too longingly of home."

The Woman's Club took up the question "How much international order can we achieve?" against the backdrop of bleak world news: Yanks fighting Japanese on Leyte Island and the "Blitzkrieg" in the Ardennes, where twenty-five divisions of three German armies pushed the Allies back fifteen miles in their advance. In the Pacific, the Allies hoped against hope that the European war would soon be over and that they would receive the reinforcements they desperately needed.

It was hard for Americans to celebrate a Prince of Peace that dark December when the *Herald*'s list of sons killed and missing was long and the list of children home from school for the holidays included only daughters and the news predicted a long war and horrible carnage and temperatures of 18 below zero. It was a suitable conclusion to a year that began with killing frosts. But there was good news too. Pat was expecting, and, after "five months of combat at the very front," Kathryn and William's son Billie was in a rest hospital in England—"apparently with no serious injury."

The Lairds were with the Epsteins on December 26. Like figures in a Chagall painting, the Epsteins lofted over their dismal experience as Polish and German Jews, and together the friends listened rapt to Elsbeth's favorite, "Die Meistersinger," and watched the real candles slowly burn on their tree decorated with real apples. Afterwards, Melvin took Helen to Chicago to see *Oklahoma*. He had already seen the musical but would see it again with Helen. She needed a break from her duties and all her sad concerns.

# CHAPTER 17

෮

# Another Ending, Another Beginning

## 1945–1946

A Knyght ther was, and that a worthy man,
That fro the tyme that he first bigan
To riden out, he loved chivalrie,
Trouthe and honour, fredom and curteisie . . .
And though that he were worthy, he was wys,
And of his port as meeke as is a mayde.
He nevere yet no vileynye ne sayde
In al his lyfe, unto no maner wight.
He was a verray parfit, gentil knyght.

—CHAUCER

As its first order of business on January 10, the state senate passed a resolution naming Jess Miller, Warren Knowles, and Melvin R. Laird to the three-member Special Committee on Committees. Melvin was elected chairman, and the powerful committee went about its business of assigning seats, rooms, and committees. Melvin became chairman of the Agriculture and Labor Committee, Gustave Buchen the Judiciary, Jess Miller the Highway, William Freehoff the Education, and Robert Robinson the Welfare. Important committees were in the hands of trusted colleagues and friends.

Melvin did well by his largely rural constituency. He succeeded in holding the 15-cent tax on oleomargarine against pressure from Milwaukee manufacturers and passed numerous bills helpful to the state's agricultural and cattle industries, including the important lime bill, a bill improving the animal species of donkeys and horses,[1] and a bill relating to bovine tuberculosis.[2] Working closely with Dean Kivlen of the University of Wisconsin's College of Agriculture, he secured a $100,000 grant for the college to study Bang's disease in cattle, from which he hoped some "splendid results."[3] Believing in miracles—and in science—he suggested that with the "great interest in the science and

Senator Melvin R. Laird Sr., ca. 1945: "I have always had a deep love for the Republican party."

the art of breeding," the university establish a corporation, without capital stock and with Kivlen as chairman, whose exclusive mission would be educational: to improve the breeding of livestock. Melvin had another ally in Edwin B. Fred, the former dean of the College of Agriculture and now president of the university.

The trio of senior "young Republicans," Laird, Miller, and Robinson, and the youthful "young Republicans" pushed through an astonishing number of progressive, socially responsible measures. They passed a controversial anti-gambling bill; Jess Miller's highway segregation bill; Robert Robinson's expanded welfare bill[4]; a resolution outlawing discrimination based on race, sex, or age in hiring[5]; and left a few measures hanging. In spite of pressure from conservationists for a selective cutting bill regulating the cutting of timber on state and private lands, no conservation measure got out of committee. Yielding legislators appointed a committee to "study the need for regulation" during the interim session and to work with the Board of Health in studying the causes of pollution of Wisconsin lakes and streams.[6] The legislators' major achievement, perhaps, was to reform the state budget system.

The budget bureau was divorced from the governor's office and established as a separate department more directly accountable to the legislature. The reform, long sought by taxpayers' groups confused by conflicting financial reports issued by the governor's office, state treasurer, and secretary of state, provided that in the future the budget director would publish a concise statement of the condition of the general treasury by the first of October and, during the first week of the legislative session, would furnish lawmakers with a "progress report" on the treasury. The new state budget bureau would also make annual audits of all state departments, something that had not been done before. A "hold-over" senator, Melvin again became chairman of the Interim Committee on the State Budget and chairman of the Interim Joint Legislative Committee. He also became chairman of the committee to plan for Wisconsin's centennial celebration.[7]

From Helen's detailed, almost daily letters, Bom thought his father must be having some fun in Madison. He was, although dealing with Goodland had been frustrating. "As you know," Melvin wrote Henry Baldwin, who was disappointed because the legislature had not been able to override the governor's veto of a summer camp for the state's National Guard, they had had "difficulties with the old Governor. He is very obstinate and very difficult to deal with at times." Reporters played up the hostile relationship between the governor and the legislators, pointing out that Goodland never entertained Republicans at dinner in the mansion. Wyngaard predicted that the antagonism between the executive and the legislative branches, if it continued, would inevitably become so violent as to mean permanent harm to the Republican Party.

The rivalry and antagonism between the governor and the legislators was not as intense as the rivalry and antagonism among the Connor brothers. Trouble began at the first directors' meeting of the new year. William rejected Gordon and Richard's proposals to limit dividends to 2 percent ("just a sop") and objected to their desire to spend the cash the war boom generated on purchasing additional timberland in Michigan. Gordon "blew his top" when William announced that he wanted his old job back in Laona after the war. "Gordon," William wrote Helen, accused him "of everything except rape and murder." Helen tried to smooth troubled waters, but William would have none of it. William wanted "to see peace in the family—but not at the price of letting G.R. and R.M. do as they please." He told Helen that his brothers had no business to take a "holier than thou" attitude; they had no right to threaten to sell Laona unless the rest of the family went along with their plans or to say "Constie should be satisfied with what she has—because she didn't pay for her stock anyway." She paid just as much as they did for the same stockholders' rights." He would not put his "head in the sand or be pushed around."[8]

"I note what you say about the all encircling personality and business head of the family," Angie wrote Helen from New Guinea. It would be "shameful" for another family feud to develop. The one between her father, Rob, and W.D. never did anyone any good. Helen would be "the one to steady the boys" and see that they were fair with one another. "I am like you—I know nothing about business and we must trust to the men to solve those problems."[9]

Melvin's vote to limit purchases to a single section in Michigan, as well as his refusal to go along with Gordon's proposals (made in private later) to grant more authority to Richard and limit William's authority,[10] probably cost him. The senator seemed, Gordon wrote Richard after the trip he made to British Columbia with Melvin to size up the CPS situation, more interested in what was going on in Madison and willing to postpone dealing with problems out West until the session concluded. "Perhaps business affairs can be carried on in that way, but I am doubtful as to whether I want to be associated with such a setup." One of the most important things in Gordon's mind was "for us to get in the balance of the outstanding preferred [CPS] stock" to put them in a position to sell the company. If in order to get it done, he had to do it himself, he doubted if he "would be in favor of splitting it all up in Connor Brothers to these other individuals who are so busy with other affairs that they cannot participate in the efforts of getting this stock bought."[11]

Gordon was forty years old and eager to pursue his ambitions for the company's future. Melvin was sixty-seven. He had worked tirelessly for the company for twenty years, but he was a humanist constitutionally unable to make business the center of his life.

Helen, the woman between, the peace-maker, seems not to have considered the possibility of a connection between her family disputes and the larger wars raging on the European Continent and in the Pacific. European cities lay in rubble, but the heavy losses in the Ardennes made it seem that victory over Hitler as well as victory in the Pacific lay well into the future. Preparing for that future remained her mission.

During the winter and spring of 1945, while Melvin was occupied with state and Connor business, she worked to arouse the public on the necessity of American participation in a world organization. History taught, she believed, that if future wars were to be avoided, Americans could not stand aside, as they had after the First War when they did not join the League of Nations or the World Court. Without a world organization, World War III could not be avoided. With the rapidity of scientific developments, we might then anticipate "generals sitting in caverns underground, pressing colored buttons to release thousands of tons of explosives thousands of miles away—robot bombs and bitter super fortresses until territory will be no defense in air raids."[12]

In 20-degrees-below-zero weather she drove to Stevens Point to deliver a "Town Meeting of the Air" address over the radio station WFHR. "'What Should Be America's War and Peace Aims' was delivered before the Big Three meeting at Yalta as preparations began for an Allied conference in San Francisco," she noted on the copy she kept and initialed. The homemaker, living in a small town in central Wisconsin, supposedly far from the centers of power, was convinced that what she said counted, and the radio gave her the biggest platform of her life.

She thought it "significant" that the subject of the speech should be addressed more than three years after America had entered the war—significant both because of the time element and because "most people decide on their aims before they go to work and not years afterwards." She listed several aims: "to defend America by keeping war as far away from her shores as possible"; to "so crush the dominant military power of Germany and Japan that it shall not rise again to threaten the peace of the world"; "to "see to it that peace shall be based on a Democratic pattern and not on a totalitarian. . . . Great masses of people are fighting against the idea of racial superiority and discrimination"; and finally, to "prevent World War III." To that end, it was "imperative" to convince people that there was no alternative to international co-operation.

The United States had "to assume spiritual as well as political leadership in the world. . . . Let us pursue the Christian principles of justice, mercy, and understanding."

In Madison, on February 1, the Council on Foreign Relations voted to continue, temporarily at least, as a branch of the Women's Action Committee for Victory and Lasting Peace. Chairing the meeting, Helen reiterated her conviction: "This may be our last chance. If the peace to come should fail, there may be no next time. The V3s, V4s, and V5s of the next war could annihilate civilization."[13] She hammered home her message again as the date for the conference to consider the Dumbarton Oaks proposals for a permanent organization to maintain peace approached, writing members that the United States was "no longer on the sidelines giving advice." America was an actual participant in world affairs, "not only in world war, but in the most gigantic effort in history toward world peace. We can't afford to side-step this second chance—the alternative is another world war."[14] She wrote personal letters to the U.S. delegates to the conference expressing the interest of the council in their deliberations and votes. Following Willkie's death from a coronary thrombosis in October 1944, she placed her hopes for an enlightened national leader in Harold Stassen, another "one worlder" and a delegate to the San Francisco conference.

When she received a letter from the commander of the Naval Reserve stating that Bom had been wounded in the service of his country,[15] her concern about him overwhelmed her concern about the world. She hoped he would ask for a leave—others had—but he had gotten "pretty well seasoned" and rejected the idea. He made little of the experience that put him on a hospital ship for two weeks, but he confided to his cousin Jean that he had been in the wardroom with nine other men when the Kamikaze attacked, and he was the only man to survive.

The *Herald* published the numbers of the battle casualties in the Pacific, horrible by themselves—averaging 20,000 a week—but even more horrible when the names, the stories, the pictures of the young men all looking so shining and strong in their military uniforms were published too, day after day, week after week in a war that broke American records for length. The high losses on Iwo Jima suffered by U.S. Marines, confronting the strongly resisting Japanese determined to hold that little island 750 miles from Tokyo, could only be justified, Harold Quirt editorialized, if the island held great strategic value.

In March, the *Maddox* put to sea in company with the Fast Carrier Task Force 58.1 headed for Japanese waters.

Our carrier planes lashed the island of Kyushu, and on the following day, more of the same treatment was given to the "home" islands of Shikoku and southern Honshu. On the 23rd, 24th, and 25th of March, the attacks were shifted to Okinawa Gunto. Our aircraft, battleships, cruisers, and destroyers bombed, strafed and bombarded enemy installations in the softening up operations in order that our landings might be successfully accomplished with a minimum of casualties. On the 27th and again on the 31st we participated in the final strikes in preparation for the Marine-Army amphibious assault on Okinawa Gunto. . . . Hostile aircraft made determined attacks on our formation on the 18th, 19th, 20th, 21st and 27th of March, but our operations were not hampered.[16]

Helen did not have the *Maddox* historian's accounts that Dick was privy to. The *Herald*'s accounts of the American advance to the Okinawa chain of islands and the extraordinarily fierce fighting by Japanese suicide troops were enough to make worry fasten on her like a leech.

Angie's letters contributed to her sharp sense of the war's reality in human not numerical terms. "Heine you could not believe all that goes on in this war unless you saw some of it. . . . It would seem that the family is really suffering—but all families are and some day we will talk it over." Angie thought often of David, in his last year of high school; she knew he chafed to get into the war, and she hoped he would not. And she thought of her mother. Florence talked about Helen in every letter she wrote, "and hence, now I, like the rest of the family know that you are seeing Mom gets what she needs while I gad about like a fool, avoiding responsibility."

Captain Angie Connor avoiding responsibility? She saw it that way. She sent Helen—who had once encouraged her to pursue her writing interests by going to the Bread Loaf summer school where Bernard DeVoto taught—verbal "snapshots" of her patients: the handsome boy who was amused because he had picked up a book about the French revolution to read in the hospital; the older Italian who regretted that he was a bachelor and believed his bowels stopped because he was lonely; the tall Australian with a high fever and yellow eyes who apologized for being "so much trouble to you Yankees"; the "bored colored soldier from Georgia" who would probably go back to "hominy grits and dirt and poverty, gallery seats, and divided street cars"; and Wung, "the China-man," who coughed and hawked up blood and, with his hands crossed on his chest, died "a dignified death without emotion as his ancestors, when old, had philosophically died for generations."

At a special assembly at the senior high school on May 8, V.E. Day, David delivered a salute to the United Nations flag. Later, Helen, David, and Melvin huddled around the radio, not to listen to President Roosevelt, who had succumbed to a massive cerebral hemorrhage on April 12, but to listen as Truman and Churchill addressed the world. The war in Europe was over. All efforts focused on ending the war in the Pacific.

The raising of the American flag on Iwo Jima, a powerful symbol of the fight for ideals, inspired David's valedictory graduation speech. The "dark days" would remain with them, but the young had "a heritage of courage" and were prepared to take on the "tasks of tomorrow": finishing the war, rehabilitating Europe, healing the wounded, feeding the starving, restoring governments, securing a "just and lasting peace." Howard Quirt, editor of the *Marshfield News Herald,* published the idealistic speech[17] along with the dispiriting news that an essential flaw had been uncovered in the organization of the new League of Nations.

Americans were told to "dump overboard any illusions [they] might have that the new league [would be] a cure-all for world trouble." Each of the five great powers in the Security Council (the British, Russians, Chinese, French, and Americans) had a veto power over action taken by the others. Contrary to the will of the four other powers, the French, in what was termed a "prelude to World War III," were fighting in Syria, their former colony. (The British sent troops in to protect the French from Bedouin attacks, fearing that the French war against Arabs in Syria might throw a united Arab world into war, distracting from the allied efforts against Japan, where the really violent loss and gain game raged.)[18]

Good news came on June 21 and June 22: after 82 days of fighting, the Okinawa campaign was over; a strategic base 325 miles from Japan had been established; the 32nd Division of the National Guard of World War I fame had won a final battle on Luzon—and a letter came from Bom. "The old *Maddox* is a red hot ship, and will ride this war out in fine shape." Bom's description of a "red hot" ship was apt (the week before, the *Maddox* had survived the coordinated attack of four Japanese planes that launched two torpedoes and a bomb); his belief that the *Maddox* would "ride this war out in fine shape" was hopeful. The belief that America would also "ride out this war in fine shape" also seemed hopeful, as strikes interfered with the war effort and demonstrated a nation not entirely united by a fervent patriotism.

A call from the admission's officer at Billington Hospital sent Helen hurrying down to Chicago, where David, having passed the navy's Eddy test but failed the physical, had begun studying for a B.A. under Hutchins's accelerated integrated program. After enduring excruciating stomach pains through a symphony concert at Ravinnia Park, he had walked over to the hospital and was immediately admitted. Helen brought him back to Wisconsin, where he slowly recuperated.

Unanimously elected chairman of the Marshfield School Board in July, Helen looked her age and more than a little severe in the family picture taken at the lake. Melvin stood in the last row, tall enough that his uncovered head rises over the others, his hair receding and gray. No year for a very long time had been without strain, but 1945 was a year of rather exceptional strain as well as accomplishment. He had always borne his many heavy and varied responsibilities uncomplainingly. He had had a fair amount of physical discomfort, intestinal pain, that year as well, sharp enough at times to make him pace restlessly at night, and perhaps that is what showed in his face. A return visit to Rochester had been in order for some time. Flanking the senator in the photograph were the Connor brothers, William, Richard, and Gordon, who again had quarreled. After the board meeting of the Connor Lumber and Land Company, both William and Gordon tendered their resignations. Neither the presence at the lake of wives and children or the participation in picnics and shared memories of early years and early events prevented the brothers from upsetting the family carriage in which they all traveled. The volatile family mended its fences, however, and both brothers withdrew their resignations within a month.

On July 22, in "one of the most daring feats of the war," the *Maddox* steamed into the outer portion of Tokyo Bay within "spittin'" distance of shore batteries on three sides, airfields, minefields, and surface vessels. The *Maddox* and eight other destroyers sank two ships, probably sank another, and damaged a fourth before withdrawing without suffering any casualties, either material or personnel. "Within thirty minutes, the engagement was over and the Nip had done nothing except fire a few ineffectual rounds at nothing in particular."[19]

Helen read the gripping UP account of the night strike inside Tokyo Bay in the *Forest Republican*[20] on July 26. On August 6, she read that America had loosed the atomic bomb on Hiroshima, the "most destructive force in the history of the world." On August 9, the U.S. dropped another bomb on Nagasaki. On August 10, the Japanese asked for an end to the war. While other people danced in the streets on V.J. Day, she clipped editorials and studied sermons in an attempt to understand the atom's implication for peace. She believed Norman Cousins was right. The development of the atom clarified, as nothing else did, the victory of science over morals.[21]

Helen celebrated September 1, a beautiful day at Birch Lake, by writing to Bom, who had "been most satisfying always, as a babe and as a grown-up." She meant it when she said she needed him. "You always give me a lift in spirit and it's fun to be with you and Barbara. It would be grand if you decide to live near us."

September 2 was another beautiful day at the lake. The family enjoyed leisurely round-robin tennis, rotating in adults and children, the skilled and the less skilled. The spectators lounged in Connor chairs talking in low voices, commenting on form, noting the occasional cheater calling an in ball out. Afterwards Gordon invited them all over to the island to enjoy brats and fresh corn. The war was over at long last, and, for the moment, at least, company business was moving along in a satisfactory manner. William agreed to locate in Marshfield, largely because Kathryn was not well and was anxious to be in the larger city. Gordon prided himself on securing CPS stock certificates in Michigan and acknowledged Melvin's hard work in accumulating shares from shareholders in other parts of the country at most attractive rates.[22]

Bom was in Tokyo Bay on September 2, where it was gray and overcast. The *Maddox* was part of the escort group for the nine submarines involved in the official surrender ceremonies. Admiral Charles Donald Brown, a graduate of Annapolis, whose beard turned white overnight after his first sighting of a Japanese submarine, was in command of one of those submarines. Over the course of many months in the Pacific, the submarine had risen in the dark to take supplies from the *Maddox*. The handsome officer, Florence Brown Connor's brother, hailed from Rhinelander. He sent Bom a message on the historic occasion: "Wouldn't this be a nice day to spend at Birch Lake?"

The two and a half weeks Helen spent on the West Coast with Melvin in late September, at the Empress in Victoria, at the Jordan River, and in Bremerton, visiting with Dick and Pat, and anticipating Bom's arrival, were the happiest she had experienced in years. Not even the fact that she had to leave before seeing Bom dampened her spirits. She had heard the joy in his voice when he called from San Francisco, and said the Witters were taking good care of him.

"Wished David were with us too," Helen wrote in her diary on October 15, as Bom and his sweetheart, Barbara Masters, were married in Indianapolis. "He's in Santa Fe," teaching at the Waring School outside of Los Alamos, a job Constance had suggested when Helen indicated he should have more time to recuperate before continuing his studies.

After a visit home, Bom and Barbara left for Cleveland, where Bom was assigned shore duty at the navy's Bureau of Supplies and Accounting. After receiving his discharge, Dick went to work for CPS and Connor Brothers and moved his family to British Columbia to live at the nearly deserted Jordan River location, a big change from the comfortable officers' quarters at the Bremerton base, with its commissary, club, tennis courts, near-by golf course, and easy sociability. There was almost nothing at the Jordan River outpost except the ocean stretching endlessly toward the Orient. Men lived most of the time in oilskin suits, since the damp permeated everything, and thousands of bats swirled in the night, suggesting that the world was a dark and sinister place. The only company for Pat was the wife of the engineer in charge of the power station at the dam on the river. In New Mexico, teaching long hours for little pay and overseeing boys just a little younger than he was, David was lonely.

Sons gone and the excitement over, Helen turned to her interests in national and international affairs. In *Capitol Hill Views the World,* a monthly journal put out by Americans United for World Organization and headed by Rachel Bell, she studied the bills and resolutions introduced in Congress. She put a checkmark next to Senator Helen Gahagan Douglas's bill to condition the tax exemption status of the DAR on nondiscrimination in Constitution Hall, a bill generated by the DAR's refusal to allow Congressman Adam Clayton Powell's wife, a black pianist, and the renowned black contralto Marian Anderson, to perform at Constitution Hall. Helen wrote a letter of protest to the DAR's national board: "Art knows no national boundaries, and to base discrimination on race, nationality, or creed, rather than on merit, we consider a grievous and short-sighted error."[23]

She wrote for the transcript of the University of Chicago Round Table discussion "Peace and the Atom Bomb," sponsored by the National Broadcasting Company and the university.[24] The three leading intellectuals, university president Robert Hutchins, university vice president Reuben Gustavson, and the dean of the Division of Social Science, Robert Redfield, believed that the nation's military and political leaders, relying on the persuasive power of "force," were heading the nation down the wrong track. A reliance on physical force and world domination was not only misguided but dangerous. Americans, under the impact of the discovery of atomic energy, had become "vulnerable from every quarter of the globe." "The air of moral superiority" with which America stated its policy disturbed the Chicago intellectuals. Truman hinted that "we are entitled to world domination because we are devoted to the Ten Commandments and the Golden Rule," but it was "a little difficult to see how dropping atomic bombs, without warning, upon the men, women, and children of Hiroshima and Nagasaki could have been suggested to us by either the Ten Commandments or the Golden Rule." To people in other countries, it had to seem that we were "preparing to dominate the world by force." To many people in the United States, the government's policy was "completely confused," threatening "while we do not really mean the threat."

Americans, the scholars said, had to contemplate a world in which every nation capable of making the effort could have atomic bombs in five years. A policy emphasizing military domination by our country would "add up to . . . [an] ultimately suicidal armament race . . . exaggerate the tensions leading to war, and create a world which must live in perpetual fear."

While the weekly New York Philharmonic Symphony broadcasts (sponsored by the United States Rubber Company) lifted her spirits, the lectures given during the intermission by the physicists instrumental in ushering in the "Atomic Age" did not. Hans Albrecht Bethe, Harold Clayton Urey, and James Franck spoke positively of science as "the hero of the day," but J. Robert Oppenheimer of the University of California and the California Institute of Technology stated flatly: "The explosion in New Mexico was neither a controlled source of power nor a research tool—it was a weapon." Atomic bombs could be "made plentifully, made cheaply, and indeed be made very much more destructive than the one we tested in New Mexico." There was "little valid foundation for the belief that in a world torn by major wars these weapons, for tactical or humane reasons, [would] be left unexploited." Our hope lay in uniting "in law, in common understanding, in common humanity, before a common peril."[25]

For Oppenheimer, technology made the humanities imperative. But Harry Emerson Fosdick, whose words had supported Helen throughout most of her life, wrote despairingly of man, who "has proved to be so insane, so corrupt, that the more power you give him the more he will destroy himself." Born into "the days of the first telephones, the first express trains, the first uses of electricity, the first internal combustion engines," their generation had had "to live through the most colossal breakdown of optimism in history." For them, there was the sense of an awful burden, a new consciousness, a new struggle, a revolution greater by far than the revolution Darwin sparked when they had stepped forth confident in their capacity to right wrongs and create a better future for mankind.

Melvin was alone aboard the *Empire Builder* on January 1, 1946. Sensing her winter mood after Christmas, he had encouraged Helen to come with him to Victoria for the CPS and Connor Brothers meetings. Constie and Ritchie Modrall, as well as William and Dick Laird, would be there to work on the terms of the sale of CPS to the Koerner Brothers. Helen, however, preferred to be alone, set her own agenda.

She attended a Missionary Society meeting where the topic was "The Spirit of Giving"; wrote checks supporting international and national organizations; visited with Kathryn, William's wife, who was recovering from surgery; gave a talk to the Rotary Club about the schools[26]; read her brother Richard's letter. His wife, Florence, was tired, having had the additional burden of taking Marian's two children after Constie, saying she was "worn to a thin nub," sent them back to Wisconsin, indicating she was no longer willing or able to care for them. They had enrolled fourteen-year-old William at Northwestern Academy. Twelve-year-old Elizabeth would go to school in Laona until she was old enough to go to boarding school. "Constance sent the kids' things up, also many *soiled* clothes which Florence *washed*! Fortunately she can get a woman to iron them. Isn't that something! Some *family*. We'll *skip* it though."

Richard's letter stirred painful memories and worried Helen. "He is usually so uncomplaining." Though the choice had been hers to remain at home, Helen felt lonely, lacked energy and enthusiasm. The tone of the long letter she wrote Melvin indicates that the days after he left were dark. She and David had just finished eating waffles and bacon in the kitchen.

> Had your note this afternoon and sorry you had the wait in St. Paul but with a day and a night in Seattle before boat leaves it won't make much difference and some time tomorrow you'll get in. Perhaps you can take night boat.
>
> . . . Another holiday season over. Only wish I didn't get so tired. Didn't want to see anyone New Year's Eve and was lazying around till noon New Years as if I had a real toot.
>
> Had I known youngsters were not coming it might have made a difference in traveling plans. Felt it was my duty to keep them at least the rest of this week if Richard wanted to send them. . . .
>
> I think too that with you *four* directors out there you should be able to come to some *decisions* yourselves. Certainly father had harder ones to make *alone* and in tougher times, with no money.
>
> David's done some skating which he enjoyed and still seems glad just to be home. . . .
>
> After thinking matter over, think I could make good talk at Rotary now. I should have gone after some of those boys hammer and tongs when I had the chance and let the chips fall.
>
> Hope you keep well and with no one to cramp your style, it should be a vacation.
>
> Love to all and tell Dick I would like to see the baby, as you casually mentioned with one foot out the door.

The international and national news was as wintry as Helen's mood with strikes at home making it seem America was on the verge of industrial civil war and reports of Soviet obstructionism in the Security Council.

Melvin had no time in Canada to ponder the news. His cryptic jottings in the two-by-three-inch "Daily Reminder" notebooks reflect an intensely busy schedule: meetings with customers, barristers, solicitors, and notaries; numerous conferences with Dick Laird and Ritchie Modrall, and other the directors; meetings with the Koerners; a supper at Dick's home with Patricia and baby Jessica; a dinner with Dick and Patricia at the Empress, with "Baby left in my room with nurse girl"; a meeting at the company office when the directors agreed to sell to the Koerner Brothers' Alaska Pine and agreed to the values of the land and equipment. His thoughts turned to politics on his return to Wisconsin. He wrote John Brynes, now a U.S. congressman: "The old man in the Executive Office is not helping the Republican Party one iota, and I feel that he is going to be a candidate again. Then too, I think we will have Robert M. La Follette on our hands as a Republican. The whole thing is a mess. We need a master strategist and I feel that he'll be hard to find on short notice."[27]

Headlines confirmed Melvin's observation that "the old man is not helping the Republican party one iota." Insisting his health was better than when he was first elected, and that he planned to run regardless of actions taken at the state Republican convention, Goodland delivered "a scathing condemnation of the Republican controlled 1945 legislature for frittering away its time and being more interested in re-election than in the welfare of Wisconsin citizens."[28] Edward Doan, the governor's former press secretary, was quoted as saying that Goodland had ordered Warren Knowles out of the office, calling him "a young squirt."[29] The papers predicted Goodland would win easily if he chose to run again. Republican power broker Thomas Coleman supported the governor in public announcements: "Despite his age, Walter Goodland is an outstanding governor who has met the challenge of the times." In his private diary, and to an inner circle of Republicans, however, he acknowledged that the governor was senile, "has no remembrance of what he does from day to day with the exception of a few isolated incidents that apparently make enough of an impression on him so that he holds the impression for a time."[30] Mrs. Goodland sat in on meetings, was fiercely supportive of her wandering husband, and helped keep conversations on track.

Melvin wrote Knowles that he hoped he "would throw his hat in the ring somewhere along the line, either as a candidate for Governor or Attorney General."[31] By return post Knowles answered that he had thought of Melvin "as a candidate for either Governor or Lieutenant Governor . . . [W]hy don't you give the matter some consideration and if you conclude to run be sure and let me know."[32]

Melvin's handwriting in his "Daily Reminder" indicates something amiss, although the letters he dictated do not. The abdominal pain from which he had suffered off and on for some time returned with far greater intensity and could not be ignored. Driving over to Rochester with Helen, the couple focused on the external news: the inflation crisis, the dishonesty and fakery in government information, the fuel shortage paralyzing New York City, the meeting of the twelve midwestern Republican state chairmen. The Republicans had come up with another American right: the right of every individual worker to have as much or as little unionism as he wants.[33]

Melvin saw his doctor, had x-rays taken, and drove to Northfield to visit David, who was enrolled at Carleton for the second semester. He returned to Rochester to talk with Dr. Norman Keith, who said more x-rays were needed. He wrote John Kissinger, suggesting that the annual stockholder meeting of CPS be postponed and advised him to consult with Richard Laird. On Tuesday, March 5, after spending a short time at the office, Helen and Melvin returned to Rochester. Helen registered at the Kahler Hotel. Melvin was assigned a room at St. Mary's Hospital. His diary entries during the six-day interim between his hospital admission and his scheduled surgery focus on facts: meals, sulfa drugs, doctors' visits, Helen's visits. On March 10, he had "dinner—not much—largely chicken leg and back with meat gone. Sulfa tablets 4 every 4 hours. Something also for bowel movements."

Helen sent a wire to Lieutenant and Mrs. M. R. Laird in Cleveland Heights, Ohio, on March 12: "Dad fairly comfortable. Some ordeal. Appreciated call and letter." She sent another wire on March 14: "Dad coming along quite well after major operation. I will be relieved when first seven days safely pass. Angie here yesterday. Doing everything possible. Love, Mother."

The pages of Melvin's life, noted in the "Daily Reminders," ended on March 10 with the trivial remarks about the pitiful chicken leg and back with meat gone, the sulfa tablets, the something for bowel movements. He survived the surgery and seemed to be recuperating; he was in good humor, joking with the nurses and visitors. Aunt Florence, Angie, and William, who had been with Helen, went back to Marshfield. David, who had come down from Carleton, went back to Northfield relieved, assuming the danger over. But a blood clot moved into the strong man's heart on March 19 and killed him. The nurse, Erdeen Brennan, did not forget Melvin's last words. He had talked to her about David, his love and his pride in him, his admiration for his qualities of intellect and sensitivity. In the letter she wrote to Helen, Mrs. Brennan recalled that conversation, recalled how Melvin had asked for Coca-Cola or 7-Up and how, after he had taken a few sips, had looked at her, smiled, and asked whether it would put him "six feet under the sod." She had reassured him it wouldn't. Undoubtedly the abrupt and painless end was a gift. From the spreading cancer in his bowel only further pain and trouble might have been anticipated in those days.

The news of Senator Laird's death flashed on the radio and made headlines, stunning friends and acquaintances who had not known he was ill.

In spite of the many difficulties, personal and financial, and the many challenges Melvin had faced in his life, he had never needed a reminder to be kind, such was the quality of his empathy, his soul's imbedded conviction of man's inherent spiritual nature. His physical strength and intellectual gifts had carried him through the myriad of business and civic duties and family problems. That his great human heart had sustained his family and touched and reassured his many friends and acquaintances is reflected in the hundreds of condolence letters Helen received by others left bereft, though not as bereft as she.

Businessmen in the lumber industry, young people in Marshfield, old friends from Melvin's ministerial days in Prairie du Sac, and schoolmates from Illinois wrote. Aunt Betty wrote of his being "so gentle and mild mannered and really good—a contrast and a welcome one to our Connor impetuosity."[34] Richard wrote that he hoped "that those of us that need it so much will inherit some of Melvin's goodness, friendliness and integrity." Esther H. de Weerdt, executive director of the Wisconsin Society for Mental Health, wrote, "The Legislature loses a valuable member and the defenseless and inarticulate of the state an understanding and generous friend." Senator Gustave W. Buchen wrote: "He possessed uncommon good sense and judgment. . . . He was, by common consent, a leader among his colleagues, . . . a great and good man." Senator Warren Knowles wrote: "Senator Laird and I had become very close friends and I came to regard him as one of the outstanding members of the legislature. His loss will be felt throughout the state of Wisconsin. . . . He has a lasting monument in all of our hearts, in his outstanding record of legislative activities. We shall miss his wisdom and guidance." Congressman John W. Byrnes wrote: "He will not soon be forgotten. All who knew the Reverend (as I like to call him) loved him. He served his God, his country and his family well. I have lost a dear friend."

A letter Helen received from one old friend, the Reverend George E. Hunt, was particularly poignant and full of the undercurrents that had pulled through Helen and Melvin's lives together.

> I cannot tell you how shocked I was listening to the radio the other noon to hear that Melvin Laird had just died in Rochester. I did not know that he was sick, and I naturally felt that he had many years left ahead of him. I have loved that

boy for forty years, since I knew him. I helped ordain him, and you know who married him. . . . I guess that everybody that ever knew him, loved him. You have been a lucky woman, you have had the privilege of living with one of God's Princes. That man was clean, as pure in heart as one of God's true children. The world is a poorer place in which to live, now that he has gone. But you are a Christian, you know that he is not dead, he has just gone on ahead of you into a better world, where he and the boy the War took, are together. By and by you will join them.[35]

Reuben Connor urged Bom to announce his decision to seek his father's seat before Assemblyman Walter E. Cook or Assemblyman W. W. Clark announced their interest.[36] On March 29, ten days after his father's death, the *Herald* announced "Laird to Seek Father's Post." Together, Bom and Dick reviewed Helen's financial situation, contacted lawyers and accountants, and concluded that she did not have sufficient liquid funds to pay the estate taxes and that for her future security she could not afford to be dependent on dividends from the family stock. She needed to diversify. Then Bom left for Cleveland to secure his separation papers, promising to return in a week or ten days, and Dick left for the coast.

When the house was quiet again, Helen could not drum up the energy to get started anywhere. When everyone else had gone, David remained in Marshfield on his spring vacation. He has no memory of this time, no memory of this spring vacation, no memory of Bom's decision to run for their father's office, no memory of his brothers' arrival or departure, no memory at all of his father's funeral.

Elsbeth Epstein went walking and driving with Helen during the hard last days of March and early April. "Is there a purpose in the things that happen?" Helen asked as they drove down Fifth Street. Elsbeth did not have an immediate answer but wrote Helen a note saying she was thoughtless not to have pondered it before but felt that was because somewhere deep inside herself she was sure of the answer. "It is our job to carry on, to give this life, so dark and hazy, so burdensome often, direction and meaning. If we bear patiently, seek deeply, we will find. It will be given to us."[37]

But it was not given to Helen then. She told David she was exhausted, could not stop her mind from going around and around in the same groove, could not pull herself on to freer ground. Intellectually she understood the wisdom in Henry James's advice to a suffering friend to "sit tight and go through the movements of life," to keep up the connection with life, the immediate and apparent life, beyond which, "all the while, the deeper and darker and the unapparent, in which things really happen to us, learns under that hygiene, to stay in its place." She had to live through this pain she knew, as she had lived through the others, but she could not. Faith that something valuable might come was absent, her loneliness unrelieved. She had, in her despair, in the absolute solitude that she felt, no hope. Her life had been given to family, father, husband, sons, beliefs—a better America, a better world. One by one by one they had been taken away.

David found her late in the morning of April 15, the day before he was to return to Carleton, and judged, seeing her profoundly sleeping and the empty pill box by her bed, that she had taken a way out. He called Stephan Epstein, who came immediately and got her drinking coffee and then called the Milwaukee Sanitarium in Wauwatosa and arranged for her admission and treatment. William dropped everything and drove her down, David going along.

It did not matter to her that Europe suffered from "a moral and spiritual collapse"; that important sections of the continent were in a "shocking state of immorality"; that the Progressives, after nearly twelve years dominating politics in Wisconsin, decided to abandon the third party and merge with Republicans; that the CPS annual stockholder meeting in Vancouver was held without Melvin; that there were riots in Butte, Montana, among the Anaconda copper miners; that there were strikes and hundreds of thousands of idle workers; that there was a booming membership in the Ku Klux Klan. To all the noisy news of the state, the nation, and the world Helen remained oblivious.

An undated letter Helen wrote to David indicates that she had been treated, quieted, and slowed down and that she was far from her usual self. "You've been good to write me and I hope all goes well with you. Maybe Bom will get to see me tomorrow. The Dr. said it would be O.K. Maybe I'll call up home tonight to see if Bom and Barbara are there and if they will soon come after me. Hope you're having fine spring days. May begins tomorrow doesn't it? Had a good letter from Dick. Victoria seems a long ways off. Will you be glad when college is over? Angie must be up home now isn't she? Hope I'll soon be there too—and when is your school out? You should be getting an allowance I'm sure."

Helen paid her bill for treatment at the sanitarium from April 15 through May 17 (treatment, room and board, and the services of the nurse came to $412.41; laundry, postage, newspapers, occupational therapy, gym socks and shoes amounted to $16.17; electric shock with curare came to $42[38]). Bom drove her home. He and Barbara had moved into her house.

Having "neither the free time nor the energy that this office merits and requires," Helen resigned from the Board of Education,[39] but she could not resign from her family, and the destructive family dynamics began almost at once. Richard's reassuring letter indicating that when the time came they would work out something in the way of a solution to her tax problems was followed by another: "Constance seemed very alarmed because she claimed that Gordon had been dealing with Dick Laird on the coast to buy part or all of your stock. I told Constance I knew nothing about it, but that I did not think you would sell your stock without consulting me. . . . . Where would Constance get the idea? Did someone tell her about it, or did she imagine it all?" He wondered if William were "telling the whole story when he said he wanted to stay in Marshfield or has he some plans of his own?"[40]

Helen drove north through the green land dotted by churches and farms, through Crandon along the winding road to attend a directors' meeting. Driving alone out into the land, she experienced a familiar sense of peace and good fortune. She took deep drafts of the sweet northern air and, until she took Melvin's chair in the basement of the Gordon Hotel on June 18, 1946, hoped, in spite of previous experience, that her brothers and she might work harmoniously for their collective good.

Determined to face the challenges of her new life as she had earlier been ready to throw the old one away, she took notes, seconded motions, approved purchases, including one for a new seat machine for use in making the reasonably priced maple dinette sets they decided to add to their juvenile furniture department. With so many returning service men and their wives getting started in life, there would be demands for products the company could produce. The June meeting of the Connor companies marked a turning point in Helen's life. Her brothers would never attempt to paint the whole picture, but she was drawn more fully into their world and would no longer flee from some of the difficult, disagreeable realities involved in running a large business enterprise.

A director determined to do her best, Helen nonetheless had limited insight into the business. Her brothers, like her father, kept secrets. Knowing her to be a "straight shooter" and sympathetic to the plight of some of the former shareholders of R. Connor Company stock, including Aunt Florence, who depended on the company dividends, they did not tell her that in transferring title of R. Connor Company property in the West to the Connor Brothers, W.D., in one of his shrewd maneuvers to avoid losing the property, might have placed them in some legal jeopardy as they now attempted to sell the partnership and merge it with the Connor Lumber and Land Company. R. B. Graves, the company lawyer, uncovered the problem.[41] Nor did Richard tell her about the letter he had received from George R. Birkelund, a member of the financial offices of Baker, Fentress & Company, Chicago, a man who had served on the court-appointed Bond Holders Protective Committee of the Connor Lumber and Land Company during the Depression and who was familiar with the company's history and its assets. Birkelund indicated that a price could be established and outside buyers found for Connor Lumber and Land Company stock should some of the stockholders "be interested in selling part—or perhaps all—of the stock they own."

Gordon, to whom Richard communicated his correspondence with Birkelund, fearing that other family members might wish to sell through the financial markets and they might lose control, rejected the idea of bringing in outsiders. Following his younger brother's lead, Richard wrote Birkelund that there had been "no definite stock proposition and apparently nothing in prospect at least for the time being. I therefore suggest that we drop the matter."[42]

By August 17, when Richard called a special directors' meeting "for the purpose of considering the purchase of a certain stock of the corporation . . . owned by Mrs. M. R. Laird," her brothers had come to the conclusion that the company would not, after all, be able to buy a substantial portion of her stock. The explanations sounded plausible—the market was vulnerable, they had only comfortable reserves should they come under an IRS audit, etc.— but they were, as explanations to female members involved in family inheritance historically almost always were, deceptive. Helen's brothers looked, as W.D. certainly did, to their own interests first. Helen raised cash to cover her estate taxes by selling 100 shares of Consolidated and 25 shares each of General Electric, ATT, and General Motors stock. When William offered her $200 a share for 500 of her CL&L Company stock, she orally agreed to sell to him at that price after Melvin's estate had been settled.

The fight for company control began in earnest among W.D.'s sons in the late summer and fall of 1946. Richard did not have the cash to buy stock, but Gordon did. He bought 50 shares from Dick, 50 from Barbara Vail Laird, and 438 from Constie. The two brothers, who had worked well together throughout the war, were eager to control and expand. When Gordon picked up a rumor at a logging congress in Houghton that the Ford Motor Company planned to dispose of a 40,000-acre timber tract in Michigan, which had been selectively logged and had 30 to 40 percent hardwood still standing, he shared the information with Richard and advised him to contact Ford's land manager in Iron Mountain, but he did not copy his letter to William or Helen.[43]

At a public hearing in Wausau regarding a popular bill scheduled for introduction in the next legislative session to limit the cutting of immature trees, Gordon proclaimed the Connor Lumber and Land Company's opposition.

"Poor politics certainly," Helen scribbled over the headline proclaiming "Timber Saving Bill Opposed by Connor." It might have been, but it didn't hurt Bom. Carrying the Laird name and reputation into the primary, he handily won over his more experienced opponent, Assemblyman Walter E. Cook. As anticipated, Goodland also won, although the party had not endorsed him.

In November, Bom swept Wood County with a vote of 11,665 to 158 for his opponent, socialist William B. Brecke, and the three-county twenty-fourth senate district by 21,841 to 799.[44] Things looked good for the Republicans in Wisconsin, who again took both the executive and legislative branches, and bad for the country, in which Christmas lights were dimmed and rail service was cut as John L. Lewis, "the domestic Hitler," called a strike of the soft coal miners. The great internecine quarrels between management and labor not only hurt the public, Senator Wiley declared, but threatened the nation's survival.[45]

The world news wasn't hopeful either. Leftists gained in the European elections; America's policy toward Russia changed from conciliatory to confrontational, and Korea loomed as the world's next danger spot. "All the signs are that the Soviet intends to stay right where she is in Korea, which is a mighty buttress to her great Siberian port of Vladivostok." Russia was also "vitally interested" in the Manchurian ports of Dairin and Port Arthur. "Just as Russia intends to stay where she is, so there are no signs that Uncle Sam intends to decamp."[46]

Ice paralyzed local traffic as Helen walked downtown to review the company statements and the correspondence. She thought the accounts receivable needed better attention[47] but was pleased that contracts for the sale of CPS with the Koerners had been signed. Dick remained in British Columbia to ensure that the terms were lived up to, but he looked forward to coming back to Wisconsin in a year or two. He envisioned that Bom, who had entered law school in September, intending to work toward a degree while serving in the legislature, and he would be able to set up an office together in Madison. With Dick's knowledge of accounting procedures and Bom's of the law and his political connections, they would be ideally situated to do business.

Bom, Barbara, and David celebrated the holidays with Helen. The familiar smells pervaded 208 as Melvin's spirit seemed to. His serene, thoughtful, changeless countenance looked out from the large black-and-white photograph Helen had placed in the rear of the long living room on top of the cherry bookcase, a long-stemmed artificial rose in front.

CHAPTER 18

༄

# In a *Man's* *World*

## *1947–1950*

All the battle flags were furled
for the Federation of the World.

—ALFRED LORD TENNYSON

A large photo in the *Capital Times* on January 12 showed Bom smiling broadly
and shaking hands at the Republican caucus with Fred Risser, the only remaining Progressive in the legislature. Warren Knowles, Robert Robinson, Jess Miller,
William Freehoff, Louis Fellenz, Gustave Buchen, and Arthur Lenroot, Jr. welcomed him warmly into their "young Republican" clique. Jess Miller assigned
him his father's chair and membership in two committees: Labor and Management and Veterans Affairs. Senator Robinson, who had delivered a eulogy
at Melvin's funeral, presented Joint Resolution No. 7 relating to the life and
public service of Melvin R. Laird, whose "dignified and considerate manner"
would "long leave an impression in these legislative halls."

With David at Carleton, and Bom and Barbara sharing a rented house in
Madison with Bob and Nancy Barnes Froehlke, Helen moved into her new life
as a widow in her staid community in which, aside from the loss of familiar
faces, so little changed from year to year. She demonstrated her interest in making a fresh start by repapering her living and dining rooms, and she depended
on Bom's weekend visits to bring life and news from Madison, a city pulsing
with life where the money flowed, aided so largely by business leaders who had
done very well in the war. A newly established University of Wisconsin Foundation helped the university expand.[1] With money available, and money to
grow, everyone was determined to push on into the perplexing, unstable future.

With the help of colleagues, and of Reuben Connor, the perennial member
from Auburndale on the Wood County board who advised him on issues and
strategies, Bom quickly developed political skills and a reputation as a capable,
conscientious, personable legislator. His career as a law student floundered,

however. He wasn't cut out to be a scholar; he couldn't give books the necessary attention and was much more interested in studying people and meeting the challenges of immediate consequence bearing issues before the legislature. In spite of the part-time remuneration ($2,400 a year), the political job became almost full time. Helen, a witness to her father's physical collapse when high political and business ambition collided, as well as to the demands a dual career placed on her husband, urged Bom to focus on government service.

Company meetings, for a time, were unusually congenial, the family buoyed by affluence and the prestige of Bom's election. Wishing to suggest harmony in the new epoch, they postponed a decision with regard to the quarterly dividend. Her siblings, recognizing her need for cash, decided to do the right thing, and a 7 percent dividend was finally agreed upon in contrast to the usual 1.5 to 3.5 percent.

Dick's letter to Helen informing her that William planned to let two long-term CPS employees go without pensions presented the inevitable jarring note. Both employees were over seventy and had been responsible for protecting the operation at the Jordan River, where they had had no available insurance protection against fire and flood. Dick's assessment that William had "no integrity" and would "use any available means to gain your confidence and then turn on you without a moment's hesitation when it suited his purpose"[2] was blunt. Advising his uncles that until all releases were in, there could be no distribution of funds, Dick secured pensions for the men on the same basis as Connor Lumber and Land Company employees.

Helen's involvement in the "man's world" increased as her work in women's organizations faded. She chaired the meeting at the YWCA library in Milwaukee at which the eighty-nine representatives from the ten women's organizations affiliated with the Council of World Affairs voted to dissolve the organization.[3]

Determined to remain engaged on the side of the committed idealists, Helen joined the largest membership organization supporting world government, the World Federation.[4] Headed by Cord Meyer Jr., a 1943 Yale graduate and marine who had lost an eye in the Guam campaign, the Federation published *The Journal of the World Republic*, taking the speech Mazzini gave to the young men of Italy in 1848 as its epigraph: "Love and venerate the ideal. The ideal is the world of God. High above every country, high above humanity, is the country of the spirit, the city of the soul, in which all are brethren who believe in the inviolability of thought and in the dignity of our immortal soul." Helen clipped it and stuck it in her diary.

In the *World Government News* she studied what national leaders were saying about the emphasis on military preparedness. Dwight Eisenhower claimed:

"For too many generations, too much of the world has taken it for granted that war is a normal part of human life, whose penalties can be lessened, not by rooting out the cause of war, but only by maintaining so large and powerful a war machine that defeat would be impossible—the equivalent, say, of maintaining fire departments on every street corner while building cities of tinder and tissue." Scientists, who had developed the atom and foresaw the "grisly possibility" of another horror, bacteriological warfare, "sure-kill bacteria and viruses," which did not require vast factories for manufacture and were probably at least as great a threat, almost unanimously agreed on the necessity of world government and world law.[5]

She underlined a passage: "this civilization . . . [might] not be capable of producing the men who can make the revolution in political organization, which the sudden and violent advance in applied science has made necessary. If so, a time worse than the Dark Ages lies ahead."[6] However, with the right leadership, man might yet master his vast, brilliant, rampant capabilities and destructive tendencies. Helen believed Harold Stassen, a member of World Federation, to be the visionary leader the nation required, and in her son's auspicious beginnings in Madison, reported throughout the state, she saw the promise of another leader in Wisconsin.

John Wyngaard proclaimed the 68th legislative session, following the death of Governor Goodland and the assumption of Lieutenant Governor Oscar Rennebohm to the position of acting governor, the most productive in years. He gave Melvin R. Laird of Wood County credit for showing "courage and enterprise."[7] Aldriv Revell, an "unreconstructed socialist," praised Bom in an article published in the *Capital Times* and other Wisconsin papers. The "left of center youngster" had "established a reputation for integrity, intelligence and fairness." He studied issues and voted his convictions. "It is easy to recognize Laird as the product of family life in the highest American tradition. He is well adjusted, tolerant and intellectually alert."[8]

Helen basked in the reflected glory and accepted the congratulations of her siblings when the families reunited at Birch Lake. Bom had been helpful. He not only secured allotments of wall-eyed pike, bass, croppies, and muskellunge for lakes the Connors were interested in (Richard complained that the Conservation Commission was routing stock to some of the active fish and game clubs, because of "some conniving on the part of individuals")[9] but persuaded Jess Miller to push forward the improvement of Highway 32 into Laona.

Corporate responsibilities consumed a good deal of Helen's time. Gordon's wife thought "she must have found the day long directors' meetings quite tiresome. . . . The Connor Lumber and Land Company meetings . . . went into all details of operations and budget forecasts."[10] The directors had advance warning about the bill Bom was going to bring up in the next session, mandating health insurance for workers and their dependents, and were prepared to meet new expenses. The Laona town board's passage of a resolution requesting expert help from the Department of Taxation in assessing all property within the town presented a potentially more expensive problem. Richard handled it the way his father would have. Believing the tax department's assessor would undoubtedly want appraisals on the plant property and also data relative to the insurance they carried on the property as "well as our estimates on our timber," he didn't "know that there would be any advantage to us in disclosing this information to the assessor, in fact, it might be used against us and I presume we could tell the party to go ahead and make the assessment based on his best knowledge and I presume we could refrain from giving the information requested."[11]

Eager to consolidate family interests in the summer of 1947, the five "brothers" involved in the Connor Brothers partnership met with their accountant, D. K. Harbinson, at the office of Edward Gore and Company in Chicago to discuss the holding company's absorption into the parent Connor Lumber and Land Company. The two female "brothers," Helen and Constie, were represented by male family members, Helen by Bom and Constie by her husband. When the conference deadlocked on the question of the share price,[12] in a rare instance of harmony William, Richard, and Gordon "excused themselves from the meeting and went into conference to determine what they would be willing to pay as majority stockholders in the CL&L Co." Within an hour they came up with a figure: $575 per share.

Bom and Dick advised Helen to go slowly.[13] When Richard received Dick's wire requesting "complete financial statements Connor Lumber and Land earning power past five years, a certified cruise summary of all Connor Lumber and Land timber showing comparison actual cut summary to be independent of book accounts," a summary of the last insurance appraisal of assets, current coverage on inventories, and details regarding recent standing timber and saw log sales, uncertain as to how to react, he wired Gordon for advice. Gordon's answer demonstrates the usual Connor determination to play the cards close: "Suggest you wire Richard Laird offering to send him balance sheet of Connor Bros. financial statement of Connor Lumber and Land Company on earnings of company over the last twenty years not only five years. Advise him we do not have recent certified cruise nor recent appraisal of assets."

Helen ignored Dick's repeated suggestion that she at least get some idea of the standing timber.[14] She wanted peace in the family and would not stand

against her brothers and brother-in-law, who were eager to dissolve the partnership whose asset acquisition and lack of adequate records had caused them
sleepless nights. As corporate secretary, Helen sent the letters to the family,
indicating that the Connor Lumber and Land Company was willing to pay
$575 per share of Connor Brothers stock, the purchase being contingent upon
all shareholders signing. Connor Brothers went out of business; its assets,
including the property around Birch Lake, were absorbed into the CL&L
Company.[15] Three years after W.D.'s death, and a year after Melvin's, the company's "perfect record" was nearly complete.

Shortly after, William stopped in to see his sister. After a few pleasantries,
he came down to business. He wanted her to honor the oral commitment she
had made to sell him 500 shares of her CL&L Company stock at $200 a share.
A verbal agreement was not enforceable, R. B. Graves informed her, but when
William refused to release her from her "moral" commitment, and give her a
more realistic price (in determining the value of Connor Lumber and Land
Company stock held by Connor Brothers, the price was fixed at $267), she
agreed to accept his offer sweetened by a "bonus" or "gift" of $5,000 and his
promise to support a Laird position on the board. Her main concern was not
so much price as to maintain harmonious relations and to secure Bom's future
should his political career falter and he needed a means of supporting a family. Besides, having received a substantial check for her 240 shares of Connor
Brothers, an amazing sum to her after the Depression years, there seemed no
reason to quarrel.

She was not concerned about Dick's future. A confident businessman,
mechanically inclined, and thoroughly dependable, and someone Gordon
looked forward to bringing into the company to help with the Michigan operation once the CPS contract with the Koerners had been fulfilled,[16] Dick was
already a good provider for his family. While looking after the CPS interests,
he developed a successful lumber equipment supply business with his friend
Newt Cameron. As for David, he was still an undergraduate. The time to worry
about his future would come later, if she had to.

After a summer hitchhiking east—an impressionable young man couldn't read
*The Great Gatsby* with Arthur Meisner and not head off on his own voyage
of discovery—and not wanting to return to Carleton after Meisner left for
Cornell and after his friends, most of them older veterans, had also left, David
enrolled at the University of Chicago. Declining the invitation to join Connor's fraternity, he took a room at International House. Promising to keep
Helen entertained with music and ideas day and night, if and when she

came for a visit, he sent the program for the San Carlo opera series and schedules for several series of public lectures offered by the university. The Charles R. Walgreen Foundation for the Study of American Institutions offered a series on "Free Speech and Justice Holmes," "The Rulers and the Ruled," "Public Speech and Private Speech," "Individualism and the Constitution." Helen recalled the hoopla when Walgreen withdrew his daughter from the University of Chicago in the thirties because of the anti-American bias of many of its professors and recognized that the drugstore magnate's money was going into providing an alternative view. David's letters provided Helen an antidote to the business-political world that now engaged so much of her attention.

After a year and a half of participating in at least some of the corporate decisions, Helen took her intense youngest son to the Northwoods Lumber Association meeting at Kings Gateway Lodge on the northern Wisconsin-Michigan border. While he skied in the bright, sharp January weather before the start of a new term, and enjoyed the plentiful food and card games around the fire, Helen visited with her brother Richard and many of Melvin's old friends. She attended meetings, studied brochures put out by equipment man-ufacturers of new high-speed machines, and listened to speeches (many of them devoted to the use of hardwoods in the production of veneer products). As she would often be in this, the third stage of her life, she was the excep-tional woman among men.

The men probably would have judged her to be acting "just like a woman" when she expressed a social conscience and protested the company's decision to raise flooring prices by 8 percent. She "had hoped," she wrote Richard, "the company would win a little extra good-will by reducing them instead, *before* such a reduction became mandatory."[17] (With the Marshall Plan and the mil-itary buildup raising the national peacetime budget to an all-time high, Tru-man had asked for laws to cope with the inflationary spiral.)

Experiencing a renewed enthusiasm for life and a need to engage in a wor-thy cause, Helen decided to run as a Stassen delegate in 1948. She had always believed, and preached, what Bom was now also preaching: "For every right there is a duty. . . . If good men won't run, we can't elect them."[18] If Helen believed in Stassen, and that she had a name and the oratorical gifts to help him, she had an obligation to fight for him. She marked her calendar to be present when Governor Stassen came to Milwaukee on February 6 to meet with fellow delegates to go over plans for a "hard-hitting, driving campaign."

Life became more exciting. She had thrown her hat into the political arena and would stand for election—and she had a grandson. Along with notices of

the February stockholders' meeting in Marshfield, she included the announcement of the birth of John Osborne Laird, Bom and Barbara's first child.

In the nomination papers Helen took out for George C. Landon and herself as the two Stassen Seventh District Delegates, she explained her interest
in Stassen because "he is a man of integrity and . . . understands the necessity
for economy and wise planning in government." She did not include the fact
that he had been president of the International Council of Religious Education, a national organization chartered by an act of Congress. David, who had
been concerned to know if his mother's life were "eventful," now found it "hard
to follow you in the various roles you play." He was sure Helen's aid would
"insure the 7th district in Stassen's behalf" but wondered if she didn't "feel that
a more conservative candidate might even now impair Republican chances."

The speeches Bom and Helen delivered in the district on behalf of Republican candidates and causes put "the family in the public eye, acceptably." Bom
was with her when Stassen campaigned in Wood County, but it was she who
introduced him at a joint meeting of the Marshfield service clubs and at a
public meeting at the Eagles Club.[19] She traveled to the Rapids with Stassen
and introduced him at a public meeting there. Her photo appeared on the
front page of the *Herald* standing beside the candidate, who urged citizens "to
have faith in the future of America" and stressed the importance of offering
the people of the world not only economic and military strength but moral
leadership as well.

She took time out of a full schedule to visit David, who was exhausted after
reading Max Weber, Thorstein Veblen, parts of Toynbee, Marx, and Tawney's
*Religion and the Rise of Capitalism* and writing his quarter exams. The most
liberal member of this liberal Republican family, he spoke of his interest in
third-party candidate Henry Wallace, who as Truman's secretary of agriculture
had so bewildered the president he finally fired him. Effusive in his thanks for
the time his mother gave him, David then set off alone for Santa Fe and Albuquerque to spend what Helen assumed would be a short break between terms,
but what turned out to be a several-month tour of the western states and
Canada. She may or may not have viewed the number of David's "moves and
changes" and his decision not to pursue his B.A. in Chicago with her "accustomed stoical resignation," as David advised her to. That she kept his letters
indicates that she found them interesting. She probably regarded them with
a mother's concern and a historian's detachment.

He wrote of running into B. B. Dunne, with whom he had become friendly
during his Waring School days. He found the journalist in his usual spot in
the lobby of the La Fonda Hotel, Santa Fe, where he gathered most of his

information. The Waring School was still operating; the country was crowded because of the government project at Los Alamos. "Still a number of artists and authors in the city and it holds its old world ways in spite of the recent influx."

The Grant Hotel, from which his next letter came, lay in the shadow of the Mark Hopkins. San Francisco seemed "traditional and very old in its ways," a "friendly city, but perhaps that is because I have heard you and the family speak of it." He walked along Montgomery Street looking "at the upper windows for some small indication of where the Witter Company might be located." That the Dean Witter firm occupied "an enormous building of its own in the heart of San Francisco business district came as quite a surprise." Ushered into the "inner sanctum," he had "a fine visit with Mr. Jean Witter and Mr. Jack Witter" and met Jean Witter's son, Bill, who insisted they have lunch together. "Certainly a fine looking group of men and carry their regards to you."

Next she heard, he was sitting in the library of "the welcomed Empress" writing enthusiastically about his reunion with Dick and Pat and little Jessica, who talked nonstop. He had visited Victoria College, gone to church with Dick and Newt Cameron, and taken a business trip with Dick to the Carrvichan Lake territory. At Crawfton, where the CPS logs were brought in from the Jordan River, Dick "sized up the booms estimating the amount of timber in the water. He certainly keeps a weary [Freudian slip or deliberate?] eye on that business as well as his own, which is quite fortunate for all concerned."

He was reading the nineteenth-century authors Helen had studied: Wordsworth, Coleridge, Lamb, De Quincey as well as Renan's *Life of Christ*, which he remembered having heard discussed at home, and Lewis Mumford's *The Condition of Man* and the constitution released by the Committee to Frame the World Constitution of which Dr. Hutchins was the leader. He was more than ever convinced that "World Federation carries with it the cure of the capitalistic ills. It is a substitute for depression within a nation and rivalries without. It is also in accord with both the physical well being and the spiritual freedom of all mankind."[20] In the beauty of Victoria he perceived "a tradition of which one can be secure and which stands firmly on its island fortress."

Responding to the factual tone of her letters, in which Helen advised him to eat and sleep well and pay his bills, he shifted the subject and submitted the kind of objective report she was accustomed to receiving from her father. Canadians seemed to "take little interest in European recovery" and were "perfectly willing to let the U.S. not only pay the bills, but go to bat for Democracy as well." In Victoria truck driver and bank president both observed the custom of afternoon tea and conversation in any number of small shops. "Only at your coffee table has the ritual been more faithfully or more graciously maintained."[21]

Helen was surprised to receive his next letter from Seattle, where he visited the university, heard Professor Heilman deliver "a fine lecture on Thoreau," and attended a Shakespeare seminar in which the professor introduced him to his class and asked for comments on what Chicago was doing in the way of interpretation. He located a room at a YMCA near campus and assured Helen he had settled in and was certain he would enjoy life around the university. He soon found a new "home," however, at Reed College, Portland, Oregon, a college with a student body of approximately 700, which he judged "one of the few—perhaps the only—school engaged in education today." He made friends among the friendly students and staff who gave him a room in the dorm and permitted him to audit classes and use the library. He was sure Helen would find the curriculum "fascinating."

Like European scholars of earlier times, he wandered from university to university absorbing what the professors and students had to offer. He could fancy walking into the Olympic dining room with her if she were there, the music playing, the lobby filled with rhododendrons. He was obviously very lonely.

His next epistle, written from the YMCA in Victoria, ran to eight pages. After delivering a lecture on the "common psychological bond existing between the medieval craftsman and some modern artists," both of whom sought "effects beyond that of the world of appearance," he turned to the poetry of Auden and Eliot, the subduing of "one's own ego—a sacrifice of independence and personal identity—to a higher impersonal calling." He quoted Eliot's "Teach me to care and not to care," "Teach me to sit still." He asked Helen to notice the resemblance of Eliot's thoughts to Dante's *Divine Comedy*, which he had been reading for the first time, and to follow him as he traced the common theme of humility and subordination—"In His will is our peace"—from the medieval period to the modern period where the pendulum had swung from the nineteenth-century Emersonian self-reliance (which became extreme in the Nietzsche "ubermensch" and in the self-glorification of the individual in fascist-Hitlerian dogma) to the opposite direction, the subordination of the individual to higher, impersonal values. "The Communists are aware of the age and seem abreast of the current away from individualism. They have chosen the glory of the group to which any human value may be sacrificed. We fear this sacrifice to the group of those very values we most firmly hold. Our political structure is designed to insure that people are politically free to make choices if they care to."

From a discussion of communism, he moved to Hamlet's "the times are out of joint. O cursed spite! That ever I was set to put them right" and suggested that Hamlet's concluding line to Act I—"Nay, Let's go together!"—carried the subtext: "Nay, let's not despair, even though his world has crumbled and his faith shakes."[22]

Helen read the papers no professor read. Intellectual discourse had been prized at 208, bonding husband and wife, but David was galloping too fast. Ideas possessed him. They interested Helen, but she was approaching her six-tieth year and was more or less satisfied now to converse with political possi-bilities and the daily mundane, the seasons of her great hopes and despairs moving like her youthful good looks into memory. Club meetings, business meetings, politics, national and international affairs, correspondence, old friends, trips to Madison and Milwaukee and West Bend, her first grandson, beds and dishes and groceries filled her days. She had neither the reins by which to steer David nor the route to set him on. Melvin, with his deeply tried but steady wisdom, could have offered the twenty-one-year-old a soul's peace and reassurance, which she was not free to give and too honest to pretend to, and could, perhaps, have pierced the shield of his protective erudition. She offered what she had: fortitude, endurance, standards.

Helen was, as anticipated, elected a Stassen delegate. Ebullient, she strode into the convention hall in Philadelphia with Bom, an alternate. Wisconsin came to the convention with nineteen delegates for Stassen, seven for Mac-Arthur, and none for Dewey. Joseph McCarthy, Arthur Lenroot Jr., Walter Kohler Jr., Warren Knowles, William Campbell, and Wilbur Renk were com-mitted to Stassen. Renk, a Willkie delegate in 1944, responded to Senator McCarthy's secretary's suggestion that it would be "inappropriate, disrespectful, look bad, for anyone, but the senator to head the delegation" by nominating Walter Kohler Jr. as chairman. Helen immediately seconded his motion,[23] thus cementing a long friendship between the farmer and the homemaker.

Ignoring both the Roper Study and the Gallup Poll, which showed Stassen the clear favorite among voters, the convention nominated Dewey.[24] When Stassen's loss became inevitable, Bom took Helen's place. Having pledged to Stassen, she could not bring herself to vote for Dewey. Too earnest, she would never make a real player in the political game, however much she loved it.

She returned home to another skirmish between her brothers. While Richard was out of town, a fire broke out in the paint room, causing a heavy loss in the Laona furniture factory. Gordon and William both showed up and assumed charge, their orders countermanding one another and confusing the managers.

Helen was drawn into the quarrel when she received a copy of the letter Richard sent to William: "There is one thing that I can assure you of and that is this—if I leave Laona again—on any extended trip, I will leave no uncertainty as to who is to issue instructions to the superintendent, the assistant manager and to the department heads. I wish to have no arguments with anyone and I wish to carry on my work, insofar as possible, in a businesslike way, without arguments with anybody as to who has the authority and who does not have authority."[25]

Richard's letter did not sit well with his older brother, who insisted that any time he wished "to stall or confine the authority of the President of the company, regardless of what question arises," all he had to do was "make the statement that the directors should act upon it." Richard had come to the conclusion that "there is no way that I can alleviate his distrust, his suspicion and his jealousy. I can prevent him, of course, from interfering here with my work and that is what I intend to do if I stay on in my present position."[26]

Peace within the family looked to be no more foreseeable in the immediate future than peace in the world. Recognizing that William would continue to frustrate them, his brothers intensified their efforts to amass the stock shares that would give them control.[27] Helen felt powerless to prevent the direction in which their antagonism was pushing them. And yet Birch Lake drew them together. For a while in summer, when the sun shone and the water shimmered, she could remember when they had been young and happy there.

Anticipating Dick's return to the Midwest with his family and the need for more space, she had a small detached guest cabin constructed next to hers. The square bed-sitting room was big enough for a chest, table, a Connor juvenile desk, and twin beds (with the mattresses purchased in Omaha years ago for Connor and Dick when they were boys). Bare light bulbs dangled from electric cords, and prints of George and Martha Washington adorned the unpainted wallboard. A narrow screened-in porch faced the lake; a narrow closet with a cold water sink faced the woods, where the old outhouse stood some twenty-five feet up the hill. She had not taken David's suggestion that she add a small kitchen and an indoor bath with an inexpensive oil heater. The primitive setup suited her. It reflected the original tone and purpose of Birch Lake, the rudimentary setting her father had placed her in when she was a girl and they all wanted to follow Thoreau's example and live simply in the woods.

She bought no additional lake frontage from the company but set the little structure within her original 100-foot lot. There was no reason to believe she needed to own more private property on those shores, where life seemed as timeless and secure as the great trees all around, which no family member, no more than any Indian once living there, considered turning into money.

Laona was, however, both lake and mill town. When another fire broke out in the "fireproof" fuel house that had brick walls and a steel roof, but contained highly flammable "hog feed" (ground up wood moved by conveyors used to heat the mill's boilers),[28] Helen's concern centered on the laid-off workers. She was not reassured that some of the men would be employed in the cleanup. She also worried about the workers' housing. "I know that you are interested in humanity," Richard wrote, "and feel that you are very sincere in your attitude. I hope that we can continue having fairly good labor relations here at Laona." He assured her that they had begun modernizing the company houses in the summer of 1947 and would be doing more. They expected to hook up the water pipe onto the old hotel well unless the directors decided to put in a new well. As soon as they could get the pipe laid up, and it shouldn't be too much of a job, as they could do the excavating with their "hoist away dragline bucket," most of the houses would have indoor plumbing. Admittedly, the houses needed work, but the rents were low: $17 or $18 for "modern" houses, $7 or $8 for houses that weren't "modern."

With her broad social concerns and inviolable sense of fairness, Helen was not the usual corporate board member. The company was operating two wood flour mills, the sawmill, and furniture departments fifty four hours a week. It was producing so much, in fact, that it had to worry about a "penalty tax." The favorable balance sheet was further augmented by the Michigan Supreme Court's decision in the company's favor in its appeal in the Porcupine condemnation case. Not only was the company's valuation of its land accepted, but court costs, including the charges of the expert witnesses, also had to be borne by the state (the people) of Michigan.[29] Helen perplexed Richard when, at the end of the company's fiscal year on August 31, 1948, she wrote that "she did not know whether she would accept the check"[30] representing the bonus the board of directors voted to give themselves.

It seemed "more fair and also more business like" to her to make "a more adequate distribution of earnings to stockholders as dividends" when they were making such large profits. She had been given to understand that dividends were based on earnings and not on the par value or even the book value of the stock. "Am I right and if so do you feel our dividend rate compares well and fairly with our profits during the past fiscal year? I say no, and this was my position in the meeting. Although out voted we may at another time want to give it some clarification."[31]

Unable to persuade her brothers to pay out a higher dividend, Helen quietly distributed gifts from her own funds to her sons, daughters-in-law, and grandchildren and made her usual large number of charitable donations.[32] She contributed to the National Mental Health Association; to many church and educational institutions, including the Near East College Association and the American School for Girls in Istanbul; and engaged in quiet personal charity in town, leaving no check stub behind and receiving no tax benefits.

National television had become a reality, but she listened to the 1948 election returns on the radio with Bom and Barbara. For her, as for most Americans, newspapers, magazines, books, and the radio still provided the news. And so much of it was bad: road blocks in Berlin, the "world fight" shifting to the far eastern theater, longshoremen tying up shipping on the East Coast. The Democrats won nationally, but the Republicans swept Wisconsin.

Speaking to the newly sworn-in legislators in January 1949, the Chief Justice of the Wisconsin Supreme Court declared that the world order was "groaning under greater stress and strain than at any previous time in recorded history." Following China's fall to the Communists and the Soviet explosion of an A-bomb in Siberia, hysteria mounted. It looked as though charges of Communist infiltration in the State Department might be justified, and Secretary of State Dean Acheson might indeed be "Red."

Yet, in Wisconsin the 1949 legislative session, during which Bom served as "right hand man" to both Governor Rennebohm and senate leader Warren Knowles, was the most productive in a decade. Unlike his predecessor, Rennebohm had no political appointees in his office, employed professional civil servants, and made appointments based on technical ability.[33] John Wyngaard called Melvin R. Laird Jr. "one of the leading figures among the young men who rule the Republican legislature."[34] Bom's introduction of a State Sickness Disability Plan was widely applauded.

While the goal of World Federation became an impossible dream in the ideologically sharply divided world,[35] Bom's future as senator from the Thirty-sixth District seemed secure. Anticipating that he would be living in Marshfield as far into the future as any of them could see, Helen and he jointly purchased the massive old Pulling house at 400 East Third Street. Later he would buy the house next to hers, a duplex, and live in the upstairs apartment. That he would be her neighbor was a dream come true—more, perhaps, Helen's dream than Barbara's.

In the fall of 1948, as a polio epidemic raged and 800 pickets surrounded the Roddis veneer plant, Dick and his family, which now included two daughters (four-year-old Jessica and one-year-old Melissa), returned to Marshfield,

Dick's employment in Canada having terminated with the completion of the CPS sale to the Koerner Brothers (Alaska Pine). They moved into the Hartl Apartments on Central Avenue, and, as Gordon had not yet come through with a job offer in Michigan, Dick began looking around the state for a place to open a lumber yard. David also returned to Wisconsin and was working toward completion of his B.A. in Madison.

Helen christened the room she kept for David at 208 "the cave." In what was to become a life-long habit, he had begun to fill it with books, pictures, and objets d'art. David thought her epithet for the room was appropriate. "In the second or sixth book of Plato's *Republic* is a wonderful myth of the cave. Where shadows play upon the wall a man goes to the entrance and sees the light, reality—the eternal goodness and truth—of which the worldly images are but reflections or shadows. So really that cave, as you kindly call it, as you raise the curtains and turn up the heat, is really an underground passage to the top of mount Parnassus. In other words to come to the point, it's not surprising that it smells to high Heaven which is what, I imagine, you meant when you said it was a cave."

His "cave" was not unlike her "mountain meadows," his manner of knocking a poetical impulse with a dose of cynicism, something Helen, her father's daughter, habitually engaged in. Her sons, so different from one another, held aspects she recognized in herself. Dick exhibited both extrovert and introvert tendencies. Bom, an extrovert, found security in society, coping and excelling through the warmth of his expansive ego, drawing in numerous friends and admirers. David survived by aligning with the things that spoke to him in private tongues, tangible things that could neither leave nor betray, and by sharing himself and his collections with a very few individuals whose natures might be sympathetic. Helen was such a one.

In one of his frequent letters, he wrote of reading Yeats's autobiography, the "most magnificent prose creation of our time." While there were other "important people in literature," there were many more "who do not write memoirs or books but wear their devotion and taste in the market place, which at least gives the buyers something at which to throw, and for these characters who throw stones such a target may someday and always does provoke sufficient curiosity for them to investigate what it is that they are destroying."

Like his deceased brother, David had a strong sense of his parents' belonging to a passing civilization. "And you, Mrs. Laird, are one of these saints who walks among the turnips and draws water as Moses struck the rock from which sprung the fountain. Your cultivation of the patch reminds me of a poem by a man who turned earthward to prune new life into form and give it direction."

Apologizing for having "gone into nothing with such completeness," he pulled back, knowing she disliked "flowery talk" and the focus on herself. He wrote of frequent sightings of Bom, whom he had heard give an excellent speech "vindicating State Republicanism"; of seeing friends from Carleton, Scott Bates and his wife Phoebe; of new friends, Werner Vortrieda, the tall, poetic, romantic professor in the German department, and the verbally brilliant, socially critical, unconventional Bostonian, Richard Roud, who later took a road away from academia and America and put his training to use as a film critic in France and later as director of the National Film Institute in London.

An undergraduate, David lived in a graduate rooming house on Langdon Street. He did not enjoy, as his mother once had, chocolate milkshakes and sodas at the Chocolate Shoppe on State Street, but hamburgers, endless cups of black coffee, and cigarettes while sitting on a stool at the counter of the White House, open twenty-four hours a day, with a book or Roud for company. There was no mention in his letters about that. He wrote about books, beauty, friendship, the party that he, the Bateses, Werner Vortriede, and the artist Dudley Huppler had been invited to at the home "of a remarkable young family, O.B. and Mary Frances Hardison. (O.B., later a professor in the English department at the University of North Carolina, Chapel Hill, became the director of the Folger Library.) They all brought records, and after a very nice dinner they pooled their music for a concert, before sitting back and reading poetry to one another "until the milk-man's horse was heard."

William Hay, his philosophy professor, suggested David apply for a scholarship to Harvard. David was not optimistic about his chances. "The scholarships all seem to have a specific stipulation which is most difficult to fill. My name is not Saltenstal or Cabot or Downer, but one I think a great deal more of. However, the generous individuals who established the scholarships were not unwise for they tagged their grants for their descendents—even Marblehead and Provincetown have special mention."

On June 4, David "read with greatest interest of my very illustrious and famous mother in the newspaper, which makes me respect the Governor for his very good taste here demonstrated."[36] Rennebohm had appointed Helen to the seven-member State Free Library Commission, a position for which she was ideally suited after many years of unobtrusive work on behalf of Wisconsin's free libraries.[37] Helen was introduced to "Wisconsin's library world" in the June 1950 Wisconsin Library *Bulletin:* "The latest appointment to the Wisconsin Free Library Commission will be welcomed by the librarians of the state, especially in those libraries which were founded by women's clubs and have a close relation to club women today. . . . She has made her home in Marshfield all her life, and is familiar with the north country and the problems of Wisconsin's sparsely populated areas. Her advice and interest will be an asset."

Commission members were not paid. Associating with recognized intellectual leaders in the state—George Watson, the state superintendent of Public Instruction; E. B. Fred, the president of the University of Wisconsin; and Clifford Lord, the director of the State Historical Society—was reward in itself. The commission employed a secretary and was charged not only with writing biennial reports and producing a monthly Wisconsin Library *Bulletin* and occasional book lists but with assisting in establishing and maintaining libraries throughout the state and advising on location and construction and book selection.

Drawing up book lists in various subject areas had never been a problem for Helen, who saw "no controversy over grouping." She liked to tell the story of Robert Ingersoll, who, asked "to settle a dispute over heaven and hell, answered that he had nothing to say. Have friends in both places." She had no apologies for bringing novels into a list, thought that fiction as a category was a "poor name in that it signifies invention, fabrication, almost falsehood. The real novel is based on life and its forces as they are in human nature, and like other forms of art, its purpose is to enlarge man's comprehension." Walter Botsford, the commission's secretary, claimed she was "invaluable in pointing out the weaknesses in our budget and in putting her finger on flaws in our methods."[38]

In the "significant and timely letter" the commission received from Dwight D. Eisenhower, then president of Columbia University, Helen recognized the thread that ran through the University of Wisconsin's history. "One principle which all free universities unfailingly must defend," Eisenhower wrote, "is the ideal of full freedom of scholarly inquiry and expression, the right of mankind to knowledge and to the free use there of." Because that principle "is now being subjected to serious and systematic attack in many lands," institutions of higher learning, museums and libraries throughout the world were asked "to join in the re-affirmations of their faith in the freedom of inquiry and expression."[39]

The Wisconsin Library Commission chose as the theme for state libraries in 1951 "The Heritage of the U.S.A. in Times of Crisis." The objective was to "stimulate thinking on the problem of how to defend our freedom by understanding its origin and its application to the great problems of today." No book should be banned, and no voice stopped, but an effort to educate in the western tradition was a legitimate undertaking.

"Things have piled up a bit recently," Helen wrote Richard on June 14, before leaving for Madison after returning from the Republican convention in Milwaukee where she and Bom had been part of the now familiar mother-son political duo. She had enjoyed talking with state chairman Cyrus Philipp, former Governor Emanuel Philipp's son, and as pleased as Bom that Warren Knowles had successfully engineered to make Walter Kohler Jr. the next governor. Preferring good manners and rational argument to hyperbole, she thought Senator McCarthy presented the only jarring note.

The lives of mother and sons moved on. With funds borrowed from Helen and the Citizen's National Bank, Dick opened a retail lumber yard. The *Manitowoc Herald-Times* announced the opening of the Laird Lumber Company on several acres of land with more than 500 feet of spur track on the Soo Line. Situating his yard in a leading industrial and agricultural area in a heavily populated section of the state, Dick anticipated the almost daily arrival of lumber in straight carload lots from the West Coast as well as from Wisconsin's northern hemlock and hardwood mills and a good volume of lumber trade.[40] On June 25, Korea intervened.

North Korea's army, some 90,000 troops, crossed the 38th Parallel into South Korea. Helen, who had cited the "secret treaties" made by the European powers as one of the causes of war, innocent of America's own involvement in secret treaties, was shocked to read Richard Oliver's history of the small nation. She had not been aware that William Howard Taft, representing Theodore Roosevelt, "in a secret conversation [in Tokyo] with Prime Minister Katsura, had agreed that Japan might have Korea in return for a Japanese promise not to attack the Philippines" and that, after incorporating Korea into its empire, Japan had ruthlessly exploited the country while converting it "into a base for attacks on Manchuria and China." Nor had she realized that, although in November 1943, Roosevelt, Churchill, and Chiang Kai-shek agreed that Korea should have its independence restored, at a subsequent meeting, because the "second front" problem in Europe was not solved and Russian demands were adamant, "a secret agreement was made between the U.S. and Russia to divide Korea into two zones along the 38th parallel," with Russian troops occupying the northern half and Americans the southern. Surrounded by Siberia, China, and Japan; with sixteen all-weather ports; with coal, mineral, timber, and hydroelectric resources, Korea had "all the potentials for becoming a highly industrialized nation." In Russian hands, it would be "the key to domination of all Asia north of Hong Kong."[41] Appalled to learn about the secret treaties that led to the current conflict, Helen grasped the strategic importance of the island to American economic interests. Her new duties had not lessened her absorption with national and international affairs.

When the Korean War broke out,[42] anticipating price regulations and priority sales, Richard Connor advised the sales office to be wary of making promises to its customers that they might not be able to keep. The Defense Production Act went into effect,[43] and the formidable undertaking of establishing a semi-mobilized economy began again. Helen raised with Bom the issues she would have raised with Melvin Sr.: MacArthur's push north of the 38th Parallel had certainly been a mistake, hadn't it? It had brought Chinese "volunteers" into the conflict and forced our soldiers to retreat. Although Truman said we had the right to use every weapon in our arsenal, there surely wasn't a possibility that the United States would use atomic power, was there?

The Lairds celebrated Walter J. Kohler's election as governor, Bom's reelection, Dick's success in establishing his company, and David's pursuit of graduate study in Madison. But other young men, William's son Andy among them, were drafted. Off to boot camp in Indiana, a foot soldier in Company K, 112th Infantry, Twenty-eighth Division, Andy was on his way to the killing hills of Korea.

❧

# CHAPTER 19

# Regent

## 1951–1959

One of Wisconsin's most talented women, . . . a woman of wisdom who knows the score.

—UNIVERSITY OF WISCONSIN NEWS SERVICE, April 7, 1951

On January 24, Helen drove to Madison over clear roads expecting to celebrate the beginning of Bom's sixth year in the senate and the conclusion of David's first semester of graduate school. She anticipated having dinner with her sons and driving David and "gear" home. "For good or for bad," he was going to Europe. It was "now or never," a pause before settling into his prelims and the dissertation grind.

Walter Kohler reached her at the Loraine Hotel and asked her to fill a vacancy on the University of Wisconsin Board of Regents. She had "a bad night deciding. Seems too big a job, but hate to say no to Governor Kohler at start of his term." Over dinner at the Madison Club, Bom and David urged her to accept. In the morning, she walked over to the governor's office, told him her sons voted "yes," and that "yes" was her answer. She visited the senate chamber, waited while David loaded his belongings, and started home.

On January 27, the governor, acknowledging "the interest of the women of Wisconsin in the University is fully as great as the interest of men, and they should have a strong voice in its affairs," announced her appointment. Helen made an entry in her diary: "News breaks. Die is cast or I'd be scared out of it even now. Maybel and Carl Pick called and the Cardinal office, etc. Aunt Florence had dinner with David and me after rather busy day. Get company minutes off. Nice winter day. Bake coffee cake to regain equilibrium and go to office. Glad David is here now."[1]

Helen was in the limelight. News reports listed her qualifications: expresident of the Marshfield Board of Education, member of the State Library Commission (from which she now had to resign), secretary of the Connor

Lumber and Land Company. The *Herald* picked up the governor's theme on the importance of the appointment to women: "Wisconsin citizens generally and Wisconsin women particularly will approve of the Governor's appointment."[2] Mrs. Yvonne Town, a Wisconsin member of the Republican National Committee, wrote, "You will bring honor and credit not only to your splendid family, but to the governor and to women everywhere in Wisconsin." Interviewed by Jean Matheson for the *Daily Cardinal*, Helen said, "I certainly have the interest of university women at heart, though I don't believe I'm on the Board of Regents solely to represent women."

The governor, who had known Helen by reputation and personally for many years, needed little prodding to make the appointment. The Kohlers and Lairds belonged to a likeminded "old family club" of first-, second-, and third-generation descendants of Republican builders in the new country. They had roots in the land and were, according to John Wyngaard, becoming increasingly rare on the political scene. "Young people interested in government careers have moved into Democratic politics, which offer the only reasonably certain avenue to preferment."[3]

Now began for Helen the Marshfield-Madison commute, often in Bom's company. Her work for the Regents became her predominant intellectual interest, intertwined as it was with state and national politics.

Zona Gale described the "naive amazement and shock" of her first meeting with the Board of Regents in 1923, when they spent the "whole morning discussing whether somebody should be engaged as foot-ball coach, and whether the university could afford to pay him six thousand dollars a year."[4] Helen's first board meeting was equally inauspicious. Because of illness or absence from the state, only Regent Daniel H. Grady showed up, and the meeting adjourned without business.

Like the journalist she had once thought of becoming, she decided to make the most of her time and get a firsthand feel for the university. She thought of herself as a "reactivated alumna seeing things from the inside out instead of outside in." She met with President Fred and faculty members of the educational committee, to which she had been assigned; lunched with the *Cardinal* staff; attended a dinner of the Matrix Society; gave a dinner for Professors Ruth Wallerstein and Werner Vortriede and graduate students Scott and Phoebe Bates.

It surprised her to learn that Professor Aaron J. Ihde thought it necessary to issue recommendations on what students and faculty should do in the event of an atomic attack: "Close eyes, cover with an arm, drop to ground, pull coat collar over head, wait for heat and shock waves to pass (2 minutes), avoid panic, be prepared to obey authorities, don't start rumors etc." Some scientific breakthroughs pleased her. Karl Paul Link's discovery of a new rat killer, warfarin, would make a major difference in farmers' ability to control the rat populations in barns. The birth of a calf through transference of a microscopic egg from one animal to another, a "scientific miracle," accomplished by work

Helen Connor Laird, ca. 1950: "A woman of wisdom, who knows the score."

done cooperatively by the American Foundation for the Study of Genetics, the university, and the U.S. Department of Agriculture's Bureau of Dairy Industry,[5] had tremendous implications for the cattle and dairy industries.

She returned home rejuvenated with a packet of material President Fred gave her to study. Her diary indicates her mind at work over a pressing issue: an American history requirement. "Enemies of our time fear and distrust, intimidation. Why increase these? Stand of Dr. Fred regarding this policy. Educational matter. Recommendation of our President should be given utmost consideration. Content? Do you [Regents] intend to audit all courses? If you compel attendance, then content is your responsibility. This group [Regents] not educators." Good citizenship "like character caught not taught." It came "by example in the home in early years formative period."

The illustrated centennial historical map detailing the University of Wisconsin's history, which President Fred gave her, indicated good citizenship was on the wane. The university had a proud history, but the "termites of corruption" had crept in. Commercialism in college sports, "rampant throughout the country," bred bribery, fraud, and forgery.[6] A "Wisconsin Code of Sportsmanship" had become necessary. "We of Wisconsin, players and partisans, yearn to win, if win we can. But fairly! In victory unvaunting . . . in defeat, proud of a game fought to the hilt. So today in sports . . . so ever in life." The "Code," together with a statement written by President Fred, speaks to ideals threatened from both within and without. The map, Fred wrote,

> brings out the original meaning "God our Light" of Numen Lumen and the eye of the University seal. . . . "God Our Light" is in direct contrast to the atheism of iron-curtain universities.
>
> One of our present day enemies is the big lie of totalitarian propaganda and the debauchery of honor in human relations. Our battle for the minds of men in a war for survival of our way of life must stand on truth and honor. The value of Wisconsin's standard of 'unlimited right of search and research' needs our enthusiastic support wherever we are. It is the character-stamp of the Wisconsin man and woman.[7]

In April, Helen parked her Chrysler New Yorker in front of Bascom Hall and met with the full board for the first time. Conservatively, professionally dressed, she sat at the large oval conference table in the president's office among the well-suited, well-groomed, prominent men seated around the table, her little hat snug on her freshly permed hair, which was no longer auburn but a mix of a deeper brown and gray. She hardly needed an introduction to fellow board members; she knew them all, some well and some principally by name and reputation.

F. J. Sensenbrenner, the president of the board, at eighty-seven was the senior member, another Republican associated with Wisconsin's timber and lumber manufacturing industry. The benign-looking, white-haired chairman of the board of Kimberly Clark, Neenah, had been a Dewey delegate in 1944.

William J. Campbell, a lumberman from Oshkosh, had a long history of involvement with Republican politics. He spearheaded the Republican-Democratic coalition in 1938. Appointed to the Board of Regents in 1943 by Walter Goodland, the elderly fireball had fizzled and now passed more than a few moments dozing through proceedings.

Leonard J. Kleczka, a Milwaukee attorney, had served an earlier term as an appointee of former Governor Schmedeman, a Democrat, but had been removed in January 1936 after the legislature mandated the presence of a representative of labor on the board. Governor Julius Heil reappointed him in 1939 and he had been serving since.

Helen Connor Laird and chairman of the board of regents, F. J. Sensenbrenner, Madison, Wisconsin, 1951.

Sixty-nine-year-old Dr. R. G. Arveson, a 1947 appointee of Governor Good-land's, was a past president of the Wisconsin State Medical Association. A highly respected physician who served as a member of the state's Board of Medical Examiners, Arveson was a good friend of Marshfield's Karl Doege. Melvin Sr. had often consulted with him in the 1930s and 1940s about public and family health issues.

Charles D. Gelatt was, at twenty-nine, was the youngest person ever named to the board when Goodland appointed him in 1947. In 1951, he was still the youngest.

Board members representing law, medicine, farming, business, industry, and, with Helen, "homemakers" came from every part of the state, from rural and urban areas. John D. Jones was from Racine; A. Matt Werner, whom Governor Kohler appointed to a third term, was an editor and publisher from Sheboygan. At the Regents' June meeting Helen nominated Werner vice president, a nomination unanimously approved by the board, which again named Sensenbrenner president. (Nine months later, Sensenbrenner, in failing health, resigned from the board and was replaced by another long-time Republican friend, former Governor Oscar Rennebohm.)

At the April meeting, Helen began to understand the extent of the federal government's involvement with the university. It included everything from paying nonresident tuition for air force military personnel to supporting research in various university departments. The Department of Army funded research in chemistry; the Atomic Energy Commission funded enzyme research and research in the Departments of Genetics and Pathology; the Office of Naval Research supported grants to the Departments of Physics, Biochemistry, Economic Entomology, Psychology, and Zoology. The government's footprints were all over. Hard to believe that twenty years before, the president of Williams College, Tyler Dennette, had refused Harry L. Hopkins's offer of federal assistance for needy students, saying he feared the consequences of acceptance would be to make the college dependent upon the federal government and change the very nature of government in the United States.[8] With all the federal money directing research, the "very nature" of the university had changed.

The former peace advocate and one-worlder noted that the U.S. Armed Forces Institute was at the university. She understood that "defense in this age [was] impossible without the great U" and that in order for the university to participate in government-sponsored research, it had to deal with costly critical needs. The dean of the law school was not the only one concerned about lopsided grants to technological projects. This was not, however, her chief concern during her first year on the board.

Rejecting as too open-ended and vague the faculty's recommendation that advisers encourage students to elect courses that would increase their effectiveness as citizens, over Helen's strenuous objection, the Regents directed the faculty to come up with a more specific proposal. Delighted to greet her friend Wilbur Renk when he joined the board in May, she made clear that she had "a mind of her own" and was "not afraid of opposition" by expressing her anger that newspaper accounts of the April meeting indicated the Regents were in favor of a history requirement for all undergraduates and insisting that "the papers should report the attitude of the regents as being that of 'some of the regents' or of the 'majority of the regents.'"[9]

In subsequent meetings, she restated her opinion that the faculty's recommendations were sufficient. Her lone voice was heard but did not carry. On January 11, 1952, with Helen the sole abstention, the Regents unanimously approved a revised faculty report. Exhibit A, Document 1032, regarding the teaching of American history, stated that "instruction at the college level in the distinctive features of American social, political and economic ideas, and their historical origins and developments, should be a part of every university student's educational experience."[10]

The liberal *Capital Times* excoriated the faculty in its editorial of January 9 for bowing to the Regents and voting 178 to 34 for the U.S. history requirement. In its editorial of January 18, it praised Helen for displaying "a far deeper appreciation of proper education procedures than her male colleagues on the board. It is a dangerous practice for the regents to set themselves up as the final arbiters of what should and what should not be taught at the university. . . . Mrs. Laird deserves a smart salute for standing alone in defense of sound principles of education." Paul Burke, Patricia Laird's father, who read about Helen's stand in the *Green Bay Gazette*, wrote that "academic freedom is integrally bound with all the other. We in Wisconsin have particular reason just now for vigilance and courage in these matters."[11] A faculty wife, Martha Linton, wrote that Helen's stand in the Board of Regents meetings has "greatly heartened many of the faculty and friends of the university—and now particularly, your refusal to vote for required American history. . . . The history department voted as a unit, but that does not mean they all approved! There is an atmosphere of fear and suspicion in our country when people fear to speak their minds. But our university should keep to its high ideals, mindful of the plaque on Bascom Hall. You have our thanks."[12]

Helen became chairman of the education committee in 1952 and served in that capacity throughout her tenure. She met regularly with student leaders and reported their belief that more attention needed to be given undergraduate teaching and advising and that too much money went into research. When John Wyngaard took the administration and the Regents to task for the "unauthorized purchase of land" through a "quasi-private instrumentality known as the University of Wisconsin Building Corporation, a legal device candidly created to circumvent the state's constitutional mandate against public debt" (the university had borrowed funds to purchase land it believed essential for further expansion), the Regents grasped both the seriousness in his prediction that the university's "whimsical and arbitrary attitudes and policies" would have consequences, and the humor in his assertion that they had been "informally, but nonetheless really spanked by a Legislative Council committee studying fiscal affairs."[13] Helen's son was chairman of the council.

The horse out of the barn, the Regents issued a statement indicating that they understood the relationship of the university to the legislature and recognized their proper function was to submit building needs to the legislature through the State Building Commission. The power of the Regents was secondary to that of the legislature.

Under extreme pressure to expand higher educational opportunity in the state, as a first matter of business in the 1952 legislative session, Governor Kohler asked the legislature to consider improvements in state financing of higher education by modifying the statutory arrangement under which the university's operations were handled. The Regents and the Madison faculty immediately released a joint position statement: any changes "in the organizational matters of higher education in the State should be taken slowly one step at a time, and not abruptly in a single all-inclusive step. Any sudden and pronounced changes in this organization might be disastrous to the University and the State."

Ignoring the Regents' offer to cooperate, the politicians presented bills calling for the integration of all state institutions of higher education, uniform degrees, and a new fifteen-member board appointed by the governor governing all state institutions. Helen immediately presented and moved the adoption of a motion expressing "at once" to the chairman of the senate Committee on Education and Public Welfare (her good friend Robert Robinson) the Regents' "opposition to Bills 275,S and 479,A relating to an integrated system of higher education, because the bills fail to promote the best interests of the University and its alumni, because they do not represent economy in higher education, and because they are not in the best interests of the people of the State in that they do not insure a higher quality of education, nor show an understanding of the true purpose of a university."

Having passed Helen's motion, the Regents declared their strenuous opposition to the bills. They went on record saying they favored some sort of integration of the various campuses, wished to work with chairmen of the appropriate legislative committees to modify the bills, and repeated their preference for excellence over size and their wish to admit all qualified students to the Madison campus and to provide them with a top-flight education.[14]

Helen battled her powerful friends: Governor Kohler, Lieutenant Governor Knowles, and Senator Robert Robinson. With his ruling on March 15 that it was "not germane," Knowles killed a university-sponsored amendment to the governor's bill, which would have retained two separate boards. The university quickly drafted a bill of its own, which called for the development of a four-year University of Wisconsin campus in Milwaukee and postponement of consideration of a united board.

The AFL backed Kohler's integration plan, believing it would broaden educational "rights" in the state and break down the "elitism" of Madison; the University of Wisconsin Student Senate favored the university's substitute bill. The governor's bill on the integration of the state and university boards, Bill 451S, came up as "a special order of business" three consecutive times and was delayed each time. Attorney General Vernon W. Thomson believed the governor's plan would be in violation of the state constitution. The fight in the legislature did not break along party lines but along place lines. Gaylord Nelson (D-Madison) introduced the substitute university bill in the Senate; Carroll Metzner (R-Madison) introduced it in the Assembly.

After weighty discussions on Bascom Hill, Helen would walk to the capitol, listen as legislators debated educational issues, collar assemblymen afterwards and argue her position: the Madison campus must not be diluted; Wisconsin could not afford the duplication of professional schools; the most advanced work, the most highly qualified administration and faculty talent, must remain in Madison.

The ball tossed back and forth between the politicians and the educators, Madison and Milwaukee, from 1952 until April 16, 1955, when the senate passed an education bill, which the Regents declared would create "revolutionary changes." It provided two seven-member boards of regents, appointed for one year only. According to university analysts, they were not true boards but committees drawn from a merged fifteen-member University and State College Board. The bill's very vague provisions were "an invitation to expend enormous sums. The result would probably be the deterioration of the quality of existing institutions."[15]

Meeting at the university the day following senate passage of the bill, the Regents drafted a compromise bill that would unite the state institutions of higher education into a single board for the purposes of presenting a single budget to the legislature. Under the compromise bill, the university system and the state college system would each maintain unique boards of regents, which would fulfill their traditional functions, but each board would elect three members to serve on a united board, which together with the superintendent of education would work out the budgets to be presented to the legislature for approval.

On August 30, 1955, Helen attended a special joint meeting of the Board of Regents of the State Colleges and the Board of Regents of the University of Wisconsin at the Schroeder Hotel in Milwaukee. The regents of both boards approved a motion to form a committee composed of fifteen members: four regents from the state board, four from the university, the presidents of each, four citizens appointed by Governor Kohler, and the state superintendent of public instruction to coordinate higher education in the state.

At the December 1955 Regents meeting, Oscar Rennebohm, in recognition of their hard work on the education committee, moved the nomination of Regents Laird, Renk, Steiger, and Werner to the Coordinating Committee for State Supported Institutions of Higher Education in Wisconsin.

Helen's selection to the committee, which was charged with supervising the merger of higher education facilities in Milwaukee on or before January 1, 1957,[16] as well as with working on budget and educational policies for all state institutions of higher learning, was front-page news in the *Herald* on December 12 and subject of an editorial the next day. Marshfield was "extremely proud" of her.

As her work became more demanding, she hoped that the Regents might handle routine matters by written ballot. University vice president Ira Baldwin squelched that hope. Statutes regulating the practices and regulations of the Regents mandated that they be present to discuss everything. Acknowledging that they had to be careful how they went about altering their prerogatives, the Regents set up a committee, with Helen a member, to review the statutes with a view to making adjustments enabling the board to focus on broad policy deliberations. Helen's proposal that they minimize the travel requirements by holding all the Coordinating Committee meetings in conjunction with the Regents meetings was also rejected. Some members could not afford an additional day's absence from their private business activities.[17]

Engaged in the serious work of setting the budget for the entire Wisconsin higher educational system by a September 1 deadline, the work to be completed over the summer of 1956, demonstrating their interest in the whole state, a sign of the state's interest in further democratization of opportunity, the Coordinating Committee met in Eau Claire, Oshkosh, Madison, Milwaukee, and other state centers.

With the anticipated increase in student enrollment the most significant factor in the higher educational system in 1956–57—almost 5,000 students were expected at the newly created four-year Milwaukee campus, an increase of more than 1,000 students, and almost another thousand, from 15,134 to 16,000, in Madison[18]—the university needed more money from the state for everything from professors to paper clips. Fiscal conservative though she was, Helen aggressively lobbied legislators for additional funding. Yet, as costs mounted year by year, she believed the Regents' request for appropriations "would be difficult to explain to people back home."

At the October 1956 Regents meeting in Madison, Helen announced that she was satisfied that the Coordinating Committee's provision of a single, consolidated biennial budget request for all state-supported institutions of higher education was "at least an approach to the solution of a complicated problem." She moved that the merger of the Milwaukee Extension Center and State College be approved and the Wisconsin State College and the University Extension Center in Milwaukee be merged to become University of Wisconsin-Milwaukee. Although opposed to the merger the year before, political reality persuaded her of its necessity. Having discharged herself of what had proved to be a heavy, time-consuming responsibility, Helen asked that she be relieved of the responsibility of serving on the Coordinating Committee.

The first commencement exercises at the Wisconsin-Milwaukee campus were held outdoors on the Kenwood campus, University Stadium (Pearse Field), on June 16, 1957. President E. B. Fred conferred the degrees, and Charles Gelatt extended greetings to the graduating class. Helen marched in the processional and sat on the platform with the other regents and dignitaries, because E. B. Fred asked her to, although she would have preferred that regents had not been asked.

While working on the integration of the state's institutions of higher learning had been her most consuming task, she dealt with many other issues, some rubber-stamp issues approving faculty leaves and appointments, others more serious. She was on the search committee, along with friends Ruth Wallerstein and Mrs. Bernard Brazeau, for a new dean of women. On March 10, 1956, she announced that Martha E. Peterson, former dean of women at the University of Kansas, had accepted the position. She was also on the search committee for a new president. E. B. Fred reached the mandatory retirement age on June 30, 1957, but because of "the critical situation" facing higher education, he agreed to remain in office until June 30, 1958.

During her tenure, Helen voted to convey title to the University Hill Farms area, "one of the most valuable pieces of property to come on the real estate market in or adjacent to any community in the Midwest in a long time,"[19] to a private nonprofit corporation;[20] to approve the purchase of the Milwaukee Downer campus and the construction of new fine arts and science buildings for the University of Wisconsin-Milwaukee; and to approve a major expansion of the Madison campus. Building plans included additions to the biochemistry building, construction of a new woman's dormitory to replace the old Chadbourne Hall, an observatory at Pine Bluff, married-student housing units at Eagle Heights, a preschool laboratory, medical genetics and poultry research buildings, a social science survey laboratory, a numerical analysis laboratory, and a new law school. Plans included set aside property in the heart of the downtown campus for religious centers.

As a member on the search committee for the new president of the university, Helen met several times during the summer of 1957 with candidates, including Cal Tech president Lee Dubridge, whom she traveled to Pasadena to interview. Two summary documents stated university objectives and the criteria for the new president. The first document addressed the twin issues of sharply increasing enrollments and the "expanding base of knowledge."[21] The second restated the problems of an enrollment "increasing by geometrical progression" and a "modern society" demanding answers to its problems: "how to cure disease, how to help people live together amicably, how to prepare young people for economic success and social adjustment." The next president had "to help the university remember that knowledge is its first concern."[22]

The development of "character" with its set of assumed values, the accepted goal of American universities when Helen was a student, is mentioned nowhere in the documents. The growing complexity of society, the competition between the world's major social systems each attempting to outdo the other in scientific "advances," called for "modern apparatuses" and "modern mentalities."

When the Russians launched the first man-made satellite and Sputnik began orbiting the earth in October 1957, panic struck. Army Chief of Staff General James Gavin claimed the Soviet launching was a "technological Pearl Harbor." CIA intelligence reports indicated Russian advances in intercontinental missile technology made a "first strike" landing of atomic warheads on American soil not only possible but likely.[23] The fear was real; the end of Western civilization was predicted. Security discussions dominated in the White House and Congress and touched every university in the country.

At their meeting in January 1958, the Regents learned how the Soviet technological breakthrough would affect the University of Wisconsin. The government would offer postdoctoral fellowships to "any person who had received a Doctor's degree in the natural sciences and who had demonstrated ability and interest in basic research in the natural sciences and an interest in doing research into the defense sciences." Recognizing "the excitement, almost hysteria, engendered by the demonstrated and rapid Russian advances in scientific and engineering fields," the engineering faculty, anticipating an enrollment increase in the School of Engineering 10–20 percent higher than for the university as a whole, prepared a statement of policy for the Regents.

The increase carried with it "several dangers," including an "over-emphasis on development and application as opposed to the need for broad and basic scientific training, and over-emphasis on science and engineering at the expense of other fields and disciplines." The School of Engineering planned to cooperate more closely with high schools, which had begun to recognize the need to better prepare its graduates; to focus on "quality of training," rather than "mere quantity of graduates"; and, in cooperation with other midwestern universities, to seek to establish joint facilities at the Argonne Laboratories. The school had pending before it "the Atomic Energy Commission requests for $160,000 for special equipment for a reactor simulator, a small sub-critical reactor of the pickle-barrel variety, and a low-power critical reactor with associated instruments and controls for use in a program at the master's level in the field of Nuclear Engineering."[24]

Helen digested the words, the implications, and returned home from the winter meetings feeling sometimes as leaden as the sky, even though the issues hadn't been all science and defense. Professor James Watrous talked to the Regents about the possibility of an art gallery on the campus, and they had heard recommendations for the development of a walkway and bicycle path along the Mendota Lakeshore, a public bathing beach and parking area at Picnic Point, and a boat landing in the Walnut Street area. Helen's motion that the development plans be accepted passed,[25] as did her motion that Dean Ingraham's request for $350 from the Anonymous Trust Fund to bring Alfred Mirovitch to the School of Music for a lecture and a recital.

Helen announced at the February 1958 meeting that C. A. Elvehjem, a biochemist, "a one hundred percent Wisconsin product," was the committee's choice for university president. The speech he gave four months later at the P.E.O. convention in Racine, an organization supporting education for women (Helen became a founding member of the Marshfield chapter in 1936) that Helen attended with Mrs. Elvehjem, confirmed the wisdom of the choice. The fifty-seven-year-old scientist made a plea for an increased interest in the humanities.

Words celebrated the humanities, but funds were channeled to the sciences. The joint staff study published by the Wisconsin Coordinating Committee for Higher Education, which Helen read before the June 1958 Regents' meeting, bluntly stated: "The propelling force is specialized talent. Freedom and perhaps even survival stand in the balance. . . . With a suddenness and might that is characterized by the burst of a sunrise, man is thrust into the space age. It appears that this will be an age in which human resources, with heavy emphasis upon specialized talent will be the all powerful key to success."[26]

President Fred's last meeting with the board was in June. On October 9, 1958, Helen attended the formal investiture of Dr. Elvehjem. On November 8, she received congratulations from her friends on the board for Bom's outstanding performance, their expressions of surprise and disappointment over the Democratic sweep, and individual expressions of regret that governor-elect Gaylord Nelson would certainly replace her when her term expired in the new year.

She had said when she joined the board in 1951 that she had the interests of women at heart. She fought for and lost a battle on their behalf when she urged that the site of the old Chadbourne woman's dormitory be used for a campus building and smaller women's dormitories be constructed along the lakeshore. She had to be satisfied with participating in the naming of the floors of the new Chadbourne Hall for Wisconsin women who had achieved public distinction, most of whom she had personally known: Zona Gale Breeze, Ruth Campbell, Abby L. Marlatt, Lois K. M. Rosenberry, Gretchen B. Schoenleber, Almere Scott, Ruth C. Wallerstein, Julia M. Wilkinson, and Charlotte R. Wood.

While the male members of the board, some of them extremely wealthy, contributed thousands and millions of dollars to the university for substantial building or scientific projects, with her smaller purse Helen made regular contributions in support of women entering the traditional fields of nursing and teaching. She also gave $100 to the David Stimple Memorial Scholarship in History fund, established by Stimple's widow and designated for majors in American or modern European history with the stipulation that those applying "must have broad interests, including philosophy and religion, must be firm exponents of the ideas on academic freedom."

Although she gave several speeches to women's groups at the university, she kept her notes for only two: one, when she acted as mistress of ceremonies in March 1955 when the Beta chapter of Theta Sigma Phi, the women's journalism society, celebrated its forty-fifth anniversary. She had been a founding member in 1910,[27] one of the thirty students, nine of them women, enrolled in the "news writing course" in the English department. She told the young women that her journalism professor, William G. Bleyer, had broken new ground by urging women to enter the field. She introduced Mrs. Glenn Miller Wise, another groundbreaker, who received her M.A. in economics from the University of Wisconsin in 1919 and after serving as secretary of the economics department at the university, became the university statistician. Governor Kohler appointed her secretary of state following Fred Zimmerman's death: "One among few women in the country to hold that position, she has long advocated greater participation in government by women." Helen introduced the guest of honor, Margaret Bourke-White, as a woman who needed no introduction. Her photography had appeared in *Look* and *Fortune.* She portrayed the faces of poverty during the Depression and the horrors of the Second World War. She was there when Hitler invaded Russia. She had "taken her camera around the globe, especially through times of change and upheaval." The reporter covering the event for the *Cardinal* quoted Mrs. Laird as saying "that she admired the members of today's Beta chapter for their facility at looking at the past, while living for the future."

In her speech to the senior women living in Bascom Hall, she did not focus on women of outstanding achievement. She said she wanted to "write from the heart." Although she joked about ideas flitting through her mind like returning birds, hard to catch, and said she wished simply to say she was "glad to be here and sit down," she did speak from her heart—and mind. They had read "at times of the President and the regents being in hot water. Just at times where they ought to be. Hot water generates steam." Their education should inform them about themselves and their world and make their potentialities their capacities. She wanted them to come back, as she had, after forty years. "There will be many whom you will recall in memory only, just as I do—the names of such professors as Turner, Fish, Bell, Dickinson, Pyre, Ross, Snow, Young, Reinsch, Kiekhofer, and others, all of whom I had, come back to me, a goodly heritage."

She stressed the importance of teachers, putting their contributions on a par or above that of researchers. She spoke of education as a continuous process enabling the adult to look at life and see it in its mystery and wonder, its contrasts, its interplay of good and evil. "The person of real education senses the vast reservoir of the world's knowledge and realizes too what a small share of it is his. He bows humbly before the creations of God and man. He realizes too the interdependence of men and nations through the years." She spoke, too, of the many new and varied careers open to women, which had not been open in her day. She said she believed with the women of her mother's and her own generation that "it takes a well rounded education certainly to prepare for marriage." She did not believe women had to marry in order to have a full life, but "if you marry and have children, please stay with them for a half dozen years at least."

Education should give the women "a good climb," add to the enrichment of life, be "a continuing process. They were living in a time of many disappointments and difficulties, challenges, and opportunities. Life had never been more complicated, nor had it ever been more necessary "to know the important and the meaningful from the superficial." As they assumed the responsibility of putting into practice the values and techniques their community had helped them to acquire, they would need, at times, to turn to nature, to live momentarily in their own Walden Ponds to renew themselves "in the gentle sounds of silence and in the beauty of nature near at hand. . . . As the eagle uses the storm to help it mount, as the tree slowly develops deeper roots on the windward side, we need to learn the patience of nature. We must learn not only to appreciate it, but to co-operate with it, to learn serenity from it and peace." While peace and patience were essential to life, she advised the women to engage, make decisions, be leaders in their communities, have convictions.

In a speech to the Marshfield Woman's Club, when her work for the Board of Regents was over, she shared her knowledge and her convictions. She described the coordinating committee's history and its battles and said the increasing enrollment was "not due to birth rate yet" but a result of accepting 25 to 30 percent more high school graduates. She spoke of the enormous appropriations necessary from the legislature, the need to remember that education was "one of numerous state agencies," and that welfare costs were up ten million in requests. Many ramifications of expansion had not been mastered. They had gone ahead, nonetheless, and worked out the Coordinating Committee compromise plan "in order to avoid a dictator in higher education." Her team had worked hard to ensure that Milwaukee with Kenosha and Racine didn't wind up "running everything in the state," and they succeeded in doing that.

❧

# CHAPTER 20

# Family Matters

## 1951–1959

I believe in aristocracy. . . . Its members are to be found in all nations
and classes, and all through the ages, and there is a secret understanding
between them when they meet. . . . Their pluck is not swankiness, but
the power to endure, and they can take a joke.

—E. M. FORSTER

William stopped by 208 South Cherry for a friendly visit and to present Helen
with copies of poems Andy had written. Participating in the spring advance
in Korea, engaged in driving back the Chinese and North Koreans to the 38th
Parallel and beyond, Andy presented a foot soldier's point of view of the war,
something to balance against General Douglas MacArthur's grand "Old Soldiers Never Die" speech.

*6 May 51*

How much longer
Are we forgotten men
That no one cares how long we've been
In this infernal, devil's den.
How much longer
Are we supposed to press the fight.
How much longer,
Will homefolks waste time giving ear
To windbags with no dead sons here?

They were fortunate, Gordon wrote Helen, as labor shortages and higher
labor costs followed the outbreak of war, in having inaugurated the "very progressive steps" of investing in new equipment. With increased mechanization,
twenty-seven men, sometimes fewer, did more work than a hundred used to.[1]

New machinery, selective cutting, and reforestation would enable the company to go on forever. The Connors' old home in Marshfield would not, however. The family elected to raze the house and sell the property as a church site for the merged congregation of Trinity and St. Matthew's Lutheran Church.

On a personal level, 1951 was a most satisfactory year for the Lairds, with Helen engaged in a new career; Dick and his family established in Manitowoc; Pat pregnant for the third time; Barbara occupied with John O. and baby Alison; Bom praised by Wyngaard as "the young man who has probably advanced more quickly, as a result of aptitude, work and a record of accomplishment, than any other relatively new personality in the legislature"; and David pursuing his master's degree in English in Madison.

David filled her in on his courses, student life, and work as Frederick Hoffman's research assistant for his book *The Twenties*. When he was not her companion, Bom often was. As the year ended, Governor Kohler praised Helen for her "excellent work as a regent," which gave him "reason to feel proud of having appointed" her. David congratulated her for another achievement: "To return to the house and find it run so well and so beautifully kept is a very great joy."

A congenial meeting of the Connor Lumber and Land Company board at the beginning of the new year augured well for the business, while "the complete moral disintegration of the Truman administration" augured well for Republicans. When Truman, confronted with an out-of-balance federal budget[2] and uncontrollable inflationary pressures, ordered the steel mills seized, Senator Robert Taft's presidential prospects became "irresistible."[3] Truman's action enabled him to keep the ammunition flowing to Korea and prevented an untenable rise in prices from affecting every industry and every worker. But the outcry of the unconstitutional assumption of power (the Supreme Court ruled the takeover illegal in June) gave Republicans grist for their mill, as did publication of Sumner Welles's book *Seven Decisions That Shaped History,* a book Helen immediately snapped up. Roosevelt's highly educated and well-regarded undersecretary of state criticized American policy in the Far East between 1945 and 1950, charging that State Department officials, ignorant of the writings of Lenin and Stalin, had expedited rather than retarded Russia's ambition of linking the billion and a half men and women in China, India, and Southeast Asia with the people of Russia "in order to insure the defeat of Western capitalism."[4]

Bom could not have chosen a more auspicious time to run for Congress. When Congressman Reid Murray's illness became known in 1951, the "booming" for Bom began by the elderly chairman of the giant paper making Marathon Corporation, D. C. Everest, the leading mover in 1929 of the founding of the University of Wisconsin's Institute of Paper Chemistry. Everest, a self-educated, powerful, behind-the-scenes Republican activist in central and northern Wisconsin,[5] well-acquainted with the family in Marshfield, managed Bom's first campaign. Bob Froehlke, who had gone to work for Carl Jacobs at Sentry Insurance in Stevens Point after graduating from law school, became campaign treasurer and managed Bom's subsequent campaigns.

While Bom and Dick were moving on in their chosen paths, David threw a curve into his. Admitted to graduate school at Harvard, he arrived on campus, located Heider Rollins, to whom Alvin Whitley had given him a letter of introduction, chatted with him, walked around, and left. He chose New York over Cambridge, Macy's over Harvard. Supplying the necessary reassurances that his life was in order, he wrote Helen of living at International House on Riverside Drive, of calling for his mail at the Plaza Hotel, and of a dinner party "at the lovely home of the Henry Flynts, which was at first quite frightening for a backswoodsman like myself. The Flynts are the people doing for Deerfield what the Rockefellers did for Williamsburg, Virginia, and the father a knowledgeable man and a scholar in American history." He explored the Metropolitan Museum and visited Caroline Rutz-Rees, a "most lovable 'grande dame,'" a classic scholar who had founded and operated the Rosemary School for girls for many years and was a friend of Eleanor Roosevelt's and a former National Committee woman. She inscribed a "very rare volume in her library— The Second Book of the Rhymer's Club—a fine Yeats item" to him. "She claims she has heard much of you and is determined to meet you."

He wrote Helen of auction houses, china shops, bookstores, parlors of the old moneyed and refined but not of the bohemian restaurants in the village where he could eat cheaply, and where the smoke was thick and manners easy.

Helen gave no sign of disapproval when he wrote of demonstrating toys at Macy's or any sign of approval when he wrote of graduating to the position of shoe salesman. She forwarded his mail and kept him current on family news. Dick and Pat had a son, Richard (Richie). William had written from Pampano Beach, expressing gratitude for her "very timely and considerate help" in securing a lease with option to purchase the Auburndale farm. William hoped to set Billie on his feet there. Wounded in WWII, divorced, and married for a second time and with young children, but with no means of a livelihood and no direction, he needed his father's help. The farm was not the major enterprise it once had been, but it could keep a small family busy. Corn and hay crops were still raised there, and a number of animals were also kept.

Andy, on leave after Korea, had spent a few days with William and Kathryn in Florida before returning to Camp McCoy. "Only time will ease the memory of all the Chinamen he has killed! After seeing so many people in Florida for enjoyment and rest, it was hard for him to believe that they recognize we are actually fighting a tough *war* in Korea." William signed his letter "with love," but it wasn't long before the old family dynamic reasserted itself. He complained about not receiving adequate compensation for the extra hours he put in at the office on the newly formed Connor Realty Company and wanted Helen to plead his case with his brothers.[6]

Throughout the spring, David's accounts of dinners, receptions (including one by Mrs. John D. Rockefeller III, the founding member of the Asian Society), museum visits, poetry readings (one by William Carlos Williams) were consistently upbeat. He wrote about his activities "not to boast, but to indicate why I like New York and perhaps why I am staying on" in spite of the fact that "I miss our home very much." He worked during the day. At night, unless otherwise engaged, he went over to the Columbia University Library, where he had a desk in the stacks, a title of "visiting scholar," and library privileges. He had attended some lectures at the university, where professors "in their tea cup chatter sometimes struck a vital chord." Columbia, however, with its "informal and messy" classes, was a "strange institution. . . . How much wiser are the ways of Wisconsin where discipline and inspiration, style of language and grace of person still can be found."

Worried about a lapse in David's letters, Helen directed him to come home. He was venturing too far from his midwestern roots. He hated to leave but knew that "the time has come. You need not worry, for I shall be very happy and content in Marshfield and to be with you the real reward of homecoming."

Helen's three sons were with her when the town of Laona celebrated its golden jubilee on July 3–6, 1952. Richard Connor gave a speech honoring the pioneers. Helen, ever the mindful historian, wrote an account of the event to be placed in the company minutes. Summer, celebration, and pride in the family's rising politician once again brought out the best in a united family.

On July 9, Bom, a Taft delegate, was in Chicago. As Governor Oscar Rennebohm's representative to the Governors' National Tax Conference in Philadelphia and to the Governors' Conference on Workmen's Compensation, Unemployment Compensation and Disability in New York (ill health prevented Rennebohm from attending), he was already a familiar figure on the national Republican scene. Arriving early to help draft the foreign policy plank and chair the platform committee's Labor and Welfare Committee, he met with Taft, Dewey, Nixon, Eisenhower, Stassen, and Lodge—as well as with AFL president William Green and Secretary-Treasurer George Meany, who submitted their proposals to him. Helen clipped an article celebrating his "important role" at the convention as "further proof that he is eminently qualified for a seat in the halls of Congress."[7]

The Chicago convention of 1952, the first televised national convention, was not nearly the stressful event the 1904 convention had been for Helen's father, but cameras caught the fist fights and hard words on the convention floor as disputed delegates (from Texas) successfully drove the nomination from Taft to Eisenhower.[8] Like most Republicans and many Democrats, Helen liked Eisenhower and believed he was a sincerely religious man and rallied behind him. She had no quarrel with the Republican promise to lead "free men . . . into a new day—a new and better day—under the guidance of Divine Providence."

The summer of 1952 marked another turning point in the stormy Laird-Connor saga. On August 1, in the basement meeting room at the Gordon Hotel, Helen submitted her resignation, effective immediately, as a director and secretary of the Connor Lumber and Land Company and left the meeting. Henceforth, while carried on the payroll at a reduced figure of $175 a month, acting as hostess to important clients, and writing an occasional letter, until August 1953, when she became eligible for Social Security benefits, she would be released from the stress of the business—and from acting as go-between for her battling brothers.

Following Dick Laird's unanimous election to fill the vacancy left by her resignation, harmony ended. Subsequent resolutions, introduced by Gordon and seconded by Dick, specified duties as they had never been specified before, significantly reducing William's power. Caught off guard, William requested the secretary, Dick Laird, take down a statement and record it in the minutes registering his opposition "to the company doing business in this manner" and his position that the resolutions should "not be made effective." He proposed a resolution declaring a special dividend since the company had funds over and above the needs for working capital. When Richard called for the vote, William alone voted for it.[9]

Helen now could focus on her regents' work and the election. With the enthusiastic support of the popular governor[10] and Bom's reputation for efficiency and probity, he piled up the largest vote ever cast for a Seventh District candidate. Dwight D. Eisenhower won by an "avalanche" over Adlai Stevenson, whom cartoonists featured riding over the world on a cloud. The GOP took thirty of the forty-eight governorships, 48 seats in the U.S. Senate to 47 for the Democrats, and 220 House seats to the Democrats' 206. They would control committee chairmanships. Congressman John Byrnes looked forward to showing Bom the ropes. The *State Journal* predicted that "in the years ahead, there may be bigger shoes to fill, and when the time comes, Melvin Laird will be one of the men well prepared to serve."[11]

Helen's three sons, two daughters-in-law, and five grandchildren celebrated the Christmas holiday in Marshfield, all sensing that this was a special time with Bom about to leave for the nation's capital, Dick for Michigan to take over managing the Connor operations there (Gordon was moving his family to Wausau to manage the Underwood Veneer Company, which the company had purchased), and David for Madison, well along the road, everyone hoped, on his academic career. They appreciated the haven of their home, Helen's stöllen, Bessie Jackson's bread, Ethel Sexton's spirited egg-nog, and Aunt Florence's lighter than air schaum tortes. Helen sat at the head of the dining room table, upright and proud as she almost always seemed to be, her fine china, crystal, and silver on display and in use. Entering her sixty-fifth year, she could hardly recognize herself as the demanding, inward, often profoundly depressed woman who had given herself and her loving family such a hard time. She could almost sometimes feel there was some design to history, some providence shaping one's end, after all.

She did not wave or smile, made no pretense of an enthusiasm she did not feel, but simply allowed the *News Herald* photographer to capture the historic moment when Bom set off for Washington, D.C., in his two-door two-tone green Plymouth. His assurances that flying home for weekends would take just about as long as driving home from Madison, that nothing would really change, were not convincing. Her life would change, and her face shows that she knew it. His apartment stood empty, waiting for the family's return at the end of the congressional session.

Helen clipped the photo from the *Milwaukee Journal* showing Bom standing next to the president in the White House with other Republican legislative leaders, their broad smiles evidence of their pleasure in being a part of the turning of history's page, their belief that the new team could steer America more directly and honestly than the entrenched Democrats had after too many years of single-party control. She listened to Eisenhower's inaugural address in which he spoke of the massed and opposing forces of good and evil as the "fact [that] defined the meaning of the day."[12]

She shared Bom's excitement when, with the help of Congressmen John Byrnes and Glenn Davis, he immediately stepped into a position on the House Appropriations Committee. She applauded his informative newsletter in which he educated her and his other constituents about the issues facing Congress.

He wrote of his hope to cut government spending but privately urged her to spend more on herself "instead of always saving every penny you get." He wrote of being escorted to the Pentagon by a colonel. "After traveling what seemed like miles of corridors and breaking into untold numbers of conference rooms, my guide finally admitted he was lost. Perhaps the story of the Western Union boy who went in the Pentagon to deliver a message and came out a full colonel is not too far-fetched!"[13] No one suspected that the Pentagon's power of transformation would touch him.

As promised, he made frequent trips back to Wisconsin, flying in to Milwaukee, Madison, Wausau, or Green Bay and driving home in a rented car from the airport almost as often as he had formerly driven home from Madison. Helen and Melvin remained the familiar duo at Republican events in Madison and throughout the district. He had his key to 208, and if late he would let himself in. She would inevitably be sitting in the kitchen the next morning, the bacon and toast crisping in the oven, waiting for him to come down and bring her up to speed on his family and the political news, while she would fill him in on the local news. His work on behalf of the Menominees got good press.[14]

Bom spoke enthusiastically about the harmonious working relationship between Taft and Eisenhower; about Stassen, who was part of the administration's team; and about the Republicans' early accomplishments: the cuts in spending, the lifting of price controls, the recognition of the nation's need for high speed interstate highways as a priority (a means of stimulating another industry besides the war industry, a way of spreading money throughout the states), the movement on a Korean armistice.

The five days of hammering blows on the Red lifeline in northwest Korea by the U.S. 5th Air Force's Sabre Jets seemed to have turned the tide and given the required evidence that Eisenhower meant business.[15] The end had to be near. That Stalin's end seemed near might also be good news. That the French, whose war in Vietnam the United States had been underwriting for years, wanted America to take a greater hand concerned them both. The exhausted French, with Algeria to worry about, were ready to pull out of Vietnam but did not want to admit free elections. If the people voted, they would undoubtedly go Communist. That was the way in the former colonies. Third World countries would almost all invariably go Communist, as Sumner Welles predicted.

Bom could "always tell" when Helen had just returned from Madison, as she seemed "to fall for the line of the liberal left-wing journalists and university crowd" afterwards. Her comments about not giving away western lands and water power were influenced by the "propaganda line" used by left-wing journalists writing in the *Capital Times* who were trying to discredit the administration. There were, he maintained, "no plans to give away any western lands." There were plans to sell mature timber on the lands before it rotted away and became economically worthless. As for water power, the administration "will not go along with the idea that the only people that can develop water power

The newly elected congressman from the Seventh District delivers a speech. Robert Froehlke and Helen are seated at the speakers' table, ca. 1952.

are certain groups and organizations here in the federal government. . . . I don't care if I never return to Congress, I will call the shots as I see them and make my decisions based upon facts, not fancy."

Bom didn't mean to be critical and did appreciate getting her "little side notes," but so far as he was concerned, the only criticism he had was that the administration was not conservative enough. He was "growing more and more conservative each day as [he] watched things in Washington." The threat of war wasn't the thing they had "to fear most. The threat of spending ourselves into bankruptcy and chaos is the greatest single thing we have to fear."[16]

It was warm, above 90 degrees, but the heat in Washington in May 1953 couldn't compare to the heat then generated in the Connor clan. "This thing is heating up," Helen wrote Dick after William filed suit against his brothers on behalf of their nephew William Connor Rhyner, a minor. He charged Richard with neglect in his duties as a trustee or guardian and Richard and Gordon of collusion in the sale by Richard to Gordon of William Rhyner's stock for an amount considerably less than its value. Helen speculated as to whether if she had sued William for giving her a price significantly below value when he purchased a third of her shares, she might have prevented the present suit.

With family tensions escalating, Dick and Bom studied Richard and Gordon's proposal to purchase the remaining Laird stock. Their mother had no interest in resuming her involvement in company affairs and Dick had begun to think he would be happier as his own boss. They concluded that, if they could work out "a satisfactory deal," they should sell out. Helen turned sixty-five on August 22 and received her last paycheck from the Connor Lumber and Land Company. She was in Madison on August 28 when the directors met in the basement of the Gordon Hotel and passed the resolution that, in the end, affected all their lives.

The resolution provided Helen, out of company funds, approximately $54,000 as additional salary for services rendered by Melvin R. Laird Sr. that he had not been able to receive due to his untimely death. As Melvin's widow, Helen was also to be paid a pension from the company in the amount of $7,200 for five years and $3,000 each year thereafter for the remainder of her life. (The $100,000 insurance policy the corporation took on her life could justify costs.) William's request for time to review the resolution because he had not had time to consider it and "did not know its provisions or its effect" was overridden by Gordon, Richard, and Dick, who, without discussion, voted for it. William was recorded as not voting.

Following the directors' meeting, Dick, Bom, Richard, and Gordon drove to Wisconsin Rapids, where they met with R. B. Graves to work out the final settlement of the sale of the Laird stock to Gordon and Richard. On August 31, Dick sent his mother a letter. Helen studied it, put it back in the envelope across which she wrote "important history," and signed it with her initials, "H.C.L." Dick thought they had made "a favorable disposition of a troublesome matter" and was pleased that Helen seemed "relieved to have it settled." He indicated that the matter of the purchaser of the stock had taken a sudden turn, with Richard and Gordon as individuals purchasing the stock rather than the Connor Lumber and Land Company, and that it was understood and reflected in the price paid for Helen's shares that the stock sale did not affect Helen's equal share in the Birch Lake property.

"You asked about the Birch Lake situation which property is of course *not owned by the purchasers*. . . . We entered into a 'gentleman's agreement' with the purchasers that this property would be dealt with as a family matter and that we would be dealt with on at least an equal basis with other members of the family. . . . We did not give up our rights to property on Birch Lake along with the stock in C.L.& L. Co. . . . We did not receive any amount of money for our stock that would represent the equity in this property. . . . Under the 'gentleman's agreement' our situation should be dealt with in respect to Birch Lake—just as though this sale had not occurred."[17]

The deed was done. The Lairds had sold their stock. Dick would remain on the board but would be free to go his own way should he so desire. The stock would be held in escrow until William's suit against Gordon and Richard for collusion in the sale of William Connor Rhyner's stock was settled.

David was in New York on his way to England on a Fulbright-Hays grant with plans to work at the University of London and the Warburg and Courtauld, the "best school of Art History in the world," on the thesis he and his adviser, Mark Eccles, had decided on: "The Inserted Mask in Jacobean Drama." Settling in the lobby of the Plaza Hotel (it had become a defining habit to locate himself in the comfortable lobbies of elegant hotels), he wrote Helen while waiting for Dick Roud to join him. He had had "splendid days, phenomenal luck." He had had dinner with Werner Vortriede's friend Mrs. Zimmer (the daughter of Hugo von Hofmanstahl), seen Jonson's *Volpone*, and seen "the magnificent premier of Swan Lake with Fontyne dancing." He hoped she would excuse his hurried letter, "too hurried to say very much except I miss you and love you very much." David did not, indeed, say much. He did not mention that Helen Lauritzen had been his almost constant companion.

Bom, traveling in October as a member of the Appropriations Committee, sent Helen a card from Cairo, Egypt. While he considered the American

University of Beirut "the greatest asset the U.S. has in the Arab world," he thought that "we have made many mistakes in the Arab states." He did not say whether the covert action that led to the overthrow of Mossadegh's government in Iran and the reestablishment of the Shah in power might have been one of the mistakes. (Fifty years later, however, he recalled that visit and was frustrated that Secretary of Defense Donald Rumsfeld's deputy and his briefers seemed to have little understanding of the politics in the area.)

When Bom stopped for meetings with Ambassador George Dillon in Paris en route home, David took the boat-train across the Channel to join him. Seeing his brother and sharing his room at the Crillon made the weekend "birthday and Christmas rolled into one" in spite of the fact that Bom left the Segovia concert at the Trocodero before the end to go to bed.

Helen's spirits, buoyed over the holidays by Bom's return and the presence of both Dick and Bom and their wives and the grandchildren, and by the appearance of an article on the front page of the *Herald* tracing her family's brilliant record of public service over half a century,[18] were abruptly shattered on New Year's Eve when the door bell rang. Answering it, she found a young man, who handed her a copy of a complaint William had filed in Wood County Circuit Court.

William named Helen and Dick as defendants along with Richard and Gordon, charging "fraud and collusion" in an "illegal transaction that transpired on August 28, 1953." The resolution that the directors of the Connor Lumber and Land Company passed on that date had been a means of concealing the true price paid for Helen's stock. William asked that she be required to restore the monies paid by the company by virtue of the Resolution, and that the Resolution be declared "illegal and null and void."[19]

On January 30, the suit made the front page of the *Herald* and, on February 4, the *Forest Republican*. Now "everyone" knew that William was suing his sister, alleging fraud. "Everyone" did not comprehend the significance of the statement that "at the last meeting of the Connor Lumber and Land Company, Richard M. Connor, Gordon R. Connor, Richard M. Laird, P. F. Taylor and Thomas L. Rasmussen were elected directors." William had been kicked out. Gordon's wife, Mary Roddis, remembered:

> It was an unpleasant time. We all liked Katie [William's wife] and this rift was hard on everybody at Birch Lake. The harassment and the newspaper publicity of William's suit against them was, of course, front page news. . . . William had a great power play trying to take over, when he came back from the service after World War II, trying to drive Gordon and Dick [Richard Connor] out of the

business. Their attorneys in Milwaukee finally said, "Why do you have to keep him"? This was a great new thought to them, previously unthinkable, and it led to Gordon's power play, when he had a meeting of all the salesmen here [in Wausau]. He, with about eight salesmen, went over to Marshfield's office one Sunday and emptied every drawer and all the machines. They took all to Wausau's office and telegraphed every employee to report to Wausau on Monday morning. There was nothing for William when he arrived at the office, but an empty space and emptied files, due to this draconian measure.[20]

The brief response Helen's lawyers R. A. Crawford and John M. Potter made to the complaint contained almost nothing of the sixteen-page history Dick Laird wrote detailing Melvin's long association with the company.[21] It indicated merely that Helen acknowledged selling her stock to Gordon and Richard, that she had not known about the resolution before it was adopted. Citing Wisconsin statutes, she denied that the company was without legal right to vote her compensation for the "loyal and valuable services" of her husband, whose salary had ranged from "nothing to $6,000 a year."[22]

William lost. He lived in Marshfield, in the house he and Kathryn built on the town's fashionable west side, but did not speak to Helen or his brothers for more than twenty years (corresponding by writing only when business necessitated contact).

As a younger person, Helen would likely have fled the state when news of William's suit hit the press. Now she made a public appearance at the dedication of the new $5 million University of Wisconsin Memorial Library, an event bringing together the state's distinguished citizens, public officials, and educators.

President Fred presided over the occasion with his usual dignity. Howard Mumford Jones (class of 1914), a professor of English at Harvard, said, "We did not fight the war this building commemorates in order that the first of the four freedoms—the freedom of speech and expression—should dwindle and die at home." It was a memorable evening with many friends among the many faces. Most of those present would surely have read the *Capital Times,* which that day carried the story of William's suit under the headline "Seek to halt $54,000 payment to Mrs. Helen C. Laird." It took some courage for Mrs. Helen C. Laird to powder her nose and quit the safety of her room at the Loraine to mingle with that large and illustrious crowd.

Helen never queried the freedom of the press, but she did query the freedom of access to the Congress when three Puerto Ricans, shouting "free Puerto Rico," fired a volley of bullets from the gallery of the House chamber wounding

five congressmen. Bom had gone out of the chamber a moment before, passing directly through the area peppered by the bullets, to speak with Captain
Jim Sigl, an air force officer from Marshfield, and a high school classmate.
Helen was "not pleased with the news that the halls of Congress are being
turned into a shooting gallery. Where were those sleepy guards who stand
around doing nothing? I can't imagine their allowing such a strange-looking
group to come into any gallery even without cards. . . . It certainly was a strange
thing to have happen in our National Capitol especially."[23]

On March 20, 1954, while William's suit proceeded through the courts,
Helen set off from Marshfield on the midnight Soo train with the bespecta-
cled gray-haired widowed sisters, the very bright and precise Ethel Sexton and
the soft-spoken Bessie Jackson, whose slow southern speech never failed to
relax her more intense companions. They had passports, indicating they could
not be used to travel to Albania, Bulgaria, China, Czechoslovakia, Hungary,
Poland, Romania, or the Union of Soviet Socialist Republics. Bom met Helen
in New York for a farewell dinner before she boarded the *Andrea Doria*. Dick
phoned to wish her "bon voyage" and to report the favorable outcome of the
suit and the birth of a fourth child and third daughter, Maggie.

Naples "surprised" Helen, being "much more interesting and beautiful than
[she] thought." David surprised her by showing up early. "Married forty one
years today," she noted in her diary on April 16. The art of Rome, its history,
her youngest son as companion, the rain, a sudden visitation of a sharp loneliness, something, many things, probably, triggered remembrance. She was "not
too pleased" with David's choice of quarters in Florence, the Palazzo Annalena.
("Stairs endless and hard to get heat.") She adjusted, however, and decided
she liked the people, the blooming wisteria outside, the breakfasts of rolls and
jam and tea in her room. And she appreciated David's stoking the tile stove. She
did not care for the big statue in her room, which at night seemed to move.

A letter from Dick brought his restlessness home. It seemed that he had been
in Wakefield a "good long time—at least long enough to deserve considering
or speculating about a change," but Pat's enthusiasm about their present situation completely stifled "even the vaguest private thought in this direction."
He had read that the New York Stock Exchange, with its ticker tapes and mes-
sengers scurrying around, was as "obsolete as a Babylonian market place. A
computer could handle the whole operation. Brokers would simply dial orders
into a machine and it would buy and sell at a specified time and price, and
then notify both parties." Like his grandfather, Dick kept a sharp eye out for
changes that had economic repercussions.

Helen did not entirely lay off old habits and abandon herself to sightseeing

in the old world. The *International Herald Tribune* which she and David read
two or three times a week, reported that Secretary of State Dulles was taking
the "Red" threat in Southeast Asia extremely seriously and that the "valiant
French" were suffering terrible loses in Vietnam in spite of the supplies America was flying in through the Philippines.

In Paris, Helen and David settled into the Albany and St. James, a comfortable hotel on the Right Bank that catered to English guests. They had
lunch with Elizabeth Debost and visited the Louvre, Notre Dame, the Bois de
Bologne, and the Tuilleries. Crossing over to the Champs Elysees, they were
startled to see an enormous black banner hanging from the Arc de Triomphe.
The ominous sign signified a day of national mourning: Ho Chi Minh's decisive victory over the French at Dien Bien Phu, ending the French empire in
Indo-China, an historic, humiliating event for the once-proud colonial power.
It did not occur to either of them just how significant that black drape would
be for their country's or their family's future.

From Paris to London, it was gray and dreary. While David was busy, Helen
lived in the room David lined up for her at the English Speaking Union. Within
walking distance of Piccadilly, it was not to her liking. The all-important bath—
shared—at the end of the corridor was difficult for an older person accustomed to privacy. She was lonely in the impersonal metropolis, having no work
to occupy her while David pursued his studies at the Courtauld. Luncheon
with him at the heated Berkeley Buttery made the days tolerable.

He explained London, its districts, its history, and entertained her with
descriptions of his sightings of T. S. Eliot on the Tube, working the crossword
puzzle, the lectures on Jacobean and Elizabethan drama given by William
Empson on leave from the University of Sheffield, and the professor of rhetoric at Thomas Gresham College in the City of London, a position once
held by the dramatist Ben Jonson. Most attending the lectures seemed to have
dropped in to get out of the cold, but David and his friend Bob O'Clair, a fellow Fulbright scholar, had gone to hear what Empson had to say. They invited
the professor to join them at the pub after the first lecture, and the pub visits
became habitual, leading finally to an invitation to dinner at Empson's flat in
Hamstead Heath, a high point of David's London experience.

He told Helen about the Lancaster pie, which Hetta, Empson's young, good-
humored, athletic wife, an Afrikaner, prepared, but not about the amount of
Retsina they put away. He described Empson as short, thin boned, clean shaven,
except for a funny chin beard he wore as "a sort of eternal muffler," and
related his interesting story: how he had gone from Cambridge to China and
participated in Mao Tse-tung's long march in the 1930s; how he had written

*Seven Types of Ambiguity*, depending on memory as he quoted from the English poets and how, consequently, so many errors had slipped into his book. Helen listened and participated by throwing in, lawyerlike, questions: "Why had Empson not corrected the errors when he got to England?" "Why didn't his editor catch them?" "Did they alter his thesis?" "Were they significant?" You could tell she did not care for the description of the unkempt scholar and admired him less than David did.

She awaited David's visits and the end of his term impatiently. Her mood darkened and then brightened again when, his classes over, he was free to be her guide and companion. He rented a car and took her into the English countryside, his friend Bob O'Clair coming along. Helen approved the curly-haired Irish American and enjoyed his flattering attention and hearing him talk about his thesis subject: George Eliot, a more congenial subject than *Seven Types of Ambiguity*. She did not care for ambiguity; it required definition. They visited Salisbury, Bath, Wells, which were "all wonderful." Dunston, a deserted place on the Cornish coast, spooked her. She did not want to linger. They drove to the east coast, to Cambridge, where O'Clair left them to return to London, and David and his mother called on E. M. Forster.

Helen's journal entry marking the occasion is perfunctory. "[Wednesday, June 2] Rainy day. Pleasant inn and grate fire after breakfast. Wrote letters and at 10:30 we go to King's College. See E. M. Forster in his quarters—gracious." David remembers particulars. They had no letter of introduction. David wrote one, saying he was a Fulbright scholar whose mother was visiting. A great admirer of Forster's work, she would very much like to greet him. The porter delivered it and returned at once with word that Mr. Forster would be glad to see them. He led them to Forster's sitting room on the second floor where the author thanked David for escorting his mother and invited him to enjoy the gardens below while he visited with his mother.

Forster was nine years older than she, almost exactly Melvin's age. His world and hers shared, in spite of the dividing sea, memories of other times, manners, expectations. Home and place featured significantly for each. Guarded and restrained, with powerful emotional natures, they were both affected by, and alert to, other life possibilities. Helen expressed her gratitude to Forster for writing *A Room with a View*. His fictional Lucy Honeychurch was key to their common ground, her entry point to their easy talk. He, no doubt, appreciated the experienced Calvinist behind his articulate visitor.

They talked of Italy, the fecundity of the American south, the color, the air, the surprise of sunshine. They talked of England and Wisconsin, the restraining effect of the cold and damp and fog, how it mangled spirit. They talked about the brutalizing twentieth century that disconnected people one from another, the simpler times they could both remember and which receded even while they talked. She drank the sherry he offered, not telling him that she did not drink. He escorted her to the gardens afterwards to meet David and bade them farewell. They returned to the Garden House Hotel on the River Cam, the "pleasant inn" where Helen enjoyed the grate fire and a warm memory of her "gracious" host.

She and David attended services at Christ Church the next day and heard a "superb" sermon in which the minister described the "suspended anxiety of the Christian," his "uneasy conscience lodged between acceptance and blasphemy."

Helen picked up her mail at the English Speaking Union and moved into a bright, spacious, yellow room with a private bath at the Connaught Hotel for her final two days in England. She had booked her return, a first-class cabin aboard the SS *Liberté* departing June 10. David saw her off on the stormy night when heavy seas prevented the *Liberté* from docking at Southhampton, watching as the passengers, taken out to sea aboard smaller crafts, boarded off-shore, cautiously wending their way up the narrow gangway slung from ship to rolling ship aided by cheerful, confident personnel. She sent him a cable when she reached New York—"Hallelujah!"

Helen returned to the usual mix of good and bad family news. The judge in the Rapids ruled that William Connor Rhyner's suit against Richard Connor, his uncle, guardian, and trustee charging fraud and collusion in the sale of his stock to Gordon R. Connor without merit.[24] (Ironically, William's refusal to offer Helen a more adequate price for her shares gave the judge grounds to rule that "the sale price of $200 a share represented the reasonable value of the stock at the time of the sale.") As for the charge of "collusion between Richard M. Connor and his brother, Gordon, to secure voting control of the Connor Lumber and Land Co.," the judge found that to be "totally lacking in probative value."[25] (Connor Lumber and Land Company papers, since deposited in the archives of the Wisconsin State Historical Library, Madison, do, however, suggest a high degree of collaboration.)

With his Uncle William urging him on and paying costs, William Connor Rhyner appealed to the Wisconsin Supreme Court. William also appealed the suit he had filed and lost against Helen, in order, Dick was convinced, to drive up the price of his stock now that he would certainly sell out. He had, however, put on a public show of family cohesion at the Republican convention (elected a delegate in absentia, an alternate took Helen's place) and at a Marshfield Chamber of Commerce meeting when Bom and Walter Kohler teamed up to discuss "Your State and Nation Today." One of the hosts at that meeting, William was photographed with his arm around Bom's shoulders.

After months of being a tourist, Helen was glad to be working and needed. When Bom reached her in Madison on July 17, with news that his third child, David Malcolm, had been born, she took his older son, John O., to Laona to lighten Barbara's load. He helped take her mind off the Connor quarrels and the horrible international problems. In the Far East, the Chinese had fired on the heavily fortified islands of Quemoy and Matsu; in Central America, it appeared the Communists were opening a path all the way from Guatemala to the Panama Canal to northern Mexico.

When the Woman's Club met in September, Ruth Doyle, former assemblywoman from Dane County, the wife of James Doyle (defeated in the gubernatorial primary by William Proxmire), presented the Democratic program for dealing with national problems. Mrs. Henry Stewart Jones (Sara Roddis Jones) spoke for the Republicans. "Both speakers did well," Helen thought. Bom did well in the election, in spite of a vituperative campaign launched by his opponent.[26] Walter Kohler won a third term by a slim margin. Nationally, however, the Republicans lost the Congress.

Occupied as she was with the regents' business, Helen volunteered as a "Gray Lady" at the hospital and wrote several speeches, including one about "Women in Modern Poetry" and another about the Romantic poets' reaction to the industrial revolution. David, who had returned to Madison, helped with the latter. "Percy Bysshe Shelley described 'Lords' as 'drones' who drained the sweat and drank the blood of the working men in his 1819 poem 'Song to the Men of England.'" The poem was a "serious statement of his view and of the view of many of the Romantic poets beginning with William Blake." David advised her to look at Elizabeth Barrett Browning's "The Cry of the Children" and Thomas Hood's "The Song of the Shirt," "The Bridge of Sighs," and "The Lay of the Labourer." His conclusion was pessimistic. "It was not until the later part of the 19th century that some of the disappointments and failures convinced many of them that their hope of human progress had been but myth and illusion. They had come down from their Olympus only to find the waste land."

A headline in the *Herald* alluded to the sense of "wasteland" abroad in America in 1954: "Christmas Season Both Fun and Annual Bore." A Christmas card from Ethel Sexton expressed the "something more" the season held for some. "Through our shared sorrows you have shown such confidence in my faith that I want you to know that without you it would not have been less, but because of you it is much stronger. You know I appreciate your friendship. My love, Ethel."

Herbert F. Margulies's letter requesting information about the Wisconsin political scene in the first decade of the century took Helen back to a simpler time
before the atom and the hydrogen bombs and competing ideologies. From
her mannered reply, Margulies, a Ph.D. candidate in history, must have realized that he had not struck a rich lode of political gossip. "I imagine the reason
Isaac Stephenson was chosen in the 1907 Senatorial contest in the legislature
was because he was an outstanding citizen of the State and perhaps had been
proposed for this crowning honor in his old age by Republican leaders." She
had "a copy of a fine speech which Mr. Connor gave at a Lincoln Day dinner
in Milwaukee in 1906, which gives some of his ideas." She had only the single
copy, but "perhaps through David" could arrange to see him sometime when
she was in Madison.[27]

"Play the Queen" was the theme of the second annual Co-Ed Week celebrated at the University Union. The four-point program covered careers, fash-
ions, travel, and marriage and did not interest Helen any more than the first
Co-Ed Week "Fashioning Your Future," which the university had sponsored
the year before. That program was "designed to show women how best to package themselves."[28] Her letter in support of her friend Norma Hoblit Woods's
nomination for the 1955 Smith College Mother of the Year award speaks to
the standards of women of their class and generation. According to Helen, the
qualities that made Norma Woods an ideal candidate for the award included
her loyalty to the college and to her many friends, "the rare hospitality offered
in her interesting home," her devotion to her three sons ("one of whom lost
his life in the World War"), the "fine character and education of the two living
sons," her "unusual determination to better conditions in her own community" as leader of the local youth center, her "great contributions in time and
money" to the Episcopalian Church of which she was "a devout and com-
municant member," her participation in the DAR as State Chaplain, and "the
sincerity of her prayers."[29]

David passed his orals, sent off applications for a teaching position, and
invited fifty friends to celebrate, a mixed group of artists, professors, undergraduates. John Wilde and wife, Alvin Whitley, Wynn Chamberlain, George
Herring, Werner Vortriede, Marshall Glasier, and Alden Thayer were among
the guests, as was Helen Lauritzen, who would receive her B.A. in June. "Miss
Lauritzen's work in the campus plays has won wide acclaim," the *Cardinal*
reported on March 29. "She was first seen in the *Madwoman of Chaillot* and
the performance won her the Madison Critic's award." The just ended production of the *Crucible* was "her last performance as a student."

David borrowed a downstairs apartment on Langdon Street from Alden

Thayer's girlfriend for the celebration and hired a burro from a local farmer. The burro wandered around carrying a tray on his back. No one remembered what was served. Martinis? Two-hundred-proof medical alcohol? Hors d'oeuvres? It was a great party. So good no one wanted it to stop. When the farmer arrived to collect his burro, David led the revelers on foot to the Madison Club, with everyone so far gone that no one minded being turned out of the bar downstairs where loud voices and raucous behavior were tolerated, but only among politicians and businessmen.

David had returned to his customary decorous self when he and his mother attended the University of Wisconsin Honor's Convocation in the Union Theater on June 17. Dean Mark H. Ingraham of the College of Letters and Science addressed the students who had achieved a grade point average of at least 3.25, Helen Lauritzen among them. Her parents, immigrants from Aalborg, Denmark, who owned a bakery in Bay Ridge, Brooklyn, had not been able to come.

David finished his dissertation over the summer. On September 10, while Helen attended a regents' meeting, he and Helen Lauritzen were married in Brooklyn, New York. Bom, who flew up from Washington to be his best man, and their cousin Elizabeth, recently graduated from Smith College and working in Manhattan, represented the family.

David wrote his mother on September 11 as he and his bride flew from New York to Cleveland en route to Oberlin, where David had accepted a position as an instructor in the English department. "It was a very lovely wedding. The ceremony at the church (Our Savior's Danish Lutheran) and the dinner after. Bom will give an eye witness account. . . . How did things go in Madison?"

On December 31, 1955, two years to the date after Helen received the summons announcing her brother's lawsuit, headlines in the *Marshfield News Herald* and the *Wisconsin Rapids Daily Tribune* reported that the litigation in the Connor cases had ended without recourse to the higher courts.[30] Henceforth, with Dick also determined to cut his ties with the Connor Lumber and Land Company, the Lairds and the Connors would, with the exception of Birch Lake, which bound them, go their separate ways.

Bom was thoroughly engrossed in the political life he loved. Dick planned to open another lumber yard at Verona and build a home in the new University Hill Farms development in Madison. And for David the world was opening. For Helen, the summer of 1956 was replete with reminders of the past and of her family's beginnings in Wisconsin. The *Stratford Journal* published a special edition recounting the origins of the town, and the *News Herald* and *Daily Tribune* jointly published a Centennial Edition to celebrate Wood County,[31] a history to which she had contributed. In Laona on her sixty-eighth birthday, she was in a deeply reflective mood as she wrote a poem, "To Father." She likened him to "the big pine that crowned the hill." He had stood "through storm and stress" to beat a trail, lonely then, to the heart of the virgin forest, to the blue lake. "What matters it now to you and me, who holds the title to all I see. . . . Whoever else may title hold, all I feel, all I see, belong to thee."[32]

She rarely allowed the past to dominate her thoughts and almost never exposed a sentimental side. Her sharp questions showed her in the current of events, not at all beached. With her sons she discussed world and national affairs: the civil rights cases coming before the Supreme Court, the appeals concerning the immediate admission of black pupils to white schools in Texas and South Carolina, and the pernicious effects of the McCarran Act, which had caused so many outstanding members of the NAACP to be fired from their jobs on the charge that they were Communists.

While regretting that Harold Stassen failed in his campaign to dump Nixon, she approved of the 1956 Republican platform, which promised to continue "sound advances in matters of basic human needs,"[33] and liked Eisenhower's acceptance speech in which he said the party was "in league with the future" but "change without principle becomes chaos."

Bom, she observed, campaigned with his usual exuberance not only for himself but for the party, seeking votes and urging citizen participation.[34] On November 4, she gathered around the television with Dick, Pat, and Barbara to watch Bom on WSAW-TV. (Even with television, campaigns were not expensive in those days. Bom reported receiving $690 and spending $715.) He "performed well," Helen thought, hammering home themes that would remain consistent throughout his years in government service: national security (on the defense subcommittee of the appropriations committee, he voted to add additional funding to an already astronomical bill in order to achieve missile warfare readiness) and the deterioration in the quality of public discourse.

With Bulganin's threat of a Third World War, following the attempt by Britain, France, and Israel to wrest control of the Suez Canal from Egypt, Eisenhower won by a landslide. Bom won by a landslide too. But the Democrats retained the majority in Congress, and it would not be friendly. The Republicans won in Wisconsin. Vernon Thomson became governor, Warren Knowles lieutenant governor, Warren Smith again was treasurer, and Robert Zimmerman, who had defeated Helen's candidate, Mrs. Glenn Wise, in the primaries, took his father's place as secretary of state. As always, no woman held high political office in Wisconsin.

Her three sons and their wives celebrated Thanksgiving with her at 208

South Cherry, while the grandchildren were fed in Bom's house next door. After grace, the festive family reunion was briefly marred when Helen, smiling warmly, asked Bom to carve. Dick abruptly pushed away from the table, stood up, and flashed a hostile look. As eldest son, the honor should have been his. In asking Bom to do the honors, Helen showed instinctive favoritism. Connor used to come first. Now Bom. Only David, the youngest, did not compete, at least not so that it showed.

Helen was partially to blame for raising a competitive family. Yet, as the Jaycees announced that they would drop the annual parade at Christmas due to a lack of interest in the event, and last year's "Keep Christ in Christmas Parade" would be the last, it was the Christian story that dominated her thoughts. On the final page of her annual journal she wrote: "Fallacy to think what helps others hurts us. Jehovah vs. universal god. Didn't want to go to Nineveh. Paul and the Jews sensed god was universal and admitted gentiles— otherwise Christianity would have been just a Jewish sect."

"All is well here in Washington. Kids are enjoying school and are well settled," Bom reported when he phoned on January 5, adding that he had brought John and Alison with him to hear the president when he addressed the joint session. She missed the children, he knew, more than she would admit. She saved her questions about America's ability to afford spreading the Marshall Plan beyond Europe and about the necessity of continuing atomic testing (eminent scientists, including Linus Pauling, claimed the fallout was danger- ous) until she saw him again. She treasured his monthly office reports, often using the back side to jot her thoughts: "World would be a wonderful place if it weren't for the people." "Leadership. Educator. In an urgent sense those nations which educate their people best will hold the strongest position in the critical ideological conflict that now grips the world."

Dick was land hunting all over southwestern Wisconsin, buying logs and stocking his yards in Manitowoc and Verona. He and Pat settled into their new two-story colonial house in Madison. Active in the Parent Teacher Association, Pat had her hands full raising four youngsters. The family joined the Congre- gational Church, Dick the Rotary. In Oberlin, David slid into the second semester of his second year and began looking for another job. His appointment had been for one of the usual three-year rotating appointments Oberlin offered to young Ph.D.'s, with tenure almost never granted, certainly not in English. His mother liked Oberlin and regretted the position had not been permanent.

She was visiting with Bom and Barbara in Washington on May 3, 1957, when Joseph McCarthy died of acute liver failure. She had never liked McCarthy, but a Marshfield man, Steve Miller, president of the Cheese Corporation, was head of the Wisconsin McCarthy Club, and Bom had, at first, supported him. Bom attended the speech Vietnam's president Ngo Dinh Diem gave, at Eisenhower's request, to the joint session of Congress asking for increased aid.[35] Helen wondered if the administration had given up on holding the line on debt. Bom assured her it hadn't. The papers reported that Harold Stassen, Eisenhower's special assistant on disarmament, was increasingly isolated, his access to the president limited.[36] Bom assured her that Stassen's report on the international talks on serious arms cutbacks would reach the president. It pleased her to know that Bom had friends on both sides of the aisle, that he enjoyed membership in the Chowder and Marching Club, a close-knit group of Republicans that included Vice President Nixon, John Byrnes, Gerald Ford, and Glenn Lipscomb, midwesterners and westerners who came together to pray, eat breakfast, and discuss issues and tactics.

"The Churches Speak," a speech he delivered in Wausau over WSAU-TV on September 14, reminded her of the address Melvin gave when he first ran for the state senate. Bom answered his own question: "Ought a Christian go into politics?" with another, "How can a Christian stay out?" The Presbyterian commitment to civic involvement ran through his answer. "To what better

Dick Laird's family, ca. 1958. From left: Dick, Jessica, Richie, Maggie, Lissa, and Pat.

source for help can politics turn than to those whose philosophy of life is Christian. Government has to do with lives. . . . In this 20th century much of our lives is shaped by government, the hands that do the shaping should be Christian hands."

Convinced "the importance of organized religion to our world will be measured . . . in terms of legislators it has socially inspired," but unshaken in her belief that religion was a profoundly private affair,[37] Helen was better satisfied when Bom spoke of his having accepted an additional assignment on the House Appropriations Committee and would be one of the five members on the subcommittee on Health, Education and Welfare. The position practically guaranteed that the National Advisory Heart Council would select the University of Wisconsin as a regional center for research and training in heart disease.

A fragile March sun filtered through the east-facing windows of her little study off her bedroom as Helen wrote "A Lenten Meditation." Lent was "a good time to eliminate some of the unnecessary 'busyness' of our lives," a good time to let the soul catch up with the body.

Across America on Easter Sunday 1958, people marched for peace and thought about Henry Luce's advice to build bomb shelters against the Soviet Union's deployment of intercontinental missiles. David, in Charlottesville, considering and being considered for a position in the University of Virginia's English department, had dinner with Floyd Stovell, an Americanist who headed the department. William Faulkner, the artist in residence, picked David up at his hotel at 6:00 A.M. the next morning. Faulkner knew the holes at a deserted lake. Since the fish weren't biting, Faulkner stopped rowing; they stopped casting, listened to the birds as the dawn brightened, and drank the coffee Faulkner brought in a thermos. As the boat drifted silently along, they talked about *The Bear* (a story David liked to teach), the disappearing American wilderness, northern Wisconsin. Most folks wouldn't know what to do in the wilderness now, Faulkner said, but he was much more comfortable there than in town and would leave Virginia and go back to Mississippi.

David did not go to Virginia, which offered no better prospects for a young instructor than Oberlin. He accepted an offer from California, where Governor Pat Brown was building up institutions of higher education to match the burgeoning population. Los Angeles State College, as California State University, Los Angeles, was then known, a "street car" college downtown with some 6,000 junior, senior, and graduate students, most of them older and many married and working, was expanding. In the process of building new quarters on the hills above the San Bernadino freeway in east Los Angeles, the college was hiring an "elite faculty" of young Ph.D.s from all over the country to develop a "correspondingly elite undergraduate and graduate curriculum." Brought in on the third step of assistant professor, David could anticipate interesting courses, and tenure was practically a given.

Helen prodded him about his appointment; she was not pleased to have him move so far away and into a school still under construction. She was correct in her belief that the college was once a state normal school, but she erroneously assumed it had become one of the University of California's many branches, not recognizing that while Wisconsin was uniting its state colleges into a university system, California was developing two separate and unequal systems.

Dick, at least, would remain in Wisconsin. Helen shifted her attention to him when he underwent prostate surgery. She visited him in the hospital, bringing pajamas, a new bathrobe, a book, and a check. "It was wonderful of you to come through like that. It is very welcomed and useful of course, but I can get by okay without it and don't qualify as an emergency in that respect." Helen's letter about Dick's hospitalization made David feel how "out of touch" the brothers were. He had had no idea Dick "was having such a bad time." They would have to "work out some system of keeping in touch."[38]

While adjusting to another shift in her life with David's move to the West Coast, Helen had to adjust to the loss of Ethel Sexton, with whom she had shared two widowhoods, the one a temporary period during the First World War when their husbands were serving abroad and the other after their husbands died. From her kitchen window, Helen looked out on other changes: a fire at St. Alban's Episcopal Church at the corner of Maple and Third Streets destroyed the Guild Hall, scene of more than a half-century of Woman's Club gatherings; Dr. Jim Vedder Sr.'s and Dr. W. S. Heaton's houses were knocked down to make way for a new telephone exchange building on Cedar and Second. Her backyard now adjoined the telephone company's large asphalt parking lot instead of Dr. Heaton's barn and garden. She recognized "progress" when Marshfield's telephone system went on dial at 1:00 A.M., on Sunday, October 5, but it was a mixed blessing.

On October 9, after attending the formal investiture of Dr. Elvehjem as the University of Wisconsin's thirteenth president, Helen sped home in order to be there when Bom and Governor Thomson arrived. The candidates, instead of standing on a street corner and using a megaphone, as they had in the last election, arrived in a well-publicized "torchlight" parade that rolled down Central Avenue at 7:30 P.M. Led by the colors, color guard, and a sound car, the parade consisted of a steam engine with the governor as engineer, Bom as

fireman, Assemblyman John Crawford as conductor, all pulling a float containing Russ Lewallen's band and fourteen handsome "Thomson Girls." A
hula-hoop float carried hula-hoop girls and a milk maid, butter maid, and
cheese maid—truly a Marshfield parade, a parade out of central Wisconsin.
Afterwards, at the Republican rally at the Eagles Hall, a sizeable, enthusiastic
crowd heard Bom speak about the need for congressional investigations of labor
racketeers, for adequate and effective federal legislation to restore and protect
the civil liberties of working people, and for fiscal responsibility. The 85th Congress had spent, or appropriated, $80 billion while anticipating $68 billion in
receipts. "Our debts of today will be passed on to later generations." Helen
wrote, "Only if Bom rolls up a bigger vote than ever, will he be satisfied. Even
that wouldn't repay me for being away from a young family four months
straight."[39]

The Democrats' massive landslide—they won all state offices with the exception of secretary of state position—made Bom's reelection, in spite of a hard
campaign mounted against him, a noteworthy exception. Wyngaard reported
his victory "when all else on his Republican ticket was going down in humiliating defeat" and the "fearful cost" of reaching "the ear and eye of the sover-
eign elector." It would "stun the old time politician."[40]

Nationally the Republican picture was not without a few bright lights: Bom's
good friend, Michigan's representative, Gerald Ford, was reelected; Arizona's senator, Barry Goldwater, also won reelection; and Nelson Rockefeller was elected
governor of New York. Those who became leading Republican figures were
on stage preparing for the next act, which Mrs. Ruth Murray, vice chairman
of the Wisconsin Republican Party, in announcing her resignation, threatened
would not go smoothly. Declaring that the GOP should "stand for something
other than a 'me too' policy," she made it clear she was "in no mood to build
an organization to elect someone like Nelson Rockefeller as president."[41]

"Bam will have to use all his good judgment in what course to pursue for
they are already suggesting that he run for governor next time. With Kohler,
Knowles, Thomson sitting on the sidelines, it doesn't look promising," Helen
wrote David. If she went to Washington over Christmas, it would be on about
the 14th or 15th, when Bom was expected to be in the district and she could
travel back to Washington with him. If his plans changed, she would wait until
the 20th. "Hardly the way to treat the old house which has served us so well, to
desert her in her old age at Christmas. It won't seem natural to me to be away."

She wrote David again from Milwaukee on December 3. She had had "to
fight so to get started." It was "never easy." The Pfister was no hotel in which
"to go modern and I'm sure my boy friend regents will be at the Schraeder,

but I like this end of town." The magazine on her desk, *Changing Times*, made her think "the times may change, but not this hotel. It looks exactly as when I saw it first as a girl about 14 years of age." Dick, who had been to a National Lumber Dealers meeting in Chicago, would write "in due time," she supposed. Bom was going to spend a week in the District and hoped she would return with him to Washington.

She did not go to Washington. Her "funny doctor" told her "You stay in the Midwest" after she experienced an "uncertain time." She would stay home and water the violet plant Elsbeth Epstein sent; and the poinsettias, azaleas, and Jerusalem cherries her sons and brothers Richard and Gordon sent; visit every day with Aunt Florence, who was ill; entertain and be entertained at teas and dinners; walk bundled and carefully down the slippery streets to Central Avenue to the bank, library, post office, drug store, grocery, and church. Then, in January 1959, she left for a regents meeting and a visit with Dick and his family in Madison.

"Such a quietness settles upon us when it is so cold—not even many cars passing," Helen wrote David and Helen L. on her return. The winter quiet led

Bom's family, ca. 1956. From left: Alison, Barbara, David M., John O., and Melvin.

to serious rumination. As she had many times before, she turned to people she considered wise, putting her questions: "How does Jesus fit into the modern world?" "Where is Christianity now; where faith, where spirit?" into a letter she wrote to the Reverend Robert McCracken, who succeeded Harry Emerson Fosdick at the Riverside Church in New York. He answered:

> Dear Friend,
>
> I am sorry not to have been able to reply to your good letter more promptly. You seem to me to be on the right track in your thinking. Concentrate on God as Spirit and on Jesus as supremely revealing the Mind and Spirit of God. The New Testament does not emphasize the physical appearance of Jesus— His face for example—but it centers attention on His spiritual attributes.
>
> I do not think of the Apostle's Creed as outmoded but as a great landmark indicating what was believed by our forebears in the faith. It needs interpretation in the light of the age in which we live and when so interpreted is far less of an intellectual problem.
>
> With warm good wishes.
> Yours faithfully,
> R. J. McCracken.[42]

She also sent for a sermon the Reverend Lawrence Lowell Gruman delivered at the First Congregational Church in Madison: "Academic Dilemma: Is God Dead." Gruman quoted George Forell of the University of Iowa School of Religion: "Man is dying," says Forell, "not God." "Man is dying because he has tried too long to live without God, and man is man only in relation to God."

She experienced dizziness, palpitations, and a blurring of vision in her left eye after returning home from the commencement, president's luncheon, and her last regents' meeting in June. "I will miss two or three on that board muchly," Helen admitted to David and Helen L., "but I feel like a hanger on now and the governor might as well appoint."[43] Dick was with her when she entered St. Joseph's hospital for a series of tests. Diagnosed as having high blood pressure and as having had, perhaps, a small stroke, she followed orders to "slow down." She began to take medication and, instructed to do so, limited her caloric intake and began to shed the accumulated pounds of many Wisconsin winters.

The "episode" made her "uncertain a bit," but she took it in stride, considering it "fortunate that only one eye went bum." Although she promised Dick to think over his proposal that she come to Madison, live near him, and his family, she had no intention of leaving her home. Her sons were concerned, she knew, and she promised to "try out a woman" to help at the house. Dick "would like to have had everything settled and tied up with a woolen string," but she couldn't "work that way just now." She had to "be patient and reasonably quiet." She had been walking around in the wet with Bessie, and wondered when David planned "to start this way" and if he planned to drive.[44] He did. In the summer of 1959, David and Helen L. made the first of what became an annual seasonal migration from California to Wisconsin.

Bom blew into town on September 10 to accompany her to the celebration honoring Stephan Epstein, the clinic's "first investigator" and a leading force behind Bom's interest in establishing the Foundation for Medical Research at the Marshfield Clinic. She felt lonely when he left, more so now that she had fewer immediate issues to tangle with and was more physically vulnerable. She tried to lift herself out of sad thoughts by writing David and Helen L. Dick said he might drive up "some day before long, hoping we could drive on north to see the leaves." Things seemed pretty slow. "Get an occasional letter from Madison, but by now, I'm not missed—replaced as well as succeeded, but no one even mentions the new man to me." She found it "amusing that Steve Miller has taken it upon himself to speak for Governor Rockefeller as to his candidacy, etc."[45]

LeRoy Luberg, assistant to the president of the university, had not forgotten her. He wrote saying they would miss her in their opening sessions, and he hoped that her not being there would not prevent them from having "a continuing exchange of information." He knew she would be pleased that during the last meeting the regents unanimously voted to provide funding for three new positions for the Counseling Center. They had all read the reports from "the Washington scene," where "Melvin continues to do his superior work for us in Wisconsin. I know you feel he is busy enough, but there are many of us who look forward to his assuming even heavier responsibilities. He is the one to do it."

David remained her contact with the creative word world on which she had always been so heavily dependent, and she wrote him about a description she read in Henry James's *The Turn of the Screw:* "'The summer had gone; the autumn had dropped upon Bly and had blown out half our lights. The place with its gray sky and withered garlands, its bared spaces and scattered dead leaves was like a theater after the performance—all strewn with crumpled play-bills.' I love that last and think of it every morning when I sweep the porch. The show is over."[46]

On November 12, Helen attended an "Appreciation Night" dinner in Bom's honor at the Field House in the Rapids. Former Governor Walter Kohler and

Lieutenant Governor Warren Knowles were among the 4,500 in attendance. Vice President Richard M. Nixon delivered the major address, praising Bom for his most "impressive" characteristic: he "studies all sides of every question." Frank Panzer, president pro-tem of the Wisconsin Senate, hailed Bom "as a rising political figure" and prophesized "you will some day come back here in a much higher capacity than you are being honored for here tonight." Representative John Byrnes, Green Bay, chairman of the Wisconsin delegation, also turned prophetic. "Mel Laird's story is only beginning—the final telling will bring glory to his state and the country he loves so well." Evident in a news photo of Helen standing beside Vice President Nixon and her son are the compressed lips with which she struggles to hold back her tears.[47]

Tears of joy for Helen. Tears of sorrow for William. His son Billie had not succeeded either as a farmer or a husband. Divorced from his second wife, separated from his children, he left Wisconsin and headed west. On December 16, headlines in the *Herald* carried shocking news: "Connor Son Found Dead Near Omaha." He was thirty-seven years old, Bom's age. His body, clad in hunting clothes, was found in a ditch in a wooded area about twelve miles west of Omaha. His car had been rifled through, but there seemed to be no other evidence of foul play.

"I depart for Madison, likely by bus tomorrow, though until the snow storm today I had expected to drive," Helen wrote David and Helen L. on December 22. "Haven't even lit up the out-door tree, nor gotten one for inside, but down-town it looks like Christmas and they play the carols and people run around with packages. . . . Don't know just what I'll do in Madison this trip— probably do penance for not getting to California. Will rest some and take it easy though I get along here without much effort and it's the place where I belong Christmas. So many memories!"

On December 29, in another letter to David and Helen L., she wrote that she'd had "a good rest at the Loraine, shut in by bad weather." Many around there knew her, which helped, and she felt comfortable. "Spent the night of Christmas Eve out at Dick's so as to see the youngsters perform and then the great unwrapping by Santa Claus and the gifts the next morning followed by much coffee and bacon and the stollen I had taken down." Jessica had come up with her by bus. "Both her parents wanted her to come." She "will get good rest here." She had started reading Allen Drury's Pulitzer Prize–winning novel, *Advise and Consent,* and was still reading it because "it is so long," over 600 pages of small print in the Doubleday first edition." It made her feel "at times as if I were in Washington. Some picture of the 'goings on' there! Exaggerated, I hope."[48]

Pat and the children rarely visited Helen. Dick usually came to Marshfield alone. Their youngest, Maggie, could not remember 208 South Cherry at all, although she remembered Helen coming to Madison and family meetings on neutral territory, at restaurants in the Rapids or Wausau. Pat thought Helen "couldn't give any warmth at all." In Madison, she heard gossip about her mother-in-law: "she had sprung very strongly to Walter Kohler's defense when someone at a dinner party at the Freds one night said something unkind about him, and Mrs. Fred had wondered afterwards: 'What kind of woman is she?'" Helen's sharp interrogations were "intrusive." Rumor had it that she was overly aggressive and unfeminine in her pursuit of answers, "a bit of a show off with the men." Helen could suddenly shift mood, deciding "I don't like it here in Madison. I want to go home." Rumor also had it that Helen was "liked by the people on the board" and was considered "an excellent regent."

Wilbur Renk, who considered her "the finest lady" he had ever met, an "excellent regent,"[49] admitted that on the rare occasions when Helen missed a meeting, the social gatherings afterwards at the university guest house were a little more relaxed. A teetotaler, and a stickler for decorum, she put a damper on their rather free and easy stag celebrations, the cigar smoking, card playing, and male gossip. Her "boy friend regents," as she privately referred to them, belonged to a generation when no lady could be considered just another fellow. Certainly not Helen, who chastised Dean Mark Ingraham for appearing before the board casually dressed without a coat and tie.

Helen had many memories from the nine years she served on the Board of Regents, most of them good. It pleased her to know that President Fred was fond of and thought well of her, that she had a reputation for being "always business," and that people "knew where she stood." Madeleine Doran, a professor in the English department, admired "the quality of her remarks—shrewdness and clarity in seeing and defining issues, good judgment and balance in her attitudes, and good humor."[50] Helen thought it had been a nice board, and they had had a fine staff.

While the loss of so many loved ones remained a wound, the decade—which saw Helen employing her energies in useful, interesting ways; participating in numerous public events; and observing her three sons successfully pursuing their different, honorable paths—had been satisfactory. If she had not often been happy, she had often been pleased.

With one son on one coast, another on the opposite, and Dick in Madison, with friends dying and her own health problematical, she cannot have faced the new decade with much enthusiasm. On December 31, William deeded five and a half acres to Marshfield in memory of his son William D. Connor and his son's grandfather, William D. Connor, in hopes that the city would practice reforestation in the wooded area in accordance with recommendations of the Wisconsin Department of Conservation. He did not call Helen to tell her about the gift. He never called. She read it in the papers. Had they been friends, they might have helped one another.

An interesting family, not an easy one. But then, the times were not easy either, nor had they ever really been, except, perhaps, when they had all been young together and Mame steered them along the right way. David's English class, she knew, was reading John Osborne's *Look Back in Anger*. It was not her way of looking.

CHAPTER 21

✌

# A Different World

## 1960–1968

If the fate of twentieth-century man is to live with death from adolescence
to premature senescence, why then the only life-giving answer is . . .
to encourage the psychopath in oneself, to explore that domain of
experience where security is boredom and therefore sickness, and one
exists in the present.

—NORMAN MAILER

"To become a regent of the University of Wisconsin is, in my opinion, about
as high an honor as a woman is likely to seek or achieve and this is only one
of the things, which you have accomplished. In looking over the record of the
Witters and the Connors one can well be proud of the distinguished record of
both families. They have indeed played an important part in the welfare and
development of that great state. . . . Please congratulate Melvin on his outstanding achievements. It is upon young men such as he that the future welfare
of our country depends."[1]

Dean Witter's letter was among the pile of mail waiting Helen's return from
southern California where she had spent a month with David and Helen L.
in their modest stucco home in San Gabriel. The home bordered the more
affluent San Marino suburb and was well situated, a twenty-minute drive
through the Alhambra commercial district to the sprawling Cal State L.A. campus and a twenty-minute walk from the Huntington Library and Gardens.
During her absence, Bessie looked after her house, piled her mail, and saved
clippings about Helen's illustrious son, one of which, a "Washington based
story," predicted, as Dean Witter had, future glory. His "many friends in the
national [Republican] committee, including Chairman Thurston B. Morton,"[2]
were boosting him for chairman of the platform committee.

Information Bom provided enabled Helen to write a speech, "Why the
Church Speaks on International Relations," in which she called attention to the

World Health Organization as a "realistic arm of the United Nations dealing with the tremendous problem of health." David helped with another: the poetry of Robert Frost. She remained active in church and club work and served on several boards: the Library Board, the Hospital Citizen's Board, and the Marshfield Research Foundation. With Bom's help, the foundation received its first federal grant of $41,219 in 1960[3] to study "farmer's lung" disease. Researchers Dean Emanuel and Fritz Wenzel traced the devastating disease to farmers' exposure to mold growing in forage. The research had worldwide implications.

From the stronghold of her well-rooted past, Helen observed and reflected on the tensions in the world and the nation. She heard Nixon, a Quaker, claim he did not hold to his religion's pacifist tenets and Kennedy claim the Republicans had allowed American military strength to slip. Like everyone else, she knew Castro was beating the Communist drum in Cuba, ninety miles off the Florida coast. She kept her cookie jar filled for the unexpected guest, for Bom, who rolled in and out of Marshfield frequently in the election year. Everyone but Bom seemed to recognize that trying to unseat "one of Wisconsin's most firmly entrenched Republicans"[4] would be a formidable task. While Nixon lost to Kennedy by less than 1 percent, Bom won the most decisive victory of all the nine Wisconsin congressional district candidates and became a leading spokesperson for the Republican view in the House. On January 25, 1961, five days after the Republican administration passed into history, in the address he read into the *Congressional Record*, Bom urged Americans never to forget "that we face the outbreak both of brush fire wars and general nuclear wars" and warned against a Munich-style appeasement.[5]

Helen kept up her personal clipping service detailing his political career, but almost never made any reference to it in the annual Wisconsin Historical Society Calendars she began keeping in 1961. There she kept track of the weather, proof that it changed and had a bearing on her moods. Year after year she noted beauty in the different seasons. Summer flowers, fall leaves, snow sparkling like diamonds in sunshine. When she was eighty-seven she laughed at herself for noting "first snowfall." She recorded trips, the small details of her daily life, significant dates and events: her father's birthday, Melvin's, Connor's, her parents' anniversary, hers. "April 16, 1963: 'My fiftieth wedding anniversary 1913–1963.'" "April 13, 1976: 'My anniversary. Thirty years alone.'" She, who had never celebrated her anniversary while Melvin lived, never failed to note the date, albeit sometimes inaccurately. Through the pages of her calendar, her beloved dead continued to live and to age. Connor became fifty-seven in 1970; Donald died in a car accident fifty-three years ago in 1966. She recorded visits to and from friends, telephone calls, jotted down verses, ideas, thoughts. "It is along the still and restful ways / Beneath the beauty of the glowing sky / That I find meaning to my earthly days / And comfort when the night draws nigh."

On April 7, 1961, she wrote "daughter born to David and Helen." On the April 8, "Bam home." She drove to Madison with him, settled in "her" room at the Loraine Hotel for a few days, had lunch with Dick and Bom and dinner with Dick and Pat and the youngsters. She sent David verbal snap shots of her grandchildren: "Lissa is the upcoming student of the family," Jess had "too many deals on"; Maggie needed "to eat and sleep"; Richie was "like a blasé Norse man."

While 25,000 people in more than a dozen cities walked for peace, in far away Vietnam American leaders quietly inaugurated a policy of "gradualism." The policy would prove as unrealistic, given the extent of corruption within the professional army and the lack of fighting fervor among the south Vietnamese,[6] as the hope that the Cubans would pick up arms against Castro. The real "gradualism" was in effect in America, where the divide between the people and the government, against which she and Melvin Sr. had so earnestly fought, had become a chasm.

She was not, however, ready to agree with the four leading Western scientists whom she heard on a CBS program celebrating MIT's centennial. Sir Eric Ashby, Isidor Isaac Rabi, Raymond C. F. Aron, and Jerrold R. Zacharias argued that the average citizen could not comprehend the science on which governmental decisions had to be based. The "scientific age" was "already too complex for 'common sense' to be an effective answer" to the questions facing national leaders.[7]

The cost of everything overwhelmed her. She took no comfort in knowing that James Doyle Sr., "the most respected private citizen among the Democrats of Wisconsin," and Philip Kuehn, a leading Republican, both believed that "the legitimate rise in public expenditures, present and prospective" required a departure from the tax policies of "more simple times."[8]

She was with Bom when he delivered a speech at the newly opened municipal airport, saying he hoped the "huge sum" necessary to "maintain freedom" would be "wasted" and observed that the "national character" appeared to be "cracking." It didn't "seem to have the driving will to maintain freedom."[9] She watched his weekly television programs taped in Washington and shown on local TV. He called almost every day, and although she suffered from dizzy spells, she didn't talk about them, nor did she tell him what she told David: she was rereading her favorite nineteenth-century novels.

She drove to Madison to celebrate "Woman's Day." Don Anderson, the Alumni Association president and publisher of the *Wisconsin State Journal*, wrote urging her to come. "Historians," he claimed, would mark "the day when the ancient and honorable Wisconsin Alumni Association decided that women are people."[10] She "didn't get too big a kick out of meeting—Too many has beens like myself."

Reluctant as she was to associate with "has beens," she spent a good deal of time with Aunt Florence, whose "has been" status had to be beyond doubt, and returned to Madison for a reunion luncheon of the Half Century Club when Maybel Pick said she was going. She enjoyed herself, even though everyone looked old. She watched an old man, Walter Lippmann on CBS television, read John Pressly Jr.'s letter saying his father had heard him preach at a meeting of Presbyterians at the Nebraska Synod in Hastings. A few months later, John Pressly Sr. followed his wife, Margaret, into the "chapter eternal."

She pictured Dean Witter as a young man; the large photo of him in the article he sent, "Montgomery, A Money-Splendid Street," showed him an old one, standing in front of skyscrapers looking back on a fifty-year career on the street. "Within the name 'Montgomery Street' are the five letters that spell the essence of the mile long way from Market Street to Pier 33 on the Embarcadero. The letters spell M-O-N-E-Y. . . . Montgomery Street remains the headquarters of the 46 nation-wide investment offices of Dean Witter and Company, which was founded there." Chosen investment banker of the year in 1959, the "huge, powerfully built sportsman" was "the personification of the ultimate ambitions of those who work in the caves of Montgomery Street."[11]

This celebration of her favorite cousin as the acknowledged King of the "M-O-N-E-Y Street" was not without its irony. Helen remembered how her husband had warned against Mammon's encroachment when she and he were newlyweds. No one now, except the society's all but disregarded, underpaid ministers and all those vocal revolutionaries and peaceful visionaries, claiming they wanted to redistribute the wealth, seemed to trouble about the "value" of men dedicated to making money and money making money, although that had once been a weighty subject in America causing much soul searching and many cautionary tales.

During a winter visit with David and Helen L. in 1962, she saw her nine-month-old granddaughter Vanessa for the first time and met David's in-laws, who had retired and settled in Santa Barbara. "Pleasant evening. A handsome couple." A railroad traveler, she broke her return trip in Albuquerque, where she was entertained by Constie and several of her friends whose lovely homes featured fine Santa Clara black pottery and the work of western artists that were beginning to be recognized and fetch high prices: Victor Higgens, Irving Couse, Oscar Berninghaus, E. Martin Hennings, and Kenneth Adams.

Constie may have come to a wilderness when she married, but it was no wilderness now, not for her, anyway.

"Aside from seeing Dick in Chicago, the biggest thrill" Helen had, she wrote in her thank-you note to David and Helen L., "was getting ahold of my car again on a nice open road with little traffic. . . . Dick seems to be getting interested in Warren Knowles' campaign for governor." She had sorted her accumulated mail and looked forward to Bom's coming "with two or three Congressmen friends on a Lincoln Day tour."

Ice cracked under her feet and she had to walk slowly against a sharp wind. She thought of warmer places and a familiar impatience set in. She hoped Dick would follow through on his offer of taking her on a "bat." He did, but not before Bom pulled in to escort her to the Republican caucus in the Rapids, where they reunited with Republican leaders and friends Warren Knowles, Wilbur Renk, and gubernatorial candidate Philip Kuehn. She told Bom she had received a letter from Walter Lippmann in answer to one of hers and that he did not think "we could promote *democracy* in India, Nigeria and Brazil" but that "these were the key countries in the three continents which could be kept non-communist."

Her sons, by an unwritten agreement, took turns visiting and providing what they knew to be essential stimulation, even though she was a determined self-starter. In addition to his summer migration, David regularly flew in to Chicago or Minneapolis from L.A. on the "red eye special," rented a car, drove to Marshfield, and usually set off with her for Laona or Madison.

Dick came for solo visits, which she sometimes found tiring, and twice he tried, not too successfully, to entertain her in New Orleans. He liked horse races; she preferred concerts. He could also be "a bit belligerent in mood. He likes to argue things out and I don't." She counted on Bom's dropping in during his frequent trips into the district, and until 1966, when the congressional sessions began to last throughout the summer, and his importance to the party compelled him to keep his base in Washington, on his family's arrival to spend the summer in their home next door. The youngsters were in and out of her house then.

Bom's son David Malcolm retained "vivid memories of the house at 208 South Cherry, so much a part of my childhood summers." He remembered "the coolness of the darkened living room, playing the piano or games with Bamma. She would often read with me so on nights when I was not feeling well, she would have me spend the night in the upstairs bedroom. I can still hear the songs she would sing as she gently stroked my head, . . . the soothing sound of the train whistles through the open window." His sweetest memory was of "being able to stand on my bed each night and call across the way to Bamma in her bedroom and say 'Good Night.'"[12]

Helen seems to have chosen to lavish affection on this grandchild. None of her other grandchildren, some of whom admired her, reported such warm feelings. One occasion, however, stands out in their minds. When Jessica, Lissa, John O. and Alison, still largely apolitical in the early sixties, came in a body to call, she was determined to give them and herself a good time. Seated at the piano, an enormous pile of sheet music beside her, she led them in singing the tunes from early revues, popular songs they had never heard and a few later ones with which they were familiar. She and her grandchildren went through a veritable history of four decades of popular songs. They belted out Gershwin's 1924 hit "Lady Be Good," sobbed with the "Chinkies" in the "Limehouse Blues" and traveled "a thousand miles," saw "a thousand sights," and met a "thousand gals." They sang about being "in big towns jazzin' a-round" and in small towns, about not being ready to "sit pat on the Bam Bam Bamy-y shore." They pressed and caressed "Ramona," "Tip-Toed through the Tulips," felt "Alone Because I Love You," "Saw Paris" for the last time, and became "Younger Than Springtime." They concluded by "dancing all night," going "around the world," and "climbing every mountain."

A number of the arrangements from the twenties were for piano and ukulele. The ukulele had been Connor's instrument, and unlike her tone-deaf younger sons, he had had a fine voice. He and she had had some good times playing and singing together, but she did not tell her grandchildren about those days.

As a grandmother, Helen was remembered more for the lessons she tried to instill. Alison recalled Helen's instructions on the art of serving and drinking afternoon tea, on good manners, and on the art of conversation. As an adult, reflecting on her grandmother's behavior, she wondered how this unbending, rigorous old woman, who pushed her carefully arranged tea cart into the living room and talked with her in such a measured, careful way, got to be the way she was.[13]

David's daughter, Vanessa, coming later, escaped the tea ritual, but as a very young child she responded to her grandmother much as Alison did. She expressed herself as a three-year-old: "Bamma treats other people down." Years later she confided that being with Helen was a little like "running a maze." You got to one point and heard "eat your peas," to another and were blocked by a "don't answer your mother back." She did not feel that her grandmother was "formidable" or "unapproachable," as some children did, but she did not expect any warmth from her either.

Dick's daughters, Jessica and Lissa, while never achieving emotional close-ness with their grandmother, admired and kept in touch with her even after she jumped on them at Birch Lake "for the disarray of the little cabin. Lissa had never heard me explode before and will remember." That the girls had the heat on full tilt in the electric board heaters she had had installed and "win-dow shades pulled down to the floor" in spite of the 70-degree temperatures outside prompted her outburst. Dick's family took their summer vacations in Door County thereafter.

"Why get lonely"? Helen asked herself when Bom and David and their fam-ilies returned to their respective coasts. "I wonder if Bam would miss me if I weren't here when he has to come back. Only time will tell, but then it's too late to say so. Still miss my old home and those in it."

Bom's book *A House Divided: America's Strategy Gap*, published in anticipa-tion of the 1962 election, dealt less with the economic threat posed by Com-munist advances in Southeast Asia and the erosion of American and Western European interests than with "the spiritual threat represented by the Com-munist system, . . . a religion of materialism and without God. . . . and by the shallow thinking of East coast positivist scholars," including the "brilliant writer" James Schlesinger. "Tomorrow, unless we act now . . . we may face the darkest age of mankind's history." The Western world was moving in a path of "suicidal decline."[14]

Helen did not believe that religion, a private matter, divided the country. Vietnam did. The Women Strike for Peace organization spread; thinkers and scholars Helen admired, Hans Morgenthau and Walter Lippmann among them, urged the administration to force reforms on the Diem regime and to seek an internally negotiated settlement in line with America's very limited interests in the area.[15] The regime was alienating people, and the war was "a losing proposition."[16] In 1962, Bom argued that survival lay not with the doves but the ready and watchful hawks. His book, Helen saw, would contribute to his steadily growing reputation as one of the nation's most visible and articu-late hawks. Having long ago abandoned her pacifist tendencies, and recogniz-ing the complexity of issues, she respected her son's more informed positions, even if she did not always agree.

Even without the help of the Democratic chairman of the Appropriations Committee, Clarence Cannon, who called Mel Laird "one of the most valu-able members of the House," Bom would have trounced his opponent in an election that brought out a record number of voters and saw Wisconsin Demo-crats taking important slots: John Reynolds became governor and Gaylord Nelson took Alexander Wiley's seat in the U.S. Senate. Wilbur Renk, Helen wrote David, to whom she sent the results, "is aiming to become head of party in Wisconsin."

For most Republicans, pacifists, the religiously inclined, and the Kennedy administration, 1962 was a bad year. Hope for a coalition government in Laos collapsed[17]; the news coming out of Vietnam was terrible, while "the hotbed of war danger in the heart of Europe [was] becoming ever more ominous in Berlin."[18] The Reverend Martin Luther King, Jr., who advocated social revolution at home through nonviolence and "had a dream," landed in jail for the third time in nine months in Albany, Georgia, arrested with nine other Negroes on disorderly conduct charges for congregating on a sidewalk and beginning a prayer vigil. The Supreme Court, in a suit brought by a New York family, struck down the legality of the state's right to mandate prayer in public schools. "In this world, it is becoming more and more unpopular to be a Christian. Soon it may become dangerous,"[19] Bom declared, his remark conveying something of the societal change since Alexis de Tocqueville observed that "there is no country in the world in which the Christian religion retains a greater influence over the souls of men than in America."[20]

America could no longer be assumed to be a Christian country—not in its great urban centers, anyway. In Marshfield, however, the chamber of commerce, reacting to the Supreme Court decision, printed cards announcing that "the Christmas Message Comes to Main Street" and set up displays emphasizing "the religious significance of Christmas."[21] Tuning out the bad news from the rest of the country and the world, Helen concluded her 1962 Calendar with a quotation "from a friend." "I get up each morning and dust off my wits / Pick up the paper and read the obits / If my name is missing, I know I'm not dead / So I eat a good breakfast, and go back to bed."

She felt a little less jaunty after suffering a heart attack in January 1963 while visiting Constie and spending a week in an unfamiliar hospital in Albuquerque. Deflecting attention from herself in her thank-you note to David for his time and attention in seeing her safely home, she asked: "Hasn't de Gaulle kicked up a row?" She had been reading about de Gaulle's playing "Parisian roulette with Europe's future," making the Communists happy and throwing the six Common Market nations into confusion by vetoing Britain's bid for membership.[22]

She did not mind being housebound while the winds howled and blizzards whitened the land, although sad news piled in. "Aunt Florence's chum Ruby Winch died and was buried." Nettie Laird, the last of Melvin's siblings, died. Margaret Schorger died. Helen understood "something of Aunt Florence's feeling as her friends are knocked off one by one."

She ventured out less and missed church three Sundays in a row, a fact remarked by herself and others. She thought, as one gray day succeeded another, "We shall soon be blind like fish." Her health uncertain, she did not attend the Republican fund-raiser in Milwaukee, although Bom, who had escorted Rockefeller into the state, was to introduce him. If she saw less of Bom as he took an increasingly prominent role in the party, she read more AP press reports quoting him.[23]

When an AP syndicated article appeared in the *Chicago Tribune*, the *Herald*, and other papers casting Melvin Sr. in the role of a "bewildered pastor" and made his son, Melvin Jr., who, "at the age of 17, . . . chose his life career, that of a professional politician," his father's superior,[24] Bom set the record straight in a letter, a copy of which he sent to Helen. "I well realize that the major reason that I was elected to the State Senate at the age of 23 was because of my father's reputation and good work as a member of the State Senate. There is no finer inheritance a father can leave to a son than a good name and my father did just that."

If Bom modestly revealed his indebtedness to his parent, he felt at liberty to brag about making more than fifty speeches on college campuses since 1961, celebrating politics as an honorable profession, and the Republican Party as responsible and forward looking. David did not talk much about the thousands of lectures he gave to increasing numbers of ill-prepared students in east Los Angeles. Open admissions, not advanced study, had become the name of the game in California's state college system. David and Dick, highly conscious of their brilliantly effective brother, loved him but realized his life had taken a public turn and did not often "bother" him. They had, in any event, always been both close and singularly private, their mother the fixed pole in their lives.

No member of the family was with her on her seventy-fifth birthday. Bessie and she celebrated with dinner out, and she talked of having another celebration "sometime with the Freds or others in Madison." She drove to Laona alone on September 21—not to stay, just to see the leaves: "brilliant—whole hill sides red with sumac and all maples aglow," all "so red and gay as they go down in defeat." She stayed at the Gordon Hotel and "went to Laona church. People faithful. Still looking for inspiration."

Recognizing that her elderly sister would henceforth avoid Albuquerque's high altitude, Constie began flying in to visit Helen in the late fall. Her welcome visits fatigued Helen, accustomed now to spending many hours alone with her letters, books, and thoughts. The sisters covered many subjects. Helen bragged about Dick, who had opened a new office in Madison, and was expanding, and Bom, of whom they were all reading, and David, who had been appointed an associate professor. They talked about William and the lawsuit he filed charging his daughter-in-law with being an unfit mother. He had gained custody of his two grandsons: Bill, eleven, and Rob, nine. History seemed to repeat itself. They felt for Thelma, Andy's wife, with three children of her own, who would be responsible for raising William's grandchildren since William and Kathryn were too old to take care of them.

She noted Constie's departure for Madison with Gordon and Mary but did not record the shocking news that Diem and his brother had been unceremoniously assassinated and stuffed into the back of an armored personnel carrier on November 9. But on November 22 she wrote: "About 12:35 came news of terrible assassination of President."

The spirit of cooperation in the Congress following Kennedy's assassination ended with Secretary of Labor Willard Wirtz's admission that the administration on the evening of the election had grossly distorted employment statistics. Bom prophesized that "the upshot of this new emerging image of official statements [would be] to undermine the American people's confidence in all official statements."[25]

Hounded by southern senators opposed to the Civil Rights Bill and by Republicans for misleading the public and for failure in foreign policy, Johnson cut off direct communication with the Republican House minority leader Charles A. Halleck and Senate minority leader Everett M. Dirksen. Milton Eisenhower, one of his brother's most trusted counselors during Dwight Eisenhower's eight years in the White House, tried to tone down the political crossfire and hard feelings, which increasingly polarized and bewildered the nation. He headed a Republican Critical Issues Council aimed at setting out Republican thinking on vital matters and stimulating public opinion—without recourse to "super-heated campaign oratory." Moderate and internationalist, the council, reflecting the views of Governors Scranton and Rockefeller, hoped to shape the 1964 platform substantially in the image of Eisenhower Republicanism.[26]

Helen wished them well, was on their side; she did not approve of the extremist oratory or of either Johnson's action in cutting off consultation with the Republican leadership or Senator Dirksen's retaliatory charge that President Johnson was an "appeaser." She hoped, for the sake of the country, that the charge would be dropped.

"Last week dragged a bit—I guess I was impatient waiting for spring, but have now given up as after winds of hurricane proportion yesterday we now have another snow fall and a white frosting. Our one really nice day—last Friday, I did drive to Wisconsin Rapids for lunch and alone. Heard the first meadow lark which was encouraging."[27] She needed an encouraging sign. While one had to "reconcile oneself to a bit of old age," she wrote David, it was "hard to agree with our friend Browning—'the best of life is yet to be'—when so many know different." She felt too many losses. The Epsteins' house was up for sale. Stephan Epstein, having reached the clinic's mandatory retirement age of sixty-five, was moving to Madison where he could continue to practice. She would no longer be able to walk and talk with Elsbeth, Bessie was "no good for walking any more," and another "dear friend," Mrs. Roddis, died while vacationing with Augusta in Pampano Beach, Florida.

Mrs. Roddis's funeral service united the Roddises and the Connors. Younger generations knew little or nothing about the fierce rivalry and animosity that had once existed between the families. The Connor office had been in Wausau for years, and the Roddis company had been sold to Weyerhaeuser following Hamilton Roddis's death in 1960. Empathizing with Augusta's loss, Helen did what she could to help the devoted daughter, now living alone in her parents' home on Fourth Street, which, like Helen's, was haunted with memories. Augusta always addressed Helen as Mrs. Laird just as Helen had always addressed her mother as Mrs. Roddis, the formality both linking and separating them, a sign of their shared heritage in a gentle world only remnants of which remained.

While she appreciated that world, Helen also, having been brought up listening to a master practitioner, appreciated wit. She vastly enjoyed Bom's reply to McNamara's assertion that he had trimmed $10 billion from the defense budget: "You know you could come up with a terrific saving figure here if you would put in the record at this point how much you have saved by not buying horses since 1899."[28] She was reminded of W.D. again when Bom escorted Robert Taft Jr. into the state.

Friendly with both Rockefeller and Goldwater, Bom was an early choice for chairman of the platform committee in 1964. "All Bam's family expects to be in California in July," Helen wrote David. "John goes early with his Dad." She read but did not refer to the speech Bom made on the floor of the House on June 2. Convinced that the administration policy of disinformation harmed the Republic, he informed the Congress—and the nation—that top administration officials were holding secret talks in Honolulu to plan America's course vis-à-vis the increased aggression in Southeast Asia and that those talks included a plan for an invasion of North Vietnam. Helen paid attention to the speech, even if most people didn't.[29]

Her heart kicked up before the convention and she didn't venture out, satisfied to read the *Los Angeles Times* article David sent. The *Times* wished "Congressman Laird every success in his Solomon endeavor"[30] to bring Republicans together on a platform. That "Laird expects the '64 plank to support the impending new federal [civil rights] law, against which Goldwater voted," was not news to Helen. "Disappointed but not surprised" when Goldwater won the nomination, Helen wrote Walter Kohler expressing her concern that the party unify behind the candidate. Kohler shared her "concern about getting us all under one tent." "Bom," he knew, "will contribute all he can to that greatly to be desired accomplishment."[31]

Unable to reach his mother by telephone, Bom wrote a rare note to let her know that his family and David's had met in Disneyland and that they "had a wonderful family time in the West." He was "glad convention is all over— I found myself in a very hot spot. Tried to keep from getting too bloody but did come out with the odd scars here and there. Great lesson in politics which will long be remembered and be most helpful in the long run." The press's interpretations of the platform amendments made him "sick and show they have not even taken the trouble to read the document."[32]

The political season was in full swing on August 3 when Vietnamese patrol boats attacked the *Maddox,* which, with the *C. Turner Joy* was in the Gulf of Tonkin, asserting the freedom of the seas. The entire outraged Congress, with the exception of two senators, united behind the president to vote the Tonkin Resolution, enabling the president "to take all necessary steps including the use of force" to assist any Southeast Asia Treaty Organization (SEATO) member "requiring assistance in defense of freedom."[33] Or, as Johnson put it, to stop playing around up there and begin "knocking hell out of them."[34] Bom predicted an increase "in all war activity in South Viet Nam in the next three or four months." The Communists wanted to provoke "an incident to force the United States into an international meeting to work out an agreement similar to that used to govern Laos," an agreement the Communists had violated "hundreds of times."[35]

"A Melvie Bird" told syndicated columnist Rowland Evans that "we had written something in our column that distressed" Helen. His description of Bom as "a 'backroom' maneuverer or party power, far from being ungracious" was "the highest encomium. . . . We love Mel—maybe not all the time, but much of the time. The only trouble with Mel is that he hardly ever tells us anything. So may I appeal to you to help in this respect? I know that you have more influence on him than any one else, even Barbara, and we need your help." He had heard "a great deal" about her from Mel, but she could tell "lots more. Please write me."[36] She didn't.

Helen could see Bom thrived as a public figure, and there was no cause for her to worry about him. She did about his family, perhaps, as he had less and less time to give to them. However a drawback that might be, his enthusiasm for political life remained boundless, as did the zeal with which he tried to enlist young people to its service. It was a fascinating job requiring brains, energy, and personality, a "Most Rewarding Career."[37]

Bom received the American Cancer Society Man of the Year award for his efforts in establishing cancer research facilities in fourteen American universities (including the University of Wisconsin) and the Albert Lasker public service award[38] for his contributions in the health field. Helen was not well enough to join the contingent of clinic physicians, including Ben Lawton, Dean Emanuel, George Magnin, Russell Lewis, Thomas Rice, and Stanley Custer, who attended the Lasker award's ceremony in New York; but she did join Bom when he came to Marshfield, bringing his colleague on the Appropriation's Welfare Committee, John Fogarty and Surgeon General Luther Terry, to celebrate the dedication of a research center at the Marshfield Clinic and the opening of the new wing at St. Joseph's Hospital. David thanked her for her "interesting account of the Clinic Research Center and Hospital" and the pictures. "How prominently Bom figured and it must be satisfying for him to get such praise from at least one Democrat—Fogarty didn't leave much doubt where he stood, did he? Sounds like much activity on the home front."

Bom reaped awards and praise, but the 1964 election was disastrous for other Republicans. Only 140 out of the 435 representatives and 32 of the 100 senators were Republicans. "Goldwater and the people who supported him before the convention have got a lot to answer for," David wrote Helen. "It is no time to review the past, though that seems a temptation these days. Where are the political passenger pigeons of yesteryear? Where the whooping crane and now the elephant? At least the Indians were retired to reservations. Maybe we should change the game laws to conserve conservatives. One for each city park like old locomotives for children to play on and to be reminded of a glorious past they never knew. Glad you retained your sense of humor through it all and know that you were helpful in helping Bom keep his."[39]

Bom was frustrated that few Republicans waged their campaigns on the platform and outraged that the Democrats deliberately misrepresented it. He thought it possible, even probable, that the American people wanted states and localities to become "mere administrative arms of the Central government," that "we are entering a new phase—a phase in which most governmental, political, economic, and social questions for the entire country are faced, diagnosed, and resolved in one manner or another at one level of government—the Federal level." If so, it was "Republican responsibility" to apprise the people of "the fundamental changes" that were taking place and being proposed "so that the people may make an informed and intelligent decision as to whether this is the road they wish to travel."

Helen wished the times had been such that he could have concluded his speech there, but his expertise in defense made it inevitable that he talk about war. In spite of the thousands of casualties caused by America's policies, he went on, "we continue a fiction that it is a South Vietnamese war, that we are only advisors." He predicted that "the conflict in Vietnam will end in the not-too-distant future in some form of compromised settlement that cannot help but lead to an eventual Communist takeover." Republicans had proposed in the past and still proposed "a positive program designed to keep our nation's sword sharp, ready and dependable,"[40] but the Eisenhower-Dulles policy had been that America "should not tie down large-scale ground forces in southeast Asia."[41] He charged the administration with not being fair with the American people or with the Congress, in not clearly setting forth their short-term aims and long-term objectives in Vietnam.

The press may not have given much coverage to that speech or to the many others Bom made on the floor of the House, but Helen read them in the *Congressional Record.* She shared his frustration at the repeated "blatant distortions" of Republican positions and his hope that "someone in the administration will recognize the value of debate" and that "members of Congress again accord to each other the respectful hearing and the reasoned response without which debate cannot be conducted."[42]

Helen sought relief from the discouraging contemporary scene by rereading Thackeray's *Vanity Fair* and relief from the raging sciatica in her right leg and the arthritis in her shoulders by swallowing aspirin, sinking into hot baths at night, and offering her pale and aching limbs to the sun whenever it shown. Having suffered a "baffling spell," when she was "afraid to lie down," she kept indoors when the weather turned hot and humid.

Aunt Florence was going to Hawaii, permanently this time. She couldn't live alone anymore and she probably didn't have long to live. Angie came for her. Another piece of the past gone.

"Welcome August," Helen wrote in her Calendar on the first day of the month, adding, "I don't know why for I'll be a year older." She confided she had not behaved well at a church committee meeting, had in fact "blown up" when a young woman glibly spoke of her absolute confidence in God, salvation through Jesus Christ, angels, the eternal life, and her certainty of meeting her loved ones after death. "Oh, I wish I had the faith of you young people," Helen angrily exploded, shocking everyone. The girl "had no experience with the trials that test faith," Joanne Lueck, who witnessed the attack, observed.

"The unrest in the nation got to her." Johnson signed a draft order for unmarried men nineteen to twenty-six, keeping quiet about it until the marriage license bureaus closed in the East on August 26.[43]

She drummed up the energy to go to Madison in October to hear John Bennett, president of the Union Theological Seminary, speak at the Congregational Church and attended the dinner in his honor afterwards. She watched as students, responding to reports of casualties in Vietnam and the draft increase, protested the war.[44] She "heard two men from State Department weakly discuss foreign policy" and studied the speech her son read into the *Congressional Record* at the conclusion of the 89th Congress. His "primary task," as chairman of the Republican conference, had been "to keep the two party government alive and the Congress independent." Congress had acted too much as a satellite of the president. Positions had been labeled good or evil without meaningful public debate. Whole segments of opinion were systematically suppressed. The "great consensus of the great planned society really boils down to a great conformity."[45]

Helen marked it a "very important speech" and kept it along with an article Dick sent: "In Melvin Laird's Washington," which floated the idea that Melvin Laird, whom few disputed was "sharper by far than his two superiors in the House Republican command—Minority Leader Gerald Ford (Mich.) and Minority Whip Les Arends (Ill.)," might be "the next GOP candidate for President."[46]

In February 1966, Helen returned to Lincoln, Illinois, with her famous son. Invited by Jim Vaughn, a trustee of Lincoln College, Bom delivered the keynote address at the college's Charter Day convocation and received the first of many honorary doctorates. Helen showed him the manse where she had lived as a bride, the church, and the village-square, which had hardly changed.

There were changes in Marshfield, however. Not only had Aunt Florence gone, but Bom and Barbara would no longer be returning to spend summers in Wisconsin, although they would be in and out of town and planned to keep their apartment in their house next door. David, who had expanded his interests to include real estate and had purchased a large piece of property along the Pecos River in New Mexico and small parcels in Wisconsin, and Helen L., who taught French at Westridge, a private girl's school in Pasadena, assumed greater responsibility for Helen during their vacations.

Bom's son, "little David," who was already taller than "big David," after a session at Camp Manitowish in Boulder Junction, would spend a week or ten days with them at the lake. His presence, the enthusiasm with which he played

tennis, sailed, and fished "all at once," and the way he settled down after Helen
L.'s dinners to enjoy the story his grandmother read aloud to him, took her
mind off national and international problems.

Bom's hope for a "big vote" in 1966 was not disappointed. "Got it!" Helen
jubilantly exclaimed in her Calendar as voters across America breathed life
into the moribund two-party system.

David thought Bom was to be congratulated for having done so well. He
had Pat's letter announcing Jessica's engagement and wedding plans. "Dick
should be very pleased that his daughter chooses such an eligible young man
[Jim Doyle] rather than becoming a nun or something like that. . . . Will of
course be a blow to the father . . . but gentle parents have survived the marriages of their children in times past and will probably continue to do so.
Obviously we must try to band together now to console and reassure Dick at
his time of difficult re-adjustment." David couldn't "help but recall Dick's
response at the time of [David's] wedding when he was so moved as to remain
absolutely motionless sinking into a profound silence that remained unbro-
ken for months." They would like to join her "in what must certainly be a
joyous, festive celebration. The marriage of your first grand-child is a great
event and I think we should try to respond accordingly—that is, to take a leaf
from your book and show, as you have always done in matters concerning your
grand-children, an abundance of love and concern and family feeling."

David relished fishing, walking in the woods, and talking trees and land
values with Dick, and Dick and Pat were always warm and welcoming when
he and Helen L. came through Madison. Dick's hurtful silence at the time of
David's marriage may well have been because he was depressed, preoccupied
with his own problems. Helen recorded "Dick's favorite detachment 'I couldn't
care less.'" He suffered, as Helen had, from extremes of mood, from periodic
depression, and from bewildering, angry explosions. David was not exempt
from mood swings either. His letter might have concerned some parents, but
Helen did not bring it up. Just another one of the things one didn't talk about.
She had long ago realized she had to take people, including herself, as they came.

Jessica's wedding, a gala affair at the Madison Club on December 21, 1966,
was one of the rare times when the Lairds were all together. Helen recorded
little about it except to say "family all there." Constie, who "looked well in
her Christmas red outfit and white fur coat," suffered from a migraine and
took to her room after the ceremony and dinner. Bom left on an early plane
on December 22, while David and his family began the long drive west and
Helen, after a visit with Elsbeth Epstein, returned to Marshfield. The "Holiday passed okay."

Friends from the past circled 'round, their shared memories uniting them in the dance of life they all recognized as ending: Edwin Phillips Kohl sent Helen a collection of seventy-five short essays, *Some Footprints on a Long Life's Journey*; Aunt Betty wrote, "I guess memory is precious to us all more and more so as we grow older"; Maybel Pick, who had moved to Woodside, California, wondered if David, "one of my special favorites, couldn't lure you out here this winter? I wish you would write me. This seems sad to have this silence."[47] Helen noted that January 31 was the "sad day those astronauts" were buried. "As has been said, there never was a replacement for a human being." In her Calendar she copied out a statement from Pearl Buck's *A Bridge for Passing:* "It is the Saints, the believers who should have the courage to urge the scientists to help them discover whether the spirit continues its life of energy when the mass we call body ceases to be the container. Faith supplies the hypothesis, but only

The Connors and Lairds at the Madison Club, celebrating the wedding of Jessica Laird and Jim Doyle, December 1966. Seated, from left: Gordon P. Connor, Sara Connor, Mel Laird, Helen, Constance Modrall, Mary Roddis Connor, Vanessa Laird, Helen L. Laird, Sigrid Connor; standing, from left: David Noel Connor, Gordon R. Connor, David Laird.

The marriage of Jim Doyle and Jessica Laird in 1966 united two political families. Standing by Jim Doyle are Judge Jim and Ruth Doyle. Standing beside Jessica are Dick and Pat Laird.

scientists can provide the computer for verification. The supremely natural not supernatural proof will be a wave-length. Then the scientist recognizing it will exclaim 'But that's someone I know, I took his wave length before he died.'"

David wrote about a "scientific" lecture he had heard at the Atheneum at Cal Tech in Pasadena. James F. Crow from Wisconsin read "a fascinating paper on the new biology. Earlier claim to be descended from monkeys broadened now. Appears plants, virus and bacteria are all close relatives. Scientists have great hopes for the world if they don't destroy it first. One biologist said we were on a fantastic streetcar named evolution and if we ever got off something else would be sure to take our place. Funny to hear test-tube breed talk like poets and scared ones at that. Hope students are treated to the excitement of discovery which some of these people really are able to generate and also to some of the anxiety."[48]

They were exciting times for scientists, but difficult times for others. David wrote about the deterioration in the state college system under the Reagan administration: the severe funding cuts; the proliferation of remedial English courses; the switch to the quarter system, which entailed a third again the paperwork involved in the semester system, along with an increase in the number of classes a professor was expected to carry per quarter. Helen shared the information with Bom, who was less than sympathetic. David responded to their joint call from 208, writing Helen afterwards: "It was good to talk with you and Bom, and I appreciate your thinking of us out here. Also, Bom's encouragement to those of us in education on grounds that things are tough all over."[49]

On May 1, Bom's colleague, Carl Steiger, son of Helen's colleague on the board of regents, rose in the House to include an "extraneous matter" in the *Congressional Record*. "Last Saturday, April 29 marked two very significant occasions. That date marked the 178th anniversary of the inauguration of our first President, George Washington. April 29 also marked the presentation of the George Washington Award by the American Good Government Society to my Wisconsin colleague, the Honorable Melvin R. Laird."

More and more people in Wisconsin were convinced Bom would become president.[50] Almost everyone in Marshfield was.

Helen suffered another dizzy spell and so began taking a new "Anti-Vert" drug. She copied a quotation to think about: "Roots that go too deep cannot be yanked up completely [and] betray a person overly committed to houses built on sand, to mortality instead of immortality." Feeling "rather let down" after finishing Thornton Wilder's *The Eighth Day*, which had been "such a treat after several disappointments in books," she pulled herself out of a tendency toward despondency by attempting to analyze the novel's effect on her. "Few of our real-life fellow creatures so persistently engage our thoughts as do these people of *The Eighth Day* . . . Ashley would have been quick to deny that he was a man of religious faith, but religions are merely the garments of faith (often ill cut). What do men of faith have faith in? I must ask Elsbeth if she finds in the silence of the Quaker service help in her self-effacement and trust. How does one make sure our lives are being used in the unfoldment of God's plan for the world? Of what use the billions of years before coming of Christ?"

Helen, the conduit between her sons, did not raise philosophical questions with them, maintaining instead a correspondence dealing with their interests and the events of their immediate lives. David appreciated the photo she sent of Bom standing in front of the Capitol Building with a group of teenage visitors from Wisconsin, but it was her "amusing account" of Dick's visit that prompted his insightful appraisal. Bom received plaudits enough. Dick, an extremely modest, successful business man, almost never got any.

David thought Dick had "wider interests than he lets on" and was "a remarkably creative person—a real builder and doer—caught up with things he does well and which interest him." He had been glad to learn of his appointment to the Conservation Commission. "Not many are able to find a frontier in their own backyard."[51]

She hung laundry in the yard and sent Lissa, who had graduated from Madison East High and would be off to Stanford in September, a silver dish and ladle, a family heirloom. She drove to Laona when Noah called to say a "suitable" room was available at the hotel, spent the day at the lake, and checked the cabins, which looked "fine but empty." On August 27, Pat and Lissa flew to New York to see Jim and Jessica Doyle, members of the Peace Corps, who were off to Tozeur in southeastern Tunisia. (Bom had tried, unsuccessfully, to have the Peace Corps named the Freedom Corps.) On August 30, "fibrillation began 8 o'clock A.M." She rested, took "green pills," called George Magnin, who came at 4 P.M. The fibrillation lasted 24 hours, but, having taken "seconal and pills," she had a fairly good night, although her eyes bothered her. No one told her that Dick had been hospitalized for depression.

"Having learned that it would please my son, Melvin, Jr.," Helen wrote Robert Froehlke, treasurer, "I want to be the first contributor to the Laird Youth Leadership Foundation, recently organized. With confidence that it will serve a useful and stimulating purpose to students of our Seventh District, and in memory of my husband, M.R. Laird, Congressman Laird's father, I am enclosing my check in the amount of $2,000."[52]

At the first biannual Laird Leadership Foundation Education Day at the University of Wisconsin-Stevens Point, university chancellor Lee Dreyfus welcomed students from sixty-three high schools in Bom's district and the national and state leaders Bom brought together to speak to them and perhaps inspire them with a higher regard for public service: John W. Gardner, secretary of Health, Education and Welfare; General Richard G. Stilwell, former chief of staff, U.S. Military Assistance Command in Vietnam; Esther Peterson, assistant secretary of Labor; Father Stephen Boehrer and the Reverend Perry Saito, members of the Governor's Commission on Human Rights; and John Bibby, professor of political science at the University of Wisconsin-Milwaukee.

When her famous son took her out to dinner at the Casa Loma, she never complained about the dim lighting, the noise, the people stopping by their table to greet them, or the late dinner hour—8:00 P.M. She did not believe Bom was angling for the presidency but did believe his assessment that Johnson would "pressure South Vietnam into negotiating with the Viet Cong in hopes of getting the war ended before the 1968 elections." She thought Republicans had a campaign issue if the Democrats declared that the Viet Cong should participate in negotiations and in a subsequent government in South Vietnam. If that was an acceptable position now, "why," as Bom said, "was it not acceptable 18 months and more than 50,000 casualties ago?"[53]

She could not drum up any enthusiasm for Harold Stassen, stirring as a peace candidate; she believed new leadership was required, but not the new leadership that came forward in Chicago. Three thousand members of American left-wing organizations, including many blacks and housewives, joined in a "New Politics" convention at the Palmer House and proposed Martin Luther King as president and Benjamin Spock as vice president. Contemporary American and British novelists, playwrights, and poets, including (among many others) Norman Mailer, Ken Kesey, Jack Kerouac, John Osborne, and Allen Ginsberg described a beatnik, hippie, acidhead revolution spreading over Western democracies that was at odds with well-established bourgeois normative values. Helen did not read that literature, one so distant from her world of Christian values. She discovered one contemporary writer, Alan Paton, for whom prayer was not outmoded: "Lord make me an instrument of thy peace. Where there is hatred, let me sow love, where there is injury, pardon; where there is doubt, faith; where there is despair hope; where there is sadness joy; where there is darkness light." She indicated the quote came from *Instrument of Thy Peace*, a book she had ordered on its publication from a Madison bookstore.

But peace was far off in October 1967, the wildest month of the wild year: the South Vietnamese provisional national assembly, denying election irregularities, installed General Nguiyen Van Thieu as its head; marines were subjected to suicide attacks; the Haiphong Port was bombed; the Turks demanded atomic mines along their border; British agent Kim Philby's thirty-four years as a "Red" spy were uncovered. The congregation of the First Congregational Church sent a letter to President Johnson calling for a ceasefire in Vietnam to be followed by a peace conference; Madison students protested the draft and burned their draft cards; 200 students took over the Commerce Building; the police moved in with clubs, arresting students employing "lie down tactics"; riot leaders were suspended, and some faced civil arrest; thousands of protesting students marched up State Street.[54] U.S. District Court Judge James E. Doyle denied a request for a temporary restraining order to bar University of Wisconsin and city officials from interfering with antiwar demonstrations on the campus. Educated in the vanishing debate tradition, Doyle would not restrain university officials without hearing both sides.

David reassured Helen that Cal State remained comparatively peaceful. Only a few antiwar "warriors" and minority students intent on publicity instigated demonstrations. A small band of blacks, charging that African Americans were not admitted in sufficient numbers, broke into the admission's office and dumped files, but there had been no major demonstrations. Students at Cal State weren't children of the privileged classes. They wanted jobs, better jobs, some sense of security. Many of them took night classes after a full day's work. Perhaps 10 percent enrolled in the campus's Center for the Study of Armament and Disarmament.

Pride in Bom's achievement in securing a $20 million food and research laboratory for the University of Wisconsin at Madison[55] was tempered by Helen's knowledge that his political ascendancy was stalked by the divisive war and civil discord and, within days, by the shock of another family tragedy.

Dick was killed in the flaming wreckage of his truck on November 8 when the boom of a log-skidding machine he was carrying struck a highway overpass in Madison. The cab, with Dick the driver and sole occupant, was thrown up and burst into flames. Would-be rescuers, observing the accident, could not reach him.

Bessie was with Helen when George Magnin rushed over. Highly agitated and suffering from transient global amnesia after receiving word of the tragedy, Helen remembered who she was but nothing else. George Magnin agreed with Bessie that she should remain home and that Bessie should spend the night. By the time David arrived the next day, Helen's memory had returned. She understood why he had come and that he would join Bom in Madison for the funeral.

The minister described Richard Laird as a man who "faced problems squarely," who did not look "for approval or reward or notoriety," but in his "natural drive towards a better community, . . . simply moved forward in his own persistent way."[56] "Persistent" was the word he had used to describe himself to Helen when he felt he could not, perhaps, be as brilliant as she may have wished him to be.

That David, Bom, and Barbara drove to Marshfield together after the funeral was "a comfort." They returned to Madison to put Barbara on the plane for Washington and be of what help they could to Pat. "Good David and Bom can be together." She thought of them, they of her. Bom would bring her to Washington for Thanksgiving, and David would bring his family and stay in Bom's apartment in Marshfield over the Christmas holidays.

She drew herself together and seemed to be handling the crisis well, had a "fine trip" to Washington, but heart palpitations set in almost immediately, and on November 23 she was admitted to George Washington Hospital where she remained for six days. After a night at his house, Bom brought her back to

Wisconsin, where she wanted to be under George Magnin's care in familiar surroundings. David and his family tried valiantly to work up some Christmas spirit, but it was not easy in spite of eight-year-old Vanessa's efforts to decorate trees at 208 and in Bom's apartment. It was lucky that Vanessa, like her grandmother, was a great reader. She needed her books in that gloomy atmosphere where Helen and Bessie, the Christmas dinner over, played bridge with David and Helen L. and listened to Christmas music on the radio. Helen concluded her annual Calendar with a brief note: "Good to have year *end.*"

Yet, the new year, the crucial 1968 election year, promised to be interesting. Reporters tried to figure out what Bom was up to. They said he was secretly working to promote Rockefeller's candidacy and that he had switched tactics vis-à-vis Vietnam. "He now says the Republican party must be the party of peace in 1968," that "peace with justice, peace with respect can be achieved with new initiatives and a new administration."[57] They said he was shrewd, wily, a king-maker, secretive, Machiavellian, ambitious, "the complete politician"— all descriptions she had been hearing for some time. He stopped in once or

Helen L., David, and Vanessa Laird on their property on the Baraboo Bluff, 1967.

twice a month to be of help to Helen and sometimes managed a much-needed "restful time in spite of our three hour dialogues."

John O., Helen observed, held his generation's profound suspicion of almost everyone involved in politics. Art and history interested him, and, no matter how often Helen might urge him on, he refused to star. Dick's son, Richie, was another quiet person; he was interested in music. He would never seek the limelight but played the bass fiddle in the Madison Youth Orchestra. Helen went to hear the orchestra when it came to Marshfield but didn't feel well afterwards. She did not go to hear Nixon speak at the armory or to the Marshfield Clinic Foundation program and so talked to David instead, and would have given up attending the Wisconsin alumni dinner as an honored guest had David not said he would fly in and go with her. They were photographed together at the ceremony when University of Wisconsin president Fred Harrington presented her with a Certificate of Appreciation for a "distinguished Record of Service and Leadership."[58]

Bom flew in before David had to leave, and, briefly, she enjoyed her two sons together. It seemed quiet after they left, but she heard Bom on *Face the Nation*. Partisan though she was, she thought the speech President Johnson made on April 1 was "a good speech, his withdrawal and move towards peace."

University of Wisconsin president Fred Harrington presenting Helen a "Certificate of Appreciation for a Distinguished Record of Service and Leadership," Marshfield, March 1968. David Laird looks on.

She had always sought to and often succeeded in drawing peace out of beauty—nature's, and some human—and that at least had not changed. Her old and ordered mind took in the "lovely flowering almond in [her] yard—at its pinkest," while the national mood turned increasingly ugly: Martin Luther King and Robert Kennedy were assassinated; American boys were still dying in Vietnam; 50,000 people joined in a poor people's march on Washington.[59] Chaos broke out in Chicago during the Democratic convention after Hubert Humphrey was nominated over war opponent George McGovern. Mayor Daley put his 12,000-man police force on twelve-hour shifts over the four turbulent days while the governor sent in 6,000 national guardsmen. Aunt Betty's grandson, George Walton, one of the nonviolent band marching behind Dick Gregory, was arrested and charged with disturbing the peace, a charge later amended to jay-walking.

Helen's youthful, quasi-religious adoration of George Washington and the Founding Fathers and her belief that her country was "a city on the hill, the wonder and blessing of the world," could not be sustained in the face of the present confusion. And yet, she maintained her house, saw that the grass was mowed, and enjoyed the celebration of her eightieth birthday in Marshfield in August when Bom hosted a dinner for his and David's families at the Charles Hotel.

Alone again, she picked up the copy of *Republican Papers,* the book Bom left with her. Prepared in anticipation of the national elections, it defined the problems and offered solutions for the "domestic crises facing today's America." In his introduction, Bom claimed that in the "summer and fall of 1967 two emerging patterns seemed discernable. One seemed well advanced while the other was in its early stages." Both, however, cast long shadows on America's future. "First, in a very real sense, American society seemed to be coming apart. Old and tired institutions were responding to old and tired solutions hardly at all. The search for scapegoats was on in earnest. Each level of government and each layer of authority within those levels seemed bent on blaming other power centers, never themselves. A sense of leadership and direction, whether from elected officials, appointed administrators, or leaders of thought, seemed everywhere absent."

He saw a more hopeful pattern emerging in a coalition, "not a political or ideological or interest group coalition in the traditional sense," but "a meeting of minds among men" who heretofore had not found common grounds. Daniel P. Moynihan and G. Robert Blakey were among those who sensed the urgent need for a new direction for America.[60] Helen's generation had also been asked to throw away "times old and rusted key." But those were slower times.

She held to life through many "uneventful days," gratefully greeted a beautiful Indian Summer day, sat out awhile, raked leaves, careful not to move her arms too suddenly for fear of stirring up the arthritis. When Nixon came into the state to campaign early in October and Bom came with him, it was "good to have Bam here," if only to watch him collapse exhausted on the sofa. On October 17, he was back in the state attending Oscar Rennebohm's funeral. The papers quoted Rennebohm as saying the university had changed—used to be "greater respect for faculty people. It was quite a bit different" than when he was a student and when he was a regent. "It saddened him."[61] Helen as well.

Radicals and pacifists protested the on-campus recruiting of the Dow Chemical Corporation in Madison; in Washington, Norman Mailer, Robert Lowell, David Bruce, Mary McCarthy, and William Sloane Coffin marched on the Pentagon to confront the "war makers," while federal marshals and troops maintained order.[62]

With his unflagging energy and enthusiasm, Bom campaigned hard to bring about a Republican victory. Helen watched the election returns with him,

Helen and Melvin, Washington, D.C., ca. 1965. Bom holds the *Congressional Record* in which his many speeches are recorded.

Barbara and John O. in Marshfield. For his sake, largely, she was glad Nixon won. But it was a bad time for Republicans to take on what had become an almost ungovernable society.

"Guess he has outgrown district," Helen wrote on December 7, when Bom flew out to join the president-elect in California. "Fear he is bound for cabinet job. Secretary of Defense?" When David, who had also heard the speculation that Bom would take the cabinet post, telephoned, she found his "comment interesting." "At least," he said, "the addiction is creative."

The word broke. Bom would be Secretary of Defense. Helen's son had taken on the world's most difficult, unsympathetic task, but the whole terrible, complex situation interested her, and it probably kept her alive. A representative from *Newsweek* called, Channel 9 breezed in, the *Herald* came out with an article saying "Mrs. Mel Laird Not One for Limelight"— about Barbara, not Helen. The reporter from the *Appleton Post-Crescent* focused on Helen. She said what most Wisconsinites thought: Bom's move from national to international prominence would mean severing links with his home town. Helen wanted it known that the job amounted to a personal sacrifice. He loved legislation. He accepted the job "because he has long been interested in ending this war" in Vietnam.[63]

Bessie came at noon on Christmas Day to eat the duck Helen baked. It was a "relief to have Christmas over." Her heart beat rapidly. Mighty snow banks grew even mightier as the snow continued to fall. "No cars or people in sight. David may come." She thought about the 540,000 American servicemen in Vietnam and about the Israeli warplanes that struck at Arab guerrillas inside Jordan.

◠

# CHAPTER 22

# The Mother, The Politician, and The Professor

## 1969–1974

In the seventies an outbreak of various mental problems reached epidemic levels.

—ALVIN KERNAN

Having celebrated two major events in one day, an early twenty-first birthday for John O. and the dedication ceremonies of the new multimillion-dollar Marshfield Senior High, at which Bom was the principal speaker, Helen was not up to the crowds gathered at the Field House in Stevens Point to honor her son or to the "good luck" dinner for the intimate group of friends and supporters afterwards. In the few quiet moments they shared before he set off, Bom reassured her that he looked forward to the new challenges. He would not have accepted the appointment had he not had Nixon's assurance, in writing, that he would have absolute control over appointments. Carl S. Wallace, his congressional assistant, a Stevens Point man, would be moving over to the Pentagon as his special assistant, and he was going to appoint Bob Froehlke his secretary of the Army.

Bom and Bob phoned her and talked "at length—like boys almost" after the Senate confirmation hearings at which William Proxmire called Bom's nomination "the top honor" to come to Wisconsin "certainly in this century."[1] Helen regretfully acknowledged that she was not up to the crowds or the "strain of getting ready and off" to the inauguration but watched some of it on television. It was better than looking outside at the "dirty and discouraging snow."

Lloyd McKool read Lincoln's Second Inaugural address at her Bible study class and Helen delivered the prayer: "In this age of anxiety may we help to raise up leaders. Strengthen the youth of our land, comfort the sorrowing, quicken our hearts, renew our minds and revive a right spirit within us." She sent for

"In the Cure of Souls: The Meeting of Psychiatry and Religion" by Ann Belford Ulanov, a professor at the Union Theological Seminary. Ulanov claimed the riots, protests, and difficulties they were all experiencing testified to the existence of "psychic epidemics" and that religion had known for centuries about "the phenomenon of projection and the phenomenon of the contagion of feeling or affect" about which the psychiatrists were talking.[2]

When she crossed the street to attend the tenth anniversary celebration of the Faith Lutheran Church, memories flooded in of the house and people who had once occupied that space. She felt tired, perhaps because she was old and her arthritis was on the move, kicking up first in her left shoulder and arm, then in the right, then "strangely in my thumbs"; or perhaps because her heart was weak and she was experiencing "strange, uncertain spells" (reflected in her sprawling, uneven handwriting); or perhaps because there wasn't much happening, just the radio, the reading group, Augusta's Sunday dinners, music on the state station, Bom's now rather routine appearance on *Face the Nation*. She was not surprised by the public announcement of his March 5 departure for Vietnam.

He called almost every day, always careful to sound more positive than he felt, since his enthusiasm for his new job began to diminish almost at once as he perceived Nixon "freezing out the more traditional government bureaucracy from the foreign policy structure" and "streamlining" government by placing responsibility on the NSC staff, with Kissinger in charge. The March 17 B-52 bombing of Communist sanctuaries inside Cambodia, kept secret from Congress, the American people, and many key military and diplomatic officials, was politically dangerous and constitutionally dubious.[3]

Helen missed his visits, but she didn't say so. She sharply felt the changed circumstances when the election was held to fill his place in the House of Representatives and David Obey, a Democrat, became her congressman. She was glad for David's call, telling of his vacation beginning March 24 and that he would, as usual, be with her.

A neighbor alerted her to the appearance of an AP article in the *Milwaukee Sentinel*: "Mrs. Melvin Laird Sr. Talks about Her Son." Helen had spoken freely with the engaging reporter, Marian McBride, believing their talk was private. But the "woman lied and printed [an] article." She did not like to read about herself as an eighty-year-old who drove her own car, played the piano "for fun" and read the *Atlantic Monthly, Harper's, Time, Newsweek,* and several newspapers "to slow down getting old" and who got "a little misty" when talking about her sons growing up in the home, which she wouldn't leave, "although its sort of on the edge of the slums now." Nor did she think it was anyone's business that she disapproved of Mel's taking the "burdensome" job, "although it's a valuable experience in a way." She kept the article, however, and some of the letters that flooded in after it appeared.

Laona's postmaster, John Irish, a World War II decorated fighter pilot, wanted "in a humble manner, to say that you are a very fine lady and it makes me feel proud that I know you." Warren Knowles wrote that Bom "seemed very relaxed and completely absorbed with the duties of his new office" when he saw him in Milwaukee at the time he received the Broadcasters Man of the Year award.[4] President Nixon wrote of understanding "how difficult it is for a family in public life." He was "sure" her "background of community participation was a major source of inspiration and strength to each of your sons and to all who know you."[5] Edmund Zawacki, a professor of Slavic languages, wrote that the article "warmed" his heart, and the "open cities" idea, in which she expressed an interest about an exchange of academics and other leaders between Communist and non-Communist countries, had made "considerable progress."[6]

That Bom was safely back in the states and David with her when *Newsweek* put him on the cover with shadowy figures of weary GIs in the background marching through brush carrying rifles and shovels made the bleak news in the feature article—"The War: Nixon's Big Test Vietnam"—easier to bear. The casualty lists from Vietnam were higher than ever in 1969 after the Tet Offensive, and "brainy, bullet headed Mel Laird . . . was catching most of the heat."[7]

Helen had not seen Bom in four months when she received the "Schedule for Sec. Def. Laird 10–11 MAY, 1969." He was coming for a "visit with Mrs. Laird Senior," a meeting of the Laird Youth Leadership Foundation at the Wausau Club, a Technical Institute luncheon, a dedication speech at the North Central Technical Institute, a ribbon-cutting ceremony, a tour of the new building, a press conference and reception. He would attend a church service at the First Presbyterian Church in Marshfield before leaving for Andrews AFB. Security was heavy in Wausau, routes checked, the six-man detective force and all regular policemen and fifty emergency police force on duty, some stationed at the entrance and intersections on the campus, in anticipation of problems with antiwar demonstrators. There were none. As the secretary delivered the dedicatory address at the Technical College, only twenty-five peaceful demonstrators stood outside, holding signs and distributing handouts calling for troop withdrawal and an immediate end to the war.[8]

Feeling "deserted after so much attention," Helen turned to the copy of the *Milwaukee Journal* Bom left. She clipped James B. Kelley's article, "Universities and the Military Tie." He had been one of a group of ten physicists and engineers during WWII who set up the navy's jet propulsion program and later supervised multimillion-dollar research programs in the field, many of them at universities; these were programs the younger generation, and Kelley, were now attacking.[9]

When Bom returned to Wisconsin in June to be best man at his son's "very nice" wedding to Nancy Huset, a fellow student at the University of Wisconsin–Eau Claire, he seemed unusually sober and preoccupied, "as if his thoughts were elsewhere, as would be a perfectly human tendency of any man with such towering responsibilities in a troubled world."[10] John O. made the victory sign to students who threw "Vietnamese rice" over the bridal couple as they emerged from the church.

Less restless than she had been in the past, not looking for or seeking greener pastures since Bom and his family would not be in and out of Marsh-field, when David's family pulled into the state she went north with them. That peaceful environment seemed, and was, a world apart from the Wood-stock Music and Art Fair, that three-day "Aquarian Exposition" that drew America's doped-out flower children to Max Yasgur's 600-acre farm in Bethel, New York, in the summer of 1969.[11]

The analysis of the Woodstock phenomenon appeared in the same August 29 issue of *Time* magazine that featured Bom on its cover and an article: "Shaking up the Pentagon. The Politician at the Pentagon."[12] He was taking the brunt of the congressional frustration that had been building for years. Helen worried about him, and with news pouring in about disruptions on college campuses throughout the nation, she worried about David as well as he returned to Los Angeles to take over as head of the sixty-member Cal State English department.

He lightly touched on the revolutionary times, describing a newly hired member of the newly created African studies department who wore a woven hat, ornate garments, and carried a walking staff. No one could understand him when he rose to speak in the Faculty Senate, but "everyone listened as if he were Sarah Bernhardt." He did not share the information that Cal State University president John Greenly was shot at. He did not tell her that he led students through pickets attempting to close down the engineering building, which housed the English department offices and many of its classes. He never missed a class, held in his anger and his fatigue from all except his immediate family. He was not in Vietnam; but he was on the battleground in America.[13] Helen feared Bom's job would change him. She did not know, from his largely humorous accounts, how much the stress of David's job affected him.

Bom sounded "tired of it all" when he called before setting off to visit the 6th Fleet, Turkey, and Greece. The tensions had been mounting. Peace advocates, hippies, communists, and loyal Americans, including many interfaith religious leaders and members of the Republican Ripon Society, had supported a nation-wide strike on October 15 to demonstrate their united stand against American policy in Southeast Asia. But Bom seemed his old buoyant self when he came home to Marshfield ten days later, bringing the secretary of Health, Education and Welfare Robert Finch with him. Helen skipped the meeting of the Clinic Foundation and the dinner following, husbanding her strength for the "Youth Leadership Conference" in Stevens Point. A relief to her that the conference focused on achievements in the fields of health and welfare and that Bom got credit for his continued interest in domestic social needs. There wasn't much of a confrontation on his arrival at the university, only a handful of students reading names of Vietnam War dead and distributing antiwar leaflets.[14] But the pictures in the *Herald,* one of Bom hugging her and the other of Bom talking with his son, who sported the era's long sideburns, were "terrible."

Not so terrible as the television pictures she saw a few days later of people marching from Arlington National Cemetery to the Capitol, each bearing a placard with the name of an American killed or a Vietnamese village destroyed. Bom called to reassure her that things were under control. They weren't. On November 15, as Alison set out by car to pick up her father, as she often did on the nights he did not sleep at the Pentagon, the police stopped her. "Are you crazy? You'll be killed if you try to go down there," they said, sending her back home to Bethesda.[15]

To distract herself, Helen "bothered about the house" and wrote Philip Drotning that she admired his books, *Black Heroes in Our Nation's History,* and *A Guide to Negro History in America.* Drotning, who had served two Wisconsin governors, acknowledged her letter, saying he remembered her well and hoped the books "did some good." She wrote David, telling him not to worry about her, "old but battling." He and his family planned to spend a few days with her after the Modern Language Association meeting in Denver. They would take her to Madison or Laona, where ever she wanted to go.

On New Year's Day 1970, they set off for Laona, where Noah Maedenwald had their rooms ready at the Gordon. Birch Lake was hauntingly beautiful. The pure air, the brilliant blue sky, the majestic snow-laden pines with their long dark shadows splayed across the white land, the lake blanketed by deep, unmarked snow, and the mysterious quiet carried them to a world apart from the peopled world of their ordinary restricted lives and the anxious present. They all felt stronger and better because they were there. Their reverence was broken by the sound of Dickens and Mary Ann Connors' three tall sons, Bryan,

Timothy, and Robert , arriving on snowmobiles. They visited, standing by the outlet, when Tim, suddenly inspired, invited his great Aunt Helen for a ride. She accepted, climbed on behind him, laced her arms around his waist, and off she went over the wide and frozen lake.

At the beginning of his second year in the "world's hardest job," on his way to present a United States Junior Chamber of Commerce award to Gale Sayers, a running-back with the Chicago Bears, Bom arrived "a bit late" to pick Helen up.[16] His military assistant, the tall, courteous, broadly educated Robert E. Pursley, and the sprightly, ingratiating, multitalented, mysterious Murdock Head rounded out the party. Helen called Constie from the air force base in Albuquerque, ate dinner on board, and arrived in Los Angeles on a balmy night with the perfume of flowers in the air. Their rooms at the Huntington Hotel, Pasadena, were "choice." David and Helen L. joined them for dinner.

Like millions of other solitary, elderly, shut-in women, Helen became addicted to a daily dose of As the World Turns on her return from the lofty heights. The postman would bring no more letters from her favorite cousin Dean Witter or her dear friend Maybel Pick. Augusta, Fanny, and Bessie, "loyal friends," came through the snow for cake and coffee. Fred Schlitz, owner of the Standard Oil station on the corner of Central and Arnold, backed her car into the garage so she would not have to back out the long winding driveway. Fred's mother, Mary Miksha, lived a block away on Cedar Street. Born and raised in Czechoslovakia, Mary, whose first husband, Fred's father, had committed suicide during the Depression, spoke English with a heavy East European accent. She was almost, but not quite, as old as Helen.

Life in Marshfield had its strange contradictions, its social stratifications, and easy crossovers. With no formal education beyond the eighth grade, Mary and Helen were not part of the same "circle," but they belonged to the same neighborhood, and it was to Mary's house that Helen came "to cry and cry" when death and life's demands were too much. Helen prized her companionship when she was younger and increasingly as she grew older.

Mary Miksha stopped by with an azalea plant when Bom left for a second trip to Vietnam, knowing how worried Helen was, how the close call he had had when the bomb exploded behind him in Turkey haunted her. Katie Aschenbrenner, another Cedar Street widow whose modest bungalow Helen could see from her kitchen window, took on Bessie's job of telephoning Helen in the morning whenever Bessie left town to visit relatives. Katie's front porch, like Helen's, and like Bessie's back porch, was one of the places where the elderly trio of widows would sit visiting on fine days. Katie and Helen shared a long history, including memories of Auburndale, where Katie's brother-in-law, Tony Aschenbrenner, had managed the Connor farm for half a century.

Bill and Sandy Eiche belonged to a younger generation but were descendants of pioneers and retained their ties to the old Pleasant Hill neighborhood. Bill's father was Helen's dentist before Bill inherited her. If Bom were speaking at a televised congressional hearing at a time when she had an appointment, Bill would carry his set down from his upstairs apartment, and they would watch together, Helen exclaiming from time to time, "I knew he would say that!" An elderly egg man, who still went around town selling eggs, was at the Eiche office one day when Helen stopped by. "I'm eighty-two," the farmer declared teasingly. "How old are you?" Helen smiled, shook her head, and refused to tell, but he persisted, and she bowed to his good natured charm and admitted to having the edge on him at eighty-four.

Her nights were "not so good." Awakening several times, she usually gave up trying to sleep at four or five, went downstairs for a cup of coffee and piece of toast, and settled down on the living room couch, the MacCallum wool plaid over her, listening to the old Grunow, hoping to doze and sometimes succeeding. She gave herself instructions the way old people do, "wiggled over" for a hair appointment, "stirred my sticks to go to dinner at noon with Bessie"—something each day to keep going until David's arrival to spend a full week over his spring break.

He drove her to Madison where she heard a good Sunday service at the Congregational Church and visited with Patricia for the first time since Dick's death. On the way home, they "made the mistake of driving on to Boscobel for the night," a poor night for Helen listening to the heavy rain beat down on the historic old sandstone Boscobel House, where a conspicuously located plaque honored the Gideon Society. It was while spending the night there that two salesmen conceived the idea of organizing a society to equip hotel rooms with a Bible so that no traveler should feel bereft of comfort in a strange place. The Bible in the night-table drawer was well and good, but small comfort for Helen, who lay awake listening as the loggers and salesmen stomped up the wooden stairs. She would have appreciated a better bed, a prettier room that was more spacious, less noisy and damp, but she knew from long experience that those things didn't count with David.

Her tension eased over a good breakfast in a small cafe where the locals, retired farmers and heavy-set widows, greeted one another familiarly. She enjoyed overhearing their good- natured banter, their original wry remarks, the kind one couldn't hear on television or read in the papers, a reminder of that older, younger America. But it wasn't until they got to Mauston for lunch and she could feel home that she really relaxed. Safely back at 208, she rested, glad to have survived.

She tried to discourage Bom when he called to say he was coming to see her on Mother's Day. She would "feel better" if he "spent a quiet Sunday at home in my honor Mother's Day rather than trying to come here for a few hours and no chance to visit. . . . Please take my suggestion. Too many other things on your mind."[17]

He "arrived with crew from Detroit" on Sunday, May 10, and was gone the next day by 7:45 A.M. "Three cars in attendance. Will stop over in Detroit for speech. Am tired and have rested most of day." The red telephone and the direct line to Washington remained in place. She suffered another "uncertain spell" but was game to join him when he returned for a luncheon for Laird Foundation Scholarship winners and for ceremonies commemorating the opening of the central Wisconsin airport in Mosinee. Warren Knowles, Lee S. Dreyfus, and Bom gave speeches. The United States Air Force Thunderbirds, a precision team, and Wayne Flinkenger, an aerobotic pilot, performed overhead. Members of the U.S. Army Golden Knights Parachute Team landed, Wausau and Mosinee bands played, student protesters numbering more than a hundred shouted "more, more" and demanded greater reductions in defense spending. Not a likely prospect with Nixon asking for a $16 billion increase in the nation's debt ceiling.

Elsewhere in America that May following the shooting of four Kent State students by a nervous National Guard, reports that 217 Americans had been killed in Vietnam in a single week (the highest number since August 1969), 77 in Cambodia, and 1281 had been wounded, there was chaos.[18] Demonstrations erupted, bombs exploded, the Bank of America was burned in Santa Barbara. (Word that Bom disagreed with the administration's policies that were helping to fuel the civil unrest came out later.)[19] In the midst of all the turmoil, flags, including Helen's, flew on Memorial Day.

After a Rip Van Winkle absence of more than twenty years, William stopped by. She accepted his appearance for what it was, an acknowledgment that she and he were old and shared a past, some of it good and some of which should be put behind them. A quiet, civil meeting between W.D.'s proud namesake and W.D.'s eldest daughter whom he had loved and respected, defrauded and sued.

More than her brother's reentry into her life, it pleased her that Bom received the Second Annual Statesmen in Medicine Award in recognition of his contribution to the Art and Science of Medicine at a black-tie event held at his friend Murdock Head's Airlie Foundation in Virginia.

Thanksgiving week, coming on the heels of the failure of a daring commando effort to rescue American POW's, was a "difficult week for Bam." Despite daily Pentagon news briefings, despite his frequent on-the-record news conferences, "the credibility issue is haunting the Defense Department, just as it did during the years of President Lyndon Johnson's administrations."[20] Not only the press but family members turned on him: Jessica and Jim Doyle, his Aunt Constie, his sister-in-law Patricia, those whom he felt should have known better, had begun to send him highly critical, accusatory, hurtful letters. His son John and daughter-in-law were among the students in Eau Claire protesting the war. He had reason to be "touchy."[21]

Helen concluded her Calendar in 1970 with two quotations. One was from the contemporary American psychologist Rollo May: "One retires to feelinglessness from where it is only a short step to apathy and from apathy only another step to violence. To avoid anonymity, some inflict pain to prove one can affect somebody." "Is apathy a step toward violence?" She identified the other quotation as something Rudyard Kipling wrote in 1872:

> When earth's last picture is painted and the tubes are twisted and dried
> When the oldest colors have faded and the youngest critic has died
> We shall rest and faith we shall need it—lie down for an aeon or two
> Till the master of all good workmen shall put us to work anew. . . .
> But each for the joy of the working
> And each in his separate star
> Shall draw the thing as he sees it
> For the God of things as they are!

There was snow and more snow in January 1971, "big drifts like early days in Auburndale. . . . Trust Bam is almost to Honolulu—a long drag both ways and I wonder how helpful. That Saigon must be a dreadful spot. . . . Vietnam situation difficult now—as ever." On his return from the far east, Bom took Helen with him to California, where he was scheduled to deliver a speech at the Commonwealth Club, San Francisco, and enjoy a brief holiday in Pebble Beach. She did not accompany him to the Commonwealth Club, although she knew she would run into some of her Witter relatives there. She read excerpts from his speech in the *Monterey Peninsula Herald* and was familiar with his arguments for increased defense spending. He wanted to achieve zero draft calls by July 1, 1973, increase military pay, and maintain the United States' "technological leadership in light of the momentum of weapons development and procurement by the Soviet Union."

While Bom played several eighteen holes at the Pebble Beach course, Helen tried the putting green and luxuriated in the sunshine and in their "lovely suite overlooking the bay" at the Del Monte Lodge. She watched the fog come in over the Pacific, wrote David and Helen L. that she was "swimming in lap of luxury. Never saw such a suite, two big bedrooms (full of flowers also fruit), a living room with grate fire and three baths with adjoining dressing rooms. Wonderful! (Except that I am also a tax-payer.) Our big windows and doors overlook the bay. My bed is seven feet wide. Know the golf is good for Bam. . . . Plane was even more luxurious than last time. (I flew in a kite to Minneapolis to get aboard it. Quite a difference but good of the army to oblige.) . . . Our plane awaits us in San Francisco on call."

March was traditionally David's time to be with his mother, and he offered to stop en route to Alison's wedding so that they could fly into D.C. together. But when Helen phoned to say he need not bother, Bom had arranged for a plane to pick her up, he cancelled plans not only to pick her up but his and Helen L.'s plans to attend the wedding.

Pleasant memories of the "very nice" occasion at the Airlie Foundation and of the luncheon with Bom at the Pentagon receded with the bad news pouring in from Vietnam. Even Helen finally joined the chorus of disapproving voices: "If the government were a bit more candid about what went wrong, it would be a great deal more credible about what went right."[22] She advised the secretary to "make sure you people there are not creating another credibility gap." She softened almost at once. Probably regretting her attack, she sent him a copy of his Washington Office Report dated May 6, 1964, with the comment: "Going at my desk furiously last night I came across this. It may amuse you and as you once said, it all depends upon what side of the table one is on."

In 1964, he had criticized Secretary McNamara's request for a defense spending increase and charged that the transcripts of the Appropriation Committee hearings released by the State Department and the Department of Defense had "been severely altered to eliminate secret and top secret testimony. . . . In some cases the deletions were made for self security rather than national security." Appropriations committee members "had a wider experience in defense matters than the Secretary of Defense has been able to acquire in the last three years. . . . Our Committee must continue to reduce funds for the Department of Defense whenever we feel waste or extravagance exists." Knowing that he could write his ticket when he left Defense, Helen pressed him on his next move. "You keep us guessing don't you? Whether 'to be or not to be,' governor? Senator?"[23]

She missed his "pleasant voice" during her ten-day stay with David and his family at the lake.[24] While she appreciated the pattern of her days with David and Helen L., the set hours for lunch and dinner, the quiet time for her after-noon nap, the walks and talks and the evening readings, she had picked up the tension in David's voice and the strained atmosphere in the cottage. She did not pry as to causes, but she resented that David never stayed overnight after driving her home and called his insistence on making the round trip "foolish." There probably was not a family in America that was not in some way affected by the social turmoil that had been swirling for too many years.

The Christmas of 1971 was probably the loneliest of Helen's life. She had had many invitations but accepted only one from the Chronquists on Christ-mas Eve. Jessica Doyle called, as she would year after year when she returned to Madison for the holidays, saying she would come to see her, but proud of Jessie though she was, year after year Helen "discouraged her coming."

The sea of ice covering three counties melted enough so that she could walk to the post office with her "forked stick and in the road" and buy stamps. The photo of Bom looking desperately tired, which appeared in the *Herald* on December 28, and the two front-page articles blaring "War the Major News" and "Laird: Hanoi Responsible for Strikes" depressed her. Bom's statement that while he could not "rule out more strikes against North Vietnam," the pri-mary emphasis of the strikes would be the protection of remaining American troops, was challenged by Democratic presidential hopeful George McGovern, who claimed the "shocking escalation . . . sinks us deeper into the quagmire of Indochine."

On New Year's Eve, Helen wrote Bom: "I'm not much good at writing sen-timental New Year's letters but this is only to say that I'm thinking of you at year's end and also beginning. I trust the next will be an easier one and hope I can rejoice with you when it is over. We haven't liked the ending of this one much and I know some things are difficult to explain. Haven't liked the insin-uation that Mr. Nixon still hankers for a military victory, nor is the sugges-tion adequate that the bombing is or was necessary to protect our men when it wasn't to protect five times as many." She had begun her letter intending to make them "all envious of us here at home for this is a day in a million. Every tree is etched in white against a clear blue sky. The Evergreens are laden with snow, all of which I can't describe—and the sun is shining but the temperature just right to prevent melting. . . . I wonder if I'll ever see again so beautiful a day. . . . Until I see you, my love and appreciation of what you are trying to do. It is all some task."

In the dead of winter, like a figure out of a fairytale, Bom descended to whisk her away and bring her to new life in a place she had never been. The "Wigwam" Country Club in Phoenix, where he brought her in 1972, was a "beautiful place," "all green grass for blocks, flowers, stock, phlox, marigolds etc. Most attractive rooms, living room with fire place and two big bed rooms off with baths and dressing rooms."

Bom was photographed in the *Phoenix Gazette* with Archie David, the chamber of commerce president. In the speech he delivered at the national chamber's meeting at the Wigwam, he stressed that the United States defenses would "be pressed as never before during the next twenty years" and would "require an increase in terms of our military commitments to our allies and an increase in our own defense spending." It had been his troubling message for some time, but it did not trouble Helen when, after a couple of rounds of golf, he returned to drink a Manhattan or two and share some easy moments with her before taking her arm and strolling, in the cool of the desert evening, to the main lodge for dinner. She observed him poring over papers with General Pursley and Admiral Murphy before she finally said goodnight and went to her bath and bed.

The inevitable thank-you note followed: "Just another note to tell you how much I appreciate your many attentions and how I loved being with you at times. Like your father you calm the whirling tensions of my mind." The "whirling tensions of her mind" may have been due to her increasingly problematical sleep. She tried codeine, which let her sleep some, but she didn't like it. She wondered if her body might not be signaling a sympathetic response to the stress she knew Bom was undergoing, although he never spoke about the indignities he and Barbara faced: the crowds in front of their home chanting and throwing feces; Allen Ginsberg urinating on their living-room picture window, hoping they would call the police, which they didn't, knowing he wanted publicity. He never told her the FBI suggested they move away from Bethesda to another undisclosed location, that Barbara adamantly resisted the idea. "This is my home."[25] Helen did not hear those things, but she read about the secret service and police escorts that surrounded him whenever he made an appearance anywhere now.

David's arrival in March "helped" her, and George Eliot was her companion afterwards. Having reread *Adam Bede, Mill On the Floss, Romola,* and finished the two volumes of *Daniel Deronda,* she began *Middlemarch.* David passed her notes comparing *Deronda* with *Middlemarch* on to Nina Auerbach, the George Eliot specialist at Cal State. "I wrote her a short note of thanks for taking time to write me. Naturally I wouldn't argue with her, but Causabon's trouble was that he was a born *pill* in the first place, and hadn't found anything *worth while* for which to strive. He was running a bluff and *failed* for understandable reasons. *Different* with Lydgate. H.C.L."[26] She did not write

David about the paragraph from *Middlemarch* she copied into her Calendar: "Will not a tiny speck very close to our margin of vision blot out the glory of the world and leave only a margin by which we see the plot? I know no speck so troublesome as self."

Driven back to the turbulent present by reports of the increasing violence in the nation following the Pentagon's announcement that it would "probably not" give information to the public on U.S. bombing raids on any "regular" basis[27] and after President Nguyen Van Thieu had declared martial law throughout South Vietnam, Helen sent Bom "just a sheet to carry my love on these trying days. Sad they had to come again." She had heard Senator Fulbright and Bom carrying on and was glad to remember they "were really friends—youth and age and both nice people. It will be good when your 'aggressive enthusiasm' as he called it can be used in a different cause."[28] She wrote David and Helen L.: "[I] know how difficult these days are [for Bom] but he seldom admits that."

When Marshfield held its centennial celebration in June 1972, a time capsule was buried at the library to which Bom contributed a letter. Sent from the Pentagon, marked "eyes only," and addressed "to the Residents of Marshfield of the year 2072 A.D.,"[29] the capsule was opened and its contents read twenty-five years later, when the library expanded. People were still alive who had vivid memories of the chaotic times Bom wrote of living through. He wrote that the values of patriotism and hope and the sense of duty, which had been his inheritance from his family and community, were the values that would sustain the nation.

They prevented him from slipping into Nixon's orbit during that bitter election year.[30] The break-in at the Democratic National Committee offices in the Watergate complex and at Daniel Ellsberg's psychiatrist's office, reports of telephone taps, and attempts by administration officials to "get at" political "enemies" drove the hysterical political climate to a new pitch. No wonder young people, Dick's daughter Lissa among them, looked elsewhere for the sustaining values their grandparents and parents had been more or less able to take for granted.

Deracinated, searching for meaning far from home after graduation from Stanford and her marriage to an equally questing classmate, Lissa wrote to her grandmother from Nepal. She wrote of the art, temples, and the myths that had evolved with the Himalayas, the warm and helpful Tibetans and Nepalese, the shockingly cheap prices, the unfathomable economics, the hungry children. In Simla, Hamachal Pradesh, India, Lissa and her husband lived in the home of the principal of a government fine arts college whose name "some monk happened to give us. . . . When we first arrived in mid-afternoon, he talked, showed us around, sang, just played with us all through the day and late into the night." The man was "quite lonely and quite misunderstood by his wife," who didn't approve of their presence, or of the monks who occasionally came to visit, but she couldn't protest. "In the [Hindu] religion if she is totally supportive she will be liberated at the end of life." With "the guy" they had developed "a frank relationship" and were "able to discuss all topics." She hoped to be able to bring back home "this strength to be frank." Lissa, whose most vivid memory of her grandmother during the Vietnam period was that she was in favor of world government, would think of her "at the lake with the pines and warm sun as we greet the monsoons in partnership with the Vietnamese."[31]

Helen was in Laona with David and his family on July 4 when the Connor Company celebrated its centennial. William, who had dominated the Auburndale centennial, was nowhere to be seen. Gordon, now president of the company, and his wife, Mary Roddis, dressed as members of the Victorian era's upper class headed the parade, seated in an open carriage pulled by an elegant team of horses. Helen and some others remembered when W.D. led the Laona parade during the fifty-year celebration. He walked, holding a rope and guiding a pair of oxen.

The news that "Nixon [was] to carry every state except Massachusetts and District of Columbia was even better" than Helen expected. "The victory wasn't for him, but against McGovern. Locally the Dems won. . . . I imagine O'Konski had a surprise. He was muchly on the air." Lissa, she knew, had visited Helen L. and David in Los Angeles. "Such globe trotting. After India, I'd think they would appreciate even U.S.A."[32]

After bidding "adieu" to 1972 on the last page of her Calendar, she corrected David's observation: "I am glad your perspective is shifting from stern, austere moralist to that of slightly jaded, amused urban philosopher." "No, instead—often amused, completely jaded, and only semi-urban philosopher. No mental agility or youthfulness. H.C.L."

From a powerless entity on the world stage, a land of plow, oxen, hard physical labor, and immense hope, her country had evolved to be a technological superpower driven by the engine of rampant materialism. While undeniably bringing benefits, the transformation had also ushered in the chaotic time. While after the Second World War, Europe, with the aid of the Marshall Plan, did not collapse into fascism or communism, the 1960s had not been the promised "Development Decade" in which the rich nations helped close the gap with the poor; the gap had widened instead. In America, the promised "Great Society" had not emerged, the phrase becoming absurd almost as soon as Johnson uttered it. Dissention and division dominated the times. Beliefs and enthusiasms, including the belief in scientific "breakthroughs," collapsed.

No wonder Helen claimed to be "completely jaded," although she was not. It was not cynicism that caused her to give up church attendance. She gave up going because listening to the new minister's sermons "irritated her," and she had not had "a happy experience" in church for some time. Arthur Oates, long retired from the ministry and living in Arizona, supported her decision. "If I have to go to church in circumstances that make me angry, or that leave me cold, I'd better stay home."[33] She did not, however, give up Lloyd McKool's Bible study classes.

David Broder, in the syndicated article he wrote for the *Washington Post* summarizing Bom's career in defense, wrote of his having "a degree of cynicism and complicity" that enabled him "to survive in the Pentagon-Congress struggle." Broder's conclusion that "American politics will be diminished by his departure," Ed Heller's editorial calling attention to the rumor that Bom was "no longer high on the list of Richard Nixon's favorites," and John K. Jessup's statement on CBS that "in a tough and thankless job, Mel Laird has done well by this republic"[34] gave Helen enormous satisfaction, but she was now as eager for him to get out of the political game as she had once been eager for him to get into it.

With offers to serve on the boards of seventeen or eighteen major corporations, Bom would almost certainly become a wealthy man. That did not mean much to Helen, but that he had begun to look relaxed and healthy when he slipped into town, "hardly noticed by anyone," in January did. He had not criticized Nixon's policies in Vietnam while the war raged. After the signing of the cease-fire, however, he wanted his mother, who had trusted him, the relatives who had condemned him, the Carleton faculty and administration who had tried to rescind his undergraduate degree, and the world to know that he had opposed the secret invasion of Cambodia and the heavy bombing Nixon ordered on North Vietnam in May and again in December 1972. He maintained, however, that he had been justified in his deep suspicion of the Soviet Union and in his "hard line approach on the antiballistic (ABM) and other weapons systems" and was proud of his record as secretary of defense. It had been an "excruciatingly tough" twenty-four-hour-a-day job.[35]

He and Helen drove to Madison, Bom chauffeuring, something he hadn't done in some time. They stopped en route for lunch at the Mead in the Rapids and for a visit to John Potter's office to see that her will was in order and to sign papers transferring her Birch Lake property: Connor's point to Bom and Barbara, who intended to build there, and the old cabins to David and Helen L.

David arrived two weeks after his brother left. Her house, which seemed "deserted without him," came briefly to life again when Bom arrived after the Laird Foundation meeting in Stevens Point and a meeting in Milwaukee. "He gets around in a hurry." She had just begun to count on his more frequent visits when speculation began as to whether he would be able to resist helping the president out now that details of the "grubby affair" at the Watergate pointed to the involvement of his White House staff.[36] Bom maintained he could not be drafted again, and she believed him even after Nixon fired John Dean and accepted resignations from John Ehrlichman and Robert Haldeman, aides who knew little "of standards of personal behavior required of men in power."[37]

With the news pouring in of a government in chaos, David wrote his brother a rare letter.

Former Secretary of Defense Melvin R. Laird enjoying a quiet moment at 208 South Cherry, following his release from official duty in February 1973.

My hunch is that you have met with various appeals to abandon Burning Tree
and to assume some sort of role in a rescue mission which even now must be
gathering along the Potomac, waiting for orders in a dozen random phone booths.
I hope you can defend against those pressures, though, if your track record is
any indication, you probably can't. You cowboyed the herd through the national
convention of 1964 and have been rough riding the face of San Juan Hill ever
since. It's probably just not in the script for you to decline the call. But I sense
something of your predicament, instructed as it must be by clearer knowledge
than that shared by the rest of us, and I would like to come down on the side
of golf. I hope you can find a way to suppress your missionary zeal and to keep
separate a hard-nosed concern for the country from a wrong-headed concern
for the shitheads who stole Christmas. Good luck and don't get off the dime—
the silver market's going up.[38]

Helen, to whom David sent a copy, added a note: "Good letter for posterity—
We'll see how affairs turn out. June 7, 1973. H.C.L."

Bom came into the White House when his whole family said "don't," convinced by friends on both sides of the aisle, including Edmund Muskie, Tip
O'Neill, Pat Moynihan, and William Proxmire, that he was the only one able
to take hold of the rudderless ship of state. He went over to the White House
determined to enlist a new team,[39] to maintain the "broadest, most open lines
of communications" with Congress, an institution "I love so much."[40] His
name floated again as a possible presidential prospect. "Mel Laird for President.
Don't bet against it."[41]

Helen expressed her anger at Bom's move in a note addressed to the "Honorable Melvin R. Laird, Counselor to the President, Domestic Affairs, The
White House, Washington D.C. 20500": "I had never been told whether the
other office to which I had directed people had been closed. Would certainly
*not* direct anyone to this new address." Her anger spilled over. "Such wandering gypsy-like grandchildren I have. No one of them stays put for a week."

Vice President Spiro T. Agnew's resignation on Columbus Day 1973,
followed by the "bad news" of the "Saturday night massacres" during which
Nixon fired independent prosecutor Archibald Cox and Elliot Richardson
resigned, made Helen wonder "if Bam can help put [the administration] back
together," but he "always seems in good spirits and says his motto is to get
some fun out of any job," Helen wrote David and Helen L. "Bam will maybe
get out when and if he gets Ford confirmed as VP."

She celebrated Thanksgiving with Augusta Roddis and Gordon and his large
family at Mary Pierce's home in Wisconsin Rapids. Neither Gordon nor Helen

brought up the subject of the transformer Helen had discovered that summer at Birch Lake, although it had made her "boil." Located almost "inside my cabin door," and giving off a loud hum, it carried power to the east shore of Birch Lake where Gordon's son David Noel was building a cabin. (After failing to get Laona Power and Light, a subsidiary of the Connor Company, to relocate the transformer, David finally went outside the family and applied to the Wisconsin Service Commission, which investigated and ordered it removed.)

In San Gabriel, David and Helen L. celebrated the holiday with Jessica and Jim Doyle and John O. and Nancy Laird. The Doyles had driven over from Chinle, Arizona, where Jessica had taken a job teaching on the Navajo reservation and Jim a job with the legal services there. John, who was gaining insight into the life of a high school substitute teacher in L.A.'s inner city, after his attempt to locate a teaching job in Marshfield failed, said his father was "ready to leave the White House, and might become a resident pundit at Readers Digest."

DeWitt Wallace, the childless eighty-four-year-old self-made multimillionaire owner and publisher of the Digest had observed Mel Laird over the years. Born and raised in Minnesota, the son of a Presbyterian minister, the Republican Wallace wanted Bom on his team as senior counselor for National and International Affairs, one of his stable of "signers," and as a member of the Digest board and the Wallace Foundations. The "signers" were famous people too busy to write but able to discuss issues with editors, provide insights, direct them toward informative sources. Editors wrote articles for "signers" the way speech writers wrote speeches for presidents, politicians, and other busy, important people. Dwight Eisenhower, General Daniel Graham, Senator James Buckley, and Billy Graham, among others, read and approved articles published under their names. Nothing went out without approval. Wallace would not impose heavily on Bom's time, nor would his work for the Digest preclude his taking positions on other boards. For the use of his name on the Digest masthead as "Senior Counselor," an occasional discreet lobbying effort (escalating postal rates were a present and continuing concern), and an occasional article on some current issue of national and international interest,[42] Wallace offered Bom financial security, an office and secretarial staff in Washington D.C., a Digest car, travel expenses, liberty.

Bom liked the Wallaces and the offer. While he did not publicly admit to having doubts about the president, he had to believe Nixon had something to hide. A guilty Nixon would bury the Republicans for a long time to come. The presidency for Melvin Laird? Not likely. But he had become addicted to Washington, and the Digest offer kept him in the center of the action.

David flew in before Christmas and was with Helen on December 19, when Bom announced his resignation as presidential counselor, effective February 1, 1974. The farewell address he delivered to the press corps on January 20 amused Helen, who observed how skillfully he directed his answers away from the scandals surrounding Nixon and toward the domestic policy achievements Congress had made during his eight-months' tenure in the White House. While Helen never tooted her own horn, Bom managed to sound like a full orchestra.[43] He could not, however, divert the pack from feeding on its prey and finally admitted that as far as the Republican Party was concerned, he had "to believe that we have some trouble. I am a realist." He hoped the party would "survive and move forward." The people wanted two strong political parties.

In Washington, that embattled and intimate circle of outsized egos, Bom was known as a wily politician who kept his cards close or, as Jerry Ford said, a man of "political and personal integrity." Henry Kissinger said he was a man "no one man can handle," an "extremely smart" man who "knows he is extremely smart" and "will let you know he is extremely smart."[44] In his home town he was the beloved native son who partook of the shrewdness for which his grandfather was both famous and infamous and enjoyed the balancing grace of Melvin Laird Sr.

Helen sent regrets to President and Mrs. Nixon's black-tie dinner honoring "the Honorable and Mrs. Melvin R. Laird" on February 26, 1974. David read aloud to her the *Herald*'s account of the event. A photo showed President Nixon presenting Melvin R. Laird with the Medal of Freedom and quoted Vice President Ford saying he could not think of a person who had made a "better record than the one Mel Laird has achieved in the federal government."[45] There wasn't the smallest hint in the photo or the article of what Henry Kissinger called Melvin Laird's "titanic struggles" with the president.[46]

Helen and David enjoyed a quiet dinner at the Casa Loma in Marshfield while Bom was being feted. The next day, David settled down at the dining room table to work on their income taxes, pausing occasionally to carry wood up from the basement, throw logs on the fire, and join her for coffee and conversation in the living room. He had taken over from Bom the handling of her portfolio when Bom became secretary of defense. She remarked on his unusual ability to combine business skill with his intellectual interests; not many could.

Thinking of David and his efforts on tax day, Helen wrote an unusually short thank-you note. Her calendar entry on April 15 explains its brevity: "Getting old and blinder. Notice latter especially." Richard's wife was in a nursing home in Antigo; William's daughter Mariana Leisch died.

Bom left for Europe, David for a Popular Culture Conference at San Diego State University. His previous nonacademic interests in popular culture and American Studies were now disciplines taught in colleges and universities. Opportunities for visiting professorships as well as Fulbright grants, almost none of which were available in the field of seventeenth-century English literature anymore, were available in the new areas, reflecting the inevitable inter-relationship between the government and the universities and America's evolution into a world power.

He sent Helen syndicated columnist Nick Thimmesch's article describing Bom as "the Master Back-Room Dealer in Waiting" who loved Washington and who, besides earning his pay from *Reader's Digest* and performing "a battery of free services," enjoyed kibitzing with old friends like Tip O'Neill or John Rhodes, playing "golf with Ken Rush and George Schultz on weekends," and helping Henry (Kissinger) "because he's got problems with our European allies."[47] The article was published on May 5, but Thimmesch's interview took place on March 25, the day before Nixon presented Bom with the Medal of Freedom. "That will be a nice gathering," Bom told the reporter. "My son, John [26] won't be there, though. He's teaching school out in the center city part of Los Angeles. Mostly Black and Chicano kids. God, that's something. He really has a fascinating experience. It's the greatest thing in the world to have experiences like that."

"Fascinating experience!" Bom had no idea. Enjoying life at the pinnacle of power,[48] not in the ghettos of the powerless, he had no time for philosophical speculation, for the vagaries of discontent so keenly felt by America's dispossessed, the humanist intellectuals, the children in the ghettos of her great cities, the underprivileged African Americans and Chicanos who provided John with the "fascinating" experiences that turned him back to the Midwest before the year was out. This was the Age of Aquarius when the alienated hearkened to Narcissus's song. In America, the world's richest nation, in England, in France, in cities all over Europe, Sartre's *Being and Nothingness* dominated the philosophical landscape in the 1970s with the siren song of the self and the dismissal of the bourgeois notion of responsibility. This was the Western world's psychic epidemic of which the theologian Ann Belford Ulanov had written, that "contagion of feeling or affect": that could spread like a virus.

Her sons' devotion saw Helen through the days it took "a lion's courage to get through." Her brother Richard and his wife, Florence, were both hospitalized. Death hung around the corner waiting for her. She looked over the "Dear Sons" letter she left in her safety box, letting stand what she had written in 1964, including her "attachment to the comfortable, old home at 208

South Cherry" and her hope that "if no one of you wants to live in it, do put it to good use otherwise and don't rent or sell to just any old body. There are many things of interest in it." She added: "I have had wonderful sons—each one different and outstanding in his way. Now you, Bam and David are left. My love and thanks. Mother."

That summer, Helen, David, and Helen L. drove to Milwaukee to talk with Catherine Cleary about her trust and its provisions. As David dedicated himself to her interests, she thought Helen L. "will be glad when this business binge is over."

For years Helen L. had felt the strain of her subordination to the strong will and mind of her mother-in-law, had felt estranged from the duo that David and Helen presented as they forged ahead in their exclusionary, formal, intellectual discourse that was at once so intimate, distant, and different from the apolitical, nonintellectual, imprecise talk in her parents' house. But that had changed over time. The women had bonded in the mysterious way some women sometimes do. Helen, who ate very little when she was alone, was grateful for Helen L.'s many good meals. "I don't know how she does it," she told Mary Miksha.

Helen gave her daughter-in-law something in return. Her resistance to change, exemplified in her ordered home, speech, dress, and manners, came to have a profound meaning for Helen L. She wanted to tell Helen she was grateful to find her there in the old home in Marshfield year after year, season after season, to see her holding steady in spite of the buffeting winds of change that had knocked so many off their moorings. The habit of silence, the unwritten rule of not speaking about feelings, however, was too deep, and she did not break it. Eyes told what words would not. Helen L. did not know that the woman, the perfect emblem of unwavering stability, had had to fight to achieve and maintain her ordered self.

Helen watched Nixon deliver his resignation speech on television on August 8. Everyone did. On August 9, Gerald Ford was sworn in as president. Newsmen called her, wanting to talk with Bom, to know where he was. She guessed he was talking with Ford about his vice presidential choice but would not tell them so.

Both sons were with her at the lake when she celebrated her eighty-sixth birthday. Gone were the days when Andy felt obliged to warn David and Helen L. that anyone standing on the hill behind the Laird cabin where the trees had been trimmed along the power line right of way had "a clear line in" and it would "be a cinch to take Bom out."

On August 25, Bom called from his other life in D.C. David, Helen L., and Vanessa stopped by on their way to Baraboo, Reedsburg, and Dodgeville where

David was eager to get into his other life in the woods in Sauk and Iowa Counties. The county foresters had marked the weed trees, the double stems, the hickory, the box elder to be destroyed so that the desirable red oak and walnut could have more of the sunlight and space in which to grow. He did not hire the work done but went into the woods himself, bringing Helen L. and Vanessa along to share in the experience and help with the work. They all took turns employing the hydro-hatchet the forester lent them. There was no need to hassle with a dangerous power saw. With a little container of arsenic worn around the waist, a hydro-hatchet with a tube running from the container into the blade, and a few arsenic releasing blows to score the offending tree, the deed was done and the trees were killed as surely as if felled by a saw. The system was employed for a time by the forest service and then quietly abandoned. Nobody in Forest County ever heard of it.

On September 8, Helen noted in her Calendar: "President Ford announces his pardon of former President Nixon." On September 9, she wrote the Honorable Melvin R. Laird at his *Readers Digest* office: "Greetings! Any credibility recently gained has been thrown out the window. Timing bad! H.C.L."[49]

In spite of the black spec moving before her eye, she felt rejuvenated—perhaps because of Bom's interest in building at the lake. Old age is, in any event, not a straight line of descent unless some galloping other disease sets in. Bad days, weeks, months when arms hurt, legs swell, eyes fail, hearts fibrillate give way to better days. Helen enjoyed a better fall than she or anyone else anticipated after the ill health she had endured, but Richard was dying. Helen baked a coffee cake to distract herself and took a piece to Mary Miksha, house-bound with a broken ankle. Bom's arrival for the Fifth Laird Youth Leadership Day and the dinner she had with him, John O., and John Dressendorfer turned her attention back to the living, but she wasn't up to going to hearing Caspar W. Weinberger, the secretary of Health, Education and Welfare, and Lee S. Dreyfus, the chancellor of the University of Wisconsin-Stevens Point, deliver speeches or attending workshops led by Tim Wyngaard, and Bob Froehlke.

"The big weekend went well," she wrote David and Helen L. From the way Bom used "the ailing mother . . . as an excuse at times to get away from places, one would think he came out here every week-end. . . . He *is* comical." He did get some rest at the house Sunday morning, "just being lazy, looking at games etc. until he joined Dressy [John Dressendorfer] and Richardson [Spring Valley man] at Inn and later out to dinner which I refused. Think Dr. Lewis joined them and they went out to Casa Loma for a stag party. I didn't even hear Bom come in but he said he slept better the night before, *naturally*." She was "almost back to normal." "Politics" was "warming up."[50]

William stopped by the day Richard passed away, thinking Helen would be glad to see him, and she was. He did not go to Laona for the funeral, but Helen attended the graveside services with David, Bom, and Barbara. On October 29, she wrote in her Calendar: "Even nature sheds tears today. David flying to L.A. and Bom and Barb to Hawaii. I am satisfied at home." She found a word in the dictionary she wanted to use in writing Dickens about his father: "He 'up-girded' the town of Laona." She wondered if the term didn't derive from the old girths belted around horses.

When bad weather foiled David's plan of returning on the "red eye" to spend a few days with her before Christmas, she urged him not to attempt the trip, but to rest instead. She visited with Fanny on Christmas Eve—"will not go out again"—and wrote David and Helen L. on Christmas Day that she had been "*bewildered* with beauty—five inches of pure white new snow and every bush, tree and twig in the backyard etched with it. I never expected to see such a sight again and hope I can remember it."

CHAPTER 23

౿

# *Past and Present*

## *1975–1979*

That which is has already been, and what is to be has already been.

—ECCLESIASTES

The snow was dirty in January when Bom arrived to take her to Minneapolis, where they shared "a grand comfortable suite" on the Marquette Hotel's seventeenth floor, overlooking the city and the new skyways. He introduced her to some "nice people," treated her to a symphony concert in the new Orchestra Hall and to "delightful, gourmet" dinners at the Hotel, the Country Club at Lake Calhoun and the Minneapolis Club. She shopped and had her hair done at Dayton's. "Same gent cut my hair as he did 15 years ago— grayer even than I." After four wonderful days, Bom drove her home in a blustery, blinding rainstorm, which delayed his flight to D.C. "Bam kept the dining room grate fire going and didn't seem to mind the lay-over. Luckily had food enough in house for week-end and thought of Emerson's poem, but why does he say 'tumultuous privacy of storm' when it is the *storm* not the privacy that is tumultuous."[1]

David thought it sounded as though they had been "on poverty row up there" at the top of the Marquette and that Emerson might be suggesting "tumult in both his privacy and the storm. Maybe the isolation of the storm puts him at the mercy of his own restless thoughts."

When Bom brought Helen to Washington in April, he tried to persuade her to move into a residence hall in his neighborhood. While Helen enjoyed her time away, and having Bom serve her breakfast in her room, being chauffeured about, eating at a "ritzy" restaurant downtown and at the exclusive Georgetown Club and the Airlie Foundation, and visiting Bom's capacious office on Rhode Island Avenue, she would not consider leaving Marshfield. Home was there, memories, dependable old friends: Fanny Purdy, Mary Miksha, and Katie Aschenbrenner in the neighborhood. Not Bessie Jackson anymore; she was in a Catholic home in Milwaukee near her children. Helen could get in even though she wasn't Catholic, Bessie said, but Helen passed on her offer.

The Khmer Rouge troops stormed into Phnom Penh and seized control of Cambodia on April 17, and the final siege of Saigon was about to begin when Bom brought her home. He stayed overnight before leaving for a Metropolitan Life board meeting in New York, where Barbara would meet him and they would enjoy some theater and have dinner at Sardi's. Helen had his number at the Waldorf where he stayed whenever he went to New York. She did not query him about the new world he had entered, an interwoven network of major corporations and politicians. She eagerly read, however, everything about him, as well as the articles he contributed to the *Reader's Digest*. She was grateful for the large print subscription he provided and did not hesitate to point out a rare dangling participle when she found one.

She received in absentia her "certificate of appreciation for devoted service to the Federation and community for over fifty years" from the Seventh District Woman's Club. What she wanted to do, she did. That was the privilege of great old age. She did not often play the piano anymore, and she almost never sang. Even her speaking voice cracked, and because she was becoming increasingly hard of hearing, she often asked "Whaaaat?" in a rather sad, whining way when someone said something to her and she missed it. In 1975, in recognition of the help she had periodically needed and received, she subscribed as a charter member to the Menninger Foundation, which promised through research to develop techniques and procedures to benefit thousands who suffered from mental illness.

While George Magnin, Tom Rice, Tony Waisbrot, and at least half the other men in town headed for the rivers and lakes when the fishing season opened, Helen prepared for the arrival of both sons. She ordered chicken and ham, so that they could enjoy a snack, supper, or lunch at home for a small family reunion, the three of them, before the Youth Leadership meeting in Stevens Point. She filled the vacuum afterwards by reading about Bom.

He didn't look to her like "the best snake oil salesman in the Republican party" or like "one of those silver-tongued political devils who can peddle bridges and Florida wetland sight unseen and leave the buyer convinced that it is his own fault if he's been taken." She could believe he was "a favorite of the Washington press corps" because he remained close to the action, was willing to share inside information, was "right more often than not," and "always sounds right." Reporters credited him with being the "main man behind Gerald Ford's campaign to stay in the White House." They said Mel Laird promoted Ford as a reasonable man against the unreasonableness of the heavily

Democratic Congress that he was behind Rockefeller and "in favor of giving the conservatives a chance to knock" him.[2] As usual, it was impossible to know where Mel really stood.

She watched him on the *Today Show* and thought he did well "advertising President Ford—and *Reader's Digest*. Latter mentioned three times." Bom hosted her birthday dinner at the Holiday Inn in Marshfield: "88th birthday over and am glad. Bom off to Hawaii and Japan. David back to lake. John and Nancy to River Falls." John, working on a graduate degree with a concentration in colonial history and teaching as an assistant in the English department, thought "they must not teach composition in any high schools anymore. I thought the kids at L.A. High were in trouble, but some of the freshman from lily white Wisconsin are in worse shape. Secondary education and education in general is in really bad shape."[3] Nancy had a "terrible job" as a nursing assistant at a local nursing home. "An experiment in hard labor. They work as hard as construction workers for $2.00 an hour."

She walked to Mary Miksha's and sat awhile on her porch with her, noting Lissa's phone call on September 7: "Hope Lissa has good Madison stay. Did not invite her here." She was expecting Bom, who had phoned her on his way to Japan from Anchorage, Alaska, saying he would arrive on the evening of the 11th. By then, Helen had said goodbye to David and his family, who were on their way to France. Helen L. had a semester's sabbatical leave from Westridge and Vanessa and David leaves of absences from their institutions, and Elizabeth Witter Debost had offered them the use of the Debost apartment in Dijon.

David wrote of calm seas and good weather, of the Debosts' warm reception and their pleasant "pied a terre" on 4 bis rue des Roses, within walking distance of the Palace of the Dukes of Burgundy. Helen L. wrote of the bomb threat David heard two employees talking about on the *Queen Elizabeth II* on which they sailed, of not feeling safe during their short stop in London, of security guards at stores and handbag searches at entrances of museums and theaters, of the high tension in the air—and of the Debosts' hospitality.

The Debosts introduced David and his family to restaurants all over Burgundy and took them to meet Henry's brother, "a genuine country squire" who lived in an old abbey on the Debost ancestral farm outside of Dijon. Elizabeth introduced David to members of the English faculty at the University of Dijon, who much preferred to speak French but would, after some wine, bread, ham, and olives, talk about Faulkner or Eudora Welty. Vanessa attended the Lycée Marcelle Pardée as a freshman. The rote learning and rude teachers amazed her. Henry Debost said the product of French education was to make anarchists or royalists of the students. Watching them tear out of the finally unlocked black iron gates at the end of the school day, flinging themselves on their motor-cycles, lighting their cigarettes, and beating it out of there as fast as they could in a great swirl of smoke, sound, and defiance, convinced Helen L. he was right. "Vanessa might lead a student uprising if she had the vocabulary. She is less than persuaded by the French method."

David wrote of the high prices, the periodic strikes that interrupted elevator service and mail delivery, and the good time they had had in Paris when Bom and Barbara arrived in October. They had drinks together at the U.S. ambassador's residence and rode in the famous elevator painted by Marc Chagall before setting off for dinner at a restaurant David knew about on the Left Bank across from the Ecole des Beaux Arts, where the tablecloths were paper, the food good, the wine cheap, and the crowd lively.

Helen followed Lissa's moves from a letter David forwarded. From Madison, where she had spent three weeks but "unfortunately wasn't able to arrange a visit with Bamma," she traveled to Guatemala, spent the summer "with a few wise people," and was now living in Clinton, Washington, where she was "working as a reader in the English department for one professor in a class of linguistically oriented topics taught to English students." He asked her to give "a lecture on Black English," which she "was thrilled about giving," in spite of all the preparation involved. "Mostly depended on the writings of Ishmael Reed and a sociologist named Paul Carter Harrison who wrote Nonuno (Non-imo), and a record of talking drums."[4] This granddaughter was an "internationalist" in a way Helen could never have dreamt of becoming, teaching an English class unimaginable in her day.

Helen roused herself for the visit of David and his family on their return to the States in December, but when they set off again, she was "glad to rest and keep quiet. Pep all gone! but house deserted." She managed a note to Vanessa: "It is not always that left behind articles give pleasure, but such is the case here. I loafed today and found how you had left the interesting and appreciative card to the 'World's greatest geometry teacher' [David] which I loved in its gratitude for everything. Much love, Bomma."

"Not feeling too well." "Hardly know one day from another." "Try out the piano this A.M." "Very little mail." "May walk to Mary's." "Have discouraged Constie's coming now. Too cold."

She was a year older and a year weaker when Bom arrived to bring her to Washington. Perhaps now he could persuade her to come and live near him. He could not. February 11: "Took early plane for home via Madison." February 12:

"Good to have Bam home here and he has given up trip into Illinois and will stay over week-end. Dr. Magnin stops in and starts antibiotic which Bam keeps track of." Bom thought Ford's challenger from the party's well-organized conservative wing, the telegenic Ronald Reagan, might win a few primaries but predicted that Ford would go to Kansas City with a majority of the delegates.

It was March before she ventured out to Karau's grocery store, walking there carefully on the snow-crusted streets and taking a taxi home. She wrote to congratulate Ben Lawton, head of the Clinic Research Foundation, on his appointment to the University of Wisconsin Board of Regents and looked forward to David's arrival on the 21st. "So good to have him here. Miss him." Bom came on the 30th, John Dressendorfer with him. Both stayed at the Holiday Inn, leaving after lunch for Appleton, where they were campaigning for Ford. Dean Emanuel said her blood pressure was high, and she was content to stay quiet at home, to sit out on the porch with Mary, who brought her some of her "Slavonic bread." Feeling stronger, she and Fanny paid a call on the recently widowed Helen Doege. When David wrote enclosing Vanessa's report card, she sent it to Bom's secretary, along with a note. "Very good report—Please return it to me! Ask Bom to write me about his being in West Bend recently. Others have! H.C.L."

"You would have had fun listening in to some of our conversations (Clay's compromise would seem simple in comparison and we ended friends)," she wrote David and Helen L. after one of Bom's short stopovers. He "looked well and still believes in looking at the sunny side. (My eyes aren't strong enough for that.)"

Aware that news of Bom fueled her quiet life, David forwarded an article from the *Los Angeles Times* in which he was named along with George Ball, Peter Peterson, Cyrus Vance, James Schlesinger, Paul Warnke, Elliot Richardson, and Zbignew Brzezinski as one of the old guard of "big eight" in the running for secretary of state. Not many in Washington thought Henry Kissinger would continue in office "even if Gerald Ford is re-elected." The foreign-policy establishment of Wall Street bankers and lawyers had been "transformed and subsumed by a new, broader grouping" comprised of professors, lawyers, businessmen, congressional aides, foundation executives, think-tank experts—even some newsmen. . . . A sign of the times is that the Council on Foreign Relations, once the elitist New York headquarters of the foreign-policy Establishment, has had to open its doors to the new crowd in order to survive as just one of the power centers of the Community. . . . Mel Laird is . . . stumping the country and writing articles about the dangers of Russian military strength."[5]

Defense policy, it seemed, would remain the area in which he would continue to exert the greatest influence. He was chairman of the newly formed Public Policy Project on National Defense, whose mission it was to examine "the many controversial issues involved in the defense of the United States" and to ensure that the collective expertise of public figures involved in the field, including Les Aspin, Jack Kemp, Clark Clifford, Admiral Thomas Moorer, Clement Zablocki, and Sam Nunn, would not be ignored.

On June 26, the family was reunited in Marshfield for the nation's bicentennial celebration. Bom shared the speakers' platform with his friend Senator John Warner. David, Helen L., Vanessa, and Helen sat out on the benches in the library parking lot in the hot sun, listening to the patriotic speeches, walking the short distance afterward to enjoy a relaxing moment in Helen's cool living room with Bom and the senator.

The talk among the Lairds when they gathered at Birch Lake later that summer was not about politics but about the plans architect Fritz Roth had prepared for Bom and Barbara's "cabin" on "Connor's point" and David and Helen L.'s renovations to Helen's old cabins. Bom and Barbara's architectural plans were grand, a match for the winterized places Gordon's children, Gordon Phelps, Cate, and David Noel, had built at the lake, symbols of the new times and the good fortune of the third generation. (Richard's son Dickens built a comfortable, attractive Montana ranch–style cabin when his sister, Jean, inherited their parents' cabins.) David and Helen L.'s additions to what was now the oldest property on the lake were modest, but there was pride in Helen's voice as she pointed out the changes to Constie: the large kitchen-dining room, the pine paneling hiding the broken-down plaster ceiling and walls in the living room, the recessed ceiling lights, the porch incorporated into the living room, the telephone, the modest shrine to W.D. In the corner of the dining room, on a "wooden horse," on a double weave Navajo blanket, David had placed his grandfather's western saddle. W.D.'s felt hat rested on the horn, his leather boots, dried and turned up at the tips, with the imprint of his feet molded in, lay on the floor beside.

David was apparently more interested in history than Constie, who had knocked down W.D.'s old cottage in the fifties, replacing it with a one-story cabin. In the sixties, preferring to spend her summers at the ranch she and Dick Modrall had bought outside of Las Vegas, New Mexico, she gave her cottage to her son Jim when he settled in Chicago with his wife, Nancy, and their three children. Flying in for brief visits with the family gave Constie all the contact she needed with the lake, which had once, she insisted, meant so much to her.

The new dock, which replaced the old wooden dock at the Modrall cabin and had to be lifted out by workmen every fall and reinstalled every summer, had its advantages: slips for boats and no possibility of splinters. Motor boats also had advantages, although Helen did not appreciate their noise when she wanted to lie down. But she could see that the younger generation enjoyed speed, the thrill of skiing on water, knew that she would once have skied herself had she had the chance, had there been the equipment and the money for such sport.

On August 15, while Bom and his son, David Malcolm, were attending the Republican Convention in Kansas City, Helen listened to the proceedings on the radio. Waking early, she studied the "wide bands of orange color clouds across the lake." She missed Richard but relished Gordon's late-afternoon visits, when they would sit on the Laird deck and engage in a duel of wits that left them both howling with laughter and exhausted her.

Bom arrived on August 21, and Helen celebrated the "finest kind of birthday" on the 22nd. "Both boys here. Helen and David out-did themselves as hosts. John, Alison and David M. phoned. Vanessa baked the cake. Helen the dinner." Three days with both boys. Then Bom had to leave. He "seemed to have enjoyed the time past three days for some rest after Kansas City." He had looked tired. He had been with Ford and the group of Ford Republicans— Nelson Rockefeller, Robert Hartman, Bryce Harlow, John Tower, Bob Teeter, Stuart Spencer, Richard Cheney—who gathered in Ford's quarters at 3:15 A.M. to decide on the vice president. At 5:00 A.M., with no conclusion reached, they caught a few hours sleep. Brent Scowcroft and Nevada senator Paul Laxalt (one of Reagan's chief strategists) joined the group, and they finally agreed, incorrectly as it turned out, that Ford's choice of Bob Dole was a good one.[6] As Bom predicted, Ford was nominated, but the convention was "a disappointment, mostly bedlam," Helen thought.

Life went its seasonal course. Goodbyes became increasingly difficult. It seemed "quite different," Helen wrote David and Helen L., "having you get farther and farther away than when you were headed in this direction. . . . You people did well in keeping lake and town too livened as well as affording me pleasure and rest. Thanks again."[7]

She took Mary Miksha for a ride in the country, warning her that she might get dizzy, instructing her to kick her foot off the gas pedal and turn the wheel towards the curb if she passed out. Fanny drove her through the park to see the leaves. She noted that Gordon had gone to Albuquerque to be with Constie before she and Dick left again for Los Angeles with diminishing hopes of effective treatment for Dick, whose phlebitis worsened, and that David was setting off for a series of meetings, delivering speeches in Sioux Falls, Iowa, in

Madison, Kansas, and Knoxville, Tennessee, on the *Great Gatsby* and another on the automobile in American culture.

Helen heard the slip Gerald Ford made during the television debate with Jimmy Carter: "There is no Soviet domination of Eastern Europe." She heard Bom on *Face the Nation* and wrote him: "I anticipated *exactly* what you would say about Eastern European slip." While she thought Bom had made "a very good presentation," he "might have picked up the last words of one questioner and said 'Yes, vote on trust'—after all, that is not such a bad idea."[8]

The election was a "strange phenomenon." Ford won in Marshfield, but farmers, women, and Bob Dole, who projected "an ogre like image,"[9] helped Jimmy Carter to a narrow victory, and the Democrats retained their overwhelming congressional majority. In Wisconsin, Patrick Lucey won another term, and the Democrats strengthened their hold in the senate. Robert Knowles, the brother of former governor Warren Knowles, lost to a twenty-nine-year-old Democrat, Michele Radosevich. Jessica's thirty-year-old husband, Jim Doyle, was elected district attorney in Madison. Helen did not mention the fact in her letters to David or in her Calendar, but she kept the clipping from the November 5 *Capital Times* Pat sent: "Doyle Brings Liberal Viewpoint, Diverse Background to D.A.'s Post," and, when Jim and Jess stopped by a few months after the election, she was glad to see them, to know they were happy to be back in Madison after Boston, Tunisia, and Chinle, Arizona.

"No hope" for Dick Modrall or Kathryn Connor. Helen's handwriting, with words and sentences crashing into one another, sometimes almost entirely superimposed on one another, indicates that she was not doing too well herself. She talked with Constie, with William, and tried to phone Elsbeth, but had "no luck." She did reach Gordon on December 12 to wish him a happy birthday.

Friends helped with groceries. Days passed, December days, with "no great accomplishment." She thought her heavy, uncurled hair made her look as if she had a wig, decided she needed a permanent, rouged her cheeks, put powder on. She thought it her duty to dress well, to make an effort, especially since Dean Emanuel's house call when he gave his okay to her plans to spend Christmas in Washington. David arrived on December 16. "Good to have car out with David to drive and having warmed up engine out to lunch." They shopped, bought a plant for Mary Miksha and a gift for Fanny. David, paying an "outrageous price," bought her a new wide-brimmed brown felt hat to wear in D.C. "I should have backed Mr. Baxter against the wall first for the high price he charged for it." But then, she came from another age and still thought a nickel was a decent tip and two dollars should cover a tank of gas even in her big gas guzzler. When David left to check on things at Laona, Bom arrived to whisk her off to Washington. On December 28, he saw her safely home.

"I must stop trying to visit by letter," Helen declared in a long letter to David, Helen L., and Vanessa.[10] David's "fine application" for a grant to the University of Chicago had arrived along with a brochure he had prepared for the American Studies department at Cal State, Los Angeles, an interdisciplinary department that he directed. "It was thrilling to see and to know it could be done," Helen wrote, demonstrating exceptional warmth. "You have been so quiet and modest about it all. I wonder how you were able to accomplish so much. The format is tops and should bring much praise and appreciation." He denigrated his efforts, as usual, said she was "a hero to work through that stuffy grant proposal." He had received the nomination from Cal State to attend a National Endowment for the Humanities Institute, "Technology and the Individual," at the University of Chicago. "If I should get the fellowship, it would mean a year's residence at the University of Chicago at the equivalent of full salary and the chance to work out a course similar to the one described in the proposal. The fellowship begins in the fall of 78."

The possibility of David's return to the University of Chicago, that "intellectual mecca" boosted David's spirits, and Helen's. She needed a boost when William called to say that Florence had died in Laona and when Andy called to say Kathryn had died. Florence and Kathryn had been first cousins and sisters-in-law; both were Smith College graduates who had probably anticipated better lots than the one fate dealt them. It was good, after all, that David insisted on coming as usual in March. Too many sad thoughts were piling on.

He came again at the end of April when Pat Laird and the widowed Roy Luberg were married in Madison. Bom and Barbara drove to Marshfield with David to give Helen the full report of the "very nice wedding" and "the very nice party also following at Madison Club, supper and dancing also. Numerous U.W. people and others there."

Doctors, she decided, "seem too slow to lay down the law or to admit they can't combat *real* old age." She felt better in Laona, where her nightmares that were induced, she thought, by her medication, which she had been told to double, ceased. The sweet air, the moon path over water, the early-morning sunrise, the company, and the care helped. Another birthday celebration: "All here," Helen noted, from Bom and David's family, "except Chip," Alison's former husband. Marriages didn't hold these days. Molly, Cate, Lissa, Alison, Helen's nieces and granddaughters, had all shed their mates and looked for and found others.

She wrote Helen L. on August 29. "I don't like to think of your closing down camp this week. It is no easy undertaking I know. You have kept so busy all along and have all given so much pleasure to so many. I for one do appreciate that and continue the enjoyment in memory. Even putting away the various little grocery items made me realize the time it took to assemble them. Thanks again and love." Appreciating a woman's work, she wrote Helen L. a second note expressing her gratitude: "I had such good 'breathers' up north with you people that the renewed energy *should* endure. You did so much for so many this summer that I hope an easier life for a time will be welcomed."[11]

As David developed his new interests, writing, traveling, and lecturing in the fields of Popular and American Studies, Helen L. increasingly took over the role as family correspondent. She wrote of the music and the many people in attendance at the memorial service for Dick Modrall, her parents' fiftieth anniversary celebration in Santa Barbara, David's quiet celebration of his fiftieth birthday in San Gabriel, his plan to stop in Marshfield on his way to an American Studies meeting in Boston to speak about the links between Mark Rothko and other modern artists and the work of early Navajo blanket weavers.

On November 17, Helen wrote Helen L. a long newsy letter recounting Alison's arrival at Houston for a National Organization for Women (NOW) meeting, her hesitation about accepting Augusta's invitation for a DAR meeting because she had dropped out of the organization years ago, and the pleasure she took in hearing about the papers Helen L. and David had read at the West Coast Philological Association meeting at University of Southern California. "An *unusual* occurrence. David enthused about *yours* but did not mention his. It was a banner day. . . . *You* must read *your* paper to me—first opportunity."

Less than two weeks after Helen L. received the controlled and newsy letter, Helen made a desperate call to Bom and Barbara. She was, Barbara wrote David and Helen L., "all shook up, not a physical thing, but little things that had gone wrong and she was determined to 'get out of this house.' . . . This could be a blessing in disguise if it means she will be more willing to spend time here—will keep you well informed."[12] Bom hurried out in a heavy snowfall to bring her to Washington.

Neither her Calendar nor her letters to David and Helen L. give any hint of the panic Barbara reported. She wrote of a fine trip, Bom's attentions, of having "to fight a bit of home-sickness (a long time weakness of mine, which not everyone understands and I am too old now to conquer it.) Everyone is very kind and I am surely having a good rest."

She was reminded of a play they read in college. "Do you know it? *A Woman Killed with Kindness*? Barbara gave me the clipping you enclosed to her, Helen.

Good picture of David, but that writer of novels [Joseph Wambaugh] sounded like a tramp to me." (A former Cal State student, policeman turned popular author, Wambaugh gave an informal lecture to David's "Popular Culture" class. The photo showed David standing beside the author as he presented the manuscript of his best selling *The Black Marble* to Cal State's head librarian, Morris Polan. A murder mystery, it would not have been a book Helen would care to read.) She looked at the nearby retirement home but was not interested in trying it. "Hope I don't have to battle with Bam over that."[13]

She had had to get out of 208 but wrote David and Helen L. of having a "deep desire to get home at times which neither height nor depth, warmth nor cold completely dislodge."[14] To please Bom and Barbara, she tried out the home, but the experiment was the failure she anticipated. Bom brought her back to Wisconsin, having had to accept her declaration that she could not be with "all those old people."

"Really hold in, tired, and weather very cold," Helen wrote on December 31, ending the calendar year with a "Good Bible quote: 'The spirit of the Lord is not of fear but of power, of love and of a sound mind.'" She was happy to be home, but her news was sad. "Martina Marsh McKinney is to be brought here for burial, Wednesday from Detroit. Guess I told you that Dr. Mason is gone, also his sister, Mrs. McCormick and her husband—none by accident." A few weeks later, she learned of the death of another old friend, Helen Doege. She did not attend the services. She was glad Fanny stopped in and had tea with her, forcing herself to connect with life.

She sent Helen L. a card with a picture of the Watergate Hotel on it. "Isn't this a ghastly looking place, all by itself, as indeed it should be, I guess. (One of a box of cards I wouldn't choose.)" She began writing about her "easy trip home" with Bom, how he stayed on for several days to settle her in and do odd jobs. "He is quite a patient man." And then, in a sudden burst of impatience, she broke her usual reserve to reveal her deep anger over what the country had been made to go through. "Feel like scribbling all over picture," she wrote, before recalling herself and politely inquiring if Vanessa got to ride horseback in Palm Springs, to indicate that that was something she would have liked to do and to recount her other news: Constie had called wanting to know where William was, but she couldn't tell her, and Augusta was "an abiding friend," a "kind and loyal friend."[15]

She called Constie on her seventieth birthday on February 13, 1978, and noted with customary disapproval that Lincoln's and Washington's birthdays were celebrated together. Mary Miksha brought a lemon pie. "Another long weekend maneuvered."

Helen L. wrote of returning to her work on a biography of the Swedish-American artist Carl Oscar Borg (1879–1947) and of having "an appointment with a Miss Judson who belonged to the Los Angeles art community at the turn of the century. She sounds charming on the phone and promises to tell me all about the women's clubs of the time. Club women were responsible for promoting art and artists and wielded quite a bit of power, quite quietly." Helen could have told her all about the women in the club wielding a "good deal of power quite quietly," but Helen L. didn't know that.

Bom stopped by in February on his way to Fort Lauderdale. He confirmed what Helen L. had written. He and Barbara had decided not to build at the lake after his cousin Cate rejected his request to tie into the underwater cable.[16] There was no other power source. Helen may have been disappointed, and probably was, and she may have wondered whether the denial was in retaliation for the Lairds having brought the illegal transformer to the attention of the Wisconsin Public Service Commission.

She did not focus on what she could not change. She sent for a copy of the poem "The Chrysanthemums in the Eastern Garden" that she heard on the state radio station.[17] The quiet poem concludes with the lines "I ask you, late Chrysanthemum-flower / At this sad season, why do you bloom alone? / Though well I know that it was not for my sake, / Taught by you, for a while I will open my face."

Helen L. arrived, filling in for David. She took her for a drive to Rozelville, to the Knight's Inn for dinner and prepared a dinner at 208 for Helen and William. Inquiring after Helen L.'s mother, as was her custom, Helen learned that she was tired of life, in pain, couldn't walk, and wished there were a pill that people who felt they had lived their lives and done what they should do, seen what they should see, could take to slip out. Helen vigorously supported the idea. "Tell her to draw up a petition. I'll put my name first on the list."

After Helen L.'s return to California, she kept Helen posted on the family news. She wrote about the combined birthday party her parents celebrated in Santa Barbara describing how, after dinner, the guests, who were feeling pretty mellow, began the traditional round-singing at the table, each person starting a song and the others joining in, seated, holding hands, swaying side to side in rhythm. They had all been Danish songs, until someone started "God Bless America." Then, everyone spontaneously rose. Standing tall, they gave a powerful rendition. "It was an experience!" "People have been poor mouthing America for so long that David, Vanessa, and I exchanged looks of amazement" at the display of patriotism.

They had been more amused than amazed at the honors convocation at Polytechnic School, Pasadena, when Vanessa was presented the Brown University Alumni Award, which was created at a time when women were excluded from higher education, and retained its original language. Vanessa received the award "in honor of his selection as the Junior who best combines a high degree of ability in English both written and oral with those outstanding personal qualities which, in the words of the Brown Charter of 1764, give promise that the student become one of the 'succession of men duly qualified for discharging the offices of life with usefulness and reputation.'" The news pleased Helen, who wrote, "Do congratulate Vanessa on her Brown University recognition. Wonderful! And always considered a good University, too."[18]

There was a strike in Laona in the summer of 1978 when David and his family arrived with Helen. "All company property involved. Even store seems deserted." She lingered in the north among W.D.'s descendants, the few of her generation, their children, and their children's children. She couldn't keep up with the expanding numbers, and didn't try to, although she recognized some faces and was invariably warm in her greetings. She stayed through rain, which in earlier years would have driven her off, and was pleased to have her brother, William, sit down with them for lunch at the hotel, which operated throughout the strike. She was pleased, too, that the oldsters in town, who knew all about the family split years ago, observed the mending.

She was not aware that troubles were brewing. She had observed a rift in the family in the summer of 1974 when she had attended her grand-nephew Jeff Connor Evans's wedding in Wausau. Observing the absence of Gordon and his family at that major gathering of the Connors, Helen had leaned over and whispered to Helen L., seated on the pew beside her, "This would have killed my mother." Helen L., who knew no more about the family quarrels than she did about the lumber business, had no idea what she was talking about. Company business had been no business of Helen's for many years. It went on behind closed doors, and she did not pry, although she perceived the obvious changes: the name change to Connor Forest Industries and the expansion in product lines. She knew that Richard's son Dickens had left the board and gone out on his own, that Gordon's sons Gordon Phelps and David Noel had become vice presidents.

What occurred in August 1978, when the board met in the basement of the Gordon Hotel, did not stay behind closed doors. A motion was made, seconded, and passed to name Gordon Phelps president and his father, Gordon Sr. chairman of the board. Gordon had no inkling of his son's plan to replace him.

Gordon had been generous over the years and had distributed large blocks of shares to his children. Following Richard's death, his stock was distributed to his children Jean and Dickens. Gordon Phelps had counted the votes. With his, his brother David Noel's, Jean's, and Dickens's stock, he had enough. He did not indicate his plans to his sisters, whom he knew to be devoted to their father, but, following his grandfather's most important principle, had kept his intentions secret. He could rationalize his action. He was forty years old. He did the work of president, made the hard decisions, oversaw the day-to-day operations, no longer respected his father's business habits and decisions. He felt entitled to pursue his ambitious plans for the company, and the majority of the board supported him, doubtless believing that under his stewardship the company could become the largest hardwood supplier in the world.

Helen, who believed in the reality underlying great stories, might well have seen in her brother's rage at thus unceremoniously being usurped, some resemblance to King Lear's titanic pain, might have recalled how George Eliot in *The Mill on the Floss* related the theme of the aged male's need to retain supremacy not to kings but to every man. "Successful fathers do not wish to be usurped by their ambitious sons," Eliot wrote. "I don't MEAN Tom to be a miller and farmer. I see no fun i' that; why, if I made him a miller an' farmer, he'd be expectin' to take to the mill an' the land, an' a-hinting at me as it was time for me to lay by an' thik o' my latter end. . . . Pretty well if he gets it when I'm dead an' gone."

Gordon's thundering rage at being usurped, dumped, outsmarted by a son who owed him life and fortune was felt throughout the lake. The air filled with the wild human emotions that eclipsed the loon call and darkened the moonlight. The whole atmosphere silently, oppressively howled. If man responds to nature's mood, nature also responds to man's when the emotions are powerful enough. Gordon rejected his election as chairman and quit the board. His daughter Cate, to whom her father was closest, who had so often received his succor and support, became her brother's most implacable enemy. Gordon's wife, Mary Roddis, resigned her position as secretary and cut her sons off. "I have no sons." "Mary is loyal," Helen said, her only remark about the whole affair.

Another era ended for the Connor clan in Forest County. The company was in the hands of another generation, but actions are like accidents: we cannot anticipate the results nor predict the ramifications. The shareholders were a small group of hostile, divided family members. The seeds of the company's dissolution had been sown. It took a few years before they would be harvested.

Gordon R. sought relief, as his father would have, in revenge. Rumors circulated that he called the IRS to inform the service that Richard's daughter Jean had underestimated the value of the stock she inherited at the time of her father's death, that he received an award for turning informant, and Jean was hit with a heavy assessment and fines, that he defended his action, saying he had not acted for the financial reward, "only" for revenge.[19] He also rewrote his will, leaving his sons a dollar and naming his daughter Cate trustee over their children's inheritance.

The shocks were not over. Helen celebrated her ninetieth birthday quietly with Bom, John, David, Helen L., and Vanessa in Marshfield and returned to the lake afterwards for a brief final look at summer. The days already seemed fall-like; the ducks, congregating on the dock, were almost grown. She was in Marshfield on Labor Day when Cate knocked on the door of the Laird cabin bearing the news that the private airplane in which her brother David Noel Connor had taken off near Laona had not been able to reach its elevation, had struck trees, and crashed. David Noel had been killed.

His parents, who, in their wounded pride, had declared they had no sons, found themselves mercilessly bereft of their sweet boy. "The Connors are jinxed," Helen told Augusta. Bom was celebrating his birthday when he heard the news. "He will come for funeral and stay here until Sunday anyway or Monday." Bom, David, and Helen L. attended the services in Wausau, heard Gordon Phelps's eulogy for his brother, his promise to care for his brother's two fatherless toddlers as if they were his own. The church was full of shocked and grieving friends and relatives. Bom drove back to Marshfield, had dinner with Helen, who could not face the funeral crowds, and stayed for the opening of the Central Wisconsin Fair, where he heard Loretta Lynn sing, before flying back to Washington on September 4. David and Helen L. returned to Laona, where they joined in a family circle with Diane, David's young wife, who stood, heavily sedated, with her two uncomprehending youngsters beside her in the living room of the magnificent home David Noel had built on the beautiful shores of Birch Lake. The Reverend Robert Roth conducted services for the family before Diane went out in the boat and spread her husband's ashes on the water.

On September 14, David, Helen L., and Vanessa stopped en route to Chicago. David had won received the National Endowment for the Humanities Institute Fellowship and would be spending the academic year at the University of Chicago. "Pleasant time together," Helen wrote after the chicken dinner at the Casa Loma. She was pleased that they were not driving 2,000 miles away. Dr. Oates was a guest at the church's 100th anniversary celebration on September 17. Helen and Fanny were now the oldest communicants, but Helen did not attend the celebration. Reverend Oates called before he left town. Helen thought it was "good to see him" but good afterwards to have "house to myself," to sit on the porch, to slowly walk over to Katie's house the next day and sit out with her for awhile.

So the good days passed, sitting out. She paid bills, read a cheerful note from Helen L., who said Vanessa was adjusting well to University School in Chicago. (She would spend the first semester there and return to California for the second in order to graduate with her class at Polytechnic School.) They liked their spacious apartment, and when David picked her up in October and drove her to Chicago for a visit, she also felt comfortable there. She liked the high ceilings, the moldings, the solid appearance of the turn-of-the-century brick building, with its location within what had become known as "the Golden Circle," so close to the university and Rockefeller Chapel. She was aware, however, that people walked quickly home in the middle of the street when it turned dark.

David pointed out the familiar buildings and told her about his colleagues, the group of diverse scholars from large and small institutions gathered to find common threads, if indeed there were any, between the ascending technological society and the declining humanistic tradition. The situation, he said, was not so unlike the one he had experienced when, as an undergraduate, he sat silently in the back of the seminar room in the social science building while distinguished professors from the different disciplines, several of whom had fled Hitler's Germany, discussed a common text.[20] The seminar in which he now participated met in the room next door to that room. It had been a long, hard journey to get back to that invigorating atmosphere—for Helen as well.

A reluctant plane traveler, Helen, unaccompanied, boarded Roy Shwery's twelve-passenger plane for the trip home. Even with the stop down at Wisconsin Rapids, the trip went "wonderfully well. Nice pilot." For a moment she felt younger.

Back home, she shared her adventure with Fanny. She voted at the library, marking her ballot, as the majority of Wisconsinites did, for Lee Dreyfus for governor. She did not have much time to "miss the nice family I left in Chicago" before Bom and Carl Wallace arrived. They had dinner at the Knight's Inn. She had coffee ready the next morning, thinking the men might come because it was too windy to play golf, but they didn't.

After several years of not feeling up to attending the Laird Youth Leadership Foundation meeting, she drove to Stevens Point with Augusta and Russ Lewis. She recorded that the "meeting went well." She continued to reach out, called Gretchen Felker, enjoyed Emily Mead Baldwin's visit, and asked Irma Jablonic to shop, cook a turkey, and bake a pie, although she knew

David, Helen L., and Vanessa had made arrangements for Thanksgiving dinner at the Inn. They would eat out, but it would be good to have food on hand, cold turkey to pick on. A woman planned, even an old one, if she still had her wits and an occasional surge of strength and renewal of interests.

Eager though he had been to distance himself from Cal State, David understood its evolved mission and wrote a letter to the editor of the *Chicago Tribune* sending a copy to Helen, challenging Roger Rapoport's condemnation of the university as an institution that "exploits and abuses its students."[21] Rapoport had to know that Cal State had not played intercollegiate football for two years and could not thus be accused of exploiting student athletes for financial gain and then throwing them overboard, ill prepared to meet the real world. Cal State's decision to withdraw from conference competition was based, at least in part, on a recognition of the problems Rapoport chose to discuss in detail "without, of course, acknowledging the remedial action taken by the university." Not only had Cal State withdrawn from conference competitions, but the university had taken steps to help students develop basic reading and writing skills at the outset of their academic careers "in the face of considerable opposition, apathy, and declining budgets." Following the passage of Proposition 13, the literacy program was under great pressure. "To ignore it altogether while deploring the consequences of a fading literacy among students at the university is ironic."[22]

Helen concluded her Calendar with a jaunty "Finis 1978" and the deeper thought: "A spark within us that will not out until we have reached our best."

Marshfield escaped the full brunt of the "great Chicago snowstorm" in January 1979, but the sidewalks were dusted with powder with treacherous patches of ice beneath, and Helen walked gingerly. Bom descended again to lift her out of winter. They flew to Fort Lauderdale in a Phillips Petroleum plane. They were golden days for Helen, who responded to the sunshine, the flowers, the sight of numerous boats of many kinds passing by her window on the Inland Water way. Murdock Head sent his secretary, Carole Fleishman, to be a companion when Bom had to make a quick flight to New York. Helen felt uneasy only once during her two-week stay, experiencing a "strange Sunday." Perhaps the pleasure-seeking atmosphere had begun to pull against her Calvinist training. "Should have found a church," she wrote.

February was half over when Bom brought her safely home. They "didn't get near Chicago coming back but flew in a company plane (2 pilots) direct from Fort Lauderdale to Mosinee in 2½ hrs. even against the wind and very comfortably." Bom got in "some good golf and likes that course in Ft. Lauderdale. . . .

Always had some time each day with Bam and evening dinner. I laughed when he said I was always trying to teach him something. I felt that farthest from my thoughts. He was most kind, thoughtful and attentive, even with many other people and things on his mind (I was really overwhelmed by the magnitude of that company)."[23]

The number of days when she felt "tired and no good" increased. Her handwriting, which had been fairly steady, flowed wildly again over the pages of her Calendar. David arrived. "Glad he came. Here Sunday and Monday." The capsules eased her pain but did not agree with her. Helen L. came. Her handwriting straightened with the coming of spring. She caught the statement read over the local radio station when Bom's portrait went up in the Department of Defense: "War colleges personnel agreed he did more to invigorate our nation than anyone since George Washington." He reformed the nation "without visibility and without much credit" in the face of a "ruthless and effective media." The chestnut tree, the lilacs and the fruit trees began budding out. Helen had other complaints, many, but never of allergies, even in the sprouting time.

She and Fanny remained faithful to Lloyd McKool's religious study classes. He no longer gave the classes in Marshfield after the new minister took over but continued to lead a small group of loyal students at his home in Arpin. Helen wrote a poem of appreciation when the meetings terminated for the summer.

> Tell me not in mournful numbers
> Life is but an empty dream
> When on every Wednesday morning
> Things become not what they seem
> There around that oaken table
> Gather friend and foe alike
> To partake of earnest learning
> From Calvin, Luther, but not Pike.
> Through the chills of snowy winter
> To the chills of another spring
> So we gather ever weekly
> With a heart for any fate
> Insured by the Lloyds of Arpin
> To reach the pearly gate
> And now we send a real petition
> To the session large or small
> That this class will be continued
> Just the same—in the fall.

"The history of man from 1750 to 1950 will be seen by historians in the 21st century to have been all of a piece," an un-Christian, secularist structure whose foundations are "pride, ambition, desire to dominate, lust for the world's goods."[24] That was the contemporary drift according to a writer in the *Atlantic* in 1942. The current had not changed its course, but not everyone bobbed along in it. Always in every age there are those who seek and find a different channel. Lloyd McKool, who found it difficult as an older man to locate a pastorate in the Presbyterian church, and his wife, Ann, who offered succor to the people she encountered at the laboring job she took to help pay the bills, numbered among them. In their quiet service they were among those Helen perceived to be the "best people," the "real leaders."

"Wonder if David will go to graduation," Helen wrote in her Calendar as his term in Chicago and Vanessa's in Pasadena ended. Feeling, not perhaps correctly, that he was needed more in Marshfield, he went north to keep his mother company, while Helen L. flew to California.

At Birch Lake in the summer of 1979, Helen observed the socially prominent weekend guests from Minneapolis, Chicago, and Wisconsin, lawyers and businessmen, visiting in the palatial homes of Gordon's children, the obligatory whites on the tennis court, the dressing up for the cocktail hour—all so different from the plain style of her day. The letter Gordon Phelps wrote his cousin David, explaining the high charges for the garden, tennis court, and firewood, suggests the new times. He suggested that he consider Birch Lake as "a kind of country club."[25]

One evening as Helen, David, and Helen L. sat together on the well-worn couch by the blazing fire, when they had had enough of reading aloud from Willa Cather's *The Lost Lady*, Helen L. told Helen a story. She had shared it with her elderly parents and a very few others and felt that as their sympathetic bond had grown strong, and since Helen, at ninety-one, could not have long to live, the time to share it with her had come.

I woke on the morning of June 2, 1976, feeling very calm and content. Usually, my inner voice has a direction, a worry, a slight edge of anxiety, something to accomplish, something more or less pressing. This morning was unusual, everything seemed remarkably easy. I drove to the Huntington Library where I had been working on a translation of George Sand's *Histoire de Ma Vie*.

I don't remember what drew me to the Sand autobiography. But in the summer of 1973, I requested the book from the Laona library. Laona wouldn't have it I knew, but Wisconsin's remarkable library system meant it would be searched for throughout the state until it was located. Much to my surprise, the *Histoire* arrived from the University of Wisconsin, Madison, in the original ten volume leather bound edition of 1854. Apparently not too many people had asked for it. I read the volumes with increasing wonder. I felt so close to Sand. I had always loved the French language, was a great admirer of Flaubert, Hugo, Stendhal, the great nineteenth-century male writers. But here was a woman writing a prose that entered my heart. She expressed so many of my feelings in a voice that moved me like music.

I thought if her autobiography meant so much to me, it would have to mean something to other women and I decided to translate an abbreviated version containing the parts that I had found most compelling. I had spent many months on the project, had read Sand's early novels, written a paper (the one I delivered to the Philological Association), because I felt such an affinity with Sand and her time, her friends, those many others in America, England, Russia, and France who admired her, who shared her Zeitgeist: Doestoevsky, Emerson, Elizabeth Barrett Browning, George Eliot, Mazzini. I had gone pretty well along in my translation when I awoke that morning feeling so completely at home in myself and drove to the Huntington Library to work at my desk in the main reading room.

Instead of writing anything new, I read over the pages I had written. My concentration was complete and I was utterly absorbed, completely given over to the world in the words. At 11:30, I had to leave my desk to drive my cleaning lady home. When I was little more than a block away from the house, having had my mind full of what I should say to Amanda Vaill, an editor to whom I had sent some pages and from whom I had not heard in several months, my ears suddenly blocked. I only had time to say to myself: "What's happening? What's going on? Am I going deaf?" when a loud, off-key sound filled my head. EHEHEHEHEHEHEHEHEHEHEHEHEHEHEHEHEHEHEHEHEHEHEHEHEHEH, and then I exploded. The sound stopped, my ears unblocked, my eyes shot to the sky where I saw George Sand floating overhead. I felt myself to be in a realm of dazzling, overwhelming power where time was backwards and forwards and one. A different dimension entirely. When I pulled to the curb, I could hardly walk out of the car. I went in the house and blurted out the experience to Vanessa, home from school as it was exam time, and the cleaning lady. Vanessa cried, "You look spacey!" and ran outside slamming the door behind her. Mrs. Diaz softly said: "You've been working too hard."

I was not surprised at Vanessa's reaction; the experience was too strong for a fifteen-year-old, but Mrs. Diaz's reaction amused me, because she was a good church-going Catholic. Mrs. Diaz did not perceive, however, what I felt had happened. A miracle. I said to myself in wonderment over and over again as I drove Mrs. Diaz the few blocks to her home: "I have been shown that the soul exists." I had experienced the truth behind the words: "the power and the glory forever and ever."

Helen sat quietly reflecting a long moment on Helen L.'s story before she quietly asked "Didn't that happen because you released your ego?"

Years and years before, in giving a speech, "Fruits of the Spirit," to the Woman's Club, Helen had said. "It is that little piece of self-will we keep even though we think it is so secret and hidden that God himself will not notice it which prevents us from receiving the infinite and complete benefits and grace of guidance." She had been a student of nineteenth-century transcendentalism, had struggled to reconcile her great religious inheritance and inclination with her strong ego needs, had sought to negotiate between the voices of memory and passion and the voice of reason. She wanted to lead but also believed she should relinquish ambition.

Interested in psychology and religion, she had read William James's *The Varieties of Religious Experience;* had talked with her husband about the Harvard professor's attempts to meld the fields of philosophy, religious experience, medicine and psychology; had attempted to work old understandings into the scheme of the new scientific age of which they were both a part. She would not have been aware of the letter William James wrote to a correspondent on psychic matters, in which, while admitting to being "permanently incapable of believing the Christian scheme of vicarious salvation," he said he nonetheless believed that "the mother sea and fountain-head of all religions lie in the mystical experiences of the individual, taking the word mystical in a very wide sense" and that "all theologies and all ecclesiasticisms [were] secondary growths superimposed." He said he attached "the mystical or religious consciousness to the possession of an extended possession of the subliminal self, with a thin partition through which messages make irruption. We are thus made convincingly aware of the presence of a sphere of life larger and more powerful than our usual consciousness."[26]

Swedenborg's notion of "spiritual energy" and Emerson's notion of the "over soul" were part of the zeitgeist of Helen's youth. In 1898, when she was ten, James delivered the Ingersoll Address at Harvard in which he used Swedenborg's term and Emerson's notion, appropriated from Hindu religion and philosophy. Helen was prepared to hear Helen L.'s story because she had studied Emerson and read James. It was not unfamiliar, but it was part of an older history which held that ever since human beings developed an urge to comprehend themselves and their position in the universe, since they had developed the language with which to recount their experiences, since they had formulated religious systems to interpret themselves, their thoughts seemed not to be bound by linear time but to emanate from a common stream flowing continuously backward and forward. What came to Helen L.'s mind in the last quarter of the twentieth century had also existed in William James's mind, in Swedenborg's, in Blake's, in so many other minds down through the centuries. The working of the human mind repeatedly suggested something that might still have to go under the unscientific designation—miraculous. You could not force a proof, but testimony proclaimed it. All this, although she did not articulate it, seemed to be part of that something Helen had wrangled with all her thinking life: her emotional self that said she was spirit and would not die, her reasoning self requiring evidence.

As she walked off to bed, Helen turned to Helen L. and said: "My mother came to me in a dream. She told me to hold my tongue." Their eyes met in silent communion. Helen's dream had been real, her mother present as her guide come to tell her to still her famous Connor tongue, the wit that outwitted others. Her long life's war at the near end was giving over to the power and the promise of a dream.

There were no answers. There were the heart's hopes and joys—and mysteries. Wasn't that what Melvin Sr. had said so long ago when his young wife was fired by a belief in reason and progress and looked for answers and when he told her that the world's greatest need was not a lesson but a miracle, the miracle of grace that, while so many were at work eliminating the mysterious out of life, life was full of mystery.

She became "too blind to see the electric bill," too blind to write much in her Calendar in September when David, Helen L., and Vanessa came for a final visit before heading west. Constie offered to spend the winter with her. "Please don't say no immediately, but think it over. You really can't live alone any longer, and I know you want to stay in your own home."[27]

Constie's letter required an answer, but Helen could "not make a definite one so early," or think of Constie staying "for so long ever." Fall was coming fast. She would "be okay. Will get back on my rather stupid old age special program which should attract no one."[28] She observed that the men delivered a supply of wood from Laona to her house just as a wedding began in the church across the street represented "conflicting interests." She was "trying to learn more of Tunis, capital of Tunisia. Seems far away." David had called to say that the Fulbright Commission had asked him to teach American Studies at the University of Tunis during the 1979–80 academic year. The professor who had been the commission's first choice to receive the award, after a few weeks on the scene, would be returning to the States because his young son could not adjust.

On the day of his scheduled departure for Tunisia, David suddenly announced that he could not go. The crisis passed. Years later he acknowledged that it occurred because he feared his mother might die in his absence. The lines etched on Helen's face as it folded into a tragic mask of grief when David and Helen L. said goodbye showed that she also feared their goodbyes might be final.

Helen did not die, as David feared she would, while he was in Tunisia. She limped along, older and blinder, and declined yet again Jessica Doyle's offer to come for a visit: "Difficult, but had to phone Jessica for I did not feel equal to visitors." She did gratefully accept an occasional visit from William and an occasional meal out with him as well as with Fanny and faithful Augusta. Bom came often, reading current events to her from the papers, reading out loud the long letters David and Helen L. sent from Tunisia.

They reported the friendliness of the people, the bureaucracy, the enormous gaps in income, Hachette's monopoly on books, the students' reluctance to memorize anything (having been forced as youngsters to memorize the Koran), the armed guards surrounding the university and positioned in the halls, the coffee houses full of unemployed male university graduates, the crowded, safe streets, and the 10:00 P.M. curfew. They wrote about their move from the noise of Tunis to the quiet of Sidi Bou Said where they lived in a house on a hill across from a Mosque and could hear the daily call to prayer and see Ambassador Steven Bosworth's residence located on the Mediterranean coast below. They wrote about the arranged marriages, the increasing number of women dressed in the traditional chodore (a long, white sheet-like garment covering head and body), the chic well-traveled and educated women wearing the latest Parisian and Italian styles, and the brisk young women in blue jeans, who in spite of their modern look would not feel comfortable entering restaurants or coffee bars alone or with other women. They wrote that the controlled Tunisian press deplored, as contrary to both Muslim and international law, Khomeini's taking of American hostages, and they told of observing Arab leaders driving past Place Pasteur near the American embassy, King Hussein of Jordan waving and smiling at the people while those in his entourage sat back in their seats and didn't look too interested.

They did not write that rumors of revolution were rife, that embassy personnel had received "evacuation plans," that an uprising, quickly squelched, occurred in Gafsa. Their life in Tunis, Helen L. wrote, was "a little like having a fever; one runs hot and cold." For ballast, they attended a little Anglican church in the Souks. Thomas Howard Payne, who wrote "There's No Place Like Home," was buried in the yard. They looked forward to Vanessa's being with them over her winter break from Williams College.

∼

# CHAPTER 24

# *Home*

## *1980–1982*

Home is a metaphor infinitely capacious; in Ecclesiastes it stands for death ("a man goeth to his long home") and in Thucydides for everlasting fame after death ("a home in the minds of men").

—BRENDAN GILL

"Not so good at writing letters anymore," Helen nonetheless wrote to "Dear David and Helen and now Vanessa too" on January 8. "Christmas and even New Years seems a long time gone. Thought of you often, but it was unusually quiet for me. Some of the 'rels' were at Birch Lake. Gordon and Mary came back from California, Phelps and family from Minnesota! etc. etc., but I didn't see them, nor did I see any of Bam's and Barbara's family." Just after New Years, Bom came with Dr. Head and "valiantly decided he wanted to make a project of getting someone to be here at the house at all times, so I would not be alone so much." It was below zero and she hadn't ventured out. "So glad you have been meeting *nice* people."

"Our mother," Bom wrote on the 9th, was "getting on well enough, but needed permanent full time help." He had established a special account at the bank for Judy Schmidt, the registered nurse he hired to oversee the household, and arranged for Varnetta Parmeter and Irma Jablonic to alternate three- and four-day shifts to live in and take care of her.

In spite of Bom's valiant efforts, Helen suffered a heart attack. She was hospitalized for five days and transferred to the Seventh Day Adventist Convalescence Center to recuperate for several more before returning home. "Bom helped me move," Bom wrote in her Calendar on January 25. "Great helper!" Helen scribbled afterwards. Dean Emanuel removed stitches from a "poor insert" of a pacemaker. Bom telephoned David and reassured him that the situation was under control.

407

From Rome, where David and Helen L. had gone with Vanessa on her return to the States, David wrote of never failing "to enter a cold church or gallery without remembering your feeling about them." From Tunisia, he telephoned almost every day and sent postcards every three or four days. He wrote of going to a reception for Donald McHenry, the U.S. ambassador to the UN at Ambassador Bosworth's home, of the pleasure it had given them to know that she had been out on the town with Bom. After their telephone went dead, he phoned home every few days from a hotel. He did not suspect that workmen on the roof might be signaling their disapproval of foreigners by cutting the wires (a young Turkish woman, an employee of Citibank, rented the upstairs apartment)—and of their landlords, members of the business and political elite, but after finding the wires cut and splicing them, he had to consider the possibility.

Helen scrawled a penciled note to David and Helen L. on March 2 "to celebrate your having phoned yesterday, and it is a celebration for I can even write more intelligently. (Must be just hearing your voices.) From the bright sunshine up-stairs here you would think it May though outside it is likely zero or below. Anyway, spring is trying to come even here. You have all done well to carry on. Love and blessings."

In another of the brief notes in her sprawling, uneven hand, she wrote that the papers were full of the presidential primary. "Nothing decisive as yet." She was "still hovering around the grate-fire" in the middle of March, although she had walked up and down outside for the first time in nearly three weeks. She was glad Vanessa was back in college; she said that she didn't think she would like their part of the country, "although your people sound nice. You are good adjusters and better than I. Old house is comfortable. Writing not conducive to more."[1] She passed time sorting through the correspondence in her drawers. "Many from years back to occupy attention now that I've leisure."

Mrs. Jablonic and Mrs. Parmeter became comfortable in their routines. Helen had someone to talk to when she wanted to talk, to do errands and read the news and letters to her, to take her driving when the weather permitted, to see that she ate nourishing meals.

David wrote of reading about Ford's withdrawal from the primaries, "Withdrawal is, I guess, not the word since he had not been an announced candidate. People here were sorry to see Reagan win in Illinois, and I hope it doesn't put an end to Anderson's chances. Wisconsin primary will be a big one this year and you must let us know how it looks from 208."[2] If he were teaching in the Schools of Engineering or Law, they would have been back a while ago. The government had closed those faculties because of dissident students.

Letters and Science was open, but there were policemen with guns in the entrance seeing that things were kept in order.

With the longer, warmer days, with the hope that she would see her wandering son again—and an effective pacemaker doing its job—Helen's health and spirits improved. Eager to show Bom that she had not entirely given up on life, she sent him a note inquiring if he knew Dr. Marshall D. Shulman. "He is over at the State Department as a special advisor on Soviet Affairs. I do know him and do not have much confidence in him."[3] Having shown herself alert to the present, she drifted into the past: "March 24, Father's birthday."

On Easter Sunday, April 6, Helen L. wrote of having enjoyed a dinner with Ambassador and Mrs. Bosworth and the ambassador's brother and sister-in-law who were visiting from the states. Barry Bosworth, an economist, "was certainly a painter of gloomy scenes." David was never "sure from week to week whether classes will meet, whether there will be a strike, whether exams will be given. The government has again closed the law faculty and said that there would be no exams. If David were teaching in that faculty we could begin to pack now. In Monastir the dental students are on strike. They claim they have no equipment and terrible teachers and that they cannot serve the people who come into the clinics."

A faculty member asked them for dinner. His French wife, "of whom the Tunisian is very proud," served "an excellent French meal. . . . His children go to the French Lycée." Another Tunisian couple was present, a young banker and his wife. They thought that their hosts were making a mistake in sending their children to the French school. They were going to send their child to Arab schools as Arabic was the language and the wave of the future and they wanted their child to be "on the right side of the changes."

When the Chicago fellows held a reunion in May, David combined a short trip to Chicago with a visit to Marshfield. He spent two days before driving to Minneapolis to have dinner with Bom and John and flying back to London.

"The family has moved about so fast lately," Helen wrote Helen L., "I can hardly keep track, but guess you and David were in London yesterday and today is Monday May 12 by my reckoning." She had had dinner with Bom the Saturday before Mother's Day. "He was off to New York today. Thought he looked well and hope same holds for you. Good idea getting to Denmark in interim, but we missed you here. Do hope things wind up in good shape and that plans work out fine. You have both adjusted so well. I send love and appreciation of David's visit once again. . . . Slow down a bit now please!"

There was no chance then for Helen L. or David to slow down. They settled into the task of grading hundreds of papers, packing, selling their car, saying farewell to friends. After another brief stopover in London, they flew into Chicago, rested overnight, and hurried on to Marshfield for a few days. Their departure for California was "too sudden" for Helen, who felt "left suddenly alone with the elements," although she knew they had to check their house, which they had rented to a couple of foreign students who had given up paying their rent many months ago, and that Helen L.'s parents were eager to see them. She had enjoyed "all of [their] visit—except end."

She made a few entries in her almost empty Calendar: nose bleeds, William's drive to Mosinee to meet Angie's plane, David and Helen L.'s return. She seemed to know the "beautiful Fourth of July fireworks" in Laona were her last. She returned to Mrs. Parmeter's care three days later, sent off her "many thanks for all helps and kindness which I appreciate mightily." Their cabin looked "so frisky and interesting" with the Tunisian accessories, and they "all looked well and making it okay and I congratulate you upon all your travels."

William and Angie asked Helen out, but it was "too hot for me." She observed that Bom wasn't at the Republican convention but in Pleasantville with *Readers Digest* people. She did not comment on Bom's trip to Hawaii or on the clipping Angie sent from the *Honolulu Sunday Star-Bulletin* with his photo and his bleak assessment of America's defense posture. The "ill prepared, ill equipped, under-manned U.S. military make it difficult for the United States to deter war, to exercise leadership and to compete successfully."[4] He proposed the country increase defense outlays by $30 billion.

She did not know that he had prepared a technical analysis, "The Problem of Military Readiness," for the American Enterprise Institute for Public Policy and that the Marshfield Free Library had a copy. She may or may not have realized that his authoritative voice charging that "our intercontinental ballistic missiles are becoming vulnerable, our submarine launched ballistic (SLBM) production is lagging, our bombers are aging and our strategic balance with the Soviets is being upset" undoubtedly contributed to the Republican decision to build up the national defense.

She existed within the frame of her personal history. The dark, rainy days in September, which made her think that much as she'd like to have David and Helen L. nearby in Laona, she couldn't wish them there, persisted into October, but "the leaves go on coloring just the same and some are quite beautiful even around here. Bam and Dr. Head were in town for most of two days and took me driving almost to Neillsville to see colors they had seen from plane, but we found some just as pretty nearer home—some red maples."[5]

David combined a conference in Minneapolis with a visit. It helped her to talk with him. "Am getting *too* old that's the real trouble," she wrote David and Helen L. as the days grew shorter. "I will go at last more slowly I fear. . . . Miss sun on porch as well as you both." In a P.S. she added that she had "just read in paper that Bam will come to Stevens Point meeting of youth Leadership, Wed. next with D.C. group and maybe speak, but I doubt if I go, a long day." She didn't. She walked a short while instead and visited with Bom at the house. Days passed, one like another, slowly. Dean Emanuel stopped in. Mrs. Jablonic wrote "Happy Thanksgiving Day," reminding Helen of that special day, which passed like the others. On November 29 she walked to Katie's; she was glad to be out, but fell getting home when she reached for a fence, which tumbled over taking her with it.

The hairdresser came to the house to give her a permanent, Judy Schmidt to take her blood pressure. "Bam," she noted, was in Florida on December 7, playing golf en route to a Phillips Petroleum board meeting in Oklahoma. She accepted Augusta's invitation to Sunday dinner and was pleased to see Gordon and Mary there. David flew in again before Christmas, Bom afterwards, and briefly mother and both sons were together. On New Year's Day she phoned them both. She wrote David that she thought of the numerous gifts, "but most remarkable of all was for both sons to come even briefly."

In her scrawling hand, Helen wrote checks, gifts to the Marshfield Medical Foundation, the Marshfield Convalescent Center "for the purpose of making the residents' lives more enjoyable," and to the North Wood County Historical Society, which had acquired William Henry Upham's home. Historical Society president, former *Marshfield News Herald* editor Ed Heller, wrote to thank her: "As time goes on the public service of your father and of Senator Laird and your own substantial contributions on the local Board of Education and as a University regent will be more and more appreciated in Marshfield. And Melvin Jr., of course, is destined to be remembered as one of the great leaders Wisconsin has produced. . . . Your sons have a heritage such as few can claim."[6]

Fatigue, increasing blindness, deafness, confusion, the pains of arthritis, the worn-out heart regulated by drugs and a pacemaker—these were the great handicaps of old age. Judy Schmidt ordered rails put on Helen's bed to prevent falls; Mrs. Jablonic and Mrs. Parmeter coped. Irma Jablonic, a woman in her late sixties, "learned a lot" from Helen, a "steady, calm, wise" woman who "goes from point A to B immediately for a solution," who was "logical, no make believe, nothing phony."[7]

Helen was, she claimed in letters to David and Helen L., "no letter writer but can enjoy them at times." She still acted as clearinghouse, passing on family news. David's visit at the end of February prompted her letter of March 3 to Helen L. "David's visit was a life saver of which I was *most appreciative* and know you must have encouraged it and helped see him off. Am glad you saw your mother, too. Our nice days went with him—the sun has rarely appeared since—that I can understand."

On April 1 she wrote again, including a clipping from the March 27 *News Herald* announcing the death Dr. Paul F. Doege, son of Marshfield Clinic co-founder Karl W. Doege, in Tucson, Arizona, where he and Erville had been living since his retirement in 1968. "Such terrible pens and pencils I never before witnessed, but will scratch forward. I do not enjoy writing anymore anyway. Bam was here yesterday and looked well." Notified of his friend De Witt Wallace's death, he "packed and left by plane this A.M. early to go back east to New York. Said that his wife, Mrs. Wallace, is now alone with many employees only. They were both only 80 years of age but the Co. will continue to be run well I am sure." She was also "sure Bam felt I was fast continuing to be and become a *disagreeable* person for numerous reasons and he senses no reason."

For the first time since 1900, Helen did not return to Birch Lake in the summer of 1981. As the days grew shorter with the coming of fall, she began to insist on going "Home." Carefully dressed with Mrs. Jablonic's or Mrs. Parmeter's help, Selby shoes, navy-blue dress and coat, gloves and purse resting in her lap and hat on her head and cane beside her, she sat erect, as she had been taught to do almost a century before, on a chair in front of the French doors in the living room facing Cherry Street. Staring at the place where once her father's house had stood, and the Faith Lutheran Church still stands, she sat waiting and repeating the single word "Home." David asked what she meant, but she could not answer. Grown to gentleness, she only asked over and over to go "Home." How much she had seen of pride and passion, war and peace; how much she had sought to shape the future, to lead, only to find herself, in the end, a humble pilgrim bent on going "Home."

Her life began in Wood County when the lights at night were starlight and candles, and it ended there in the same mystery in spite of electric wires. She had been a little girl in the deep woods when wolves and still-wilder animals threatened and were subdued. She experienced the ravages of the wild beasts of war and hoped the wilderness in man might be subdued through intelligence and dedicated enterprise. She witnessed that hope buckle before man's relentless ambition and the enormous, perplexing complexity of everything.

She had thought death was coming for many years but did not think of death now, only of going "Home."

The old battles were behind. She had accomplished her life's tasks, the ones set early by her ample inheritance from the Victorian world now seemingly so largely extinguished but whose embers certainly glowed ready to ignite when the time came to serve: to be one's best, to lead, to raise one's self, children, and community. Right hand–left hand, Ying-Yang, sun-moon, light-dark, winter thoughts—spring hopes, her brilliant mind and her passionate heart, anxious and divided through so much of her life, had grown together in her great old age when, accepting her human limits, she came to terms with her condition at the long, long last and asked again and again and again to go "Home."

The care she needed finally exceeded the women's ability to provide it. They were powerless to take her "Home," and they let Bom know she needed more help than they could give. He saw her installed in a room of her own at the convalescent center, where Judy Schmidt continued to look after her. He bought a sky-blue rug, her favorite color, to cover the cold linoleum floor and chose the furniture and the pictures from 208 he thought should be in the room. Mary Miksha came to see her; Gordon and Mary came; her granddaughter Jessica and her husband, Jim Doyle, came with their son, Gus, her first great-grandchild, an African American adopted at birth. Gus gave her a picture he had painted and chatted with her as he carefully pushed her in her wheelchair down the long corridor. Bom came. David and Helen L. came, stopping off in Marshfield in January 1982 en route to Washington, D.C., where David had a grant to join Inge-Stina Ewbank's Jacobean seminar at the Folger Library.

The snow lay high on the ground, covering all but the bare brown tips of the shrubs surrounding the convalescent center. Inside it was very warm, a requirement for the old and frail, whose blood runs cold. Helen was dressed, prepared for the visit, glad to see them. She paid no attention to the nurse walking by with her medication cart ready to distribute a multitude of different drugs prescribed by doctors for a variety of ailments. The cart symbolized a revolution, the passing of an era she had known when Merchant's Gargling Oil sufficed in different wrappers for all ailments: yellow for man, white for beast.

Wearing the elegant, expensive, broad-brimmed, velvet-trimmed brown felt hat David bought her, her heavy cloth coat and warm boots, Helen went out for a drive and a second breakfast with David and Helen L. She sat beside them at the counter at the busy Patio Cafe, one of her brother William's properties, and ordered toast, regretting only momentarily that it was not crisp like zwieback, which was the way she liked it but never got it anymore. She did not ask to drive by her house at 208 South Cherry. She had gone from there but was glad for the short ride around town, glad to be back afterwards in the surroundings and among the people she accepted, those on stretchers, those who made sense, those who didn't. "Does Adolph know where I am," a woman anxiously asked, while the old man near her ceaselessly scraped an invisible something off the floor. "He's crazy," Helen announced matter-of-factly.

Winter is not "winter" for the young. Great age brings the real frost, tearing down boundaries, breaking lines between time present, time past. The mind moves. Helen, suddenly anxiously, asked David and Helen L. as they walked toward the door preparing to leave: "Is Father home? Is he cold? Is he wet?" Her past was present. Love would not let it die. W.D., long gone, went out again from Auburndale in the dark night into the wolf-infested northwoods while his little girl worried at home.

She fell a week or so later. The neurosurgeon, who called Bom, told him she would not survive if he did not remove the clot that had formed in her brain. Bom agreed to the immediate operation. She did not awaken from the coma into which she slipped after surgery. She lingered for weeks, a white towel wrapped around her head, shaved of its thick tresses. The doctors finally removed the feeding tubes, and still she lingered. Mary Miksha came to see her and claimed the silent woman whose eyes were shut had communicated by pressing her hand when she asked if she were hungry and thirsty. The nurse told her she could give her nothing. But still she lingered. Perhaps Mary applied a damp cloth to her lips.

208 South Cherry, Marshfield, 1982.

Bom, David, and Helen L. flew in to see her in St. Joseph's Hospital during the long wait for her final passing. David spent ten days in Marshfield in April, anticipating the end, which would not come; he was there when, baffled by her long coma, the persistence of life in spite of the lack of nourishment, the doctors said she would have to be transferred to the convalescent center. David accompanied her in the ambulance and then returned to Washington. He and Helen L. had a late, subdued dinner at the Kennedy Center with Bom and Barbara.

That night, the night of April 23, 1982, in the little apartment David had rented from the Folger Library, Helen L. could not sleep. As the hours passed and she tossed and turned and could find no cause for her restlessness, she said to herself in words she never used: "Something is happening in the psychic sphere." Toward dawn, she finally dozed and dreamt that she was standing in line behind three tall men dressed in gray. They were standing motionless in the hospital corridor silently waiting, looking through a small window in the center of the door into Helen's room. A nurse was in the room gathering up sheets from the empty bed. A beautiful female toddler came out from under the bed striding confidently toward them.

The vivid dream ended with the ringing of the telephone. David answered. It was Bom calling to say their mother had died in the night.

She had grown up under a set of two laws: constancy and change, the soul's permanence and the world's transience. In the end, if dreams provide clues, she could claim the grace of release from her worn out body and the permanence of something we might as well call soul.

# *Postscript*

Four months after Helen's death, shareholders of Connor Forest Industries sold the company to a Swiss family investment group headed by Stephan Schmidheiny and Hans Peter Hoffmann. The mill and timber in Michigan's Upper Peninsula became their property. Because Wisconsin law prohibited the sale of more than a section to a foreign entity and carried a penalty of confiscation, Swiss ownership in Wisconsin was limited to the Laona mill and 640 acres. The shareholders of Connor Forest Industries formed a partnership, Wisconsin Timber Associates, Gordon Phelps Connor as general partner, to take title to Connor timberlands in Wisconsin except for those sections surrounding Birch Lake. Those 1,600 acres of old growth timber and property fronting the lake not already owned by family were divided among the Gordon and Richard Connor families. While communal use of lake property ended and family divisions persist, W.D.'s descendants preserve Birch Lake in something like the pristine state in which W.D. found it.

The Swiss stayed in Laona less than three years before shutting down. In 1995, Bridgewater Associates, a global investment company engaged by the Swiss, liquidated operations in the Midwest. By then, the Michigan timber had been clear-cut.

The logging museum that Gordon Robert and Mary Roddis Connor established on the site of the old company farm and Camp 5 in Laona, originally run the Connor Lumber and Land Company as a tourist attraction, is managed by their daughters, Mary Pierce, Catherine C. Dellin and Sara Connor, as an educational foundation. The old Laona and Northern runs in the summers from a depot just off Highway 8 taking tourists to the attraction. People come to see the old saws, the old engines, the old cook shanty and to learn about tree harvesting, selective cutting, the wild plants that grow in the sandy soil, and the wild birds and animals that inhabit the area. But Laona itself? Russell and Cate Collins's statement of April 11, 2000, is posted in the town hall: "The last thing my grandpa told me was Laona had everything: two doctors, a dentist, a lawyer, two barber shops (one uptown and one down town), at one time they had thirteen taverns, a full-time town cop, their own jail house. Today their ain't nothing here." Kevin Koepke, the postman, maintains that even though not everyone has put a for-sale sign on his house in Laona, everything is for sale. Just knock on the door and ask. The Gordon Hotel and the hospital are gone.

There are, however, signs of economic activity. A reorganized Wisconsin Timber Associates, with Gordon Phelps Connor remaining as general partner, bought the mill and formed a new operating corporation, Nicolet Hardwoods. Gordon's son Peter has formed a company, W.D. Flooring, LLC. The Laona State Bank in which Richard Connor Jr. has an interest has expanded and has several branches in the area.

The Potawatomi and Mole Lake Sokaogan Chippewa (Ojibwe) have found their voice in northern Wisconsin and through the courts have won the significant hunting, fishing, and harvesting rights established by treaty in 1837 and 1842 when they ceded their lands to the United States. These days, with casinos and motels, they take credit for creating jobs and bringing tourists into the area. They're the ones who advertise the north as "a place surrounded by inherent beauty" with "ample out-door recreational opportunities." With their purchase from Nicolet Mining of the acreage containing the "Crandon Mine" in Forest County, the area's "ample out-door recreational opportunities" looked secure into the foreseeable future. Forest County Potawatomi vice chairman Al Milham has declared, however, that mining is not a dead issue. If modern technology shows there would be a safe way to mine, and forestry issues and rights are settled (Exxon and some members of the Connor family continue to hold rights) plans for the mine might proceed.

The immaculate farms, horse ranches, and large homes on the outskirts of Marshfield signal the prosperity of the "City in the Center." The Marshfield Medical Complex can be seen from miles around. A regional and national center for the study of bovine and farm-related diseases and an internationally recognized center for rural health, the complex supports not only a clinic with more than 700 physicians but also the Ben Lawton and the Melvin R. Laird Research Centers, where cutting-edge genetic research is conducted.

The Laird house at 208 South Cherry is listed on the Municipal, State, and

National Registers of Historic Places. David and Helen L. have lived there since David's retirement from Cal State and have established a Laird Foundation for Historic Preservation, deeding the house to the foundation. A Fine Arts Building at the University of Wisconsin, Marshfield/Wood County, bears Helen Connor Laird's name.

For many years Melvin R. Laird, who divides his time between his home in Florida and Washington, D.C., has supported activities in the theater, honoring his mother's interest in the arts. He returns periodically to Wisconsin for meetings of the Marshfield Clinic Foundation and the Laird Leadership Foundation at the University of Wisconsin-Stevens Point, which has benefited from the scholarships he has endowed and the programs he has initiated. He maintains his interest in national politics and as an "old timer" still works behind the scenes to point out when the party he loves neglects the lessons of history he recalls only too well.

# Notes

### 1. To Wisconsin

1. Joseph Wood was a pioneer and state legislator from the heavily wooded central Wisconsin region.

2. Jeremiah Witter to George Witter. Oct. 4, 1858, Helen Connor Laird Family Collection (hereafter cited as HCL).

3. Edwin Witter Jr., "A Witter Family History: The Ancestors of Dr. George Franklin Witter 1830–1910," 1988; "A Phelps Family History: The Ancestors of Francis Louisa Phelps (1835–1900) Wife of Dr. George Franklin Witter," 1992, typescript, HCL.

4. *Milwaukee Journal,* Jan. 6, 1896.

5. Oral history, John Berg, "The Wood County Railroad: A Chronology, 1883–1894. "Forest History Association of Wisconsin Nineteenth Annual Meeting," Marshfield, Wisc., Oct. 1, 1994.

6. November 28, 1893, HCL.

### 2. Getting Ahead

1. Unidentified Forest County newspaper clipping, HCL.

2. *Marshfield News,* Nov. 9, 1893.

3. Len Sargent, "Saw-Dust," typescript, Archives University of Wisconsin, Stevens Point, 46.

4. Sargent, "Saw Dust," 41.

5. *Marshfield News,* Aug. 24, 1893.

6. The mill ran eleven-hour night and day shifts, six days a week. Crews worked days one week, nights the next.

7. Sargent's son tells the story of how the black sheep of the extended Hughes family offered to deliver some white pine to W.D.'s mill for a ridiculously low price, no questions asked as to its origin. W.D. him took up on the offer and agreed to pay cash on delivery. The next summer a cruiser noted that most of the best white pine in a

tract owned by W.D. was missing. W.D. had been bilked, but "this time, he was a good sport and said nothing." Sargent also tells the story of how W.D. managed to block construction of a new county road that would have run through his lumber yard by sending his agent to bury the Carlsons, a recently deceased impoverished elderly couple, in the yard. Law prohibited building roads through cemeteries. Pete Kafka remembered the words of "The Connor Script Line," made up by the "hoboes" working in Stratford. The song provides another account of conditions:

We got agents in Liverpool, London, and Park,
sixteen in Boston and Twelve in New York,
eight in Chicago and six in Des Moines,
all chasing the hoboes for the Connor Script Line.

*Chorus:* TIMBER, TIMBER. GET OFF OF THAT CONNOR SCRIPT LINE.

Where the boys from Saint Paul for Stratford were bound,
to work for Bob Connor and sleep on the ground,
our coats and our satchels is all we can find,
to make up our bed on the Connor Script Line.

*Chorus*

We arrived at Marshfield one morning 'twas fine,
the agent said, "Boys, you're a little behind,"
the train left for Stratford exactly at nine,
with two hundred hoboes for the Connor Script Line.

Interview, Wally Ives, May 26, 2005, Marshfield, Wisc. Wally Ives made a Mercury label recording of the song in 1947.

8. *Forest Republican,* undated clipping.

9. *Forest Republican,* Nov. 22, 1912.

10. Interview, Charlie Barney's daughter and son-in-law, Alice and Bud Hansen, Laona, Wisc., July 1991.

11. Sargent, "Saw Dust," 94.

12. *Marshfield Times,* Sept. 27, 1895.

### 3. Marshfield

1. City Hall Papers, North Wood County Historical Society, Upham Mansion, Wisc (hereafter cited as NWCHS).

2. City Hall Papers, NWCHS.

3. City Hall Papers, NWCHS.

4. William G. Hinman, a Civil War veteran, railroad engineer, and lumberman, and perhaps also a physician, built the house.

5. Helen, school assignment, 1900, HCL.

6. Helen, December 1964, HCL.

7. Mmes. Connor, Upham, Lathrop, Pors, Elvis, Wahle, Deming, Finney, Williams, Pulling, Doege, Vollmar, Kraus, Cady, and Roddis; the wives of Marshfield's leading citizens, were members of the Ladies' Travel Class.

8. Selma Bartman, "A 70 Year Chronology of the Marshfield Woman's Club" (1967), pp. 7–8, typescript, NWCHS.

9. W.D. Connor to Fred Vollmar, HCL.

10. The library became known for its fine, permanent collection of several thousand volumes, extensive magazine collection (it subscribed to the *Century, Harper's, McClure's, Scribners, The Forum, The Outlook, Great Round World, St. Nicholas, Youth's Companion*), interlibrary loan of Norwegian and German books, twenty-two-volume set of the International Encyclopedia (donated by Mr. Connor), and its "most remarkable collection of children's books." Cornelia Marvin, "Wisconsin Free Library Commission," in *A History of the Marshfield Free Library*, ed. George O. Jones et al. (Winona, Minn.: H. C. Hooper Jr. and Co., 1923).

## 4. Laona

1. Robert Connor to Florence Glasner, Aug. 6, 1902, Angie Connor Collection, Honolulu, Hawaii.

2. *Forest Republican*, Nov. 12, 1902.

3. W.D. to Richard, May 21, 1941. Connor Lumber and Land Company Collection, Historical Society of Wisconsin Archives, Madison (hereafter cited as CL&L Co. Collection).

4. Interview, W.D. Connor Jr., July 1982, Laona, Wisc.

5. Sargent, "Saw Dust."

6. Interview, Marian Hansen, July 1982, Laona, Wisc.

## 5. A Meeting of Titans

1. The district included Wood, Portage, Waupaca, Outagamie, Brown, Kewaunee and Door Counties.

2. Stanley P. Caine, *The Myth of a Progressive Reform: RR Legislation in Wisconsin 1903–1910* (Madison: State Historical Society of Wisconsin, 1970), 96.

3. *Fond du Lac Bulletin*, Mar. 17, 1905.

4. *Milwaukee Free Press*, Mar. 17, 1905.

5. Albert Barton, *La Follette's Winning of Wisconsin 1894–1904* (Madison: A. O. Barton, 1922), 431.

6. Ibid., 331.

7. Sargent, "Saw Dust," 102.

8. Ralph Plumb, *Badger Politics 1836–1930* (Manitowoc: Brandt Printing and Binding Co., 1930), 139.

9. *St. Croix Observer*, L. B. Naegle to Hon. Samuel A. Cook, W.D. clipping scrapbook, Microfilm, State Historical Society Archives, Madison (hereafter cited as SHSW). The *Milwaukee Sentinel*, owned by Charles Pfister, published Stalwart propaganda

while the *Milwaukee Free Press,* owned by Isaac Stephenson, pushed the Half-Breed cause.

10. *Milwaukee News,* July 26, 1904.

11. Ibid., July 9, 1904.

12. The term "Half-Breed" implied the admission of newcomers into Republican ranks. To Connor's surprise, Teddy Roosevelt pulled the time-honored trick of the bureaucrat and passed him along to an elderly, reactionary senator from Connecticut, Charles Booker, a close friend of Stalwart senators Spooner and Quarles, the very delegates Connor hoped to unseat. After a day on the hill, Connor, trotting out his finest histrionic manner, insisted he was stymied. He didn't know what to do "unless it be to go on a spree, as they say, and try to forget it." Barton, *La Follette's Winning of Wisconsin,* 380. Those who knew Connor knew he never went on sprees, and he never forgot.

13. *Milwaukee News,* June 21, 1904.

14. Dispatch to the *Milwaukee Free Press,* Aug. 10, 1904.

15. Mary Kelley Upham, Aug. 10, 1904, "Journal," NWCHS.

16. Barton, *La Follette's Winning of Wisconsin,* 404.

17. *Milwaukee Free Press,* , Oct. 11, 1904.

18. "Praise for Party Manager," *Milwaukee Journal,* Nov. 10, 1904.

19. Letters to W.D. Connor, Nov. 10, 1904, Melvin R. Laird Collection, Archive, SHSW, cited here with permission.

20. Glove, *Democrat,* Nov. 10, 1904; *La Crosse Leader Press* Nov. 12, 1904.

21. G. E. Vandercook, Dec.6, 1904, Connor scrapbook, microfilm, State Historical Society of Wisconsin.

22. *Milwaukee Sentinel,* Jan. 3, 1905.

23. Belle C. La Follette and Fola La Follette, *Robert M. La Follette,* vol. 1 (New York: Macmillan, 1953).

24. Caine, *Myth of a Progressive Reform,* 94.

25. Isaac Stephenson, *Recollection of a Long Life, 1825–1915* (Chicago: R. R. Donnelly & Sons, 1915), 253.

26. Connor had helped with the financing that enabled Bill Mead to fulfill his father-in-law Jeremiah Witter's visionary project of constructing the dam across the Wisconsin River at Wisconsin Rapids.

27. "When Mr. Connor ships lumber to Chicago over the North-Western railroad and secures a rebate, drawback or rate apportionment of 25% of the tariff rate he is, according to the decision of the commission, a lawbreaker." *Milwaukee News,* Mar. 17, 1905.

28. W.D. to Irvine Lenroot, July 11, 1905, Melvin R. Laird Archive, SHSW, cited with permission.

29. In 1896, W.D.'s sister, Molly, read Burns's poetry aloud to their father as he lay dying in Auburndale.

30. Caine, *Myth of a Progressive Reform,* 81.

31. *Milwaukee Free Press,* Dec. 17, 1905.

### 6. Business, Politics, and Family

1. *Milwaukee Free Press*, Feb. 17, 1906.

2. *Milwaukee Journal*, May 16, 1906.

3. W.D. was inconsistent. As a businessman he used the patronage system; as a would-be politician he insisted that "personal preference" be removed from public service and replaced by civil service examinations to ensure "each man a fair chance." In 1904, fearing the Wisconsin Supreme Court might reject the Half-Breed claim to be the legitimate representative of the Republican Party, he declared that "no court has the power to decide who will be governor." In his Lincoln Day speech, he said, "The safety of the individual as well as the security of property depends upon the wholesome regard in the minds of the people for the majesty of the law and respect for the honesty and integrity of our courts" (pamphlet, May 15, 1906, HCL).

4. Letter from Headrick Allan to Jack Anderson, Archivist, Jan. 10, 1985, Ontario Historical Society, Stratford, photocopy in author's collection. Mrs. Allan wrote that "they were all strong Presbyterians even in those days."

5. *Milwaukee Journal*, Sept. 5, 1906.

6. W.D. Connor, "Lincoln Day Speech," pamphlet, HCL.

7. *Marshfield Times*, Aug. 8, 1906; *Milwaukee Journal*, Aug. 10, 1906.

8. *Milwaukee Journal*, May 28, 1906.

9. *Ladysmith Journal*, Nov. 17, 1906.

10. Aug. 10, 1906, pamphlet, HCL.

11. *Milwaukee Sentinel*, Nov. 3, 1906.

12. *La Crosse Leader Press*, Aug. 25, 1906.

13. *Racine Times*, May 22, 1907. The same criticism was later leveled against La Follette, a "surly, contentious, and vituperative" man "eaten up and consumed with ambition" whose "biggest weakness has been his hostility toward his opponents and critics." John Strange, "Autobiography," M64018, Archive, SHSW. Loren H. Osman, *W. D. Hoard: A Man for His Time* (Fort Atkinson, Wisc.; W. D. Hoard, 1985), 434. The list of former La Follette supporters who felt betrayed, abused, or outraged by La Follette grew long. To the names W.D. Connor, Isaac Stephenson, and James Davidson must be added those of other leading Republicans: Irvine Lenroot, John Strong, William D. Hoard, Nils Haugen, Emanuel Philipp, James McGillivray, and William Van Hise. See Herbert F. Margulies, *The Decline of the Progressive Movement in Wisconsin 1890–1920* (Madison: State Historical Society of Wisconsin, 1968), 96.

14. Max Otto Papers, MS. 101, Series 3, Box 12, Archive, SHSW.

15. *Beloit Free Press*, May 16, 1907.

16. *Milwaukee Journal*, May 17, 1907.

17. *Antigo Journal*, May 20, 1907.

18. *Ashland News*, May 20, 1907.

19. MS., W.D. Connor, author's collection. The bill had twice passed the Assembly and twice been defeated in the Senate. Senator Spooner led the opposition attempting "in every way to prevent the measure from coming to a vote." Railway attorneys and

lobbyists flagrantly disregarding the anti-lobby law packed the chamber. "Every conceivable argument was resorted to in order to influence the vote and all sorts of tactics technical and delatorian were used to confuse and delay the course of the measure." When an attempt was finally made to move a call of the House, "the President of the Senate held the motion was not in order as it was offered too late, since the vote was already being taken on the measure." The bill passed the Senate, was returned to the Assembly where it met a "fierce fight," and was amended to strike out a clause permitting the roads to collect three cents per mile if the passenger wished to pay cash on the train. The amendment forced the bill back to the Senate and Senator Sanborn moved to lay the amendment on the table which, under the rules, would mean the defeat of the entire measure. "Senator Munson was on his feet promptly and in no uncertain words explained what was attempted to be accomplished by sharp practice. The move met with such a reception that Sanborn asked permission to withdraw his motion and then moved that the amendment be nonconcurred in. The vote on the role call stood a tie: eight for and eight against, several of the senators having gone home thinking the matter closed. The clerk, as usual in such cases, called the President of the Senate and Mr. Connor voted for the measure."

20. *Reeseville Review*, Oct. 11, 1906.

21. *Appleton Crescent*, Aug. 19, 1907.

22. *Milwaukee Journal*, Aug. 16, 1907.

23. Occasionally a man too independent to submit to W.D.'s "law" made local history by standing up to him. Leon Webb and his wife, Cecilia McCue, were among the first settlers in Laona. Cecilia's father and brothers hauled supplies to the camps, and Leon worked a number of jobs, including that of conductor on Connor's Laona and Northern Railroad. One day Mrs. Joe Dennee was on the train with a guest, Mrs. Anderson. Mrs. Dennee, as wife of the mill superintendent, was entitled to ride free, and Leon didn't collect the 16-cent fare from her or her guest. When word got to W.D. that Webb had let Mrs. Anderson ride free, he called him into his office and "chewed him out." Mr. Webb handed W.D. 16 cents from his own pocket, quit the Connor Lumber and Land Company, and went to work for the Chicago and Northwestern for forty years. Interview, Agnes Carter, Aug. 1991, Laona, Wisc.

24. *Monroe Times*, July 20, 1907.

25. *Eau Claire Leader*, July 20, 1907.

26. *Rhinelander New North*, July 25, 1907; Viroqua *Censor*, July 25, 1907.

27. *Milwaukee Free Press*, Sept. 10, 1907.

28. *Grand Rapids Daily Herald* and *Grand Rapids Reporter*, Nov. 27, 1907.

29. George and Willis Witter began their careers as teachers in Marshfield and Wausau. After obtaining law certificates in Madison, they accepted their Uncle Timothy Guy Phelps's invitation to join him in California. A childless and wealthy widower, Phelps offered to help his nephews make their way in the world and hoped his sister Frances and her husband, George, would also migrate. After receiving enthusiastic reports from their sons, they did.

30. *Contemporary Biographies of Representative Men* (San Francisco: Bancroft, 1882).

31. Edwin Witter Jr. "A Phelps Family History," MS., 1992, HCL.

## 7. Risky Business

1. Bartman, "History of the Marshfield Woman's Club," 18.

2. *Milwaukee Journal*, Apr. 30, 1908.

3. *Manitowoc Tribune*, Feb. 1, 1908.

4. *Milwaukee Wisconsin*, Feb. 18, 1908.

5. *Forest Republican*, July 3, 1908.

6. *Marshfield News*, July 2, 1908; *Milwaukee News*, July 2, 1908.

7. John Gregory, *History of Milwaukee* (Chicago: S. J. Clarke Co. 1931), 2:1169–70.

8. *Milwaukee Sentinel*, Nov. 4, 1908, 6.

9. Stephenson and Connor cooperated behind the scenes to defeat Backus. On July 31, 1908, Stephenson, grateful for Connor's support in his bid to return to the Senate for a full term, wrote W.D.: "You and I did more than anyone else, financially, to help put these reforms upon the statute books and Wisconsin to-day stands first in the country. Now Connor, I feel very grateful to you for what you did to help me secure the nomination for the U.S. Senate last year. You have a friend in me and anything that I can do in the future for you I shall be glad to do." He "should have been glad" if W.D. had been a delegate to the national convention and regretted that he had not been able "to suggest or do anything in that direction. As I said to you in Chicago—there is a future when things will be different," HCL.

10. *Milwaukee Sentinel*, Nov. 4, 1908, 7. See also *Cumtux*, the Milwaukee Downer yearbook, 1909.

11. Sept. 25, 1908, HCL.

12. Sept. 26, 1908, HCL.

13. The *Manitowoc Herald, Oshkosh Northwestern, Beloit Free Press, Janesville Recorder, Eau Claire Telegram, Appleton Post, Sheboygan Telegram, Berlin Journal, Fond du Lac Reporter, Ashland Press, Green Bay Gazette, Green Bay Record Herald,* and *Watertown Times* all carried the story. The $4,000 W.D. received from the insurance came in handy as he threw his formidable energies into expanding in the north. Fires, accidental and deliberate, were still endemic in Wisconsin in both residential and forested areas, while the techniques to investigate and establish cause were undeveloped. W.D. may or may not have had anything to do with the fire.

14. In 1904, Addams and Sabin were among the six women invited to join 145 distinguished national and foreign educators as official delegates to the celebration commemorating the fiftieth anniversary of the University of Wisconsin's first commencement.

15. Established in 1889 and modeled after Toynbee Hall, which was founded in 1884 in London's East End by a group of Oxford men, Hull House was located in the Nineteenth Ward, one of Chicago's poorest districts. Immigrants from Italy, Germany, Sicily, Russia, Greece, and other countries, lived there in crowded tenements in unsanitary conditions.

16. Jane Addams Correspondence, McCormick Collection, microfilm 118, SHSW.

17. Len F. Sargent recounts how a seemingly natural decision to transfer the county seat to Laona, which had connections with major rail lines running north, south, east, and west, while Crandon had only a spur track with one train running from Pelican Lake to Crandon once a day, was thwarted by lawyers living in Crandon. "Making good from Forest County residents," and determined to block W.D. Connor's efforts, they followed the advice of a disbarred lawyer by the name of Cash. He advised the lawyers to meet with "trusted" members of the county board in absolute secrecy, out in the woods at night, and to bring the county clerk along with his record book. "By lantern light the county clerk made the entries in the book"; an architect drew up plans, and bids for the building were advertised. "All was done according to law, as the records in the new court house will show." The lawyer offered his conviction: "It makes no difference how an incident took place, when it took place, where it took place and even if it never took place, just so long as the records show that it took place according to law." "Saw-Dust," 114.

## 8. Promising Years

1. O. G. Munson, the governor's private secretary, informed W.D. of the governor's appointment on October 1, 1909. Melvin R. Laird Collection, Archive, SHSW, cited with permission.

2. Merle Curti and Vernon Carstensen, *The University of Wisconsin, 1848–1925* (Madison: Univ. of Wisconsin Press, 1949), 2:85.

3. *Daily Cardinal,* Nov. 4, 1910, 4.

4. Unidentified newspaper clipping, HCL.

5. HCL quoted by Marian McBride in "Melvin Laird's Mother Earned Her Own Fame," *Milwaukee Sentinel,* Mar. 13, 1969, 8.

6. In public lectures Ross warned that the standard of living of American workers was threatened by a policy that allowed great numbers of "Orientals" into the country before they had raised their own standard of living and lowered their birth rate. Dependent on cheap labor, Colis B. Huntington and other railroad magnates urged Mrs. Stanford to have him fired. Professors were, after all, "mere hired men." Ross's discharge, illustrative of the dangerous stifling of the power of thought by the power of wealth, eventually led to the formation of the tenure-track system in American universities and the formation of the Association of University Professors. See Edward A. Ross, *Seventy Years of It* (New York: Appleton-Century Co., 1936).

7. Emma Goldman, *Living My Life: An Autobiography* (1931; reprint, Salt Lake City, Utah: Peregrine Smith Books, 1982), 462.

8. *Daily Cardinal,* Nov. 5, 1910, 5.

9. *Milwaukee Sentinel,* June 9, 1910, 1.

10. Ibid., June 10, 1910, 1.

11. *Milwaukee Journal,* Nov. 22, 1944.

12. *Milwaukee Sentinel,* June 9, 1910.

13. Curti and Carstensen, *University of Wisconsin*, 2:53.

14. *Forest Republican*, Dec. 31, 1909.

15. J. O. Boswell to James O. Davidson, Jan. 5, 1906, Box 4, Davidson Collection, Archive, SHSW.

16. George E. Hunt, Madison, Wisc., to P. L. Jonson, Hastings, Neb., Sept. 12, 1912, NWCHS.

17. Bartman, "A Seventy Year Chronology."

18. Bartman, "A Seventy Year Chronology," 33–34.

19. W.D. Connor scrapbook, microfilm, SHSW.

20. Jennie A. Keysan to HCL, Apr. 11, 1913, HCL.

### 9. Melvin Robert Laird

1. George Hunt, Sept. 25, 1912, HCL.

2. John Leonard Conger, *The Illinois River Valley* (Chicago: S. J. Clarke Publishing Co., 1932).

3. *Prairie du Sac News*, N.D., Laird Prairie du Sac scrapbook, HCL.

4. *Prairie du Sac News*, N.D., Laird Prairie du Sac scrapbook, HCL.

5. *Prairie du Sac News*, Aug. 15, 1907, Laird Prairie du Sac scrapbook, HCL.

6. Few places in Palestine made a stronger impression on Melvin than Jacob's Well, "the very spot where Jesus sat and talked with the woman of Samaria." He found it highly significant that Jesus preached His Gospel "first of all" to the Samaritan woman, from a tribe despised by the "good" people of the time. She was an ignorant woman who "had neither education, nor character, nor reputation." By preaching to her, Jesus taught that "every man in the eyes of Jesus, no matter what his race, his nationality, his color, his rank or social condition is the child of God, created in His image, fitted for communion with Him, entrusted with vast responsibilities, the heir of an immeasurable destiny. This was the belief of Jesus. The foundation truth of Christianity is the infinite worth of man." Sept. 2, 1909, Laird Prairie du Sac scrapbook.

7. George Hunt to P. L. Jonson, Hastings, Neb., 1912, HCL.

### 10. Illinois versus Wisconsin

1. Andrew Lindstrom and Olive Curruthers, *Lincoln: The Namesake College* (Lincoln, Ill.: Lincoln College, 1965).

2. Donald to Helen, May 25, 1913, HCL.

3. *Marshfield News*, June 11, 1913. W.D. never learned to drive. He used travel time to attend to his voluminous correspondence.

4. Dana Bartlett, *The Better City* (Los Angeles: Neuer Co. Press), 291.

5. Elizabeth Jozwiak, "Politics in Play, Socialism, Free Speech, and Social Centers in Milwaukee," *Wisconsin Magazine of History* (Spring 2002): 10–21.

6. Mary Eliott Seawell, "The Ladies' Battle," *Atlantic Monthly* (Sept. 1910): 291.

7. W.D. to Helen, July 6, 1913, HCL.

8. "Education and a Cash Age," *The Lincolnian* (Dec. 1911).

9. *A Study of Child Nature* (Chicago: Kindergarten Training School, 1891) 13.

10. Restlessness of workers vied with the restlessness of women who agitated for the vote, respect, and a more engaged life as the major social issue. *Harper's* and the *Atlantic Monthly* abounded in stories in which the "woman question" was raised. Was woman primarily a "person" or a "woman"? Stories supporting the "person" view alternated with those supporting the traditional "woman" view. Karin, an artist, tells the man who implores her not to leave him: "I must have myself, Legien. The growth-strength is in me." *Harper's* (Feb. 1913): 414–15. Elsa, a medical student, "struggling to give woman her place in the world against poverty, against ridicule, against even–love!" surrenders to Mr. Fitch: "She lifted her [face] and her spirit left her and was his. They stood, his great-coat about her, their lips close; and she knew that she was woman of woman, the mate, the mother. This was her doom, and she accepted it." *Harper's* (Apr. 1913): 724–29.

11. Some in the crowd listening to La Follette wanted to know about the senator's "having accepted campaign funds from such prominent lumbermen as Isaac Stephenson, W.D. Connor, W.H. Hatton and others who are no longer adherents." *Marshfield Times*, Jan. 11, 1916.

12. *Marshfield Times*, Feb. 16, 1916, 1.

13. Ibid., Apr. 19, 1916.

14. Rob to Helen, June 28, 1916, HCL.

15. *Marshfield Times*, June 28, 1916, 8.

16. Ibid., Apr. 28, 1916, 13.

17. Rob to Helen., June 28, 1916.

18. Russell Lewis, Marshfield Clinic physician and clinic historian, reports that Henry Wahle, another prominent physician at the time, did not join the clinic, claiming it to be a communistic endeavor.

19. W.D. to Helen, Dec. 19, 1916, HCL.

## 11. War

1. Newspaper reports indicated that 600,000 Armenians had been slaughtered in Turkey, 30,000 French soldiers killed in the battle of Morhange, 20,000 British troops in a single day in France, tens of thousands of Russians in East Prussia, and thousands in Syria, Belgium, Italy, Serbia, Bulgaria, and Romania.

2. Ray Stannard Baker, *Woodrow Wilson Life and Letters: War Leader* (Garden City, N.Y.: Doubleday Page Co., 1939), 6.

3. Rob to Helen, April 10, 1917, HCL.

4. *Marshfield Times*, May 9, 1917.

5. "What manner of man is this," Nolan queried, "who allows his substitute go forth to fight and die for him without giving liberally and adequately of his vast income to buy food, clothing, life insurance and ammunition for that boy? Do the people of Marshfield look on that kind of conduct with approval? What say the mothers and fathers of these boys who have gone to the front for McMillan and protect McMillan

in his smooth easy life at the rear." Julian S. Dolan to W.D. Connor, Oct. 31, 1917, HCL.

6. Rob to Florence, 1917, Angie Connor Collection, Honolulu, Hawaii.

7. Another member of the extended Kohl family, a painter-decorator, scrawled on the second- floor hall wall of Judge Eli Winch's house "papered last by Lorenz Kohl, June 6, 1917 when the Germans licked the world" before plastering floral paper over it.

8. Rob to Helen, Dec. 23, 1917, HCL.

9. W.D. to Helen, Nov. 19, 1917, HCL.

10. Rob to Helen, May 21, 1918, HCL.

11. *Marshfield News*, Apr. 17, 1918.

12. *Marshfield Times*, May 1, 1918, 1.

13. Rob to Florence, June 30, 1918, Angie Connor Collection.

14. Rob to Helen, July 7, 1918, HCL.

15. Rob to Florence, Aug. 15, 1918, Angie Connor Collection.

16. Helen to Rob, May 22, 1918, HCL.

17. Rob to Florence, Dec. 14, 1917, Angie Connor Collection.

18. From Connor's "Baby Book," HCL.

19. Rob to Florence, Nov. 6, 1918, Angie Connor Collection.

20. W.D. to Helen, Sept. 10, 1922, HCL.

21. W.D. Jr. (William) to Helen, Mar. 4, 1943, HCL.

22. Rob to W.D., Oct.1, 1918, HCL.

23. A Marshfield boy, Wallie Mueller, had been wounded but was "getting on OK and he got eight before they got him, and should be decorated for bravery." Glen Kraus was also wounded and sent home.

24. Ira Berlin, ed., "A Wisconsinite in W.W.I, Reminiscences of Edmund P. Arpin, Jr.," *Wisconsin Magazine of History* (Spring 1968): 232.

25. William Francis. Raney, *Wisconsin: A Story of Progress* (Appleton, Wisc.: Perin Press, 1963), 310.

26. Rob to Florence Dec. 22, 1918, Angie Connor Collection.

27. *Marshfield Times*, Nov. 13, 1918. 1.

28. Rob to Florence, Nov. 23, 1918, Angie Connor Collection.

29. Interview, Angie Connor, n.d.; note in Connor's "Baby Book," HCL.

30. From Connor's "Baby Book," HCL.

31. F. K. Schuh, a mechanic with the 168th Infantry stationed near Coblenz, also found the Germans "awfully good to us. They respect the U.S. troops more than any other soldiers because of the way we handled this great German bunch of cowardly soldiers." He went on to say that the German soldiers were "great" as long as they were licking the French and English around, "but when we started to punish them, they were ready to quit because they can't stand punishment. From childhood up they are knocked around, first by their teacher, and later by their officer, who actually hit men in the face. So if that kind of treatment don't make cowards, I don't know human

nature. These people are actually afraid of an officer and don't see how we can stand and talk to our officers and joke with them. Several have asked me about them and I told them our officers were human beings and not idols." *Marshfield Times*, Mar. 5, 1919.

32. Rob to Florence, Mar. 13, 1919, Angie Connor Collection.

33. Rob to Florence, Feb. 4, 1919, Angie Connor Collection.

34. *Marshfield Times*, Jan. 15, 1919.

35. Melvin took the train to Chateau Thierry and the Bellum Woods, "two names which will become very familiar in American history." He followed the battle line to Soissons, down along the Vesle River "where the 32nd did some fine work," and saw the damaged Cathedral and buildings in Reims. With the chaplain of the 29th Division, he spent "a night in a German dugout in what was once a woods, but now a barren shell-ridden waste" of barbed-wire entanglements, trenches, and camouflaged machine gun nests and larger guns. "Rusty German guns, hand grenades, helmets, bullets, blankets, uniforms and a few unburied bodies of Germans covered the ground." The 29th had "met fearful resistance" near the Ormond woods and "showed most magnificent courage." He got a truck ride out to Varennes, in the heart of the Argonne Forest, near which he saw "the wonderful German dugouts built of cement having all the conveniences of a modern home, bath tub and electric lights." With a driver of a Winston limousine, who was driving the car back from Germany, he "rode like a general all the way down the east side of the Meuse River to St. Mihiel, pretty well fed up on battle fronts, dugouts and trenches with barbed wire entanglements." HCL

36. Melvin to Helen, Mar. 4, 1919, HCL.

37. Rob to Florence, Jan. 19, 1919. Angie Connor Collection.

38. Apr. 14, 1919, HCL.

### 12. Omaha

1. MRL sermon, May 2, 1920, HCL.

2. *Omaha Bee*, Oct. 3, 1919, 8.

3. Harvey Newbranch, *Evening World Herald*, Sept. 30 1919.

4. William Klingaman, *The Year Our World Began* (New York: St. Martin's Press, 1987), 582.

5. *Marshfield News*, Nov.27, 1919.

6. Klingaman, *The Year Our World Began*, 598.

7. *Omaha Bee*, Jan. 2, 5, 1920, SHSW.

8. Sept. 18, 1919, HCL.

9. Robert M. Miller, *American Protestantism and Social Issues* (Chapel Hill: Univ. of North Carolina Press, 1958), 258.

10. Jan. 1920, HCL.

11. Herbert Croly, "Behaviorism in Religion," *New Republic* (Feb. 22, 1922): 368.

12. Helen's speech to Ladies Society of the Westminster Presbyterian Church, Omaha, n.d., MS., HCL.

13. W.D. to William, Mar. 3, 1921, CL&L Co. Collection .

14. In 1909, forty-two fires in Forest County, the most heavily forested county in the state, with only 20 percent cut-over land as opposed to the 50 percent to 95 percent of other northern counties, burned 7,263 acres destroying 2,170,000 board feet. "Report of State Forester of WI for 1909–1910, Madison 1910," MS 246576, Huntington Library, San Marino, Calif.

15. W.D. to William, Jan. 1, 1923. CL&L Co. Collection.

16. J. F. Hooper to W.D. Jr., n.d., CL&LCo. Collection.

17. *Marshfield News Herald,* Nov. 3, 1922.

18. W.D. wanted 48,000 in preferred CPS stock in 1919–20; $15,000 cash (if the company had money to pay in cash) of 60,000 preferred stock in 1921; 200,000 in preferred stock set aside that he could purchase for cash at $30 flat at any time prior to the date when the bonds came due, which would be in four years. W.D. to Helen, June 12, 1920, HCL.

19. CPS, Annual Report, Sept.11, 1920, HCL.

20. Dec. 8, 1920, HCL.

21. Nov. 22, 1922, HCL.

22. Oct. 29, 1919, HCL

23. *Marshfield News Herald,* Sept. 30, 1921.

24. Sept. 20, 1922, HCL.

25. Quotations from Melvin's sermons written in Omaha, 1919–1923, HCL.

26. Quotations from Melvin's sermons written in Omaha, 1919–1923, HCL.

27. William Chalmers Cover, "Voices that Call," pamphlet (New York: General Board of Education of the Presbyterian Church, 1922).

28. Westminster Presbyterian Church calendar, Feb. 23, 1923, HCL.

29. Frederick M. Davenport, "Something Brewing in the Middle West," *Outlook,* Nov. 1, 1922, 369.

30. Ibid., Nov. 22, 1922, 555.

31. Oct. 11, 1923, HCL,

32. *Omaha Bee,* Mar. 15, 1921; Oct. 20, 1921.

33. Ibid., Apr. 11, 1922.

34. Ibid., Oct. 12, 1922.

35. Ibid., Oct. 8, 1919.

36. Zona Gale, *Portage Wisconsin and Other Essays* (New York: Alfred A. Knopf, 1928), 136. The printed edition of Gale's play contained two endings. In the one, the main character, Lulu Bett, a spinster, leaves her brother-in-law's "protection," declaring, "I want to see out of my own eye. I'm going, I don't know where—to work at I don't know what. But I'm going from choice." The alternative ending suggests a public not ready to abandon traditional social roles and romantic solutions. In it, Lulu Bett, who hated making her sister's house "go round," her inability to "earn anything," and dependence on her brother-in-law's charity, happily becomes a wife and triumphantly strides off stage on her husband's arm.

37. "What Women Won in Wisconsin, pamphlet, Huntington Library, San Marino, Calif., MS 259085, 1922, 4.

38. *Omaha Bee*, Oct. 31, 1919, Jan. 6, 1920, Dec. 12, 1921, July 1, 1922, Feb. 10, 1923.

39. Ibid., Aug. 31, 1922

40. W.D. to HCL, Sept. 9, 1922, HCL.

41. Rev. W. M. Hunter, in *Associate Reformed Presbyterian Church 1803–1903* (Charleston, S.C.: Presbyterian Synod, 1905), 637.

42. Oct. 24, 1923, HCL.

43. Dec. 10, 1923, HCL.

### 13. The Return

1. *Milwaukee Sentinel*, Feb. 11, 1923. Mrs. Ritt claimed she signed the complaint because of her indignation that "more than a dozen prominent Marshfield business men are living dual lives and maintaining 'love nests' in Milwaukee, Chicago and other large cities," and these same men have "controlled the courts in Marshfield for more than ten years thereby obstructing justice and saving themselves from arrest."

2. *Marshfield News Herald*, Dec. 24, 1927.

3. Ibid., Nov. 6, 1924.

4. W.D. to William, June 2, 1924, CL&L Co. Collection.

5. W.D. did not "believe that any construction company or any sawmill construction people or machinery makers would take the contract to replace that plant unless they added 30% to 50% to what it actually has cost us." He had been "on the job [himself] month after month and looked after the labor especially and looked after the buying of a lot of the material." He was sure they had in Laona, and had had "for the last three months, the best lumber this Company ever had to sell. Made in the best way." W.D. to Rob, Nov. 10, 1926, CL&L Co. Collection.

6. Robert C. Nesbit, Wisconsin: A History (Madison: Univ. of Wisconsin Press, 1973), 465.

7. Bringing Sarett to Laona was William's idea. He had heard the poet at a Chautauqua in Madison. Recognizing the value of the publicity should he be able to persuade the poet to abandon the "jazz filled big city," he offered to build him a house in Laona and rent it to him for a dollar a year should he promise to stay for a year. Sarett was then at the peak of his celebrity: in 1925, the Poetry Society of America voted his book of poems *Slow Smoke* the finest book of poems published in America; schoolchildren across America read and memorized his poem "Four Little Foxes"; Harriet Monroe celebrated him in her book *The Poets and Their Art*; Harry Hansen devoted a chapter to him in his book *Midwest Portraits;* and *The American Magazine* featured his life and work. When he accepted the offer to go to Forest County, the Connors—and the poet—reaped the publicity they hoped for. Newspapers across America reported the popular nature poet's decision to renounce civilization, flee to the wilds, and seek the only "true life" buried in the primeval forests of Laona. Regular train

service on the Chicago and Northwestern allowed him easy access to Chicago, where he could spend four days a week and teach his classes while his wife and eight-year-old son remained in Laona in the "idyllic" north. See Lyn Miller, "Lew Sarett" (Ph.D. diss., Northwestern University, 1978), 148.

8. Albert Douglas Bolens claimed that La Follette's domination of state politics had destroyed not only the old "boss system" but both the Democratic and Republican Parties in Wisconsin. "Today we have a bureaucratic form of government, responsible to nobody, pursuing its wasteful course by this power of cohesive spoils, self-perpetuating, each part thereof a law unto itself, yet in its political aspect reaching into every factional camp and personal following—strictly non-partisan in the sense that whatever takes place in any camp that may adversely affect the security of said system instantly is known to all parts and an united front immediately is in evidence that that security shall remain undisturbed." *Port Washington Star*, July 16, 1925, Bolen Papers, Wisconsin Historical Society, Milwaukee.

9. Interview, Agnes Carter, Aug. 1989, Laona, Wisc.

10. Otto Olson, the Laona constable wrote: "No wonder that corruption and greed is rampant in our country when our public officials sworn to uphold the Constitution of the U.S.A. and The State of Wisconsin is engaged in such nefarious work." Otto Olson to William, Oct. 23, 1926. CL&L Co. Collection.

11. Kronschnabl gave as an example the island on W.D.'s "private lake," which "no one could touch for less than $10,000." It was assessed at $70 before—and after—"a very beautiful cottage" was built on it. *Forest Republican*, Dec. 12, 1929.

12. William to W.D., copy to Melvin, Aug. 21, 1927, HCL.

13. W.D. to William, Apr. 2, 1926, CL&L Co. Collection.

14. *Marshfield News Herald*, Apr. 22, 1927.

15. Ibid., Nov. 25, 1927.

16. The board had previously passed a resolution providing for the appointment of a grievance committee to hear charges against any county supervisor or officer appointed by the board before ouster proceedings could begin.

17. *Marshfield Daily News*, Nov. 25, 1927.

18. *Marshfield News Herald*, Nov. 25, 1927.

19. Feb. 16, 1928, HCL.

20. Henry Seidel Canby, "The Promise of American Life," *Saturday Review of Literature*, Nov. 8, 1930.

21. *Marshfield News Herald*, Jan. 2, 1929.

22. Ibid., Apr. 30, 1929, 4.

23. Interview, Angie Connor, n.d..

24. *Marshfield News Herald*, Oct. 25, Oct. 30, 1929, 1.

25. By 1930, Lew Sarett had left Laona and given up writing nature poetry.

26. Raymond H. Palmer, "The Nobel Jury Judges America," *The Christian Century*, Nov. 26, 1930, 1448–50.

14. Surviving Losses

1. *Marshfield News Herald,* Jan. 28, 1932.

2. *Forest Republican,* July 21, 1932.

3. Ibid., Apr. 7, 1932.

4. Ibid., Nov. 28, 1932.

5. Ibid., Dec. 15, 1932.

6. W.D. to Helen, Mar. 13, 1933, HCL.

7. W.D. to Gordon, May 25, 1931, CL&L Co. Collection.

8. W.D. to Melvin, Oct. 17, 1935, HCL.

9. Richard to Melvin, June 4, 1936, HCL.

10. *Marshfield News Herald,* May 6, 1936.

11. Ibid., Sept. 16, 1933.

12. Ibid., Sept. 28, Oct. 4, 1933.

13. Angie Connor to author, Jan. 1, 1991.

14. Chesterfield ads depicted an affluent, clearly independent-minded woman hold-ing a cigarette. "Your town and city authorities see to it that the water you drink is pure. An eminent scientist has said: 'Chesterfields are as pure as the water you drink.'" *Marshfield News Herald,* Apr. 23, 1934.

15. W.D. to Helen, Sept. 26, 1935, HCL.

16. W.D. had "planted" $370,000 during the years 1920–30 in a purchase contract he entered into with the Miami Lumber Company, Los Angeles. His contract with Merrill and Ring Lumber Company, Ltd., to cut and sell "merchantable" timber esti-mated at between 65 and 70 million feet on a lease held by the Canadian Puget Sound Lumber Company on the Theodosia River provided the money enabling him to hang onto the Miami contract in 1935. W.D. to Melvin, Oct. 29, 1935, HCL.

17. W.D. to William, Feb. 6, 1936, CL&L Co. Collection.

18. W.D. to Melvin, Feb. 18, 1936, HCL.

19. June 14, 1936, HCL.

20. Wilder did not assign a letter grade to Connor's essay but commented that the treatise "should be either treated at greater length or left alone. Very risky this glancing through generalizations. But this was interesting just the same," HCL.

21. Melvin to W.D. and T.W. Brazeau, May 13, 1936, HCL.

22. W.D. to Melvin, June 26, 1936, HCL.

23. William to W.D., Oct. 8, 1936, CL&L Co. Collection.

24. William to W.D., Oct. 8, 1936, CL&L Co. Collection. W.D. was "certain that McReady and Peotter were working together trying to get in all the cheap bonds." Gardiner Dalton, First Wisconsin Bank Buildings, Milwaukee, apologized to W.D. when an error in their files prevented them from offering W.D. the $2,000 bonds that they sold elsewhere and promised that in the future W.D. would get all offerings of R. Connor six and a half bonds that came to market.

25. Mar. 8, 11, 1937, HCL. The seventy-two-year-old minister, who wrote of his "hard circuit with long drives," appreciated receiving "an encouraging word regarding

the bond." He could "get along at present" but might need money in a few months' time. "They are retiring ministers at the age of sixty eight, and I know the sword will fall on me before long." He would "need every dollar" he could get hold of.

26. Mar. 7, 1936, CL&L Co. Collection.

27. W.D. listed other lies: Peotter and Smith said they were buying about 5 percent of the logs they were sawing when they were really buying 95 percent and were "dealing with as crooked a Finlander as there is in Gogebic County." They claimed the mill had run steadily since the first of October; it ran "three days the first week in October; the second week two days; and from that time to January 6, never run a day, and when it is running it is operating on logs that they are buying. They are not cutting and realizing from Connor Company timber." More infuriating to the lumberman even than the lies and the costly, wasteful mismanagement of company assets was Peotter's attempt to confuse the "little red book" W.D. had carried with him for forty years with "regular" office books. "There is in that book Florence County, Forest County, Sawyer County, Arkansas lands that I owned a large tract, property in several states during that period that I have been interested in, and included in that is the Michigan lands for my own convenience. Might just as well call on me to leave my watch down there or my jackknife." He congratulated Melvin for "making such success," in working out "in the most concise form possible a reasonable fair explanation" of the indebtedness of the R. Connor Company, a difficult job because of the interrelation of the R. Connor Company with the Connor Lumber and Land Company going back many years. Gordon credited him with being "the champion fixer," HCL.

28. W.D. to William, Sept. 7, 1936, Box 7, CL&L Co. Collection.

29. W.D. to William, Oct. 21, 1936, CL&L Co. Collection.

30. Sept. 26, 1936, HCL.

31. Sept. 23, 1936, HCL.

32. Oct. 12, 1936, HCL.

33. W.D. to Helen, Oct. 12, 1936, HCL.

34. May 31, 1936, HCL.

35. In anticipation of the bankruptcy of the Connor Lumber and Land Company and his personal bankruptcy, W.D. had transferred the sections surrounding the lake to Mame. Anticipating her death, Mame deeded the lots by quit claim to her children. In November 1936, their application to the State of Wisconsin Conservation Department to place the land within "a state refuge for the protection and propagation of the natural game resources of Wisconsin" was granted, and the refuge was to be called "The Laona Refuge." On November 26, 1936, Helen received the certificate from H. W. MacKenzie, director of the Conservation Commission of the State of Wisconsin, indicating the granting of refuge status to the property to which she held exclusive title—the 100 feet of Government Lot 5 (NE SW) Section 29–36–15 on which her cabin stood—and the balance of Lot 5 in which she shared record title with her siblings, as well as Government Lot 6 (SE SW) Section 29–36–15, in which she and her siblings shared title (with the exception of the plot containing her brother Richard's

cabin, which was in Florence Brown Connor's name). The Connor Lumber and Land Company held title to Government Lot 4, which was also listed in the State's Exhibit A designating "The Laona Refuge."

## 15. The Divided House

1. *Forest Republican*, Mar. 11, 1937.

2. E. W. Meeker, president and editor of the *Hardwood Record*, to Melvin, Apr. 21, 1937, HCL.

3. William insisted that the company's position was vulnerable; they were still operating under an agreement with creditors and bondholders. Because the Connor Lumber and Land Company had rarely held directors' meetings in the past, that was no reason why they should continue on in that unbusinesslike basis. As long as he was a director, he was "determined" that that situation was going to change. He was now forty years old, Richard thirty-eight. "If we are ever going to be able to take responsibility, we are now. We have all worked so hard the last seven years to save the Laona operation, that we must not now, with the first pick-up in business, get so optimistic we place additional burden on the operation that will sink it if another depression comes in four years and finds us unprepared." William to W.D., copy to Melvin, Apr. 6, 1937, HCL.

4. "I have your letter of April 19 criticizing the dimension and furniture department," William wrote his father on April 20. "As Mr. Birkelund said in the recent meeting, "you're a great maneuverer." But don't throw too much dust in our eyes as we want to keep our eyes on the main question, the Michigan operation. Naturally, this sudden counter attack on my management here at Laona arouses me, but does not deter me from objecting to any further expenditures at Connorville," HCL.

5. Apr. 11, 1937, HCL.

6. Melvin R. Laird to Karl H. Doege, Apr. 30, 1937, HCL.

7. Stephen L. Tanner, *Paul Elmer More: Literary Criticism as the History of Ideas* (Provo, Utah: Brigham Young University, 1987), 1

8. Peace Campaign pamphlet, Apr. 6, 1937, HCL.

9. Robert M. Miller, *Henry Emerson Fosdick: Preacher, Pastor, Prophet* (New York: Oxford Univ. Press, 1985), 495, 499, 483.

10. W.D. to William, Jan. 26, 1937, CL&L Co. Collection.

11. William to Gordon, copy to Melvin, June 23, 1937, HCL.

12. June 10, 1938, HCL.

13. G. W. Dishong to Helen, Jan. 3, 1933. Helen copied out Fosdick's phrases as she always copied down words and ideas that helped her or that she found pertinent or beautiful or both: "The only realists are idealists with long term faiths"; "need an inner sanctuary where one can stand aside from the world and in solitude recover faith in life. There rise from the unreal to the real, from the transient to the eternal, from trivial to the significant, from short views to long views, from fear to faith lest the music in you die," HCL.

14. June 20, 1937, HCL.

15. June 18, 1937, HCL.

16. Constie to Melvin, n.d., Melvin R. Laird Collection, Archives, SHSW, printed with permission.

17. The League of Women Voters, the YWCA, the Association of University Women, the Federation of Business and Professional Women, and the Federation of Women's Clubs sent representatives.

18. The women agreed with Mrs. Phillip F. La Follette that "if we are to meet our obligations as citizens our research and study must lead to action." They had work to do to "make Democracy work at home." Wis. Mss. OA, Wis. Council on World Affairs, records of Wisconsin Conference on the Cause and Cure of War, Papers 1937–1941, Archives, SHSW.

19. Melvin to W.D., June 26, 1937, HCL.

20. "Complaint: Henry Paull, Plaintiff, vs. Connor Lumber and Land Company et al., Oct. 3, 1938," CL&L Co. Collection.

21. July 12, 1937, HCL.

22. The demands they presented to the superintendent included: single bunks with four-inch spacing, windows at each bunk, pillows, pillow cases and sheets, shower baths, laundry facilities, hot and cold water, granite ware in the kitchen, and fruit on the table three times a week.

23. J.V.Q. to O. T. Swan, July 14, 1937, Box 34, Folder 7, CL&L Co. Collection.

24. Fehl to William, July 14, 1938, CL&L Co. Collection.

25. Dec. 17, 1937. CL&L Co. Collection.

26. *Forest Republican*, Nov. 11, 1937.

27. W.D. to Melvin, Nov. 18, 1937, HCL.

28. William to O. T. Swan, Secretary Manager, Northern Hemlock and Hardwood, Nov. 23, 1937, CL&L Co. Collection.

29. Feb. 7, 1938, HCL.

30. *Midwest Labor*, Apr. 15, 1938, 1.

31. Interview, Walt and Agnes Carter, July 1990, Laona, Wisc.

32. George C. Prouty, Secretary, Gasoline Station Employees Union Local No. 19802, notarized statement to Harley F. Nickerson, Milwaukee, Wisc., Nov. 12, 1936, Box 34, Folder 23, CL&L Co. Collection. A member of the People's Party, Mayville had been arrested in April 1937, tried, and found guilty of intimidating a Minnesota legislator.

33. W.D. to Thomas Rasmussen, Apr. 8, 1938, CL&L Co. Collection.

34. William to Richard, Feb. 14, 1938. CL&L Co. Collection.

35. W.D. to John Kissinger, July 13, 1938, Box 9, Folder 3, CL&L Co. Collection.

36. W.D. to William, July 1, 38, CL&L Co. Collection.

37. Letters circulated among mill owners indicating that the CIO was at the very least Communist infiltrated. Notarized documents established that some of the strike leaders in Laona were Communists. Harry Mayville was not only a Communist himself

but, as long-time Connor employee Frank Sturzl, the undersheriff of Forest County, learned from the sheriff of Ramsey County, Saint Paul, Minnesota, Mayville's estranged wife claimed that Maysville had been "living somewhere in Wisconsin with a woman named Jenny, one of the girls in the Communist Party that belongs to the Worker's Alliance." Thomas J. Gibbons, Sheriff, by Harold St. Martin, Deputy, to Frank R. Sturzl, June 2, 1938, CL&L Co. Collection.

38. Jerold Auerbach, *Labor and Liberty: The La Follette Committee and the New Deal* (Indianapolis: Bobbs-Merrill Co., 1966), 152–53, 160.

39. Ibid., 164, 166.

40. W.D., Aug. 1, 38, Box 34, Folder 4, CL&L Co. Collection.

41. Interview, Anderson (Andy) Connor, Aug. 1992, Laona, Wisc.

42. Workers did not realize that if they shut down the power at the plant, the power in the village would be affected. Concerned that the union might go ahead and turn off the power, William made arrangements with the Wisconsin Public Service Corporation, whose high line ran half a mile east of town, to connect up and furnish current for the village should they require it. Worried that if the company were forced in this instance to take current from the Wisconsin Public Corporation's high line, the State Public Service Commission might require them to continue to do so or "else meet the very low wholesale rate that they will sell the current at," he was relieved when the union agreed, temporarily at least, to let them keep the boiler and engine room going and to furnish teamsters and men to supply fuel.

43. *Marshfield News Herald,* Oct. 20, 1938, 1.

44. Kenneth A. Allen to William, Sept. 13, 1938, CL&L Co. Collection.

45. W.D. to William, Sept. 13, 1938, CL&L Co. Collection.

46. K. K. Du Vall to L. D. Beard, Dec. 15, 1938, Box 9, Folder 1, CL&L Co. Collection.

47. That La Follette left the incoming administration with a hefty problem by granting pay increases to two thousand secretaries, stenographers, and other assistants and created a staggeringly expensive Department of Social Adjustments in the last few weeks of his administration did not dampen Republican enthusiasm for the chance to get back in the game.

48. The American Association of University Women, General Federation of Women's Clubs, National Board of the Young Women's Christian Associations, National Committee of Church Women, National Council of Jewish Women, National Federation of Business and Professional Women's Clubs, National Home Demonstration Council, National League of Women Voters, National Woman's Christian Temperance Union, National Women's Conference of American Ethical Union, and the National Women's Trade Union League sent representatives to the Cause and Cure meeting in Washington, D.C., 1939.

49. James G. McDonald, former high commissioner for refugees in the League of Nations; Major George Fielding Eliot, author of *The Ramparts We Watch;* Dr. Walter Judd; Lady Layton; Vera Michelas Dean, author of *Europe in Retreat;* Professor Charles

A. Fenwick of Bryn Mawr; and Hans Kohn of Smith College, author of *Force or Reason*, gave speeches.

50. *Marshfield News Herald,* May 19, 1939, 1.

51. *Forest Republican,* July 20, 1939.

52. Ibid., 676.

53. *Marshfield News Herald,* Oct. 11, 1939, 8; Oct. 14, 1939, 11.

### 16. Endings and Beginnings

1. Mar. 21, 1940, HCL.

2. Elizabeth Cushman, "Office Women and Sex Antagonism," *Harpers,* Mar., 1940, 356–63.

3. *Marshfield News Herald,* Catherine Curtis, national director, Women Investors in America, Inc., "When the Women Wake Up," *Marshfield News Herald,* n.d., clipping, HCL.

4. W.D. to Richard, Mar. 3, 1940, CL&L Co. Collection.

5. Melvin's publicity card read: "Past 12 years member of Wood County Board of Supervisors—unanimously re-elected Chairman in 1940. Active in County Welfare Work; Champion of the rights of local communities to govern themselves—the American way. Member of Wood Co. agricultural committee with sincere interest in farming. Served in American troops. Interested many years in educational work," HCL.

6. W.D. to Constance, copy to Helen, July 31, 1940, HCL.

7. Oct. 6, 1940, HCL.

8. Oct. 31, 1940, HCL.

9. *Daily Cardinal,* Jan. 1, 1941, 1.

10. Ibid., Jan. 11, 1941, editorial page.

11. Ibid., Jan. 23, 1941, 1.

12. *Wisconsin State Journal,* Jan. 23, 1941, 1.

13. Angie Connor, experiences in Labrador, 1941, HCL.

14. Miller, *American Protestantism and Social Issues,* 523.

15. Nadine Roberts, Secretary to Dean Acheson, Reader's Digest, Pleasanton, N.Y., letter to Helen, Feb. 27, 1941, HCL.

16. In an "Easy Chair" article that Melvin pasted in his scrapbook, marking the subject "Education," DeVoto sharply criticized the manner in which American history was taught. The "debunkers and fellow travelers" showed that Andrew Jackson spelled badly, his wife used tobacco, the Constitution safeguarded property, the pioneers cut down the forests, Marx expected finance capitalism to collapse—all demonstrations going to prove "that our civilization was low, our past ignoble, and our great men corrupt." The "science of pedagogy" had taken the drudgery out of study by inventing games. Packed with goodwill, the teaching methods produced illiteracy. On the university level, all students, whether they intended to be research scholars or high school teachers, learned "to subdivide research into progressively smaller areas of progressively more trivial and useless facts." Professional historians became convinced

they were "natural scientists" and the public did not read their "history." Melvin's scrapbook, HCL.

17. W.D., who blamed the First Wisconsin for many of his problems in the Depression, was nonetheless surprised when the bank took part in the tenders, canceling the "considerable interest, possibly up to 40% on a large note." That made "a very favorable result for the Connor Lumber and Land Company." W.D. to Melvin, copy to Richard, July 8, 1941, Box 10, Folder 27, CL&L Co. Collection.

18. Contrary to the case W.D. prepared for government lawyers, he did not want to see all the timber around Laona cut off. He gave orders not to touch their best timber there. The large camps in Michigan, where they had timber "in abundance for the present purposes and for a good many years to come," and logs purchased from Federal Lands in Forest County should provide the Laona mill. W.D. to William, Richard and Melvin, July 8, 1941, CL&L Co. Collection.

19. Kohl hoped W.D. would write the history, "since history is said to repeat itself, perhaps the statesmen of today could avoid *some* of past mistakes by listening to the Voice of Experience." Kohl to W.D., Aug. 10, 1941, HCL.

20. W.D. to Edwin P. Kohl, Jan. 2, 1941, HCL.

21. W.D. to Richard, Feb. 19, 1940, Jan. 26, 28, 1941, CL&L Co. Collection.

22. Aug. 28, 1941, HCL.

23. W.D. to William, copies to Richard, Gordon, and Melvin, Sept. 3, 1941; W.D. to Gordon, copies to William, Richard and Melvin, Sept. 9, 1941, Box 10, Folder 27, CL&L Co. Collection.

24. W.D. to William, Oct. 17, 1941, Box 10, Folder 27, CL&L Co. Collection.

25. W.D. to William copies to Richard, Gordon, and Melvin, Nov.10, 1941, Box 10, Folder 27, CL&L Co. Collection.

26. *Marshfield News Herald,* Dec. 29, 194, 6.

27. Jan. 19, 1942.

28. Jan. 30, 1942.

29. W.D. to Richard, Feb. 7, 1942, Box 11, Folder 7, CL&L Co. Collection.

30. Published in 1941 by Midwest Labor in Duluth, *We're the People* included the essays attacking the Connors published in the Duluth labor paper in 1937 at the height of the Midwest labor wars as well as an essay written in 1941 by Irene Paull, "Calamity Jane," the CIO propagandist. In her "Open Letter to Lindbergh's Dad," written in 1941, Paull accused Chamberlain, Deladier, and Lindbergh of being racists, white supremacists in the same league as Spanish and German fascists, who were determined to save their world from "oriental guns." She likened dying American lumberjacks to dying Spanish peasants; called European leaders "vultures"; attacked Martin Dies's committee; and celebrated the Soviet army that "smashes back the Fascist machine rumbling desperately toward the green Ukraine."

31. Franklin D. Roosevelt, "Fireside Chat on the Seven Point Program," Apr. 28, 1942, in *Ah, That Voice,* ed. Kenneth D. Yielding and Paul Carlson (Odessa, Tex.: Ben Shepperd Jr. Library of the Presidents, 1974), 329.

32. *Marshfield News Herald,* Jan. 27, 1942, 7.

33. July 24, 1942, HCL.

34. Forum topics included "Japan's Desperate Attack," "The Battle of Russia," "The War in the Middle East," "The Battle of the Atlantic," "Our War Economy," "The President's Foreign Policy."

35. *Marshfield News Herald,* Jan. 7, 1942, 9.

36. Ibid., Dec. 31, 1941. 9.

37. Connor to Helen, Sept. 4, 1942, HCL.

38. In April manufacturers had reluctantly gone along in Roosevelt's attempts to stabilize prices by fixing ceilings on commodities, rents, and services, but his attempt to set a $25,000 ceiling on net income to "prevent incomes from getting too high" met with an avalanche of protests. "A political measure first proposed by the CIO, then Mrs. Roosevelt, and finally discovered as a plank in the Communist platform of 1928," it was an instance of "creeping collectivism one more proof of the fact that our Government has been captured by a minority of European-minded Social Democrats—more intent upon winning the class war at home than the world war abroad." The president had no authority broad enough to issue such an order. *Hartford Courant,* Nov. 15, 1942.

39. Helen listed books and articles she read and wanted to discuss: Robert Bendiner's *The Riddle of the State Department,* Edward Hallett Carr's *Condition of Peace,* Julian Huxley's "Conduct of War" in *Fortune,* the autumn issue of the *Yale Review,* Lin Yutang and Upton Close on India. Speech notes, HCL.

40. Willkie, a lawyer, had defended William Schneiderman, a naturalized German the government wanted to strip of his citizenship and deport because he was a member of the Communist Party.

41. Melvin trusted Senator William Freehoff to let him know what transpired when a group of Republican leaders met in Madison on November 17. He advised him that H. M. Jacklin, a newly elected senator on the Democratic ticket, was "very anxious to co-operate and go along with any reasonable program" and that Senator J. H. Carroll had solicited his support for a place on the Committee on Committees. He did not believe Carroll should have a place on that committee. Senators anticipated that "war bills would undoubtedly complicate matters in the 1943 session making it a long one. The Republicans needed to caucus, and as Senator Rudolph M. Schlabach, member of the Committee on State and Local Government, wrote Melvin on November 18, "take the initiative and work out a good liberal constructive program of our own, so as to be ready when the session starts."

42. Madison industrialist Thomas Coleman, together with at least two influential Republican newspapers, the *Wisconsin State Journal* and *Janesville Gazette,* and an angry group of voters who called themselves "conservationists," including F. G. Kilp, were determined "to bend every effort possible" to defeat Governor Heil. F. G. Kilp to M. R. Laird, May 27, 1942, HCL. Heil believed two bills brought about his downfall: the bill creating the labor board and a bill eliminating a certain kind of picketing. Others believed his dominating manner brought his downfall.

43. *San Francisco Examiner*, Nov. 28, 1942, 1.

44. D. W. Dishong to Helen, Feb. 27, 1943, HCL.

45. Helen arranged for speakers to address the council. Madame Chiang Kai-shek could not accept her invitation because she was convalescing from a long illness. She would make only one address at the Chicago Stadium on the evening of January 13, 1943. Tickets were available at Marshall Field's.

46. *Capital Times*, Feb. 2, 1943, 3. The bill guaranteed them the right to return to their other civil service positions in government when the legislature adjourned.

47. The *Herald* ran the story on the front page on February 23 under the headline "Son of State Senator Lost as Minesweeper Capsizes in Pacific." Sixteen men were picked up, five of whom died of exposure during the night. Connor was not among them.

48. Hazel and Chester Newhun to Mr. and Mrs. Laird, Feb. 23, 1943, HCL.

49. *Marshfield News Herald*, May 21, 1943, 6.

50. April 6, 1943, HCL.

51. On April 1, Senators Warren Knowles, Louis Fellenz Jr., John Byrnes, Melvin Laird, and Jess Miller along with Assemblymen Ora Rice, Vernon Thomson, Alfred Ludvigsen, James Fitzen, and nonelected Republican leaders C. A. Dawson, Maurice Coakley, and T. E. Coleman met in the governor's office. The legislative program and appointments procedure were "discussed and partially agreed to, with arrangements made to have frequent meetings to develop these matters suitably." MS. T. E. Coleman Collection, Box 7, Folder 7, Archive, SHSW.

52. *Marshfield News Herald*, Apr. 3, 1943.

53. *Journal of the Senate*, Apr. 8, 1943, 628–31, SHSW.

54. *Marshfield News Herald*, June 17, 1943, 6.

55. Other members of the committee were Senator Robert P. Robertson (vice chairmen); Senator Taylor G. Brown, and Assemblymen Arthur R. Lenroot Jr. (secretary), Paul A. Luedtke, Frederick S. Pfennig, and Randoph H. Runden. The committee, meeting throughout the summer and fall and into the interim year, "unanimously agreed that a coordinating agency should be established to control expenditures." *Journal of the Senate*, Jan. 25, 1945, 84.

56. John Wyngaard, "State Capital Closeup," *Marshfield News Herald,*, Sept. 13, 1943. The review involved studying the literature on state budgets and the budget systems of other states, as well as the budgets of the university, the conservation department, and the highway department,

57. *Marshfield News Herald*, Feb. 2, 1943,1. Presented by William Freehoff, when Acting Governor Goodland refused to take action against Director Klode, the bill also provided that the part-time welfare advisory board would retain the right to discharge the director without any intervention from the Bureau of Personnel.

58. The bill had been killed in every session of the legislature since 1937. *Capital Times*, Feb. 19, 1943.

59. M. R. Laird to Col. F. B. Andreen, July 18, 1943, HCL.

60. Quotations are from the scrapbook Melvin Laird Sr. kept in the 1940s, unidentified as to source and date, HCL. Columnist David Lawrence thought Congress should debate whether the United States should enter into a postwar alliance with Great Britain. The proposal "looked innocent enough," but the United States had never entered into a peacetime alliance with any nation since George Washington warned against permanent alliances.

61. World problems, Taylor warned, were astronomical and rooted in historic tensions. Most of "the colonials of the world" could not, or would not, use freedom to maintain freedom. America had to recognize her "limitations and abandon the impertinent idea that a world is to be built in the American concept." A "policy of exaggerated internationalism" was "as dangerous, fool-hardy and destructive as narrow isolationism." *Readers Digest,* Aug. 1943.

62. At the conclusion of a special three-week session in July, Melvin confided to Earl C. Kidd that "the Republican members of the legislature were very much disgusted with the veto messages of the acting Governor. Many of the bills were passed in the first place with a large vote. It would appear to some of us that no matter how meritorious a bill may have been, through the influence of Frank Graass and others the bill was vetoed. I am happy to report to you that we overrode the veto on seventeen bills. The legislature will return to Madison on August 3rd, and I hope we can keep up the good record," HCL.

63. Arthur W. Prehn to M. R. Laird, Sept. 1, 1943, HCL.

64. Oct. 2, 1943, HCL.

65. W.D. addressed his grandchildren William and Elizabeth as "dear son" and "dear daughter."

66. Melvin received outstanding cooperation from the director of welfare, the tax commissioner, and other officials as he worked on the new budget system, but his relationship with the governor continued to deteriorate. Offended when the governor's secretary, Roy Brecke, led him to believe his candidate to fill a vacancy on the tax appeal board would be considered when the position had already been filled, Melvin explained to Earl C. Kidd: "The thing that aggravates the situation is that the Governor has repeatedly declared that he will consult the members of the State Senate before any appointments are made to these various State Agencies, and in nearly every case he has ignored them. He may find it more difficult than ever to obtain the confirmation of some of these appointments." Melvin expressed the same thought to Al Devos, the lawyer from Neillsville, whom he had put forward. The governor would not consult. M. R. Laird to Earl Kidd and to Al Devos, Oct. 28, 1943, HCL.

67. Nov. 3, 1943. Goodland's antagonism toward the "young Republicans" was such that he did not name a single legislator to the official committee celebrating the launching of the new battleship *Wisconsin* until reporters brought the snub to public attention. Goodland then included Speaker of the House Vernon Thomson and the senate president pro tem, Conrad Shearer, into the ceremonies. Reporters also pointed out that Goodland's guest list for the dinner and reception he hosted in the governor's

mansion for Wendell Willkie included three Progressives but no Republicans. This time he did not amend his list.

68. W.D. to Ray Graves, Feb. 22, 1944, Box 11, Folder 21, CL&L Co. Collecton.

69. C. A. Dawson, chairman of the Public Policy Committee of the State Medical Society of Wisconsin, wrote thanking Melvin for his work on behalf of public health. While Dawson expressed the appreciation of the State and County Medical Societies for Melvin's attitude on matters pertaining to the public health of the state of Wisconsin, he could not publicize his support for fear that the medical society would be accused of "getting into politics." He wanted Melvin to have his letter to show in private whenever he felt it might be useful. Apr. 8, 1944, HCL.

70. *Marshfield News Herald,* Mar. 31, 1944, 2.

71. Ibid., Apr. 11, 1944.

72. Sept. 1, 1944. OA, Wisconsin Council on World Affairs 1937–1947, Archives, SHSW.

73. *Forest Republican,* Aug. 9, 1944, 1.

74. Comprised of four districts, Laona, Florence, Argonne, and Eagle River, in 1944 the Nicolet National Forest stretched a distance of approximately forty-two miles from the Oconto County line on the south end of the county to the Michigan state line at the Brule on the north and thirty-six miles west from the Marinette County line to Oneida and Langlade Counties. Timberlands in the Laona district were 40 percent government owned and 30 percent county and privately owned, 15 percent by the Consolidated Light and Power Company of Wisconsin Rapids and 15 percent by the Connor Company. In September, northern and central Wisconsin received the good news that the counties would be the prime beneficiaries of an enormous postwar reforestry program involving two million acres of state land. Deemed necessary to prevent soil erosion and to add to the state's heavily depleted timber supply—and to provide jobs and quell any possible labor unrest on the part of returning military—the postwar planting program promised to furnish spring and fall labor for nearly 2,000 men for at least twenty years. The government's reforestation program was a boon to the population and the company, as was the state's decision to straighten and make Highway 8 a major road. Helen was almost alone in opposing the new road, writing the Highway Commission of her disapproval. The narrow, winding old road was beautiful.

75. W.D. to Helen, October 4, 1944, HCL.

76. Melvin sent a congratulatory letter to John Byrnes, the newly elected congressman from the Eighth District of whom Wisconsin "expected great things," and identical telegrams to Senators William A Freehoff, Jess Miller, Frank E. Panzer, and Conrad Shearer: "Can you meet with certain state senators Madison Saturday morning 11th." It was important that they pull together. Melvin to Panzer, Nov. 15, 1944, HCL.

77. Resolution, Northern Hemlock and Hardwood Association, Milwaukee, Wisc., Jan. 31, 1945, HCL.

78. Nov. 29, 1944, HCL.

79. The Zells' claim that it was W.D.'s wish that, if anything happened to him, they remain as the children's caregivers, could not be substantiated by any letter of instruction. Harvey Zell suspected that Gordon had found such a letter in W.D.'s safety deposit box and had destroyed it. Interview, Harvey Zell, May 1986, Marshfield, Wisc.

80. Dec. 15, 1944. Christians, once considered the most liberal of Americans, have been lumped together in a "Christian Right" label, a catch-phrase for extreme conservatism and narrow-minded bigotry. The church movement was, and many Christians remain, socially progressive.

81. Nov. 22, 1944. Melvin also received word that Governor Goodland wanted to see him, a sign, perhaps, that the old man recognized he needed a better relationship with the senate.

82. The *Maddox*, assigned to Task Group 38, conducted strikes against Luzon and Leyte on December 14, 15, and 16. A typhoon, during which three destroyers were lost, gave them a harder fight.

### 17. Another Ending, Another Beginning

1. Detailed provisions in bills coming out of the legislature regulating the public sale of mares, jennies, stallions, and jacks indicates a determination to improve the species by breeding. The animals had to be certified sound by a veterinarian and registered with the agriculture department. The presence of a cataract, St. Vitus's dance, moon blindness, roaring or whistling, crampiness, shivering disqualified a mare or jennie for breeding. A stallion or jack of inferior type or conformation, or lacking in size, height, or weight for the breed or classification to which it belonged, was also disqualified. The legislature further authorized the department to adopt regulations to supplement existing statutes "to provide for a necessary amount of elasticity to meet all conditions in protecting the health of domestic animals, and in doing this to employ the most efficient and practical means known to modern science." An authorized agent was authorized to enter the premises of any building or place where he had reason to suspect there were diseased animals and examine and test them. Pamphlet, HCL.

2. Feb. 15, 1945. No 130S, *Index to Journals of Legislature*, (Madison: State Historical Society of Wisconsin), 1945, 65.

3. "As you know, I was active in securing an appropriation of $100,000 for a special study [of Bang's disease] and experimentation to be conducted by the University," Melvin wrote Professor V. E. Kivlen, dean of the College of Agriculture. "I want to keep in touch with the program you have adopted." Kivlen's report of the Bang's disease conference held at the University shows the disease as a problem in the process of solution without any clear solution on the horizon, HCL.

4. The welfare bill provided funds for new buildings and repairs at institutions caring for lawbreakers, the insane, the feeble minded, and dependent as well as funds for the construction of a diagnostic center in Madison to be run in cooperation with the University of Wisconsin Medical School at which inmates of penal institutions and criminals about to be sent to prison would receive mental, physical, and character

examinations and recommendations would be made as to their treatment. A bill provided pensions for totally and permanently disabled persons between seventeen and sixty-five years who had lived in the state a year and had no relatives to support them. A new law guaranteed free sanitarium care for the state's 5,500 tuberculosis sufferers and for future victims of the "white plague." Any legal resident or person who had lived in Wisconsin for five years might be treated without cost at a public institution, but the patient had to turn in any insurance he might have. *The 1945 Legislature on the Record,* prepared and circulated by the Republican Party of Wisconsin, reprinted from the editorial columns of the *Wisconsin State Journal,* HCL.

5. Joint Resolution 48, which would have made a law degree a requirement for election to the Wisconsin Supreme Court (drafted to block Fred Zimmerman's run for the office), was nonconcurred, but Melvin promised to use his influence to secure Judge Elmer Barlow's election. Barlow was elected.

6. Anticipating that a conservation bill would be brought forward in the next session, Melvin contacted Michigan legislator George P. McCallum, who was working on such legislation in Michigan, asking for "any information you may have regarding the work of your committee and also your thoughts in regard to the regulations which should be imposed upon timber owners," HCL.

7. *Wisconsin Blue Book,* 1948, 77–79.

8. Jan. 22, 1945, HCL.

9. Jan. 11, 1945, HCL.

10. MSS. Letters, 1945, Box 14, Folder 15, CL&L Co. Collection.

11. Gordon to Richard, Apr. 6, 1945, CL&L Co. Collection.

12. From Helen's "Town Meeting of the Air Address," Jan. 1945, HCL.

13. *Marshfield News Herald,* Feb. 28, 1945, 7.

14. Helen urged leaders to reread in their groups the "Atlantic Charter, the Fulbright and Connally resolutions, the Dumbarton Oaks proposals, and the report of the Crimean conference." She pointed out that "one woman, Doctor Virginia Gildersleeve, Dean of Barnard College," was among the bi-partisan group of conference delegates, HCL.

15. Feb. 10, 1945, HCL.

16. "Ship's History," USS *Maddox* (DD731), HCL.

17. *Marshfield News Herald,* May 31, 1945.

18. Ibid., June 4, 1945, 1

19. Horace Nealy, USS *Maddox,* War Communique No. 5., HCL.

20. Following the successful engagement, "'Bull' Halsey messaged 'You are unpopular with the Emperor—good work' to Captain T. H. Hedreman, who commanded the raid, the first in history inside Toyko Bay. Hederman replied 'So are you.'" *Forest Republican,* July 26, 1945, 1.

21. Norman Cousins, "Modern Man Is Obsolete," *Saturday Review of Literature,* Aug. 18, 1945, reprinted in *Herald Tribune,* Aug. 23, 1945, 34.

22. With Fred Taylor's help, Melvin accumulated more than the required number

of shares of both preferred and common stock as well as bonds to ensure the family's position as majority stockholders of CPS. He planned to take the stock certificates with him and have them transferred equally among Gordon, Richard, and himself. Melvin to Richard, Aug. 29, 1945, HCL.

23. Nov. 15, 1945, HCL.

24. Nov. 11, 1945, HCL.

25. "The Atomic Age," in "Serving Through Science" (United States Rubber Company, 1945), HCL.

26. The Marshfield school system was "big business" with a budget of $216,000, of which $124,000 was raised by local taxes. While school buildings were maintained as well as could be expected, Helen insisted new schools were needed. *Marshfield News Herald,* Jan. 2, 1946.

27. Feb. 27, 1946, HCL.

28. *Capital Times,* Mar. 15, 1946, 1.

29. Ibid., Feb. 13, 1946, 4.

30. Thomas Coleman Papers, Box 4, Archives, SHSW.

31. Feb. 22, 1946, HCL.

32. Feb. 23, 1946, HCL.

33. *Capital Times,* Feb. 4, 1946, 5.

34. Betty Connor Graham to Helen, Mar. 24, 1946.

35. Mar. 25, 1946.

36. W.D.'s half-brother, Reuben Connor, active in Wood County politics for more than forty years and one of the five members of the Wisconsin State Central Committee of the Republican Party from the Seventh District, became Melvin Jr.'s political mentor.

37. Mar. 27, 1946, HCL.

38. Electric shock, a comparatively new treatment, became standard procedure for severe depression in sanitariums in 1946. In 1941 Dr. Edward F. Dombrowski, managing officer of the Illinois State Hospital, reported "temporary successes with an electric shock at a cost of one cent per 100 patients." A thirty-second charge of 110 volts shot through the temple resulted in a noticeable change. "We don't know exactly what happens, but there are beneficial reactions." The doctor also noted "preshock fear and anxiety" in patients. The "pre-shock fear and anxiety" lay buried in Helen until some thirty years later, when, following a stroke, she underwent a CT scan on her brain and reacted to the procedure with a panic that only David understood.

39. *Marshfield News Herald,* June 12, 1946.

40. June 7, 1946, HCL.

41. In researching the history of the California property that had passed to Connor Brothers, Inc., on July 2, 1938, by order of the court, R. B. Graves discovered the "conveyance was entered in the United States District court on June 27, 1937." Mr. Grubb, then the attorney for R. Connor Co., claimed the land was "burdensome" because of excessive taxes, that a substantial amount of taxes were delinquent, the land

not saleable, and that "it is to the interest of R. Connor Company that it abandon any interest in the land." Graves could discover "nothing in the records in the United States Court showing that the stockholders of R. Connor Company, who would have the beneficial interest in any assets consented or agreed to the transfer of the absolute title of the California land to Connor Brothers, Inc."

42. Richard to Birkelund, Aug. 1946, Box 12, Folder 13, CL&L Co. Collection.

43. Nov. 4, 1946, Box 12, Folder 23, CL&L Co. Collection.

44. *Marshfield News Herald,* Nov. 6, 1946.

45. Ibid., Nov. 13, 1946, 2; Alexander Wiley's speech to the Business and Professional Women's Club in Racine, HCL.

46. *Marshfield News Herald,* Nov. 12, 1946, 6.

47. Helen noted total current assets of more than $1.5 million. (Dick Laird put it at $5 million.) Current liabilities, including the $192,150.90 reserve for federal and state income taxes, amounted to $309,015.48. 1946, Box 13, Folder 6, CL&L Co. Collection.

## 18. In a Man's World

1. F. J. Sensenbrenner, retired president of Kimberly Clark Corp., Neenah, and chairman of the University of Wisconsin Board of Regents, raised $5 million. Walter J. Kohler, chairman of the Centennial Fund Committee, raised more millions.

2. Mar. 18, 1947. Dick wrote Helen that William's statement that Taylor and Sager would be rewarded for representations made in connection with the CPS sale was false. "No arrangements were made either directly, or by the remotest implication, to reward any of the CPS employees for help in connection with the sale," HCL.

3. Mrs. Norbert Klein sketched the organization's history, "stressing especially its auspicious beginning and the havoc that the war had brought to the organization." Mrs. W. Phelps, the first vice president, told of the death of the organization's "faithful Secretary, Miss Almere Scott, and the great loss that this was not only to our organization but to all women's organizations in the state." Miss Scott's association with the university extension division had enabled the women to hold their meetings at the Union. HCL.

4. *World Government News,* June 1947, HCL.

5. Federalists cited the report of Truman's Advisory Commission on Universal Military Training, which acknowledged that it was essential to abolish war and establish a reign of law among nations. Harold C. Urey was quoted in the *Bulletin of the Atomic Scientist (Apr./May 1947)*: "If some nation or nations refuse to go along, then the partial world government should be started anyway, including all countries that are able to agree on necessary principles and some adequate mechanical structure to implement those principles. I should like to see the principles include an adequate bill of rights for world citizens."

6. Thomas Finlater, "Timetable for World Government," *Atlantic Monthly,* June 1946, 60; the offprint published and distributed by Americans United for World Government.

7. On May 26, Paul Reynolds, executive director of the Wisconsin Taxpayers Alliance, sent Helen the quotation from Wyngaard's syndicated column on government and politics.

8. Revell praised Laird for voting with the cooperatives on most measures and for his vote in favor of natural gas. His votes for a bill outlawing strikes in public utilities and for outlawing jurisdictional disputes "were cast after a searching study of the problem." They were not antilabor. Laird had tried to get the AFL representatives in Madison to draft a bill that would prohibit such strikes and not touch other labor controversies, but the AFL refused. Their unwillingness to draft a bill was "stupid." Laird consulted with professors at the university versed in labor legislation who drafted the bill for which he voted. (Edwin Witte, on whose expertise President Franklin Delano Roosevelt depended and who had been involved as an arbitrator in settling Connor labor disputes, was almost certainly among those Bom consulted.) "To date, no one can tell whether this will react in favor of labor or the employer." *Capital Times,* June 3, 1947, 4; *Marshfield News Herald,* June 9, 1947, 2.

9. Richard Connor to Melvin, Oct. 22, 1948, HCL.

10. Mary Roddis Connor to the author, Dec. 7, 1988.

11. Richard to R. B. Graves, copy to Helen, Gordon, and William, Aug. 13, 1947, HCL.

12. The Connor Brothers partnership, whose "books" had been maintained by W.D., held diverse assets—real estate in several states, stock in Consolidated Water Power and Connor Lumber and Land, along with a scattering of other assets not listed in the books for which proper title transfers were not always available.

13. Dick and Bom, letters to Helen, July 16, 1947, HCL.

14. Dick to Helen, Aug. 7, 1947.

15. On August 20, the day before the close of the CL&L Co. fiscal year, F. P. Aschenbrener, vice president and cashier of the Laona State Bank, sent Helen a check drawn on the Connor Lumber and Land Co. for her 200 shares of Connor Brothers and the forty shares held in the Estate of M. R. Laird.

16. Dec. 21, 1946, Box 12, Folder 26, CL&L Co. Collection.

17. Jan. 5, 1948, HCL.

18. *Marshfield News Herald,* Jan. 7, 1948, 10.

19. Mar. 22, 1948, HCL.

20. David to Helen, July 28, 1948, HCL.

21. April 28, 1948, HCL.

22. May 19, 1948, HCL.

23. Interview, Wilbur Renk, 1992, Maple Bluff Country Club, Madison, Wisc.

24. The Roper study showed Stassen pulling 10,440,000 votes over Truman against Dewey's 5,160,000. The Gallup Poll had Stassen winning by 15 million votes against Dewey's 5.4 million. Coleman Papers, Box 7, Folder 3, Archives, SHSW Library.

25. Richard to William, copy Helen and Gordon, , June 1, 1948, Box 13, Folder 18, CL&L Co. Collection.

26. Nov. 6, 1948. Box 13, Folder 17, CL&L Co. Collection.

27. Anticipating the need for a paper trail and, perhaps, the law suit that eventually took place, Gordon wrote a formal letter to Richard M. Connor, president, Connor Lumber and Land Company, Laona: "On November 18, 1947, I purchased 150 shares of Connor Lumber and Land Company stock at a cost of $40,050.00. Before that date, I believe it was in 1946, I made another purchase from you as guardian of a block of stock. Would you please give me the number of shares in that transaction and the price that was paid for them?" He also wrote Mrs. M. R. Laird, secretary, Connor Lumber and Land Company, Marshfield. "Back, I believe, in 1946, I purchased fifty shares of Connor Lumber and Land Company stock from Richard M. Laird. Would you please look up the record and see what the date of this purchase was and also give me the information as to how the certificates were made out that replaced this fifty shares that I purchased from him." G. R. C. Manager, Michigan Division, CL&L Co. Collection.

28. *Forest Republican*, May 4, 1948, 1.

29. R. B Graves to Richard, Box 13, Folder 19, CL&L. Co. Collection.

30. Richard to William and Gordon. Aug. 31, 1948, CL&L Co. Collection.

31. Helen to Richard, copies to Gordon and William, Sept. 17, 1948, HCL.

32. Helen made donations to local organizations, church groups, schools, the Wisconsin Taxpayers Alliance, the Phillips Andover Academy Scholarship Fund, the Near East College Association, the Albert Schweitzer Fellowship, the Emergency Committee of Atomic Scientists, the National Mental Health Association, the Seaman's Institute, the American Printing for Blind, National Vespers, March of Dimes, American Red Cross, CARE, Women's Action Committee, American Association of the United Nations, and the International Recovery and Relief.

33. "In previous administrations," Wyngaard wrote, "executive secretaries were politicians first, experienced and schooled tacticians. Their successors are to all intents and purposes non-partisans. There isn't a political advisor in the lot." *Marshfield News Herald*, Sept. 9, 1949, 14.

34. Ibid., Dec. 2, 1948, 18. "Sickness disability benefit payments as a third prong in the State's pioneering and liberal workmen's security program will be one of the main topics among the new legislative proposals considered and debated in the legislative session this winter. Senator Melvin R. Laird, Jr. Marshfield, one of the leading figures among the young men who rule the Republican legislature, announced that he would sponsor his personal version of a desirable sickness disability plan when the Legislature reconvenes."

35. Ibid., Dec. 19, 1949: "U.S. Shapes New Policy to Halt Reds in Far East Area."

36. June 4, 1950, HCL. Thrilled with his mother's appointment, David volunteered an achievement of his own. He had received the highest score for the university—99 percent—on the standard test for progress in language given all first- and second-year students. Having claimed an achievement, he immediately destroyed it. "All bunk."

37. In 1933, when the legislature threatened to cut funding for the university's

Library School, throwing the weight of the Woman's Club behind her, Helen wrote Walter J. Rush, then her state senator, declaring the women's opposition to the cut. "We were able to amend it as to restore the appropriation for the Library School. Amendment passed and now part of the budget bill." Rush to Helen, Mar. 31, 1933, HCL.

38. Apr. 7, 1951, University of Wisconsin News Service, clipping, HCL.

39. Wisconsin Library *Bulletin* 46, no. 6 (June 1950): 3.

40. *Manitowoc Herald Times,* June 22, 1950, 6.

41. Robert T. Oliver, "Korean Powder Keg," in *Freedom and Union,* pamphlet, June 1947, 9–11.

42. The UN Security Council, with the exception of the Soviet Union, voted unanimously to send troops to South Korea. The United States supplied 50 percent of the ground troops, 80 percent of the navy, and more than 90 percent of the air force.

43. The act had been fiercely debated by Robert Taft and other Republicans, who claimed that with its sweeping grant of powers to set price controls and rationing, to control credit and provide financing for defense programs, it menaced economic freedom in the United States. Donald O. Bacon et al., *Encyclopedia of the U.S. Congress* (New York: Simon & Schuster, 1995) 2:623.

## 19. Regent

1. HCL diary, Jan. 27, 1951, HCL.

2. *Marshfield News Herald,* Jan. 27, 1951, editorial page.

3. Ibid. Apr. 6, 1951, 16.

4. *The Badger* (University of Wisconsin yearbook), 1933.

5. *Daily Cardinal,* Feb. 27, 1951.

6. Emma Goldman, *Living My Life* (1931, reprint, Layton, Utah: Peregrine Smith, 1982), 188.

7. On October 25, 1952, the *Daily Cardinal* published "Is There No Way? The Wisconsin Story," in which journalism major Richard Schickel traced the history of free speech at the university. Helen kept his essay with the her limited edition centennial historical map. Schickel's essay perfectly encapsulated her experience.

8. Dennette was quoted saying, "Freedom is now in some danger." It had been "a great shock to lovers of liberty to see with what content the American people, in the years since the war, have permitted the state to retain or to resume the control of public opinion." Newspaper clipping, n.d., HCL.

9. *Minutes of the Regents,* May 12, 1951, 12:24, University of Wisconsin Archives, University Library, Madison.

10. The American history and values requirement, established "in a time of conflicting social and political ideologies," was for "education not indoctrination." Students could meet the requirement by courses or by an attainment examination in U.S. history taken at the beginning of his junior year. As Helen anticipated, no regent heard a professor in the history department suggest to hundreds of naive incoming students that Lincoln was not only, or even primarily, a self-serving individual.

11. Feb. 1, 1952, HCL.

12. Jan. 15, 1952, HCL.

13. *Marshfield News Herald,* Apr. 19, 1952, 12.

14. *Minutes of the Regents,* Apr. 11, 1953, 14:19, 20–24.

15. *Minutes of the Regents,* Apr. 16, 1955, 16:2–4.

16. *Minutes of the Regents,* Aug. 30, 1955, 17, "Recommended Plan for Coordination of Higher Education," n.p.

17. *Minutes of the Regents,* January 7, 1956, 17:3,4,7. Also see working papers of the Regents, Series 1/1/7, Box 14, University of Wisconsin Archives.

18. "Highlights of University of Wisconsin Budget, 1956–57," HCL.

19. Minutes of the Regents, April 7, 1956, 17:5–8, 10, 12–13.

20. Minutes of the Regents, July 1956, 18:4–8. Subject to real estate taxes, both city and university benefited from the sale of lots at the University Hill Farms. The project, which Oscar Rennebohm had been instrumental in developing, soon became a major money maker. Before Helen's term as regent expired, the net return to the university on the land exceeded $3.5 million.

21. The university believed that "the interdependence and exchange of knowledge and experience between undergraduate and graduate students" should not be weakened and that "highly specialized courses should be avoided." It conceded that the goal of integrating of "all branches of knowledge" had become increasingly difficult and recognized that the university should "be aware of the various sources of research support" and "help the faculty to secure such support." It should maintain a community of scholars engaged in fundamental research and support excellence in teaching as an "inspiration for men in all walks of life."

22. "Working papers of the Regents," series 1/1/17, Box 15, File 6.

23. Mark Perry, *Four Stars* (Boston: Houghton Mifflin Co., 1989), 78.

24. *Minutes of the Regents,* Mar. 15, 1958, 19:8, 10, 11.

25. *Minutes of the Regents,* Feb. 1, 1958. 19:12, 22, 23.

26. "Wisconsin Co-ordinating Committee For Higher Education," June 1958, 20–32, series 1/3/1 M 354, University Archives, Memorial library, Madison.

27. *The Matric Midget* (Newsletter of the Woman's Journalism Society), Mar. 15, 1955, Number 21.

### 20. Family Matters

1. Feb. 27, 1951, HCL.

2. "We are sitting on economic dynamite, and unless we accept high taxes and tight controls on prices and wages, the fuse is in the Politburo's hands." John Harriman, "We All Want Inflation," *Atlantic Monthly,* Jan. 1952, 41.

3. Taft Committee Campaign Flier, Jan. 2, 1952, HCL.

4. Sumner Welles, *Seven Decisions That Shaped History* (New York: Harper, 1951), 218.

5. D. C. Everest was a member of the advisory council of the State Conservation

Commission, a member of the board of the State Historical Society of Wisconsin, and president of the Marathon Historical Society. *Wisconsin Historical Magazine*, June 1952.

6. William to Helen, May 9, 1952, HCL.

7. "His chairmanship of the Wisconsin Legislative Council and of the state GOP platform committee, both in 1950 and 1952, and the numerous hearings he has conducted in the state—32 in the past year—on both state and national platform issues provide a solid background for the task entrusted to him at Chicago." Unidentified newspaper article, July 9, 1952, HCL.

8. Stephen Ambrose, *Eisenhower, 1890–1952* (New York: Simon and Schuster, 1983), 1:535–37. Television cameras caught Minnesota changing its vote from Robert Taft to Dwight Eisenhower, but it was Texas that gave the nomination to Eisenhower on the first ballot. Taft supporters, outraged that the election had been swept from under their candidate by the dirty tricks of Eisenhower's people who had engineered the seating of "illegal" Texas delegates, refused to make the vote unanimous.

9. Company minutes, Aug. 1, 1952, CL & L Co. Collection. The *Forest Republican*, Aug. 24, 1952, 1, published the changes in the Connor Company management.

10. *Marshfield News Herald*, "The Obvious Choice," Sept. 13, 1952, editorial page. Walter Kohler wrote that the success of the 1951 legislative session was due in large part to Melvin's work. "Your thorough knowledge of legislative problems and constant willingness to work diligently for a just cause were great assets to me, to the people of your district, and the people of your state." Much as Kohler regretted losing his services in Madison, he recognized that "your value to the state will be substantially increased if you can serve it in the broader field of the United States Congress."

11. *Wisconsin State Journal*, Nov. 19, 1952, editorial page.

12. Stephen Ambrose, E*isenhower: The President* (New York: Simon and Schuster, 1984), 93.

13. "Washington Office Report," Mel Laird Newsletter, Feb. 14, 1953, HCL

14. "In my many years as a tribal representative in Washington, I have never observed a congressman, particularly a freshman, discharge his duties so competently." Gordon Dickie, newspaper clipping, Shawano, Apr. 8, 1953, HCL.

15. *Marshfield News Herald*, Mar. 2, 1953, 1.

16. May 12, 1953, HCL.

17. Dick Laird to Helen, Aug. 31, 1953, HCL.

18. *Marshfield News Herald*, Dec. 12, 1953, 1.

19. The complaint, drawn up by R. C. Dempsey of the Brazeau and Brazeau law firm in Wisconsin Rapids was sworn to and notarized on December 30, 1953.

20. Mary Roddis Connor to author, Dec. 7, 1988.

21. In the sixteen-page "Confidential Memorandum Re the Suit Brought by W.D. Connor, Jr. Against the Connor Lumber and Land Company and Others," Dick pointed out that "prior to the date of his death, he [Melvin R. Laird] had the longest continuous service of any living officer of the Connor Lumber and Land Company." Dick described the meeting at Wisconsin Rapids, which followed the August 28, 1953,

at which the pension plan for Helen was agreed on. He noted that Attorney R. B. Graves, Richard Laird, Melvin Laird Jr., Gordon R. Connor, and Richard M. Connor were present; that William had acquired 500 shares, approximately a third of the Laird shares, at a price of $200 per share. "It was her intention to sell an approximately equal amount to each of her other two brothers. Her chief concern and reluctance in making the sale was the fact that the family property, apart from that owned by individual members of the family, at Birch Lake near Laona, Wisconsin, was now in the hands of The Connor Lumber and Land Company and she did not want to do anything that would interfere with her rights to the use of this property or with her rights with respect to the acquisition of additional property on Birch Lake. G.R. Connor stated that the value of the lake frontage on Birch Lake as well as other lake frontage owned by The Connor Lumber and Land Company was not included on the books of the company and it would be difficult, if not impossible, for them to compute a value of the lake frontage in arriving at value, the per share value, of stock of the Connor Lumber and Land Company. He stated that the matter of stock ownership and stock value was not involved with respect to this family property on Birch Lake and that a program should be worked out wherein the property would be divided fairly among members of the family. He stated that our [Laird] rights would be equal with those of other members of the family regardless of stock ownership. With these assurances, the sale of the balance of the stock held by Helen C. Laird to Richard Connor and Gordon Connor was concluded."

22. *Marshfield News Herald,* Feb. 1, 1954, 1.

23. Mar. 2, 1954, courtesy Melvin R. Laird.

24. Following nine days of testimony, Judge Arthur M. Scheller filed a nineteen-page decision in the Wood County Court rejecting charges that "Richard M. Connor, Laona, President of the Connor Lumber and Land Company, had perpetuated a fraud in the handling of guardianship funds of William Connor Rhyner, formerly of Marshfield. The testimony failed to disclose that the personal interests of the guardian were in any way promoted by this sale to his brother, Gordon R. Connor, to defraud the ward, nor was there a fraud committed upon the court or the ward in obtaining the orders authorizing the sale."

25. *Forest Republican,* June 10, 1954.

26. Bom's opponent, Kenneth E. Anderson of Stevens Point, circulated a "malicious and vituperous four page Pictorial Report on how the 7th District Has Been *Mis*-Represented by Melvin Laird." The strongest bit of negative advertising ever seen in the district, it deeply offended Helen and many others and backfired. (In spite of her feeling that the publication smacked of "depravity," Helen was too good a historian to destroy it.) Set up as a report card, "Susie Q. Public," gave Mel Laird for his actions in the 83rd Congress "100% for Foreign Travel, 100% for Texas Oil Interests, and 100% for Tax Relief for Millionaires." "Susie Q" commented, "Melvin shows little aptitude for representation in the public interest. I suggest that he be enrolled in a good school for lumber executives." Cartoons depicted Laird (his large, domed

balding head already a target for caricature) rejecting the agriculture committee for the appropriation committee so "I can see the world," receiving the congratulations of a Texas millionaire for the "right patriotic job" he did on behalf of the oil interests, and driving a large convertible with three passengers, "Stock Holders, Big Industry, Special Interests," HCL.

27. Jan. 6, 1955, HCL.

28. *Daily Cardinal,* Feb. 9, 1954.

29. Helen to Mrs. Robert W. Roper, Mar. 7, 1955, HCL. Adlai Stevenson delivered the commencement address to the Smith class of 1955, the class from which Elizabeth (Rhyner) Connor graduated. About the twentieth-century collision between individualism and collectivism, he said, "this crisis we are forever talking about, will be won not on the battlefield but in the head and heart." The Smith graduates' "important work" was to pull all together into a meaningful whole in the home, supporting the "specialized work" the men performed "at the front." Norma Woods to Helen, quoting Stevenson, HCL.

30. *Wisconsin Rapids Daily Tribune,* Dec. 31, 1955, 1.

31. June 21, 1956, Aug. 5–11, 1956, HCL.

32. Following settlement of William's suits, the Laird stock had been released to Richard and Gordon. R. A. Crawford of Superior, Wisconsin, secured the title in Helen's name for an additional 200 feet at Connor's point for $10 a foot, the price Richard paid for additional frontage on which to build a guest cabin. Her brothers' "gentleman's agreement" seemed binding then, although the poem implies a lingering concern.

33. The platform called for the expansion of Social Security, broadened coverage in unemployment insurance, improved housing, and better health protection for all our people.

34. In "Congress Is Listening, But It Hasn't Heard Much Yet," Melvin claimed that proposals to effect change and savings by adopting recommendations made by the Second Hoover Commission on Governmental Reorganization had been frustrated by citizen inaction.

35. May 8, 1957, HCL.

36. *Marshfield News Herald,* May 16, 17, 1957, 1.

37. Puffed by the media since 1949, when he first mounted a major tent revival in Los Angeles and William Randolph Hearst decided he should be puffed, Billy Graham had gained the support of the local council of churches, an organization that included a number of Protestant liberals. His revivalist campaign in New York in 1957 was highly successful. Helen preferred the intellectual Reinhold Niebuhr.

38. May 7, 1958, HCL.

39. Helen to David and Helen L., Oct. 12, 1958, HCL.

40. *Marshfield News Herald,* Nov. 7, 1958, 14, Nov. 6, 1958.

41. Ibid., Dec. 9, 1958, l.

42. Robert J. McCracken to Helen, June 24, 1959, HCL.

43. June 11, 1959, HCL.

44. Helen to David, June 23, 1959, HCL.

45. Sept. 12, 1959, HCL.

46. Sept. 28, 1959, HCL.

47. *Wisconsin Rapids Daily Tribune,* Nov. 13, 1959, 1.

48. In his novel *Advise and Consent,* Drury described Washington as "a city where you didn't have to be born into anything, you could just buy your way in," where politicians' families suffered the "heavy price exacted by public office" because they understood their husbands and fathers were "political animals" who thrived on the pressures and the quickly shifting daily dramas which absorbed them.

49. Interview, Wilbur Renk, Aug. 1994, Maple Bluff Country Club, Madison.

50. Madeleine Doran to David Laird, Sept. 12, 1969, HCL.

## 21. A Different World

1. Feb. 15, 1960, HCL.

2. *Marshfield News Herald,* Feb. 23, 1960, 4.

3. Bom and John Fogarty, a liberal Democrat from Rhode Island who served with Bom on the Health, Education and Welfare subcommittee, worked together to develop and expand the activities and funding for the National Institutes of Health.

4. *Milwaukee Journal,* Oct. 27, 1960.

5. Melvin Laird accused the Democratic administration of "lullabying" itself to sleep following World War II by putting the Atomic Energy Commission into the hands of those against the military uses of atomic energy, while the Soviet Union searched for "atomic means to dominate a sleeping America. Dr. Klaus Fuchs' confession that he had been leaking atomic secrets finally awoke the slumbering White House." Eisenhower inherited an "equally dangerous lag in guided missiles from the Truman administration, which impounded the $75 million appropriated for research and development, $17 million of which was specifically to have been for missile development." The Russians, meanwhile, succeeded in building an intercontinental rocket. Under Eisenhower's administration the United States "came from behind to race ahead of Russia by placing 32 satellites in orbit, obtaining a vast variety of scientific knowledge, and obtaining a remarkable series of 'firsts' in exploration areas where Russia lags in her space program." *Congressional Record,* Jan. 25, 1961, HCL.

6. Alistair Cooke, *America Observed* (New York: Alfred A. Knopf, 1988), 127–28.

7. Apr. 2, 1961, typescript from CBS program, HCL.

8. *Marshfield News Herald,* Apr. 3, 1961, 4.

9. Ibid., July 5, 1961, 10.

10. May 3, 1961, HCL.

11. Rick Setlowe, *San Francisco Examiner,* Oct. 29, 1961, pictorial section, 16.

12. David M. Laird to David Laird, Feb. 13, 2000, HCL.

13. Interview, Alison Laird Large, July 2000, Laona, Wisc..

14. Melvin R. Laird, *A House Divided* (Chicago: Henry Regnery Co., 1962), 113, 165, 170–71.

15. Charles DeBenedetti, *An American Ordeal: The Antiwar Movement in the Vietnam Era* (Syracuse, N.Y.: Syracuse Univ. Press: 1990), 374.

16. *New York Times*, July 25, 1962, 1.

17. *Marshfield News Herald*, June 12, 1962.

18. Ibid., July 9, 10, 1962, 1.

19. Ibid., July 10, 1964.

20. Ann E. Weiss, *God and Government: The Separation of Church and State* (Boston: Houghton Mifflin, 1982), 33.

21. *Marshfield News Herald*, Nov. 2, 1962.

22. Helen remembered when the general sought American aid for French troops fighting in Indochina, threatening that without such aid the French public would be so disappointed France might even fall into the Russian orbit. Now, almost twenty years later, De Gaulle wanted to distance himself from American power. He planted a kiss on Chancellor Konrad Adenauer's German cheek, signaling forgiveness and future alliance, and was even willing to join with his old enemy Russia. He was unwilling, however, to give up the centuries old rivalry with Britain and accept a diminished role for France. He strenuously rejected British membership in the Common Market because it would create "a colossal Atlantic community under American dependence and direction," clipping, n.d., HCL.

23. Bom charged that Secretary of Defense Robert McNamara had not told the truth when he said there was "no evidence of export of Communist subversion from Cuba to Central and South America." John McCone, the director of the Central Intelligence Agency, had supplied "detailed data on the number of trained Latin American guerrillas, running into the hundreds, who have left Cuba for other countries." *Marshfield News Herald*, Mar. 11, 1963, 1.

24. William Edward, "Rep. Laird Bright GOP Star," *Marshfield News Herald*, June 23, 1963.

25. Wirtz stated that 4,500,000 more Americans had jobs than when the administration took office in January 1961 and that unemployment was more than 2,000,000 fewer jobs. The actual figures were 1,224,000 more jobs, and a reduction in unemployment of 784,000. *Marshfield News Herald*, Dec. 21, 1963, 5.

26. Ibid., Apr. 11, 1964, 1.

27. Helen to David and Helen L., Apr. 15, 1964, HCL.

28. *Marshfield News Herald*, Apr. 16, 1964.

29. See Michael R. Beschloss, *Taking Charge: The Johnson White House Tapes, 1963–1964* (New York: Simon and Schuster, 1997), 379–83. Laird charged that "McNamara has given [Vietnam Ambassador Henry Cabot Lodge and others with whom McNamara is meeting in Honolulu] a plan for invasion of the North." Concerned about the effect of Laird's remarks, Johnson told McGeorge Bundy, "I approved no plan to invade anything." Bundy advised the president to "just leave it alone. I wouldn't get into an argument with Laird. He's too small."

30. June 21, 1964, HCL.

31. Walter Kohler to Helen, July 20, 1964, HCL.

32. July 27, 1964, HCL.

33. Beschloss, *Taking Charge,* 510. Republican senators H. R. Gross and Wayne Morse were the only senators to vote against the Tonkin Resolution, which passed the House unanimously.

34. Ibid., 494. Deciding (incorrectly) that the attack was a new Communist strategy and not an isolated attack, Johnson gave shoot-to-kill orders to the navy. Equating national honor with personal honor and political survival, he committed the United States to escalating an engagement he hated and had been repeatedly warned against.

35. Aug. 7, 1964, HCL.

36. Aug. 15, 1964, HCL.

37. According to the article he contributed to the Carleton College magazine *The Voice* (Sept. 1964), Melvin Laird's decisions on the Appropriation's Committee "directly affected research in cancer and heart disease" and "the number of Polaris submarines" on station, which, without an amendment he introduced five years before, would now have been "far fewer." He never regretted his "early choice to enter politics." Few politicians did, because "the deeper [the politician] feels the continuing challenge it poses, the greater his satisfaction as his responsibilities grow and widen. The elected officeholder is the one who *makes* the decisions. The appointee, or government worker, merely carries out the decisions."

38. *Marshfield News Herald,* May 14, 1964, editorial page.

39. Nov. 9, 1964, HCL.

40. Perry, *Four Stars,* 148–50.

41. *Marshfield News Herald,* June 17, 1965.

42. *Congressional Record,* Cong. 1, sess. 1, Nov. 15, 1965, A6618–6619. Senate majority leader Mike Mansfield and Senator Frank Church claimed Republicans wanted to bomb missile sites, raise the level of conflict, expand the war, and that Republicans advocated "the indiscriminate slaughter of Vietnamese," that they were "air hawks [whose] challenge should be ignored." The truth was quite different. "Republicans who speak out on Vietnam are pointing out the course of action, which they believe will promote the security of our Nation. If they were motivated by considerations of political gain, they would offer no suggestions. They would simply criticize the consequence of administration policy."

43. Cooke, *America Observed,* 160, 162.

44. Antiwar and anti-American sentiments dominated most, but not all, campuses. The "duly elected representatives of the Clemson University student body" supported "the U.S. Government in its announced foreign policy to utilize such force as necessary to assist the South Vietnamese Government in the protection of its freedom from external political and ideological domination." *Congressional Record,* Cong. 89, sess. 1, Nov. 15, 1965, A6625.

45. Ibid., A6610–A6615.

46. Alfred Mauer, "Window on Washington," *Capital Times,* Sept. 27, 1965. The

article covered Laird's work on the defense budget but ignored his support of water pollution and medical complex bills.

47. Oct. 3, 1966, HCL.

48. Oct. 30, 1966, HCL.

49. Feb. 17, 1967, HCL.

50. A reporter for the *Appleton Post-Crescent* thought it "unlikely that even the mature citizens of Wisconsin familiar with the political history of their state can recall any Wisconsin member of the United States Congress who has risen to such prominence and influence in the councils of his party as the comparatively youthful Rep. Melvin R. Laird of Wisconsin's Seventh District," the Republican party's "theoretician." Undated clipping, HCL.

51. The frontier David refers to was located in southwestern Wisconsin where Dick was actively engaged in surveying and buying timberland.

52. Helen to Robert Froehlke, treasurer, Laird Leadership Foundation, Nov. 8, 1967, HCL. The Laird Youth Leadership Foundation not only provided financial support for talented students in the district seeking to enter the University of Wisconsin-Stevens Point, but educated young people and the public about the issues politicians faced.

53. John H. Averille, *Los Angeles Times*, Sept. 18, 1967, 16.

54. Madison *Capital Times*, Oct. 6, 10, 17, 19, 20, 21, 1967.

55. Declaring "there's too much concentration of research in coastal cities," with a resultant brain drain from the Midwest, Bom attached an amendment to the funding bill stipulating that the lab could not be built within fifty miles of Washington, eliminating Beltsville, Maryland, the FDA's first choice. David Lawrence, *Wisconsin State Journal*, Oct. 30, 1967, 8.

56. Lawrence Lowell Gruman, notes, HCL.

57. William Randolph, *Milwaukee Journal*, undated clipping, HCL. "The Republican co-ordinating committee proposed by Laird after the Republican rout in 1964 and composed of congressional leaders, former presidential nominees, some governors and members of the Republican national committee came into being in 1965. Its purpose was to formulate positive alternatives to administration policies." The "high powered house conference research staff," which Laird developed, "produced much of the ammunition for the co-ordinating committee's position papers," which hit hard on "some of Laird's favorite themes": proposals for federal tax sharing with the states, tax credits and block grants to states instead of earmarked funds which often required matching by state or local governments. Tax sharing "might be years in the offing," but it provided the Republicans "a positive sounding program, to offset their negative demands for cuts in Great Society programs."

58. Earl Nelson received an award for his service on the university center commission and for his support of the center as a member of the Wood County board of supervisors.

59. The *Report of the National Advisory Commission on Civil Disorders* "discovered"

housing as a major issue and advised a massive expansion of the housing supply for low-income families.

60. John F. Bibby, associate professor of political science at the University of Wisconsin–Milwaukee, contributed an essay to the *Report of the National Advisory Commission on Civil Disorders*. See "Oversight and the Need for Congressional Reform," 477–88, HCL. Bibby quoted Daniel Patrick Moynihan (D-N.Y.), who, in the wake of the urban riots of 1967, wrote: 'In our desire to maintain public confidence in [social welfare] programs, we have tended to avoid evidence of poor results. These failings have been accompanied by a formidable capacity for explaining them away." Bibby stressed the crucial importance of oversight committees as congressmen "established mutually rewarding relationships with agency people reluctant to become actively engaged in a close review of that agency's affairs."

61. *Capital Times*, Oct. 16, 1968, 1.

62. *Marshfield News Herald*, Oct. 21, 1968.

63. *Marshfield News Herald*, Dec.15, 1968.

## 22. The Mother, the Politician, and the Professor

1. Following Senator Proxmire's introduction, Laird took questions. Asked about his opinion on the theory that we should cut down our military capability to a parity with that of Russia as the best insurance to prevent the outbreak of nuclear general war, he answered that he disagreed with that theory, "and I believe it is absolutely important that the United States maintain a superior position." He spoke of his hope that we could move toward a volunteer army and acknowledged that the situation with regard to the super powers had changed since 1961 when he wrote *A House Divided*. That was a period of confrontation with the Soviet Union. "We are moving from a period of confrontation to a period of negotiation, and I would hope that all Americans would favor moving into this period of negotiations." Container D3, Department of Defense Letters, Gerald R. Ford Library, Lansing, Mich.

2. The lecture was part of the Monday-morning series of lectures sponsored by the Women's Committee of the Seminary.

3. Stephen Ambrose, *Nixon: Ruin and Recovery, 1973–1990* (New York: Simon and Schuster, 1991), 392. Bom had spoken against the bombing. His push to "Vietnamize" the war, to "train, equip, and inspire the South Vietnamese to fill the gaps left by departing American forces," eventually became policy. "It was largely on the basis of Laird's enthusiastic advocacy that we undertook the policy of Vietnamization." But it took some months before the policy went into effect.

4. Mar. 13, 1998, HCL.

5. Apr. 29, 1969, HCL.

6. Zawacki remembered Helen telling him at a U.W. Alumni dinner-meeting in Marshfield that his "open cities" idea made sense. "We exchanged letters afterward." Zawacki included an eleven-page document describing his correspondence with Nixon during the years 1956–60, the proposals and memos he had written to Raymond Price

Jr., Nixon's "special assistant," and his criticism of Henry Kissinger's two major books, *Nuclear Weapons and Foreign Policy* (1957) and *The Necessity for Choice* (1960). Kissinger's books constituted "a quite exhaustive statement of the revolutionary situation in the world today" but contained a critical flaw: "Nowhere in either book does he probe into the intuitable dynamics of nuclear peace at all." Kissinger's "blind spot" might be, Zawacki thought, "the very place where the imaginative breakthrough might be made." HCL.

7. Mar. 31, 1969.

8. "Laird Advises Nixon on Domestic Affairs Too," *Merrill Daily Herald*, May 12, 1969, 3.

9. James Kelley provides an interesting account of the relationship of the military, the universities, and the government following World War II and the effects of that relationship on the society. Government contracts enabled graduate students to get "free rides on research." The universities waxed strong on government contracts after the war; graduate students, who "never had it so good," went into highly paid military-oriented industries after commencement or into universities to teach (reluctantly) and do research. With material affluence the measure of success, "who was going to be the first to cast a stone at the idol which produces billions of dollars? We Americans, in and out of the universities, put this monster together; a monster which sooner or later had to threaten to devour us. Isn't it time we asked ourselves, 'What is a university?'" 'What is its relevance to life?'" James Kelley, "Universities and the Military Tie," *Milwaukee Journal*, May 11, 1969.

10. *Marshfield News Herald*, June 21, 1969.

11. "All over America psychologists, philosophers, sociologists studied Woodstock. Some saw in Woodstock youth's search for community; others, like Columbia Sociologist Amitai Etzioni, while applauding the idealism of the young, argued that the flight from reason was ultimately dangerous as was its exaltation of self." Historian Theodore Roszak pointed out that the rock revolutionaries bore a "certain resemblance to the early Christians, who, in a religious cause, rejected the glory that was Greece and the grandeur of Rome. Ultimately, they brought down a decaying pagan empire and built another in its place. But the Second Comings of history carry with them no guarantees of success, and a revolution based on unreason may just as easily bring a New Barbarism rather than the New Jerusalem. As Yeats so pointedly asked: 'And what rough beast, its hour come round at last, Slouches toward Bethlehem to be born?'" "The Message of History's Biggest Happening," *Time*, Aug. 29, 1969.

12. "It is the task of lifelong politician Melvin Laird to preside over the Pentagon at the most critical and criticized era for the U.S. military in many years. He must manage America's withdrawal from Viet Nam in such a way that an unsatisfactory war does not turn into a debacle. He must find ways to reduce sharply military spending in a time of rising costs at home, continuing challenges to U.S. power abroad, and changing definitions of America's role in the world. He must shake up a Pentagon grown sluggish and wasteful. And he must do it all under the aroused and hostile

scrutiny of a Congress and public now convinced that for too long the generals and the admirals have got too much of what they wanted." "The Politician at the Pentagon," *Time*, August 29, 1969.

13. Protests of the old order came not only from blacks and students. *Oh, Calcutta*, a revue made up of a series of sketches by a dozen writers, including Samuel Beckett, Jules Feiffer and the English critic Kenneth Tynan, and dealing with such controversial subjects as wife-swapping, rape, masturbation, and a takeoff on Masters and Johnson type of sex research, presented by a "frequently nude cast," employing "some of the most uninhibited dialogue heard currently on any stage," and played on stages across America adding to the social pathology.

14. *Marshfield News Herald*, Oct. 27, 1969, 1.

15. Interview, Alison Laird Large, August 1999, Laona, Wisc.

16. Diary entry, Jan. 15, 1970, HCL.

17. Helen to Melvin, Apr. 30, 1970, courtesy Melvin R. Laird.

18. *Marshfield News Herald*, May 21, 1970, 1.

19. See Perry, *Four Stars*, 232–33. Perry writes, "A backchannel link housed in the Pentagon's underground Relay Center, under twenty-four-civilian guard, had instructions from Kissinger that specifically denied access to the Secretary of Defense. Using the Relay Center, Nixon pushed Abrams to approve the Cambodian invasion, which enraged Laird and his top military aide, Robert Pursley. This White House policy of bypassing Laird, first used by Kissinger and Nixon to initiate the April-May Cambodian incursion, remained the unstated policy of administration insiders."

20. "Laird Touchy on Credibility," *Marshfield News Herald*, Dec. 2, 1970.

21. The reasons behind the "touchiness" of the "devious dove" (Bob Schieffer's name for Mel Laird) have been well documented. See Perry, *Four Stars*, and Stanley I. Kutler, *Abuse of Power: The New Nixon Tapes* (New York: Free Press, 1997).

22. Mar. 31, 1971, HCL.

23. Apr. 21, 1971, HCL.

24. Aug. 14, 1971, HCL.

25. Interview, Alison Laird Large, August 1999, Laona, Wisc.

26. Apr. 29, 1972, HCL.

27. *Daily Cardinal*, Apr. 24, 1972, 3.

28. Apr. 20, 1972, HCL.

29. Melvin Laird wrote from his office in the Pentagon "at a time in our nation's history when the winds of peace seem to be stirring." He summarized his family background, his deep roots in Wood County. "The people of Marshfield—friendly, frank, open and generous people—taught me what I know of life and its purpose, of God and country. By word and deed they impressed on me the duty that one owes to his fellowmen." He could wish no greater blessing for any future generation "than to have such people as friends and neighbors." Marshfield Library Archives.

30. On the morning of August 3, in Washington D.C., the president worried aloud to Haldeman and Ehrlichman: "We have all the power. And we aren't using it."

Ehrlichman agreed. The "grief" he had taken trying to get McGovern's service jacket from the Department of Defense was "unbelievable." "Guys like Laird, like Shultz, like Kleindienst, are just as touchy as hell about cooperating with us on this kind of thing." Kutler, *Abuse of Power*, 113.

31. June 22, 1972, HCL.

32. Nov. 11, 1972, HCL.

33. May 11, 1973, HCL.

34. *Marshfield News Herald,* Jan. 20, 1973.

35. Ibid.

36. Stewart Alsop, "Our Supererogatory President," *Newsweek,* Apr. 9, 1973, 120.

37. Ambrose, *Nixon,* 126.

38. June 5, 1952, HCL.

39. Laird's popularity among Republicans and some Democrats, his ability "to leak and everything," which "he loves to do," would be "an enormous assistance." Haig thought, "We made a helluva move [in getting Laird to come on board] and I think [Melvin] Laird's gonna be a big asset around here." He's "a tough political in-fighter. He knows where all the monkeys are. These guys on the Hill are just uniformly excited about it. Well, I'll tell you, there isn't a guy on the Hill who doesn't know that a shrewd sonofabitch like Mel Laird would never have entered your staff if he wasn't very convinced that this was a viable option for him." Kutler, *Abuse of Power*, 582, 586, 587, 593.

40. Anthony Ripley, "Skilled Presidential Assistant Melvin Robert Laird," *New York Times,* June 7, 1973, 37. Ripley believed Laird's appointment put "at the right hand of the President a skilled, hard-working and respected politician, in sharp contrast to what one Republican Senator called the "faceless ghosts" of the President's past four years."

41. "Laird Tackles Tough Job," *Eau Claire Leader-Telegram,* n.d., clipping, HCL.

42. Samuel Agnew Schreiner, *The Condensed World of the Reader's Digest* (New York: Stein and Day, 1977), 95–96, 167.

43. Melvin Laird cited domestic achievements and achievements in the area of national defense for which he had had a direct responsibility: the ending of the draft, the ending of the war, getting Americans out of Vietnam, increasing opportunities for blacks and women, moving those qualified into flag and general officer ranks. "We have a long ways to go here." He got in a plug for his friend Vice President Jerry Ford, said he had not talked with the president about the eighteen-minute gap in the tape. Nixon had been given him assurances, "and there is nothing that has happened that would change my mind about his having no knowledge of the coverup until March," HCL.

44. Dedication of the Melvin R. Laird Center, Marshfield, Sept. 12, 1997, George Magnin Library, Marshfield Clinic.

45. Senate Democratic leader Mike Mansfield, House Republican whip Leslie C. Arends, Senate Republican leader Hugh Scott, Republican senator Barry Goldwater, and former Secretary of State William P. Rogers were among those present.

46. Dedication Melvin R. Laird Center, Marshfield, Sept. 12, 1997.

47. Bom claimed friendships with Helmut Schmidt and Dennis Healey because they were "all politicians. Henry doesn't know them like I do. They're upset because Henry believes it is easier to deal with dictators and Communist leaders than elected officials in democratic countries. You know, politicians have a constituency, and that's the way it goes. We MUST maintain democratic forms of government. They have elections in Europe. They speak out and express opinions. Is that BAD?" HCL.

48. Praise for Melvin Laird was not unanimous in 1974. The Carleton faculty, after a heated meeting, rejected the trustees' proposal to award Melvin R. Laird an honorary degree. A faculty member later explained that "there was such distrust of everything that we heard from the government, there had been so many lies, that there was this suspicion that Laird's reputation as a moderate was just another lie—that Laird was really an evil genius." Laird took the slight to heart and former Governor Lee Sherman Dreyfus, as chancellor of the University of Wisconsin-Stevens Point, benefited. "Mel Laird connected me with leaders like Henry Kissinger; generals William West-moreland, Creighton Abrams and Alexander Haig, as well as presidents Nixon and Ford. [He] also led me to money for my campus and students. His alma mater, Carleton College, alienated him by passing faculty and student resolutions condemning him for the Vietnam War, ignoring the fact that he inherited that mess from Secretary Robert McNamara and President Johnson. The more Carleton attacked him, the more he helped Stevens Point." *The Freeman*, Mar. 1, 2001. In June 1981, the Carleton College Alumni Association presented Melvin R. Laird the Distinguished Service Award for three decades of public service.

49. Bom was playing golf with President Ford at Burning Tree after Ford's Sunday-morning televised broadcast announcing the Nixon pardon. He kept his answer to Ford's question as to his opinion of his action until after the game. Tip O'Neill, another golfing buddy, said, when Ford told him of his determination to issue a pardon, that he was crazy and predicted the move would cost him the election. Barry Goldwater told him the pardon didn't make sense. Not political sense, anyway. Gerald Ford, *A Time to Heal* (New York: Harper and Row, 1979), 128.

50. Oct. 9, 1974, HCL.

### 23. Past and Present

1. Jan. 13, 1975, HCL.

2. Jim Squires, Washington, May 13, 1975. In his autobiography, Ford described Mel Laird as the "most political" of the group of close friends: John Byrnes, William Scranton, David Packard, Bryce Harlow, William Whyte, and Melvin Laird constituted the "kitchen cabinet" with whom he met informally but regularly in the Oval Office. Ford regretted that Melvin's business commitments prevented him from managing his reelection campaign.

3. John O. to David and Helen L., Mar. 2, 1975, HCL.

4. Nov. 9, 1975, HCL.

5. Leslie Gelb, *Los Angeles Times*, May 23, 1976, 1.

6. Ford, *A Time to Heal,* 401, 404.

7. Sept. 9, 1976, HCL.

8. Oct. 10, 1976, HCL.

9. Evans and Novak, *Marshfield News Herald,* July 2, 1976, 7.

10. Helen to David, Helen L., and Vanessa, Jan. 2, 1977, HCL.

11. Oct. 15, 1977, HCL.

12. Barbara Laird to David and Helen L., Nov. 28, 1977, HCL.

13. Helen to David and Helen L., Dec. 9, 1977, HCL.

14. Helen to David and Helen L., Dec. 11, 1977, HCL.

15. Helen to David and Helen L., Feb. 1, 1978, HCL.

16. Barbara may also have worried about being stranded in Forest County while Bom maintained a hectic schedule.

17. "Glad you liked the poem: found in Arthur Waley's *Translations from the Chinese*; Alfred A. Knopf—a wonderful book! yours! Steve Miller." Apr. 22, 1978, HCL.

18. June 20, 1978, HCL.

19. Interview, Jean Connor Evans, June 1979, Laona, Wisc.

20. David recalled when members of the Committee on Social Thought discussed *King Lear.* Those discussing the text included Morton Zabel, an early-twentieth-century Joyce and Conrad scholar; Peter Heinrich Blanckenhagen, an emaciated, arthritic German refugee who "probably knew more about Medieval Europe than anyone in the world"; Otto von Simson, another refuge and a distinguished art historian; Eugene Neff, a sociologist and chairman of the Committee on Social Thought; Richard McKeon, a member of the philosophy department; David Grene, a translator of Greek classics; Napier Wilt, Henry James's amanuensis; and Ronald Crane, a professor in the English department.

21. Nov. 5, 1978, HCL.

22. Nov. 25, 1978, HCL.

23. Helen to David and Helen L., Feb. 17, 1979. Friends in the business community recognized Mel Laird for his brilliant skills and commitment as a "conservative in Congress" and as a "shameless liberal" on the compensation committees of the many boards on which he served. Oral history, General John Walker and Wheelock Whitney, Wausau, Wisconsin, May 11, 1998.

24. Bernard Iddings Bell, "Will the Christian Church Survive," *Atlantic,* Oct. 1942, 106–12.

25. Aug. 13, 1979, HCL.

26. Gay Wilson Allen, *William James* (New York: Viking Press, 1967), 425.

27. To David, Sept. 8, 1979, HCL.

28. Sept. 24, 1979, HCL.

## 24. Home

1. Mar. 15, 1980, HCL.

2. Mar. 20, 1980, HCL.

3. Mar. 17, 1980, HCL.

4. Mike Feinsilber, "Assessment Bleak," *Honolulu Star,* Sept. 21, 1980, HCL.

5. Oct. 2, 1981, HCL.

6. Jan. 8, 1981, HCL.

7. Interview, Irma Jablonic, July 1983, Marshfield, Wisc.

# Selected Bibliography

A Note on the Archival Sources

The Helen Connor Laird Family collection [HCL], author's possession, Marshfield, Wisconsin, and the Connor Lumber and Land Company papers [CL&L Co.], Archives, State Historical Society of Wisconsin, Madison, are major sources. (References to the CL&L Co. papers that do not include box numbers were reviewed in Laona or at the University of Wisconsin–Stevens Point before they were inventoried.)

Additional manuscript sources located in the State Historical Society, Madison, include: Melvin R. Laird, personal letters, Melvin R. Laird Collection; Max Otto papers; Jane Addams Correspondence, microfilm, in the McCormick Collection; John Strange, Autobiography in John G. Strange Papers; Wisconsin Council on World Affairs Papers.

Other manuscript sources include: Charles H. Bolen Papers, Archives, University of Wisconsin Library, Milwaukee; City Hall Papers, North Wood County Historical Society, Marshfield, Wisconsin; Selma Bartman, "A Seventy Year Chronology of the Marshfield Woman's Club," North Wood County Historical Society, Marshfield, Wisconsin; Mary Upham diary, North Wood County Historical Society, Marshfield, Wisconsin; Robert Connor letters from World War I, Angie Connor Collection, Honolulu, Hawaii; Leonard Sargent, "Sawdust," Archives, Library, University of Wisconsin, Stevens Point; Constance C. Modrall, "Birch Lake in the Olden Days," monograph, author's possession; Edwin D. Witter, Jr. "A Witter Family History," and "A Phelps Family History," typescripts, author's possession.

Published Sources

Aikens, Andrew J., and Lewis A. Proctor. *Men of Progress*. Milwaukee: The Evening Wisconsin Company, 1897.

Allen, Gay Wilson. *William James*. New York: Viking Press, 1967.

Ambrose, Stephen. *Eisenhower, 1890–1952*. New York: Simon and Schuster, 1983

———. *Eisenhower: The President*. New York: Simon and Schuster, 1984.

———. *Nixon: Ruin and Recovery, 1973–1990.* New York: Simon and Schuster, 1991.

Auerbach, Jerold. *Labor and Liberty: The La Follette Committee and the New Deal.* Indianapolis: Bobbs-Merrill Co., 1966.

Baker, Ray Stanley. *Woodrow Wilson, Life and Letters: War Leader.* Garden City, N.Y.: Doubleday Page Co., 1939.

Bartlett, Dana W. *The Better City.* Los Angeles: Neuer Co. Press, 1907

Barton, Albert O. *La Follette's Winning of Wisconsin, 1894–1904,* Madison: A. O. Barton, 1922.

Beschloss, Michael R., *Taking Charge: The Johnson White House Tapes, 1963–1964.* New York: Simon and Schuster, 1997.

Boynton, Percy. *Literature and American Life.* Boston: Ginn and Co., 1936.

Busby, Katherine G. *Home Life in America.* London: Methuen and Co., 1910.

Caine, Stanley. *The Myth of a Progressive Reform: Railroad Regulation in Wisconsin, 1903–1910.* Madison: State Historical Society of Wisconsin, 1970.

Carter, Paul A. *Another Part of the Fifties.* New York: Columbia Univ. Press, 1983.

Conger, John Leonard. *The Illinois River Valley.* Chicago: S. J. Clarke Publishing Co., 1932.

*Contemporary Biographies of Representative Men.* San Francisco: Bancroft Publishing, 1882.

Cooke, Alistair. *America Observed.* New York: Alfred A. Knopf, 1988.

Cowley, Malcolm. *Exile's Return.* New York: W. W. Norton and Co., 1934.

Curti, Merle, and Vernon Carstensen. *The University of Wisconsin, 1848–1925,* Madison: Univ. of Wisconsin Press, 1949.

DeBenedetti, Charles. *An American Ordeal: The Antiwar Movement in the Vietnam Era.* Syracuse, N.Y.: Syracuse Univ. Press: 1990.

Ford, Gerald. *A Time to Heal.* New York: Harper and Row, 1979.

Fosdick, Harry Emerson. *On Being Fit to Live With.* New York: Harper and Brothers, 1946.

Gale, Zona. *Portage Wisconsin and Other Essays.* New York: Alfred A. Knopf, 1928.

Garment, Leonard. *Crazy Rhythm.* New York: Random House, 1997.

Goldman, Emma. *Living My Life.* 1931. Layton, Utah: Peregrine Smith, 1982.

Goldman, Eric F. *The Crucial Decade, America 1945–1955.* New York: Alfred A. Knopf, 1956.

Gregory, John. *History of Milwaukee.* Chicago: S. J. Clarke Co., 1930.

Hull, Cordell. *Memoirs of Cordell Hull.* New York: Macmillan Co. 1948.

Hunter, W. M. *Associate Reformed Presbyterian Church, 1803–1903.* Charleston, S.C.: Presbyterian Synod, 1905.

Klingaman, William. *The Year Our World Began.* New York: St. Martin's Press, 1987.

Kutler, Stanley I. *Abuse of Power: The New Nixon Tapes.* New York: Free Press, 1997.

La Follette, Belle C., and Fola La Follette. *Robert M. La Follette.* New York: Macmillan, 1953.

Laird, Melvin R. *A House Divided.* Chicago: Henry Regnery Co., 1962.

Leighton, George. *Five Cities.* New York: Harper Brothers, 1939.

Margulies, Herbert F. *The Decline of the Progressive Movement, 1890–1920.* Madison: State Historical Society of Wisconsin, 1968.

Marsden, George M. *Religion and the American Culture.* Fort Worth, Tex.: Harcourt College Publishers, 2001.

Marsh, C. W. *Recollections, 1837–1910.* Chicago: Farm Implement News Co., 1910.

Miller, Robert M. *American Protestantism and Social Issues.* Chapel Hill: Univ. of North Carolina Press, 1958.

———. *Henry Emerson Fosdick: Preacher, Pastor, Prophet.* New York: Oxford Univ. Press, 1985.

Nagel, Paul C. *John Quincy Adams.* New York: Alfred A. Knopf, 1997.

Nesbit, Robert C. *Wisconsin: A History.* Madison: Univ. of Wisconsin Press, 1973.

Nixon, Richard. *The Memoirs of Richard Nixon.* New York: Simon and Schuster, 1990.

Paull, Henry. *We're the People.* Duluth, Minn.: Midwest Labor, 1941.

Perry, Lewis. *Intellectual Life in America,* New York: Franklin Watts, 1984.

Perry, Mark. *Four Stars,* Boston: Houghton Mifflin Co., 1989.

Plumb, Ralph. *Badger Politics, 1881–1916.* Manitowoc, Wis.: Brandt Printing and Binding Co., 1936.

Raney, William F. *Wisconsin: A Story of Progress.* New York: Prentice-Hall, 1940.

Ross, Edward A. *Seventy Years of It.* New York: Appleton-Century Co., 1936.

Schreiner, Samuel Agnew. *The Condensed World of the Reader's Digest.* New York: Stein and Day, 1977.

Stephenson, Isaac. *Recollections of a Long Life, 1825–1915.* Chicago R. R. Donnelly & Sons, 1915.

Tanner, Stephen L. *Paul Elmer More: Literary Criticism as the History of Ideas.* Provo, Utah: Brigham Young University, 1987.

Weiss, Ann E. *God and Government: The Separation of Church and State.* Boston: Houghton Mifflin, 1982.

Welles, Sumner. *Seven Decisions That Shaped History.* New York: Harper, 1951.

Williams, William Appleman et al. *America in Vietnam: A Documentary History.* New York: Anchor Press/Doubleday, 1985.

Woodward, Bob, and Carl Bernstein. *All the President's Men.* New York: Simon and Schuster, 1974.

Yielding, Kenneth D. and Paul H. Carlson. *Ah, That Voice.* Odessa, Tex.,: Ben Shepperd Jr. Library of the Presidents, 1974.

# Index